# Handbook of
# Pattern Recognition
# and Image Processing

# Handbooks in Science and Technology

Edited by

NORMAN G. EINSPRUCH

College of Engineering
University of Miami
Coral Gables, Florida

NORMAN G. EINSPRUCH (ed.). VLSI Handbook, 1985

TZAY Y. YOUNG and KING-SUN FU (eds.). Handbook of Pattern
Recognition and Image Processing, 1986

# Handbook of Pattern Recognition and Image Processing

Edited by

TZAY Y. YOUNG

Department of Electrical and Computer Engineering
University of Miami
Coral Gables, Florida

KING-SUN FU

School of Electrical Engineering
Purdue University
West Lafayette, Indiana

ACADEMIC PRESS, INC.
Harcourt Brace Jovanovich, Publishers
San Diego   New York   Berkeley   Boston
London   Sydney   Tokyo   Toronto

ACADEMIC PRESS, INC.
1250 Sixth Avenue, San Diego, California 92101


*United Kingdom Edition published by*
ACADEMIC PRESS INC. (LONDON) LTD.
24-28 Oval Road, London NW1 7DX


LIBRARY OF CONGRESS CATALOGING-IN-PUBLICATION DATA


Main entry under title:

Handbook of pattern recognition and image processing.

    Includes index.
    1. Pattern recognition systems.    2. Image
processing.    I. Young, Tzay Y., Date
TK7882.P3H36    1986    621.3819'598    85-13381
ISBN 0-12-774560-2 (alk. paper)


PRINTED IN THE UNITED STATES OF AMERICA

88 89      9 8 7 6 5 4 3

# Contents

## Part I   PATTERN RECOGNITION

### Chapter 1   Statistical Pattern Classification
KEINOSUKE FUKUNAGA

### Chapter 2   Cluster Analysis
ANIL K. JAIN

### Chapter 3   Feature Selection and Extraction
J. KITTLER

            KING-SUN FU

     I.    Introduction                                                      85
     II.   Primitive Selection and Pattern Grammars                          87
     III.  High-Dimensional Grammars for Pattern Description                 90
     IV.   Syntactic Recognition                                            100
     V.    Error-Correcting Parsing                                         102
     VI.   Clustering Analysis for Syntactic Patterns                       107
     VII.  Syntactic Approach to Shape and Texture Analysis                 112
     VIII. Syntactic Image Analysis and Image Database Management           113
     IX.   Concluding Remarks                                               113
           References                                                       114


Chapter 5   Syntactic Pattern Recognition: Stochastic Languages
            MICHAEL G. THOMASON

     I.    Basic Definitions                                                119
     II.   Derivations as Realizations of a Stationary Stochastic Process   123
     III.  Inference                                                        128
     IV.   Classification via p-Grammars                                    132
     V.    Stochastic Automata                                              137
     VI.   Semantics                                                        139
     VII.  Stochastic Tree Grammars                                         140
           References                                                       141


Chapter 6   Problem Solving Methods for Pattern Recognition
            LAVEEN N. KANAL AND G. R. DATTATREYA

     I.    Introduction                                                     143
     II.   Problem Solving Models                                           146
     III.  Problem Solving Algorithms                                       150
     IV.   Primitive Extraction and Waveform Analysis                       162
     V.    Summary                                                          164
           References                                                       165


Part II    IMAGE PROCESSING AND UNDERSTANDING

Chapter 7   Image Coding
            ALI HABIBI

     I.    Introduction                                                     169
     II.   Digital Imagery                                                  170
     III.  Image Bandwith Compression                                       174
           References                                                       188

## Chapter 17    Cellular Logic Arrays for Image Processing
### KENDALL PRESTON, JR.

## Chapter 18    Parallel Architectures for Image Processing, Computer Vision, and Pattern Perception
### LEONARD UHR

## Chapter 19    VLSI Array Architecture for Pattern Analysis and Image Processing
### TZAY Y. YOUNG AND PHILIP S. LIU

Part IV    APPLICATIONS

Contents                                                                                  xi

# Contributors

Numbers in parentheses indicate the pages on which the authors' contributions begin.

J. K. AGGARWAL (311), Laboratory of Image and Signal Analysis, College of Engineering, The University of Texas at Austin, Austin, Texas 78712

JOHN R. BOURNE (545), Department of Electrical and Biomedical Engineering, Vanderbilt University, Nashville, Tennessee 37235

SHI-KUO CHANG (371), Information Systems Laboratory, Illinois Institute of Technology, Chicago, Illinois 60616

C. H. CHEN (527), Department of Electrical and Computer Engineering, Southeastern Massachusetts University, North Dartmouth, Massachusetts 02747

ROLAND T. CHIN (587), Electrical and Computer Engineering and Computer Sciences, University of Wisconsin, Madison, Wisconsin 53706

G. R. DATTATREYA (143), Machine Intelligence and Pattern Analysis Laboratory, Department of Computer Science, University of Maryland, College Park, Maryland 20742

LARRY S. DAVIS (233), Computer Vision Laboratory, University of Maryland, College Park, Maryland 20742

RENATO DE MORI (499), Department of Computer Science, Concordia University, Montreal, Quebec, Canada H3G 1MB

KING-SUN FU (85), School of Electrical Engineering, Purdue University, West Lafayette, Indiana 47907

KEINOSUKE FUKUNAGA (3), School of Electrical Engineering, Purdue University, West Lafayette, Indiana 47907

R. C. GONZALEZ (191), Electrical Engineering Department, University of Tennessee, Knoxville, Tennessee 37996-2100

ALI HABIBI (169), The Aerospace Corporation, El Segundo, California 90245

ROBERT M. HARALICK (247), Machine Vision International, Ann Arbor, Michigan 48104

THOMAS S. HUANG (333), Coordinated Science Laboratory, University of Illinois, Urbana, Illinois 61801

ANIL K. JAIN (33), Department of Computer Science, Michigan State University, East Lansing, Michigan 48824

A. C. KAK (649), School of Electrical Engineering, Purdue University, West Lafayette, Indiana 47907

LAVEEN N. KANAL (143), Machine Intelligence and Pattern Analysis Laboratory, Department of Computer Science, University of Maryland, College Park, Maryland 20742

R. L. KASHYAP (281), School of Electrical Engineering, Purdue University, West Lafayette, Indiana 47907

J. KITTLER (59), SERC Rutherford Appleton Laboratory, Chilton, Didcot OX11 OQX, England

PHILIP S. LIU (471), Department of Electrical and Computer Engineering, University of Miami, Coral Gables, Florida 33124

AMAR MITICHE* (311), Laboratory of Image and Signal Analysis, College of Engineering, The University of Texas at Austin, Austin, Texas 78712

R. NEVATIA (215), Intelligent Systems Group, University of Southern California, Departments of Electrical Engineering and Computer Science, Los Angeles, California 90089-0272

KENDALL PRESTON, JR. (395), Department of Computer and Electrical Engineering, Carnegie-Mellon University, Pittsburgh, Pennsylvania 15213

DAVID PROBST (499), Department of Computer Science, Concordia University, Montreal, Quebec, Canada H3G 1M8

B. A. ROBERTS (649), School of Electrical Engineering, Purdue University, West Lafayette, Indiana 47907

AZRIEL ROSENFELD (355), Center for Automation Research, University of Maryland, College Park, Maryland 20742

P. V. SANKAR (629), University of California, Irvine, California 92717

RICHARD G. SHIAVI (545), Department of Electrical and Biomedical Engineering, Vanderbilt University, Nashville, Tennessee 37235

J. SKLANSKY (629), University of California, Irvine, California 92717

CHING Y. SUEN (569), Department of Computer Science, Concordia University, Montreal, Quebec, Canada H3G 1M8

PHILIP H. SWAIN (613), School of Electrical Engineering and Laboratory for Applications of Remote Sensing, Purdue University, West Lafayette, Indiana 47907

MICHAEL G. THOMASON (119), Department of Computer Science, University of Tennessee, Knoxville, Tennessee 37996

LEONARD UHR (437), Department of Computer Sciences, University of Wisconsin, Madison, Wisconsin 53706

R. J. WALTER, JR. (629), University of California, Irvine, California 92717

TZAY Y. YOUNG (471), Department of Electrical and Computer Engineering, University of Miami, Coral Gables, Florida 33124

* Present address: Institut National de la Recherche Scientifique, Université du Québec, Verdun, Quebec, Canada H3E 1H6

# Preface

During the past 20 years, there has been a considerable growth of interest in problems of pattern recognition and image processing. This interest has created an increasing need for theoretical methods and experimental software and hardware for use in the design of pattern recognition and image processing systems. Over 25 books have been published in the field of pattern recognition and image processing. In addition, a number of edited books, conference proceedings, and journal special issues have also been published. There are four specialized journals in the field: (1) *IEEE Transactions on Pattern Analysis and Machine Intelligence,* (2) *Pattern Recognition,* (3) *Pattern Recognition Letters,* and (4) *Computer Vision, Graphics, and Image Processing.* Some special pattern recognition machines and image processing systems have been designed and built for practical use. Applications of pattern recognition and image processing include character recognition, target detection, medical diagnosis, analysis of biomedical signals and images, remote sensing, identification of human faces and fingerprints, reliability analyses, socioeconomics, archaeology, speech recognition and understanding, machine part recognition, and automatic inspection. Within the length limitations of this handbook, we provide a broad overview of the major elements of pattern recognition and image processing.

Pattern recognition is concerned primarily with the description and analysis of measurements taken from physical or mental processes. In order to provide an effective and efficient description of patterns, preprocessing is often required to remove noise and measurement redundancy. Then a set of characteristic measurements, which could be numerical and/or nonnumerical, and relations among these measurements are extracted for the representation of patterns. Analysis (classification and/or description) of the patterns with respect to a specific goal is performed on the basis of the representation.

In order to determine a good set of characteristic measurements and their relations for the representation of patterns so that good recognition performance can be expected, a careful analysis of the patterns under study is necessary. Knowledge about the statistical and structural characteristics of patterns should be fully utilized. From this point of view, the study of pattern recognition includes both the analysis of pattern characteristics and the design of recognition systems.

There are many mathematical methods proposed for solving pattern recognition problems. These methods can primarily be grouped into two major approaches: (1) decision-theoretic or statistical and (2) syntactic or structural. From a more general point of view, these approaches can be discussed within a common framework in terms of pattern representation and decision-making and structural analysis (based on a given pattern representation).

A quick scan of the recent publications of pattern recognition and image processing reveals that the majority of the papers deal with the analysis of images and scenes. The general goal of image processing is to analyze images of a given scene and to recognize the content of the scene. Many types of scenes are essentially two dimensional (documents are an obvious example); and two-dimensional treatment is often quite adequate in applications such as remote sensing (flat terrain is seen from very high altitudes), radiology (where the image is a "shadow" of the object), or microscopy (where the image is a cross section of the object). In such situations, the image analysis process is basically two dimensional. One extracts "features" such as edges from the image, or segments the image into regions, thus obtaining a map-like representation, consisting of image features labeled with their property values. Grouping processes may then be used to obtain improved maps. The maps can be represented by abstract relational structures in which, for example, nodes represent regions, labeled with various property values (color, texture, shape, etc.) and arcs represent relationships among regions. Finally, these structures can be matched against stored models, which are generalized relational structures representing classes of maps that correspond to general types of images. Successful matches yield identifications for the image parts and a structural description of the image in terms of known entities.

In other situations, notably in robot vision applications, the scenes to be described are fundamentally three dimensional, involving substantial surface relief and object occlusion. Successful analysis of images of such scenes requires a more elaborate approach in which the three-dimensional nature of the underlying scenes is taken into account. Here the key step in the analysis is to infer the surface orientation at each image point. Clues to surface orientation can be derived directly from shading (i.e., gray-level variation) in the image. Alternatively, two-dimensional segmentation and feature extraction techniques can first be applied to the image to extract such features as surface contours and texture primitives, and surface orientation clues can then be derived from contour shapes or from textural variations. Using the surface orientation map called the "$2\frac{1}{2}$-D sketch," feature extraction and segmentation techniques can once again be applied to yield a segmentation into (visible parts of) bodies or objects, and these can in turn be represented by a relational structure. Finally, the structure can be matched against models to yield an interpretation of the scene in terms of known objects. Note that the matching process is more difficult in the three-dimensional case, since the image shows only one side of each object and since objects may partially occlude one another. We are not simply "matching" a model with the observed structure but, rather, are verifying that the model could give rise to that structure under appropriate viewing conditions.

This handbook consists of four parts. Part I is devoted to the major techniques in pattern recognition. Part II summarizes developments in image processing and understanding. Part III describes several computer systems and architectures for pattern recognition and image processing. Part IV contains chapters demonstrating major applications of pattern recognition and image processing. The contents of this volume should be useful for both college students and industrial engineers. It will serve as a technical reference as well as a broad source of general information in pattern recognition and image processing.

# In Memoriam

**King-sun Fu**
**(1930 – 1985)**

Professor King-sun Fu, coeditor of this Handbook, passed away April 29, 1985. He received the B.S. degree from National Taiwan University, Taipei, in 1953, and the Ph.D. degree from the University of Illinois, Urbana, in 1959. He joined the faculty of the School of Electrical Engineering at Purdue University in 1960, and at the time of his death was Goss Distinguished Professor of Engineering at Purdue.

King-sun was a leading authority in the field of pattern recognition. His early research efforts at Purdue were in statistical pattern classification and feature selection. When the patterns are complex and/or the number of classes is very large, the idea of describing a complex pattern in terms of a composition of simple subpatterns and their relations becomes very attractive. Several researchers recognized the importance of structural information and proposed various grammars for pattern analysis in the 1960s. It was King-sun who combined these ideas to formulate a coherent theory of syntactic pattern recognition that included the use of stochastic grammars and languages to deal with ambiguities and uncertainties in the patterns. His two books on syntactic pattern recognition are often quoted classics in the field.

As a teacher, scholar, and researcher, King-sun's contributions and influence pervade almost all aspects of pattern recognition and image processing. He collaborated with his colleagues and students in applying syntactic techniques to practical problems such as fingerprint analysis, texture modeling, shape and waveform analysis, and medical images. In recent years, he contributed significantly to image database systems, VLSI architecture for pattern analysis, and computer vision for robotic systems.

King-sun received many honors, including the 1981 ASEE Senior Research Award, the 1982 IEEE Education Medal, the 1982 AFIPS Harry Goode Memorial Award, and the 1977 Outstanding Paper Award of the IEEE Computer Society. He was a fellow of the IEEE, a Guggenheim Fellow, and a member of the National Academy of Engineering and of Academia Sinica. He was the first president of the International Association for Pattern

Recognition (IAPR), and the founding editor of *IEEE Transactions on Pattern Analysis and Machine Intelligence.*

I have known King-sun for almost twenty years, and I have kept close contact with him in recent years. His death was a personal loss as well as a great loss to the PRIP community. His leadership, dedication, versatility, and friendship will be missed by students and fellow researchers alike.

*Coral Gables, Florida*                                          TZAY Y. YOUNG

# Part I

# Pattern Recognition

# Chapter 1

# Statistical Pattern Classification*

KEINOSUKE FUKUNAGA

School of Electrical Engineering
Purdue University
West Lafayette, Indiana

## INTRODUCTION    I

The purpose of statistical pattern classification is to determine to which category or class a given sample belongs. Through an observation and measurement process, we obtain a set of numbers which make up the

* This work was supported in part by the National Science Foundation under Grant ECS 83-00536.

HANDBOOK OF PATTERN RECOGNITION
AND IMAGE PROCESSING

measurement vector. The vector is a random vector and its conditional density function depends on its class.

The design of a classifier consists of two parts. One is to collect data samples from various classes and to find the boundaries which separate the classes. This process is called *classifier design, training,* or *learning*. The other is to *test* the designed classifier by feeding the samples whose class identities are known.

Figure 1 shows a breakdown of the design process. First, the data is gathered and properly normalized. Then, the *Bayes error*, the overlap among different class densities, is estimated. The Bayes error is the smallest possible error in the current measurement space. In the later stages, selecting features and designing a classifier will always result in increased error. Therefore, if the error is unacceptably high at this stage, there is no use in processing the data further. We must return to data gathering and find alternative measurements in order to obtain acceptable error. Also, the estimated Bayes error could serve as a reference for future operations. For example, when features are extracted, the Bayes error in the feature space must be estimated and compared with the one in the original measurement space in order to

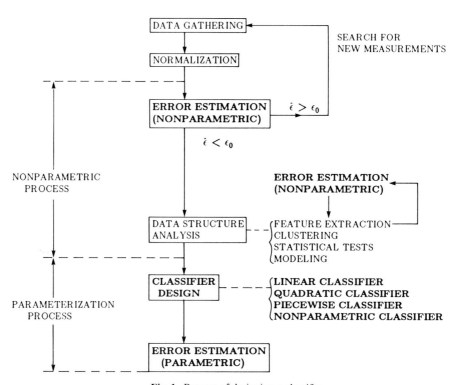

**Fig. 1.** Process of designing a classifier.

determine whether the extracted features are acceptable or not. The same is true for the error of the final classifier.

Once the estimated Bayes error is acceptable, we can move to data structure analysis, which includes many operations, such as feature extraction, clustering, statistical tests, and modeling. Based on these studies, we may choose a proper classifier for the given data. The final stage is the evaluation of the classifier.

When the Bayes error is estimated in either measurement or feature space, it is not appropriate to assume any mathematical form (such as Gaussian) for the class density functions. Therefore, a nonparametric technique must be used. Data structure analysis combined with classifier design is considered to be a parameterization process.

In this chapter, only the boldfaced portions of Fig. 1 will be discussed. Clustering and feature extraction are discussed in detail in other chapters. Also, unless otherwise stated, only the two-class problem is discussed in this chapter, although the results for a more general multiclass problem are listed whenever available.

## THE BAYES CLASSIFICATION    II

In this section, the classification algorithms and the resulting errors are presented, based on the assumption that $p_i(X)$ and $P_i$ are known. The classification algorithms are also known as *hypothesis tests*.

### Likelihood Ratio Classifier [1, 2]    A

The probability of the classification error can be minimized by classifying $X$ into either $\omega_1$ or $\omega_2$, depending on whether $q_1(X) > q_2(X)$ or $q_1(X) < q_2(X)$ is satisfied. That is,

$$q_1(X) \underset{\omega_2}{\overset{\omega_1}{\gtrless}} q_2(X) \qquad \text{(Bayes classifier)} \qquad (1)$$

The resulting risk at $X$ is

$$r^*(X) = \min[q_1(X), q_2(X)] \qquad \text{(Bayes risk)} \qquad (2)$$

The overall error is obtained by taking the expectation of (2) over $\mathbf{X}$:

$$\epsilon^* = \mathrm{E}\{r^*(\mathbf{X})\} = P_1 \int_{\Gamma_2} p_1(X)\,dX + P_2 \int_{\Gamma_1} p_2(X)\,dX \qquad \text{(Bayes error)} \qquad (3)$$

where $\epsilon_1 = \int_{\Gamma_2} p_1(X)\,dX$ and $\epsilon_2 = \int_{\Gamma_1} p_2(X)\,dX$ are called the $\omega_1$ and $\omega_2$

errors, respectively. $\Gamma_i$ is the region where $X$ is classified to $\omega_i$.
For the multiclass problem,

$$q_k(X) = \max_i q_i(X) \to X \in \omega_k \tag{4}$$

$$\epsilon^* = \mathrm{E}\left\{1 - \max_i q_i(\mathbf{X})\right\} \tag{5}$$

A more convenient form of the Bayes classifier is obtained by applying the Bayes theorem, $q_i(X) = P_i p_i(X)/p(X)$, and taking negative logarithm:

$$h(X) = -\ln[p_1(X)/p_2(X)] \underset{\omega_2}{\overset{\omega_1}{\lessgtr}} \ln[P_1/P_2] \tag{6}$$

The $h(X)$ combined with a threshold is called the *likelihood ratio classifier*. When $\mathbf{X}$ is distributed Gaussianly with $M_i$ and $\Sigma_i$ for $\omega_i$,

$$-\ln p_i(X) = \tfrac{1}{2}(X - M_i)^{\mathrm{T}}\Sigma_i^{-1}(X - M_i) + \tfrac{1}{2}\ln |\Sigma_i| + (n/2)\ln 2\pi \tag{7}$$

The threshold of the classifier could be changed according to various requirements as follows:

## 1   Bayes Classifier for Minimum Cost [2, 3]

Let $c_{ij}$ be the cost of classifying a $\omega_i$ sample into $\omega_j$. The expected cost of classifying $X$ into $\omega_i$ is

$$c_i(X) = \sum_{j=1}^{L} c_{ji} q_j(X) \tag{8}$$

The classification rule and the resulting cost are

$$c_k(X) = \min_i c_i(X) \to X \in \omega_k \tag{9}$$

$$c^* = \mathrm{E}\left\{\min_i c_i(\mathbf{X})\right\} \tag{10}$$

For the two-class problem,

$$h(X) = -\ln[p_1(X)/p_2(X)] \underset{\omega_2}{\overset{\omega_1}{\lessgtr}} \ln[(c_{12} - c_{11})P_1/(c_{21} - c_{22})P_2] \quad (11)$$

This is a likelihood ratio classifier with a new threshold.

### Neyman–Pearson Test [1]   2

Let $\epsilon_1$ and $\epsilon_2$ be the error probabilities from $\omega_1$ and $\omega_2$, respectively, as shown in (3). The likelihood ratio classifier minimizes $\epsilon_1$ subject to $\epsilon_2$ being equal to a given constant, say, $\epsilon_0$. The threshold value must be selected to satisfy $\epsilon_2 = \epsilon_0$ and is normally determined empirically. A plot of $\epsilon_1$ vs. $1 - \epsilon_2$ for the likelihood ratio classifier with varying threshold is shown in Fig. 2. This plot is called the *operating characteristic* and is used frequently as a visual aid to see how two errors are traded by changing the threshhold. In the

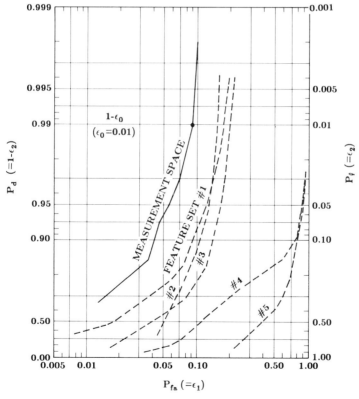

**Fig. 2.** Operating characteristics.

Neyman–Pearson test, the dot mark of Fig. 2 is the operating point and the corresponding threshold value is chosen. When $\omega_2$ represents a target to be identified against the other $(\omega_1)$, $c_1$, $c_2$, and $1 - c_2$ are called the *false alarm*, the *leakage*, and the *detection probability*, respectively.

## 3  Minimax Test [1]

We can make the expected cost invariant for the change of $P_i$ by selecting the threshold of the likelihood ratio classifier to satisfy

$$(c_{11} - c_{22}) + (c_{12} - c_{11})c_1 - (c_{21} - c_{22})c_2 = 0 \tag{12}$$

Particularly, when $c_{11} = c_{22}$ and $c_{12} - c_{11} = c_{21} - c_{22}$, the threshold is chosen to satisfy $c_1 = c_2$. This classifier eliminates the possibility of having an unexpected large error due to the unexpected variation of $P_i$.

In all of these three cases, the likelihood ratio classifier is commonly used, and only the threshold varies. This can be interpreted as replacing the true $P_i$'s of (6) by artificial $P_i$'s. Therefore, theoretically all these cases may be treated as the Bayes classifier, leaving the meaning of $P_i$ to each application. Some of the related subjects are presented as follows.

**a. Independent Measurement Sets.** When $\mathbf{X}$ consists of statistically independent measurement sets as $\mathbf{X}^T = [\mathbf{X}_1^T \mathbf{X}_2^T \cdots \mathbf{X}_M^T]$, the Bayes classifier becomes

$$-\ln[p_1(X)/p_2(X)] = \sum_{i=1}^{M} -\ln[p_1(X_i)/p_2(X_i)] \underset{\omega_2}{\overset{\omega_1}{\lessgtr}} \ln(P_1/P_2) \tag{13}$$

This suggests how to combine, for classification, seemingly unrelated information such as radar and infrared signatures.

**b. One-Class Classifier.** When one clearly defined class is classified against all other (sometimes not well-defined) possibilities, the boundary may be determined from the knowledge of one class only. A typical example is a hyperspherical boundary around a Gaussian distribution with $M = 0$ and $\Sigma = I$. However, this concept must be adopted cautiously, particularly for high-dimensional cases. Let us examine the marginal density of radius $l$ for a Gaussian distribution with $M = 0$ and $\Sigma = I$:

$$p_l(l) = \frac{n}{2^{n/2}\Gamma(1 + n/2)} l^{n-1} e^{-l^2/2} \tag{14}$$

where $\Gamma(\cdot)$ is the gamma function. Figure 3 shows the plot of this density function for $n = 5$, 10, and 20. The densities are concentrated around relatively large $l$'s. Thus, if the boundary is set, say, at $l = 1$, most samples from this class will be located outside the hypersphere and misclassified to the other class. The boundary $l = 1$ corresponds to the standard deviation of $\mathbf{x}_i$.

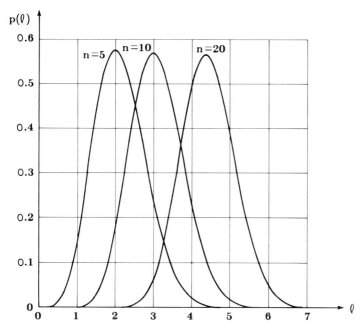

**Fig. 3.** The marginal density of radius for a Gaussian distribution.

**c. Reject [3, 4, pp. 218, 231].** When $X$ falls in the region where the Bayes risk $r^*(X)$ is high, we may decide not to classify the sample. This concept is called *reject*. The *reject region* $\Gamma_r(t)$ and the resulting *probability of rejection* $R(t)$ are specified by the threshold $t$ as

$$\Gamma_r(t) = \{X : r^*(X) > t\} \tag{15}$$

$$R(t) = \Pr\{r^*(\mathbf{X}) > t\} = 1 - \Pr\{r^*(\mathbf{X}) \leq t\} \tag{16}$$

Note that $\Pr\{r^*(\mathbf{X}) \leq t\}$ is the distribution function of a random variable $r^*(\mathbf{X})$. The probability of error with reject is the integration of $r^*(X)p(X)$ in $\bar{\Gamma}_r$, outside $\Gamma_r$, and thus depends on $t$. The error may be evaluated directly from the reject probability as

$$\varepsilon(t) = -\int_0^t \xi \, dR(\xi) \tag{17}$$

The error decreases as the reject probability increases, and vice versa. With the largest possible $t = 1 - 1/L$ for the $L$-class problem, $R(1 - 1/L) = 0$ and $\varepsilon(1 - 1/L)$ is equal to the Bayes error, $\varepsilon^*$.

**d. Model Validation [4, pp. 218, 231].** The distribution function of the random variable $r^*(\mathbf{X})$ is a simple and good parameter to characterize the classification environment, determining both $\varepsilon(t)$ and $R(t)$. Thus, when samples are drawn and a mathematical model is assumed, two distribution functions of $r^*(\mathbf{X})$ may be obtained: one empirically from the samples and the other theoretically from the model. The comparison of these two distribution functions could be used to test the validity of the mathematical model.

## B  The Bayes Error

The Bayes error of (3) is generally hard to compute, except for the following two cases.

(1)  *Gaussian* $\mathbf{X}$ *with* $\Sigma_1 = \Sigma_2 = \Sigma$ [1]. For this case, the Bayes classifier becomes

$$h(X) = (M_2 - M_1)^{\mathrm{T}}\Sigma^{-1}X + \tfrac{1}{2}(M_1^{\mathrm{T}}\Sigma^{-1}M_1 - M_2^{\mathrm{T}}\Sigma^{-1}M_2) \lessgtr t \quad (18)$$

Since $\mathbf{X}$ is Gaussianly distributed, $h(\mathbf{X})$ is also a Gaussian random variable. Therefore,

$$\epsilon_1 = \int_{(t-m_1)/\sigma_1}^{+\infty} \frac{1}{\sqrt{2\pi}} e^{-\xi^2/2}\, d\xi \quad \text{and} \quad \epsilon_2 = \int_{-\infty}^{(t-m_2)/\sigma_2} \frac{1}{\sqrt{2\pi}} e^{-\xi^2/2}\, d\xi \quad (19)$$

where

$$m_1 = E\{h(\mathbf{X})|\omega_1\} = -\tfrac{1}{2}(M_2 - M_1)^{\mathrm{T}}\Sigma^{-1}(M_2 - M_1) \tag{20}$$

$$m_2 = E\{h(\mathbf{X})|\omega_2\} = +\tfrac{1}{2}(M_2 - M_1)^{\mathrm{T}}\Sigma^{-1}(M_2 - M_1) \tag{21}$$

$$\sigma_i^2 = \mathrm{Var}\{h(\mathbf{X})|\omega_i\} = (M_2 - M_1)^{\mathrm{T}}\Sigma^{-1}(M_2 - M_1) \quad (i = 1, 2) \tag{22}$$

(2)  *Gaussian* $\mathbf{X}$ *with* $\Sigma_1 \neq \Sigma_2$ [1]. The Bayes classifier for this case is

$$h(X) = \frac{1}{2}(X - M_1)^{\mathrm{T}}\Sigma_1^{-1}(X - M_1) - \frac{1}{2}(X - M_2)^{\mathrm{T}}\Sigma_2^{-1}(X - M_2)$$

$$+ \frac{1}{2}\ln\frac{|\Sigma_1|}{|\Sigma_2|} \lessgtr t \tag{23}$$

The distribution of $h(\mathbf{X})$ is no longer Gaussian, but the errors can be computed as follows:

$$\epsilon_1 = \frac{1}{2} + \frac{1}{\pi}\int_0^\infty \frac{\prod_{i=1}^n |\phi_{1i}(\omega)|}{\omega} \sin\left\{\left[\sum_{i=1}^n \angle\phi_{1i}(\omega)\right] - \omega t\right\} d\omega \tag{24}$$

$$\epsilon_2 = \frac{1}{2} - \frac{1}{\pi}\int_0^\infty \frac{\prod_{i=1}^n |\phi_{2i}(\omega)|}{\omega} \sin\left\{\left[\sum_{i=1}^n \angle\phi_{2i}(\omega)\right] - \omega t\right\} d\omega \tag{25}$$

where

$$|\phi_{ji}(\omega)| = (1 + \omega^2 a_{ji})^{-1/4} \exp[\tfrac{1}{2}(-b_{ji}^2\omega^2)/(1 + \omega^2 a_{ji}^2)] \tag{26}$$

$$\angle\phi_{ji}(\omega) = \tfrac{1}{2}\tan^{-1}(a_{ji}\omega) - \tfrac{1}{2}\omega[c_{ji} + (a_{ji}b_{ji}^2\omega^2)/(1 + \omega^2 a_{ji}^2)] \tag{27}$$

$$a_{1i} = 1 - \frac{1}{\lambda_i}, \qquad b_{1i} = \frac{d_{2i} - d_{1i}}{\lambda_i}, \qquad c_{1i} = \frac{b_{1i}^2}{1 - a_{1i}} + \ln\lambda_i \tag{28}$$

$$a_{2i} = \lambda_i - 1, \qquad b_{2i} = \sqrt{\lambda_i}(d_{2i} - d_{1i}), \qquad c_{2i} = \frac{-b_{2i}^2}{1 + a_{2i}} + \ln\lambda_i \tag{29}$$

The $\lambda$'s are the eigenvalues of the simultaneous diagonalization

$$A^T\Sigma_1 A = I \qquad \text{and} \qquad A^T\Sigma_2 A = \Lambda \tag{30}$$

and the $(d_{2i} - d_{1i})$ is the $i$th component of the vector $A^T(M_2 - M_1)$. Equations (24) and (25) must be integrated numerically, but they are one-dimensional integrations.

Frequently, the *upper and lower bounds* of the Bayes error are used for convenience. Some of popular bounds are listed as follows [1, 3]:

$$\mathrm{E}\{q_1(\mathbf{X})q_2(\mathbf{X})\}: \qquad \text{2 nearest-neighbor error} \tag{31}$$

$$\mathrm{E}\{\min[q_1(\mathbf{X}), q_2(\mathbf{X})]\}: \qquad \text{Bayes error} \tag{32}$$

$$2\,\mathrm{E}\{q_1(\mathbf{X})q_2(\mathbf{X})\}: \qquad \text{Nearest-neighbor error} \tag{33}$$

$$-\frac{1}{2\ln 2}\,\mathrm{E}\{q_1(\mathbf{X})\ln q_1(\mathbf{X}) + q_2(\mathbf{X})\ln q_2(\mathbf{X})\}: \qquad \text{Equivaction} \tag{34}$$

$$\mathrm{E}\{\sqrt{q_1(\mathbf{X})q_2(\mathbf{X})}\}: \qquad \text{Bhattacharyya bound} \tag{35}$$

The inequalities $(31) \le (32) \le (33) \le (34) \le (35)$ hold regardless of the distributions.

One of the popular bounds is the *Bhattacharyya bound*, which has an explicit expression for *Gaussian distributions* as

$$\mathrm{E}\{\sqrt{q_1(\mathbf{X})q_2(\mathbf{X})}\} = \sqrt{P_1 P_2}\, e^{-J_B} \tag{36}$$

$$J_B = \frac{1}{8}(M_1 - M_2)^T\left[\frac{\Sigma_1 + \Sigma_2}{2}\right]^{-1}(M_1 - M_2) + \frac{1}{2}\ln\frac{|(\Sigma_1 + \Sigma_2)/2|}{\sqrt{|\Sigma_1|}\sqrt{|\Sigma_2|}} \tag{37}$$

The first term of (37) indicates the class separability due to the mean difference, and the second term gives that due to the covariance difference.

A similar upper bound of the Bayes error is the *Chernoff bound*, which also has an explicit expression for *Gaussian distributions* as

$$E\{q_1^s(\mathbf{X})q_2^{1-s}(\mathbf{X})\} = P_1^s P_2^{1-s} e^{-J_{c(s)}} \tag{38}$$

$$J_c(s) = \frac{s(1-s)}{2}(M_1 - M_2)^{\mathrm{T}}[s\Sigma_1 + (1-s)\Sigma_2]^{-1}(M_1 - M_2)$$
$$+ \frac{1}{2}\ln\frac{|s\Sigma_1 + (1-s)\Sigma_2|}{|\Sigma_1|^s|\Sigma_2|^{1-s}} \tag{39}$$

The Chernoff bound is larger than the Bayes error for any $s$ in $0 \leq s \leq 1$. However, the inequalities with the others do not exist. The Bhattacharyya bound is a special case of the Chernoff bound with $s = 0.5$. With the optimized $s$, the Chernoff bound can be made smaller than the Bhattacharyya bound. However, in practice, their difference is small in most of the cases, and $s = 0.5$ is commonly used.

## III   ESTIMATION OF THE BAYES ERROR

In this section, nonparametric techniques to estimate the Bayes error are presented. They are used on the estimation of density functions by the $k$-nearest-neighbor ($k$NN) and Parzen approaches.

## A   Density Estimation

There are two approaches for density estimation, as follows.

## 1   *Parzen Approach*

Set a local fixed region $\Gamma(X)$ around $X$ with volume $v$, and count the number of samples in $\Gamma(X)$, $\mathbf{k}(X)$. The density function is estimated by

$$\hat{\mathbf{p}}(X) = \frac{\mathbf{k}(X)}{Nv} \quad \text{with} \quad \Pr\{\mathbf{k} = k\} = \begin{bmatrix} N \\ k \end{bmatrix} u^k(1-u)^{N-k} \tag{40}$$

where $u = \int_{\Gamma(X)} p(X)\,dX$ is the *probability of a sample falling in the $\Gamma(X)$*. The $\hat{\mathbf{p}}(X)$ of (40) is asymptotically unbiased and consistent $[\lim_{N\to\infty}\mathrm{Var}\{\hat{\mathbf{p}}(X)\} = p^2(X)(1-k/N)/k \simeq p^2(X)/k]$ if $\lim_{N\to\infty}k = \infty$ and $\lim_{N\to\infty}k/N = 0$ [6]. Equation (40) is also expressed for available samples, $X_1,\ldots,X_N$, as

$$\hat{\mathbf{p}}(X) = \frac{1}{N}\sum_{i=1}^{N} g(X - \mathbf{X}_i) \tag{41}$$

where $g(X - X_i)$ is a uniform kernel function with $g = 1/v$ in $\Gamma(X_i)$ and 0 outside. Once the form of (41) is adopted, the kernel function is not required to be uniform. The easiest one for practical implementation is a *Gaussian kernel* as

$$g(X - X_i) = \frac{1}{\sqrt{(2\pi)^n h^n}\sqrt{|\Sigma|}} \exp\left[ -\frac{1}{2h^2}(X - X_i)^T \Sigma^{-1}(X - X_i) \right] \quad (42)$$

where $h$ must satisfy $\lim_{N \to \infty} h^n = 0$, $\lim_{N \to \infty} N h^n = \infty$, and $\lim_{N \to \infty} N h^{2n} = \infty$ for asymptotic unbiasedness, consistency, and unform consistency, respectively [1]. The $\Sigma$ determines the shape of the kernel function, but it is unknown how to select $\Sigma$.

### kNN Approach 2

For this approach, $k$ is fixed and $\Gamma(X)$ is extended until the $k$th NN is found. The $v$ is a random variable. Then

$$\hat{p}(X) = \frac{k-1}{Nv(X)} \quad \text{with} \quad p_u(u) = \frac{N!}{(k-1)!(N-k)!} u^{k-1}(1-u)^{N-k} \quad (43)$$

If $p(X)$ can be assumed to be linear in a small local region $\Gamma(X)$, $u$, and $v$ are related by $u(X) = p(X)v(X)$. The $\hat{p}(X)$ of (43) is asymptotically unbiased and consistent $[\lim_{N \to \infty} \mathrm{Var}\{\hat{p}(X)\} = p^2(X)\{(k - 1)(N - 1)/(k - 2)N - 1\} \simeq p^2(X)/(k - 2)]$ under conditions $\lim_{N \to \infty} k = \infty$ and $\lim_{N \to \infty} k/N = 0$ [6]. The variance of the Parzen estimate is smaller than the one of the $k$NN for the same $k$. Also, in the $k$NN density estimate, $k$ must be larger than 2 in order to avoid large variance. However, the Parzen density estimate has trouble in low-density areas, where samples are sparse. With a fixed kernel function, the estimate varies considerably depending on whether any sample is nearby or not. On the other hand, the $k$NN approach adopts variable kernel size, depending on the sample density.

The $m$th-order moments of the distance to the $k$NN can be computed by assuming that $\Gamma(X)$ is a hyperspherical region with radius $d_{kNN}$ and that $u(X) = p(X)v(X)$:

$$E\{\mathbf{d}_{kNN}^m | X\} = \frac{\Gamma(k + m/n)}{\Gamma(k)} \frac{\Gamma(N + 1)}{\Gamma(N + 1 + m/n)} \frac{\pi^{n/2}}{\Gamma(1 + n/2)} p^{-m/n}(X) \quad (44)$$

$$E\{\mathbf{d}_{kNN}^m\} = \frac{\Gamma(k + m/n)}{\Gamma(k)} \frac{\Gamma(N + 1)}{\Gamma(N + 1 + m/n)} \frac{\pi^{n/2}}{\Gamma(1 + n/2)} \int p^{1 - m/n}(X)\,dX \quad (45)$$

The integral of (45) can be computed for some $p(X)$'s as follows:

$$\text{Gauss:} \quad (2\pi)^{m/2}|\Sigma|^{m/2n}(1 - m/n)^{-n/2} \quad (46)$$

$$\text{Uniform:} \quad (2\pi)^{m/2}|\Sigma|^{m/2n}\Gamma^{-m/n}(1 + n/2)(1 + n/2)^{m/2} \quad (47)$$

When $m/n$ is small, only $n$ and $|\Sigma|$ affect the moments and the effects of $k$, $N$, and $p(X)$ are minimal.

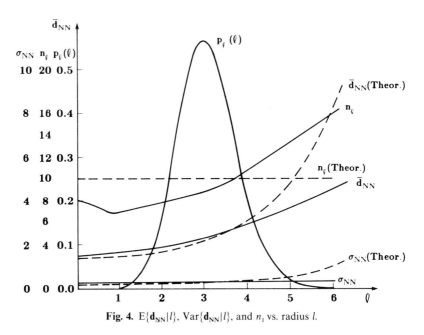

**Fig. 4.** $E\{\mathbf{d}_{NN}|l\}$, $Var\{\mathbf{d}_{NN}|l\}$, and $n_1$ vs. radius $l$.

The ratio of two consecutive averaged $k$NN distances depends only on $k$ and $n$ and is independent of $N$ and $p(X)$ as follows:

$$\frac{E\{\mathbf{d}_{(k+1)NN}|X\}}{E\{\mathbf{d}_{kNN}|X\}} = \frac{E\{\mathbf{d}_{(k+1)NN}\}}{E\{\mathbf{d}_{kNN}\}} = 1 + \frac{1}{kn_1} \qquad (48)$$

The $n_1$ computed by (48) depends only on neighboring information and thus indicates the *local dimensionality* (or *intrinsic dimensionality*).

Figure 4 shows how these moments and $n_1$ vary, depending on the location (specified by the radius $l$), for a 10-dimensional Gaussian distribution with $M = 0$ and $\Sigma = I$. Theoretical curves are computed from (44) and empirical curves are obtained by generating samples. Both $E\{\mathbf{d}_{NN}|l\}$ and $Var\{\mathbf{d}_{NN}|l\}$ are not sensitive to $l$.

## B   Asymptotic *k*NN Errors

The $k$NN classification for the two-class problem is performed as follows.

(1)   For odd $k$'s; Find the $k$NN of $X$, $X_{NN}, \ldots, X_{kNN}$ and classify $X$ according to the majority of the classes to which the neighbors belong [4, pp. 261, 280, 333].

(2)   For even $k$'s: Do the same as (1) but, when the number of $\omega_1$ neighbors is the same as the number of $\omega_2$ neighbors, $X$ is rejected. This case is not counted as a misclassified case [6]. For extended discussion of reject, see Ref. 3.

Assuming $q_i(X_{kNN}) = q_i(X)$ for a large sample size, the *asymptotic risks* at $X$ are expressed as [4, p. 235].

$$r_{2k}(X) = \sum_{i=1}^{k} \frac{1}{i}\binom{2i-2}{i-1}[q_1(X)q_2(X)]^i \qquad \text{for even NNs} \qquad (49)$$

$$r_{2k-1}(X) = r_{2k}(X) + \frac{1}{2}\binom{2k}{k}[q_1(X)q_2(K)]^k \qquad \text{for odd NNs} \qquad (50)$$

On the other hand, the *Bayes risk* of (2) is

$$r^*(X) = \frac{1}{2} - \frac{1}{2}\sqrt{1 - 4q_1(X)q_2(X)} = \sum_{i=1}^{\infty} \frac{1}{i}\binom{2i-2}{i-1}[q_1(X)q_2(X)]^i \quad (51)$$

Figure 5 shows these risks as functions of $q_1(X)q_2(X)$, which varies between 0 and 0.25. These curves indicate the following inequalities regardless of $X$:

$$\tfrac{1}{2}r^*(X) \leq r_2(X) \leq r_4(X) \leq \cdots \leq r^*(X) \leq \cdots \leq r_3(X) \leq r_1(X) \leq 2r^*(X) \quad (52)$$

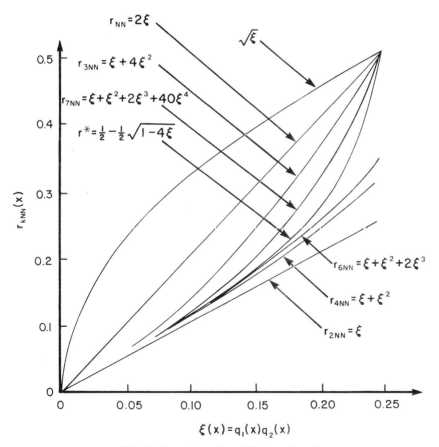

**Fig. 5.** Comparison of $r_{kNN}(X)$ for various $k$.

Since $c_{kNN} = E\{r_k(\mathbf{X})\}$, the same inequalities hold for the *asymptotic* $k$NN *errors* as

$$\tfrac{1}{2}c^* \leq c_{2NN} \leq c_{4NN} \leq \cdots \leq c^* \leq \cdots \leq c_{3NN} \leq c_{NN} \leq 2c^* \qquad (53)$$

Figure 5 also includes $\sqrt{q_1(X)q_2(X)}$ because $E\{\sqrt{q_1(\mathbf{X})q_2(\mathbf{X})}\}$ is the Bhattacharyya bound as shown in (35).

When a sample size is finite, the above inequalities may not hold. If the inequalities of (53) are observed, it may mean that the $k$NN approach seems to be working. Also, note that $c_{NN} = 2c_{2NN}$ [and $r_1(X) = 2r_2(X)$]. This relationship could be used as another check for the validity of the $k$NN approach.

The equality $c_{NN} = 2c_{2NN}$, can be extended to general multiclass problems by counting $c_{2NN}$ as follows:

(1) Count 1 error at $X$ if $X_{NN}$ and $X_{2NN}$ agree in class but disagree with $X$.

(2) Count $\frac{1}{2}$ error at $X$ if $X_{NN}$ and $X_{2NN}$ disagree in class and neither one agrees with $X$.

## C  *k*NN Errors for a Finite Sample Size

When a sample size is finite, the $k$NN errors, $\hat{c}_{kNN}$, may vary considerably, depending on $N$, $n$, $p_i(X)$, the metric, and so on. This is due to the fact that the estimation is based on the small number of local samples.

(1) *Selection of N.* It is difficult to determine theoretically how many samples are needed to obtain the reliable bounds of the Bayes error. But, in practice, the plots of $\hat{c}_{2k-1}$ (upper bound) and $\hat{c}_{2k}$ (lower bound) as functions of $N$ will give a reasonable feeling as to where the Bayes error is located and whether or not the available $N$ is adequate. Figure 6 shows such a plot for a 256-dimensional data set. With 1000 samples available, $\hat{c}_3$ and $\hat{c}_2$ are obtained. Then, the 1000 samples are divided into two groups of 500 samples. For these two groups, two $\hat{c}_3$'s and $\hat{c}_2$'s are obtained. Figure 6 shows the two curves bounding the supposed-to-be Bayes error. Also, this figure gives the impression that, even if we add more samples, say, 1000 more, probably we cannot expect a much more accurate estimate of the Bayes error. As this example indicates, it has been found that only small sample sizes relative to the dimensionalities are needed to get flat bounds, although this depends very much on the structure of the distribution.

(2) *Selection of k.* Theoretical treatment to find the optimal $k$ is very difficult and very little is known on this subject. However, experience tells us that the Bayes error is reasonably well estimated by selecting as large a $k$ as possible until the inequalities of (53) are violated.

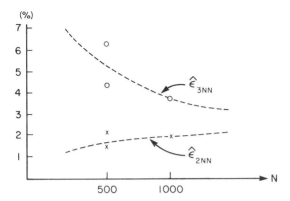

**Fig. 6.** An example of $\hat{\epsilon}_{3NN}$ and $\hat{\epsilon}_{2NN}$ vs. $N$.

(3) *Selection of a metric.* The metric to measure nearness must be selected properly in order to obtain a reliable $\hat{\epsilon}_{kNN}$. The use of a conventional Euclidean distance for significantly different class distribution could result in $\hat{\epsilon}_{kNN}$ far different from $\epsilon_{kNN}$, in which case $\hat{\epsilon}_{kNN}$ would no longer be guaranteed to be a bound of the Bayes error.

For the simplest case of $k = 1$, the optimal metric which minimizes $E\{[\hat{r}_{NN}(X) - r_{NN}(X)]^2|X\}$ is [6]

$$\nabla^T q_1(X)(\mathbf{X}_{NN} - X) \tag{54}$$

That is, the local samples in $\Gamma(X)$ must be mapped down on a vector $\nabla q_1(X)$, the gradient of $q_1(X)$, and the neighbor which has the smallest component on $\nabla q_1(X)$ is selected as the NN. The $\nabla q_1(X)$ is proportional to the gradient vector of the likelihood ratio $-\ln[p_1(X)/p_2(X)]$, that is, $\nabla q_1(X) \sim [-\nabla p_1(X)/p_1(X) + \nabla p_2(X)/p_2(X)]$.

If both $p_1(X)$ and $p_2(X)$ are Gaussian [6], then

$$\nabla q_1(X) \sim \Sigma_1^{-1}(X - M_1) - \Sigma_2^{-1}(X - M_2) \tag{55}$$

This vector could be used for many distributions in which the surface structure of the boundary is similar to the Gaussian case.

When the distributions are far different from Gaussian, $\nabla q_1(X)$ must be estimated from samples. For this purpose, the following equation is used [6]:

$$\nabla q_1(X) \sim E\{(\mathbf{Y} - X)|\Gamma(X), \omega_1\} - E\{(\mathbf{Y} - X)|\Gamma(X), \omega_2\} \tag{56}$$

In order to estimate $\nabla q_1(X)$, the expectations in (56) are replaced by the corresponding sample means. Equation (56) is based on the knowledge that

$$E\{(\mathbf{Y} - X)|\Gamma(X), \omega_i\} = \frac{2d^2}{n+2} \frac{\nabla p_i(X)}{p_i(X)} \tag{57}$$

where $d$ is the radius of $\Gamma(X)$, assuming $\Gamma(X)$ is a local hyperspherical region around $X$. Equation (57) is used to estimate the gradient of a density function for clustering and other applications.

(4)   *Polarized 2NN.* For $k = 2$, the Taylor series for $\hat{r}_{2NN}(X) - r_{2NN}(X)$ does not have the first-order term and starts from the second-order term. This suggests that the estimation of $\epsilon_{2NN}$ is fundamentally more reliable than the one of $\epsilon_{NN}$. The same property is observed in general $2kNN$ errors.

Furthermore, the $\hat{\epsilon}_{2NN}$ could be made closer to $\epsilon_{2NN}$ by choosing $X_{NN}$ and $X_{2NN}$ as follows:

Find the best pair $X_j$ and $X_k$ among the local samples in $\Gamma(X)$ by minimizing the polarized Euclidean distance, $\|(X_j - X) + (X_k - X)\|$.

This procedure is called a *polarized* 2NN *selection rule.* The Euclidean distance could be replaced by the optimal metric to add more reliability. Since the polarized $\hat{\epsilon}_{2NN}$ is more reliable than the conventional $\hat{\epsilon}_{NN}$, we could replace $\hat{\epsilon}_{NN}$ by $2\hat{\epsilon}_{2NN}$ to obtain the upper bound of the Bayes error.

## D   Use of Distances to the *k*NN

Up to now, the $k$NN approach was treated as a counting process, that is, the numbers of $\omega_1$ and $\omega_2$ neighbors were compared. A modification can be made to use the distance information to the $k$th NN.

Since $v = cd^n$, (43) is rewritten as

$$-\ln \hat{\mathbf{p}}_i(X) = n \ln \mathbf{d}_i(X) + \ln \frac{cN_i}{k - 1} \tag{58}$$

where $\mathbf{d}_i(X)$ is the distance from $X$ to the $k$th NN from $\omega_i$, $X_{kNN}^{(i)}$. The comparison of (58) with (7) indicates that $n \ln \mathbf{d}_i(X)$ is the *nonparametric version of the Mahalanobis distance,* $\frac{1}{2}(X - M_i)^T\Sigma_i^{-1}(X - M_i)$. Substituting (58) into (6), the Bayes classifier becomes

$$n \ln d_2(X) \mathop{\gtrless}^{\omega_1}_{\omega_2} n \ln d_1(X) + \ln \frac{N_1 P_2}{N_2 P_1} \tag{59}$$

Thus, $X$ is classified to the class of the smallest $d_i(X)$. Since (59) can be rewritten as $d_2(X) \gtrless d_1(X)(N_1 P_2/N_2 P_1)^{1/n}$, the constant term of (59) indicates how the *scales of distances* must be adjusted for various $N_i$'s and $P_i$'s.

## 1   Two-Dimensional Display of X [6]

Selecting $n \ln d_1(X)$ and $n \ln d_2(X)$ as $x$ and $y$ axes, $X$ may be plotted as shown in Fig. 7. In Fig. 7, 50 samples from $\omega_1$ and 150 samples from $\omega_2$ are generated according to eight-dimensional Gaussian distributions used in [1].

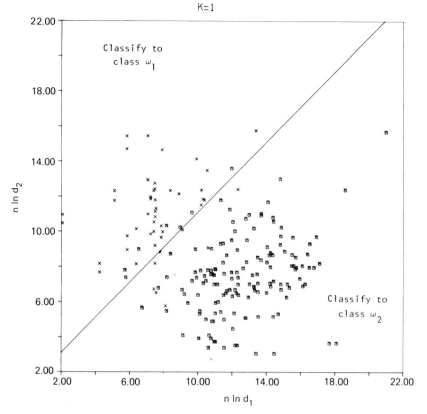

**Fig. 7.** Nonparametric display for $P_1 = P_2 = 0.5$, and $N_1 = 50$, $N_2 = 150$.

The proper weighting to the distances could be found from this display by shifting the 45° line. The power of the display is in its flexibility. Once samples are displayed, we could change the slope of the boundary line, shift the line, and even select a more complex curve for the boundary.

Also, the boundaries for the *Neyman–Pearson* and *minimax tests* can be found by shifting the 45° line to satisfy $\epsilon_2 = \epsilon_0$ and $\epsilon_1 = \epsilon_2$, respectively. The threshold value could be determined theoretically, but selecting the position of the line visually on the data display gives more flexibility, a better understanding of what we are doing, and even a better result in many cases.

**Bayes Risk Contour [6]    2**

Combining (2) and (43), the Bayes risk is related to $d_1(X)$ and $d_2(X)$ as

$$n \ln d_2(X) = n \ln d_1(X) + \ln \frac{N_1 P_2}{N_2 P_1} \pm \ln \frac{r^*(X)}{1 - r^*(X)} \qquad (60)$$

where $+$ and $-$ are used for $q_1(X) < q_2(X)$ and $q_1(X) > q_2(X)$, respectively. Hence, for a given level of $r^*(X)$, the contour becomes a $45°$ line. Figure 8 shows these constant risk lines for various values of $r^*(X)$. These risk lines are symmetric about the Bayes classifier $[r^*(X) = 0.5]$. In Fig. 8, the contours of the mixture density function, $p(X)$, are also plotted.

When we want to *reject* samples with, say, $0.4 \leq r^*(X) \leq 0.5$, the samples between two 0.4 risk lines are rejected. The number of the rejected samples divided by $N$ is $R(0.4)$ of (16). $\epsilon(0.4)$ of (17) is also obtained by counting the number of misclassified samples outside two 0.4 risk lines.

## 3 Bayes Error Estimation [6]

Using the distance information to the $k$th NN, the Bayes error itself could be estimated as follows:

$$\hat{r}^*(X) = \min\left[\frac{\hat{P}_1\hat{p}_1(X)}{\hat{P}_1\hat{p}_1(X) + \hat{P}_2\hat{p}_2(X)}, \frac{\hat{P}_2\hat{p}_2(X)}{\hat{P}_1\hat{p}_1(X) + \hat{P}_2\hat{p}_2(X)}\right]$$

$$= \min\left[\frac{v_2(X)}{v_1(X) + v_2(X)}, \frac{v_1(X)}{v_1(X) + v_2(X)}\right] \tag{61}$$

where $\hat{P}_i = N_i/N$ and (43) is used for $\hat{p}_i(X)$ with $k_1 = k_2$. The estimate of the Bayes error is obtained by replacing the expectation by a sample mean as

$$\hat{\epsilon}^* = \frac{1}{N}\sum_{i=1}^{N}\hat{r}^*(X_i) \tag{62}$$

This estimate is known to have a smaller variance than the conventional error counting. Although this is not guaranteed to bound the Bayes error, it has been experienced that the estimate gives a closer value to the Bayes error than $\hat{\epsilon}_{NN}$ and $\hat{\epsilon}_{2NN}$. The selection of a proper metric to measure nearness is important to obtain a reliable estimate.

## E Parzen Approach

When the Parzen density estimate is used for classification, there is no known relationship between the error due to the Parzen approach and the Bayes error. However, we know a more general guideline to find the bounds of the Bayes error as follows.

Let $S = \{P_1, p_1(X), P_2, p_2(X)\}$ be a set of all true distribution information, and let $\hat{S} = \{\hat{P}_1, \hat{p}_1(X), \hat{P}_2, \hat{p}_2(X)\}$ be a set of their estimates. The classification error depends on two sets and is written as $\epsilon(S_D, S_T)$. It means that the Bayes classifier is designed for $S_D$ and the error is computed by testing $S_T$. $S_D$

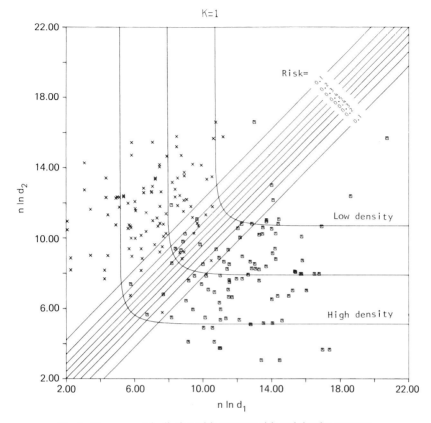

**Fig. 8.** Nonparametric display with constant risk and density contours.

and $S_T$ are not necessarily the same. Then, the Bayes error, $\varepsilon(S, S)$, is bounded by [1]

$$\mathrm{E}\{\varepsilon(\hat{\mathbf{S}}, \hat{\mathbf{S}})\} \leq \varepsilon(S, S) \leq \mathrm{E}\{\varepsilon(\hat{\mathbf{S}}, S)\} \tag{63}$$

This bound is based on the assumption that $\mathrm{E}\{\varepsilon(S, \hat{\mathbf{S}})\} = \varepsilon(S, S)$, that is, the error estimate is unbiased for test densities.

The lower bound is obtained by testing the same data used for design, and this testing procedure is called the *resubstitution method*. For the upper bound, the true distribution must be tested for the Bayes classifier designed by a given data set. Since the true distribution is never known, $S$ is often replaced by a data set $\hat{\mathbf{S}}_T$ which is not used for design. Although $\mathrm{E}\{\varepsilon(\hat{\mathbf{S}}, \hat{\mathbf{S}}_T)\}$ is not guaranteed to bound the Bayes error, it is generally accepted that the error of this procedure is larger than the Bayes error. This procedure is called the *hold-out method*. Another approach to the upper bound is the *leaving-one-out method*. With $N$ samples available, each sample is tested for the classifier designed by $N$-1 samples, excluding the tested sample. This is repeated $N$

times. Thus, in this method, the available samples are more effectively utilized. Also, we do not need to worry about how to divide samples, which is a problem in the hold-out method.

When the above test procedures are combined with the Parzen density estimate of (41), we obtain the following equations [1].

(1) *Resubstitution method:*

$$\frac{N_1}{N} \frac{1}{N_1} \sum_{i=1}^{N_1} g(X_k - X_i^{(1)}) \underset{\omega_2}{\overset{\omega_1}{\gtrless}} \frac{N_2}{N} \frac{1}{N_2} \sum_{j=1}^{N_2} g(X_k - X_j^{(2)})$$

(64)

$$\text{for testing } X_k \in \{X_1^{(1)}, \ldots, X_{N_1}^{(1)}, X_1^{(2)}, \ldots, X_{N_2}^{(2)}\}$$

where $X_j^{(i)}$ is the $j$th sample from $\omega_i$.

(2) *Leaving-one-out method:*

$$\frac{N_1 - 1}{N - 1} \frac{1}{N_1 - 1} \left[ \sum_{i=1}^{N_1} g(X_k - X_i^{(1)}) - g(0) \right] \underset{\omega_2}{\overset{\omega_1}{\gtrless}} \frac{N_2}{N - 1} \frac{1}{N_2} \sum_{j=1}^{N_2} g(X_k - X_j^{(2)})$$

(65)

$$\text{for testing } X_k \in \{X_1^{(1)}, \ldots, X_{N_1}^{(1)}\}$$

$$\frac{N_1}{N - 1} \frac{1}{N_1} \sum_{i=1}^{N_1} g(X_k - X_i^{(1)}) \underset{\omega_2}{\overset{\omega_1}{\gtrless}} \frac{N_2 - 1}{N - 1} \frac{1}{N_2 - 1} \sum_{j=1}^{N_2} [g(X_k - X_j^{(2)}) - g(0)]$$

(66)

$$\text{for testing } X_k \in \{X_1^{(2)}, \ldots, X_{N_2}^{(2)}\}$$

The leaving-one-out method lowers the $\omega_i$ density when a $\omega_i$ sample is tested and always has more error than the resubstitution method. Also, note that the additional computation in the leaving-one-out method is to subtract a constant $g(0)$. Thus, when the error is counted by the resubstitution method, the leaving-one-out error is also computed simultaneously with a negligible additional computation time.

The critical parameters for the Parzen approach are the mathematical form and the size of the kernel function. It is not well known how to choose these parameters.

## IV  CLASSIFIER DESIGN

Once the structure of data is studied thoroughly, it is easy to select a proper classifier for the data. This section presents how to design several typical classifiers.

The Bayes classifier becomes linear for the following two cases.

(1) *Gaussian* $\mathbf{X}$ *with* $\Sigma_1 = \Sigma_2 = \Sigma$ [1]. For this case, the Bayes classifier is expressed by (18), which is linear. In particular, when $\Sigma = I$,

$$h(X) = (M_2 - M_1)^{\mathrm{T}} X + \tfrac{1}{2}(M_1^{\mathrm{T}} M_1 - M_2^{\mathrm{T}} M_2) \underset{\omega_2}{\overset{\omega_1}{\lessgtr}} t \qquad (67)$$

This classifier is also known as the *distance classifier* in which $(X - M_1)^{\mathrm{T}}(X - M_1) \overset{\omega_1}{\underset{\omega_2}{\lessgtr}} (X - M_2)^{\mathrm{T}}(X - M_2)$, or the *correlation classifier* in which $M_1^{\mathrm{T}} X \overset{\omega_1}{\underset{\omega_2}{\gtrless}} M_2^{\mathrm{T}} X$ with an energy constant condition $M_1^{\mathrm{T}} M_1 = M_2^{\mathrm{T}} M_2$. In both cases, $P_1 = P_2$ and thus $t = 0$ is assumed. When $\Sigma \neq I$, the distance or correlation classifier must be applied, but only after $\mathbf{X}$ is linearly transformed to $\mathbf{Y} = A^{\mathrm{T}} \mathbf{X}$ in order to make $\Sigma_Y = A^{\mathrm{T}} \Sigma A = I$.

(2) *Binary independent* $\mathbf{x}_i$'s [1]. For independent $\mathbf{x}_j$'s taking either $+1$ or $-1$,

$$p_i(X) = \prod_{j=1}^{n} w_{ij}^{(1 + x_j)/2}(1 - w_{ij})^{(1 - x_j)/2}[\delta(x_j - 1) + \delta(x_j + 1)] \qquad (68)$$

where $w_{ij} = \mathrm{Pr}\{x_j = +1 | \omega_i\}$. Sunstituting (68) into (6),

$$h(X) = -\frac{1}{2}\left\{ \sum_{j=1}^{n}\left[ \ln \frac{w_{1j}(1 - w_{2j})}{w_{2j}(1 - w_{1j})} \right] x_j + \sum_{j=1}^{n}\left[ \ln \frac{w_{1j}(1 - w_{1j})}{w_{2j}(1 - w_{2j})} \right] \right\} \qquad (69)$$

For Gaussian $\mathbf{X}$ with $\Sigma_1 \neq \Sigma_2$ and more general non-Gaussian $\mathbf{X}$, a linear classifier is not the best one. However, because of its simplicity, a linear classifier is frequently adopted. The design procedure is as follows [1].

$$h(X) = V^{\mathrm{T}} X \overset{\omega_1}{\underset{\omega_2}{\lessgtr}} t \qquad (70)$$

Equation (70) indicates that $\mathbf{X}$ is linearly mapped down to a variable $\mathbf{h}$ and the distributions of $\mathbf{h}$ for $\omega_1$ and $\omega_2$ are separated by a threshold $t$. Thus, the optimum $V$ is found by minimizing the probability of error in the $h$ space. Because of complexity in the error computation, simpler criteria such as $f(m_1, m_2, \sigma_1^2, \sigma_2^2)$ are often used, where $m_i = \mathrm{E}\{h(\mathbf{X}) | \omega_i\} = V^{\mathrm{T}} M_i$ and $\sigma_i^2 = \mathrm{Var}\{h(\mathbf{X}) | \omega_i\} = V^{\mathrm{T}} \Sigma_i V$. The typical examples are

$$f = \frac{(m_1 - m_2)^2}{\sigma_1^2 + \sigma_2^2} \qquad \text{Fisher's criterion} \qquad (71)$$

$$f = \frac{P_1(m_1 - m_0)^2 + P_2(m_2 - m_0)^2}{P_1 \sigma_1^2 + P_2 \sigma_2^2} \qquad \left( \frac{\text{between class scatter}}{\text{within class scatter}} \right) \qquad (72)$$

$$(m_0 = P_1 m_1 + P_2 m_2 : \text{mixture mean})$$

These criteria measure the class separability of the distributions of $\mathbf{h}$. The solution of $\partial f/\partial V = 0$ is

$$V \sim [s\Sigma_1 + (1 - s)\Sigma_2]^{-1}(M_2 - M_1) \tag{73}$$

where

$$s = \frac{\partial f/\partial \sigma_1^2}{\partial f/\partial \sigma_1^2 + \partial f/\partial \sigma_2^2} \tag{74}$$

That is, the optimum $V$ always takes the form of (73) regardless of the functional form of $f$. The effect of $f$ is observed only in the averaging coefficient of covariance matrices, $s$. For example, $s = 0.5$ for (71) and $s = P_1$ for (72).

$V$ can be found even without specifying $f$. Since the form of $V$ is known as in (73), we change $s$ from 0 to 1 with a certain increment, say, 0.1, compute the empirical distribution functions of $\mathbf{h} = V^T\mathbf{X}$ for $\omega_1$ and $\omega_2$ from the given data set, set a threshold, and count the number of misclassified samples. The optimum $s$ is the one which gives the smallest error in this operation.

The Bhattacharyya bound of (37) gives a simple test to decide whether or not a linear classifier is appropriate. When the first term of (37) is dominant, the classifiability comes mainly from the mean difference. Therefore, a linear classifier is a proper choice. However, if the second term is significant, the covariance difference plays an important role, and a quadratic classifier is called for.

## B  Quadratic Classifiers

For Gaussian $\mathbf{X}$, the Bayes classifier becomes quadratic, as shown in (7) or (23). However, in practice, the quadratic classifier of (23) has been widely adopted in many applications, even without checking the Guassianness of $\mathbf{X}$, and with much success. Probably, this is the classifier everyone may try first, even before conducting data structure analysis.

However, it is not known how to design the optimum quadratic classifier as the linear classifier was designed. The optimization of $f(m_1, m_2, \sigma_1^2, \sigma_2^2)$ for $\mathbf{h} = \mathbf{X}^T Q \mathbf{X} + V^T\mathbf{X}$ with respect to a matrix $Q$ and a vector $V$ is too complex. If quadratic terms $\mathbf{x}_j\mathbf{x}_k$'s are treated as new variables $\mathbf{y}_i$, $\mathbf{h} = \Sigma\Sigma q_{jk}\mathbf{x}_j\mathbf{x}_k + \Sigma v_i\mathbf{x}_i$ can be considered as $\mathbf{h} = \Sigma a_i\mathbf{y}_i + \Sigma v_i\mathbf{x}_i$, which is a linear equation. However, for high-dimensional cases, the number of $\mathbf{y}_i$'s become prohibitively large.

## 1  Two-Dimensional Display

One of the procedures used to improve the performance of the quadratic classifier is to plot $\mathbf{X}$ in a two-dimensional display where $d_i^2(X) = (X - M_i)^T\Sigma_i^{-1}(X - M_i)$ for $i = 1, 2$ are used as the $x$ and $y$ axes. This is the

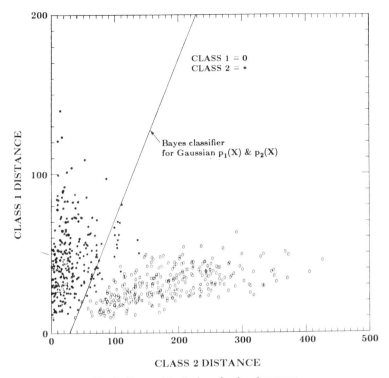

**Fig. 9.** Parametric display of radar signatures.

parametric version of Fig. 7. If $X$ is Gaussian, the Bayes classifier becomes a 45° line with a proper $y$-crossing point. Figure 9 shows the plot of samples taken from 40-dimensional radar signatures. Because the distribution in this case is not perfectly Gaussian, we can find a better line to classify samples by changing the slope and the $y$-crossing point of the line. It corresponds to adjusting $\alpha$ and $\beta$ of the following quadratic classifier:

$$d_2^2(X) \overset{\omega_1}{\underset{\omega_2}{\gtrless}} \alpha d_1^2(X) + \beta \qquad (75)$$

Once samples are plotted and examined, the boundary in the display need not be restricted to a line. Any curve could be drawn. This flexibility is the advantage of seeing the data in the display.

### *Stationary Random Processes* 2

The quadratic classifier is popular for classifying a stationary random process $\mathbf{x}(t)$. The process is normally converted to the absolute value square of the Fourier transform. The classification is carried out by comparing the weighted distances from an unknown $|X(\omega)|^2$ to the class means in the frequency domain. This corresponds to designing a quadratic classifier in the (sampled) time domain.

## C  Sequential Classifiers

When $m$ consecutive observation vectors, $X_1, \ldots, X_m$, are known as coming from the same class, we can use this additional information to reduce the classification error. That is, the number of variables is extended from $n$ for one vector to $m \times n$ for $m$ vectors. Thus, we can form a new random vector with $m \times n$ components and design a classifier in the $(m \times n)$-dimensional space. However, when these vectors are *statistically independent*, a simpler formula could be adopted as

$$-\ln[p_1(X_1, \ldots, X_m)/p_2(X_1, \ldots, X_m)] = \sum_{i=1}^{m} \{-\ln[p_1(X_i)/p_2(X_i)]\} \lessgtr t \quad (76)$$

That is, the likelihood ratio classifier is applied to the incoming sample $X_i$, and the output is accumulated. Rewriting the left-hand side of the inequality as

$$\mathbf{s} = \frac{1}{m} \sum_{i=1}^{m} h(\mathbf{X}_i) \quad (77)$$

the expected values and variances of $\mathbf{s}$ and $\mathbf{h} = h(\mathbf{X})$ are related by

$$\mathrm{E}\{\mathbf{s}|\omega_i\} = \mathrm{E}\{\mathbf{h}|\omega_i\} \quad \text{and} \quad \mathrm{Var}\{\mathbf{s}|\omega_i\} = \frac{1}{m}\mathrm{Var}\{\mathbf{h}|\omega_i\} \quad (78)$$

Thus, we can reduce the variances of $\mathbf{s}$ by increasing $m$, while maintaining the expected values of $\mathbf{s}$. Furthermore, the density function of $\mathbf{s}$ becomes close to a Gaussian by the central limit theorem.

Two important properties of the sequential classifier emerge from the above discussion. One is that we can make the error as small as we like by increasing $m$. The other is that the error is determined by a small number of parameters, $\mathrm{E}\{\mathbf{h}|\omega_i\}$, $\mathrm{Var}\{\mathbf{h}|\omega_i\}$, and $m$, and is little affected by the higher-order moments of $\mathbf{h}$.

In practice, the true $p_i(X)$'s are never known, and $h(X) = -\ln[p_1(X)/p_2(X)]$ must be replaced by some function $\hat{h}(X)$. A desired property for $\hat{h}(X)$ is

$$\mathrm{E}\{\hat{h}(\mathbf{X})|\omega_1\} \leq 0 \quad \text{and} \quad \mathrm{E}\{\hat{h}(\mathbf{X})|\omega_2\} \geq 0$$
$$\text{regardless of the distribution of } \mathbf{X} \quad (79)$$

As long as (79) is satisfied, the random variable $\hat{h}(\mathbf{X})$ carries classification information, however small, regardless of the distribution of $\mathbf{X}$. The classifiable information can be enhanced as much as we like by increasing $m$ in the sequential operations. Two $\hat{h}(X)$'s are known to satisfy (79) for all distributions of $X$, whose expected vectors and covariance matrices are $M_1$ and $\Sigma_1$ for $\omega_1$ and $M_2$ and $\Sigma_2$ for $\omega_2$:

$$\hat{h}(X) = (M_2 - M_1)^{\mathrm{T}}\Sigma^{-1}X + \tfrac{1}{2}(M_1^{\mathrm{T}}\Sigma^{-1}M_1 - M_2^{\mathrm{T}}\Sigma^{-1}M_2) \qquad (80)$$

$$\Sigma = s\Sigma_1 + (1 - s)\Sigma_2 \qquad (0 \le s \le 1) \qquad (81)$$

$$\hat{h}(X) = \tfrac{1}{2}(X - M_1)^{\mathrm{T}}\Sigma_1^{-1}(X - M_1)$$
$$- \tfrac{1}{2}(X - M_2)^{\mathrm{T}}\Sigma_2^{-1}(X - M_2) + \tfrac{1}{2}\ln(|\Sigma_1|/|\Sigma_2|) \qquad (82)$$

Equation (80) could be used, if the first term is dominant in the Bhattacharyya bound (37), and (82) is more appropriate otherwise. Note that these equations are the same as (18) and (23), respectively.

One of the most important aspects in classifier design is to make the classifier *robust*. That is, the performance of the classifier must be maintained, even if the distribution of test samples becomes somewhat different from the one used for design. The sequential technique can compensate the degradation of the performance of $h(X_i) \lessgtr t$ by increasing $m$.

One of the questions frequently asked about the sequential classifier is whether the averaging should be performed after or before the classifier. The theory of (76) dictates that the output of the Bayes classifier must be averaged. However, in practice, the quadratic classifier of (82) is often used in place of the Bayes classifier. Then, the averaging before the classifier gives, in many experiments, more or less the same or a slightly better performance than averaging after the classifier. This may be due to the fact that, by averaging, the input becomes more Gaussian in nature by the central limit theorem and is better suited to the quadratic classifier.

### Piecewise Classifiers   D

For the *multiclass problem*, the boundary must have a piecewise structure as follows.

(1) *Piecewise quadratic classifiers.* If $X$ is Gaussian, the classifier becomes piecewise quadratic as

$$\min_i[\tfrac{1}{2}(X - M_i)^{\mathrm{T}}\Sigma_i^{-1}(X - M_i) + \tfrac{1}{2}\ln|\Sigma_i|] \qquad (83)$$

Equation (83) is one of the most popular classifiers and is used widely even for non-Gaussian distributions.

(2) *Piecewise linear classifiers.* When $\Sigma_i$'s are similar, the quadratic term $X^{\mathrm{T}}\Sigma_i^{-1}X$ is eliminated from (83) to get a piecewise linear classifier as

$$\min_i[- M_i^{\mathrm{T}}\Sigma_i^{-1}X + \tfrac{1}{2}M_i^{\mathrm{T}}\Sigma_i^{-1}M_i + \tfrac{1}{2}\ln|\Sigma_i|] \qquad (84)$$

Or, replacing $\Sigma_i$ by the averaged covariance, $\Sigma = (\Sigma_1 + \cdots + \Sigma_L)/L$,

$$\min_i [-M_i^T \Sigma^{-1} X + \tfrac{1}{2} M_i^T \Sigma^{-1} M_i] \tag{85}$$

Another possibility is to design the optimal linear classifier for each pair of classes. In this case, $L(L-1)/2$ classifiers must be designed, instead of $L$ in (84) or (85).

(3) *Clustering.* In some applications, each class distribution had better be handled by dividing it into several clusters. For example, take the signatures of a target viewed from the front and side. Since they are so different, it may be more appropriate to separate them to two clusters rather than to treat all of them as one class.

Considering each cluster as a class, we can form a new multiclass problem with a significantly increased number of classes. However, the details of designing such a classifier depend so much on how clusters are defined and obtained and how many classes are generated. Therefore, although important, the subject is not discussed in this chapter.

(4) *k*NN. The *k*NN classifier forms a piecewise linear boundary, although it is very complex and data dependent. The simpler boundary could be obtained by merging samples into a smaller number of representatives.

## E   Nonparametric Classifiers

Although nonparametric techniques are important for the estimation of the Bayes error (an off-line computation), they are not popular as classifiers in practice. One of the reasons is that the classifier is too complex and time consuming for on-line operation. In addition to this, the performance of a nonparametric technique is not necessarily better than the one of a parametric classifier. Take the NN classifier for an example. It is known that $\epsilon_{NN}$ is between $\epsilon^*$ and $2\epsilon^*$, and that sometimes $\epsilon_{NN}$ is close to $2\epsilon^*$. In many applications, it is not difficult to find a proper parametric classifier which gives much closer error to $\epsilon^*$ than $\epsilon_{NN}$. Despite these disadvantages, a nonparametric classifier could still be adopted as the last resort when no mathematical structure can be found for the given data.

(1) *Edited* NN [3]. If we want to modify the NN classifier, the first goal must be to reduce the error. This can be achieved by editing the training samples as follows: for a given data set, perform the NN classification among them and store only correctly classified samples. Then, an unknown sample is classified according to the class of the nearest stored sample. The editing operation could be repeated to obtain a better set of stored samples.

(2) *Condensed* NN [3]. By storing only samples around the boundary, we can reduce the number of stored samples. Again, an unknown sample is

classified by the class of the nearest stored sample. The performance of this algorithm is close to the one of the NN classifier, and yet we can save the storage space and the computation time.

## CLASSIFIER EVALUATION   V

When a classifier is designed from a given data set, the classifier is normally tested by a different data set. This corresponds to the *hold-out method* of Section III.E and is supposed to give a pessimistic evaluation of the classifier error rate. On the other hand, an optimistic evaluation is obtained by using the same data set for both design and test (the *resubstitution method*). Thus, the true performance of the designed classifier is likely to be bounded by these two evaluations. The hold-out method can be replaced by the *leaving-one-out method*, in which the available data set is more effectively utilized.

In general, the computation time to perform both the resubstitution and leaving-one-out methods simultaneously is almost equivalent to the one for the resubstitution method alone. This was shown for the Parzen approach in Section III.E. In this section, the parametric version will be presented. Since the quadratic classifier of (23) is one of the most popular parametric classifiers, we show how to evaluate the performance of this classifier [1].

### *Resubstitution Method*   1

All available samples, $X_1^{(1)}, \ldots, X_{N_1}^{(1)}$ from $\omega_1$ and $X_1^{(2)}, \ldots, X_{N_2}^{(2)}$ from $\omega_2$, are used to estimate $\hat{M}_i$, $\hat{\Sigma}_i$, and $\hat{P}_i (i = 1, 2)$. Then, the same samples are tested as to whether or not the following inequality is satisfied:

$$h_r(X_k) = \frac{1}{2}(X_k - \hat{M}_1)^T \hat{\Sigma}_1^{-1}(X_k - \hat{M}_1) - \frac{1}{2}(X_k - \hat{M}_2)^T \hat{\Sigma}_2^{-1}(X_k - \hat{M}_2)$$

$$+ \frac{1}{2} \ln \frac{|\hat{\Sigma}_1|}{|\hat{\Sigma}_2|} - \ln \frac{\hat{P}_1}{\hat{P}_2} \underset{\omega_2}{\overset{\omega_1}{\lessgtr}} 0 \qquad (86)$$

for testing $X_k \in \{X_1^{(1)}, \ldots, X_{N_1}^{(1)}, X_1^{(2)}, \ldots, X_{N_2}^{(2)}\}$

where

$$\hat{M}_i = \frac{1}{N_i} \sum_{j=1}^{N_i} X_j^{(i)}, \qquad \hat{\Sigma}_i = \frac{1}{N_i - 1} \sum_{j=1}^{N_i} (X_j^{(i)} - \hat{M}_i)(X_j^{(i)} - \hat{M}_i)^T$$

$$\hat{P}_i = N_i/(N_1 + N_2) \qquad (87)$$

Then, the number of misclassified samples is counted. This error is supposed to be smaller than the true error of the classifier.

## 2   Leaving-One-Out Method

When $X_k^{(1)} \in \omega_1$ is tested, $X_k^{(1)}$ is excluded from the computations of $\hat{M}_1$, $\hat{\Sigma}_1$, and $\hat{P}_1$, and the modified $\hat{M}_1$, $\hat{\Sigma}_1$, and $\hat{P}_1$ are used in (86). Similarly, $\hat{M}_2$, $\hat{\Sigma}_2$ and $\hat{P}_2$ are modified for testing $X_k^{(2)} \in \omega_2$. The resulting quadratic equation, $h_l(X_k)$, becomes

$$h_l(X_k) = h_r(X_k) + \begin{cases} +g(N_1, \hat{d}_1^2(X_k)) & \text{for} \quad X_k \in \omega_1 \\ -g(N_2, \hat{d}_2^2(X_k)) & \text{for} \quad X_k \in \omega_2 \end{cases} \tag{88}$$

where

$$g(N_i, \hat{d}_i^2(X_k)) = \frac{1}{2} \frac{(N_i^2 - 3N_i + 1)\hat{d}_i^2(X_k)/(N_i - 1) + N_i\hat{d}_i^4(X_k)}{(N_i - 1)^2 - N_i\hat{d}_i^2(X_k)}$$

$$+ \frac{1}{2} \ln\left[ 1 - \frac{N_i}{(N_i - 1)^2} \hat{d}_i^2(X_k) \right] + \ln \frac{N_i}{N_i - 1} + \frac{n}{2} \ln \frac{N_i - 1}{N_i - 2} > 0 \tag{89}$$

and

$$\hat{d}_i^2(X_k) = (X_k - \hat{M}_i)^{\mathsf{T}}\hat{\Sigma}_i^{-1}(X_k - \hat{M}_i) \tag{90}$$

Equation (88) indicates that, for $X_k \in \omega_1$, $h_l(X_k)$ is larger than $h_r(X_k)$, and the chance of $X_k$ being misclassified is increased. The same is true for $X_k \in \omega_2$. Therefore, the leaving-one-out error is always larger than the resubstitution error.

When the resubstitution method is used to count the error, $h_r(X_k)$ and $\hat{d}_i^2(X_k)$ $(i = 1, 2)$ must be computed for all $(N_1 + N_2)X_k$'s. The leaving-one-method requires an additional computation of (89) for each $k$. However, since (89) is a scalar function, the computation time for this part is negligibly small. Thus, when $h_r(X_k)$ is computed and tested for each $X_k$, $h_l(X_k)$ is also computed and tested at the same time.

## 3   Comparison of Parametric and Nonparametric Error

The errors of the parametric classifier must be compared with the upper and lower bounds of the Bayes errors, computed by a nonparametric technique. Figure 10 shows such plots for three cases. In Fig. 10B, the classifier error is much higher than the Bayes error of the given data. Therefore, the mathematical form of the classifier is not appropriate, and a better classifier should be found. In Fig. 10A, the classifier error seems close to the Bayes error, although the exact value of the Bayes error is unknown. This classifier is acceptable. The classifier error should not be smaller than the Bayes error, as in Fig. 10C. However, this often happens in practice. In this case, the nonparametric error bounds should be reexamined, since the

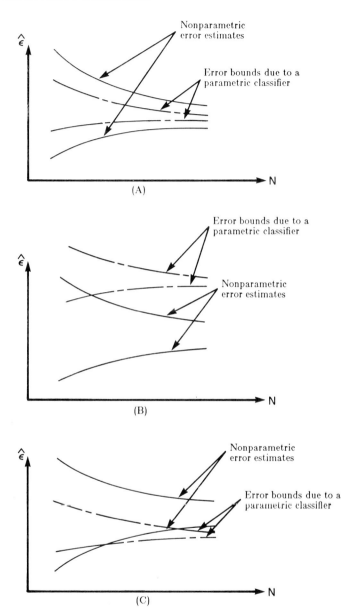

**Fig. 10.** Parametric and nonparametric error bounds. (A) Acceptable classifier, (B) unacceptable classifier, (C) the case in which something is wrong with the nonparametric error estimates.

parametric operation is, in general, much more reliable than the nonparametric one. Improper selection of metric often results in higher bounds than the true ones.

## NOTATION

| | |
|---|---|
| $n$ | Dimensionality |
| $L$ | Number of classes |
| $N$ | Number of total samples |
| $N_i$ | Number of class $i$ samples |
| $\omega_i$ | Class $i$ |
| $P_i$ | *A priori* probability of $\omega_i$ |
| $X = [x_1 x_2 \cdots x_n]^T$ | Vector |
| $\mathbf{X} = [\mathbf{x}_1 \mathbf{x}_2 \cdots \mathbf{x}_n]^T$ | Random vector |
| $p_i(X) = p_i(x_1, x_2, \ldots, x_n)$ | Conditional density function of $\omega_i$ |
| $p(X) = \sum_{i=1}^{L} P_i p_i(X)$ | Density function |
| $q_i(X) = P_i p_i(X)/p(X)$ | *A posteriori* probability of $\omega_i$ given $X$ |
| $M_i = \{\mathbf{X} \mid \omega_i\}$ | Expected vector of $\omega_i$ |
| $M = E\{\mathbf{X}\} = \sum_{i=1}^{L} P_i M_i$ | Expected vector |
| $\Sigma_i = E\{(\mathbf{X} - M_i)(\mathbf{X} - M_i)^T \mid \omega_i\}$ | Covariance matrix of $\omega_i$ |
| $\Sigma = E\{(\mathbf{X} - M)(\mathbf{X} - M)^T\}$ | |
| $\quad = \sum_{i=1}^{L} \{P_i \Sigma_i + P_i(M_i - M)(M_i - M)^T\}$ | Covariance matrix |

## REFERENCES

1. K. Fukunaga, "Introduction to Statistical Pattern Recognition." Academic Press, New York, 1972.
2. R. O. Duda and P. E. Hart, "Pattern Classification and Scene Analysis." Wiley, New York, 1973.
3. P. R. Devijver and J. Kittler, "Pattern Recognition: A Statistical Approach." Prentice Hall, Englewood Cliffs, New Jersey, 1982.
4. A. K. Agrawala (ed.), "Machine Recognition of Patterns." IEEE Press, New York, 1977.
5. L. N. Kanal, Patterns in pattern recognition: 1968–1972. *Trans. IEEE Information Theory* **IT-20,** 697–722 (November 1974).
6. K. Fukunaga, The estimation of the Bayes error by the $k$-nearest neighbor approach, in "Progress in Pattern Recognition" (L. N. Kanal and A. Rosenfeld, eds.), Vol. 2, North-Holland Publ., Amsterdam, 1985.
7. "Handbook of Statistics 2: Classification, Pattern Recognition and Reduction of Dimensionality." North-Holland Publ., Amsterdam, 1982.

# Chapter **2**

# Cluster Analysis

ANIL K. JAIN
Department of Computer Science
Michigan State University
East Lansing, Michigan

## INTRODUCTION   I

A number of scientific disciplines classify data according to measured or perceived similarities. However, in many classification and decision-making problems, there is little prior information available about the data and the decision-maker wishes to make as few assumptions about the data as possible. This restricts one to studying the interrelationships among the data points to make a preliminary assessment of their structure. Such situations come under the domain of exploratory data analysis. Cluster analysis is one tool of exploratory data analysis that attempts to assess the interaction among patterns by organizing the patterns into groups or clusters such that patterns within a cluster are more similar to each other than are patterns belonging to different clusters. Cluster analysis, along with the techniques of

33

intrinsic dimensionality, ordination, projection, feature extraction, and decision-making, allows a scientist to get acquainted with data at a preliminary stage of inquiry. The results of cluster analysis can be used to initiate hypotheses about the data, to classify new data, to test for homogeneity of the data, and to compress the data.

The field of cluster analysis is not new. While the use of clustering in pattern recognition and image processing is relatively recent, it has long been used in other disciplines, such as biology, psychiatry, psychology, archaeology, geology, marketing, and information retrieval [1]. Other terms used to describe clustering include numerical taxonomy, morphometrics, botryology, nosology, and systematics. The context usually suggests an appropriate choice of terminology. A recent review of clustering by Dubes and Jain [2] contains 250 citations from 77 journals along with 40 books. This vast literature on clustering emphasizes its importance and interdisciplinary nature. A number of software packages for cluster analysis are now commercially available, which will undoubtedly lead to further applications of cluster analysis.

Figure 1 shows a number of data sets in two dimensions. While each data set reveals two clusters, there is no single clustering technique currently available that can uncover all these structures. A majority of the clustering algorithms find clusters of a particular shape. Humans are the best cluster seekers in two dimensions, but most real problems involve clustering in higher dimensions. The difficulty with an intuitive interpretation of data embedded in high-dimensional space is obvious. In addition, data hardly ever follow the ideal structures shown in Fig. 1. This explains the large number of clustering algorithms which continue to appear in the literature; each new clustering algorithm performs slightly better than the existing ones on a specific data structure. Nevertheless, a systematic categorization of large volumes of multidimensional data necessitates the use of clustering algorithms.

The literature teems with clustering algorithms for exploring data but is deficient in objective procedures for verifying results, comparing algorithms, and answering specific questions about the gross structure of data. One of the serious drawbacks of clustering algorithms is that they will find clusters even if the data set is entirely random. Recent concerns about questions like "Are the data random?" and "How many clusters?" have led to the emerging discipline of clustering tendency and cluster validity [3]. The framework for clustering proposed by Dubes and Jain [3] consists of testing for the tendency of data to cluster before applying a clustering algorithm, and then verifying the clusters generated by the algorithm.

This chapter will provide a brief overview of cluster analysis. Our objective is to highlight the techniques available and the problems which a user is likely to face in applying clustering algorithms. For more details, we refer the user

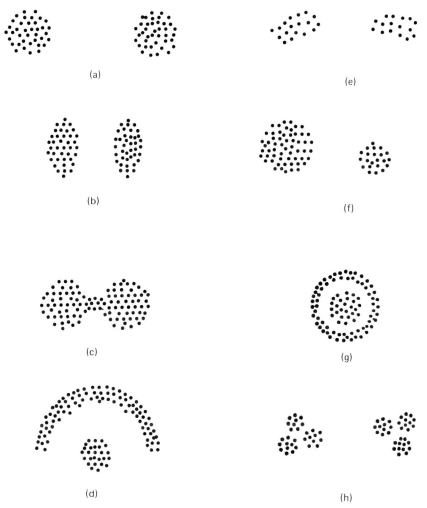

**Fig. 1.** Data sets exhibiting different clustering structures: (a) compact and well-separated clusters, (b) elongated clusters, (c) touching clusters, (d) linear nonseparable clusters, (e) noncompact clusters, (f) unequal cluster size, (g) concentric clusters, and (h) clusters within clusters.

to the excellent textbooks by Anderberg [1] and Everitt [4]. Dubes and Jain [2] provide a good tutorial that emphasizes clustering tendency and cluster verification, which is not summarized elsewhere, as well as a rich source of references for major and influential papers in the field of clustering. A user interested in obtaining a clustering package should consult Blashfield *et al.* [5]. Everitt [6] summarizes the difficulties and problems in cluster analysis.

## A Relationship to Statistical Pattern Recognition

Cluster analysis is closely related to statistical pattern recognition. The paradigm of statistical pattern recognition can be summarized as follows. A given pattern is to be assigned to one of $C$ categories $w_1, w_2, \ldots, w_C$ based on a feature vector $\mathbf{x} = (x_1, x_2, \ldots, x_p)$ measured on the pattern. The decision rule involves the class-conditioned densities $p(\mathbf{x}|w_i)$ and the a priori probabilities $p(w_i)$, $i = 1, 2, \ldots, C$. The class-conditional densities are never known in practice, so the strategies utilized to design a classifier in statistical pattern recognition depend on what kind of information is available about the class-conditional densities [7]. If it is assumed that the form of the class-conditional densities is known, then we have a parametric decision problem. Otherwise, we must either estimate the density function or use some nonparametric decision rule. The estimation of either parameters or the density function requires the availability of learning or training samples. Another dichotomy in statistical pattern recognition is that of supervised learning (labeled training samples) versus unsupervised learning (unlabeled training samples). The label on each training pattern represents the class or category to which that pattern belongs.

The various dichotomies which appear in statistical pattern recognition are shown in the tree structure of Fig. 2. The classification problems get more difficult as one traverses the tree from top to bottom and left to right. In cluster analysis, since very little information is available about the data, we are essentially working in the nonparametric and unsupervised learning mode. Further, in cluster analysis we often have no knowledge about the number of categories present in the data. Clustering methods have been touted as tools for discovery, rather than ends in themselves. Therefore, we tend to search for more descriptive structures when evaluating a clustering than we would, for example, when evaluating a decision rule for discriminating between two Gaussian distributions.

## B Data

Clustering algorithms organize data, and data are collected in several formats, sizes, and shapes. There are two popular forms of data representation: the pattern matrix and the proximity matrix. Proximity data occurs as an $n \times n$ proximity matrix whose rows and columns both represent patterns and whose entries measure proximity (similarity or dissimilarity) between all pairs of patterns. This type of data occurs most frequently in applications from the social and behavioral sciences. A pattern matrix is an $n \times p$ matrix, where each row is a pattern and each column denotes a feature. The $p$ features are viewed as a set of orthogonal axes, and each pattern is represented as a

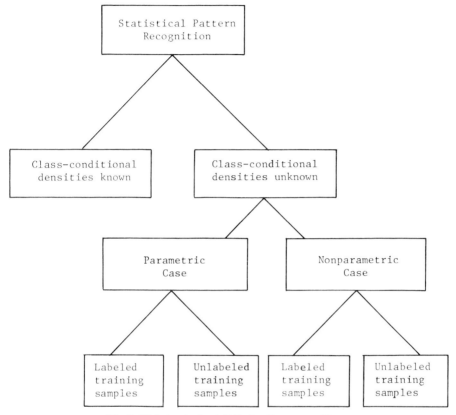

**Fig. 2.** Dichotomies in statistical pattern recognition.

point in this $p$-dimensional space, called the pattern space. A proximity matrix can be derived from a pattern matrix using Euclidean distance techniques, but ordination techniques [8] are needed to create a pattern matrix from a proximity matrix. We will concentrate only on the pattern matrix representation of the data since in various pattern recognition and image processing applications, data is available in this form. While one is usually interested in clustering the patterns, some feature-selection techniques are based on clustering the features.

The choice of variables or measurements or features to describe the patterns is very important. While this is dictated by the application area and the perception and prior experience of the investigator, it is important to keep the number of features small for ease in computation and interpretation of results. Another important consideration in cluster analysis is whether or not the data should be normalized. Often the features are measured on different units, and the patterns need to be normalized so that no single feature

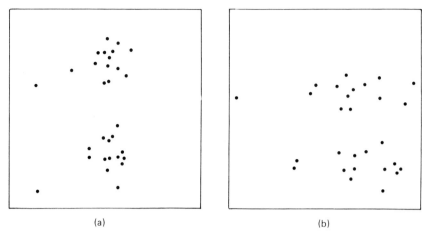

**Fig. 3.** Effect of scaling on cluster structure: (a) original data; (b) scaled data.

overwhelms the data merely because of scale. The most commonly used normalization replaces each feature with a new one whose mean value is zero and standard deviation is one. This normalization, however, should be used with caution since it can distort the clustering structure present in the data, as is demonstrated by Fig. 3.

Clustering algorithms group patterns based on some measure of similarity or dissimilarity between the patterns. Everitt [4] correctly points out that the output of a clustering algorithm will only be as meaningful as the input distances among the patterns. Euclidean distance is the most popular distance measure. In many situations, Mahalanobis distance is preferred because it takes into account the correlation among features and is unaffected by a change of scale of the features [4]. However, it is important to note that different distance measures can lead to different partitions of the same data.

## C   Ideal Cluster

A number of definitions for a cluster have been proposed, but no single definition of cluster is adequate, as seen from Fig. 1. Everitt [4] provides a number of these definitions, some of which are reproduced below.

(1)   A cluster is a set of entities which are *alike*, and entities from different clusters are not alike.

(2)   A cluster is an aggregation of points in the test space such that the *distance* between any two points in the cluster is less than the distance between any point in the cluster and any point not in it.

(3)   Clusters may be described as connected regions of a $p$-dimensional space containing a relatively *high density* of points, separated from other such regions by a region containing a relatively low density of points.

Michalski and Stepp [9] criticize these traditional definitions because they do not take into consideration any "Gestalt" concepts which people seem to use in grouping objects.

It is clear that the user's prior ceonception determines what a cluster means and sets the goal for a clustering method. One can formulate an idea of a cluster from an assumed mathematical model for data generation or from prior work in the subject matter. For example, one can picture each cluster as a single point to which measurement noise has been added in the direction of each feature. A reasonable idea of a cluster would then be a spherical or hyperellipsoidal swarm of patterns. Several partitional clustering methods proposed in the literature are based on idealized clustering structures of this type and essentially fit a mixture of Gaussian distributions to the given data. Some clustering algorithms always place the two patterns which are closest in the same cluster.

The clustering method chosen should depend on the notion of an ideal cluster. For example, the single-link hierarchical method generates loosely connected, or straggly, clusters, while the complete-link method generates compact clusters. However, if the data do not satisfy the assumptions made by a clustering technique, then it may impose a structure on the data instead of uncovering the true structure.

## CLUSTERING TECHNIQUES    II

The large number of clustering algorithms available in the literature can be broadly classified into one of two types: (i) hierarchical or (ii) partitional. A hierarchical clustering technique imposes a hierarchical structure on the data which consists of a sequence of clusterings. We will only treat the case when each clustering is a partition and the partitions are nested. The resulting hierarchical structure is pictorially represented as a tree diagram or a dendrogram. Depending on the algorithmic approach taken, a hierarchical structure begins with $n$ clusters, one per pattern, and grows a sequence of clusterings until all $n$ patterns are in a single cluster (agglomerative approach), or begins with one cluster containing all $n$ patterns and successively divides clusters until $n$ clusters are achieved (divisive approach). Hierarchical techniques are more popular in the biological sciences, where the data (e.g., plants, animals) often represent a taxonomy.

A partitional clustering technique organizes the patterns into a small number of clusters by labeling each pattern in some way. Unlike hierarchical techniques, which give a sequence of partitions, a partitional clustering technique gives a single partition. A pattern matrix is usually clustered in this way, which explains the popularity of these techniques in pattern recognition and image processing. Partitional techniques make use of criterion functions (square error), density estimators (mode seeking), graph structures, and nearest neighbors. Fuzzy partitional clustering deals with the overlapping case in which each pattern is allowed to belong to several classes with a measure of "belongingness" to each [10, 11].

It is important to distinguish between clustering techniques or methods and clustering algorithms or programs [12]. The same clustering technique can be implemented differently, resulting in several clustering algorithms. For example, a number of popular partitional clustering algorithms, such as ISODATA, FORGY, WISH, and CLUSTER [12], are essentially based on the technique of finding clusters that minimize the square error of the partition.

We will present a few of the more popular clustering algorithms, along with their performance on the well-known *Iris* data set. This data set contains measurements on three species of *Iris*. There are 50 patterns from each species, and four features (petal length, petal width, sepal length, and sepal width) are measured on each pattern. Figure 4 shows a projection of the data to the two eigenvectors corresponding to the two largest eigenvalues using the principal component method [8]. The points in this plot are labeled by category information (1, *I. setosa*; 2, *I. versicolor*; 3, *I. virginica*).

## A   Hierarchical Clustering Techniques

A hierarchical clustering technique essentially transforms a proximity matrix into a dendrogram. These techniques expect that the data are available in the form of a proximity matrix. In general, an agglomerative hierarchical technique consists of the following steps.

(1)   Assign each pattern to a unique cluster.
(2)   Find the smallest entry in the dissimilarity matrix and merge the corresponding two clusters.
(3)   Update the dissimilarities between the new cluster and other clusters.
(4)   Return to step (2) until all patterns fall into one cluster.

Various algorithms can be constructed depending on the procedure used to update the dissimilarities in step (3) above. Most of the commonly used updating procedures can be expressed in a single formula which gives the dissimilarity between a cluster $k$ and a cluster $i + j$ formed by the merger of clusters $i$ and $j$:

$$d(i + j, k) = a_i d(i, k) + a_j d(j, k) + bd(i, j) + c|d(i, k) - d(j, k)|$$

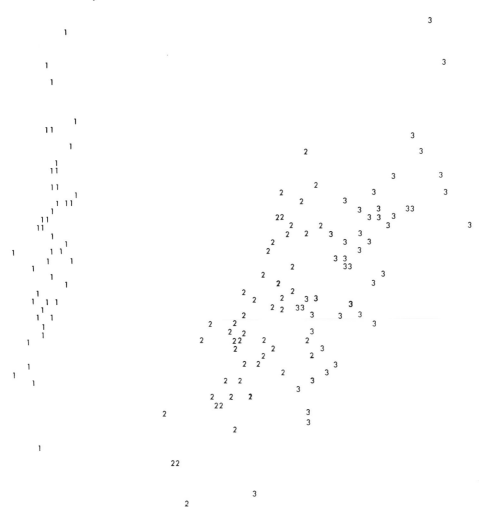

**Fig. 4.** Principal component projection of *Iris* data.

where $d(i, j)$ is the distance between clusters $i$ and $j$ and $a_i$, $a_j$, $b$, and $c$ are parameters whose values depend on the clustering strategy used. This updating formula is not suitable if the entries in the proximity matrix are on an ordinal scale. Table I gives the values of these parameters for some of the popular algorithms. These agglomerative algorithms are easy to implement and are available in most clustering packages.

Single-link and complete-link dendrograms for the *Iris* data are shown in Figs. 5 and 6, respectively. For ease in the presentation of the dendrograms, only a subset of the *Iris* data (total of 60 patterns, 20 per category) has been considered. This highlights one of the disadvantages of the hierarchical

**TABLE I**

**Properties of Six Hierarchical Clustering Algorithms**

| Clustering algorithm | Dissimilarity update formula[a] |
|---|---|
| Single-link (nearest neighbor) | $a_i = a_j = 0.5; \quad b = 0; \quad c = -0.5$ <br> $d(i + j, k) = \min\{d(i, k), d(j, k)\}$ |
| Complete-link (diameter) | $a_i = a_j = 0.5; \quad b = 0; \quad c = 0.5$ <br> $d(i + j, k) = \max\{d(i, k), d(j, k)\}$ |
| Centroid | $a_i = \dfrac{n_i}{n_i + n_j}; \quad a_j = \dfrac{n_j}{n_i + n_j}; \quad b = -\dfrac{n_i n_j}{(n_i + n_j)^2}; \quad c = 0$ |
| Median | $a_i = a_j = 0.5; \quad b = -0.25; \quad c = 0$ |
| Group average (average link, UPGMA) | $a_i = \dfrac{n_i}{n_i + n_j}; \quad a_j = \dfrac{n_j}{n_i + n_j}; \quad b = c = 0$ |
| Ward's method (minimum variance) | $a_i = \dfrac{n_k + n_i}{n_k + n_i + n_j}; \quad a_j = \dfrac{n_k + n_j}{n_k + n_i + n_j}; \quad b = -\dfrac{n_k}{n_k + n_i + n_j}; \quad c = 0$ |

[a] $n_i$ is the number of patterns in cluster $i$.

techniques. Even though the tree diagram shows the relationship among the patterns, it can be effectively used only for a small number ($<200$) of patterns. The numbers in the top row of Figs. 5 and 6 are the pattern numbers, which range from 1 to 60 (1–20 for *I. setosa*, 20–40 for *I. versicolor*, and 40–60 for *I. virginica*). The numbers along the column indicate some of the dissimilarity values where patterns or clusters merge to form new clusters. Both dendrograms show that pattern numbers 1 and 6, and 11 and 12 are the most similar and hence they group together first to form two clusters.

Various partitions from these dendrograms can be obtained by cutting the dendrogram at some level of dissimilarity. In Fig. 5, cutting the dendrogram at a dissimilarity value of 1.30 results in a partition containing two clusters. One of these clusters has all the 20 patterns belonging to *I. setosa*, and the other cluster, containing 40 patterns, groups together the remaining two categories. In order to get three representative clusters, one per category, we will have to cut the dendrogram at a dissimilarity value of approximately 0.78. Of course, a priori, we don't know how many clusters are present in the data. So where should we cut the dendrogram? A heuristic used is to choose that value of dissimilarity where there is a large vertical "gap" in the dendrogram. In other words, meaningful clusters are those which have a large "lifetime," where the lifetime of a cluster is the difference between the dissimilarity value at which the cluster merges with another cluster and the dissimilarity value at which the cluster is formed. Based on this heuristic, it is more reasonable to cut the single-link dendrogram in Fig. 5 at a level of 1.3 than at the level of 0.78.

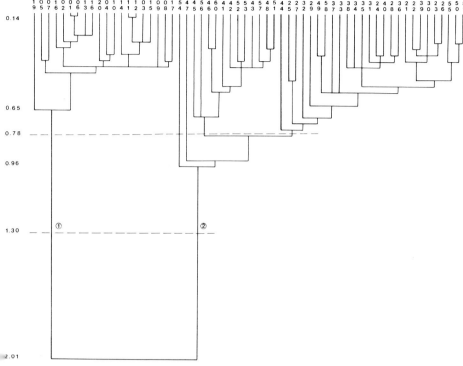

**Fig. 5.** Single-link dendrogram of *Iris* data.

The complete-link dendrogram (Fig. 6) gives a better clustering than the single-link method. Cutting the dendrogram at a dissimilarity value of 3.48 appears reasonable and results in three clusters. Since we do have category information about the patterns, we can construct a cluster by a category table or a confusion matrix to see how good this partition is in terms of grouping patterns which belong to the same category. Note that the category information was not used in forming the clusters. Table II shows that cluster 1 contains all the patterns from *I. setosa*, cluster 2 contains most of the patterns from *I. versicolor*, and cluster 3 contains a mixture of patterns from *Iris versicolor* and *I. virginica*. This grouping is supported by the two-dimensional plot of *Iris* data shown in Fig. 4, which shows that *I. setosa* is well separated from the other two categories.

Given the fact that the single-link and complete-link dendrograms are different and hence lead to different clusterings for the same data, which method should be used? Unfortunately, no guidelines are available for a potential user. Several attempts have been made to justify the use of the single-link method on a mathematical basis but, in practice, this method suffers from a "chaining" effect, whereby points which are further removed

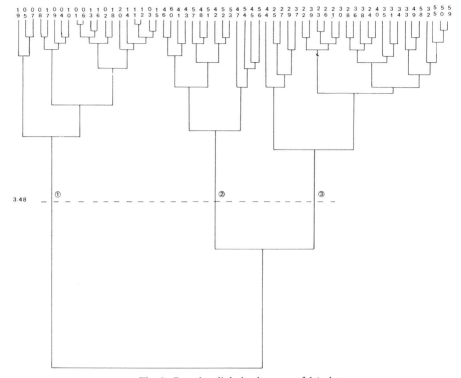

**Fig. 6.** Complete-link dendrogram of *Iris* data.

from each other are put in the same cluster because they share a neighbor. The relationship between the single-link method and the minimal spanning tree [13] has also been established.

In many applications, the given data is in the form of an ordinal proximity matrix. This is especially true when the data is collected in the social and behavioral sciences. In these situations, hierarchical clustering can be posed in terms of threshold and proximity graphs [2]. Clusters can be defined which

TABLE II

**Cluster-by-Category Table for Complete-Link Clustering**

| Cluster number | Category | | |
|---|---|---|---|
| | *I. setosa* | *I. versicolor* | *I. virginica* |
| 1 | 20 | 0 | 0 |
| 2 | 0 | 14 | 0 |
| 3 | 0 | 6 | 20 |

satisfy the properties of $k$-node connectivity, $k$-edge connectivity, $k$-minimum degree, $k$ diameter, and $k$ radius.

### Partitional Clustering Techniques   B

Partitional clustering techniques partition the given set of $n$ patterns into $C$ clusters, where $C \ll n$. The desired number of clusters, $C$, is usually specified by the user. Partitional techniques usually operate on a pattern matrix and result in a single partition. Unlike hierarchical techniques, partitional techniques allow patterns to move from one cluster to the other so that a poor initial partition can be corrected later. A majority of partitional techniques obtain that partition which maximizes some criterion function. However, finding an optimal partition is not computationally feasible (e.g., there are $1.93 \times 10^8$ different partitions of 19 patterns into 3 clusters). Therefore, most partitional techniques use some heuristics to cut down the amount of computation, but then they usually give only suboptimal partitions. Among all the criteria used to generate a partition, the square-error criterion is the most popular. Of course, using this criterion implies that one is interested in seeking hyperellipsoidal-shaped clusters.

The partitional clustering techniques based on mode seeking and mixture resolving also assume hyperellipsoidal-shaped clusters (Gaussian-based model). Techniques using minimal spanning trees, relative neighborhood graphs, or near neighbors are capable of finding clusters of various shapes (nonhyperellipsoidal), but their results are difficult to interpret [2]. We will only describe the square-error clustering methods.

Given a set of $n$ patterns in $p$ dimensions and a partition of this data into $C$ clusters, we define the square error for cluster $k$ as

$$e_k^2 = \sum_{i \in I_k} (x_i - m_k)^t (x_i - m_k)$$

where $x_i$ is the $i$th pattern, $m_k$ the mean vector of the patterns belonging to cluster $k$, and $I_k$ the set of integers corresponding to the subscripts of the patterns in cluster $k$. The square error for the clustering is

$$E_C^2 = \sum_{k=1}^{C} e_k^2$$

The objective is to obtain that partition which minimizes $E_C^2$ for a given $C$. It can be shown that $E_C^2$ is a monotonically decreasing function of $C$. The square error is zero when the number of clusters equals the number of patterns.

Clusterings obtained by minimizing the square error are also referred to as

**TABLE III**

**Criterion Functions Based on Scatter Matrices**[a]

| Criterion function | Property |
|---|---|
| (1)  Minimize $\text{Tr}(S_W)$ | $\text{Tr}(S_W) = E_C^2$ |
| (2)  Minimize $|S_W|/|S|$ | Partition that minimizes $|S_W|$ is similar to one that minimizes $E_C^2$. Criterion is invariant to nonsingular linear transformations of the data |
| (3)  Maximize $\text{Tr}(S_W^{-1}S_B)$ | Equivalent to minimizing the square error under the Mahalanobis metric |
| (4)  Minimize $\text{Tr}(S^{-1}S_W)$ | Identical to minimizing $E_C^2$ for normalized data (so that $S$ becomes an identity matrix) |

[a] Tr denotes the trace of a matrix.

minimum variance partitions. In spite of the popularity of square error as a criterion function, it is suitable primarily when the clusters form essentially compact clouds that are rather well separated from one another [7]. Another problem occurs when the number of patterns in two clusters are quite different. Quite often the square error is smaller for a partition that splits the large cluster.

The square-error criterion is related to another class of criterion functions derived from the scatter matrices used in discriminant analysis [7]. A number of these criteria based on the within-cluster scatter matrix $S_W$, the between-cluster scatter matrix $S_B$, and the total scatter matrix $S$ are given in Table III along with their properties. Note that partitions obtained based on minimizing square error when Euclidean distance is used are not invariant to linear transformation of the data. However, criteria 2–4 in Table III are invariant under nonsingular linear transformations of the data. Even these statistical criterion functions generate clusters that are essentially hyperellipsoidal in shape.

The square error is minimized iteratively but there is no guarantee of obtaining the global minimum. A partitional technique utilizing this approach consists of the following steps.

(1)  Initiate the cluster centers, or establish the first partition.
(2)  Update cluster membership, or allocate patterns to clusters.
(3)  Delete and merge clusters and identify outliers.
(4)  Stop when the error is below a threshold or the number of iterations has exceeded a prespecified limit.

Various algorithms which implement the square-error strategy differ in the heuristics used in the above steps. However, these heuristics are critical to the success or failure of a clustering program on a given data set. We will briefly describe two of the square-error clustering programs [12].

This program starts with $C$ randomly chosen patterns, where $C$ is the number of clusters desired by the user. An initial partition is obtained by assigning patterns to the closest cluster center. The Euclidean metric is used to compute the distances. The new cluster center is simply the average of all the patterns assigned to that cluster. The iteration continues until either the cluster labels do not change or the number of iterations exceeds a user-supplied limit $T_1$. Once convergence has been achieved for a given $C$, a new cluster can be created or an existing cluster can be deleted. Let $d_k(i)$ be the distance between pattern $x_i$ and cluster center $k$, and define

$$\bar{d}(i) = \frac{1}{C} \sum_{i=1}^{C} d_k(i)$$

A new cluster is created at pattern $x_i$ if

$$|d_{k_0}(i) - \bar{d}(i)| \le |\bar{d}(i)| T_2$$

where $k_0$ is the cluster center closest to pattern $x_i$ and $T_2$ is a user-supplied threshold between 0 and 1. As the value of $T_2$ increases, more clusters are created. An existing cluster can be deleted if it contains fewer than $T_3$ patterns. These patterns are treated as outliers and are not considered in further iterations [2]. A simplified flowchart of the FORGY algorithm is given in Fig. 7.

The FORGY algorithm was run on the *Iris* data. The values of the parameters provided to the algorithm are (i) $C$ (numbers of clusters desired) = 3. (ii) $T_1$ (maximum number of iterations) = 20, (iii) $T_2$ (criterion to create new clusters) = 0.0, and (iv) $T_3$ (minimum number of patterns in a cluster) = 5.

The output of FORGY includes the cluster number for each pattern, the square error for each cluster, distances between cluster centers, and the ratios of the within-cluster distances to the between-cluster distances. Since for *Iris* data we know the true category of each pattern, the program also prints out the cluster membership according to category, which is shown in Table IV.

**TABLE IV**

Cluster-by-Category Table Produced by FORGY

| Cluster number | Category | | |
|---|---|---|---|
| | *I. setosa* | *I. versicolor* | *I. virginica* |
| 1 | 50 | 0 | 0 |
| 2 | 0 | 2 | 36 |
| 3 | 0 | 48 | 14 |

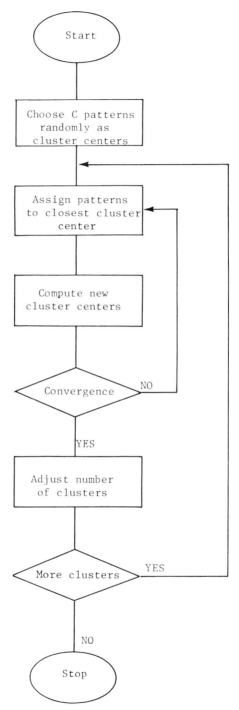

**Fig. 7.** Flowchart for FORGY.

Cluster 1 captures all patterns belonging to *I. setosa*, which is to be expected based on the two-dimensional plot of the data shown in Fig. 4. The overlap between the two categories of *I. versicolor* and *I. virginica*, apparent from Fig. 4, is reflected in the membership of the remaining two clusters. The program converged in two iterations. Various values for the parameter $T_2$ were tried. Three clusters were generated for $T_2$ in the range $0 \le T_2 \le 0.75$, and four clusters resulted when $T_2$ was increased to 0.8. The fourth cluster was obtained as a result of splitting cluster 1 of Table III. Even for the same value of $T_2$, different initial configurations (chosen randomly) resulted in slightly different clusterings. How does one specify the desired number of clusters? There is no answer to this question except to repeat the clustering algorithm for different values of $C$ and choose one which makes sense for the data under consideration. The computational requirement for each iteration of FORGY is proportional to $nC$, so this program can easily be run for different values of $C$.

### CLUSTER 2

This program generates an entire sequence of clusterings containing 2, 3,..., $C$ clusters which are not hierarchically related [12]. The program is based on a "hill-climbing" technique, where a pattern is moved from one cluster to another only if it results in a decrease of the square error. It starts with a two-cluster solution where the initial cluster centers are the centroid of the patterns and the pattern furthest removed from the centroid. After many hill-climbing passes, a "single-move local maximum" is obtained whereby moving a single pattern does not decrease the error. Given a clustering with $k$ clusters, a clustering with $k + 1$ clusters is obtained by choosing the pattern most removed from the clustering as a new cluster center. Patterns are then placed in the new cluster to minimize the square error.

Once the sequence of clusterings has been obtained, a pair of clusters is merged at a time to produce a sequence of clusterings containing $C - 1$, $C - 2, ...,$ 2 clusters. The cluster splitting and merging process continues until there is no change in square error. The best clustering obtained for each

**TABLE V**

**Cluster-by-Category Table Produced by CLUSTER**

| Cluster number | Category | | |
|---|---|---|---|
| | *I. setosa* | *I. versicolor* | *I. virginica* |
| 1 | 50 | 0 | 0 |
| 2 | 0 | 2 | 36 |
| 3 | 0 | 48 | 14 |

**TABLE VI**

**Cluster-by-Category Table Produced by CLUSTER**
**with Normalization Option**

| Cluster number | Category | | |
|---|---|---|---|
| | *I. setosa* | *I. versicolor* | *I. virginica* |
| 1 | 0 | 11 | 36 |
| 2 | 50 | 0 | 0 |
| 3 | 0 | 39 | 14 |

$k, k = 2, \ldots, C$, is stored. The main advantage of this clustering program is that the user does not have to specify any parameters, except for the value of $C$. Table V gives the cluster-by-category results obtained for a three-cluster solution from the CLUSTER program for *Iris* data. Surprisingly, the cluster memberships obtained from FORGY and CLUSTER are identical. Anytime two different clustering programs give the same clusters, it should increase our confidence in the significance of the partition. The program CLUSTER has the option of first scaling the data so that it has mean zero and unit standard deviation for each feature. The three-cluster solution obtained with scaled data is shown in Table VI. The important point to note is that the clusterings with scaled and unscaled data are different.

## III   CLUSTER ANALYSIS SOFTWARE

A variety of clustering algorithms have been reported in the literature and continue to appear regularly in the journals. A new clustering method is often motivated by deficiencies in existing methods. However, this does not mean that all the available clustering methods are "different." A clustering method developed under one theoretical framework may turn out to be identical to another clustering method based on an entirely different framework. Unfortunately, very little work has been done to objectively compare clustering methods. It is important to realize that no single clustering method is best for all data. This makes the choice of a clustering method for a given data set a difficult problem. Some practical comparisons of clustering methods have been reported [12]. Everitt [6] and other researchers suggest that several clustering methods should be used on the same data. Therefore, it is important for the user of cluster analysis to be aware of the various software packages which contain clustering algorithms.

Blashfield *et al.* [5] give an excellent review of the cluster analysis software. They divide the available software into five categories.

(1) *Collections of subroutines and algorithms.* Two such collections are found in books by Anderberg [1] and Hartigan [14]. The third collection is contained in the popular International Mathematical and Statistical Library of Scientific Subroutines (IMSL). Only the IMSL subroutines are updated and maintained.

(2) *General statistical packages which contain clustering methods.* Three general statistical packages, SAS, OSIRIS, and BMDP, contain a limited selection of hierarchical and partitional clustering algorithms. These packages are readily available with excellent documentation at most computer centers.

(3) *Cluster analysis packages.* CLUSTAN is the most versatile of the six cluster analysis packages available. The others are NT-SYS, CLUS, TAXON, BC-TRY, and CLAB. The only interactive package is CLAB.

(4) *Simple cluster analysis programs.* This category contains some popular clustering programs like ISODATA and hierarchical clustering program JCLUST written by Johnson which are not available in other software.

(5) *Special-purpose clustering programs.* There are many clustering programs which have been developed to handle the large data sets which arise in LANDSAT applications. A number of projection algorithms are also available to visualize the multivariate data, and they should be used in conjunction with cluster analysis.

The choice of a particular software package will depend on the needs of the user. However, the package CLUSTAN (developed at Edinburgh University) appears to have an edge over the other packages. Computational consideration is also an important issue in the choice of a clustering program or package. For example, single-link hierarchical clustering can be efficiently implemented using the recently available fast algorithms for computing the minimal spanning tree. Concerns about computational requirements of square-error clustering algorithms on large data sets have led to their implementation on special-purpose VLSI architectures. Ni and Jain [15] have designed a two-level pipelined systolic array for square-error clustering techniques. The National Aeronautic and Space Administration (NASA) has implemented the ISODATA program on the massively parallel processor (MPP). Preliminary runs of ISODATA on MPP show that a $512 \times 512$ multispectral image containing 4 channels can be partitioned into 16 clusters in 18 sec.

## CLUSTER VALIDITY  IV

Cluster validity deals with the significance of the structure imposed by a clustering method. One of the fundamental questions a user of a clustering algorithm is interested in can be stated as follows: Are the clusters achieved in a particular clustering significant enough to provide evidence for hypotheses about the underlying structure of the data? In other words, is the clustering "real" or merely an artifact of the clustering algorithm? The difficulty of validating clusters lies in our inability to agree on the definition of "cluster" and the meaning of validity. The problem is further compounded by the difficulty of determining the statistical distribution of the validity measure. The engineering literature has paid very little attention to the cluster validity issues, being content to present new clustering algorithms which perform reasonably well on a few data sets (usually in two dimensions). However, much more attention must be paid to fundamental questions of cluster tendency and cluster validity if cluster analysis is to make a substantial contribution to engineering applications.

The literature available on cluster validity tries to answer the following four questions [3].

(1)  Is the data matrix random? We want to determine if the data tend to cluster before applying any clustering algorithm to it.

(2)  How well does a hierarchy fit a proximity matrix? This is applicable when a hierarchical clustering algorithm is applied to data. The fit between the dendrogram and the proximity matrix is established.

(3)  Is a partition valid? The partition may be found either by applying a square-error clustering algorithm to a pattern matrix or from one level of a hierarchy constructed from a proximity matrix. Answers are based on measures of separation among clusters and measures of cohesion within clusters.

(4)  Which individual clusters are valid? If a hierarchical structure is fit to the data, then we want to determine if some of the clusters formed are "real." The compactness of a cluster is measured by its "birth time" and size, while the isolation is measured by "lifetime" in the dendrogram.

Dubes and Jain [3] provide a comprehensive review of the approaches and specific tests available for cluster validity. They emphasize the use of external criteria for validation purposes which are independent of the data being clustered. Any validity approach which uses the same criterion for forming the cluster as well as for testing its validity is not appropriate. For example, using the technique of multivariate analysis of variance to test the null hypothesis that all cluster centers are equal is not correct, because the cluster members were not chosen randomly! We will briefly review the validity tests available in the literature which are applicable to data in the form of a pattern matrix. While a number of heuristics and ad hoc tests are available, our emphasis will only be on the quantitative results.

## A  Tests for Clustering Tendency

The term "clustering tendency" refers to the problem of deciding whether the data exhibit a predisposition to cluster. These tests do not check the validity of a specific cluster or clustering. Instead, the null hypothesis is that the data have a continuous uniform distribution over some compact convex set $S \subset R^p$. The set $S$ is called the sampling window, which is defined as the compact convex support set for the underlying distribution (Smith and Jain, 1984).

The concept of a sampling window is fundamental to the notion of clustering tendency. The same data can appear as random or nonrandom depending on the choice of the sampling window. Ideally, the sampling window for the data under consideration should be known a priori. In many practical situations, however, the sampling windows must be estimated from the data. Smith and Jain [16] restrict the sampling window to compact, convex sets in pattern space. They also show that the convex hull of the data is a reasonable sampling-window estimator.

A number of clustering-tendency tests have been reported in both the ecological and the geographical literature. Ripley [17] provides a good overview of the statistical methods used. These tests are intuitively appealing, but they deal only with points in two dimensions and normally assume that the sampling window is known. Extension of these tests to higher dimensions presents tremendous computational difficulties. A few of these tests are mentioned below.

(1)  *Scan test.* An unusually large count of number of patterns in the most populous region of the sampling window indicates the presence of clustering. The size of the region must be fixed a priori.

(2)  *Quadrat analysis.* The sampling window is divided into squares of equal size, called quadrats. Under the null hypothesis of uniform data, the number of points falling in each quadrat follows a Poisson distribution.

(3)  *Distance-based tests.* The set of interpattern distances reflects the structural relationships among the patterns. Some tests incorporate only the "small" interpoint distances, others use only the nearest-neighbor distances. Various graphs, such as the minimal spanning tree, the Delaunay tesselation, and the relative neighborhood graph, have also been proposed to capture structural information. Ripley [17] describes many tests utilizing "sampling origins," which are distiguished points fixed by the researcher in the sampling window.

(4)  *Second-moment estimators.* Ripley [17] emphasized the role of the second-moment structure in characterizing a spatial point process and defined a function to capture this information. Deviations from the function known to represent a Poisson process lead to tests for randomness.

The above-mentioned tests for clustering tendency have been demonstrated to have good performance in two dimensions. However, most of them are inadequate for high-dimensional data or for situations where the sampling window is unknown. In addition, many of these test statistics have an unknown null distribution.

Smith and Jain [16] have recently proposed a clustering-tendency test which does not explicitly require any knowledge of the sampling window. The test essentially determines if two sets of high-dimensional sample points belong to the same distribution. For the problem at hand, the given set of patterns $\{x_i\}$ constitutes one sample. The other sample $\{y_i\}$ needed is obtained by generating points uniformly over the convex hull of $\{x_i\}$. A minimal spanning tree (MST) of the pooled sample points is constructed. The test statistic $T$ is the number of $x-y$ joins in this MST. The distribution of $T$ is known to be asymptotically normal. If the given data set $\{x_i\}$ is clustered, then most of the $y$ points generated will lie between the clusters of $\{x_i\}$, resulting in an unusually high number of $x-x$ and $y-y$ joins and thus reducing the value of the $T$ statistic. The performance of this clustering-tendency test has been evaluated on a large number of data sets. It gives acceptable performance on several real data sets, including the *Iris* data. These data, as well as a subset containing the two categories (*I. versicolor* and *I. virginica*) which are not well separated (see Fig. 4), are rejected as being uniform using this test.

## B   Validity of Partitions

Here we assume that the partitions have been obtained from a pattern matrix where the features are all quantitative. A large body of cluster-validity literature deals with data presented in the form of an ordinal proximity matrix and will not be considered here. The validity problem addresses the following two questions: (i) How many clusters are present in the data? (ii) Are the clusters obtained real? Since most partitional clustering algorithms are based on minimizing the square error, the ideal clusters under this approach have hyperellipsoidal shape. This right away establishes the relationship to multivariate Gaussian distributions. In spite of this, testing the validity of partitions is a difficult problem, and only a few quantitative results are available in the literature. We present some of these tests and emphasize caution in using these tests because of the underlying assumptions needed to derive the necessary distributions.

(1)   The square error in a partitional clustering algorithm always decreases as the number of clusters is increased. The objective of this test is to determine if the decrease in error is "significant." The null hypothesis is that the given data are a random sample from a Gaussian distribution with mean vector $\mu$ and a covariance matrix $\sigma^2 I$. Under the null hypothesis, the decrease in error when the unimodal Gaussian data are split into two clusters is

known. The test involves comparing the observed decrease in error for a given data set with that expected under the null hypothesis.

(2)   One popular model of clustering assumes that the patterns are drawn from a mixture of multivariate Gaussian distributions. A likelihood ratio test is available to test the hypothesis of $k$ components against $k - 1$ components in the mixture. The test statistic has a chi-square distribution asymptotically. The clustering should be repeated with $k = 1, 2,...$ until the observed chi-square value is below some critical threshold.

(3)   The ratio of between-cluster sum of squares (SSB) and within-cluster sum of squares (SSW) is an important criterion in defining a good clustering. Under the null hypothesis that the patterns belong to a multivariate Gaussian distribution, the expected value and the variance of SSB/SSW are known asymptotically. The partition will be considered valid, or, alternatively, clusters will be distinct, if the observed value of SSB/SSW is several standard deviations away from its expected value under the null hypothesis.

The ratio SSB/SSW has also been used to compare different partitions which have the same number of clusters as well as to determine the number of clusters based on the maximum value of SSB/SSW.

(4)   The amount of overlap between the cluster members when they are projected onto the intercentroid axis of the two clusters forms another basis for a test. The null hypothesis is that the two clusters are formed by splitting an essentially uniform swarm of patterns. Under the null hypothesis, the expected value of an index of overlap is known. Again, using this expected value as a threshold, the distinctiveness of clusters can be established.

Once a partition has been established to be valid, we would like to determine how "good" the individual clusters are. A cluster is good if the distances between the patterns inside the cluster are small and the distances between those patterns inside the cluster and those outside the cluster are large. The notions of "compactness" and "isolation" have been proposed to characterize a cluster. For a cluster $k$ of $n$ points, an intuitively appealing definition is

$$\text{compactness} = \frac{\text{total number of } n - 1 \text{ nearest neighbors of each point in } k \text{ which belong to } k}{n(n - 1)}$$

$$\text{isolation} = \frac{m(m - 1) - \text{total number of times points in } k \text{ are } m - 1 \text{ nearest neighbors of points which do not belong in } k}{m(m - 1)}$$

where $m$ is the number of points in the data which do not belong in cluster $k$. A compactness and isolation value of 1 means that the cluster is extremely compact and very well isolated from the rest of the points in the data. Unfortunately, no sampling theory is available for these statistics.

## V  SUMMARY

Cluster analysis is viewed as a process of partitioning a collection of patterns into groups such that patterns belonging to the same group are more similar to each other than are patterns belonging to different groups. A number of clustering techniques have been developed, each utilizing its own notion of similarity and concept of cluster. We have briefly reviewed the hierarchical and partitional techniques which by far are the most popular in pattern recognition and image processing applications. The choice of a clustering technique is data dependent. No single clustering technique meets the requirements of all the users, thus leading to a proliferation of clustering algorithms.

The user of a clustering algorithm often must provide the values of a number of parameters which affect the resulting partition. This can cause problems in interpreting the results. Some knowledge about the data, viewing various two-dimensional projections of the data, and integrating the results of various clustering algorithms applied to the same data may alleviate these problems. Another difficulty in using cluster analysis is to determine the significance or the validity of the resulting partition. A clustering algorithm always generates clusters whether or not they exist in the data. Only a few objective measures are available to determine if the data has a tendency to cluster and to evaluate the validity of clusters. A cluster is considered valid or significant if it is compact and well separated.

Cluster analysis has been used extensively in many applications of pattern recognition and image processing. In statistical pattern recognition, cluster analysis is utilized for dimensionality reduction (clustering the features), for data reduction (patterns in a compact cluster can be represented by the cluster center), and in numerous applications involving unsupervised learning (classification of multispectral data, nondestructive testing, analysis of seismic data), where it is difficult to assign a category label to each of the training patterns. In syntactic pattern recognition, patterns are represented as strings, trees, or graphs. These data structures have been clustered by defining appropriate similarity measures. Many approaches to image segmentation cluster the pixels based on their similarities on attributes like gray level, color, texture, and gradient. Detection of lines and curves in images and the problem of image registration have also been posed in terms of cluster analysis.

### ACKNOWLEDGEMENTS

I want to thank Richard Hoffman for his careful reading of this chapter and his suggestions for improving the presentation. This research is supported in part by NSF Grant ECS 8300204.

## REFERENCES

1. M. R. Anderberg, "Cluster Analysis for Applications." Academic Press, New York, 1973.
2. R. Dubes and A. K. Jain, Clustering methodologies in exploratory data analysis, *in* "Advances in Computers" (M. C. Yovits, ed.), pp. 113–228. Academic Press, New York, 1981.
3. R. Dubes and A. K. Jain, Validity studies in clustering methodologies, *Pattern Recognition* **11**, 235–254 (1979).
4. B. Everitt, "Cluster Analysis." Wiley, New York, 1974.
5. R. K. Blashfield, M. S. Aldenderfer, and L. Morey, Cluster analysis software, *in* "Handbook of Statistics 2" (P. R. Krishnaiah and L. N. Kanal, eds.), pp. 245–266. North Holland Publ., New York.
6. B. S. Everitt, Unresolved problems in cluster analysis, *Biometrics* **35**, 169–181 (1979).
7. R. O. Duda and P. E. Hart, "Pattern Classification and Scene Analysis." Wiley, New York, 1973.
8. B. S. Everitt, "Graphical Techniques for Multivariate Data." North Holland Publ., New York, 1978.
9. R. S. Michalski and R. E. Stepp, Automated construction of classification: Conceptual clustering versus numerical taxonomy, *IEEE Trans. Pattern Anal. Mach. Intell.* **5**, 396–410 (1983).
10. E. Backer, "Cluster Analysis by Optimal Decomposition of Induced Fuzzy Sets." Delft University Press, Delft, The Netherlands, 1978.
11. J. C. Bezdek, "Pattern Recognition with Fuzzy Objective Function Algorithms." Plenum, New York, 1981.
12. R. Dubes and A. K. Jain, Clustering techniques: The user's dilemma, *Pattern Recognition* **8**, 247–260 (1976).
13. C. T. Zahn, Graph-theoretical methods for detecting and describing Gestalt clusters, *IEEE Trans. Comput.* **20**, 68–86 (1971).
14. J. A. Hartigan, "Clustering Algorithms." Wiley, New York, 1975.
15. L. Ni and A. K. Jain, Design of a pattern cluster using two-level pipelined systolic array, *in* "VLSI for Pattern Recognition and Image Processing" (K. S. Fu, ed.), pp. 65–83. Springer-Verlag, New York, 1984.
16. S. P. Smith and A. K. Jain, Testing for uniformity in multidimensional data, *IEEE Trans. Pattern Anal. Mach. Intell.* **6**, 73–81 (1984).
17. B. D. Ripley, "Spatial Statistics." Wiley, New York, 1981.

# Chapter **3**

# Feature Selection and Extraction

J. KITTLER

SERC Rutherford Appleton Laboratory
Chilton
Didcot, England

**HANDBOOK OF PATTERN RECOGNITION
AND IMAGE PROCESSING**

# I INTRODUCTION

## A Role of Feature Selection and Extraction

The subject of feature selection and extraction in pattern recognition is concerned with mathematical tools for reducing the dimensionality of pattern representation. Pattern descriptors constituting the lower-dimensional representation are referred to as features because of their fundamental role in characterizing the distinguishing properties of pattern classes.

The purpose of feature selection and extraction is multifold. Its primary justification stems from engineering considerations. As the complexity of a classifier and the complexity of its hardware implementation grow rapidly with the number of dimensions of the pattern space, it is important to base decisions only on the most essential, so-called discriminatory information, which is conveyed by features.

Dimensionality reduction may also be motivated by other factors. For instance, if the pattern information to be interpreted is received over a long-distance communication channel, it may be desirable to extract the important features at the sensor and transmit only the discriminatory information. Such information compression may facilitate a considerable reduction in the required communication-channel capacity. Furthermore, identification of measurements which are redundant or irrelevant with regard to a particular classification task may be important for reducing the overall cost of measurement extraction.

Apart from engineering constraints, dimensionality reduction may prove beneficial from the classification performance point of view. The design of a recognition system is normally based on a set containing a finite (usually small) number of training patterns. Small sample problems are manifested in the so-called peaking phenomenon, which characterizes the relationship between the dependence of probability of correct recognition and the number of features used. Initially performance improves as new features are added, but at some point inclusion of further features will result in performance degradation. Thus dimensionality reduction may achieve an actual decrease in recognition error rates.

**Fig. 1.** Partitioning of a pattern recognition problem by inclusion of a feature selection and extraction stage.

Finally, a useful by-product of feature evaluation is that it provides the means for assessing the potential of a given pattern representation space for discriminating between elements of different classes. If the class overlap is too high even in the representation space, then new sources of information will need to be sought to enhance the class separability.

The inclusion of the feature selection and extraction stage effectively partitions the pattern recognition problem into two subproblems, as illustrated in Fig. 1. This model of the machine pattern recognition process appears to be consistent with the mechanisms involved in human perceptual processes.

## Problem Formulation  B

Dimensionality reduction can be achieved in two different ways. One approach is to identify measurements which do not contribute to class separability, as illustrated in the example in Fig. 2. The problem is then one of selecting a small subset of $d$ features $x_j, j = 1, 2, \ldots, d$, out of the available $D$ measurements (sensor outputs) $y_k, \; k = 1, 2, \ldots, D$. This dimensionality reduction process is referred to as *feature selection*. Note that no computation is required during routine pattern processing. The redundant and irrelevant sensor outputs are simply ignored.

The other approach is to use all the sensor outputs and map the useful information content into a lower-dimensional feature space, as shown in Fig. 3. This method is referred to as *feature extraction*.

To solve a feature selection or a feature extraction problem, we need to specify three ingredients: the feature evaluation criterion, the dimensionality

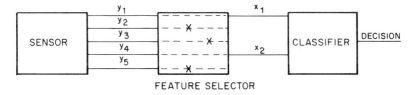

FEATURE SELECTOR

**Fig. 2.** Dimensionality reduction by feature selection.

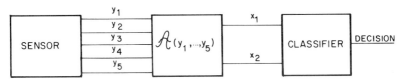

**Fig. 3.** Dimensionality reduction by feature extraction.

of the feature space, and the optimization procedure. In addition, in feature extraction we also need to specify the form of mapping $\mathscr{A}$.

These issues will be discussed in detail in the remaining sections of this chapter. In Section II we shall introduce feature-evaluation criteria in the context of feature selection. Section III reviews feature-set search algorithms. Next, in Section IV the problem of feature extraction is addressed, covering both feature evaluation criterion functions and their optimization. Some concluding remarks are offered in Section V.

The factors governing the choice of dimensionality of the feature space are common to both dimensionality reduction approaches. They include hardware or computational constraints, the peaking phenomenon, or permissible information loss.

## C   Preliminaries

Before discussing feature selection and extraction methods in detail, it will be useful to introduce some notation. We shall denote the sensor outputs (available measurements) by $y_k$, $k = 1, 2, \ldots, D$, or in a vector form by $\mathbf{y}$, that is,

$$\mathbf{y} = [y_1, \ldots, y_D]^\mathrm{T} \tag{1}$$

Each representation pattern $\mathbf{y}$ belongs to one of $m$ possible pattern classes $\omega_i$, $i = 1, 2, \ldots, m$. It will be assumed that patterns are generated by a random process and that the model of the process can be characterized by class-conditional density functions $p(\mathbf{y}|\omega_i)$ and a priori class probabilities $P(\omega_i)$, $i = 1, 2, \ldots, m$.

A set of candidate features $\xi_j$, $j = 1, 2, \ldots, d$, will be denoted by $\chi$, while $X = \{\mathbf{x}_j | j = 1, \ldots, d\}$ will designate the set of optimal features in the sense of some criterion function $J$. In the case of feature selection, optimization is carried out over all possible candidate feature sets, that is,

$$J(X) = \max_{\chi} J(\chi) \tag{2}$$

In feature extraction, on the other hand, the optimization is performed over all admissible, mappings, that is,

$$J(A) = \max_{\mathscr{A}} J\{\mathscr{A}(\mathbf{y})\} \tag{3}$$

where $A$ is an optimal feature extractor. Once $A$ is determined, the feature vector

$$\mathbf{x} = [x_1, x_2, \ldots, x_d]^\mathrm{T} \tag{4}$$

is then given by

$$\mathbf{x} = \mathscr{A}(\mathbf{y}) \tag{5}$$

We shall see in the following sections that criterion functions are defined in terms of the model characteristics $P(\omega_i)$ and $p(\mathbf{y}|\omega_i)$ or the conditional density function marginals $p(\xi|\omega_i)$. In practice, these density functions will not be known. The information on which the recognition system design can be based is normally a set of training patterns $\mathbf{y}_l$, $l = 1, 2, \ldots, N$, with the corresponding labels $\theta_l$, $l = 1, 2, \ldots, N$, which define the class membership of the training patterns. The relevant conditional density functions can be inferred from the training set using, for instance, the Parzen approach introduced in Section III.D.3.

## FEATURE SELECTION CRITERIA   II

### Error Probability   A

When solving a pattern recognition problem, the ultimate objective is to design a recognition system which will classify unknown patterns with the lowest possible probability of misrecognition. Since classification probability is the design criterion for the whole recognition system, it is naturally also the ideal objective function for designing the feature selection–extraction subsystem.

In the $d$-dimensional feature space defined by a candidate set of features $\chi = [\xi_1, \ldots, \xi_d]$, the error probability $e$ is given as

$$e = \int \left[ 1 - \max_i P(\omega_i|\xi) \right] p(\xi) \, d\xi \tag{6}$$

where $\xi$ is the feature vector composed of candidate features $\xi_j$, that is,

$$\xi = [\xi_1, \ldots, \xi_d]^{\mathrm{T}} \tag{7}$$

$P(\omega_i|\xi)$ is the a posteriori probability of the $i$th class and $p(\xi)$ denotes the mixture density function satisfying

$$p(\xi) = \sum_{i=1}^{m} p(\xi|\omega_i)P(\omega_i) \tag{8}$$

The *a posteriori* probability function $P(\omega_i|\xi)$ is related to the $i$th class-conditional density as

$$P(\omega_i|\xi) = \frac{p(\xi|\omega_i)P(\omega_i)}{p(\xi)} \tag{9}$$

Since error probability, in general, is not easy to evaluate, a number of alternative feature evaluation criteria have been suggested in the literature. The most important measures and their concepts are discussed in the following sections.

## B  Probabilistic Distance Measures

The concept of probabilistic distance can best be introduced by considering the error probability $e$ in the two-class case. It is easy to show that for $m = 2$,

$$e = 0.5 \left[ 1 - \int |p(\xi|\omega_1)P(\omega_1) - p(\xi|\omega_2)P(\omega_2)| d\xi \right] \tag{10}$$

Now the error will be maximum when the integrand is zero, that is, when density functions are completely overlapping, and it will be zero when the functions $p(\xi|\omega_i)$ do not overlap. The integral in (10) can be considered to quantify the "probabilistic distance" between the two density functions. The greater the distance, the smaller the error and vice versa.

By analogy, any other measure of "distance" between the two density functions, that is,

$$J(\chi) = \int f\left[ p(\xi|\omega_i), P(\omega_i), i = 1, 2 \right] d\xi \tag{11}$$

satisfying $J \geq 0$, $J = 0$ when $p(\xi|\omega_i)$, $i = 1, 2$ are overlapping, and $J$ is maximum when $p(\xi|\omega_i)$, $i = 1, 2$ are nonoverlapping, can be used as a feature evaluation criterion. The most commonly used probabilistic distance measures are given in Eqs. (12)–(21). The averaged forms of the measures take into account the *a priori* probabilities.

$$J_C = -\ln \int p^s(\xi|\omega_1)p^{1-s}(\xi|\omega_2)\, d\xi, \qquad s \in [0, 1]: \quad \text{Chernoff} \tag{12}$$

$$J_B = -\ln \int \left[ p(\xi|\omega_1)p(\xi|\omega_2) \right]^{1/2} d\xi: \qquad\qquad \text{Bhattacharyya} \tag{13}$$

$$J_T = \left\{ \int \left[ \sqrt{p(\xi|\omega_1)} - \sqrt{p(\xi|\omega_2)} \right]^2 d\xi \right\}^{1/2}: \qquad \text{Matusita} \tag{14}$$

$$J_D = \int \left[ p(\xi|\omega_1) - p(\xi|\omega_2) \right] \ln\left[ \frac{p(\xi|\omega_1)}{p(\xi|\omega_2)} \right] d\xi: \qquad \text{Divergence} \tag{15}$$

$$J_P = \left\{ \int \left[ p(\xi|\omega_1) - p(\xi|\omega_2) \right]^2 d\xi \right\}^{1/2}: \qquad\qquad \text{Patrick–Fisher} \tag{16}$$

$$\bar{J}_C = -\ln \int [p(\xi|\omega_1)P(\omega_1)]^s [p(\xi|\omega_2)P(\omega_2)]^{1-s}\, d\xi:$$
$$\text{Averaged Chernoff} \qquad (17)$$

$$\bar{J}_B = -\ln \int [p(\xi|\omega_1)P(\omega_1)p(\xi|\omega_2)P(\omega_2)]^{1/2}\, d\xi:$$
$$\text{Averaged Bhattacharyya} \qquad (18)$$

$$\bar{J}_T = \left\{ \int [\sqrt{p(\xi|\omega_1 P(\omega_1)} - \sqrt{p(\xi|\omega_2)P(\omega_2)}]^2\, d\xi \right\}^{1/2}:$$
$$\text{Averaged Matusita} \qquad (19)$$

$$\bar{J}_D = \int [p(\xi|\omega_1)P(\omega_1) - p(\xi|\omega_2)p(\omega_2)]\ln\left[\frac{p(\xi|\omega_1)P(\omega_1)}{p(\xi|\omega_2)P(\omega_2)}\right]\, d\xi:$$
$$\text{Averaged Divergence} \qquad (20)$$

$$\bar{J}_P = \left\{ \int [p(\xi|\omega_1)P(\omega_1) - p(\xi|\omega_2)P(\omega_2)]^2\, d\xi \right\}^{1/2}:$$
$$\text{Averaged Patrick–Fisher} \qquad (21)$$

The relationship between a probabilistic distance measure and error probability can be expressed in terms of error bounds afforded by the measures. The upper bound, which is particularly relevant, can easily be established for a given averaged probabilistic distance criterion provided the measure is expressable in the form of the averaged $f$ divergence $J_F$, that is,

$$J_F(\chi) = \int f\left(\frac{P(\omega_1|\xi)}{P(\omega_2|\xi)}\right)P(\omega_2|\xi)p(\xi)\, d\xi \qquad (22)$$

where $f(u)$ is a convex function. The error probability can then be bounded from above as

$$e < \frac{f(0)P(\omega_2) + f_\infty P(\omega_1) - J_F(\chi)}{f(0) + f_\infty - f(1)} \qquad (23)$$

where $f_\infty$ denotes

$$f_\infty = \lim_{u \to \infty} [f(u)/u] \qquad (24)$$

For example, the convex function which defines the averaged $f$ divergence corresponding to the averaged Matusita distance is easily shown to be

$$f(u) = [u^{1/2} - 1]^2$$

Then

$$J_F(\chi) = \bar{J}_T^2(\chi)$$

$$f(0) = 1, \qquad f(1) = 0, \qquad f_\infty = \lim_{u \to \infty} (u^{1/2} - 1)^2/u = 1$$

and from (23) the upper bound of the error probability in terms of the averaged Matusita distance is given as

$$e \le \tfrac{1}{2}[1 - \bar{J}_{\mathrm{T}}^2(\chi)]$$

The probabilistic distance measures listed in Eq. (12)–(21) play a very important role when the class-conditional probability distributions are parametric and in particular normal (Gaussian), that is, when the density function $p(\xi|\omega_i)$ is defined as

$$p(\xi|\omega_i) = [(2\pi)^d|\Sigma_i|]^{-1/2} \exp\{-\tfrac{1}{2}(\xi - \mu_i)^{\mathrm{T}}\Sigma_i^{-1}(\xi - \mu_i)\} \tag{25}$$

where $\mu_i$ and $\Sigma_i$ are the mean vector and covariance matrix of the $i$th class distribution, respectively. For normally distributed classes the multivariate integrals in the measures can be evaluated analytically, thus obviating a tedious numerical integration. Examples of the resulting probabilistic distance measures in their parametric form are given in Eqs. (26)–(34). An important advantage of these parametric measures is that they can be computed recursively.

$$J_{\mathrm{C}} = \frac{1}{2}s(1-s)(\mu_2 - \mu_1)^{\mathrm{T}}[(1-s)\Sigma_1 + s\Sigma_2]^{-1}$$
$$\times (\mu_2 - \mu_1) + \frac{1}{2}\ln\left[\frac{|(1-s)\Sigma_1 + s\Sigma_2|}{|\Sigma_1|^{1-s}|\Sigma_2|^{s}}\right]: \qquad \text{Chernoff} \tag{26}$$

$$J_{\mathrm{B}} = \frac{1}{4}(\mu_2 - \mu_1)^{\mathrm{T}}[\Sigma_1 + \Sigma_2]^{-1}(\mu_2 - \mu_1) + \frac{1}{2}\ln\left[\frac{|\tfrac{1}{2}(\Sigma_1 + \Sigma_2)|}{\sqrt{|\Sigma_1||\Sigma_2|}}\right]:$$
$$\text{Bhattacharyya} \tag{27}$$

$$J_{\mathrm{T}} = \{2[1 - \exp(-J_{\mathrm{B}})]\}^{1/2}: \qquad\qquad\qquad \text{Matusita} \tag{28}$$

$$J_{\mathrm{D}} = \tfrac{1}{2}(\mu_2 - \mu_1)^{\mathrm{T}}(\Sigma_1^{-1} + \Sigma_2^{-1})(\mu_2 - \mu_1) + \tfrac{1}{2}\operatorname{tr}\{\Sigma_1^{-1}\Sigma_2 + \Sigma_2^{-1}\Sigma_1 - 2I\}:$$
$$\text{Divergence} \tag{29}$$

$$J_{\mathrm{M}} = (\mu_2 - \mu_1)^{\mathrm{T}}\Sigma^{-1}(\mu_2 - \mu_1) \qquad \text{if} \quad \Sigma_1 = \Sigma_2 = \Sigma:$$
$$\text{Mahalanobis} \tag{30}$$

$$\bar{J}_{\mathrm{C}} = J_{\mathrm{C}} - s\ln P(\omega_1) - (1-s)\ln P(\omega_2): \qquad \text{Averaged Chernoff} \tag{31}$$

$$\bar{J}_{\mathrm{B}} = J_{\mathrm{B}} - \tfrac{1}{2}\ln[P(\omega_1)P(\omega_2)]: \qquad \text{Averaged Bhattacharyya} \tag{32}$$

$$\bar{J}_{\mathrm{T}} = [1 - 2\exp(-\bar{J}_{\mathrm{B}})]^{1/2}: \qquad\qquad \text{Averaged Matusita} \tag{33}$$

$$\bar{J}_{\mathrm{P}} = \{P^2(\omega_1)[(2\pi)^d|2\Sigma_1|]^{-1/2} + P^2(\omega_2)[(2\pi)^d|2\Sigma_2|]^{-1/2}$$
$$- 2P(\omega_1)P(\omega_2)[(2\pi)^d|\Sigma_1 + \Sigma_2|]^{-1/2}$$
$$\times \exp[-\tfrac{1}{2}(\mu_2 - \mu_1)^{\mathrm{T}}(\Sigma_1 + \Sigma_2)^{-1}(\mu_2 - \mu_1)]\}^{1/2}$$
$$\text{Averaged Patrick–Fisher} \tag{34}$$

A multiclass feature evaluation criterion can be defined in terms of any of the above two-class probabilistic distance measures as, for instance, a weighted average of the pairwise distances $J_{ij}(\chi)$, that is,

$$J(\chi) = \sum_{i=1}^{m} \sum_{j=i+1}^{m} P(\omega_i)P(\omega_j)J_{ij}(\chi) \tag{35}$$

Note that such a criterion will not retain a close relationship with the error probability.

## Probabilistic Dependence Measures   C

The pattern recognition process can be considered to involve two random variables: the pattern vector $\xi$ and the class $\omega$. The observation of an outcome of the former enables us to make a decision about the latter. The dependence of the two variables is embodied in the conditional density functions $p(\xi|\omega_i)$, $i = 1, 2, \ldots, m$. If $\xi$ and, say, $\omega_i$ are independent, then $p(\xi|\omega_i) = p(\xi)$, that is, the $i$th class-conditional density function will be identical to the mixture density. In such a situation, by observing the pattern vector $\xi$ we do not learn anything about its class membership.

It is apparent that the degree of dependence between the variable $\xi$ and a particular realization $\omega_i$ can be measured by the "distance" between the conditional density $p(\xi|\omega_i)$ and the mixture density $p(\xi)$. Recalling the previous subsection, there exist several measures which are suitable for this purpose. Any of the probabilistic distance measures listed in Eq. (12)–(21) can be used for evaluating the probabilistic dependence between $\xi$ and $\omega_i$ simply by replacing one of the class-conditional density functions with the mixture density. The overall dependence can be assessed by computing the weighted average of these class-conditional distances, thus yielding a multiclass criterion of feature effectiveness. Equations (36) and (37) contain examples of probabilistic dependence measures:

$$J_J = \sum_{i=1}^{m} P(\omega_i) \int [p(\xi|\omega_i) - p(\xi)] \ln\left[\frac{p(\xi|\omega_i)}{p(\xi)}\right] d\xi: \qquad \text{Joshi} \qquad (36)$$

$$J_R = \sum_{i=1}^{m} P(\omega_i) \left\{ \int [p(\xi|\omega_i) - p(\xi)]^2 \, d\xi \right\}^{1/2}: \qquad \text{Patrick–Fisher} \qquad (37)$$

## Entropy Measures   D

The concept on which entropy measures are based is similar to that of probabilistic dependence. We observe $\xi$ and compute the *a posteriori* probabilities $P(\omega_i|\xi)$ to determine how much information has been gained from the experiment. If all classes become equally probable, then the information gain is minimal or uncertainty (entropy) is maximum. Thus entropy measures can be used to assess the dependence between pattern vector $\xi$ and classes $\omega_i$, $i = 1, 2, \ldots, m$. The list of entropy measures given in Eqs. (39)–(41) has been derived from the average generalized entropies of degree $\alpha$ defined as

$$J_E^\alpha = \int (2^{1-\alpha} - 1)^{-1} \left[ \sum_{i=1}^{m} P^\alpha(\omega_i|\xi) - 1 \right] p(\xi) \, d\xi \tag{38}$$

$$J_S = - \int \sum_{i=1}^{m} P(\omega_i|\xi) \log_2[P(\omega_i|\xi)] \, p(\xi) \, d\xi: \qquad \text{Shannon} \tag{39}$$

$$J_Q = \int \sum_{i=1}^{m} P^2(\omega_i|\xi) p(\xi) \, d\xi: \qquad \text{Bayesian distance (quadratic)} \tag{40}$$

$$J_K = \int \sum_{i=1}^{m} P(\omega_i|\xi)[1 - P^2(\omega_i|\xi)] p(\xi) \, d\xi: \qquad \text{Cubic} \tag{41}$$

## E  Interclass Distance Measures

A number of popular feature selection criteria are based on the heuristic notion of interclass distance. Given a set of patterns which is representative of the mixture distribution (training set), it is reasonable to assume that pattern vectors of each class occupy a distinct region in the observation space. The average pairwise distance between the patterns in the set is then a measure of class separability in the space. Denoting by $\delta(\xi_{ik}, \xi_{jl})$ a metric for measuring the distance between the $k$th pattern of the $i$th class and the $l$th pattern of the $j$th class, the average distance can be defined as

$$J_\delta = \frac{1}{2} \sum_{i=1}^{m} P(\omega_i) \sum_{j=1}^{m} P(\omega_j) \frac{1}{N_i N_j} \sum_{k=1}^{N_i} \sum_{l=1}^{N_j} \delta(\xi_{ik}, \xi_{jl}) \tag{42}$$

where $N_i$ is the number of pattern vectors belonging to class $\omega_i$. Equations (43)–47) list common metrics that can be used in association with the criterion $J_\delta$.

$$\delta_C(\xi_k, \xi_l) = \sum_{j=1}^{d} |\xi_{kj} - \xi_{lj}|: \qquad \text{City block} \tag{43}$$

$$\delta_E(\xi_k, \xi_l) = \left[ \sum_{j=1}^{d} (\xi_{kj} - \xi_{lj})^2 \right]^{1/2}: \qquad \text{Euclidean} \tag{44}$$

$$\delta_T(\boldsymbol{\xi}_k, \boldsymbol{\xi}_l) = \max_j |\xi_{kj} - \xi_{lj}|: \qquad \text{Chebyshev} \qquad (45)$$

$$\delta_Q(\boldsymbol{\xi}_k, \boldsymbol{\xi}_l) = (\boldsymbol{\xi}_k - \boldsymbol{\xi}_l)^T Q (\boldsymbol{\xi}_k - \boldsymbol{\xi}_l): \quad \text{Quadratic} \qquad (46)$$

where $Q$ is a symmetric positive definite matrix

$$\delta_N(\boldsymbol{\xi}_k, \boldsymbol{\xi}_l) = \begin{cases} \text{constant}, & \delta(\boldsymbol{\xi}_k, \boldsymbol{\xi}_l) > \text{threshold} \\ 0, & \delta(\boldsymbol{\xi}_k, \boldsymbol{\xi}_l) \leq \text{threshold} \end{cases} \quad \text{Nonlinear} \quad (47)$$

The choice of a metric will depend on factors such as computational complexity, analytical tractability, and reliability. The nonlinear metric is likely to reflect class separability most reliably.

The city block and Chebyshev metrics are relatively easy to evaluate. The Euclidean and quadratic metrics allow analytical simplifcation of the average distance criterion. Equations (51)–(54) give examples of parametric measures derived from the criterion $J_\delta$ using the (squared) Euclidean metric under some constraints imposed on the effect of average intraclass distances. In these equations $\Sigma$, $M$, and $\boldsymbol{\mu}$, denote

$$\Sigma = \sum_{i=1}^{m} P(\omega_i)\Sigma_i \qquad (48)$$

$$M = \sum_{i=1}^{m} P(\omega_i)(\boldsymbol{\mu}_i - \boldsymbol{\mu})(\boldsymbol{\mu}_i - \boldsymbol{\mu})^T \qquad (49)$$

$$\boldsymbol{\mu} = \sum_{i=1}^{m} P(\omega_i)\boldsymbol{\mu}_i \qquad (50)$$

$\boldsymbol{\mu}$ is the mixture mean.

$$J_1 = \text{Tr}(\Sigma + M) \qquad (51)$$

$$J_2 = \text{Tr}(M/\Sigma) \qquad (52)$$

$$J_3 = \text{Tr}(\Sigma^{-1}M) \qquad (53)$$

$$J_4 = |\Sigma + M|/|\Sigma| \qquad (54)$$

## Comments  F

The usefulness of the various class separability measures will become apparent from the ensuing sections of the chapter. However, some general comments can be made now. Interclass distance measures are the only family of feature selection criterion functions which do not involve the estimation of probability density functions. These heuristic measures are therefore attractive mainly for computational reasons. Their relationship to error probability, in general, is very loose. Probabilistic distance measures are particularly useful in their parametric form when classes are normally distributed. For nonparametrically distributed classes, the Partick–Fisher separability measures (distance for two-class problems, dependence for multiclass problems) have a convenient form which is amenable to analytical simplification in conjunction with the Parzen probability density function estimator employing a Gaussian kernel.

Entropy measures are natural functions for multiclass problems. They can be estimated using the $k$-nearest-neighbor approach (see Chapter 1). Estimation of these measures is not necessarily easier than that of error probability itself. However, the variance of their estimates may be lower.

## III   FEATURE-SET SEARCH ALGORITHMS

### A   Feature Selection on the Individual Merit Basis

Given a set of measurements $y_j, j = 1, \ldots, D$, the problem of selecting the optimal subset of $d < D$ of these measurements as features involves the evaluation of effectiveness of all the possible candidate feature sets $\chi$ of cardinality $d$ that can be constructed from measurements $y_j$. The search for the optimum is a combinatorial problem, that is, the number of sets that need to be considered equals $D!/(D - d)!d!$. This number is excessive even for moderate values of $D$ and $d$. Moreover, referring to Eqs. (12)–(21) and (36)–(41), the assessment of each set $\chi$ may involve probability density function estimation in a multivariate space, the computation of the function defining the separability measure used, and numerical integration. In summary, the feature selection problem can very quickly cease to be computationally feasible.

In the very special case of two normally distributed classes with equal diagonal covariance matrices (the measurements are conditionally independent), the Mahalanobis distance given in Eq. (30) can be expressed as

$$J_{\mathrm{M}}(\chi) = \sum_{j=1}^{d} \frac{(\mu_{1j} - \mu_{2j})^2}{\sigma_{jj}} \tag{55}$$

where $\mu_{ij}$ is the $j$th component of the $i$th class mean vector and $\sigma_{jj}$ is the $j$th diagonal element of the covariance matrix. In these circumstances the contribution of class separability of one measurement is independent of all the other measurements. Hence the optimal set of $d$ features can be determined by selecting $d$ individually best measurements.

*Procedure*   Compute $J_M(y_j), j = 1, 2, \ldots, D$, and rank the measurements in the order of decreasing magnitude of the criterion function, that is,

$$J_M(y_1) > J_M(y_2) > \cdots > J_M(y_D) \tag{56}$$

The best feature set $X$ is then defined by the first $d$ measurements $y_j$, that is,

$$X = \{y_j | j = 1, \ldots, d\} \tag{57}$$

Unfortunately, in general, even if measurements are independent, features cannot be selected on the basis of their individual effectiveness.

### Branch-and-Bound Algorithm   B

Feature-set selection via exhaustive search can become computationally prohibitive. However, it may be possible to determine the optimal feature set without explicit evaluation of all the possible combinations of $d$ measurements with the help of the branch-and-bound algorithm. The algorithm is applicable under the assumption that a feature selection criterion satisfies the monotonicity property. Denoting by $\chi_j$ a candidate feature set containing $j$ features, the monotonicity property implies that for nested feature sets $\chi_j$ related as

$$\chi_1 \subset \chi_2 \subset \cdots \subset \chi_j \subset \cdots \chi_D \tag{58}$$

the criterion function $J(\chi_j)$ satisfies

$$J(\chi_1) \leq J(\chi_2) \leq \cdots \leq J(\chi_D) \tag{59}$$

To introduce the basic idea behind the branch-and-bound algorithm, let us consider the problem of selecting two features out of five measurements. All the possible triplets of measurements, which include the ones that have to be discarded to obtain the optimal set of two features, are represented by the tree in Fig. 4. Each node designates an eliminated measurement.

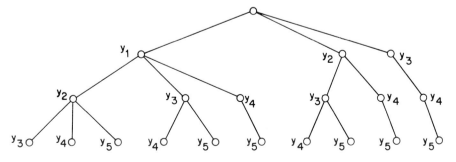

**Fig. 4.** Tree representation of a branch-and-bound algorithm.

Now suppose we evaluate our feature selection criterion at every node of the tree in a top-down manner starting with the right-most branch. At each node we compare the criterion function value with that of the current best feature set, denoted $J_0$. If the value exceeds $J_0$, then there is still a chance that a better feature set will be discovered, and the search must therefore continue along the right-most unexplored branch. If we reach the bottom of the tree and the corresponding criterion value is greater than $J_0$, then this node defines the new best feature set and $J_0$ is updated accordingly.

If, on the other hand, the value of the criterion function at some node is less than $J_0$, then the branches originating from that node need not be explored, since by virtue of the monotonicity property the elimination of additional measurements will only result in a further decrease of the function value. The search will be particularly efficient if the measurements $y_j$ for the successor nodes to each node of the tree are selected from left to right in the order of increasing magnitude of the criterion function.

## C   Sequential Forward and Sequential Backward Selection

In many situations the determination of the optimum feature set will not be computationally feasible even with the branch-and-bound algorithm. The only alternative is to seek a suboptimal solution. The simplest suboptimal procedures are the sequential forward and sequential backward selection algorithms.

Sequential forward selection is a bottom-up process. Starting from an empty set, we select as the first feature the individually best measurement. At each subsequent stage the next feature is picked from the remaining available measurements so that in combination with the features already selected it yields the best value of the criterion function.

*Sequential forward selection (SFS) algorithm.* Suppose $k$ features have been selected from the set of measurements $Y = \{y_j | j = 1, \ldots, D\}$ to form feature set $X_k$. The $(k + 1)$st feature is then chosen from the set of available measurements, $Y - X_k$, so that

$$J(X_{k+1}) = \max J(X_k \cup y_j), \qquad y_j \in Y - X_k \qquad (60)$$

$$\text{Initialization:} \quad X_0 \equiv \phi$$

Sequential backward selection is a top-down process. Starting from the complete set of available measurements *Y*, we eliminate one measurement at a time. At each stage the measurement selected for elimination is the one that results in the lowest decrease in the value of the criterion function.

*Sequential backward selection (SBS) algorithm.* Suppose $k$ measurements have been removed from the set of measurements $Y = \{y_j | j = 1, 2, \ldots, D\}$ to form feature set $X_{D-k}$. The $(k + 1)$st measurement to be eliminated is then chosen from the set $X_{D-k}$ so that

$$J(X_{D-k-1}) = \max J(X_{D-k} - y_j), \qquad y_j \in X_{D-k} \tag{61}$$

$$\text{Initialization:} \quad X_D \equiv Y$$

A few comments are in order at this point. The main source of suboptimality of SFS is that it has no mechanism for removing from the feature set the features which have become superfluous as a result of including other measurements. Similarly, once measurements have been discarded, SBS does not allow any revision of their merit. From the point of view of computational complexity, SFS is simpler than SBS since it requires that the criterion function be evaluated at most in $d$-dimensional spaces. In contrast, in SBS the criterion function must be computed in spaces of the dimensionality ranging from $d$ to $D$. However, the advantage of the top-down process is the ability to monitor continuously the amount of information loss incurred.

### Plus *l*–Take Away *r* Algorithm    D

The nesting of feature sets, which may quickly result in suboptimality of the sequential selection algorithms, can be partially overcome by alternating the process of augmentation and depletion of the feature set. After adding $l$ measurements to the current feature set, $r$ features are then removed. Thus the net change in the feature-set size is equivalent to $l - r$. This process is continued until the feature set reaches the required size. If $l > r$, the feature selection procedure operates bottom up, and for $l < r$, it operates top down.
*Plus l-take away r algorithm (l, r) for $l > r$.* Let $X_k$ be the current feature set.

> *Step 1*  Apply SFS $l$ times to generate feature set $X_{k+l}$
> *Step 2*  Apply SBS $r$ times to obtain feature set $X_{k+l-r}$
> *Step 3*  Stop if $k + l - r = d$ else return to Step 1

$(l, r)$ *algorithm for $l < r$.* The same as above with Step 1 and Step 2 interchanged.
Note that the $(l, r)$ algorithm with $r = 0$ is the SFS algorithm and with $l = 0$ it is the SBS algorithm.

### Max–Min Feature Selection    E

The main motivation behind this algorithm is to base feature selection on the individual and pairwise merit of measurements. The criterion function then need be evaluated in one- and two-dimensional spaces only.

The heuristic basis for the selection process is the following. Suppose that $k$ features have already been selected. The set of available measurements is then $Y - X_k$. The merit of these measurements can be assessed by measuring the amount of new information they would contribute if added to the feature set.

Now measurement $y_j \in Y - X_k$ relative to feature $x_l \in X_k$ conveys new information $\Delta J(y_j, x_l)$ that can be measured by

$$\Delta J(y_j, x_l) = J(y_j, x_l) - J(x_l) \tag{62}$$

Naturally we would like to find the $y_j$ whose information content is maximum. However, it will not contribute to the feature set as a whole unless its complementary content is large with respect to all features in the set $X_k$. Hence we must find the measurement $y_j$ which maximizes, over all $j$, the minimum of $\Delta J(y_j, x_l)$ over all $l$.

*Max–min algorithm.* Let $X_k$ be the current feature set. Select as the $(k + 1)$st feature that measurement $y_j \in Y - X_k$ which satisfies

$$\Delta J(x_{k+1}, x_r) = \max_j \min_l \Delta J(y_j, x_l), \qquad x_l \varepsilon X_k \tag{63}$$

## IV   FEATURE EXTRACTION

## A   Introduction

As pointed out in Section III.A.2, in feature extraction we use all the available measurements to find a lower-dimensional feature space. Information compression is achieved by a mapping process the goal of which is to project useful information contained in the original observations onto a very few composite feature variables, while ignoring redundant and irrelevant information.

In general the mapping required to achieve high-discriminatory information compression

$$\mathbf{x} = \mathscr{A}(\mathbf{y}) \tag{64}$$

may be nonlinear. An obvious theoretical possibility, for instance, is to map pattern vectors into the space defined by the *a posteriori* probability functions. However, such an objective would hardly simplify the problem of pattern recognition system design, since the computational burden would simply be shifted from the classification stage to the feature extraction stage.

In some instances a more intimate knowledge of the pattern-generating process may suggest the natural form of nonlinear mapping. For instance, if the components of the pattern vector are generated by an autoregressive moving average process, then the actual observations can be transformed into the lower-dimensional space of parameters defining the process. Similarly, any known functional relationships between measurements can be exploited in defining the appropriate form of nonlinear mapping for the feature extractor.

In the majority of situations, however, the natural form of mapping will be unknown. It may then be worth considering the effectiveness of some form of linear mapping. Linear mappings have the advantage of having at least some degree of analytical tractability and of being computationally feasible. The latter aspect may be the decisive factor in opting for a linear mapping, even in preference to a natural nonlinear mapping. In certain cases, of course, a linear mapping may even constitute the optimal form.

For the above reasons we shall concentrate in this chapter on linear mapping only, that is, we shall be looking for a feature extractor $A$, where $A$ is a $D \times d$ matrix, to transform the pattern vector $\mathbf{y}$ into a feature vector $\mathbf{x}$ according to

$$\mathbf{x} = A^T\mathbf{y} \tag{65}$$

The feature extractor should be optimal in the sense of a suitable criterion function $J(A)$. In contrast to the problem of feature selection, where optimization procedures and criterion functions are independent, here the actual optimization scheme will be closely linked with the criterion used. In special cases the optimal solution can be found analytically.

## Parametric Measures    B

The parametric measures introduced in Section III.B.2 can readily be used for feature extraction by expressing the mean vectors and covariance matrices of the class-conditional distributions in terms of the distribution parameters in the observation space $\tilde{\boldsymbol{\mu}}_i$ and $\tilde{\Sigma}_i$, $\forall i$. Note that the relevant relationships are

$$\boldsymbol{\mu}_i = A^T\tilde{\boldsymbol{\mu}}_i \tag{66}$$

and

$$\Sigma_i = A^T\tilde{\Sigma}_i A \tag{67}$$

In the following, specific feature extraction measures will be considered.

Using (66) and (67), the *Chernoff measure* in (26) can be rewritten as

$$J_C(A) = \frac{1}{2}s(1-s)(\tilde{\boldsymbol{\mu}}_2 - \tilde{\boldsymbol{\mu}}_1)^T A[(1-s)A^T\tilde{\Sigma}_1 A + sA^T\tilde{\Sigma}_2 A]^{-1}A^T(\tilde{\boldsymbol{\mu}}_2 - \tilde{\boldsymbol{\mu}}_1)$$

$$+ \frac{1}{2}\ln\left[\frac{|(1-s)A^T\tilde{\Sigma}_1 A + sA^T\tilde{\Sigma}_2 A|}{|A^T\tilde{\Sigma}_1 A|^{1-s}|A^T\tilde{\Sigma}_2 A|^s}\right] \tag{68}$$

The first derivative of (68) is then

$$J'_C(A) = (\tilde{\mathbf{\mu}}_2 - \tilde{\mathbf{\mu}}_1)(\tilde{\mathbf{\mu}}_2 - \tilde{\mathbf{\mu}}_1)^\mathrm{T} A - [(1-s)\tilde{\Sigma}_1 A + s\tilde{\Sigma}_2 A]$$
$$\times [(1-s)A^\mathrm{T}\tilde{\Sigma}_1 A + sA^\mathrm{T}\tilde{\Sigma}_2 A]^{-1} A^\mathrm{T}(\tilde{\mathbf{\mu}}_2 - \tilde{\mathbf{\mu}}_1)(\tilde{\mathbf{\mu}}_2 - \tilde{\mathbf{\mu}}_1)^\mathrm{T} A \qquad (69)$$
$$+ \tilde{\Sigma}_1 A[I - (A^\mathrm{T}\tilde{\Sigma}_1 A)^{-1}(A^\mathrm{T}\tilde{\Sigma}_2 A)] + \tilde{\Sigma}_2 A[I - (A^\mathrm{T}\tilde{\Sigma}_2 A)^{-1} A^\mathrm{T}\tilde{\Sigma}_1 A]$$

In general, the optimal solution can be found by searching in the direction of gradient $J'_C(A)$ using numerical methods. Analytical solutions can be obtained for a number of special cases. For instance, when the covariance matrices are identical, that is, when

$$\tilde{\Sigma}_1 = \tilde{\Sigma}_2 = \tilde{\Sigma} \qquad (70)$$

the optimal feature extractor is a $D \times 1$ matrix (vector) defined as

$$A = \tilde{\Sigma}^{-1}(\tilde{\mathbf{\mu}}_2 - \tilde{\mathbf{\mu}}_1) \qquad (71)$$

When the mean vectors are identical, that is, when $\tilde{\mathbf{\mu}}_1 = \tilde{\mathbf{\mu}}_2$, the optimal solution $A$ is the matrix of $d$ eigenvectors of the matrix product $\tilde{\Sigma}_2^{-1} \times \tilde{\Sigma}_1$. The eigenvectors $\mathbf{u}_j$ must be selected so that the corresponding eigenvalues $\lambda_j$ satisfy

$$(1-s)\lambda_1^s + s\lambda_1^{s-1} \geq \cdots \geq (1-s)\lambda_d^s + s\lambda_d^{s-1} \geq \cdots \geq (1-s)\lambda_D^s + s\lambda_D^{s-1} \qquad (72)$$

The feature extractor is then given as

$$A = [\mathbf{u}_1, \ldots, \mathbf{u}_d] \qquad (73)$$

A suboptimal solution for the general case of distinct mean vectors and covariance matrices can be obtained by combining the two special-case solutions. In particular, the feature extractor can be formed by the vector in (71) and the first $d - 1$ columns of the matrix in (73).

Feature extractors based on other measures in Eqs. (26)–(34) can be obtained in a similar manner. These two class separability measures can also be used for extracting features in *multiclass problems* as follows. A set of candidate feature space axes $\mathbf{u}_j$ can be generated by considering the separability of all the $m(m-1)/2$ possible class pairs. A candidate axis $\mathbf{u}_j$ transforms the observation vector $\mathbf{y}$ into a candidate feature $\xi_j$. In order to find a low-dimensional feature space, we need to select the most effective subset of $d$ candidate features using the multiclass feature selection criterion in (35). In this manner the feature extraction problem will be converted into a feature selection problem, which has already been covered in the preceding sections. Note that since the candidate axes may be linearly dependent, bottom-up search algorithms should be used to find the best feature set to avoid computational problems. The feature extractor will then be defined by the axes corresponding to the features contained in the best feature set.

The feature extraction equivalents of the *interclass distance measures* of Eqs. (51)–(54) are listed in Eqs. (74)–(77), where $\tilde{\Sigma}$ and $\tilde{M}$ are the matrices defined in (48) and (49) relating to the complete observation space.

$$J_1(A) = \text{Tr}[A^{\text{T}}(\tilde{\Sigma} + \tilde{M})A] \tag{74}$$

$$J_2(A) = \text{Tr}(A^{\text{T}}\tilde{M}A)/\text{Tr}(A^{\text{T}}\tilde{\Sigma}A) \tag{75}$$

$$J_3(A) = \text{Tr}(A^{\text{T}}\tilde{\Sigma}A)^{-1}(A^{\text{T}}\tilde{M}A) \tag{76}$$

$$J_4(A) = |A^{\text{T}}(\tilde{\Sigma} + \tilde{M})A|/|A^{\text{T}}\tilde{\Sigma}A| \tag{77}$$

All these measures can be optimized analytically with appropriate constraints, which are necessary to prevent a meaningless scaling of the feature space. Interestingly, the optimal feature extractors derived from these measures are identical. They are defined by the $d$ eigenvectors $\mathbf{u}_j$ of the matrix product $\tilde{\Sigma}^{-1}\tilde{M}$ selected in descending order of the corresponding eigenvalues $\lambda_j$,

$$\lambda_1 \geq \lambda_2 \geq \cdots \lambda_d \geq \cdots \lambda_D \tag{78}$$

### Nonparametric Measures   C

For *normally distributed classes* the feature extraction form of *error probability* in (6) becomes

$$e(A) = 1 - \sum_{i=1}^{m} P(\omega_i) \int_{Y_i} [(2\pi)^d |A^{\text{T}}\tilde{\Sigma}_i A|]^{-1/2}$$

$$\times \exp\{-\tfrac{1}{2}(\mathbf{y} - \boldsymbol{\mu}_i)^{\text{T}} A(A^{\text{T}}\tilde{\Sigma}_i A)^{-1} A^{\text{T}}(\mathbf{y} - \boldsymbol{\mu}_i)\} \, d\mathbf{y} \tag{79}$$

where $Y_i$ is the region of the observation space associated with class $\omega_i$ by the Bayes decision rule, that is, a pattern $y \in Y_i$ is assigned to class $\omega_i$. Minimization of $e(A)$ is equiavelent to maximization of the summation term denoted by $J_e(A)$. Differentiating $J_e(A)$, we find

$$J_e'(A) = \frac{1}{2} \sum_{i=1}^{m} P(\omega_i)[\gamma_i \tilde{\Sigma}_i + \Theta_i - \tilde{\Sigma}_i A(A^{\text{T}}\tilde{\Sigma}_i A)^{-1}A^{\text{T}}\Theta_i]A(A^{\text{T}}\tilde{\Sigma}_i A)^{-1}$$

where $\gamma_i$ and $\Theta_i$ can be estimated, respectively, as

$$\hat{\gamma}_i = \frac{1}{N_i} \sum_j 1 \quad \forall_j \quad \text{such that} \quad \mathbf{y}_j \in \omega_i \quad \text{and} \quad \mathbf{y}_j \varepsilon Y_i \tag{80}$$

$$\hat{\Theta}_i = \tilde{\Sigma}_i - \frac{1}{N_i} \sum_j (\mathbf{y}_j - \tilde{\boldsymbol{\mu}}_i)(\mathbf{y}_j - \tilde{\boldsymbol{\mu}}_i)^{\text{T}} \quad \forall_j \quad \text{such that} \quad y_j \in \omega_i, \quad y_j \notin Y_i \tag{81}$$

The gradient can be used in numerical optimization of the error criterion. Note that region $Y_i$ and therefore $\gamma_i$ and $\Theta_i$ are functions of matrix $A$ via the Bayes decision rule. The estimates of $\gamma_i$ and $\Theta_i$ need to be updated at every iteration of the optimization algorithm.

In the case of *two nonparametrically distributed classes*, the application of any of the probabilistic separability measures discussed in Section III.B will require an estimate of the class-conditional probability density functions (PDFs) involved. The assessment of various PDF estimators and feature evaluation functions rapidly leads to the conclusion that the only combination that will leave a scope for an analytical simplification is the *Patrick-Fisher probabilistic distance* and the Parzen estimator employing a Gaussian kernel. The latter is defined as

$$\hat{p}(A^{T}\mathbf{y}|\omega_i) = \frac{1}{N_i} \sum_{j=1}^{N_i} K(A^{T}\mathbf{y}, A^{T}\mathbf{y}_j^i), \qquad \mathbf{y}_j^i \varepsilon \omega_i \tag{82}$$

where $K(A^{T}\mathbf{y}, A^{T}\mathbf{y}_j^i)$ is a normal density function centered at the *i*th class sample point $A^{T}\mathbf{y}_j^i$ and with a diagonal covariance matrix $\Sigma = \delta^2 I$.

Owing to the convenient form of the kernel, the Patrick–Fisher distance

$$J_{\mathrm{P}}(A) = \left\{ \int [P(\omega_1)p(A^{T}\mathbf{y}|\omega_1) - P(\omega_2)p(A^{T}\mathbf{y}|\omega_2)]^2 \, d\mathbf{y} \right\}^{1/2} \tag{83}$$

can be integrated analytically to yield

$$J_{\mathrm{P}}(A) = \left\{ (2\delta\sqrt{\pi})^{-d} \sum_{h=1}^{2} \sum_{i=1}^{2} \sum_{j=1}^{N_h} \sum_{k=1}^{N_i} (-1)^{h+i} \frac{P(\omega_h)P(\omega_i)}{N_h N_i} \right.$$
$$\left. \times \exp\left\{ \frac{-1}{4\delta^2} (\mathbf{y}_j^h - \mathbf{y}_k^i)^{T} A A^{T} (\mathbf{y}_j^h - \mathbf{y}_k^i) \right\} \right\}^{1/2} \tag{84}$$

The gradient of $J_{\mathrm{P}}(A)$, which is required for numerical optimization of the criterion function, is given as

$$J_{\mathrm{P}}'(A) = \frac{1}{2J(A)(2\delta\sqrt{\pi})^d} \sum_{h=1}^{2} \sum_{i=1}^{2} \sum_{j=1}^{N_h} \sum_{k=1}^{N_i} (-1)^{h+i} \frac{P(\omega_h)P(\omega_i)}{N_h N_i}$$
$$\times \exp\left\{ \frac{-1}{4\delta^2} (\mathbf{y}_j^h - \mathbf{y}_k^i)^{T} A A^{T} (\mathbf{y}_j^h - \mathbf{y}_k^i) \right\} \left[ -\frac{1}{4\delta^2} (\mathbf{y}_j^h - \mathbf{y}_k^i)(\mathbf{y}_j^h - \mathbf{y}_k^i)^{T} A \right] \tag{85}$$

The same approach can be used in *m-class problems*, with the Patrick–Fisher probabilistic distance being replaced by the Patrick–Fisher probabilistic dependence.

## D   Karhunen–Loeve Expansion

The Karhunen-Loeve (K–L) coordinate axes are defined by eigenvectors of the matrix of second-order statistical moments of the probability distribution of pattern vector **y**. The projection of pattern vector **y** onto the K–L coordinate system has a number of desirable properties. First of all, the components of the transformed pattern vector are uncorrelated. Second, the information contained in **y** is compressed into a small number of K–L axes, that is, into only a few coefficients of the K–L expansion. Both properties can be exploited in feature extraction.

*Method 1.* Most of the discriminatory information is usually contained in first-order statistical moments. The objective of feature extraction is to project this information into a subspace of the observation space. However, the subspace effectiveness cannot be assessed without reference to second-order statistical moments, since the first-order information can be completely obliterated by large variances of pattern vector components and their covariances. Because of their decorrelating properties, the K–L axes defined by the eigenvectors of the average within-class covariance matrix $\tilde{\Sigma}$ offer an ideal system for assessing the first-order discriminatory information content. The feature extractor is then formed by the eigenvectors $\mathbf{u}_j, j = 1, \ldots, d$, providing the largest signal-to-noise ratio, that is, satisfying

$$\frac{\mathbf{u}_1^\mathsf{T} \tilde{M} \mathbf{u}_1}{\lambda_1} \geq \cdots \geq \frac{\mathbf{u}_d^\mathsf{T} \tilde{M} \mathbf{u}_d}{\lambda_d} \geq \cdots \geq \frac{\mathbf{u}_D^\mathsf{T} \tilde{M} \mathbf{u}_D}{\lambda_D} \tag{86}$$

where $\lambda_j$ is the eigenvalue of matrix $\tilde{\Sigma}$ associated with the $j$th eigenvector $\mathbf{u}_j$.

*Method 2.* In addition to any discriminatory information contained in the class mean vectors, some useful information may be present in second-order statistical moments. This discriminatory information can also be best assessed in the K–L coordinate system defined by eigenvectors $\mathbf{u}_j$ of matrix $\tilde{\Sigma}$. The information content is manifested in the distribution of magnitudes of the class-conditional contributions $\lambda_{ji}, i = 1, 2, \ldots, m$ to each of the eigenvalues $\lambda_j, j = 1, 2, \ldots, D$, that is,

$$\lambda_{ji} = P(\omega_i)\mathbf{u}_j^\mathsf{T} \tilde{\Sigma}_i \boldsymbol{\mu}_j \tag{87}$$

$$\sum_{i=1}^{m} \lambda_{ji} = \lambda_j \tag{88}$$

To convey useful information, the contributions $\lambda_{ji}$ must differ from each other. The extent of these differences can be objectively measured by the entropy function

$$H_j = -\sum_{i=1}^{m} \frac{\lambda_{ji}}{\lambda_j} \ln \frac{\lambda_{ji}}{\lambda_j} \tag{89}$$

where the normalization by $\lambda_j$ is required to ensure that the class-conditional contributions satisfy the axioms of probabilities. The axes yielding low entropy values are then selected to form the feature extractor $A$.

*Method 3.* In Method 1 the first-order discriminatory information conveyed by matrix $\tilde{M}$ is potentially spread over all the axes of the K–L coordinate system. Since the rank of the matrix is at most $m - 1$, it should be possible to project all this information into an $(m - 1)$-dimensional space. This objective can be achieved by first prewhitening the covariance matrix $\tilde{\Sigma}$ by diagonalizing it and then normalizing all the eigenvalues to unity. The prewhitening transformation $W$, which is formally defined as

$$W = U\Lambda^{-1/2} \tag{90}$$

where

$$\Lambda = \begin{bmatrix} \lambda_1 & \cdots & 0 \\ \vdots & \ddots & \vdots \\ 0 & \cdots & \lambda_D \end{bmatrix} \tag{91}$$

will, of course, also affect matrix $\tilde{M}$, yielding a new matrix $W^T\tilde{M}W$. The application of the K–L expansion to compress the information contained in $W^T\tilde{M}W$ then provides the required feature extractor $A$, that is, the columns of $A$ satisfy

$$W^T\tilde{M}W\mathbf{a}_j - \alpha_j\mathbf{a}_j = 0, \qquad j = 1, 2, \ldots, m - 1 \tag{92}$$

where $\alpha_j$, $j = 1, 2, \ldots, m - 1$ are the nonzero eigenvalues of the matrix $W^T\tilde{M}W$.

*Method 4.* When the class labels are not available (*nonsupervised learning*) and matrix $\tilde{\Sigma}$ cannot be computed, we can apply the K–L expansion to compress information in the unlabelled observations **y**. The K–L feature extractor $A$ is then defined by the $d$ eigenvectors of the mixture covariance matrix $\Phi$, associated with the largest eigenvalues, that is,

$$A = (\mathbf{a}_1, \ldots, \mathbf{a}_d) \tag{93}$$

where $\mathbf{a}_j$ satisfy

$$\Phi\mathbf{a}_j - \beta_j\mathbf{a}_j = 0 \tag{94}$$

and

$$\beta_1 \geq \beta_2 \cdots \beta_d \geq \cdots \beta_D \tag{95}$$

## V  CONCLUDING REMARKS

This chapter covers the fundamental methodology of feature selection and extraction in pattern recognition. It cannot be overemphasized that the limited scope of the chapter precluded a more detailed and exhaustive treatment of the subject. A number of important issues have necessarily been omitted, such as the problem of selecting features for sequential or tree classifiers where the cost of measurement extraction is also to be considered in the selection process.

When applying the tools described in this chapter it is important to remember the various sources of suboptimality affecting the results. They include

1. Use of suboptimal criterion functions
2. Use of suboptimal search strategies
3. PDF estimation errors due to small sample sizes
4. Numerical errors
5. Fitting errors

Constant awareness of these problems will allow the user of the presented systematic methodology to view the results in the correct perspective.

## BIBLIOGRAPHY

J. Aczel and Z. Daroczy, "On Measures of Information and Their Characterization." Academic Press, New York, 1975.

B. P. Adhikari and D. D. Joshi, Distance discrimination et resume exhaustif, *Publ. Inst. Statist.* **5**, 57–74 (1956).

A. Bhattacharyya, On a measure of divergence between two statistical populations defined by their probability distributions, *Bull. Calcutta Math. Soc.* **35**, 99–109 (1943).

D. E. Boekee and J. C. A. Van Der Lubbe, Some aspects of error bounds in feature selection, *Pattern Recognition* **11**, 353–360 (1979).

C. H. Chen, On information and distance measures, error bounds, and feature selection, *Inform. Sci.* **10**, 159–171 (1976).

H. Chernoff, A measure of asymptotic efficiency for tests of a hypothesis based on a sum of observations, *Ann. Math. Statist.* **23**, 493–507 (1952).

Y. T. Chien and K. S. Fu, On the generalized Karhunen–Loeve expansion, *IEEE Trans. Inform. Theory* **13**, 518–520 (1967).

T. M. Cover, The best two independent measurements are not the two best, *IEEE Trans. Systems Man Cybernet.* **4**, 116–117 (1974).

T. M. Cover and J. M. Van Campenhout, On the possible orderings in the measurement selection problem, *IEEE Trans. Systems Man Cybernet.* **7**, 657–661 (1977).

P. A. Devijver and J. Kittler, "Pattern Recognition: A Statistical Approach." Prentice-Hall, Englewood Cliffs, New Jersey, 1982.

R. J. P. de Figueiredo, K. C. Pau, A. D. Sagar, S. A. Starks, and D. L. Van Rooy, An algorithm for extraction of more than one optimal feature from several Gaussian pattern classes. *Proc. Third Internat. Conf. Pattern Recognition, Coronado, California, Nov. 1976*, 793–796 (1976).

P. A. Devijver, On a new class of bounds on Bayes risk in multihypothesis pattern recognition, *IEEE Trans. Comput.* **23**, 70–80 (1974).

J. D. Elashoff, R. M. Elashoff, and G. E. Goldman, On the choice of variables in classification problems with dichotomous variables, *Biometrika* **54**, 668–678 (1976).

R. A. Fisher, The use of multiple measurements in taxonomic problems, *Ann. Eugenics* **7**, 179–188 (1936).

H. P. Friedman, On some invariant criteria for grouping data, *J. Am. Statist. Assoc.* **62**, 1159–1178 (1967).

K. S. Fu, "Sequential Methods in Pattern Recognition and Machine Learning." Academic Press, New York, 1968.

K. Fukunaga, "Introduction to Statistical Pattern Recognition." Academic Press, New York, 1972.

K. Fukunaga and T. F. Krill, Calculation of Bayes recognition errors for two multivariate Gaussian distributions, *IEEE Trans. Comput.* **18**, 220–229 (1969).

T. L. Henderson and D. G. Lainiotis, Comments on linear feature extraction, *IEEE Trans. Inform. Theory* **15**, 729–730 (1969).

W. Hoeffding, Stochastische abhangigkeir und funktionaler zusammenhang, *Skand. Aktuarietidskr.* **25**, 200–227 (1942).

M. Ichino and K. Hiramatsu, Suboptimal linear feature selection in multiclass problems, *IEEE Trans. Systems Man Cybernet.* **4**, 28–33 (1974).

A. K. Jain, On an estimate of the Bhattacharyya distance, *IEEE Trans. Systems Man Cybernet.* **6**, 763–766 (1976).

H. Jeffreys, An invariant form for the prior probability in estimation problems, *Proc. Roy. Soc. A* **186**, 453–461 (1946).

A. K. Joshi, A note on a certain theorem stated by Kullback, *IEEE Trans. Inform. Theory* **10**, 93–94 (1964).

T. T. Kadota and L. A. Shepp, On the best set of linear observables for discriminating two Gaussian signals. *IEEE Trans. Inform. Theory* **13**, 278–284 (1967).

T. Kailath, The divergence and Bhattacharyya distance measures in signal selection, *IEEE Trans. Commun. Technol.* **15**, 52–60 (February 1967).

J. Kittler and P. C. Young, A new approach to feature selection based on the Karhunen–Loeve expansion, *Pattern Recognition* **5**, 335–352 (1973).

J. Kittler, A nonlinear distance metric criterion for feature selection in the measurement space, *Inform. Sci.* **9**, 359–363 (1976).

J. Kittler, Methods of feature selection in the measurement space based on interclass distance measures, *Proc. 8th Internat. Congress on Cybernetics, Namur, 1976*, pp. 330–342 (1976).

J. Kittler, Mathematical methods of feature selection in pattern recognition, *Internat. J. Man Mach. Stud.* **7**, 609–637 (1975).

J. Kittler, A review of feature extraction methods based on probabilistic distance measures, *Proc. SITEL-ULG Seminar on Pattern Recognition, Liege, Belgium, Nov. 1977*, pp. 2.2/1–2.2/10 (1977).

J. Kittler, Feature selection methods based on the Karhunen–Loeve expansion, *in* "Pattern Recognition Theory and Application" (K. S. Fu and A. B. Whinston, eds.), pp. 61–74. Noordhoff, Leyden, 1977.

S. Kullback, "Information Theory and Statistics." Wiley, New York, 1959.

P. M. Lewis, The characteristic selection problem in recognition systems, *IRE Trans. Inform. Theory* **8**, 171–178 (1962).

P. C. Mahalanobis, On the generalized distance in statistics, *Proc. National Inst. Sci. (India)* **12**, 49–55 (1936).

T. Marill and D. M. Green, On the effectiveness of receptors in recognition systems, *IEEE Trans. Inform. Theory* **9**, 11–17 (January 1963).

K. Matusita, Decision rules based on the distance for problems of fit, two samples and estimation, *Ann. Math. Statist.* **26**, 631–640 (1955).

W. S. Meisel, "Computer Oriented Approaches to Pattern Recognition." Academic Press, New York, 1972.

M. Michael and W. C. Lin, Experimental study of information measures and inter–intra class distance ratios on feature selection and ordering, *IEEE Trans. Systems Man Cybernet.* **3**, 172–181 (1973).

P. M. Narendra and K. Fukunaga, A branch and bound algorithm for feature subset selection, *IEEE Trans. Comput.* **26**, 917–922 (September 1977).

E. A. Partick and F. P. Fisher, Nonparametric feature selection, *IEEE Trans. Inform. Theory* **15**, 557–584 (1969).

G. Sebestyen, "Decision Making Processes in Pattern Recognition." Macmillan, New York, 1962.

C. E. Shannon, A mathematical theory of communication, *Bell. Syst. Tech. J.* **27**, 379–423, 623–656 (1948).

S. D. Stearns, On selecting features for pattern classifiers, *Proc. Third Internat. Conf. Pattern Recognition, Coronado, California, Nov. 1976*, pp. 71–75 (1976).

J. T. Tou and R. P. Heydorn, Some approaches to optimum feature extraction, *in* "Computer and Information Sciences II" (J. T. Tou, ed.), pp. 57–89. Academic Press, New York, 1967.

G. T. Tousaint, Note on the optimal selection of independent binary features for pattern recognition, *IEEE Trans. Inform. Theory* **17**, 618 (1971).

G. T. Toussaint, On the divergence between two distributions and the probability of misclassification of several decision rules, *Proc. 2nd Internat. Conf. Pattern Recognition, Copenhagen, 1974*, pp. 27–34 (1974).

S. Watanabe, Karhunen–Loeve expansion and factor analysis, *Trans, 4th Prague Conf. Information Theory, 1965* (1965).

S. Watanabe, P. S. Lambert, C. A. Kulikowski, J. L. Buxton, and R. Walker, Evaluation and selection of variables in pattern recognition, *in* "Computer and Information Sciencies II" (J. T. Tou, ed.), pp. 91–112. Academic Press, New York, 1967.

S. Watanabe, "Knowing and Guessing." Wiley, New York, 1969.

A. Whitney, A direct method of nonparametric measurement selection, *IEEE Trans. Comput.* **20**, 1100–1103 (1971).

S. Wilks, "Mathematical Statistics." Wiley, New York, 1962.

T. R. Vilmansen, Feature evaluation with measures of probabilistic dependence, *IEEE Trans. Comput.* **22**, 381–388 (1973).

# Chapter **4**

# Syntactic Pattern Recognition

KING-SUN FU

School of Electrical Engineering
Purdue University
West Lafayette, Indiana

## INTRODUCTION   I

The many different mathematical techniques used to solve pattern analysis (description and interpretation) problems may be grouped into two general approaches [1-3]. They are the statistical approach and the syntactic (or structural) approach [4, 5]. In the statistical approach, a set of characteristic measurements, called features, is extracted from the images. Each pattern is represented by a feature vector, and the recognition of each pattern is usually made by partitioning the feature space. On the other hand, in the syntactic approach each pattern is expressed as a composition of its components, called subpatterns and pattern primitives. This approach draws an analogy between the structure of patterns and the syntax of a language. The

HANDBOOK OF PATTERN RECOGNITION
AND IMAGE PROCESSING

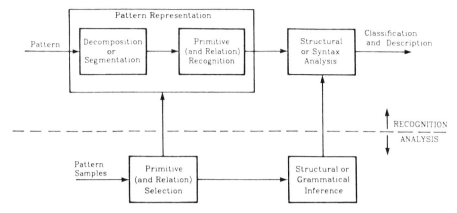

**Fig. 1.** Block diagram of a syntactic pattern analysis system.

recognition of each pattern is usually made by parsing the pattern structure according to a given set of syntax rules. In this chapter we briefly review the recent progress in syntactic approaches to pattern analysis.

A block diagram of a syntactic pattern analysis system is shown in Fig. 1. The system consists of segmentation or decomposition, primitive recognition (including relations among pattern primitives and subpatterns), and syntax (or structural) analysis.

In syntactic methods a pattern is represented by a sentence in a language, which is specified by a grammar. The language that provides the structural description of patterns, in terms of a set of pattern primitives and their composition relations, is sometimes called the "pattern description language." The rules governing the composition of primitives into patterns are specified by the "pattern grammar." An alternative representation of the structural information of a pattern is to use a "relational graph," in which the nodes represent the subpatterns and the branches represent the relations between subpatterns [4–8].

Following the notations used in Aho and Ullman [9], the definition of grammars and languages is now briefly reviewed.

*Definition* 1. A grammar is a 4-tuple $G = (V_N, V_T, P, S)$, where

(1)   $V_N$ is a finite set of nonterminal symbols,
(2)   $V_T$ is a set of terminal symbols disjoint from $N$,
(3)   $P$ is a finite subset of

$$(V_N \cup V_T)^* V_N (V_N \cup V_T)^* \times (V_N \cup V_T)^*$$

An element of $(\alpha, \beta)$ in $P$ will be written $\alpha \to \beta$ and called a production[†],

(4)   $S$ is a distinguished symbol in $V_N$ called the start symbol

[†] $(V_N \cup V_T)^*$ denotes the set containing all strings over $(V_N \cup V_T)$.

*Definition* 2. The language generated by a grammar $G$, denoted $L(G)$, is the set of sentences generated by $G$. Thus,

$$L(G) = \{\omega | \omega \text{ is in } V_T^* \text{ and } S \overset{*}{\Rightarrow} \omega\}$$

where a relation $\Rightarrow$ on $(V_N \cup V_T)^*$ is defined as follows: if $\alpha\beta\gamma$ is in $(V_N \cup V_T)^*$ and $\beta \to \delta$ is a production rule in $P$, then $\alpha\beta\gamma \Rightarrow \alpha\delta\gamma$ and $\overset{*}{\Rightarrow}$ denotes the reflexive and transitive closure of $\Rightarrow$.

If each production in $P$ is of the form $A \to \alpha$, where $A$ is in $V_N$ and $\alpha$ is in $(V_N \cup V_T)^*$, then the grammar $G$ is a context-free grammar. The languages generated by context-free grammars are called context-free languages.

Figure 2 gives an illustrative example for the description of the boundary of a submedian chromosome image. The hierarchical structural description is shown in Fig. 2a, and the context-free grammar generating submedian chromosome boundaries is given in Fig. 2b. Figure 3b shows a structural representation of the scene in Fig. 3a in terms of a hierarchical relational graph.

## PRIMITIVE SELECTION AND PATTERN GRAMMARS    II

Since pattern primitives are the basic components of a pattern, presumably they are easy to recognize. Unfortunately, this is not necessarily the case in some practical applications. For example, strokes are considered good primitives for script handwriting; however, strokes cannot easily be extracted by machine. A compromise between its use as a basic part of the pattern and its easiness for recognition is often required in the process of selecting pattern primitives.

There is no general solution for the primitive selection problem at this time [4–6]. For line patterns or patterns described by boundaries or skeletons, line segments are often suggested as primitives. A straight line segment can be characterized by the locations of its beginning (tail) and end (head), its length, and/or its slope. Similarly, a curve segment can be described in terms of its head and tail and its curvature. The information characterizing the primitives can be considered as their associated semantic information or as features used for primitive recognition. Through the structural description and the semantic specification of a pattern, the semantic information associated with its subpatterns or the pattern itself can then be determined. For pattern description in terms of regions, half-planes have been proposed as primitives. Shape and texture measurements are often used for the description of regions.

After pattern primitives are selected, the next step is the construction of a grammar (or grammars) that will generate a language (or languages) to describe the patterns under study. It is known that increased descriptive

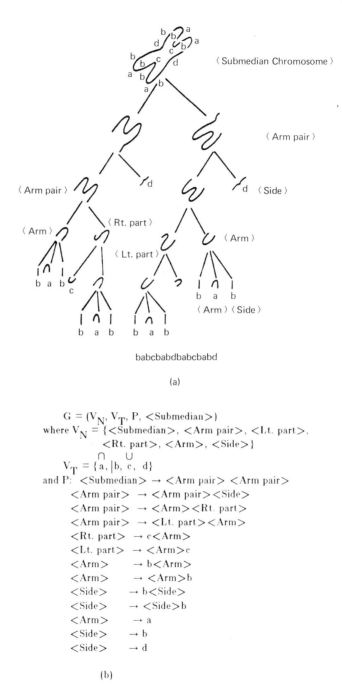

babcbabdbabcbabd

(a)

$$G = (V_N, V_T, P, <\text{Submedian}>)$$
where $V_N = \{<\text{Submedian}>, <\text{Arm pair}>, <\text{Lt. part}>,$
$<\text{Rt. part}>, <\text{Arm}>, <\text{Side}>\}$

$$V_T = \{a, |b, c, d\}$$

and P:  $<\text{Submedian}> \rightarrow <\text{Arm pair}> <\text{Arm pair}>$
$<\text{Arm pair}> \rightarrow <\text{Arm pair}><\text{Side}>$
$<\text{Arm pair}> \rightarrow <\text{Arm}><\text{Rt. part}>$
$<\text{Arm pair}> \rightarrow <\text{Lt. part}><\text{Arm}>$
$<\text{Rt. part}> \rightarrow c<\text{Arm}>$
$<\text{Lt. part}> \rightarrow <\text{Arm}>c$
$<\text{Arm}> \quad\rightarrow b<\text{Arm}>$
$<\text{Arm}> \quad\rightarrow <\text{Arm}>b$
$<\text{Side}> \quad\rightarrow b<\text{Side}>$
$<\text{Side}> \quad\rightarrow <\text{Side}>b$
$<\text{Arm}> \quad\rightarrow a$
$<\text{Side}> \quad\rightarrow b$
$<\text{Side}> \quad\rightarrow d$

(b)

**Fig. 2.** Syntactic representation of a submedian chromosome: (a) hierarchical structural description and (b) context-free grammar generating submedian chromosome boundaries.

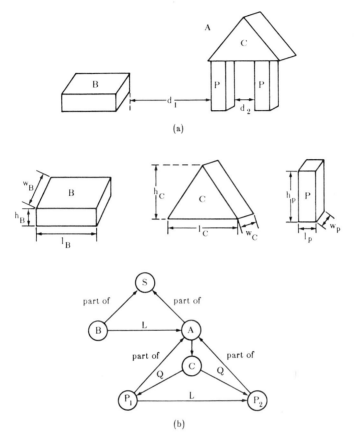

**Fig. 3.** (a) Scene $A$ and (b) its attributed relational graph representation. Attributes of brick B: $l_B$, $w_B$, $h_B$. Attributes of triangular prism C: $l_C$, $w_C$, $h_C$. Attributes of pillars $P_1$ and $P_2$: $l_p$, $w_p$, $h_p$. Attributes of relation "left of" $L$: distance $d$. Relation $Q$: "supported by."

power of a language is paid for in terms of increased complexity of the syntax analysis system (recognizer or acceptor). Finite-state automata are capable of recognizing finite-state languages, although the descriptive power of finite-state languages is also known to be weaker than that of context-free and context-sensitive language. On the other hand, nonfinite, nondeterministic procedure are required, in general, to recognize languages generated by context-free and context-sensitive grammars. The selection of a particular grammar for pattern description is affected by the primitives selected and by the trade-off between the grammar's descriptive power and analysis efficiency.

If the primitives selected are very simple, more complex grammars may have to be used for pattern description. On the other hand, use of sophisticated primitives may result in rather simple grammars for image description, which in turn would result in fast recognition algorithms. The interplay between the complexities of primitives and of pattern grammars is certainly very important in the design of a syntactic pattern analysis system. Context-free programmed grammars, which maintain the simplicity of context-free grammars but can generate context-sensitive languages, have recently been suggested for pattern description [4].

A number of special languages have been proposed for the description of patterns such as English and Chinese characters, chromosome images, spark chamber pictures, two-dimensional mathematics, chemical structures, and fingerprint patterns [5, 6]. For the purpose of effectively describing image patterns, high-dimensional grammars such as web grammars, array grammars, graph grammars, tree grammars, and shape grammars have been used for syntactic image analysis [5, 6, 10–13].

Ideally speaking, it would be nice to have a grammatical (or structural) inference machine which could infer a grammar from a given set of image patterns. Unfortunately, not many convenient grammatical inference algorithms are presently available for this purpose [6, 7, 14–19]. Nevertheless, recent literature has indicated that some simple grammatical inference algorithms have already been applied to syntactic pattern analysis, particularly through man–machine interaction [19–21].

## III   HIGH-DIMENSIONAL GRAMMARS FOR PATTERN DESCRIPTION

### A   Tree Grammars for Syntactic Pattern Analysis

This section presents a brief introduction to tree grammars and their application to syntactic pattern analysis [4, 6, 10].

*Definition* 3.  Let $N^+$ be the set of strictly positive integers. Let $U$ be the universal tree domain (the free semigroup with identity element "0" generated by $N^+$ and a binary operation "·"). Figure 4 represents the universal tree domain $U$.

*Definition* 4.  A ranked alphabet is a pair $\langle \Sigma, r \rangle$ where $\Sigma$ is a finite set of symbols and

$$r: \quad \Sigma \to N = N^+ \cup \{0\}$$

For $a \in \Sigma$, $r(a)$ is called the rank of $a$. Let $\Sigma_N = r^{-1}(n)$.

*Definition* 5.  A tree over $\Sigma$ (i.e., over $\langle \Sigma, r \rangle$) is a function

$$\alpha: \quad D \to \Sigma$$

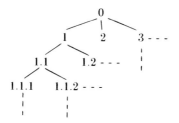

**Fig. 4.** Universal tree domain.

such that $D$ is a tree domain and

$$r[\alpha(a)] = \max\{i \mid a \cdot i \in D\}$$

The domain of a tree $\alpha$ is denoted by $D(\alpha)$. Let $T_\Sigma$ be the set of all trees over $\Sigma$.

*Definition 6.* let $\alpha$ be a tree and $a$ be a member of $D(\delta)$; $\alpha/a$, a subtree of $\alpha$ at $a$, is defined as

$$\alpha/a = \{(b, x) \mid (a \cdot b, x) \in \alpha\}$$

*Definition 7.* A regular tree grammar over $\langle V_T, r \rangle$ is a 4-tuple

$$G_t = (G, r', P, S)$$

satisfying the following conditions:

(a)   $\langle V, r' \rangle$ is a finite ranked alphabet $V_T \subseteq V$ and $r'/V_T = r$; $V - V_T = V_N$, the set of nonterminals.
(b)   $P$ is a finite set of productions of the form $\Phi \rightarrow \psi$, where $\Phi$ and $\psi$ are trees over $\langle V, r' \rangle$.
(c)   $S$ is a finite subset of $T_V$, where $T_V$ is the set of trees over alphabet $V$.

*Definition 8.* $\alpha \overset{a}{\Rightarrow} \beta$ is in $G_t$ if and only if there exists a production $\Phi \rightarrow \psi$ in $P$ such that $\Phi$ is a subtree of $\alpha$ at $a$ and $\beta$ is obtained by replacing the occurrence of $\Phi$ at $a$ by $\psi$. We write $\alpha \Rightarrow \beta$ in $G_t$ if and only if there exists $a \in D(\alpha)$ such that $\alpha \overset{a}{\Rightarrow} \beta$.

*Definition 9.* $\alpha \overset{*}{\Rightarrow} \beta$ is in $G_t$ if and only if there exists $\alpha_0, \alpha_1, \ldots, \alpha_m, (m > 0)$ such that

$$\alpha = \alpha_0 \Rightarrow \alpha_1 \Rightarrow \cdots \Rightarrow \alpha_m = \beta$$

in $G_t$. The sequence $\alpha_0, \ldots, \alpha_m$ is called a derivative or deduction of $\beta$ from $\alpha$, and $m$ is the length of the deduction.

*Definition 10.* $L(G_t) = \{\alpha \in T_{V_T} \mid$ there exists $Y \in S$ such that $Y \overset{*}{\Rightarrow} \alpha$ in $G_t\}$ is called the (tree) language generated by $G_t$.

*Definition 11.* A tree grammar $G_t = (V, r, P, S)$ is expansive if and only if each production in $P$ is of the form

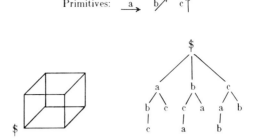

Primitives:   $\xrightarrow{a}$   $b\nearrow$   $c\uparrow$

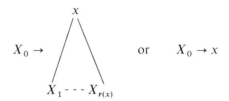

**Fig. 5.** Tree representation of a square object.

$$X_0 \to \overbrace{\underset{X_1 - - - X_{r(x)}}{\bigwedge}}^{x} \qquad \text{or} \qquad X_0 \to x$$

where $x \in V_T$ and $X_0, X_1, \ldots, X_{r(x)}$ are nonterminal symbols. For each regular tree grammar $G_t$, we can effectively construct an equivalent expansive grammar $G_{t'}$, that is, $L(G_{t'}) = L(G_t)$.

*Example* 1. The square object in Fig. 5 can be described by the tree shown in Fig. 5.

*Example* 2. The tree grammar

$$G_t = (V, r, P, S)$$

where $V = (S, a, b, \$, A, B)$

$$V_T = \{\xrightarrow{a}, \uparrow b, \cdot\$\}$$

$$r(a) = \{2, 1, 0\}, \qquad r(b) = \{2, 1, 0\}, \qquad r(\$) = 2$$

and $P$:

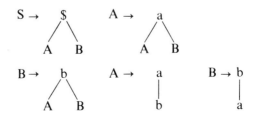

generated the patterns such as:

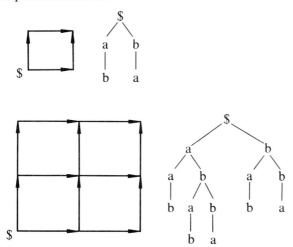

Tree automata are the recognizers (or acceptors) of regular tree languages.

*Definition* 12. A tree automaton over $\Sigma$ is a $(k + 2)$-tuple

$$M_t = (Q, f_1, \ldots, f_k, F)$$

where (i) $Q$ is a finite set of states, (ii) for each $i$, $1 \leq i \leq k$, $f_i$ is a relation on $Q^{r(\sigma_i)} \times Q$, $\sigma_i \in \Sigma$, that is,

$$f_i: \quad Q^{r(\sigma_i)} \to Q$$

and (iii) $F \subseteq Q$ is a set of final states.

*Definition* 13. The response relation $\rho$ of a tree automaton $M_t$ is defined as

(a)  if $\sigma \in \Sigma_0$, $\rho(\sigma) \sim X$ if and only if $f_\sigma \sim X$, that is, $\rho(\sigma) = f_\sigma$;

(b)  if $\sigma \in \Sigma_n$, $n > 0$, $\rho(\sigma, x_0, \ldots, x_{n-1}) \sim X$ if and only if there exists $x_0, \ldots, x_{n-1}$ such that $f_\sigma(x_0, \ldots, x_{n-1}) \sim X$ and $\rho(x_i) \sim X_i$, $1 \leq i \leq n$, that is, $\rho(\sigma, x_0, \ldots, x_{n-1}) = f_\sigma(\rho(x_{n-1}))$.

*Definition* 14. $T(M_t) = \{\alpha \in T_\Sigma | \text{ there exists } X \in F \text{ such that } \rho(\alpha) \sim X\}$ is called the set of trees accepted by $M_t$. For every regular tree grammar $G_t$, we can effectively construct a tree automaton $M_t$ such that $T(M_t) = L(G_t)$ [4, 6]. The construction procedure is summarized as follows:

(a)  Obtain an expansive tree grammar $G_{t'} = (V', r, P', S)$ for the given regular tree grammar $G_t = (V, r, P, S)$ over alphabet $V_T$.

(b)  The equivalent (nondeterministic) tree automaton is

$$M_t = (V' - V_T, f_1, \ldots, f_k, \{S\})$$

where $f_X(X_1, \ldots, X_n) \sim X_0$ if $X_0 \to xX_1, \ldots, X_n$ is in $P'$.

The tree automaton which accepts the set of trees generated by $G_t$ in Example 2 is

$$M_t = (A, f_a, f_b, f_{\$}, F)$$

where

$$Q = \{q_a, q_b, q, q_F\}, \qquad F = \{q_F\}$$

and

$$f: \quad f_a \sim q_a, \qquad f_a(q, q) \sim q, \qquad f_a(q_b) \sim q$$

$$f_b \sim q_b, \qquad f_b(q, q) \sim q, \qquad f_b(q_a) \sim q, \qquad f_{\$}(q, q) \sim q_F$$

*Example* 3. The following tree grammar can be used to generate trees representing $L$–$C$ networks:

$$G_t = (V, r, P, S)$$

where

$$V = \{S, V_{in}, L, C, W, \$\}$$

$$r(V_{in}) = 1, \qquad r(L) = \{2, 0\}, \qquad r(C) = 1, \qquad r(W) = 0, \qquad r(\$) = 2$$

and $P$:

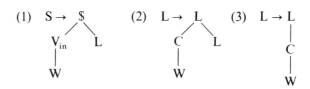

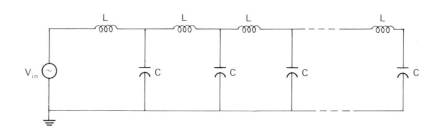

For example, after applying productions (1), (2), and (3), the tree in Fig. 6 is generated.

The tree automaton which accepts the set of trees generated by $G_t$ is

$$M_t = (Q, f_{V_{in}}, f_L, f_C, f_W, f_{\$}, F)$$

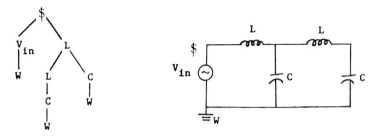

**Fig. 6.** An $L$-$C$ network and its tree representation.

where

$$Q = \{q_1, q_2, q_3, q_4, q_F\}$$

$$F = \{q_F\}$$

and

$$f: \quad f_{V_{in}}(q_1) \sim q_4, \qquad f_L \sim q_2, \qquad f_L(q_2, q_3) \sim q_2$$

$$f_C(q_1) \sim q_3, \qquad f_W \sim q_1, \qquad f_\$(q_2, q_4) \sim q_F$$

### Web Grammars for Pattern Description  B

One of the two-dimensional grammars is the web grammar proposed by Pfaltz and Rosenfeld [11]. Sentences generated by a web grammar are directed graphs with symbols at their vertices ("webs").

*Definition* 15. A web grammar $G$ is a 4-tuple

$$G = (V_N, V_T, P, S)$$

where $V_N$ is a set of nonterminals, $V_T$ is a set of terminals, $S$ is a set of "initial" webs, and $P$ is a set of web productions or writing rules. A web production is defined as[†]

$$\alpha \rightarrow \beta, E$$

where $\alpha$ and $\beta$ are webs and $E$ is an embedding of $\beta$. If we want to replace the subweb $\alpha$ of the web $\omega$ by another subweb $\beta$, it is necessary to specify how to "embed" $\beta$ in $\omega$ in place of $\alpha$. The definition of an embedding must not depend on the host web $\omega$, since we want to be able to replace $\alpha$ by $\beta$ in any web containing $\alpha$ as a subweb. Usually $E$ consists of a set of logical functions which specify whether or not each vertex of $\omega - \alpha$ is connected to each vertex of $\beta$.

---

[†] In a most general formulation, the contextual condition of the production is added [11, 22].

*Example* 4. Consider a web grammar

$$G = (V_N, V_T, P, S)$$

where

$$V_N = \{A\}, \qquad V_T = \{a, b, c\}, \qquad S = \{\dot{A}\}$$

and

P:   (1)   $\dot{A} \to a$  $\begin{matrix} b \\ \\ c \end{matrix}$     $E \doteq \{(p, a)|(p, A)$ an edge in the host web$\}$

(2)   $\dot{A} \to a$  $\begin{matrix} b \\ \\ c \end{matrix}$  $A$     $E$ is the same as in (1)

The language of this grammar is the set of all webs of the form

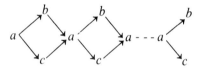

It is noted that web grammars are vertex- or node- oriented compared with the branch- or edge-oriented grammars (e.g., PDL, Plex grammars, etc.) [23]. That is, terminals or primitives are represented as vertices in the graph rather than as branches.

   An important special case of a web grammar is that in which the terminal set $V_T$ consists of only a single symbol. In this case, every point of every web in the language has the same label, so that we can ignore the labels and identify the webs with their underlying graphs. This type of web grammar is called a "graph grammar," and its language is called graph language [24]. A web production is context sensitive if there exists a point $a$ of $\alpha$ such that $\alpha - \{a\}$ is a subweb of $\beta$ and all edges between points of the host web and points of $\alpha - \{a\}$ are in $E$. In particular, the production will be context free if $\alpha$ has only a single point. Thus, a web grammar is called context sensitive (context free) if all its productions are context sensitive (context free). The web grammar in Example 4 is context free since only one-point webs are rewritten. Figure 7c shows the context-free web grammar productions to characterize the scene in Fig. 7a. These productions can be easily obtained from the derivation diagram of the relational graph shown in Fig. 7b.

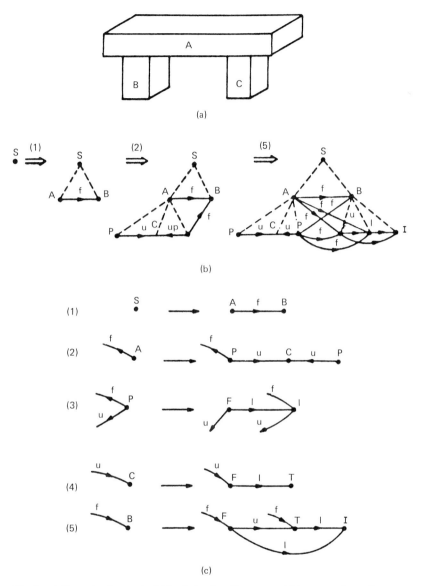

**Fig. 7.** (a) Example of an arch, (b) its derivation diagram, and (c) context-free web grammar productions. S, start symbol; A, arch; B, block; P, pillar; C, crossbar; F, front; I, side; T, top; f, in front of; u, under; l, left of.

In comparison with the plex grammar, we can consider the $N$ attaching-point entity (NAPE) in a plex grammar as webs in which one point is labeled with the name of the NAPE and the others with the identifiers of its attaching points. The joint lists in a plex grammar, which describe how sets of NAPEs are interconnected, correspond to the edges internal to the subwebs $\alpha$ and $\beta$ in a web production, while the tie point list corresponds to the embedding $E$ of $\beta$ in the host web.

*Example* 5. Consider the context-free graph grammar

$$G = (V_N, V_T, P, S)$$

where

$$V_N = \{A\}, \qquad V_T = \{a\}, \qquad S = \{\dot{a}, \dot{a} \to A\}$$

and

$P$:  (1)  $\dot{a} \to \dot{a} \to A$    $E = \{(p, a)|(p, A) \text{ an edge in the host web}\}$

    (2)  $\dot{A} \to \dot{\underset{\dot{A}}{A}}$    $E = \{(p, A)|(p, A) \text{ an edge in the host web}\}$

    (3)  $\dot{A} \to \dot{a}$    $E = \{(p, a)|(p, A) \text{ an edge in the host web}\}$

The language generated by this web grammar consists of all directed trees which have least elements.

*Example* 6. The following context-free graph grammar generates the set of all basic two-terminal series–parallel networks (TTSPN):

$$G = (V_N, V_T, P, S)$$

where

$$V_N = \{A\}, \qquad V_T = \{a\}, \qquad S = \{\dot{a} \to a, \dot{a} \to A \to a\}$$

and

$P$:  (1)  $\dot{A} \to A_{(1)} \to A_{(2)}$    $E = \{(p, A_{(1)})|(p, A) \text{ an edge in the host web}\}$
                                           $U \{A_{(2)}, p)|(A, p) \text{ an edge in the host web}\}$

    (2)  $\dot{A} \to \dot{\underset{\dot{A}}{A}}$    $E = \{(p, A)|(p, A) \text{ an edge in the host web}\}$
                                           $U \{(A, p)|(A, p) \text{ an edge in the host web}\}$

    (3)  $\dot{A} \to \dot{a}$    $E$ is the same as in (2).

A typical TTSPN generated, for example, would be

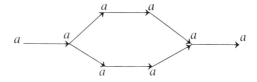

*Example* 7. Consider the context-sensitive web grammar

$$G = (V_N, V_T, P, S)$$

where

$$V_N = \{B, Z, Z', W, W', X\}$$

$$V_T = \{a, b, c, w, x, y, z\}$$

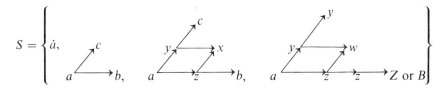

and

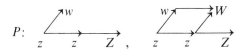

where the embedding of the "new" vertex (labeled $W$) is as shown; the attachments or connections of the other vertices in the rewritten web remain unchanged. Similar embeddings occur in the remaining rules.

The grammar generates "directed triangles" of the form

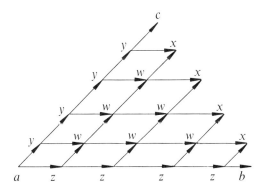

The syntax analysis (parsing) for the grammar generating all TTSPNs was implemented using the language GIRL (graph information retrieval language) [22]. GIRL is a SLIP-like extension of FORTRAN which allows a programmer to store a directed graph data structure in the computer using a few basic instructions. The analysis of a set of black-and-white images simulating neural nets in terms of web grammar was implemented using a system of FORTRAN programs collectively called NRNTST (for neuron test). NRNTST would accept pictures of simulated neural nets and produce corresponding picture description webs [22].

**Fig. 8.** Photograph of Marion County imagery from digital display.

*Example* 8. Multispectral signals measured by LANDSAT over Marion County, Indiana were analyzed using clustering analysis [2, 25]. Fourteen clusters were found, and the data from the metropolitan area were accordingly classified using a Bayes classifier. The classification result of each pixel (picture element) from the Bayes classifier provides the basic pattern primitives (Fig. 8). A hierarchical relational graph model for the spatial relationships between various classes can be constructed as shown in Fig. 9. Relations between each pair of entities are shown only at the level they first occur, although if a pair of entities are related, their descendants are also related. The form of the hierarchical graph model is the same as the derivation diagram for the web grammar with some of its productions shown in Fig. 9.

The hierarchical relational graph model shown in Fig. 9 describes the spatial or contextual relationships between primitives (spectral classes) and subpatterns (land-use classes). The spatial relations represented by web (or graph) grammar productions have been used to identify highway patterns and to improve the accuracy of cloud classification in the LANDSAT image [5, 26].

## IV  SYNTACTIC RECOGNITION

Conceptually, the simplest form of recognition is probably "template matching." The sentence describing an input pattern is matched against

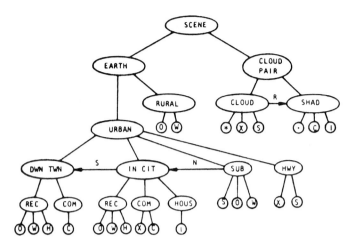

**Fig. 9.** Hierarchical graph model of the scene in Fig. 8.

sentences representing each prototype or reference pattern. Based on a selected "matching" or "similarity" criterion, the input pattern is classified in the same class as the prototype pattern which is the "best" to match input. The structural information is not recovered. If a complete pattern description is required for recognition, a parsing or syntax analysis is necessary. In between the two extreme situations, there are a number of intermediate approaches. For example, a series of tests can be designed to test the occurrence or nonoccurrence of certain subpatterns (or primitives) or certain combinations of them. The result of the tests, through a table lookup, a decision tree, or a logical operation, is used for a classification decision. Recently, the use of discriminant grammars has been proposed for the classification of syntactic image patterns [27].

There are many parsing algorithms proposed for context-free languages [9]. For the class of general context-free languages, Earley's parsing algorithm is briefly described in this section.

*Algorithm* 1. Earley's parsing algorithm [9]:

*Input*: A context-free grammar $G = (N, \Sigma, P, S)$ and an input string $x = a_1 a_2 \cdots a_n$ in $\Sigma^*$.

*Output*: The parse lists $I_0, I_1, \ldots, I_n$

*Method*:

(A) Construction of $I_0$:

Step 1. If $S \to \alpha$ is in $P$, add $[S \to \cdot \alpha, 0]$ to $I_0$. Perform Steps 2 and 3 until no new items can be added to $I_0$.

Step 2. If $[B \to \gamma \cdot, 0]$ is on $I_0$, add $[A \to \alpha B \cdot \beta, 0]$ for all $[A \to \alpha \cdot B\beta, 0]$ on $I_0$.

Step 3. Suppose that $[A \rightarrow \alpha \cdot B\beta, 0]$ is an item in $I_0$. Add to $I_0$, for all productions in $P$ of the form $B \rightarrow \gamma$, the item $[B \rightarrow \cdot\gamma, 0]$, provided this item is not already in $I_0$.

(B) Construction of $I_j$ from $I_0, I_i, \ldots, I_{j-1}$:

Step 4. For each $[B \rightarrow \alpha \cdot a\beta, i]$ in $I_{j-1}$ such that $a = a_j$, add $[B \rightarrow \alpha a \cdot \beta, i]$ to $I_j$. Perform Steps 5 and 6 until no new item can be added.

Step 5. Let $[A \rightarrow \alpha\cdot, i]$ be an item in $I_j$. Examine $I_i$ for items of the form $[B \rightarrow \alpha \cdot A\beta, k]$. For each one found, add $[B \rightarrow \alpha A \cdot \beta, k]$ to $I_j$.

Step 6. Let $[A \rightarrow \alpha \cdot B\beta, i]$ be an item in $I_j$. For all $B \rightarrow \gamma$ in $P$, add $[B \rightarrow \cdot\gamma, j]$ to $I_j$.

Note that $x$ is in $L(G)$ if and only if there is some item of the form $\{S \rightarrow \alpha\cdot, 0]$ in $I_n$. An algorithm is available to recover the pattern structure or the parse of $x$ from the parse lists [9]. It can be shown that the time complexity of Algorithm 1 is in general $O(n^3)$, that is, Algorithm 1 can be executed in $O(n^3)$ suitably defined elementary operations when the input is of length $n$. If the underlying grammar $G$ is unambiguous, the time complexity reduces to $O(n^2)$.

A parsing procedure for recognition is, in general, nondeterministic and, hence, is regarded as computationally inefficient. Efficient parsing could be achieved by using special classes of languages such as finite-state and deterministic languages for pattern description. Special parsers using sequential procedures or other heuristic means for efficiency improvement in syntactic pattern recognition have recently been constructed [28–30].

## V  ERROR-CORRECTING PARSING

In practical applications, pattern distortion and measurement noise often exist. Segmentation errors and misrecognitions of primitives (and relations) and/or subpatterns will lead to erroneous or noise sentences rejected by the grammar characterizing the image class. Recently, the use of an error-correcting parser as a recognizer of noisy and distorted patterns has been proposed [28, 31–34]. In the use of an error-correcting parser as a recognizer, the pattern grammar is first expanded to include all the possible errors into its productions. The original grammar is transformed into a covering grammar that generates not only the correct sentences, but also all the possible erroneous sentences. For string grammars, three types of error—substitution, deletion, and insertion—are considered. Misrecognition of primitives (and relations) is regarded as substitution errors, and segmentation errors are regarded as deletion and insertion errors.

The distance between two strings is defined in terms of the minimum number of error transformations used to derive one from the other by Aho and Peterson [35]. When the error transformations are defined in terms of substitution, delection, and insertion errors, the distance measurement coincides with the definition of the Levenshtein metric [36]. For a given input string $y$ and a given grammar $G$, a minimum-distance error-correcting parser[†] (MDECP) is an algorithm that searches for a sentence $z$ in $L(G)$ such that the distance between $z$ and $y$, $D(z, y)$, is the minimum among the distances between all the sentences in $L(G)$ and $y$. The algorithm also generates the value of $d(z, y)$. We simply define this value to be the distance between $L(G)$ and $y$ and denote it as $d_1(L(G)\,y)$.

When a given grammar is a context-free grammar (CFG), its MDECP can be implemented by modifying Earley's parsing algorithm. We also extend the definition of the distance between $L(G)$ and $y$, $d_1(L(G), y)$, to the definition of $d_K(L(G), y)$, the average distance between $y$ and the $K$ sentences in $L(G)$ that are the nearest to $y$. The computation of $d_K(L(G), y)$ can be implemented by further modification of the algorithm of the MDECP.

*Definition* 16. For two strings $x, y \in \Sigma^*$, we can define a transformation $T: \Sigma^* \to \Sigma^*$ such that $y \in T(x)$. The following three transformations are introduced.

(1) Substitution error transformation:

$$\omega_1 a \omega_2 \left|\frac{T_S}{}\right. \omega_1 b \omega_2 \qquad \text{for all} \quad a, b \in \Sigma, \quad a \neq b,$$

(2) Deletion error transformation:

$$\omega_1 a \omega_2 \left|\frac{T_D}{}\right. \omega_1 \omega_2 \qquad \text{for all} \quad a \in \Sigma$$

(3) Insertion error transformation:

$$\omega_1 \omega_2 \left|\frac{T_I}{}\right. \omega_1 a \omega_2 \qquad \text{for all} \quad a \in \Sigma$$

where $\omega_1, \omega_2 \in \Sigma^*$.

*Definition* 17. The distance between two strings $x, y \in \Sigma^*$, $d^L(x, y)$, is defined as the smallest number of transformations required to derive $y$ from $x$.

---

[†]If the pattern grammar is stochastic, the maximum-likelihood and Bayes criteria can be applied [28, 33].

*Example* 8. Given a sentence $x = cbabdbb$ and a sentence $y = cbbabbdb$, then

$$x = cbabdbb$$

$$\left| \frac{T_S}{} cbabbbb \right| \frac{T_S}{} cbabbdb \left| \frac{T_I}{} cbbabbdb = y \right.$$

The minimum number of transformations required to transform $x$ to $y$ is three; thus, $d^L(x, y) = 3$.

The metric defined in Definition 17 gives exactly the Levenshtein distance between two strings [36]. A weighted Levenshtein distance can be defined by assigning nonnegative numbers $\sigma$, $\gamma$, and $\delta$ to transformations $T_S$, $T_D$, and $T_I$, respectively. Let $x, y \in \Sigma^*$ be two strings, and let $J$ be a sequence of transformations used to derive $y$ from $x$; then the weighted Levenshtein distance between $x$ and $y$, denoted as $d^w(x, y)$, is

$$d^w(x, y) = \min_j \{\sigma \cdot k_j + \gamma \cdot m_j + \delta \cdot n_j\} \tag{1}$$

where $k_j$, $m_j$, and $n_j$ are the number of substitution, deletion, and insertion error transformations, respectively, in $J$.

A weighted metric has been proposed to reflect the difference of the same type of error made on different terminals. Let the weights associated with error transformations on terminal $a$ in a string $\omega_1 a \omega_2$, where $a \in \Sigma$, $\omega_1$ and $\omega_2 \in \Sigma^*$, be defined as follows:

$$(1) \quad \omega_1 a \omega_2 \left| \frac{T_S, S(a, b)}{} \omega_1 b \omega_2 \right. \quad \text{for} \quad b \in \Sigma, \quad b \neq a,$$

where $S(a, b)$ is the cost of substituting $a$ for $b$. Let $S(a, a) = 0$.

$$(2) \quad \omega_1 a \omega_2 \left| \frac{T_D, D(a)}{} \omega_1 \omega_2 \right.$$

where $D(a)$ is the cost of deleting $a$ from $\omega_1 a \omega_2$.

$$(3) \quad \omega_1 a \omega_2 \left| \frac{T_I I(a, b)}{} \omega_1 b a \omega_2 \right. \quad \text{for} \quad b \in \Sigma,$$

where $I(a, b)$ is the cost of inserting $b$ in front of $a$.

We further define the weight of inserting a terminal $b$ at the end of a string $x$ to be

$$(4) \quad x \left| \frac{T_I, I'(b)}{} xb \right. \quad \text{for} \quad b \in \Sigma.$$

Let $x, y \in \Sigma^*$ be two strings, and let $J$ be a sequence of transformations used to derive $y$ from $x$. Let $|J|$ be defined as the sum of the weights associated with transformations in $J$; then the weighted distance between $x$ and $y$, $d^W(x, y)$, is defined as

$$d^W(x, y) = \min_J \{|J|\} \qquad (2)$$

Let $L(G)$ be a given language and let $y$ be a given sentence; the essence of MDECP is to search for a sentence $x$ in $L(G)$ that satisfies the minimum-distance criterion, as follows:

$$d(x, y) = \min_z \{d(z, y) | z \in L(G)\} \qquad (3)$$

We note that the minimum-distance correction of $y$ is $y$ itself if $y \in L(G)$.

The MDECP proposed by Aho and Peterson [35] is now extended to all three types of metric; $L$, $w$, and $W$. In Aho and Peterson [35], the procedure for constructing an ECP starts with the modification of a given grammar $G$ by adding the thre types of error transformations in the form of production rules, called error productions. The grammar $G$ is now expanded to $G'$ such that $L(G')$ includes not only $L(G)$ but all possible sentences with the three types of errors. The parser constructed according to $G'$ with a provision added to count the number of error productions used in a derivation is the error-correcting parser for $G$. For a given sentence $y$, the ECP will generate a parse $\Pi$, which consists of the smallest number of error productions. A sentence $x$ in $L(G)$ that satisfies the minimum-distance criterion (measured by using Levenshtein distance) can be generated from $\Pi$ by eliminating error productions. With some modifications, this minimum-distance ECP can easily be extended to the three metrics proposed. We first give the algorithm of constructing an expanded grammar, in which the nonnegative numbers associated with error productions are the weights associated with their corresponding error transformations with respect to the metric used.

*Algorithm* 2. Construction of expanded grammar:

*Input*: A CFG $G = (V_N, V_T, P, S)$
*Output*: A CFG $G' = (V_N', V_T', P', S')$, where $P'$ is a set of weighted productions

*Method*:
Step 1. $V_N' = V_N \cup \{S'\} \cup \{E_a | a \in V_T\}$, $V_T' \supseteq V_T$
Step 2. If $A \rightarrow \alpha_0 b_1 \alpha_1 b_2 \cdots b_m \alpha_m$, $m \geq 0$ is a production in $P$ such that $\alpha_i \in V_N^*$ and $b_i \in V_T$, then add $A \rightarrow \alpha_0 E_{b_1} \alpha_1 E_{b_2} \cdots E_{b_m} \alpha_m$, 0 to $P'$, where each $E_{b_i}$ is a new nonterminal, $E_{b_i} \in V_N'$, and 0 is the weight associated with this production
Step 3. Add the following productions to $P'$:

|                      |        | Weight |                |                                              |
|----------------------|--------|--------|----------------|----------------------------------------------|
| Production rule      | $L$    | $w$    | $W$ (metric)   |                                              |
| (a) $S' \to S$       | 0      | 0      | 0              |                                              |
| (b) $S' \to Sa$      | 1      | $\delta$ | $I'(a)$      | for all $a \in V'_T$                         |
| (c) $E_a \to a$      | 0      | 0      | 0              | for all $a \in V_T$                          |
| (d) $E_a \to b$      | 1      | $\sigma$ | $S(a, b)$    | for all $a \in V_T$, $b \in V'_T$, and $b \neq a$ |
| (e) $E_a \to \lambda$| 1      | $\gamma$ | $D(a)$       | for all $a \in V_T$                          |
| (f) $E_a \to bE_a$   | 1      | $\delta$ | $I(a, b)$    | for all $a \in V_T$, $b \in V'_T$            |

In Algorithm 2 the production rules added in Steps 3b,d,e, and f, are called error productions. Each error production corresponds to one type of error transformation on a particular symbol in $V_T$. Therefore, the distance measured in terms of error transformations can be measured by error productions used in a derivation. The parser is a modified Earley's parsing algorithm with a provision added to accumulate the weights associated with productions used in a derivation. The algorithm is as follows.

*Algorithm 3.* Minimum-distance error-correcting parsing algorithm.

*Input:* An expanded grammar $G' = (V'_N, V'_T, P', S')$ and an input string

$$y = b_1 b_2 \cdots b_m \quad \text{in} \quad V'^*_T$$

*Output:* $I_0, I_1, \ldots, I_m$, the parse list for $y$, and $d(x, y)$, where $x$ is the minimum-distance correction of $y$

*Method:*

Step 1. Set $j = 0$. Then add $[E \to \cdot S', 0, 0]$ to $I_j$.

Step 2. If $[A \to \alpha \cdot B\beta, i, \xi]$ is in $I_j$, and $B \to \gamma, \eta$ is a production rule in $P'$, then add item $[B \to \cdot \gamma, j, 0]$ to $I_j$.

Step 3. If $[A \to \alpha \cdot i, \xi]$ is in $I_j$ and $[B \to \beta \cdot A\gamma, k, \xi]$ is in $I_i$, and if no item of the form $[B \to \beta A \cdot \gamma, k, \phi]$ can be found in $I_j$, then add an item $[B \to \beta A \cdot \gamma, k, \eta + \xi + \zeta)$ to $I_j$, where $\zeta$ is the weight associated with production $A \to \alpha$. If $[B \to \beta A \cdot \gamma, k, \phi]$ is already in $I_j$, then replace $\phi$ by $\eta + \xi + \zeta$ if $\phi > \eta + \xi L\zeta$

Step 4. If $j = m$, go to Step 6; otherwise, $j = j + 1$

Step 5. For each item in $I_{j-1}$ of the form $[A \to \alpha \cdot b_j\beta, i, \xi]$, add item $[A \to \alpha b_j \cdot \beta, i, \xi]$ to $I_j$; go to Step 2

Step 6. If items $[E \to S', 0, \xi]$ is in $I_m$, then $d(x, y) = \xi$, where $x$ is the minimum-distance correction of $y$; exit

In Algorithm 3, the string $x$, which is the minimum-distance correction of $y$, can be derived from the parse of $y$ by eliminating all the error productions. The extraction of the parse of $y$ is the same as that described in Earley's algorithm.

We define the distance between a string and a given language based on any one of the three metrics as follows [6].

*Definition* 18. let $y$ be a sentence, and let $L(G)$ be a given language; the distance between $L(G)$ and $y$, $d_K(L(G), y)$, where $K$ is a given positive integer, is

$$d_K(L(G), y) = \min\left\{ \sum_{i=1}^{K} \frac{1}{K} d(z_i, y) \mid z_i \in L(G) \right\} \qquad (4)$$

In particular, if $K = 1$, then

$$d_1(L(G), y) = \min\{d(z, y) \mid z \in L(G)\} \qquad (5)$$

is the distance between $y$ and its minimum-distance correction in $L(G)$.

Since the distance between a string (a syntactic pattern) and a language (a set of syntactic patterns) is defined, a minimum-distance decision rule can be stated as follows. Suppose that there are two classes of patterns, $C_1$ and $C_2$, characterized by grammars $G_1$ and $G_2$, respectively. For a given syntactic pattern $y$ with unknown classification, decide $y \in \begin{smallmatrix} C_1 \\ C_2 \end{smallmatrix}$ if $d(L(G_1), y) \lessgtr d(L(G_2), y)$.

The sequential parsing procedure suggested by Persoon and Fu [30] has been applied to error-correcting parsers to reduce the parsing time [28]. By sacrificing a small amount of error-correcting power (that is, allowing a small error in parsing), a parsing can be terminated much earlier before a complete sentence is scanned. The trade-off between the parsing time and the error committed can be easily demonstrated. In addition, error-correcting parsing for transition network grammars [33] and tree grammars [34] has also been studied. For tree grammars, five types of error—substitution, deletion, stretch, branch, and split—are considered. The original tree pattern grammar is expanded by including the five types of error transformation rule. The tree automaton constructed according to the expanded tree grammar and the minimum-distance criterion is called an error-correcting tree automaton (ECTA). When only substitution errors are considered, the structure of the tree to be analyzed remains unchanged. Such an error-correcting tree automaton is called a "structure-preserved" error-correcting tree automaton (SPECTA). Another approach to reducing the parsing time is the use of parallel processing [37].

## CLUSTERING ANALYSIS FOR SYNTACTIC PATTERNS   VI

In statistical pattern recognition, a pattern is represented by a vector, called a feature vector. The similarity between two patterns can often be expressed by a distance, or more generally speaking, a metric in the feature space. Cluster analysis can be performed on a set of images on the basis of a selected similarity measure [2, 25]. In syntactic pattern analysis, a similarity measure between two syntactic image patterns must include the similarity of both their structures and primitives. In Section V we have proposed distance measures for strings, which leads to the study of clustering analysis for syntactic patterns. The conventional clustering methods, such as the minimum spanning tree, the nearest- (or $k$-nearest-) neighbor classification rule, and the method of clustering centers, can be extended to syntactic patterns.

The studies described in Section VI.A are mainly on the sentence-to-sentence basis [38]. An input sentence (pattern) is compared with sentences in a formed cluster, one by one, or with the representative (cluster center) of the cluster. In Section VI.B we use the distance measure between a sentence and a language [39]. The proposed clustering procedure is combined with a grammatical inference procedure and an error-correcting parsing technique. The idea is to model the formed cluster by inferring a grammar which implicitly characterizes the structural identity of the cluster. The language generated by the grammar may be larger than the set consisting of the members of the cluster, and it includes some possible similar image patterns due to the recursive nature of grammar. Then the distance between an input sentence (an image pattern) and a language (a group of image patterns) is computed by using an ECP. The recognition is based on the nearest-neighbor rule.

## A    Sentence-to-Sentence Clustering Algorithms

### 1    A Nearest-Neighbor Classification Rule

Suppose that $C_1$ and $C_2$ are two image sets, represented by sentences $X_1 = \{x_1^1, x_2^1, \ldots, x_{n_1}^1\}$ and $X_2 = \{x_1^2, x_2^2, \ldots, s_{n_2}^2\}$, respectively. For an unknown image pattern $y$, decide that $y$ is in the same class as $C_1$ if

$$\min_j d(x_j^1, y) < \min_l d(x_l^2, y)$$

and $y$ is in class $C_2$ if

$$\min_j d(x_j^1, y) > \min_l d(x_l^2, y)$$

In order to determine $\min_j d(x_j^i, y)$ for some $i$, the distance between $y$ and every element in the set $X_i$ must be computed individually. The string-to-string correction algorithm proposed in Lu and Fu [38] yields exactly the distance between two strings defined in Definition 17.

The nearest-neighbor classification rule can be easily extended to the $K$-nearest-neighbor rule. Let $\tilde{X}_i = \{\tilde{x}_1^i, \tilde{x}_2^i, \ldots, \tilde{x}_{n_i}^i\}$ be a reordered set of $X_i$ such that $d(\tilde{x}_j^i, y) \leq d(\tilde{x}_l^i, y)$ iff $j < l$, for all $1 \leq j, l \leq n_i$; then

$$\text{decide} \quad y \in \begin{smallmatrix} C_1 \\ C_2 \end{smallmatrix} \quad \text{if} \quad \sum_{j=1}^{K} \frac{1}{K} d(\tilde{x}_j^1, y) \lessgtr \sum_{j=1}^{K} \frac{1}{K} d(\tilde{x}_j^2, y) \tag{6}$$

We shall describe a clustering procedure in which the classification of an input pattern is based on the nearest (or $K$-nearest) neighbor rule.

*Algorithm* 4.

*Input*: A set of samples $X = \{x_1, x_2, \ldots, x_n\}$ and a design parameter, or threshold, $t$

*Output*: A partition of $X$ into $m$ clusters $C_1, C_2, \ldots, C_m$

*Method*:

Step 1. Assign $x_1$ to $C_1$, $j = 1$, $m = 1$

Step 2. Increase $j$ by one. If $D = \min_i d(x_i^i, x_j)$ is the minimum, $1 \leq i \leq m$, and (i) $D \leq t$, then assign $x_j$ to $C_i$; (ii) $D > t$, then initiate a new cluster for $x_j$ and increase $m$ by one

Step 3. Repeat Step 2 until every string in $X$ has been put in a cluster

Note that in Algorithm 4, a design parameter is required. A commonly used clustering procedure is to construct a minimum spanning tree. Each node on the minimum spanning tree represents an element in the same set $X$. Then partition the tree. Actually, when the distances between all of the pairs $d(x_i, x_j)$, $x_i, x_j \in X$, are available, the algorithm for constructing the minimum spanning tree is the same as that for the case in which $X$ is a set of feature vectors in the statistical pattern recognition [2, 25].

### The Cluster Center Techniques    2

Let us define a $\beta$-metric for a sentence $x_j^i$ in cluster $C_i$, as follows:

$$\beta_j^i = \frac{1}{n_i} \sum_{l=1}^{n_i} d(x_j^i, x_l^i) \tag{7}$$

Then $x_j^i$ is the cluster center of $C_i$, if $\beta_j^i = \min_l \{\beta_l^i | 1 < l < n_i\}$; $x_j^i$ is also called the representative of $C_i$, denoted $A_i$. The following clustering algorithm is given in Fu [2] and Lu and Fu [38].

*Algorithm* 5.

*Input*: A sample set $X = \{x_1, x_2, \ldots, x_n\}$

*Output*: A partition of $X$ into $m$ clusters

*Method*:

Step 1. Let $m$ elements of $X$, chosen at random, be the "representatives" of the $m$ clusters. Let them be called $A_1, A_2, \ldots, A_m$

Step 2. For all $i$, $x_i \in X$ is assigned to cluster $j$, iff $d(A_j, x_i)$ is minimum

Step 3. For all $j$, a new mean $A_j$ is computed; $A_j$ is the new representative of cluster $j$

Step 4. If no $A_j$ has changed, stop. Otherwise, go to Step 2

## B    A Proposed Nearest-Neighbor Syntactic Recognition Rule

With the distance between a sentence and a language defined as in Section V, we can construct a syntactic recognizer using the nearest- (or $K$-nearest) neighbor rule. Suppose that we are given two classes of images characterized by grammars $G_1$ and $G_2$, respectively. For an unknown image pattern $y$, decide that $y$ is in the same class as $L(G_1)$ if

$$d(L(G_1), y) < d(L(G_2), y)$$

and decide that $y$ is in the same class as $L(G_2)$ if

$$d(L(G_2), y) < d(L(G_1), y) \tag{8}$$

The distance $d(L(G_i), y)$ can be determined by a minimum-distance ECP constructed for $G_i$. Consequently, a grammatical inference procedure is required to infer a grammar for each class of image pattern samples. Since the parser also gives the structural description of $y$, the syntactic recognizer gives both the classification and description of $y$ as its output. We shall summarize the procedure in the following algorithm.

*Algorithm 6.*

*Input*: $m$ sets of pattern samples

$$X_1 = \{x_1^1, x_2^1, \ldots, x_{n_1}^1\}, \ldots, X_m = \{x_1^m, x_2^{2m}, \ldots, x_{n_m}^m\}$$

and pattern $y$ with unknown classification

*Output*: The classification and structural description of $y$

*Method*:

Step 1. Infer $m$ grammars $G_1, G_2, \ldots, G_m$ from $X_1, X_2, \ldots, X_m$, respectively

Step 2. Construct minimum-distance ECPs, $E_1, E_2, \ldots, E_m$ for $G_1, G_2, \ldots, G_m$, respectively

Step 3. Calculate $d(L(G_k), y)$ for all $i = 1, \ldots, m$. Determine $l$ such that

$$d(L(G_l), y) = \min_k d(L(G_k), y)$$

$y$ is then classified as being from class $l$. In the meantime, the structural description of $x$ can be obtained from $E_l$

Using the distance defined in Section V as a similarity measure between a pattern and a set of image patterns, we can perform a cluster analysis to syntactic patterns. The procedure again involves error-correcting parsing and grammatical inference. In contrast to the nearest-neighbor rule in Algorithm 6, which uses a supervised inference procedure, the procedure described in this section is basically nonsupervised. When the image pattern samples are observed sequentially, a grammar can be easily inferred for the sample observed at each stage of the clustering procedure. We propose the following clustering procedure for image patterns.

*Algorithm 7.*

*Input*: A set of pattern samples $X = \{x_1, x_2, \ldots, x_n\}$, where $x_i$ is a string of terminals or primitives. A threshold $t$

*Output*: The assignment of $x_i$, $i = 1, \ldots, n$, to $m$ clusters and the grammar $G^{(k)}$, $k = 1, \ldots, m$, characterizing each cluster

*Method*:

Step 1. Input the first sample $x_1$; infer a grammar $G_1^{(1)}$ from $x_1$, $L(G_1^{(1)}) \supseteq \{x_1\}$.

Step 2. Construct an error-correcting parser $E_1^{(1)}$ for $G_1^{(1)}$

Step 3. Input the second sample $x_2$; use $E_1^{(1)}$ to determine whether or not $x_2$ is similar to $x_1$ by comparing the distance between $L(G_1^{(1)})$ and $x_2$, that is, $d(x_2, L(G_1^{(1)}))$, with a threshold $t$. (i) If $d(x_2, L(G_1^{(1)})) < t$, $x_1$ and $x_2$ are put into the same cluster (Cluster 1). Infer a grammar $G_2^{(1)}$ from $\{x_1, x_2\}$. (ii) If $d(x_2, L(G_1^{(1)})) \geq t$, initiate a new cluster for $x_2$ (Cluster 2) and infer a new grammar $G_1^{(2)}$ from $x_2$. In this case, there are two clusters characterized by $G_1^{(1)}$ and $G_1^{(2)}$, respectively

Step 4. Repeat Step 2, construct error-correcting parsers for $G_2^{(1)}$ or $G_1^{(2)}$, depending upon $d(x_2, L(G_1^{(1)})) < t$ or $d(x_2, L(G_1^{(1)})) \geq t$, respectively

Step 5. Repeat Step 3 for a new sample. Until all the pattern samples are observed, we have $m$ clusters characterized by $G_{n_1}^{(1)}, G_{n_2}^{(2)}, \ldots, G_{n_m}^{(m)}$, respectively

The (non-error-correcting) parsers constructed according to $G_{n_1}^{(1)}, G_{n_2}^{(2)}, \ldots, G_{n_m}^{(m)}$ could then form a syntactic recognizer directly for the $m$-class analysis problem.

The threshold $t$ is a design parameter. It can be determined from a set of pattern samples with known classifications. For example, if we know that the sample $x_i$ is from class 1 characterized by $G^{(1)}$ and the sample $x_j$ is from class 2 characterized by $G^{(2)}$, then $t < d(x_i, x_j)$. Or, more generally speaking,

$$t < \min\{d(L(G^{(2)}), x_i), d(L(G^{(1)}), x_j)\} \tag{9}$$

For $m$ classes characterized by $G^{(1)}, G^{(2)}, \ldots, G^{(m)}$, respectively, we can choose

$$t < \min_{k, l}\{d(L(G^{(l)}), x^{(k)})\}, \qquad k \neq l \tag{10}$$

where $x^{(k)}$ is a pattern sample known from class $k$ and $L(G^{(l)})$ is the grammar characterizing class $l$ $(l \neq k)$. If the above-required information is not available, an appropriate value of $t$ will have to be determined on an experimental basis until a certain stopping criterion is satisfied (for example, with a known number of clusters).

## VII SYNTACTIC APPROACH TO SHAPE AND TEXTURE ANALYSIS

Shape and texture are the two major properties of image patterns. Recently, syntactic methods have been applied to both shape description and recognition. Pavlidis and Ali [40] have proposed a general model for a syntactic shape analyzer. The first major component of the model is a curve-fitting algorithm which achieves the noise elimination and data reduction. The split-and-merge algorithm is used to obtain a polygonal approximation of the boundary of the original image pattern. It is assumed that the boundaries of the objects of interest consist of concatenations of the following subpatterns or nonterminals: QUAD (arcs approximated by a quadratic curve), TRUS (sharp protrusions or intrusions), LINE (long line segments), and BREAK (short segments with no regular shape). Each of the nonterminals has a set of attributes as its semantic information. The production rules of the proposed general shape grammar consist of both syntactic and semantic rules. Stochastic finite automata are used as parsers for shape recognition.

Another method recently proposed for syntactic shape description and recognitions is the use of attributed grammars [21, 41]. Two types of primitives with attributes are proposed. The first type is a curve segment with its direction (the vector from the starting point to the end point), total length, total angular change, and a measure of its symmetry as the four attributes. The second type of primitive is an angle primitive with its attribute specified by the angular change at the concatenating point of two consecutive curve segments. Finite-state and context-free attributed grammars are used for shape description and recognition. Each production rule of the attributed grammar has a symbolic part like the conventional grammar rule and a semantic part for processing the attributes of the terminals and nonterminals in the symbolic part. The primitive extraction process is embedded in the parsing of the strings describing the boundaries of objects. Modified Earley parser and finite automata are used as shape recognizers.

Recently, a syntactic approach to texture analysis and discrimination has been proposed [42]. A texture pattern is divided into fixed-size subpatterns or windows. Using the gray level of a pixel or of a small array of pixels as primitives, we can represent each window by a tree with a prespecified tree structure. A tree grammar is used to characterize windowed patterns of the same texture. Since the windowed patterns are also a part of the global structure of the texture, one or more higher-level tree structures can be employed to describe the arrangement of windowed patterns. Error-correcting tree automata (SPECTRA) constructed according to the texture (tree) grammars can be applied for texture discrimination [42]. Stochastic tree grammars have been suggested for the modeling of noisy and distorted texture patterns [13, 43].

## VIII  SYNTACTIC IMAGE ANALYSIS AND IMAGE DATABASE MANAGEMENT

Recently, the problem of image database management has attracted increasing attention [44–47]. Almost all image database management systems use the relational database model [48]. In the meantime, relational structures are used in syntactic image analysis to represent the structural information of given images [4, 6, 7]. Attributed relational graphs have been proposed to describe image pattern structure with semantic information [8]. The relations in relational databases can be considered as data structures for representing relational graphs. The corresponding relationships between relational graphs and the relations in relational databases are as follows. For a relational graph, each set of branches with the same label corresponds to a relation of degree two (binary relation) in relational databases. A branch label corresponds to the name of a relation, and each tuple of this relation corresponds to a pair of nodes connected by a branch with this label. Consequently, the conversion of a relational graph to its corresponding relations becomes rather straightforward [46]. Furthermore, the transformation of a generalized attributed relational graph into relational databases has been proposed.

## IX  CONCLUDING REMARKS

We have briefly reviewed some recent advances in the area of syntactic pattern analysis. Due to noise and distortions in real-world patterns, the syntactic approach to pattern analysis was regarded earlier as only effective in handling abstract and artificial patterns. However, with the recent development of distance or similarity measures between syntactic patterns and error-correcting parsing procedures, the flexibility of syntactic methods has been greatly expanded. Errors occurring at the lower-level processing of an image (segmentation and primitive recognition) can be compensated at the higher level using structural information. Using a distance or similarity measure, nearest-neighbor and $K$-nearest-neighbor classification rules can be easily applied to syntactic patterns. Furthermore, with a distance or similarity measure, a clustering procedure can be applied to syntactic patterns. Such a nonsupervised learning procedure can also be very useful for grammatical inference in syntactic image analysis [39, 43]. Application of syntactic methods to time-varying image analysis and three-dimensional object recognition has recently been studied [49–52].

It has been noted from the recent advances that semantic information has been used more and more with syntax rules in characterizing patterns. Quite often, semantic information involving spatial information, such as attributed grammars and attributed relational graphs, can be expressed syntactically [5, 7, 8, 15, 21, 53–55]. Parsing efficiency has become a concern in structural analysis. Special grammars and parallel parsing algorithms have been suggested for speeding up the parsing time [56]. Structural information of a pattern can also be used as a guide in the segmentation process through the syntactic approach [57, 58]. On the other hand, simple fixed-size segmentation procedures are often used in syntactic pattern analysis, in spite of the fact that the application of these extremely simple procedures may result in unnatural subpatterns and primitives [5, 6, 13]. Syntactic representation, of patterns such as hierarchical trees and relational graphs should also be very useful for database organization. Several recent publications have already shown such a trend [45–47].

## REFERENCES

1.  K. S. Fu and A. Rosenfeld, Pattern recognition and image processing, *IEEE Trans. Computers* **C-25**, No. 12. (1976).
2.  K. S. Fu, "Digital Pattern Recognition." Springer-Verlag, Berlin and New York, 1976.
3.  A. Rosenfeld and A. C. Kak, "Digital Picture Processing," Chap. 10—Description. Academic Press, New York, 1976.
4.  K. S. Fu, "Syntactic Pattern Recognition and Applications." Prentice-Hall, Englewood Cliffs, New Jersey, 1982.
5.  K. S. Fu, "Syntactic Pattern Recognition Applications." Springer-Verlag, Berlin and New York, 1977.
6.  K. S. Fu, "Syntactic Pattern Recognition and Applications." Prentice-Hall, Englewood Cliffs, New Jersey, 1981.
7.  J. M. Brayer and K. S. Fu, Some Multidimensional Grammar Inference Methods *in* "Pattern Recognition and Artificial Intelligence." (C. H. Chen, ed), Academic Press, New York, 1976.

8. W. H. Tsai and K. S. Fu, Error-correcting isomorphisms of attributed relational graphs for pattern analysis, *IEEE Trans. Systems Man Cybernetics* **SMC-9**, 757–768 (December 1976).
9. A. V. Aho and J. D. Ullman, "The Theory of Parsing, Translation, and Compiling," Vol. 1. Prentice-Hall, Englewood Cliffs, New Jersey, 1972.
10. K. S. Fu, Tree languages and syntactic pattern recognition *in* "Pattern Recognition and Artificial Intelligence" (C. H. Chen, ed.). Academic Press, New York, 1976.
11. J. L. Pfaltz and A. Rosenfeld, Web grammars, *Proc. 1st International Joint Conference Artificial Intelligence, Washington, D.C.* (1969).
12. A. Rosenfeld, "Picture Languages." Academic Press, New York, 1979.
13. K. S. Fu, Syntactic image modeling using stochastic tree grammars, *Computer Graphics Image Processing* **12**, 136–152 (1980).
14. K. S. Fu and T. L. Booth, Grammatical inference—introduction and survey, *IEEE Trans. Systems Man Cybernetics* **SMC-5** (January and July 1975).
15. S. M. Chou and K. S. Fu, Inference for transition network grammars, *Proc. 3rd International Joint Conference on Pattern Recognition, Nov. 8–11, 1976, Coronado, California* (1976).
16. G. B. Porter, Grammatical inference based on pattern recognition, *Proc. 3rd International Joint Conference on Pattern Recognition, Nov. 8–11, 1976, Coronado, California* (1976).
17. J. M. Brayer and K. S. Fu, A note on the $k$-tail method of tree grammar inference, *IEEE Trans. Systems Man Cybernetics* **SMC-7**, No. 4, 293–299 (April, 1977).
18. A. Barrero and R. C. Gonzalez, A tree traversal algorithm for the inference of tree grammars, *Proc. 1977 IEEE Computer Society Conference Pattern Recognition Image Processing, June 6–8, Troy, New York* (1977).
19. H. C. Lee and K. S. Fu, A syntactic pattern recognition system with learning capability, *proc. 4th International Symposium Computer Information Sciences (COINS-72), Dec. 14–16, 1972 Bal Harbour, Florida* (1972).
20. J. Keng and K. S. Fu, A system of computerized automatic pattern recognition for remote sensing, *Proc. 1977 International Computer Symposium, Dec. 27–29, Taipei, Taiwan* (1977).
21. K. C. You and K. S. Fu, A syntactic approach to shape recognition using attributed grammars, *IEEE Trans. Systems Man Cybernetics* **SMC-9**, 334–345 (June 1979).
22. J. L. Pfaltz, Web grammars and picture description, Computer Science Center, University of Maryland *Tech. Rept.* **70-138** (1970).
23. A. C. Shaw, Picture graphs, grammars and parsing, *in* "Frontview of Pattern Recognition" (S. Watanabe, ed.). Academic Press, New York, 1972.
24. T. Pavlidis, Linear and Context-free graph grammars, *J. ACM* **19**, 11–12 (1972).
25. R. O. Duda, and P. E. Hart, "Pattern Classification and Scene Analysis." Wiley, New York, 1972.
26. J. M. Bayer, and K. S. Fu, Application of a web grammar model to an ERTS picture, *Proc. 3rd International Joint Conference Pattern Recognition, Nov. 8–11, 1976 Coronado, California* (1976).
27. C. Page and A. Filipski, Discriminant grammars, an alternative to parsing for pattern classification, *Proc. 1977 IEEE Workshop Picture Data Description Management, April 20–22, Chicago* (1977).
28. S. Y. Lu and K. S. Fu, Stochastic error-correcting syntax analysis for recognition of noisy patterns, *IEEE Trans. Computers* **C-26**, No. 12, 1268–1276 (December 1977).
29. T. Pavlidis, Syntactic features extraction for shape recognition, *proc. 3rd International Joint Conf. Pattern Recognition, Nov. 8–11, 1976, Coronado, California*, pp. 95–99 (1976).
30. E. Persoon and K. S. Fu, Sequential classification of strings generated by SCFG's, *International Journal Computers Information Sciences* **4** (September 1975).
31. L. W. Fung and K. S. Fu, Stochastic syntactic decoding for pattern classification, *IEEE Trans. Computers* **C-24**, No. 6, 662–667 (June 1975).
32. M. G. Thomason and R. C. Gonzalez, Error detection and classification in syntactic pattern structures, *IEEE Trans. Computers* **C-24**, No. 1, 93–95 (January 1975).

33. K. S. Fu, Error-correcting parsing for syntactic pattern recognition, *in* "Data Structure, Computer Graphics and Pattern Recognition" (A. Klinger *et al.*, eds.). Academic Press, New York, 1977.
34. S. Y. Lu and K. S. Fu, Error-correcting tree automata for syntactic pattern recognition, *IEEE Trans. Computers* **C-27**, No. 11, 1040–1053 (November 1978).
35. A. V. Aho and T. G. Peterson, A minimum distance error-correcting parser for context-free languages, *SIAM Journal Computing* **4** (December 1972).
36. V. I. Levenshtein, Binary codes capable of correcting deletions, insertions and reversals, *Sov. Phys. Dokl.* **10** (February 1966).
37. N. S. Chang and K. S. Fu, Parallel parsing of tree languages, *Proc. 1978 IEEE Computer Society Conference Pattern Recognition Image Processing, May 31–June 2, Chicago* (1978).
38. S. Y. Lu and K. S. Fu, A sentence-to-sentence clustering procedure for pattern analysis, *IEEE Trans. Systems Man Cybernetics* **SMC-8**, No. 5, 381–389 (1978).
39. K. S. Fu and S. Y. Lu, A clustering procedure for syntactic patterns, *IEEE Trans. Systems Man Cybernetics* **SMC-7**, No. 10, 734–742 (October 1977).
40. F. Ali and T. Pavlidis, Syntactic recognition of handwritten numerals, *IEEE Trans. Systems Man Cybernetics* **SMC-7**, No. 7, 537–541 (July 1977).
41. K. C. You and K. S. Fu, Distorted shape recognition using attributed grammars and error-correcting techniques, *Computer Graphics Image Processing* **13**, 1–16 (1980).
42. S. Y. Lu and K. S. Fu, A syntactic approach to texture analysis, *Computer Graphics Image Processing* **7**, No. 3 (June 1978).
43. S. Y. Lu and K. S. Fu, Stochastic tree grammar inference for texture synthesis and discrimination, *Computer Graphics Image Processing* **9**, 303–330 (March 1979).
44. A. Blaser, (ed.), "Data Base Techniques for Pictorial Applications." Springer-Verlag, Berlin and New York, 1980.
45. T. Kunii, S. Weyle, and J. M. Tenenbaum, A relational data base scheme for describing complex pictures with color and texture. *Proc. 2nd International Joint Conference Pattern Recognition, August 13–15, 1974, Copenhagen, Denmark* (1974).
46. N. S. Chang and K. S. Fu, An integrated image analysis and image database management system, *Purdue University Tech. Report* **TR-EE 80-20,** (May 1980).
47. S. K. Chang and K. S. Fu, (eds.), "Picture Information Systems." Springer-Verlag, Berlin and New York, 1980.
48. C. F. Codd, A relational model of data for large shared data banks, *Comm. ACM* **13**, No. 6 (June 1970).
49. T. I. Fan and K. S. Fu, A syntactic approach to time-varying image analysis, *Computer Graphics Image Processing* **11**, 138–149 (1979).
50. T. I. Fan and K. S. Fu, Tree translation and its application to traffic image sequence analysis, *Proc. 1981 IEEE Computer Society Conference Pattern Recognition Image Processing, August 3–5, Dallas, Texas* (1981).
51. W. C. Lin and K. S. Fu, A syntactic approach to 3D object representation, *IEEE Trans. Pattern Analysis Machine Intelligence* **PAMI-6**, No. 3, 351–364 (May 1984).
52. W. C. Lin and K. S. Fu, A syntactic approach to 3D object recognition, *Proc. IEEE Workshop Languages Automation, Nov. 1–3, 1984, New Orleans, Louisiana* (1984).
53. K. S. Fu, A step towards unification of syntactic and statistical pattern recognition, *IEEE Trans. Pattern Analysis Machine Intelligence* **PAMI-5**, No. 2, 200–205 (March 1983).
54. Q. Y. Shi and K. S. Fu, Parsin and translation of (attributed) expansive graph languages for scene analysis. *IEEE Trans. Pattern Analysis Machine Intelligence*, **PAMI-5**, No. 5, 472–485 (September 1983).
55. M. A. Eshera and K. S. Fu, A graph distance measure for image analysis, *IEEE Trans. Systems Man Cybernetics*, **SMC-14** (May/June 1984).
56. Y. T. Chiang and K. S. Fu, Parallel parsing algorithms and VLSI implementations for syntactic pattern recognition, *IEEE Trans. Pattern Analysis Machine Intelligence* **PAMI-6**, No. 3, 302–314 (May 1984).

57.  J. Keng and K. S. Fu, A syntax-directed method for land-use classification of LANDSAT images, *Proc. Symposium Current Mathematical Problems Image Science, Nov. 10–12, 1976, Monterey, California* (1976).

58.  S. Tsuji and R. Fujiwana, Linguistic segmentation of scenes into regions, *Proc. 2nd. International Joint Conference Pattern Recognition, August 13–15, 1974, Copenhagen, Denmark* (1974).

# Chapter **5**

# Syntactic Pattern Recognition: Stochastic Languages

MICHAEL G. THOMASON

Department of Computer Science
University of Tennessee
Knoxville, Tennessee

## BASIC DEFINITIONS   I

As indicated in Chapter 4, the discrete mathematical models of formal language theory [1–3] are useful descriptions of structure on which to base effective algorithms in certain areas of pattern recognition. Stochastic language theory extends the models by incorporating probabilities needed to study the expected characteristics of pattern classes and the impact of random noise or distortion. Figure 1 is a block diagram of a complete system.

Familiarity with the conventional theory of string languages is assumed. Let $\Sigma$ be a finite alphabet of terminals (pattern primitives). $\Sigma^*$ denotes the

HANDBOOK OF PATTERN RECOGNITION
AND IMAGE PROCESSING

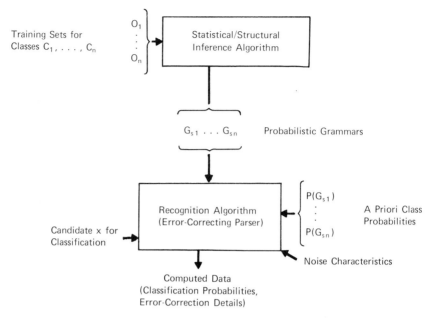

**Fig. 1.** Syntactic pattern recognition system using stochastic grammars.

denumerably infinite set of all finite-length strings of symbols from $\Sigma$, including the empty string $e$ with length 0. A *probabilistic language* over $\Sigma$ (a p-language) is a pair $(L, f)$ where $L$ is a subset of $\Sigma^*$ and $f: \Sigma^* \to [0, 1]$ is a function satisfying these requirements:

(a)   $x$ in $\Sigma^* - L$ implies $f(x) = 0$;

(b)   $\sum_x f(x) = 1$.

Here $f$ is called a probabilistic word function. For practicality, only those p-languages that can be generated by a grammar with stochastic productions are of interest. A *probabilistic* or *stochastic grammar* (p-grammar), $G_s$, is a pair $(G, F)$ where $G = (N, \Sigma, P, S)$ is a conventional grammar with nonterminal set $N$, terminal set $\Sigma$, productions $P$, and starting nonterminal $S$, and $F$ is a function assigning probabilities to the productions in $P$.

Although the production probabilities could be conditioned on various events, they are usually taken to be unconditional. A p-grammar is *unrestricted* if the probability assigned to each production $x \to y$ is the simple probability of rewriting $x$ as $y$, that is, if the rewriting of $x$ is not conditioned on events such as how $x$ itself is generated. An unrestricted p-grammar is often denoted simply as $G_s = (N, \Sigma, P_s, S)$, where the productions in $P_s$ are listed with their weights attached; for example, a production $x \to y$ for which

**TABLE 1**

**Forms of Productions to Classify a Grammar $G = (N, \Sigma, P, S)$ in the Chomsky Hierarchy**

| Type | Forms of productions | Illustration of stochastic productions |
|---|---|---|
| 0 | $\alpha \rightarrow \beta$ for $\alpha$ in $(N \cup \Sigma)^* N (N \cup \Sigma)^*$ and $\beta$ in $(N \cup \Sigma)^*$, so that $\alpha$ contains at least one nonterminal | $p: aAAb \rightarrow BAa$ for $A, B$ in N and $a, b$ in $\Sigma$ |
| 1 (context sensitive) | $\alpha A \beta \rightarrow \alpha \theta \beta$ for $A$ in $N$ and $\alpha, \beta$ in $\Sigma^*$ | $p: \alpha A \beta \rightarrow \alpha \omega \beta,\quad 1\text{-}p: \alpha A \beta \rightarrow \alpha \delta \beta$ |
| 2 (context free) | $A \rightarrow \alpha$ for $A$ in $N$ and $\alpha$ in $(N \cup \Sigma)^*$ | $p: A \rightarrow \omega,\quad 1 - p: A \rightarrow \delta$ |
| 3 (regular) | $A \rightarrow aB$ or $A \rightarrow a$ for A, B in $N$ and $a$ in $\Sigma$ | $p: A \rightarrow aB,\quad 1 - p: A \rightarrow a$ |

$F(x \rightarrow y) = p_{x,y}$ is denoted as $p_{x,y}: x \rightarrow y$. Such a p-grammar is *proper* if, for each $x$,

$$\sum_y p_{x,y} = 1$$

A p-grammar $G_s = (G, F)$ is classified as *regular* (*type* 3), *context free* (*type* 2), *context sensitive* (*type* 1), or *general phrase structure* (*type* 0) according to the form of the productions in its underlying grammar $G$. Table I defines these forms and gives illustrations of them. Types 0 and 1 remain primarily of theoretical interest, while types 2 and 3 (or variants thereof, such as stochastic programmed grammars [4]) are virtually always the forms used in practice.

Unrestricted, proper p-grammars of types 2 or 3 are considered in detail here. The rewritings of the nonterminals are independent stochastic events. When the rightmost or the leftmost derivation is designated as the standard or canonical derivation process [1], a specific derivation is naturally interpreted as the intersection of a sequence of independent events, and the probability of generating a specific string is computed over the union of the string's distinct canonical derivations; that is, given $G_s = (N, \Sigma, P_s, S)$, the probability of a derivation of string $x$ is the product of the probabilities of the productions used in that derivation, and the *probability of string $x$ in the language $L(G_s)$* is

$$p(x | G_s) = \sum_j p_j$$

where $p_j$ is the probability of the $j$th canonical derivation of $x$.

Thus, a p-grammar $G_s$ induces a function $p(-|G_s): \Sigma^* \rightarrow [0, 1]$, but it is not the case that every p-grammar generates a p-language. A p-grammar $G_s$ is *consistent* if

$$\sum_x p(x | G_s) = 1$$

## TABLE II

### Illustrations of Requirements for Consistency of Unrestricted, Proper p-Grammars

| p-Grammar $G_s$ | Example of leftmost derivations | Induced word function $p(x\|G_s): \Sigma^* \to [0,1]$ | Requirement for $\sum_x p(x\|G_s) = 1$ |
|---|---|---|---|
| $G_{sr} = (N, \Sigma, P_{sr}, S)$ <br> $N = \{S\}$ <br> $\Sigma = \{a, b\}$ <br> $P_{sr} = \{p: S \to aS, q: S \to b\}$ <br> where $p + q = 1$ <br> $L(G_r) = \{x \| x = a^n b, n \geq 0\}$ | $S \overset{p}{\Rightarrow} aS \overset{p}{\Rightarrow} aaS \overset{p}{\Rightarrow} aaaS \overset{q}{\Rightarrow} aaab$ <br> $p(aaab \| G_{sr}) = p^3 q$ | $p(x\|G_{sr}) = \begin{cases} p^n q & \text{if } x = a^n b, n \geq 0 \\ 0 & \text{otherwise} \end{cases}$ | $p < 1$ |
| $G_{scf} = (N, \Sigma, P_{scf}, S)$ <br> $N = \{S, A\}$ <br> $\Sigma = \{a, b\}$ <br> $P_{scf} = \{1: S \to Ab,\, p: A \to AA,\, q: A \to a\}$ <br> where $p + q = 1$ <br> $L(G_{cf}) = \{x \| x = a^n b, n \geq 1\}$ | $S \overset{1}{\Rightarrow} Ab \overset{p}{\Rightarrow} AAb \overset{q}{\Rightarrow} aAb \overset{p}{\Rightarrow} aAAb \overset{q}{\Rightarrow} aaAb \overset{q}{\Rightarrow} aaab$ <br> and <br> $S \overset{1}{\Rightarrow} Ab \overset{p}{\Rightarrow} AAb \overset{p}{\Rightarrow} AAAb \overset{q}{\Rightarrow} aAAb \overset{q}{\Rightarrow} aaAb \overset{q}{\Rightarrow} aaab$ <br> $p(aaab \| G_{scf}) = pqpq^2 + p^2 q^3 = 2p^2 q^3$ | $p(x\|G_{scf}) = \begin{cases} \dbinom{2n}{n} \dfrac{1}{n+1} p^n q^{n+1} & \text{if } x = a^{n+1} b, n \geq 0 \\ 0 & \text{otherwise} \end{cases}$ | $p \leq \frac{1}{2}$ |

Table II illustrates consistent and inconsistent p-grammars. Important characteristics of a grammar and general tests for consistency are obtained by using the appropriate stochastic processes as models of the derivation process. Stationarity is assumed.

## DERIVATIONS AS REALIZATIONS OF A STATIONARY STOCHASTIC   II
## PROCESS

### Context-Free p-Grammars as Branching Processes   A

A context-free p-grammar (p-CFG), $G_{scf} = (N, \Sigma, P_{scf}, S)$, is an instance of a multitype branching process [6] in which the terminals $\Sigma$ and nonterminals $N$ are the "types" of the process. Once generated, the terminal types are not subject to further change, but the stochastic productions $P_{scf}$ incorporate the probability laws whereby nonterminal types branch into (are rewritten as) occurrences of themselves or other types. (More general definitions would also allow a starting symbol to be randomly selected from $N$.)

#### Expectation Matrices   1

Given a p-CFG $G_{scf}$ with $n$ nonterminals and $m$ terminals, its *first-moment nonterminal matrix* is the $n \times n$ matrix $B$, where entry $b_{ij}$ is the expected number of occurrences of nonterminal $A_j$ in one step as nonterminal $A_i$ is rewritten, and its *first-moment terminal matrix* is the $n \times m$ matrix $D$ for which $d_{ij}$ is the expected number of occurrences of terminal $a_j$ in one step as nonterminal $A_i$ is rewritten.

The characteristic polynomial of $B$ is obtained by setting the determinant of the matrix $(B - \rho I)$ equal to 0, where $I$ is the $n \times n$ identity matrix. The characteristic roots or eigenvalues of $B$ are the $n$ roots of this polynomial. Let $\rho(B)$ be the modulus of the largest-magnitude eigenvalue of the characteristic polynomial of $B$. $G_{scf}$ can be tested for consistency as follows [5–7]: $G_{scf}$ is consistent if $\rho(B) < 1$ and inconsistent if $\rho(B) > 1$; if $\rho(B) = 1$, then $G_{scf}$ is inconsistent if and only if there is a subset $C$ of $N$ such that (i) there is nonzero probability of an element of $C$ appearing in a derivation and (ii) at least one element of $C$ is always introduced whenever any nonterminal in $C$ is rewritten.

A useful property of a square matrix of reals is the fact that $\rho(B) < 1$ if and only if for some power $k$ ($k > 0$), each row in $B^k$ sums to less than 1 [8]. The element $b_{ij}^{(k)}$ in a power $B^k$ ($k \geq 0$) is the expected number of occurrences of nonterminal $A_j$ in a $k$-step derivation from nonterminal $A_i$; thus, all derivations are taken into account in the matrix sum of all the powers of $B$. This *nonterminal expectation matrix*,

$$B^\infty = \sum_{k \geq 0} B^k$$

exists with finite-valued entries if $G_{scf}$ is consistent, in which case it may be computed as

$$B^\infty = (I - B)^{-1}$$

The *expected derivation length* (i.e., the mean number of nonterminals rewritten in deriving a terminal string) is the sum of the elements in the row of $B^\infty$ for the starting nonterminal $S$; note also that any column with a zero entry in this row signifies a "useless" nonterminal never used in any derivation. The $i - j$ entry in the *terminal expectation matrix* $B^\infty D$ is the expected number of occurrences of terminal $a_j$ in all derivations from $A_i$, so the grammar's *expected word length* (i.e., the mean number of terminals in a completed derivation) is the sum of the elements in the row of $B^\infty D$ for $S$.

*Example* 1. The following illustrates an inconsistent p-grammar, one that may be either consistent or inconsistent, and one that is consistent.

(a) Stochastic grammar $G_{scf} = (N, \Sigma, P_{scr}, S)$ with $N = \{S, X, Y\}$, $\Sigma = \{a, b\}$, and productions

$$\tfrac{4}{7}: S \to aSbS, \qquad \tfrac{3}{7}: S \to bXb$$

$$\tfrac{1}{35}: X \to aba, \qquad \tfrac{16}{35}: X \to aSbYb$$

$$\tfrac{18}{35}: X \to XbXb$$

$$\tfrac{3}{7}: Y \to abX, \qquad \tfrac{4}{7}: Y \to YabY$$

First-moment nonterminal matrix $B$ with rows and columns ordered as $S, X, Y$:

$$B = \begin{bmatrix} \tfrac{8}{7} & \tfrac{3}{7} & 0 \\ \tfrac{16}{35} & \tfrac{36}{35} & \tfrac{16}{35} \\ 0 & \tfrac{3}{7} & \tfrac{8}{7} \end{bmatrix}$$

$\rho(B) = \tfrac{12}{7} > 1$ means that $G_{scf}$ is inconsistent.

(b) Stochastic grammar $G_{scf} = (\{S, A\}, \{c, d\}, P_{scf}, S)$ with productions

$$p_1: S \to cSA, \qquad q_1: S \to d, \qquad p_1 + q_1 = 1$$

$$p_2: A \to cAA, \qquad q_2: A \to cc, \qquad p_2 + q_2 = 1$$

First-moment nonterminal matrix $B$ with rows and columns ordered as $S, A$:

$$B = \begin{bmatrix} p_1 & p_1 \\ 0 & 2p_2 \end{bmatrix}$$

Characteristic equation of $B$: $(\rho - p_1)(\rho - 2p_2) = 0$. $G_{scf}$ is consistent if $p_2 < \frac{1}{2}$. First-moment terminal matrix $D$ with rows $S$, $A$ and columns $c$, $d$:

$$D = \begin{bmatrix} p_1 & q_1 \\ p_2 + 2q_2 & 0 \end{bmatrix}$$

(c)   Stochastic grammar $G_{scf} = (\{S, A\}, \{a, b, c\}, P_{scf}, S)$ with productions

$$0.1: S \to aSSA \qquad 0.9: S \to A$$

$$0.5: A \to bS \qquad 0.5: A \to c$$

First-moment nonterminal matrix $B$ with rows and columns ordered as $S$, $A$:

$$B = \begin{bmatrix} 0.2 & 1 \\ 0.5 & 0 \end{bmatrix}$$

$\rho(B) < 1$ means that this $G_{scf}$ is consistent. First-moment terminal matrix $D$ with rows $S$, $A$, and columns $a$, $b$, $c$:

$$D = \begin{bmatrix} 1 & 0 & 0 \\ 0 & 0.5 & 0.5 \end{bmatrix}$$

Nonterminal expectation matrix $B^\infty$ and terminal expectation matrix $B^\infty D$:

$$B^\infty = \begin{bmatrix} \frac{10}{3} & \frac{10}{3} \\ \frac{5}{3} & \frac{8}{3} \end{bmatrix}, \qquad B^\infty D = \begin{bmatrix} \frac{1}{3} & \frac{5}{3} & \frac{5}{3} \\ \frac{1}{6} & \frac{4}{3} & \frac{4}{3} \end{bmatrix}$$

Expected derivation length $= \frac{10}{3} + \frac{10}{3} = \frac{20}{3}$. Expected word length $= \frac{1}{3} + \frac{5}{3} + \frac{5}{3} = \frac{11}{3}$.

### Generating Functions   2

Generating functions for the levels of derivation trees can also be used to study the derivation process of $G_{scf}$ [2]. Let $C_i$ denote the set of all productions for rewriting nonterminal $A_i$. For each $i$, the $n$ argument *generating function* (for $n$ nonterminals in $N$) is

$$f_i(s_1, s_2, \ldots, s_n) = \sum_{c_i} p_{ir} s_1^{\mu_{i1}(y_r)} s_2^{\mu_{i2}(y_r)} \cdots s_n^{\mu_{in}(y_r)}$$

where $A_1$ is the grammar's starting symbol and $\mu_{ij}(y_r)$ is the number of occurrences of nonterminal $A_j$ in $y_r$ in the production $p_{ir}: A_i \to y_r$. The $g$th-*level generating function* is defined recursively:

$$F_0(s_1, \ldots, s_n) = s_1$$

$$F_1(s_1, \ldots, s_n) = f_1(s_1, \ldots, s_n)$$

$$F_g(s_1, \ldots, s_n) = F_{g-1}(f_1(s_1, \ldots, s_n), \ldots, f_n(s_1, \ldots, s_n))$$

The p-CFG $G_{\text{scf}}$ is consistent if and only if

$$\lim_{g \to \infty}(K_g) = 1$$

where $K_g$ is the constant term in the expression

$$F_g(s_1, \ldots, s_n) = H_g(S_1, \ldots, s_n) + K_g$$

and is the probability of all strings derivable in no more than $g$ steps. The entries in the first-moment nonterminal matrix $B$ may be computed as

$$b_{ij} = \frac{\partial f_i(s_1, \ldots, s_n)}{\partial s_j}\Bigg|_{s_1 = \cdots = s_n = 1}$$

*Example* 2. Consider the p-CFG $G_{\text{scf}} = (\{S, A\}, \{c, d\}, P_{\text{scf}}, S)$ with productions as in Example 1(b). The generating functions are

$$f_1(s_1, s_2) = p_1 s_1 s_2 + q_1$$
$$f_2(s_1, s_2) = p_2 s_2^2 + q_2$$
$$F_0(s_1, s_2) = s_1$$
$$F_1(s_1, s_2) - f_1(s_1, s_2)$$
$$F_2(s_1, s_2) = F_1(f_1(s_1, s_2), f_2(s_1, s_2))$$
$$= p_1^2 p_2 s_1 s_2^2 + p_1^2 q_2 s_1 s_2 + p_1 q_1 p_2 s_2^2 + p_1 q_1 q_2 + p_2$$

Values in the first-moment nonterminal matrix $B$ are

$$b_{11} = \frac{\partial f_1(s_1, s_2)}{\partial s_1}\Bigg|_{s_1 = s_2 = 1} = p_1$$

$$b_{12} = \frac{\partial f_1(s_1, s_2)}{\partial s_2}\Bigg|_{s_1 = s_2 = 1} = p_1$$

$$b_{21} = \frac{\partial f_2(s_1, s_2)}{\partial s_1}\Bigg|_{s_1 = s_2 = 1} = 0$$

$$b_{22} = \frac{\partial f_2(s_1, s_2)}{\partial s_2}\Bigg|_{s_1 = s_2 = 1} = 2p_2$$

## B   Regular p-Grammars as Markov Chains

Since a regular p-grammar (p-RG) is a special case of a p-CFG, the preceding results are applicable; however, calculations based on the theory of Markov chains [9, 10] are often more convenient. A chain can be drawn explicitly with nodes and arcs for a clear representation of a p-RG, $G_{\text{sr}} =$

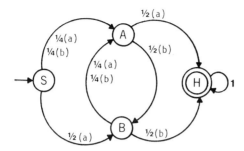

**Fig. 2.** Markov chain for p-RG.

$(N, \Sigma, P_{sr}, S)$. There is a unique starting state (corresponding to $S$) and a unique absorbing state $H$ (a new state for convenience, not representing an actual nonterminal); the arcs, labeled with probabilities and terminals, correspond directly to the productions. The $n$ nonterminals, plus $H$, yield $n + 1$ states. With these states ordered so that $S$ is the first row and $H$ is the last row in the $(n + 1) \times (n + 1)$ transition matrix $A$, the powers $A^k$ are tested for consistency as follows [2, 3]:

$$G_{sr} \text{ is consistent iff } \lim_{k \to \infty} (a_{1,n+1}^{(k)}) = 1$$

Deleting the $(n + 1)$th row and column from $A$ yields the $n \times n$ first-moment nonterminal matrix $B$ for the p-grammar $G_{sr}$. The chain's *fundamental matrix* [9] is

$$B_f = \sum_{k \geq 0} B^k = (I - B)^{-1} = B^\infty$$

for which the sum of the entries in the first row is the expected derivation and word length.

*Example* 3. Consider the p-RG $G_{or} = (\{S, A, B\}, \{a, b\}, P_{sr}, S\}$ with productions

$$\tfrac{1}{4}: S \to aA, \qquad \tfrac{1}{2}: S \to aB, \qquad \tfrac{1}{4}: S \to bA$$

$$\tfrac{1}{2}: A \to bB, \qquad \tfrac{1}{2}: A \to a,$$

$$\tfrac{1}{4}: B \to aA, \qquad \tfrac{1}{4}: B \to bA, \qquad \tfrac{1}{2}: B \to b$$

The Markov chain for $G_{sr}$ is given in Fig. 2. Chain transition matrix $A$ and its limit matrix for states ordered as $S, A, B, H$:

$$A = \begin{bmatrix} 0 & \tfrac{1}{2} & \tfrac{1}{2} & 0 \\ 0 & 0 & \tfrac{1}{2} & \tfrac{1}{2} \\ 0 & \tfrac{1}{2} & 0 & \tfrac{1}{2} \\ 0 & 0 & 0 & 1 \end{bmatrix}, \qquad \lim_{k \to \infty} A^k = \begin{bmatrix} 0 & 0 & 0 & 1 \\ 0 & 0 & 0 & 1 \\ 0 & 0 & 0 & 1 \\ 0 & 0 & 0 & 1 \end{bmatrix}$$

First-moment nonterminal matrix $B$ and fundamental matrix $B_f$ for non-terminals $S, A, B$:

$$B = \begin{bmatrix} 0 & \frac{1}{2} & \frac{1}{2} \\ 0 & 0 & \frac{1}{2} \\ 0 & \frac{1}{2} & 0 \end{bmatrix}, \qquad B_f = \begin{bmatrix} 1 & 1 & 1 \\ 0 & \frac{4}{3} & \frac{2}{3} \\ 0 & \frac{2}{3} & \frac{4}{3} \end{bmatrix}$$

Expected derivation length = expected word length = 3.

## III  INFERENCE

Inference of a p-grammar $G_s = (G, F)$ for a class of patterns involves the development of (i) a syntactic model $G$ which generates a given sample set $O$ and other elements with a "similar" structure and (ii) an assignment $F$ of production probabilities, usually obtained by estimation of parameters by statistical methods. Structural inference is a major consideration in syntactic pattern recognition, even with conventional (nonstochastic) grammars. This section mainly discusses methods of estimating probabilities for stochastic grammars.

## A  p-CFGs

At this time, a CFG $G_{cf}$ offers few options other than counting the usage of productions by sequentially parsing the strings in a finite, ordered set $O$ of samples from the desired language. Repetitions are allowed in this training set $O$. For an *unambiguous* $G_{cf}$, the maximum-likelihood estimate of $F(A \to y)$ is the number of uses of production $A \to y$ divided by the number of rewritings of nonterminal $A$. These estimates converge by a weak law of large numbers, provided that the sample set contains $L(G_{cf})$ and the relative frequency of each string $x$ in $O$ approaches $p(x|G_{scf})$ [2]. In this case, $\chi^2$ goodness-of-fit tests are applicable.

There are problems in maintaining correct frequency counts if a string has more than one canonical derivation (i.e., if $G_{cf}$ is *ambiguous*). One heuristic for this case is to divide the counts into noninteger frequencies. Another is to update the counts in a single maximum probability derivation for each string in an attempt to make some derivations substantially more likely than alternative derivations.

*Example* 4.

(a)  Unambiguous stochastic grammar $G_{sr} = (\{S\}, \{a, b\}, P_{sr}, S)$ with productions and their current frequencies

$$f_1: S \to aS, \qquad f_2: S \to bS, \qquad f_3: S \to b$$

Single derivation of sample string $aab$: $S \Rightarrow aS \Rightarrow aaS \Rightarrow aab$. New frequencies:

$$(f_1 + 2): S \to aS, \qquad f_2: S \to bS, \qquad (f_3 + 1): S \to b$$

New estimates of probabilities: $F = (f_1 + 2) + f_2 + (f_3 + 1)$:

$$\frac{f_1 + 2}{F}: S \to aS, \qquad \frac{f_2}{F}: S \to bS, \qquad \frac{f_3 + 1}{F}: S \to b$$

(b)   Ambiguous p-CFG $G_{scf} = (\{S\}, \{a, b\}, P_{scf}, S)$ with productions and their current frequencies

$$f_1: S \to Sb, \qquad f_2: S \to aS, \qquad f_3: S \to a, \qquad f_4: S \to b$$

Derivations of sample string $aab$: $S \Rightarrow aS \Rightarrow aaS \Rightarrow aab$, $S \Rightarrow Sb \Rightarrow aSb \Rightarrow aab$. New frequencies by dividing the counts by the number of derivations, 2:

$$f_1 + \tfrac{1}{2}: S \to Sb, \qquad f_2 + \tfrac{3}{2}: S \to aS, \qquad f_3 + \tfrac{1}{2}: S \to a, \qquad f_4 + \tfrac{1}{2}: S \to b$$

New frequencies by reenforcing one derivation of maximum probability: if $(f_2 + 2)(f_4 + 1) \geq (f_1 + 1)(f_2 + 1)(f_3 + 1)$, then the new frequencies are

$$f_1: S \to Sb, \qquad (f_2 + 2): S \to aS, \qquad f_3: S \to a, \qquad (f_4 + 1): S \to b$$

Otherwise, they are

$$(f_1 + 1): S \to Sb, \qquad (f_2 + 1): S \to aS, \qquad (f_3 + 1): S \to a, \qquad f_4: S \to b$$

### p-RGs   B

On a practical level, inference of a p-RG as an instance of a finite-state Markov chain offers more options than inference of a p-CFG. Three general methods are available for the estimation of chain probabilities as relative frequencies of events for a finite set of samples; the first two require an initial structure (i.e., a p-RG represented by a chain's nodes and arcs) already in place, while the third attempts to infer a constrained form of structure as well as the probabilities.

### *Unique Starting State, Unambiguous Samples, and Known Syntax*   1

If the chain has a unique starting state and the state occurrences can be matched to the terminals in scans of the sample strings without ambiguity, then the maximum-likelihood estimate of the transition probability

$$a_{ij} = (\text{next state } j | \text{current state } i)$$

is

$$a'_{ij} = n_{ij} / \sum_j n_{ij}$$

where $n_{ij}$ is the number of transitions from state $i$ directly to state $j$. Since maximum-likelihood estimates and asymptotic normal distributions are obtained, $\chi^2$ goodness-of-fit tests are applicable [11]. For instance, testing the null hypothesis that $a'_{ij} = a_{ij}$ for a specific $i$ is based on the relative squared residuals for the $j$'s,

$$\sum_{k=1}^{m} \left[ \left( \sum_{j=1}^{m} n_{ij} \right) \frac{(a'_{ik} - a_{ik})^2}{a_{ik}} \right]$$

which have asymptotic $\chi^2$ distributions with $m - 1$ degrees of freedom, where $m$ is the number of states; forming the sum of the residuals over all $i$ yields a $\chi^2$ distribution with $m(m - 1)$ degrees of freedom and a test for the fit of all the transition probability estimates.

## 2  Random Starting State, Stochastic Output Function, and Known Syntax [12].

In addition to its transition probabilities, the most general Markov chain model allows a random selection of the starting state (an initial state vector) and the generation of outputs (one element in $\Sigma \cup \{e\}$ per state occurrence) via a stochastic output function for each state. Although this is not the conventional model of a p-RG, Baum's algorithm can be used if this model is deemed appropriate in an application. The method is an iterative, gradient-climbing technique guaranteed to converge to a local maximum of the probability $p(O|M')$ for a fixed sample set $O$ by adjusting the probabilities in an initially imposed chain $M$ to create $M'$. "Forward–backward" calculations are used to reestimate the probabilities in $M$ as follows.

*Baum's Algorithm.*

Let $V = \Sigma \cup \{e\}$ and let $m$ be the number of states in Markov chain $M$. Define $\Pi_i = p(\text{starting in state } i)$, $a_{ij} = p(\text{transition to state } j | \text{current state } i)$, $b_{ij} = p(\text{output } v_j | \text{current state } i)$, $v_j$ in $V$. Let $x = x_1 \cdots x_T$ denote a sample string with $x_i$ in $V$, $1 \leq i \leq T$. Let $b_i(x_j) = b_{ik}$ iff $x_j = v_k$.

(1)  Compute the "forward probabilities"

$$\alpha_{t+1}(j) = \left[ \sum_{i=1}^{m} \alpha_t(i) a_{ij} \right] b_j(x_{t+1}), \qquad 1 \leq t \leq T - 1$$

and the "backward probabilities"

$$\beta_t(i) = \sum_{j=1}^{m} a_{ij}b_j(x_{t+1})\beta_{t+1}(j), \qquad T-1 \geq t \geq 1$$

(2)  Compute

$$P = p(O|M) = \sum_{i=1}^{m}\sum_{j=1}^{m} \alpha_t(i)a_{ij}b_j(x_{t+1})\beta_{t+1}(j)$$

for any $t$, $1 \leq t \leq T-1$; for instance, for $t = T-1$,

$$P = \sum_{i=1}^{m} \alpha_T(i)$$

(3)  Reestimate $a_{ij}$, $b_{ij}$, and $\Pi_i$, respectively, as

$$\bar{a}_{ij} = \frac{\sum_{t=1}^{T-1} \alpha_t(i)a_{ij}b_j(x_{t+1})\beta_{t+1}(j)}{\sum_{t=1}^{T-1} \alpha_t(i)\beta_t(i)}$$

$$\bar{b}_{jk} = \frac{\sum_{t \ni x_t = v_k} \alpha_t(j)\beta_t(j)}{\sum_{t=1}^{T} \alpha_t(j)\beta_t(j)}$$

$$\bar{\Pi}_i = \frac{1}{P}\alpha_1(i)\beta_1(i)$$

Iterative reestimation through the entire sample set $O$ increases $P$ to a local maximum.

### Unique Starting State, Deterministic Output Function, 3
### and Unknown Network [13].

A *network* is a Markov chain with a unique starting state, a unique absorbing state, a deterministic assignment of one element of $\Sigma \cup \{e\}$ to each state, and no loops or cycles before absorption. *Dynamic programming* is a reasonably efficient method for computing string-to-network alignments optimally according to various criteria. The trace of an optimal alignment can be interpreted as edits of the string (to make it match a path already in the network) or as adjustments to the network (to install the string explicitly by making changes in the local neighborhoods of individual nodes), as illustrated below.

*Example* 5. Suppose an optimal alignment of string $x = adcaf$ with existing network path $y = abcda$ has been computed to be

$$
\begin{array}{cccccc}
a & d & c & e & a & f \\
| & | & | & | & | & | \\
a & b & c & b & a & e
\end{array}
$$

Then an optimal sequence to edit $x$ into $y$ is

[match $a$][substitute $b$ for $d$][match $c$][insert $b$]

[match $a$][delete $f$]

An optimal adjustment of the path $y$ on a node-by-node basis so as to incorporate $x$ is

[match $a$][substitute $d$ for $b$][match $c$][delete $b$]

[match $a$][insert $f$]

which gives the new network structure

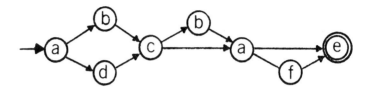

with eight paths which include the path $y$, the new $x$, and six others induced by the modifications. Figure 3a represents a dynamic programming matrix with the network nodes as the row labels and the symbols in the input string $x$ as the column labels. Assume an additive cost function (e.g., the logarithms of probabilities), and let $d_{ij}$ denote the cost computed for the matrix entry at row $i$ and column $j$; then an optimal alignment to edit the string to fit the existing network is found by the calculation in Fig. 3b, while an optimal alignment to modify the network is found by the calculation in Fig. 3c.

In stochastic languages, the cost function is based on relevant probabilities or frequency counts as estimates thereof. A network can be inferred by installing the samples from $O$ sequentially, using dynamic programming with a cost function of frequency counts on the arcs to find optimal alignments for the network node adjustments (as in Example 5) to give each sample a maximum probability derivation in the updated network (see Fig. 4). The final network is dependent on the order of the samples but preserves such sample expected values as the number of occurrences of a terminal, string length, and waiting time for a terminal to recur [13].

## IV  CLASSIFICATION VIA p-GRAMMARS

Given pattern p-grammars $G_{s1}, G_{s2}, \ldots, G_{sn}$, defining $n$ classes that have the a priori class probabilities $p(G_{s1}), p(G_{s2}), \ldots, p(G_{sn})$, and given a candidate $x$, then in the simplest cases $p(x|G_{sj})$ can be computed for $1 \le j \le n$ and

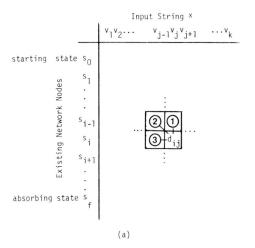

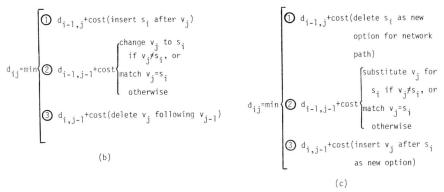

**Fig. 3.** (a) Dynamic programming matrix. (b) Modifying $x$ to fit the existing network path. (c) Modifying the network to incorporate string $x$.

$x$ can be classified according to the maximum value of

$$p(G_{sj}|x) = p(x|G_{sj})p(G_{sj})/p(x)$$

That is, according to the maximum of $p(x|G_{sj})p(G_{sj})$ or of $p(x|G_{sj})$ if the classes are equally likely. As an approximation, the probability of a single most likely derivation of $x$ is often computed in lieu of $p(x|G_{sj})$ in ambiguous grammars.

In practice, however, it often occurs that $p(x|G_{sj}) = 0$ because $x$ is a noisy or imperfectly formed string. In this case, *error-correcting parsing* can be employed to attempt a reasonable classification, provided that a representation of error probabilities (explicitly or implicitly defined) is available. The errors usually considered are independent, terminal-by-terminal occurrences of deletions, substitutions, and insertions [2, 3, 14, 15] and classification is usually based on nearest-neighbor rules [16].

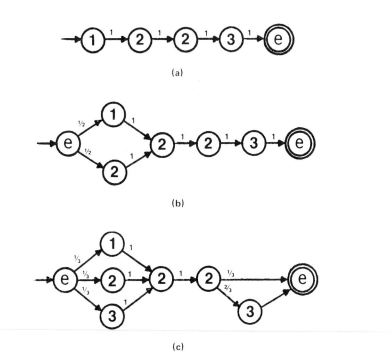

(a)

(b)

(c)

**Fig. 4.** Markov network inference by dynamic programming. (a) First network, sample string 1223; (b) second network, sample string 2223; (c) third network, sample string 322. The substring 223 occurring with high probability in all strings generated by the final network is a "landmark" substring for the set of three samples. The substring 22 occurs with probability 1, that is, all samples and all realizations (paths) of the network include this substring.

## A  Nearest Neighbors and Clusters

Concepts of distances and clusters in stochastic languages are generally based on weighted, terminal-by-terminal edit operations which transform one string into another according to maximum-likelihood calculations [16]. If for terminals $a$ and $b$ the probabilities

$$p_S(b|a) = p(\text{substitution of } b \text{ for } a \text{ or match if } b = a), \qquad b \text{ in } \Sigma$$

$$p_D(e|a) = p(\text{deletion of } a)$$

$$p_I(ba|a) = p(\text{insertion of } b \text{ before } a), \qquad b \text{ in } \Sigma$$

$$p_I(a|e) = p(\text{insertion of } a \text{ at end of string}), \qquad a \text{ in } \Sigma$$

are such that

$$\sum_b p_S(b|a) + \sum_b p_I(ba|a) + p_D(e|a) = 1$$

then the probability that terminal $a$ is transformed into string $x$ is

$$
p_t(x|a) = \begin{cases}
p_D(e|a) & \text{if } x = e \\
\max[p_S(b|a), p_I(ba|a)p_D(e|a)] & \text{if } x = b \\
p_I(b_1a|a)\cdots p_I(b_{j-1}a|a) & \\
\quad \max[p_S(b_j|a), p_I(b_ja|a)p_D(e|a)] & \text{if } x = b_1b_2\cdots b_j, j > 1
\end{cases}
$$

and the probability of inserting $x$ at the end of a string is

$$
p_I(x|e) = \begin{cases}
1 - \hat{p}_I & \text{if } x = e \\
(1 - \hat{p}_I)p_I(b_1|e)p_I(b_2|e)\cdots p_I(b_j|e) & \text{if } x = b_1b_2\cdots b_j, j > 0
\end{cases}
$$

where

$$
\hat{p}_I = \sum_b p_I(b|e)
$$

and

$$
\sum_x p_t(x|a) = \sum_x p_t(x|e) = 1
$$

The probability of transforming string $a_1a_2\cdots a_m$ into string $x$ is

$$
p_t(x|a_1\cdots a_m) = \max_j \left[ \prod_{k=1}^m p_t(z_k^j|a_k)p_t(z_{m+1}^j|e) \right]
$$

computed over all partitions $z_1^j\cdots z_m^j z_{m+1}^j$ of $x$ into $m + 1$ substrings.

Given classes $G_{s1}, \ldots, G_{sn}$, a *probabilistic nearest-neighbor rule* assigns candidate $x$ to a class $G_{sk}$ for which $L(G_{sk})$ contains a string $y_i$, achieving the maximized probability

$$
\max_{k=1}^n \left[ \max_{y_i \in L(G_{sk})} p(y_i, G_{sk}|x) \right]
$$

where the transform probability $p_t$ is used to compute

$$
p(y_i, G_{sk}|x) = \frac{p_t(x|y_i, G_{sk})p(y_i|G_{sk})p(G_{sk})}{\sum_{j=1}^n \left[ \sum_{y_i \in L(G_{sj})} p(y_i|G_{sj})p(G_{sj}) \right]}
$$

This may be extended to the $k$-nearest neighbors by computing the average of the largest values of the terms $p(y, G_{sk}|x)$ for $k$ strings $y$ in each class $G_{sk}$. Heuristic *clustering* with a control threshold $t$ can also be based on these calculations: given a new string $x$, if $\max_i [p(y_i, G_{sk}|x)] < t$ for all $G_{sk}$, then create a new class by inferring a grammar for $x$; otherwise, place $x$ into a class $G_{sk}$ for which $p(y_i, G_{sk}|x)$ is largest by updating (re-inferring) $G_{sk}$ to include $x$ in its language.

## B   Error-Correcting Parsing

A version of Earley's parsing algorithm [1], essentially a dynamic programming parser for arbitrary CFGs as modified to incorporate probabilities for maximum-likelihood error correction (to the nearest neighbor), can be used [14]. For each terminal $x_i$, in a candidate string $x = x_1 \cdots x_m$, a list $I_i$ is computed with entries of the form $[A \to y \cdot z, k, p]$, where $A \to yz$ is a production, $k$ and "." are bookkeeping items, and $p$ is a running computation of probability.

*Modified Earley Parsing Algorithm.*

Expand a p-CFG, $G_{\text{scf}} = (N, \Sigma, P_{\text{scf}}, S)$, into a new grammar, $G'_{\text{scf}} = (N', \Sigma, P'_{\text{scf}}, S')$, which has explicit "error productions" as follows.

(1)   Let $N' = N \cup \{S'\} \cup \{E_a | a \text{ in } \Sigma\}$.
(2)   For each production $p: A \to \alpha_0 b_1 \alpha_1 b_2 \alpha_2 \cdots \alpha_{m-1} b_m \alpha_m$ $(m \geq 0)$ in $P_{\text{scf}}$, where $\alpha_i$ is in $N^*$ and $b_i$ is in $\Sigma$, add to $P'_{\text{scf}}$ the production $p: A \to \alpha_0 B_{b_1} \alpha_1 E_{b_2} \cdots E_{b_m} \alpha_m$, where $E_{b_i}$ is a new nonterminal.
(3)   Add to $P'_{\text{scf}}$:

$$p_{\text{I}}(a|e): S' \to Sa \quad \text{for each } a \text{ in } \Sigma$$

$$\left(1 - \sum_a p_{\text{I}}(a|e)\right): S' \to S$$

(4)   For each $a$ in $\Sigma$, add to $P'_{\text{scf}}$:

$$p_{\text{S}}(a|a): E_a \to a$$

$$p_{\text{S}}(b|a): E_a \to b \quad \text{for each } b \text{ in } \Sigma - \{a\}$$

$$p_{\text{D}}(e|a): E_a \to e$$

$$p_{\text{I}}(ba|a): E_a \to bE_a \quad \text{for each } b \text{ in } \Sigma$$

Then a candidate $x = x_1 \cdots x_m$ and the expanded grammar $G'_{\text{scf}}$ are processed by the following steps to compute a string $y$ which maximizes $p(x|y, G'_{\text{scf}})p(y|G'_{\text{scf}})$ for the most likely derivation of $y$.

(1)   Set $j = 0$. Add $[E \to \cdot S', 0, 1]$ to $I_j$.
(2)   (a)   If $[A \to \alpha \cdot B\beta, i, p]$ is in $I_j$ and $q: B \to \gamma$ is in $P'_{\text{scf}}$, add $[B \to \cdot \gamma, j, q]$ to $I_j$.
      (b)   If $[A \to \alpha \cdot, i, p]$ is in $I_j$ and $[B \to \beta \cdot A\gamma, k, q]$ is in $I_j$, and if no item of the form $[B \to \beta A \cdot \gamma, k, r]$ can be found in $I_j$, add a new item $[B \to \beta A \cdot \gamma, k, pq]$ to $I_j$. If $[B \to \beta A \cdot \gamma, k, r]$ is already in $I_j$, then replace $r$ by $pq$ if $pq > r$.
(3)   If $j = m$ and $[E \to S' \cdot, 0, p]$ is in $I_m$, then $p(x|y, G'_{\text{scf}})p(y|G'_{\text{scf}}) = p$; otherwise, $j = j + 1$ and continue with step 4.

(4)   For each item of the form $[A \rightarrow \alpha \cdot b_j \beta, i, p]$ in $I_{j-1}$, add $[A \rightarrow \alpha b_j \cdot \beta, i, p]$ to $I_j$. Go to step 2.

A sequential classification technique, often less costly in computation, is available [14, 17]. *Stochastic syntax-directed translation* can also be considered as a model of error correction [3, 15]. A syntax-directed translation uses a finite set of rules which are essentially the productions of two context-free grammars tied together so that two derivations are developed in parallel. Specifically, a translation rule is of the form $A \rightarrow \alpha, \beta$, where $A \rightarrow \alpha$ and $A \rightarrow \beta$ are conventional context-free productions; each nonterminal in $\alpha$ has an identical, associated nonterminal in $\beta$, and both associated nonterminals must be rewritten simultaneously. The translation is made to be probabilistic by assigning a probability to these rules, that is, a stochastic translation rule has the form $p: A \rightarrow \alpha, \beta$. If the probabilities of various errors in terminals are known for independent events, then these error probabilities may be incorporated into a p-CFG to give an error-correcting translation model.

*Example* 6.   The p-productions in a p-CFG may be incorporated into p-translation rules for error correction, as shown here. Production in p-CFG: $q: S \rightarrow aAS$. Translation rules for independent errors in terminal $a$:

$$q p_S(b|a): S \rightarrow bAS, aAS$$

$$q p_D(e|a): S \rightarrow AS, aAS$$

$$q p_I(ba|a): S \rightarrow baAS, aAS$$

Part of derivation using original grammar (rewriting $S$ twice):

$$S \overset{q}{\Rightarrow} aAS \overset{q}{\Rightarrow} aAaAS$$

Part of translation to correct one deletion and one substitution error using syntax-directed translation rules:

$$[S, S] \xrightarrow{q p_D(e|a)} [AS, aAS] \xrightarrow{q p_S(b|a)} [AbAS, aAaAS]$$

Directly implemented dynamic programming, illustrated in Fig. 3, is a convenient error-correcting method for many regular grammars. Reasonable classification error rates have also been obtained by computing as though $x$ would be installed as a new sample, but using these values only for classification purposes [13].

## STOCHASTIC AUTOMATA   V

Many of the one-to-one correspondences between grammars as generators and automata as recognizers of languages in conventional language theory

TABLE III

Correspondences between p-Grammars and p-Automata

| Type of language | p-Grammar | p-Automaton |
|---|---|---|
| 3 | p-RG (regular) | p-FA (finite automaton) |
| 2 | p-CFG (context free) | p-Pushdown automaton |
| 1 | p-CSG (context sensitive) | Linearly bounded p-Turing machine |
| 0 | General phrase structure | p-Turing machine |

extend in a straightforward way to p-languages [2, 3], as indicated in Table III. This means that practical algorithms in important areas like error correction and inference are expressible with respect to either model of a language, although the p-grammar appears generally more convenient than the p-automaton in syntactic pattern recognition.

As an illustration of p-automata, a Markov chain for a p-RG may be expanded to define a *probabilistic finite automaton* (a p-FA). The automaton's states correspond to the nodes ($S$ is the starting state and $H$ is the "accepting" state, termination in which signifies acceptance of an input string); the transitions correspond to the arcs and must be such that, for each terminal symbol and each state, the probabilities on the exiting arcs labeled with that symbol sum to 1. Figure 5 is the p-FA obtained from the p-RG in Example 3. The trap state is used for exiting arc probabilities to sum to 1, for example,

$$p(S|S, a) + p(A|S, a) + p(B|S, a) + p(H|S, a) + p(\text{trap state}|S, a)$$
$$= 0 + \tfrac{1}{4} + \tfrac{1}{2} + 0 + \tfrac{1}{4} = 1$$

The probability that this p-FA accepts the string *abb* is

$$p(abb|A_s) = p(A|S, a)p(B|A, b)p(H|B, b)$$
$$= (\tfrac{1}{4})(\tfrac{1}{2})(\tfrac{1}{2}) = \tfrac{1}{16}.$$

Since a p-automaton may recognize or reject a given input string probabilistically, one potential use is in stochastic classification experiments, for example, to test whether a string $x$ which can be recognized by two different p-FAs will be recognized by either with probability exceeding a threshold or "cut point" $t$ in the long run. A specific p-automaton $A_s$ is caused to scan $x$ for $n$ independent trials. Let $m$ denote the number of times $x$ is accepted; then $m/n$ is an asymptotically unbiased estimate of the probability $p(x|A_s)$ of the recognition of $x$ by $A_s$. Using $c/\sqrt{n}$ in Chebyshev's inequality [11] to establish confidence intervals gives

$$p\left[\left|\frac{m}{n} - p(x|A_s)\right| \leq \frac{c}{\sqrt{n}}\right] \geq 1 - \frac{1}{4c^2}$$

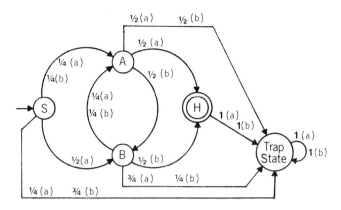

**Fig. 5.** Probabilistic finite automaton $A_s$.

so that at the end of the $n$th trial,

$$(m/n - c/\sqrt{n}) > t$$

implies $p(x|A_s$ at cut point $t) \geq 1 - 4/c^2$ and

$$(m/n - c/\sqrt{n}) < t$$

implies $p(x|A_s$ at cut point $t) \leq 1 - 4/c^2$.

## SEMANTICS   VI

In a pattern grammar, *semantics* usually means an assignment of values to the features or attributes of the terminals in a string $x$ and thence to the nonterminals in a derivation of $x$ via semantic rules [4]. If probabilities are computed on the values, the semantic rules must indicate how they are combined with the syntactic productions of a p-grammar (e.g., as stochastically independent events) as used in a derivation. For example, a p-production $p: A \rightarrow ab$ could have an associated semantic rule

   if val($a$) = val($b$),
      then val($A$) = 2 val($a$);
   otherwise,
      val($A$) = max[val($a$), val($b$)]

where val($X$) is the numerical value of the single feature of symbol $X$. However, if uncertainty in features yields $q = P[\text{val}(a) = \text{val}(b)]$ as an unconditional probability, then

$$pq = P[A \rightarrow ab, \text{val}(A) = 2 \text{ val}(a)]$$

and

$$p(1 - q) = P[A \rightarrow ab, \text{val}(A) = \max(\text{val}(a), \text{val}(b))]$$

are probabilities for two computations of val($A$) when $A \rightarrow ab$ is used in a derivation. The interaction of semantic rules and syntactic productions is often subtle.

## VII   STOCHASTIC TREE GRAMMARS

Grammars generating higher-order structures than strings are used at times in syntactic pattern recognition [18, 19, 2, 3]; in particular, tree grammars which generate trees directly have been successfully employed. Every regular tree language can be generated by an *expansive tree grammar*, $G_{et} = (N, \Sigma, P_{et}, S)$, where $N$ and $\Sigma$ are the sets of nonterminals and terminals, respectively, $P_{et}$ is a set of expansive tree productions of the forms

$$A \rightarrow a \qquad \text{or} \qquad A \rightarrow a$$

for $A, A_1, \ldots, A_k$ in $N$ and $a$ in $\Sigma$, and $S$ is a set of starting trees. A *stochastic expansive tree grammar* $G_{set}$ is one in which probabilities are assigned to the productions. Other definitions (e.g., *unrestricted*, *proper*, *consistent*) then parallel those given earlier for string grammars, and computations are based on the results of multitype branching processes, as for p-CFGs.

*Example* 7.   Consider   the   p-tree   grammar   $G_{set} = (\{S, A, B, C\}, \{\$, a, b\}, P_{set}, \{S\})$ with expansive productions

1 : $S \rightarrow \$$ ,          $p$ : $A \rightarrow a$ ,     $(1 - p)$ : $A \rightarrow a$

$q$ : $B \rightarrow b$,     $(1 - q)$ : $B \rightarrow b$,                1 : $C \rightarrow a$

Illustration of a derivation:

with probability

$$p\left(\begin{array}{c} \$ \\ \diagup\diagdown \\ a \quad b \\ | \\ a \end{array} \;\middle|\; G_{\text{set}}\right) = (1)(1 - p)(q)(1)$$

First-moment nonterminal matrix with rows and columns ordered as $S, A, B, C$:

$$B = \begin{bmatrix} 0 & 1 & 1 & 0 \\ 0 & p & p & 0 \\ 0 & 0 & 0 & q \\ 0 & 0 & 0 & 0 \end{bmatrix}$$

Characteristic equation: $(\rho - p)\rho^3 = 0$. $G_{\text{set}}$ is consistent for $0 \le p < 1$.

## REFERENCES

1.  A. V. Aho and J. D. Ullman, "The Theory of Parsing, Translation and Compiling," Vol. I. Prentice-Hall, Englewood Cliffs, New Jersey, 1972.
2.  K. S. Fu, "Syntactic Methods in Pattern Recognition." Academic Press, New York, 1974.
3.  R. C. Gonzalez and M. G. Thomason, "Syntactic Pattern Recognition: An Introduction." Addison-Wesley, Reading, Massachusetts, 1978.
4.  J. W. Tai and K. S. Fu, Inference of a class of CFPG by means of semantic rules, *Intl. J. Comp. Info. Sci.* **11**, 1–23 (1982).
5.  T. L. Booth and R. A. Thompson, Applying probability measures to abstract languages, *IEEE Trans. Comp.* **C-22**, 442–450 (1973).
6.  T. E. Harris, "The Theory of Branching Processes." Springer-Verlag, New York, 1963.
7.  D. Sankoff, Branching processes with terminal types: application to context-free grammars, *J. Appl. Prob.* **8**, 233–240 (1971).
8.  C. S. Wetherell, Probabilistic languages: a review and some open questions, *ACM Comp. Surveys* **12**, 361–379 (1980).
9.  J. G. Kemeny and J. C. Snell, "Finite Markov Chains." Van Nostrand-Reinhold, Princeton, New Jersey, 1960.
10. E. Parzen, "Stochastic Processes." Holden-Day, San Francisco, California, 1962.
11. H. Cramer, "The Elements of Probability Theory." Wiley, New York, 1954.
12. L. E. Baum, An inequality and associated maximization technique for probabilistic functions of finite state Markov chains, *Inequalities* **3**, 1–8 (1972).
13. M. G. Thomason and E. Granum, Dynamically programmed inference of Markov networks from finite sets of sample strings, *IEEE Trans. PAMI* in press (1985).
14. S. Y. Lu and K. S. Fu, Stochastic error-correcting syntax analysis and recognition of noisy patterns, *IEEE Trans. Comp.* **C-26**, 1268–1276 (1977).
15. M. G. Thomason, Stochastic syntax-directed translation schemata for correction of errors in context-free languages, *IEEE Trans. Comp.* **C-24**, 1211–1216 (1975).

16. S. Y. Lu and K. S. Fu, A sentence-to-sentence clustering procedure for pattern analysis, *IEEE Trans. SMC* **SMC-8,** 381–389 (1978).

17. E. Persoon and K. S. Fu, Sequential classification of strings generated by SCFG's, *Intl. J. Comp. Info. Sci.* **4,** 205–217 (1975).

18. K. S. Fu, Syntactic image modeling using stochastic tree grammars, *Comp. Graphics Image Proc.* **12,** 136–152 (1980).

19. K. S. Fu, "Syntactic Pattern Recognition and Applications." Prentice-Hall, Englewood Cliffs, New Jersey, 1982.

# Chapter 6

# Problem Solving Methods for Pattern Recognition

LAVEEN N. KANAL
and
G. R. DATTATREYA

Machine Intelligence and Pattern Analysis Laboratory
Department of Computer Science
University of Maryland
College Park, Maryland

## INTRODUCTION I

Pattern recognition concerns itself with the description, identification, classification, and extraction of patterns in data. Practical examples of such data include waveforms, images, characteristic data sets of social and economic systems, measurements on plants and animals, psychological data, and census data. Originally focused primarily on the methodology of multivariate statistical classification, pattern recognition now encompasses a

143

**HANDBOOK OF PATTERN RECOGNITION**
**AND IMAGE PROCESSING**

**TABLE I**

**A Comparison of Pattern Analysis Methods**

| PA methodology | Specific techniques | Representation | | Tasks | Applications |
|---|---|---|---|---|---|
| | | Input | Output | | |
| Signal processing | Time/space, frequency-domain analysis, linear prediction, random-field models, median filtering, analysis by synthesis | Real/complex-valued functions of one or two discrete variables | Same as input, estimated parameters, computed curve fits | Preprocessing, parameter estimation, parametric representation, synthesis, extraction of primitives | Speech analysis, synthesis, radar, sonar, medical waveform processing, image smoothing and enhancement, computer graphics |
| Decision theoretic (statistical and fuzzy) | Bayes, maximum likelihood, and fuzzy max–min classifiers using functional representation of individual categories | Vector of cardinal, ordinal, nominal, interval, cyclic, and finite set points | Category label | Classification, training via parametric functions, and error estimation | Remote sensing, blood cell, radar, sonar, and low-level speech and image classification |
| Nonparametric techniques | k-nearest neighbor, linear, piecewise linear, and dynamic linear data splitting using labeled training samples | Vector of cardinal, ordinal, nominal, interval, cyclic, and finite set points | Subsets of the feature space as categories | Classification, discriminant computation, and error estimation | Remote sensing, blood cell, radar, sonar, and low-level speech and image classification |
| Exploratory data analysis | Scatter plots, factor analysis, variance analysis, Karhunen–Loeve expansion | Real vector | Real vector | Feature selection and transformation | Remote sensing, blood cell, radar, sonar, and low-level speech and image classification |

| Method | Techniques | Input representation | Output | Process | Applications |
|---|---|---|---|---|---|
| Unsupervised methods | Hierarchical clustering, iterative optimization, unsupervised parameter estimation, $k$-means, and isodata algorithms | Real vector | Groups of patterns, category parameters | Clustering, unsupervised learning | Remote sensing, blood cell, radar, sonar, and low-level speech and image classification |
| Decision trees | Minimum cost classifiers, hierarchical classifiers, independent subrecognition, dynamic data splitting | Vector of cardinal, ordinal, nominal, interval, cyclic, and finite set points | Category, group of categories | Development of tree frameworks, feature allocation, and classification | Remote sensing, blood cell, radar, sonar, and low-level speech and image classification |
| State space models for classification | $S$- and $B$-admissible search strategies, nearest-neighbor search | Discrete feature states | Goal state, category label | Searching for a goal state with a minimum of feature cost | General model encompassing more practical methods like hierarchical classification |
| Syntactic PR | Syntax analysis, error-correcting parsing, tree automata | String and high-dimensional language | Grammar category | Parsing to recognize the grammar generating the language, grammatical inference | Character, finger print recognition, EEG analysis |
| Problem reduction representation | AND/OR graph searching, min-max tree searching, general nondirectional analysis, state-space search for primitives | Raw waveforms | Linguistic representation and recognition | State-space search for morphs in raw data, structural analysis via AI | Representation and parsing of carotid pulse waves and EKG |

wide range of techniques and principles drawn from exploratory statistical
data analysis; formal language theory and parsing methodology; geometry,
physics, and other classical sciences; and problem solving methods of
artificial intelligence. Table I lists some general methodologies currently
being employed for analyzing and recognizing patterns and displays typical
tasks, input–output representations, and specific techniques used by each
approach. Theory and applications of statistical and syntactic approaches to
pattern recognition are available in books by Krishnaiah and Kanal [1] and
Fu [2].

In this chapter we describe the use of some artificial intelligence (AI)
problem solving models and search techniques in pattern classification and
description. Section II describes two basic problem solving models of AI, viz.,
the state–space and problem reduction representations, abbreviated hence-
forth as SSR and PRR, respectively. The state-space search algorithms are
presented in Section III with an application to statistical pattern classification. A transformation of PRR to SSR is also described which allows
searching PRRs for candidate structural representations of patterns, using
key features only, in a model-directed–data-confirmed, data-directed–model-
confirmed manner. Section IV briefly describes an application of this search
paradigm in a structural waveform analyzer. Section V summarizes the
chapter.


## II  PROBLEM SOLVING MODELS


The paper by Slagle and Lee [3] represents an early effort connecting
pattern recognition (PR) with an AI search technique. They used a one-step
look-ahead approach to determine the next feature to be measured in
sequential pattern recognition. The use of AI ideas of state–space and
problem reduction representations and ordered search for statistical pattern
classification and structural analysis, respectively, is presented in Kanal [4].
Related work on the combination of statistical and syntactic approaches and
on searches in data and model domains include Duerr et al. [5] and Tropf
[6]. The following sections briefly define the key concepts involved. Detailed,
informal descriptions are available in Nilsson [7], Barr and Flegenbaum [8],
and other books on AI.

A state–space representation can be depicted as a directed graph in which
the nodes represent states and the arcs represent state transitions. The task of
statistical pattern recognition may be modeled as a search for a goal state in
an acyclic state–space graph. A state consists of the measured features and the
possible categories representing the pattern. A state transition occurs when a

specified subset of features is measured to gain further knowledge about the pattern under consideration. The interconnections of states, features to be measured to effect particular state transitions, and state-transition policies reflect the knowledge about the pattern analysis model and data. A PRR of pattern description and recognition is of interest since it can deal with the data in its raw form as well as with its higher-level structural relations. This aspect is embodied in the following definition: a PRR recursively tries to solve a problem by transforming it into several simpler equivalents, any of which, if solved, solves the problem, or transforming it into several subproblems, all of which, if solved, solve the original problem. Using vertices to represent problems and subproblems, a PRR is modeled by AND/OR graphs in which equivalent problems are represented by OR nodes and subproblems are represented by AND nodes.

## State–Space Search Models    A

In the directed acyclic graph, a terminal node provides the class label if there is a path to it from the initial (start) node. In many cases, the state–space graph is not explicitly defined. Transition operators are used to expand the states of this implicitly defined graph, that is, to get the successors of the tip nodes of an existing subgraph. Let us examine how this state–space representation and ordered search may be used in pattern classification. A fundamental problem in pattern classification is the assignment of a pattern sample to one of a prespecified set of categories. Notice that we might not have a completely defined model, such as a Bayesian model. Therefore, the approach is to measure a subset of features and move a step in an appropriate state–space graph. The newly occupied state could represent

(1)  a better knowledge of which categories the sample belongs to,
(2)  a better knowledge of which categories the sample does not belong to,
(3)  a better knowledge of which features to measure next, or
(4)  none of the above.

If this approach is to be profitable, it is clear that the state–space graph and the control strategy should be good for the problem at hand. How does one come up with good state–space graphs and control strategies for pattern recognition? If the control strategy can guide us to the solution directly, that is, through a minimum number of steps or a minimum cost, it would amount to having known the solution beforehand! Therefore, practical control strategies use what are known as *heuristics*. Heuristic information is some task-dependent information to help reduce search on the average. In many cases, heuristic information takes the form of evaluation functions. A formal definition of the state–space representation clarifies some of these ideas.

*Definition.* A state–space representation is a 4-tuple $\{S, I, F, q\}$, where $S = \{s_i\}$ is an enumerable set of state descriptions, $I \subseteq S$ is the set of initial states, $F \subseteq S$ is the set of final (goal) states, $q: S \times N \to S$ is the ordered successor function with $q(s_i, j) = s_k$ interpreted as $s_k$ being the $j$th successor of $s_i$, and $Q(s_i) = \{s_k: s_k = q(s_i, j) \text{ for some } j\}$.

A completely specified control strategy over the preceding state–space graph determines a state–space search algorithm. A good heuristic procedure for search is by use of the following evaluation functions. Let

$$f(s_i) = g(s_i) + h(s_i) \tag{1}$$

where $g(s_i)$ is the cost of the path taken from the initial state to $s_i$ and $h(s_i)$ is a lower bound on the cost of all the paths from $s_i$ to any goal node. That is, if $h^*(s_i)$ is the minimum of the cost of all paths from $s_i$ to all the goal nodes, then

$$h(s_i) \leq h^*(s_i) \tag{2}$$

And $h(s_i) > 0$ should come from the problem domain and satisfy (2). In Section III, we present a version of the $A^*$ algorithm (Nilsson [7]) which uses this evaluation function. A related algorithm for pattern recognition along with an explicit evaluation function satisfying (2) is also presented.

## B   Problem Reduction Representation

The problem reduction approach for solving a problem establishes sub-problems and sub-subproblems until, finally, the original problem is reduced to a set of primitive solvable problems. Initially, there will be several (possibly only one) descriptions of the problem, only one of which is required to be solved. The successor function generates equivalent sets of subproblems. A successor could generate

(1)   a set of problems such that any one of this set needs to be solved for solving the original problem (these are known as OR subproblems or OR successors);

(2)   a set of subproblems such that all the subproblems should be solved for solving the overall problem (these are known as AND subproblems or AND successors).

A graph of such reductions is known as an AND/OR graph. In general, mixtures of these two kinds of problem sets may be generated. However, it is simple to modify the generation such that a problem description has only AND successors or only OR successors. For example, let problems (($x$ AND $y$) OR $z$) be required to be solved for solving some problem $A$. Then $x$ and $y$ can be preceded by another node $u$ such that we have OR successors $u$ OR $z$. Here $u$ itself will have two AND successors $x$ and $y$. Thus, it is possible to generate an AND/OR graph in which nodes have pure AND successors or pure OR successors. Furthermore, it is possible to ensure that an OR successor has only AND successors and vice versa.

*Definition.* A problem reduction representation is a 5-tuple $\{P, r, t, u, B\}$, where $P = \{P_i\}$ is an enumerable set of problem descriptions; $B \subseteq P$ is a set of initial problems any one of which is needed to be solved; $r: P \times N \to P$ is the ordered successor function, with $r(p_i, j) = p_k$ interpreted as $p_k$ is the $j$th successor of the problem $p_i$. The set of all $m$ successors of problem $p_i$ is $R(p_i)$. $N$ is the set of natural numbers; $t: P \to \{\Lambda V\}$ is the node type function, with $\Lambda$ denoting AND and $V$ denoting OR problems; for example, if a problem is an AND problem, it should be solved along with its siblings to guarantee the solution of its parent. Clarifying further, if a problem is of type OR, its parent has OR successors; $u: P \to \{L, S, D\}$ is the node solution function interpreted as *live*, *solved*, and *dead* (unsolvable). A solved problem is known to have a solution, while a dead problem is known not to have one. A problem is live when it is not known to be solved or dead.

The definitions are dynamic since the major purpose of problem reduction search is to implicitly develop as little of the problem space as is necessary to conclude that the initial problem is solved, unsolved, or yet live.

Before we develop solution methodologies for the problem reduction representation, let us explore the possible applications of this representation in pattern analysis. A direct application is in syntactic pattern recognition. Hall [9] observed a simple correspondence between AND/OR graphs and context-free grammars. Hall's example to demonstrate this correspondence is given by the grammar

$$G = (\{S, A\}, \{a, b\}, P) \tag{3}$$

$$P = \{p_1: S \to aAS,\ p_2: S \to a,\ p_3: A \to SbA,\ p_4: A \to ba,\ p_5: A \to SS\}$$

with the usual notation: $S$ is the starting symbol, $P$ is the set of production rules, nonterminal symbols are represented by uppercase letters, such as $A$ in the preceding example, and terminal symbols are represented by lower case letters, such as $a$ and $b$. An equivalent AND/OR graph can be worked out as follows. From nonterminal nodes, corresponding production rule nodes appear as OR successors. The productions themselves (sequences of symbols) appear as AND successors to the production rule nodes. The reverse correspondence is completed by merely specifying a convention for the sequence in which AND successors are read. Figure 1 shows the corresponding AND/OR graph of the context-free grammar of (3). Branches leading to AND successors are tied together by a directional arrow across the branches. This also uniquely defines the string of symbols generated by the production.

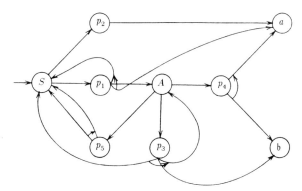

**Fig. 1.** AND/OR graph for the context-free grammar in Eq. (3).

## III  PROBLEM SOLVING ALGORITHMS

Several search algorithms have been developed for searching state–space and problem reduction representations. The canonical algorithm $A^*$ searches a state-space graph for a goal state (solution) making use of an evaluation function with a heuristic component. If the heuristic satisfies certain conditions, $A^*$ is guaranteed to find an optimal path to a goal node. The algorithm $A^*$ may be stated as follows.

*Algorithm $A^*$*

(1)  Place all the initial nodes, the elements of $I$, on a list called *OPEN*, along with their respective evaluation functions $f(\ )$.

(2)  If *OPEN* is empty, exit with failure; no solution exists.

(3)  Select from *OPEN* a node with a minimum $f(\ )$. Let this be $s_i$.

(4)  Remove node $s_i$ from *OPEN* and place it on a list called *CLOSED*. This is a list of generated nodes.

(5)  If $s_i$ is a goal node, exit with success.

(6)  Generate $Q(s_i)$, the set of all successors of $s_i$. Compute $f(s_k)$ for every node $s_k \in Q(s_i)$. Attach a pointer from each $s_k$ back to $s_i$ (to be able to trace the solution path at the end). Place all the successors on the *OPEN* list.

(7)  Go to Step 2.

This algorithm assumes that the state–space graph is a tree. If the state–space model is a graph rather than a tree, a node can be a successor of two or more nodes. Therefore, if a node is generated a second time, the graph search algorithm should update its $f(\ )$ value and also facilitate generating its successors again for possible correction of $f(\ )$ values. This additional feature is not required for searching pattern recognition state–space graphs, since they will be trees.

How do we use these ideas in pattern classification? The costs involved are (1) that of feature measurement at every measurement state and (2) classification risk at goal states.

A state-space representation was defined as a 4-tuple $\{S, I, F, q\}$ in Section II.A. For pattern recognition, $S$ is the set of states. $I$, the set of initial states, usually contains only one state called the *ROOT* state. $F$, the set of final (goal) states, has elements from $\Omega$, the class set. The set of goal states can also contain a reject state to facilitate rejection of a pattern as unclassifiable. Here $q$, the ordered successor operator, generates $s_k = q(s_i, j)$, where $s_k$ is the $j$th successor of $s_i$. Several other attributes are associated with the elements of this 4-tuple notation: $C$ is a nonnegative real-valued function on the edges generating the successors; $c(s_j, s_k)$ is the cost of features measured during the transition from $s_j$ to $s_k$; $R$ is a real-valued function on the goal states representing the expected value of the cost or loss incurred in making the classificatory decision associated with the goal state.

A classification process is a global control strategy for searching in the state–space graph for the optimal assignment of a test sample to a pattern class, represented by a goal node. In conventional AI problems, at the goal state, the heuristic component becomes zero, leaving only the cost of the path to the goal. In pattern clsassification, once a goal is reached, there is an associated cost of misclassification. This cost or risk could depend on the values of all feature measurements and not just those along the path to the goal. Also, associated with each feature measurement is a measurement cost. Thus, in general, the cost of reaching a goal could also depend on features not along the path to the goal. If, in an interactive design phase, one can obtain a good state–space graph, in the form of a skeleton of a hierarchical classifier, then the search strategy for assigning a test sample to a class can be simple. That is, it is possible to work out a state–space graph in which the risk is not much influenced by measurements at nodes not along the path to the optimal goal node. Furthermore, if a good heuristic function is employed, the number of nodes explored outside the optimal path will be small and the cost of measurements made at those nodes can be treated as search overhead and essentially ignored. Under these assumptions, one obtained a class of search strategies, termed $S$-admissible. This is the strategy primarily considered here. The more complex set of strategies obtained when the above assumptions do not hold are called $B$-admissible strategies. They are mentioned here only in passing. Further details can be found in Kulkarni and Kanal [10]. Let $c(s_i, s_j)$ be the cost of all features measured along any path from the state $s_i$ to $s_j$. In pattern recognition state–space graphs, if there are two or more paths from $s_i$ to $s_j$, they will require the measurement of the same subset of features between $s_i$ and $s_j$ (though they may measure them in different sequences).

Due to this property, the history at any state is independent of the path taken to reach the state, and, therefore, the state–space graph can be essentially dealt with as a tree. Let $y(s_i)$ be the ordered set of all the observed measurement outcomes at state $s_i$. Let $s_f$ be any goal (final state). The risk at a goal state is conditioned on the measurements up to the goal state: $R(s_f | y(s_f))$. Thus, we are interested in a search strategy that minimizes the total cost at a goal state

$$t(s_f) = c(s_f) + R(s_f | y(s_f)) \qquad (4)$$

over all $s_f \in F$.

A conceptually simple technique to realize this is by measuring all the features, computing the total cost function for each $s_f \in F$ in the state–space graph and choosing that goal state for which the total cost is minimum. However, this implies the measurement of many features not along the path to the finally selected goal state. This is analogous to searching along all possible paths in the state–space graph to choose the best goal state. The idea of searching a pattern classification state–space graph is to minimize $t(s_f)$ in (4) with as few feature measurements outside the path to $s_f$ as possible. This depends on the effectiveness of the heuristic function to be used in the search algorithm. Algorithm- $S$ describes this search procedure. An explicit heuristic evaluation function is worked out later.

*Algorithm S*

(1)   Place the *ROOT* state on the list *OPEN*. Empty a list called *CLOSED*.
(2)   For each $s_i \in OPEN$, evaluate

$$t(s_i) = c(s_i) + h(s_i) + r(s_i)$$

where

$$h(s_i) \begin{cases} = 0 & \text{if} \quad s_i \in F \quad \text{(goal state)} \\ \leq \min_{s_f \in F} c(s_i, s_f) & \text{if} \quad s_i \notin F \end{cases}$$

$$r(s_i) \begin{cases} = R(s_i | y(s_i)) & \text{if} \quad s_i \in F \\ = \min_{s_f \in F} \min_z \{R[s_f | y(s_i)]\} & \text{if} \quad s_i \notin F \end{cases}$$

(3)   Let $s_k$ be the state among all the states in *OPEN* with the minimum $t(\ )$. Remove $s_k$ from *OPEN* and add it to *CLOSED*. If $s_k$ is a goal state, exit with $s_k$ as the solution. Else, apply the successor operator to $s_k$ and place all its successors in *OPEN* and go to Step 2.

In this algorithm, if $s_i$ is not a goal state, $t(s_i)$ is a lower bound on the total cost of a goal state with a path to it through $s_i$. The algorithm is therefore admissible in the sense that it exits with that goal node $s_f$ with a minimum $t(s_f)$. Furthermore, the closer the functions $h(\ )$ and $r(\ )$ are to their true evaluations, the better will be the search efficiency of the algorithm. Formal proofs are available in Kulkarni [11]. In principle, the S-admissible strategy is applicable in problems with continuous feature distributions. However, the minimization required in Step 2 is easily carried out for discrete features only.

To utilize algorithm S for practical pattern classification problems, we need the following.

(1)   The directed acyclic state–space graph (the skeleton).
(2)   Feature subsets to be measured at each nonterminal node and class assignment at terminal nodes. Along a path from the ROOT node to a goal node, a feature may not be required to be measured more than once.
(3)   Costs of feature measurements and the loss function associated with the misclassification.
(4)   The required probabilistic structure. Note that the joint class-conditional distributions of all the features may not be required for certain state–space configurations. This is one of the advantages of the state–space model for pattern classification when the complete probabilistic structure of the problem is unknown.
(5)   The evaluation function $h(\ )$ and $r(\ )$.

The details (1)–(4) are problem specific. We need a general procedure to compute the evaluation functions from the problem data. It is important to note that there exist many heuristic functions satisfying the admissibility criteria. We present a $k$-step look-ahead procedure for computing the heuristic for a node in the OPEN list. This is a lower bound on the additional cost incurred in going up to $k$ levels beyond the present node. Let $s_i$ be the node at which the $k$-step look-ahead heuristic

$$d_k(s_i, s_i) = h(s_i) + r(s_i) \tag{5}$$

is required. Here $d_k(s_i, s_i)$ is recursively computed as follows:

$$d_k(s_i, s_i) = \min_{s_j \in Q(s_i)} \{c(s_i, s_j) + d_k(s_i, s_j)\} \tag{6}$$

Recall that $Q(s_i)$ is the set of successor nodes of $s_i$ and $c(s_i, s_j)$ is the cost of features measured at $s_j$ when descending from $s_i$. We have

$$d_0(s_i, s_l) = \begin{cases} 0 & \text{if } s_l \text{ is not a goal node} \\ R(s_l | y(s_i)) & \text{if } s_l \text{ is a goal node} \end{cases} \tag{7}$$

The notation using $s_i$ twice in $d_k(\ )$ is intended to facilitate recursive computation in (7). With positive measurement cost and misclassification functions, the preceding heuristic function is monotonic in the sense that

$$d_{k+1}(s_i, s_i) \geq d_k(s_i, s_i) \tag{8}$$

Therefore, the performance (total expected cost of search per sample pattern) of the S-admissible strategy with a $(k + 1)$-step look-ahead heuristic is no worse than and can be better than that with a $k$-step look-ahead heuristic.

The $S$-admissible strategy and the associated heuristic function were worked out under the assumption that the state–space graph is such that the feature measurements conducted at nodes outside the path from $ROOT$ to a goal node do not influence the goal node risk. There may be problems in which this assumption is not realistic. Kulkarni [11] and Kulkarni and Kanal [10] develop another state–space pattern classification algorithm, referred to as the $B$-admissible strategy for such problems. This uses an additional upper bounding function. Development of problem-specific state-space graphs and related hierarchical classification schemes are discussed in Kulkarni [11], Kulkarni and Kanal [12], and Dattatreya and Kanal [13].

## B   Problem Reduction Approach to Structural Pattern Analysis

The relation between context-free grammars and AND/OR graphs is useful in utilizing heuristic search methods for structural pattern analysis. While the state–space model requires a search for a path to the goal state, the problem reduction model requires us to find a solution tree the leaves of which are solved primitive problems. Concepts from state–space ordered search are useful in finding the solution tree. If primitives are available without ambiguity, a straightforward parsing will help in obtaining the correct representation. However, with raw pattern data, the best primitive for each segment may not yield the overall best representation. What is required is the utilization of information about good primitive fits to guide the search for a good representation based only on key features. Ideally, we would like to use both a top-down or a model-directed approach and a bottom-up or data-directed approach. It is further desirable to relax restrictions of left-right parsing in the domain of primitive strings. This would allow the use of primitives detected anywhere in the data sequence to guide the bottom-up search. To utilize these ideas, we need an appropriate transformation from the PRR to the SSR. The resulting state space should allow the available information from the model space and the data space to guide the search for a goal node.

Stockman [14] has developed a good transformation amenable to top-down and bottom-up search. This transformation requires definition of problem structures, solution structures, primary problems, successors, and solutions. A problem structure is a specific vertex in the AND/OR PRR. In addition to the index (number) of the node in the AND/OR graph, the number of the node in the sequence of successors of its parent is important. Thus, if a problem $p_i$ is the $j$th successor of some higher-level problem $h$, then the problem structure of the node $p_i$ under consideration is $(i, j)$. If $p_i$ is a solved problem and is the $j$th successor of $h$, it is denoted by $[i, j]$ and is called

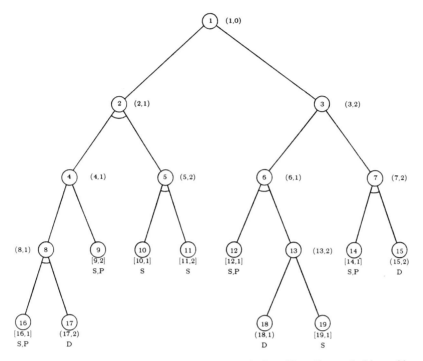

**Fig. 2.** A problem reduction AND/OR graph. S, solved problem; D, unsolvable problem; and P, primary problem.

a solution structure. Figure 2 shows a PRR example in which problem structures and solution structures corresponding to different problems are marked at a stage when only tip problems are solved. Note that AND and OR problems do not necessarily alternate in the example PRR of Fig. 2. In the following presentation of PRR and the associated search methodology, strictly alternating AND and OR problems are not a necessary constraint. Recall that a PRR is $\{P, r, t, u, B\}$ and an SSR is $\{S, I, F, q\}$. To define a transformation from PRR to SSR, we need to specify $S, I, F,$ and $q$ as functions of elements from $\{P, r, t, u, B\}$. Here $S$ is a subset of all strings of pairs of the form

$$\langle (i_1, j_1) \cdots (i_{n-1}, j_{n-1})(i_n, j_n) \rangle$$

or

$$\langle (i_1, j_1) \cdots (i_{n-1}, j_{n-1})[i_n, j_n] \rangle$$

where $(i_k, j_k)$ is a problem structure and $[i_k, j_k]$ is a solution structure; $I = \{\langle (i, 0) \rangle : i \in B\}$ is the set of initial states. An initial state is a string of only one problem structure in the set of initial problems $B$. It is not a successor of any problem and by convention is taken as the zeroth successor of some problem; $F = \{\langle[i, 0]\rangle : i \in B\}$. A final state is a solved problem from the set of implicit initial problems.

A definition of ordered successor function $q$ will allow the generation of other states recursively from $I$. Recall that $q$ is a function from $S \times N$ to $S$. Certain *primary* quantities need to be defined first. A primary path from problem $i$ in PRR is defined as a sequence of descendant problems from problem $i$ such that if any problem is an AND problem, it is the first (leftmost) successor of its parent problem. Similarly, a primary successor of problem $i$ is its first AND successor (if the successors of problem $i$ are AND problems) or any of its OR successors (if the successors of problem $i$ are OR successors). All the problems along the sequence of a primary path from a problem $i$ are known as primary descendants of $i$. Some of the primary terminal problems are indicated in Fig. 2. Parents of these primary problems are also primary. Note that these definitions of primary quantities apply within the PRR only. Successors of a state in the SSR depend on several factors in the corresponding PRR. Let $\alpha$ and $\beta$ be arbitrary strings made of elements of the form $\alpha(i, j)$. If a state $s$ is of the form $\langle\alpha(i, j)\rangle$, then the problem $i$ may be solvable, unsolvable, or live, that is, the function $u(i)$ is $S$, $D$, or $L$. If it is unsolvable, there are no successors. If it is solvable, the successor state is a string ending with the solution structure. If the problem $i$ is live, the successors are all the strings formed by concatenating the existing string with the primary successors of the problem $i$. If the present state is a string ending in a solution structure of the form $\langle\beta(k, l)[i, j]\rangle$, the successor states depend on whether the problem $i$ is an AND problem or an OR problem. If it is an OR problem, its solution solves the previous problem so that the only successor state generated is $\langle\beta[k, l]\rangle$. If problem $i$ is an AND problem and is solvable, the successor state in SSR is the string ending with the next AND successor of the same parent problem.

If the present state is a string of one solution structure, that is, $\langle[i, l]\rangle$, its successor in SSR is the solution structure of the primary parent if $i$ is an OR problem. If $i$ is an AND problem, then the solved $i$ should attempt to solve its possible primary parent so that the successor state in PRR is $\langle(k, j)[i,l]\rangle$, where $k$ is a (possible) primary parent. In this case, only if $l$ is 1 will problem $i$ be the primary successor of problem $k$. mathematically, we have three cases.

Case 1: state $s = \langle\alpha(i, j)\rangle$

(a)  If $u(i) = S$, then $Q(\langle\alpha(i, j)\rangle) = \{\alpha[i, j]\}$, that is, if a problem $i$ is solvable, the successor structure is the solution structure.

(b)  If $u(i) = D$, then $Q(\langle\alpha(i, j)\rangle) = \varnothing$, that is, unsolvable problems in PRR yield dead-end paths in SSR.

(c)  If $u(i) = L$ and $t(r(i, 1)) = \Lambda$, then $Q(\langle\alpha(i, j)\rangle) = \{\alpha(i, j)(r(i, 1), 1)\}$, that is, search for the first AND subproblem. If $u(i) = L$ and $t(r(i, 1)) = V$, then $Q(\langle\alpha(i, j)\rangle) = \{\langle\alpha(i, j)(r(i, k), k)\rangle\}$, $k = 1, n$, that is, successors are a set of subproblems, one for each OR subproblem.

Case 2: state $s = \langle \beta(k, l)[i, j] \rangle$

(a)   If $t(i) = V$, then $Q(\langle \beta(k, l)[i, j] \rangle) = \{\beta[k, l]\}$, that is, solution of an OR subproblem solves the predecessor problem.

(b)   If $t(i) = \Lambda$, then $Q(\langle \beta(k, l)[i, j] \rangle) = \{\langle \beta(k, l)(n, j + 1) \rangle\}$ if $r(k, j + 1) = n \neq \emptyset$, that is, search for the next AND successor of the parent of problem $i$. $Q(\langle \beta(k, l)[i, j] \rangle) = \{\langle \beta[k, l] \rangle\}$ if $r(k, j + 1) = \emptyset$, that is, solution of the last AND subproblem solves the predecessor problem.

Case 3: state $s$ is of the form $\langle [i, l] \rangle$ and $i$ does not belong to $B$ ($B$ is the set of initial problems)

(a)   If $t(i) = V$, then $Q(\langle [i, l] \rangle) = \{\langle [k, n] \rangle : r(k, n) = i$ for some $n$, and if $k$ is primary in PRR$\}$, that is, a solved OR problem solves its possible primary parent.

(b)   If $t(i) = \Lambda$ and $l = 1$, then $Q(\langle [i, 1] \rangle) = \{\langle (k, n)[i, 1] \rangle : r(k, 1) = i$, for some $l$, and $k$ primary in PRR$\}$, that is, a solved AND problem attempts next to solve its possible primary parent.

The state space will be dynamically developed by generating successors of an existing state, whenever required by the problem solving algorithm. These state-successor operators in SSR are best understood by examples. Figures 3a–3j show a sequence of state expansions. These are worked out on the PRR of Fig. 2 (by the nondirectional search algorithm presented later). In the depicted partial trees, one problem–solution structure in each tree has a period to its left. The state in SSR corresponding to this problem in PRR is the one to be expanded next. The state encodings resulting from the expansions are shown next to the trees. In practical problems, we require the best problem reduction tree of the PRR and not just any solution tree. The criterion depends on merits of fits of primitives to the raw data and how the merits are carried over toward the root of the tree. In structural pattern analysis, we are interested in representing the data by a string of primitives with the maximum merit among possible strings within the model. This is achieved by defining a merit of a solution as the maximum of the merits of the OR successors and as the minimum of the merits of AND successors. Thus, the merit of a solution tree is at least as large as the minimum of the merits of the leaf nodes. The true merit value of the solution to problem $i$ is denoted by $f(i)$. Its estimate is denoted by $\hat{f}(i)$. The following algorithm performs top-down and bottom-up searches to achieve the best solution tree. The search is guided by solved primary descendants of the initial problem and by the initial problem structure itself.

*Nondirectional Search Algorithm*

*Step* 1.  For every primary path from the initial problem $p$, place one state on an initially empty list called the *OPEN* as follows: $\langle [i, 1] \rangle$, where $i$ is a solved primary descendant of the initial problem $p$. Supply the merit value of

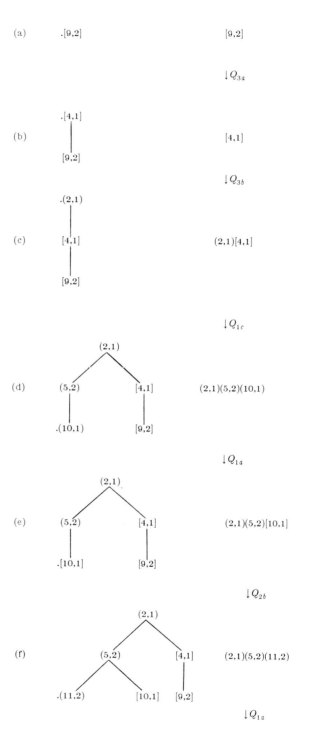

**Fig. 3.** Development of the solution tree for the PRR shown in Fig. 2 (*continues*)

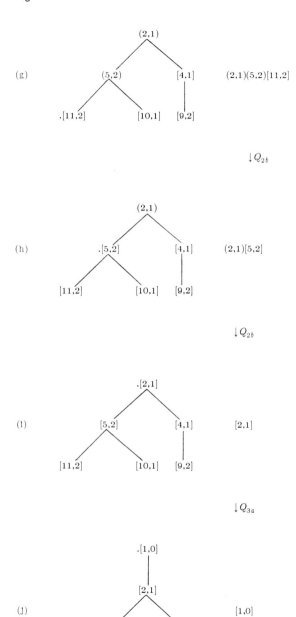

Fig. 3. *(continued)*

this solved problem: $\langle (i, 1) \rangle$, where $i$ is any primary descendant of the initial problem $p$, or $i = p$ itself. The estimate of the merit value of the initial problem is $\infty$.

*Step* 2. Remove from *OPEN* that state $n$ such that $\hat{f}(n)$ is the largest. If *OPEN* is empty, exit with failure ($f = -\infty$).

*Step* 3. If $n$ is a final state, exit with $f(n) = \hat{f}(n)$. Else, continue.

*Step* 4. Expand the state $n$, generating all successors $n_j, j = 1, \ldots, m$ using the three cases of the successor function $Q$. Compute $\hat{f}(n_j)$ as follows. If Case 1(a) applies, $\hat{f}(n_j) = \min\{f(i), \hat{f}(n)\}$; $f(i)$ is the true merit of the solution of the problem in the PRR represented by the state $n_j$ in SSR. If Case 1(a) does not apply, $\hat{f}(n_j) = \hat{f}(n)$. Place the generated states $n_j, j = 1, \ldots, m$ on *OPEN* in order of their merit and go to Step 2.

The algorithm overestimates the merit value of a goal state when it carries down the estimate of an intermediate problem to its successor. Since we attempt the maximization of merit function of the solution, this ensures admissibility. Details may be found in Stockman [14]. In practice, many solution trees above a certain threshold merit can be produced by removing the solved final state along with its merit and continuing until a final state below the specified threshold is found and rejected.

## C  Nondirectional Parsing and Its Application in Pattern Analysis

The top-down and bottom-up search algorithm in the previous section finds out if the problem is solvable and returns the merit value of the solution. However, it does not return the explicit solution tree. To be able to obtain the solution tree, we need to modify slightly the state descriptions to include the entire partial parse tree and the portion to be expanded next. This is achieved by using the parenthesized state description. The problem to be expanded next is denoted by a period to its left. Formally, $S$, the search space, is the set of all parenthesized encodings implicitly defined by the initial state encodings and the ordered state-space operator $q$; $I$, the set of initial states, is a set of states of the form $\langle . [i, 1] \rangle$ or $\langle .(i, 1) \rangle$, where $i$ is primary in PRR; $F$, the set of final states, is a set of states of the form $\langle . [i, 1\alpha] \rangle$, where $i \in B$ of PRR and $\alpha$ encodes the solution structures of $i$; and $q$, the state-space operator, is defined on $S \times N$ in terms of Cases 1, 2, and 3 of $Q$ defined in Section III.C.

As an example to illustrate these developments, Fig. 3 shows a possible sequence of partial trees ending in the final solution tree (Fig. 3j) for the solution of the PRR in Fig. 2. Figure 4 shows the sequence of tree encodings generated by the search procedure. The node descriptions are the same as in the PRR of Fig. 2. Note, however, that in the solution tree encoding, the AND

$$<.[9,1]>$$
$$\downarrow Q_{3a}$$
$$<.[4,1[9,2]]>$$
$$\downarrow Q_{3b}$$
$$<.(2,1[4,1[9,2]]>$$
$$\downarrow Q_{2b}$$
$$<(2,1).(5,2)[4,1[9,2]])>$$
$$\downarrow Q_{1c}$$
$$<(2,1(5,2.(10,1))[4,1[9,2]])>$$
$$\downarrow Q_{1a}$$
$$<(2,1(5,2.[10,1])[4,1[9,2]])>$$
$$\downarrow Q_{2b}$$
$$<(2,1(5,2.(11,2)[10,1])[4,1[9,2]])>$$
$$\downarrow Q_{1a}$$
$$<(2,1(5,2.[11,2][10,1])[4,1[9,2]])>$$
$$\downarrow Q_{2b}$$
$$<(2,1.[5,2[11,2][10,1]][4,1[9,2]]>$$
$$\downarrow Q_{2b}$$
$$<(.[2,1[5,2[11,2][10,1]][4,1[9,2]]]>$$
$$\downarrow Q_{3a}$$
$$<.[1,0[2,1[5,2[11,2][10,1]][4,1[9,2]]]]>$$
$$\downarrow$$
Solution

**Fig. 4.** The sequence of partial solution tree encodings obtained by the search procedure in Fig. 3.

successors show up in the reverse order from that in the original PRR since the problem to be expanded is added to the left in the subtree description.

In pattern analysis, each of a set of objects to be recognized would be defined by a PRR. Primitive detectors should be constructed to solve the primitive problems defined by the PRRs. The operator $Q$ in SSR is then the union of the three cases of each of the operators in all the PRRs. The initial problems of all the PRRs should be placed in the final state set. Whichever initial problem gets solved with the highest merit solution tree is recognized as the pattern category. Furthermore, the solution tree along with its merit value is the representation of the pattern worked out by the PRR methodology. In the next section we outline how several candidate solutions for each primitive can be developed along with their merits by a search procedure for use in the nondirectional search algorithm.

## IV   PRIMITIVE EXTRACTION AND WAVEFORM ANALYSIS

The potential of the nondirectional search procedure described in the previous section depends on many candidate fits of morphs of vaying merits. In contrast, syntactic pattern recognition systems expect strings (or other structures) of primitives (morphs) in a deterministic fashion. Several techniques to fit line and arc segments to the raw data are available. However, these do not interact with the structural knowledge, although structural knowledge is considered when defining primitives. This problem of ambiguity in primitives may be avoided by defining primitives on very small segments of data. However, this passes on the burden of sorting out the possibilities to the structural analysis procedure.

Search procedures can be used to seek morphs on large intervals by scanning the data with a window and perturbing the window to search for better merit curve fits. Merits of curve fits may be interpreted as the probability of how well the curve under consideration fits the data interval. Gaussian noise is assumed in computing these merits. All fits above a threshold merit are initial states in an *OPEN* list. State–space search is then used with state–transition operators represented by perturbations (shift, compress, expand) in the window of fit length. The heuristic of not expanding a fit below a certain threshold is not admissible. However, it is useful in limiting the search when a desired morph is not present.

The preceding methods have been applied to the analysis of carotid pulse waves and electrocardiograms (Stockman and Kanal [15] and Xiong *et al.* [16]). Properties of the carotid pulse wave in the artery of the human neck are related to aging, atherosclerosis, and hypertension. Figure 5a shows several variations in original carotid pulse waveforms. Figure 5b shows the result of application of the PRR approach to a data segment. Some of the key morphs are up slope (UPSLOP), trailing edge (TREDGE), local minimum (LOC-MIN), global minimum GLBMIN), maximum (CAP), large negative drop (LN), systolic complex (SSPLX), and diastolic complex (DIAPLX). Some of the intermediate problems are the joint between the two cycles of the waveforms (JYNT) and the repetitive train of pulses (TRAN). A typical PRR is shown in Fig. 6. The pair of numbers in each node indicates the interval of possible location for that structure.

All the procedures for primitive curve fits by state–space search and nondirectional analysis for PRR are integrated into a software system known as WAPSYS (waveform parsing systems). The input to the system is a digitized waveform. The user must define the PRR which is input to the system. The output consists of a few of the top candidate solution trees, rank ordered by their merit. The SSR and RPP search and analysis portions of WAPSYS are applicable across waveform domains. The primitive feature detection algorithms are also general. Thus, by providing descriptions of the

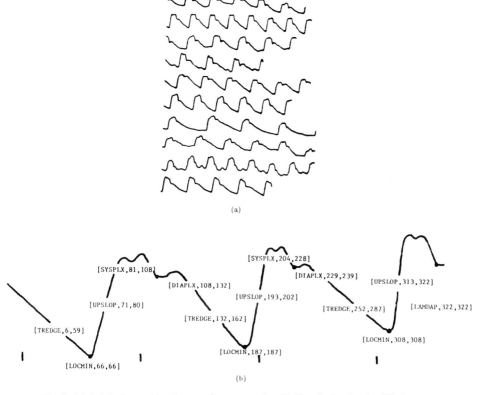

**Fig. 5.** (a) Original carotid pulse waveform examples. (b) Terminals of a simplified grammar identified on a carotid pulse wave sample.

special (problem domain specific) features and the details of structural descriptions of a waveform domain, the system can be used for the structural analysis of different types of waveforms. As an example, see Xiong *et al.* [16], which describes the use of **WAPSYS** on electrocardiograms. The advantages of the waveform parsing techniques are the following.

(1)    It is possible to develop the **PRR** model based on structural representations without being constrained by the ambiguities of data fits.

(2)    Data segmentation can be coupled with structural analysis and primitive fits can be achieved with moderate computation using state-space search.

(3)    Nondirectional analysis can concentrate on key features and avoid working on portions of data which are not critical.

(4)    If the **PRR** model is initially inadequate, it can be modified to incorporate additional structural details based on deficiencies revealed by the analysis.

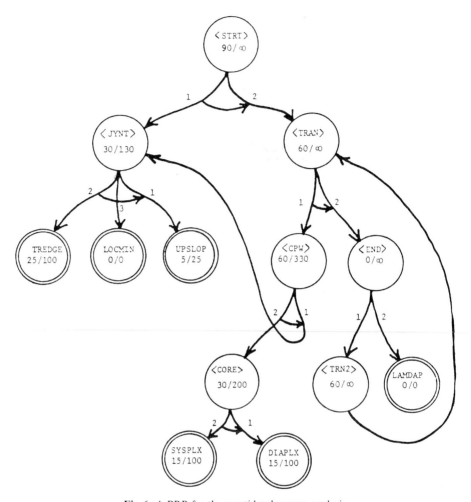

**Fig. 6.** A PRR for the carotid pulse wave analysis.

## V  SUMMARY

This chapter outlines the development of a state–space paradigm for statistical pattern classification, briefly describes the use of state–space search for primitive detection, and sketches the nondirectional analysis of problem reduction representations for the structural analysis of waveforms. This methodology led to the development of a general waveform parsing system which couples data segmentation with structural data analysis so that each phase can benefit from the other. Applications of this methodology to certain biomedical waveforms are cited. Potential areas for further investigations of the nondirectional search paradigm for pattern analysis include parallel implementations of the search procedure and applications in two- and three-dimensional scene analysis and computer vision.

## REFERENCES

1. P. R. Krishnaiah and L. N. Kanal (eds.), "Handbook of Statistics," Vol. 2. North-Holland Publ., New York, 1982.
2. K.-S. Fu, "Syntactic Pattern Recognition and Applications." Prentice-Hall, Englewood Cliffs, New Jersey, 1982.
3. J. R. Slagle and R. C. T. Lee, Applications of game-tree searching techniques to sequential pattern recognition, *Commun. Assoc. Comput. Machinery* **14**, 103–110 (February 1971).
4. L. N. Kanal, Problem-solving methods and search strategies for pattern recognition, *IEEE Trans. Pattern Analysis Machine Intelligence* **PAMI-1**, 193–201 (April 1979).
5. B. Duerr, W. Haettich, H. Tropf, and G. Winkler, A combination of statistical and syntactical pattern recognition applied to classification of unconstrained handwritten numerals, *Pattern Recognition* **12**, 189–199 (1980).
6. H. Tropf, Analysis by synthesis search for semantic segmentation applied to workpiece recognition, *5th Intl. Joint Conf. Pattern Recognition, Miami, Dec. 1980* (1980).
7. N. J. Nilsson, "Principles of Artificial Intelligence." Tioga, Palo Alto, California, 1980.
8. A. Barr and E. A. Fiegenbaum, "The Handbook of Artificial Intelligence," Vol. 1. William Kaufmann, Inc., Los Altos, California, 1981.
9. P. A. V. Hall, Equivalence between *AND/OR* graphs and context-free grammars, *Commun. Assoc. Comput. Machinery* **16**, 444–445 (July 1973).
10. A. V. Kulkarni and L. N. Kanal, Admissible search strategies for parametric and nonparametric hierarchical classifiers, *Proc. 4th Intl. Joint Conf. Pattern Recognition, Kyoto 1978* (1978).
11. A. V. Kulkarni, Optimal and heuristic synthesis of hierarchical classifiers, Ph.D. dissertation, Univ. of Maryland, Dept. of Computer Science, August 1976.
12. A. V. Kulkarni and L. N. Kanal, An optimization approach to hierarchical classifier design, *Proc. 3rd Intl. Conf. Pattern Recognition, San Diego, California, 1976*, pp. 459–466 (1976).
13. G. R. Dattatreya and L. N. Kanal, Decision trees in pattern recognition, *in* "Progress in Pattern Recognition" (L. N. Kanal and A. Rosenfeld, eds.), Vol. 2. North-Holland Publ., Amsterdam, in press.
14. G. C. Stockman, A problem-reduction approach to the linguistic analysis of waveforms, Ph.D. dissertation, Univ. of Maryland, Dept. of Computer Science, May 1977.
15. G. C. Stockman and L. N. Kanal, Problem reduction representation for the linguistic analysis of waveforms, *IEEE Trans. Pattern Analysis Machine Intelligence* **PAMI-5**, 287–298 (May 1983).
16. F.-L. Xiong, B. A. Lambird, and L. N. Kanal, An experiment in recognition of electrocardiograms using a structural analysis algorithm. *Proc. IEEE Intl. Conf. Syst., Man, Cybern., Bombay and New Delhi, India, Dec. 1983, and Jan. 1984*, pp. 383–387 (1984).

# Part II

# Image Processing
# and Understanding

# Chapter **7**

# Image Coding

ALI HABIBI

The Aerospace Corporation
El Segundo, California

## INTRODUCTION  I

The steady growth of modern communication requirements has resulted in a steady increase in the volume of pictorial data that must be transmitted from one location to another. In some cases, although image transmission to a remote location is not necessary, one does need to store the images for future retrieval and analysis.

In previous years, most of the image transmission has been accomplished through the conventional analog technique. Today, the trend in image transmission and storage is to use digital instead of analog techniques. In digital imagery the analog signal is sampled, and each sample is digitized

169

using a pulse code modulation (PCM) code. The PCM signal can be applied to the input of a digital-to-analog converter to reconstruct the analog signal. The fidelity of the reconstructed video signal is a function of the sampling frequency and the radiometric resolution of the digitizer, as discussed in Section II. To maintain the same fidelity as that of analog video, the digital imagery requires an analog bandwidth[†] approximately eight times that of the original analog video.

Aside from the large bandwidth (which is a clear disadvantage of digital imagery), the advantages of digital video representation are

(a)   no signal conditioning is needed to accomplish encryption and coding for secured communications;

(b)   precise repeatable picture definition;

(c)   color fidelity (color modulation is bypassed in color television);

(d)   noise removal is possible by error correction and coding;

(e)   protection against multipath and radio frequency interference achievable by spread spectrum coding;

(f)   variable resolution, picture insets, composites, and split frames;

(g)   variable frame rate;

(h)   computer compatibility;

(i)   restoration and enhancement of images by digital processing;

(j)   signal-to-noise ratio (SNR) is largely a matter of design rather than chance.

In the following sections we discuss the resolution and fidelity of digital imagery and describe the various image bandwidth compression techniques. In describing these techniques, we have made an attempt to explain the principles involved as well as to tell the reader how to design a bandwidth compression algorithm for a specific application. Compressing the bandwidth of digital television is used as a common application because of the future importance of digital TV and teleconferencing systems.

## II   DIGITAL IMAGERY

To achieve digital representation of imagery data, it must be converted to a set of binary integers, which in turn can be operated on to recover the picture with minimum possible degradation. The continuous image is first sampled

---

[†] The analog bandwidth is obtained by using a sampling frequency twice the signal bandwidth, using a radiometric resolution of 8 bits per sample, and assuming a QPSK modulation of binary data that results in 2 binary digits per hertz.

in the spatial domain to produce an $M \times N$ array of discrete samples, which are then quantized in brightness utilizing $K$ bits per sample. Then, using $F$ frames/sec, the data rate $B$ (bits per second) is

$$B = NMKF$$

The trade-off between spatial, temporal, and gray-level resolutions that would result in the best video quality at the lowest data rate is application dependent. In the following we discuss various factors that limit the resolution of digital imagery.

### Spatial and Gray-Level Resolutions of Digital Imagery    A

The spatial resolution of digital imagery is related to image sharpness, the gray-level resolution is related to the dynamic range of the analog signal, and the frame rate is related to the amount of perceptible motion between the frames.

In image bandwidth compression, one maintains the system resolution and reduces the digital image bandwidth by exploiting the spectral, interframe, and intraframe signal correlation; however, when large bandwidth compressions are required, a combination of bandwidth compression and resolution reduction may be used.

In reducing the gray-level resolution, there is no absolute minimum and the lower limits are application dependent. For monochrome television, the lower limit is 6 bits per sample before serious contouring (or breakup of the picture into patches) occurs. Some of the contouring effect is eliminated by adding pseudonoise before quantization and subtracting it afterward [1].

The lower limit on spatial resolution (or the minimum number of samples required to express a specified contrast change) depends on the minimum size of the object which needs to be detected. This, in turn, is related to the projected size of the object upon the scanning raster and, hence, to the distance from the camera and the lens focal length. Other factors, such as the actual contrast and lighting conditions at the object and the resolution properties of the imaging optics, also impact object detectability.

The lower limits on the frame rate are directly proportional to the expected motion in a frame time. A higher frame rate results in less smearing due to movements in a picture, which in turn improves object recognition. Higher frame rates help human vision to integrate the system noise and result in a higher effective SNR even for stationary background. In reducing the frame rate, the critical region is around 4 frames/sec. This frame rate is known to have some undesirable visual effects and is avoided in many applications.

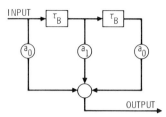

**Fig. 1.** Block diagram of the temporal filter. $\tau_B$ = one frame delay time. $2a_0 + a_1 = 1$; $a_0 = 0.25$.

## B  Spatial and Temporal Filtering of TV Signals

Due to the integrating effect of the eye, a sequence of television frames is physiologically perceived as a continuous scene. Thus, the eye works like a temporal low-pass filter having a rise time of about 60–80 msec. If, however, the frame frequency of a television signal is reduced from 30 to 15 Hz by deleting every second frame at the transmitter and by interpolating these frames at the receiver, the movement of displayed objects looks jerky. These distortions can be avoided to a certain extent if the television signal is band limited with the help of a temporal low-pass filter before the temporal sampling frequency, called the frame frequency, is reduced. The temporal filter mainly reduces the aliasing errors. With decreasing bandwidth, however, another kind of distortion is introduced, for example, moving objects appear blurred. Therefore, if temporal subsampling with 15 Hz is applied, both kinds of distortion must be balanced.

Because of the linear phase required for television signals, only symmetrical finite-response filters have been investigated as temporal filters. For reasons of implementation complexity, the order of the filters considered has been restricted to two. The structure of such a filter is shown in Fig. 1. In order not to change the average luminance level of the television signal, the sum of the coefficients must be equal to 1. Thus, there is only one parameter, $a_0$ or $a_1$, which can be optimized to minimize the picture quality degradations. Assuming temporal subsampling with 15 Hz and frame interpolation at the receiving end, it could be shown [2, 3] that the subjectively optimized temporal filter is close to that having the minimum mean-square aliasing error. The optimum value for $a_0$ is about 0.25. This makes for a rise time of the filter of 80 msec, similar to that of the eye. As a result of this temporal filter, no jerkiness but a blurring of rapidly moving objects can be observed.

It is not so much the temporal subsampling but another advantage that can be gained from temporal filtering. The blurring of moving objects has already indicated that the temporal filter influences the spatial resolution. This effect of the temporal filter can be explained as a velocity-dependent spatial low-pass filtering of moving objects. Figure 2 demonstrates this effect for a moving object represented by the luminance amplitudes $A$, $B$, $C$, and $D$.

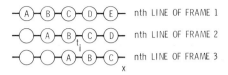

**Fig. 2.** Picture elements of one line with a moving objective *A*, *B*, *C*, *D*, *E*, shown for three consecutive frames. The object moves in the *x* direction with a speed of one picture element per frame.

At time $t_i$ a temporal filter, shown in Fig. 2, generates an output signal that is a function of the amplitudes *A*, *B*, and *C* of frames 3, 2, and 1. The same output signal can be generated with the help of a corresponding spatial finite-response filter of order two whose output is a function of the amplitudes *A*, *B*, and *C* from the *n*th line of frame 2. The corresponding spatial filter has the same coefficients as the temporal filter. The delay time of the delay elements of the spatial filter is dependent on the speed of the moving object. In the example shown in Fig. 2, the delay time corresponds to the time interval of one picture element. The speed-dependent delay time causes a speed-dependent filtering of moving objects. The static background is not affected.

By adapting the spatial sampling frequency to the actual bandwidth of a moving object, a further reduction of the bit rate can be achieved without introducing additional picture quality degradations. Only one subsampling mode with a frequency ratio of 1:2 in the horizontal and vertical directions needs to be implemented in order to avoid complex control and coding procedures. The spatial subsampling mode can be switched in when the error produced by the interpolation of the omitted samples descreases below a specific threshold.

## Image Quality and Signal-to-Noise Ratio in Digital and Analog TV Systems   C

The effects of noise upon images is different for various modulation systems. Viewers of commercial TV are familiar with noise with definite periodic components, causing herringbone, moires, and flutter, depending upon the frequency content and the part of the circuit which is affected. Many of these latter types of effects are not found in digital TV images because of the rejection of amplitude modulation.

Random noise causes snow to appear in the background and reduces contrast uniformly in amplitude-modulated TV. The performance of an analog TV system with a 48-dB unweighted SNR is termed excellent in reports [4] submitted to the FCC in 1959 by the Television Allocations Study Organization (TASO). According to TASO, an SNR ranging from 48 to 25 dB represents an image ranging from excellent to just passable, as listed on

TABLE I

**Picture Quality versus Signal-to-Noise Ratio**

| Picture rating (Television Allocations Study Organization) | Signal-to-noise ratio (dB) |
|---|---|
| Excellent (no perceptible snow) | 48 |
| Fine (snow just perceptible) | 35 |
| Passable (snow definitely perceptible but not objectionable) | 29 |
| Marginal (snow somewhat objectionable) | 25 |

Table I. An image with an SNR less than 25 dB is termed objectionable by viewers.

Digital systems experience a completely different set of phenomena in noisy images. The noise is of two types: quantization noise and interference with the signal, which results either in the generation or the annihilation of a bit. Quantization noise is generated by the discrete steps in the analog-to-digital conversion of the original signal. As discussed in previous sections, the quantization levels required for acceptable images are known; therefore, this type of noise does not enter our discussion.

Bit errors can occur at any place in the digital word which represents the signal. Losing a bit can cause an additive change in the value of the $k$-bit binary number of $1, 2, 4, 8, \ldots$, or $2^k$. The effect upon the image is to cause an individual pixel to stand out in the pattern with respect to its neighbors. If the bit is in the most significant position, the intensity or color of the pixel is most noticeable. Assuming that the bit error can involve any bit with equal probability, the SNR of digital imagery is related to BER as

$$\text{SNR} = 10 \log\left[\frac{3K(2^k - 1)}{(\text{BER})(2^k + 1)}\right]$$
$$\cong 4.77 + 10 \log(K/\text{BER}) \tag{1}$$

Although the distortion introduced by the random bit error has a different effect upon the observers from the distortion affecting the analog signal, the SNR equivalent to a BER of $10^{-4}$ (for a 6-bit PCM signal) is approximately 4.5 dB better than the 48-dB SNR sought as the level for excellent imagery in analog systems.

## III   IMAGE BANDWIDTH COMPRESSION

Although a rather high sampling rate and quantization is required to obtain subjectively high-quality pictures, statistical analysis of images indicates that the entropy of most pictures is substantially less than what these high sampling and quantization rates require. Therefore, it should be possible to compress the bandwidth of imagery data, at high compression ratios, using statistical methods of image bandwidth compression. Table II classifies the various image bandwidth compression techniques into four general classes. The following paragraphs briefly discuss the characteristics of the different techniques.

Statistical measurements on images indicate that the brightnesses of pixels within a cluster are highly correlated. Entropy calculations of information theory further indicate the statistical coding can be performed on relatively small pixel clusters at an average coding rate of about 1 bit/pixel, or less, without any loss of information. Entropy coding techniques are used routinely for coding facsimile data. They have also been combined with transform, differential pulse code modulation (DPCM), and delta modulation techniques for compressing the bandwidth of digital television.

The intraframe predictive coding and transform coding methods have proved to be practical for television bandwidth reduction. These methods are described in greater detail in the following subsections, and their characteristics are summarized in Table II.

There is considerable temporal redundancy in a television source, which can potentially lead to a significant bandwidth reduction. With the frame replenishment method, coding with an average of 1.0 bits/pixel has been achieved by transmitting only the pixels that significantly change within a frame. Some effort has been made toward the development of interframe predictive coding and transform coding techniques. These methods also perform at 1 bit/pixel, thus giving a compressed TV signal with almost no noticeable degradation. The disadvantage of any of these methods is that the frame storage is required.

## Mathematical Models in Image Coding   A

Images are often modeled as random processes $u(x, y)$, where $x$ and $y$ refer to continuous or discrete spatial variables. For the purpose of analysis, the random signal $u(x, y)$ is characterized by its second-order statistics, namely, its autocorrelation function or its power spectra. Two commonly used model for autocorrelation functions of images are $R_1(\tau_x, \tau_y)$ and $R_2(\tau_x, \tau_y)$, where

$$R_1(\tau_x, \tau_y) = \exp(-\alpha|\tau_x| - \beta|\tau_y|) \tag{2}$$

$$R_2(\tau_x, \tau_y) = \exp[-\sqrt{(\alpha\tau_x)^2 + (\beta\tau_y)^2}] \tag{3}$$

Both models imply stationarity. The first autocorrelation is separable in both the horizontal and vertical directions and implies the Markov property

**TABLE II**

**Characteristics of Image Bandwidth Compression Techniques**

| Bandwidth compression methods | Compression ratio | System complexity | Effect of bandwidth compression | Effect of channel error | Type of Process at the receiver |
|---|---|---|---|---|---|
| Entropy coding: run-length coding, Huffman coding, bit plane, universal codes | No degradation for 2.0 bits/sec | Moderate | None for errorless coding; contouring effect for large degradation | Isolated errors for simple entropy coding; error propagation in difference entropy coding | Table look-up decoder |
| Predictive coding: delta modulator, DPCM | Best performance for >1.5 bits/sec | Small | Slope overload or granular noise | Severe; error propagation is present | A simple feedback receiver |
| Transform coding: Fourier, Hadamard, slant, cosine | Best performance for <1.0 bits/sec | Large | Loss of high-frequency components (smooth edges); good subjective quality | Minimal; error is distributed over a block picture | A system performing inverse transform |
| Cluster coding: contour tracing, vector quantization, clustering | Best performance for <0.5 bits/sec | Very large (an order of magnitude more than DPCM) | Image quality related to viewing distance; contouring effect may be present | Severe: causes artifacts | Picture reconstruction from clusters (complex) |

in all directions, whereas the second model implies that the data is only Markov along the rows and the columns. In this respect the first model is less realistic but is easier for analysis. Specifically, it allows fairly simple solutions to the second-order differential equations that can be used to describe $u(x, y)$ [5]. Both models have been utilized in bandwidth compression of imagery data to develop optimum transform coding and bit assignment procedures [5, 6].

## Optimum Transform Coding    B

Assuming that images can be modeled by stationary random processes as in (2) or (3), one can pose the image bandwidth compression problem as finding the optimum processing that would convert the process $u(x, y)$, over a certain domain, to a set of binary digits which can be used to reconstruct the images with minimal distortion. Then, using mean-square error as the fidelity criterion, it is shown that the optimum processing is the Karhunen–Loéve (KL) transformation followed by block quantization [7, 8]. The KL transformation is defined as

$$u_i = \int_A \int_B u(x, y)\phi_i(x, y)\, dx\, dy \tag{4}$$

where $\phi_i(x, y)$ are the basis functions of the KL transform, the eigenfunctions of the autocorrelation function of $u(x, y)$.

In block quantization the transform coefficients $u_i$ are quantized such that there is equal quantization distortion ($\Delta$) for each coefficient. Obviously, since the energy content of transform coefficients $u_i$ is monotonically decreasing for $i = 1, 2, \ldots$, the coefficients with energy contents less than $\Delta$ need not be transmitted. Therefore, one needs to transmit only $M$ coefficients $u_i, i = 1, 2, \ldots, M$, which have energy contents larger than $\Delta$.

The discrete counterpart of the KL transform is known as the *method of principal components*, which is developed for sampled imagery [5, 9]. A practical way of using discrete KL transform for imagery is to scan the data to a one-dimensional format, then generate the covariance matrix of the one-dimensional data. The eigenvectors of this covariance matrix will give the discrete KL transform coefficients.[†] The practical difficulties with this approach are estimating the covariance matrix of a large dimension (256 × 256 for KL transform of 16 × 16 imagery) and calculating its eigenvectors. However, one still faces the fundamental problem that images are nonstationary and the covariances that determine the basic vectors are changing. As a

---

[†] Here a one-dimensional KL transform is utilized. However, since the one-dimensional data is generated by scanning the two-dimensional signal, its covariance matrix possesses the characteristics of the covariance of the two-dimensional signal.

result, the optimum solution to the bandwidth compression problem (KL transform with block quantization) is of limited practical value, since it is obtained using inaccurate assumptions of stationarity and restrictive models for the imaging data [5]. For this reason the optimum solution is only slightly better than the result one obtains using deterministic transforms such as cosine, Fourier, slant, or Hadamard transforms. Indeed, more efficient transform coding algorithms are the adaptive techniques that assume non-stationary data and vary the encoder parameters to accommodate signal nonstationarity.

## C   Adaptive Transform Coding

In adaptive methods, we assume that the analog picture is raster scanned so that is converted to a one-dimensional signal, and we are concerned with the adaptive operations of sampling, transformation, sample selection, and quantization. Changing the parameters in each of the preceding operations, such as sampling rate, the size or the type of the transformation, and the method of sample selection and quantization, affects the overall performance of the encoder. In an optimal adaptive system, one would like to have all these parameters change in response to the variations in image statistics. In the following paragraphs, we consider each of the parameters individually and discuss the feasibility of their utilization in an adaptive transform coding system.

### 1   Adaptive Sampling

In sampling an image, ideally one would want to sample more finely in areas of high detail and sharp changes and more coarsely in areas of low detail and slow variations. This assigns a larger number of samples (bits) to areas of high detail, thus improving the picture definition in these areas while still keeping the number of total samples at a relatively low level. In a variable sampling rate system, the receiver must be synchronized with the transmitter to know which areas are sampled at what resolutions.

### 2   Adaptive Quantization and Sample Selection

In adaptive transform coding, a deterministic transformation such as a Hadamard or cosine transform on a fixed block size is used, and an adaptive procedure for sample selection and quantization is utilized. The most frequently used measures for sample selection and quantization are the variances of the elements in the transform domain, the sum of the absolute values of the ac coefficients, and the ac energy of the transform coefficients.

*Use of the Activity Index.* The sum of the squares of the coefficients in the transform domain or the sum of absolute values in the transform domain, referred to as the activity index [9], can be used to classify each block to one of $M$ possible classes. It requires $M - 1$ threshold values, which can be chosen experimentally. One can choose these threshold values to have approximately a fixed number of bits per sample averaged over a number of blocks. However, in a practical situation, one would use a set of $M - 1$ threshold values that would be controlled by the fullness of the buffer. Each class would use a different sample selection and quantization procedure. The class with high activity index employs more binary digits than the class with low activity index. Use of the activity index with a block size of $8 \times 8$ samples and 4 possible activity indexes is discussed by Chen and Smith [10] and Habibi [11].

The relative size of different transform coefficients indicates the degree of image activity in various directions and frequencies. In a three-dimensional transformation of television signals, the relative amplitudes of three coefficients (vectors) adjacent to the dc term reflect the image activity in the horizontal, vertical, and temporal directions. The accuracy of the quantization of vectors corresponding to the image activity in various directions can be used to control the coding fidelity in these directions. This approach is used by Knauer [12] to encode various degrees of movement in television using a $4 \times 4 \times 4$ Hadamard transform. For rapid movements, an option giving high temporal and low spatial fidelity is utilized. For slow movements, an option giving high spatial but low temporal fidelity is utilized. These options improve the subpicture quality of the encoded imagery since human vision is very insensitive to spatial fidelity for rapidly moving objects but its sensitivity improves at slower motion.

*Recursive Quantization.* Variances of the transform coefficients can be used as an "activity index" for adaptive sample quantization. In an approach discussed by Tescher [13], the image is divided into blocks of $16 \times 16$ samples. A zig-zag scanning pattern is used for a smoother decay in the relative size of the variances of the transformed coefficients. Next the variance of the data sequence is estimated and a bit assignment in proportion to the logarithm of the estimated variances is made. When the variance of a coefficient is so small that the number of binary digits assigned for its quantization falls below 1.0 bit, the processor stops, and the remaining samples in that block are substituted with zeros at the receiver. The estimate of the variance of the $n$th transform coefficient $\hat{\sigma}_n^2$ is

$$\hat{\sigma}_n^2 = A\hat{\sigma}_{n-1}^2 + (1 - A)\hat{X}_{n-1}^2 \tag{5}$$

where $\hat{X}_{n-1}$ is the quantized form of the $(n - 1)$th transform sample (in a one-dimensional sequence) and $A$ is a weighting factor which is chosen rather arbitrarily to be equal to 0.75 in the experiments.

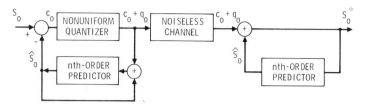

**Fig. 3.** Block diagram of a DPCM modulation system.

## D  Predictive Coding

In predictive coding systems, the correlated data is processed to generate a set of uncorrelated signals which is referred to as the differential signal. This signal is quantized by a memoryless quantizer. At the receiver, the inverse of the predictor operation is performed to obtain a replica of the original signal from the quantized differential signal. In designing predictive coding systems, the predictor and the quantizer are optimized individually, ignoring the effects of one on the other. This approach is due to the nonlinear nature of the quantizer, which makes an overall system optimization impossible. The most commonly used form of predictive coding systems are DPCM and delta modulators. The DPCM system uses a linear predictor which predicts the value of an incoming signal based on a weighted sum of the adjacent elements. The quantizer is either a uniform or nonuniform quantizer that maps the differential signal to one of two possible levels for a system using $k$ bits/sample. A delta modulator is a simple form of a predictive coder in which the quantizer is substituted by a comparator and the predictor is substituted by an integrator (summer). Block diagrams of both DPCM and delta modulators are shown in Figs. 3 and 4.

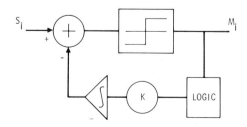

**Fig. 4.** Adaptive delta, modulation system.

## Adaptive Delta Modulators **1**

Adaptive delta modulators have received more attention than other adaptive systems for coding both speech and video signals. One reason for this may be that the performance of delta modulators can be improved significantly without introducing much additional complexity to their simple design.

In a delta modulator, each sample is compared to an estimate of it, and a positive or negative signal is produced depending upon the comparative value of the incoming sample. The output of the comparator is multiplied by a constant in the feedback loop and is used as an input to an integrator. The output of the integrator is an estimate of the incoming signal. The value of the constant in the feedback loop controls the step size of the delta modulator. A large step size introduces granular noise in the reconstructed signal over the region that the signal is changing gradually, while a small step size limits the ability of the encoder to follow large signal variations, thus resulting in slope-overload noise.

Adaptive delta modulators have been considered by a number of authors in recent years. The most widely used approach is to change the step size of the system according to signal variation. An indication of the type of signal variation is the polarity of the modulator output levels. Output levels of the same polarity indicate large signal variations, whereas output levels of alternating polarities indicate smooth signal variations. Therefore, increasing the step size when output levels of like polarity are present and reducing it for outputs of unlike polarity reduces both granular and slope-overload noise. This type of adaptive system does not require additional overhead information for synchronizing the receiver with the transmitter.

An alternative approach to designing adaptive delta modulators with variable step size is to use a variable sampling rate. This method is based on the fact that slowly varying signals convey less information than rapidly changing signals, thus fewer samples (or equivalent bits) are needed for their transmission. This approach can also be combined with the one using variable step size for maximum adaptability to signal variation. These approaches are used to design a number of different delta modulators. The characteristics and principals of operation of the three most basic adaptive delta modulators are listed in Table III.

## Adaptive DPCM Encoders **2**

In a DPCM system, the predictor uses a weighting of adjacent samples to generate an estimate of the incoming signal value. The difference between the predicted and the actual signal value, known as the differential signal, is

**TABLE III**

**Characteristics and Principal of Operation for Three Basic Delta Modulators**

| Principal of operation | Characteristics |
| --- | --- |
| *Asynchronous delta modulator* [14] | |
| Polarity of 3 consecutive outputs (8 possible combinations) is used to utilize one of 8 possible step sizes of $\pm 1 \; \pm 2, \; \pm 4$ | Transmitter and receiver are synchronized to be at the same state at the same time |
| *Song delta modulator* [15] | |
| The current step size $\Delta_k$ is generated as | Utilized for coding both voice and video data |
| $$\Delta_k = \begin{cases} 2De_{k-1} & \text{for} \quad |\Delta_{k-1}| < 2D \\ |\Delta_{k-1}|(e_{k-1} + \tfrac{1}{2}e_{k-2}) & \text{for} \quad |\Delta_{k-1}| > 2D \end{cases}$$ | |
| $D$ is a constant equal to the minimum step size; $e_k$ is the polarity of the output for the $k$th sample | |
| *Modified high-information delta modulator* [16] | Utilized for coding both voice and video data; optimal value of $p$ is 1.5; an improvement of 10 dB over nonadaptive delta modulator |
| The current step size $\Delta_k$ is generated as | |
| $$\Delta_k = p \, \Delta_{k-1} \qquad \text{if} \quad e_k = e_{k-1}$$ $$= -\frac{1}{p} \Delta_{k-1} \qquad \text{if} \quad e_k \neq e_{k-1}$$ | |
| $p$ is a constant; $e_k$ is the polarity of the output for the $k$th sample | |

encoded using a nonlinear quantizer. A nonlinear predictor involves conditional expectation values, which are difficult to implement. Instead, in most coding systems, a linear combination of adjacent samples is included. These weightings are related to the signal correlation by a set of algebraic equations. Experimental results have shown that by using the adjacent sample along the same line, the adjacent sample on the previously scanned line and the diagonal sample of the previously scanned line is sufficient for predicting the incoming sample for most pictorial data [17]. DPCM systems have an advantage over PCM systems because the differential signal has a smaller variance and a well-behaved probability density function, which allows one to design a nonlinear quantizer matched to the error-signal statistics.

In designing an adaptive DPCM system, one must either use a predictor with variable parameters such that the parameters would change generating a stationary differential signal or use a fixed predictor with a variable quantizer to accommodate the resultant nonstationary differential signal.

Experimental results show little improvement due to variable predictors, thus most adaptive systems utilize fixed predictors with a variable quantizer.

*DPCM Systems with Adaptive Quantizers.* A DPCM system with a fixed predictor has a nonstationary differential signal, which causes an abnormal saturation or a frequent utilization of the smallest level in the fixed quantizer. To remedy this situation, the threshold and the reconstruction levels of the quantizer must be made variable to expand and contract according to signal statistics. Adaptation of the quantizer to signal statistics is accomplished using various approaches.

In one approach, a number of samples in the differential signal are stored and are used to find a local variance, which is then used to design a quantizer [18] or select one of $M$ possible quantizers for this block of data [19]. Obviously, this approach requires transmitting some overhead information.

A different approach is a DPCM system with a variable set of threshold and reconstruction levels. The set of threshold and reconstruction levels would contract and expand depending upon the sequential utilization of inner or outer levels of the quantizer. For instance, a variable quantizer can be designed in which all reconstruction levels expand by a factor of $P$ (for some optimum value of $P$) upon two sequential occurrences of the outermost level, and they would contract by a factor of $1/P$ upon sequential happening of the smallest levels with opposite polarities. This system has the advantage that it is completely adaptive and does not require any overhead information, because the receiver is self-synchronizing.

## Cluster Coding (Vector Quantization)    E

Cluster coding (or vector quantization) techniques have been considered more recently for coding voice or video data. In these techniques the data are grouped to form a number of clusters. Each cluster is then represented by a number of variants which must be quantized and transmitted. In adaptive cluster coding methods, two processes can be made adaptive. One is the operation of the classifier, and the other is the operation of the quantizer. In the following we discuss applications of cluster coding to multispectral and monochrome images.

### Cluster Coding of Multispectral Images    1

Multispectral clustering has been used for bandwidth compression and classification of multispectral data [11, 20, 21]. In multispectral images each picture element is represented by $k$ measurement values, which are represented by a $k$-tuple in a $k$-dimensional space called the *measurement space.*

The location in $k$-dimensional space of the center of the mass of the sample values belonging to a cluster is called the *centroid* of that cluster. Clusters are generated as follows: initial centroid values are arbitrarily assumed, and then all samples are assigned to the cluster containing the closest centroid. The centroids of each cluster are then replaced by the center of mass of samples in that cluster. This procedure is iterated until a small percentage of samples change cluster.

Identifying all the picture elements corresponding to one centroid with one class, one obtains a classified image which consists of as many gray levels as there are classes in the measurement space. For $n$ possible classes this image requires $\log n$ binary bits per sample for its transmission using a PCM system. The centroid values require $km$ bits per block per centroid for $m$ bits of amplitude resolution.

In a multispectral cluster coding algorithms [21], the multispectral data are first divided into small blocks of fixed size (e.g., $16 \times 16$ picture elements). Then the elements in each block are clustered into a variable number of classes. Using a fixed threshold value generates a larger number of classes in blocks with high details and a small number of classes in blocks with low details.

The receiver reconstructs each block of the multispectral imagery by generating the individual bands in each block from the classified image and the corresponding centroids of those clusters. The procedure is to examine each point in the classified image and specify to what class it belongs. Then individual bands corresponding to the particular picture location are reconstructed by choosing values equal to the centroid of that particular class.

Bandwidth compression is achieved if the number of binary digits needed to transmit the classified image and the centroids are smaller than the number of digits required to represent the multispectral data. Experimental results using a fixed number of classes in each block and PCM coding of the classified image and centroids have shown that large compression ratios can be obtained at relatively low distortion levels [11]. Additional compression is obtained by using an adaptive method, such as an entropy coding technique, to encode the centroids and the classified imagery.

## 2    Cluster Coding of Monochrome Images

Cluster coding (vector quantization) [22] can be utilized to code monochrome images by taking a number of adjacent samples and considering them as picture elements from the various bands. Then the procedure outlined in section III.E.1 can be used to encode the monochrome imagery. For instance, by considering four adjacent samples, a monochrome image of $n \times n$ picture elements is encoded as a multispectral image of four bands of $n/2 \times n/2$ picture elements. Cluster coding can also be combined with other coding techniques for improved performance. For example, it can be combined with a DPCM technique in which the bandwidth of the mono-chrome image is first reduced (using a DPCM system) from 8 to 4 bits/sample. Then, using 4 adjacent samples, each quantized to 4 bits/sample, one has 256 possible combinations. The domain of the 256 combinations can be classified to 8 clusters (using 3 bits/picture element) or 4 clusters (using 2 bits/picture element) using an appropriate classification algorithm. The combined technique may give better results than using each technique individually.

### Entropy Coding and Related Techniques   F

To utilize entropy coding methods in compressing the bandwidth of images, one can measure the histogram of the data and use the optimum code word for the distribution of the gray levels. This method is efficient in reducing the bandwidth of the imagery if the distribution of data samples is peaked at certain gray levels. For a uniform histogram, the entropy coding does not offer any advantage over the PCM system. To make effective use of entropy coding, one may process the data through a reversible process such that the histogram of the output samples is highly peaked. One such process is the operation of differencing of adjacent elements. Since spatial correlation exists in most imagery, the difference between adjacent elements tends to be small. Hence, the frequency of occurrence of small differences is much larger than the frequency of occurrence of large differences. Experiments with various types of imagery have shown that the histogram of the difference signal is a highly peaked, double-sided exponential function about zero [17]. A modified form of the difference entropy coding method is used for compression ratios of about 2:1 involving absolutely no degradation. This system uses entropy coding for transmitting differences that are smaller than a prespecified value and uses a PCM code word for transmitting the actual value of the sample if the difference is larger than a prespecified value. Similar results have also been obtained using differential entropy coding and adaptive differential entropy coding for multispectral data [23, 24].

Differencing is not the only process that can be used to increase nonuniformity of the histogram of data samples. Other operations, such as transforming the data using Hadamard or Haar transforms, can also be used for this purpose [25].

In adaptive entropy coding, one assumes that the statistics of an image change significantly from block to block so that the code words which are optimum for one block do not perform as well for the others. To adapt to the changing statistics, one must change the code words accordingly. This is a difficult task since, in addition to measuring the statistics for each block and assigning the code words, one must transmit this information to the receiver so that individual blocks are decoded properly. An alternate approach is to classify each block of data to one of a limited number of classes. Then the proper code word for that class is used to encode the data in that block. Of course, additional information is required to inform the receiver which class of code words have to be used for decoding each individual block. This overhead information is small for small numbers of classes and large block sizes.

A general treatment of universal codes (block codes which adapt to obtain a performance measure arbitrarily close to the signal entropy with increasing block length) is given by Davison [26].

Various bandwidth compression techniques that are used to decorrelate imagery data in spatial, temporal, or spectral directions can be combined with entropy coding techniques if the residual signal at the output of the bandwidth compressor possesses a non-flat histogram. Combining entropy coding with other bandwidth compression techniques will make the output data rate variable, which requires buffer memory and a buffer control algorithm to transmit the variable-rate data over a fixed-rate channel [27].

## G   Hybrid Image Coding

Bandwidth compression of digital imagery is achieved by processing the sampled data to eliminate or reduce its inherent correlation in various domains (spatial, temporal, and spectral) and then using a quantizer to code the processed data for transmission. In general, different processing methods can be utilized to uncorrelate the data in various domains. One such example is the technique known as hybrid coding, in which the correlation of the data in one spatial direction is exploited by taking a one-dimensional transform of each line (or column) of the picture, then using a DPCM system to utilize the correlation of the transformed data in the other spatial direction. This approach has resulted in a bandwidth compression technique with unique characteristics since it combines the attractive features of transform coding with those of DPCM. Also, since it involves a one-dimensional transformation of individual lines of the pictorial data, the equipment complexity and the number of computational operations are considerably less than that involved in a two-dimensional transformation, thus making the system particularly desirable for on-board applications [28].

A block diagram of the hybrid coding system is shown on Fig. 5. The optimal design requires that the weight functions $A_i$ and the quantizer structure in DPCM be matched to picture statistics. However, experimental results have shown small losses in system performance due to the use of fixed coefficients and fixed quantizers [29].

Adaptive forms of the hybrid coding algorithm have been developed that use an entropy coder at the system output for further bandwidth compression [30]. In addition, three-dimensional hybrid encoders have been developed

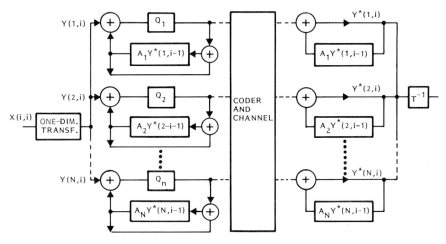

**Fig. 5.** Block diagram of a hybrid encoder.

that use two-dimensional transformation to uncorrelate a television signal in the spatial domain and a DPCM coder to uncorrelate the data in the temporal direction [31].

### Image Coding Based on Extrapolation from Image Boundaries  H

Coding by extrapolation of image boundaries is based on the assumption that images can be modeled by a second-degree Gaussian–Markov process that satisfies a second-order differential equation with a solution of the form

$$U(x, y) = U_B(x, y) + U_D(x, y) \tag{6}$$

where $U_B(x, y)$ is a solution due to the boundary conditions and $U_D(x, y)$ is a solution due to signal fluctuation for zero boundary values.

This formulation implies that if the boundary values can be used to generate a partial solution $U_D(x, y)$, then one can subtract this field from the original field $U(x, y)$. The result is a random process $U_D(x, y)$ which has a much smaller variance and vanishes at the boundaries. Thus, it could be expanded in terms of sine-transform basis functions and be represented by fewer binary digits than the original signal due to its smaller variance [32].

The preceding argument can be used to develop a fairly simple coding technique in which imagery data is divided into blocks of $(N + 1) \times (N + 1)$ samples. For each block, two edges need to be transmitted (in addition to the first row and the first column). Using these edges, the $N \times N$ samples in each block are interpolated at both the receiver and the transmitter. Next, the differences between the interpolated and actual values of picture elements are generated and transmitted. The boundary values and the differential signal can then be encoded using various bandwidth compression techniques. The author has used entropy coding (with first differencing) to encode boundary values and a rate-adaptive, two-dimensional discrete cosine transformation [27] to encode the differential signal for $N = 16$. the results are particularly pleasing since block boundaries are not visible even at low data rates.

## REFERENCES

1. L. G. Roberts, Picture coding using pseudo-random noise, *IRE Trans. Information Theory* **IT-8**, 145-154 (February, 1962).
2. H. Musmann and J. Klie, TV transmission using a 64 kbits/s transmission rate, *Proc. ICC 79*, 23.3.1-23.3.5 (1979).
3. B. G. Haskell and R. L. Schmidt, A low bit rate interframe coder for video telephone, *Bell Syst. Tech. J.* **54**, 1475-1495 (1975).
4. K. Simons, "Technical Handbook for CATV Systems," 3rd Ed. Jerrold Electronics Corp., Philadelphia, Pennsylvania.
5. A Habibi and P. A. Wintz, Image coding by linear transformation and block quantization, *IEEE Trans. Commun. Technol.* **COM-19** (1), 50-63 (1971).
6. W. K. Pratt, "Digital Image Processing." Wiley, New York, 1978.
7. T. T. Y. Huang and P. M. Schulthesiss, Block quantization of correlated Gaussian random variables, *IRE Trans. Commun. Syst.* **CS-11** (3), 289-296 (1963).
8. A. Habibi and R. S. Hershel, A unified representation of differential pulse-code modulation (DPCM) and transform coding systems, *IEEE Trans. Commun. Technol.* **COM-22**, (5), 692-696 (1974).
9. H. Hotelling, Analysis of complex of statistical variables into principal components, *J. Educational Psychology* **24**, 417-441, 498-520 (1933).
10. W. H. Chen and C. H. Smith, Adaptive coding of monochrome and color images, *IEEE Trans. Commun. Technol.* **COM-25**, 1285-1291 (1977).
11. A. Habibi, Survey of adaptive image coding techniques, *IEEE Trans. Communications* **COM-25** (11), 1275-1284 (1977).
12. S. C. Knauer, Real-time video compression algorithm for Hadamard transform processing, *Proc. SPIE* **66**, 58-69 (1975).
13. A. G. Tescher, Transform image coding, "Image Transmission Techniques," pp. 113-155. Academic Press, New York, 1979.
14. T. A. Hawkes and P. A. Simonpieri, Signal coding using asynchronous delta modulation, *IEEE Trans. Commun. Technol.* **COM-22** (3), 346-348, (1974).
15. C. L. Song, J. Garodnic, and D. K. L. Schilling, A variable step size robust delta-modulator, *IEEE Trans. Commun. Technol.* **COM-19**, 1033-1099 (1971).
16. M. R. Winkler, High information delta modulation, *IEEE Int. Conv. Rec.* **8**, 260-265 (1963).
17. A. Habibi, Comparison of $n$th order DPCM encoder with linear transformations and block quantization techniques *IEEE Trans. Commun. Technol.* **COM-19**, No. 6 948-956 (1971).
18. K. Virupaksha and J. B. O'Neal, Jr., Entropy-coded adaptive differential pulse-code modulation (DPCM) for speech, *IEEE Trans. Comm. Technol.* **COMM-22**, (6) 777-798, (1974).
19. P. J. Ready and D. J. Spencer, Block adaptive DPCM transmission of image, *NTC 75 Conference Record* **2**, 22.10-22.17 (1975).
20. E. E. Hilbert, Joint pattern recognition data compression concept for ERTS multispectral imaging, *Proc. SPIE* **66**, 122-137 (1975).
21. A. Habibi and A. S. Samulon, Bandwidth compression of multispectral data, *Proc. SPIE* **66**, 23-35 (1975).

22.  A. Gersho, On the structure of vector quantizers, *IEEE Trans. Information Theory* **IT-28** (2), 157–166 (1982).

23.  R. F. Rice and J. R. Plaunt, Adaptive variable-length coding for efficient compression of space craft television data, *IEEE Trans. Commun. Technol.* **COM-19** (6), 889–897 (1971).

24.  C. L. May and D. J. Spencer, ERTS image data compression technique evaluation, Final Report for NASA Contract NASS-21746, April 1974.

25.  R. F. Rice, An advanced imaging communication system for planetary exploration, *Proc. SPIE* **66**, 70–89 (1975).

26.  L. D. Davison, Universal noiseless coding, *IEEE Trans. Information Theory* **19**, 783–795 (1973).

27.  A. G. Tescher, Transform coding strategies at low rates, *Conference Record, National Telecommunications Conference, Nov. 1981*, pp. 9.2.1–9.2.3 (1981).

28.  A. Habibi, Hybrid coding of pictorial data, *IEEE Trans. Commun. Technol.* **COM-22** (5) 614–624 (1974).

29.  L. C. Chan and P. Whiteman, Hardware constrained hybrid coding of video imagery, *IEEE Trans. Aerospace and Electronic Systems* **AES-19** (1) 71–84 (1983).

30.  A. Habibi, An adaptive strategy for hybrid image coding, *IEEE Trans. Commun. Technol.* **COM-29** (12) 1736–1740 (1981).

31.  A. Habibi, W. K. Pratt, *et al.*, Real time image redundancy reduction using transform coding techniques, *Proc. 1974 Intl. Conference Communications* (June 1974).

32.  A. Z. Meiri and E. Yudilevich, A pinned sine transform image coder, *IEEE Trans. Commun. Technol.* **COM-29** (12) 1728–1736 (1981).

# Chapter **8**

# Image Enhancement and Restoration

R. C. GONZALEZ

Electrical Engineering Department
University of Tennessee
Knoxville, Tennessee

## BACKGROUND   I

Image enhancement and restoration techniques are formulated in either the spatial or transform (principally the Fourier transform) domains. This section establishes the fundamental ideas underlying these approaches.

191

**HANDBOOK OF PATTERN RECOGNITION**
**AND IMAGE PROCESSING**

## A    Spatial-Domain Methods

The term *spatial domain* refers to the aggregate of pixels composing an image, and spatial-domain methods are procedures that operate directly on these pixels. Preprocessing functions in the spatial domain may be expressed as

$$g(x, y) = h[f(x, y)] \qquad (1)$$

where $f(x, y)$ is the input image, $g(x, y)$ is the resulting image, and $h$ is an operator on $f$ defined over some neighborhood of $(x, y)$. It is also possible to let $h$ operate on a *set* of input images, such as performing the pixel-by-pixel sum of $K$ images for noise reduction.

The principal approach used in defining a neighborhood about $(x, y)$ is to use a square or rectangular subimage area centered at $(x, y)$, as shown in Fig. 1. The center of the subimage is moved from pixel to pixel starting, say, at the top left corner, and we apply the operator at each location $(x, y)$ to yield $g(x, y)$. Although other neighborhood shapes, such as a circle, are sometimes used, square arrays are by far the most predominant because of their ease of implementation.

The simplest form of $h$ is when the neighborhood is $1 \times 1$ and, therefore, $g$ depends only on the value of $f$ at $(x, y)$. In this case $h$ becomes an intensity mapping or transformation $T$ of the form

$$s = T(r) \qquad (2)$$

where, for simplicity, we have used $s$ and $r$ as variables denoting, respectively, the intensity of $f(x, y)$ and $g(x, y)$ at any point $(x, y)$.

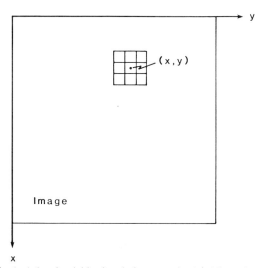

**Fig. 1.** A $3 \times 3$ neighborhood about a point $(x, y)$ in an image.

Fig. 2. A mask for detecting isolated points different from a constant background.

One of the spatial-domain techniques used most frequently for enhancement and restoration is based on the use of so-called *convolution masks* (also
referred to as *templates, windows*, or *filters*). Basically, a mask is a small (e.g.,
$3 \times 3$) two-dimensional array, such as the one shown in Fig. 1, whose
coefficients are chosen to detect a given property in an image. As an
introduction to this concept, suppose that we have an image of constant
intensity that contains widely isolated points whose intensities are different
from the background. These points can be detected by using the mask shown
in Fig. 2. The procedure is as follows. The center of the mask (labeled 8) is
moved around the image, as indicated above. At each pixel position in the
image, we multiply every pixel that is contained within the mask area by the
corresponding mask coefficient, that is, the pixel in the center of the mask is
multiplied by 8, while its 8-neighbors are multiplied by $-1$. The results of
these nine multiplications are then summed. If all the pixels within the mask
area have the same value (constant background), the sum will be zero. If, on
the other hand, the center of the mask is located at one of the isolated points,
the sum will be different from zero. If the isolated point is in an off-center
position, the sum will also be different from zero, but the magnitude of the
response will be weaker. These weaker responses can be eliminated by
comparing the sum against a threshold.

As shown in Fig. 3, if we let $w_1, w_2, \ldots, w_9$ represent mask coefficients and
consider the 8 neighbors of $(x, y)$, we may generalize the preceding discussion
as performing the following operation,

$$h[f(x, y)] = w_1 f(x - 1, y - 1) + w_2 f(x - 1, y) + w_3 f(x - 1, y + 1)$$
$$+ w_4 f(x, y - 1) + w_5 f(x, y) + w_6 f(x, y + 1)$$
$$+ w_7 f(x + 1, y - 1) + w_8 f(x + 1, y) + w_9 f(x + 1, y + 1)$$

$$(3)$$

on a $3 \times 3$ neighborhood of $(x, y)$. This type of processing can be considerably more powerful than the simple example of point detection discussed

| $w_1$ $(x-1, y-1)$ | $w_2$ $(x-1, y)$ | $w_3$ $(x-1, y+1)$ |
|---|---|---|
| $w_4$ $(x, y-1)$ | $w_5$ $(x, y)$ | $w_6$ $(x, y+1)$ |
| $w_7$ $(x+1, y-1)$ | $w_8$ $(x+1, y)$ | $w_9$ $(x+1, y+1)$ |

**Fig. 3.** A general 3 × 3 mask showing coefficients and corresponding image pixel locations.

above. For instance, neighborhood operations can be used for noise reduction, to obtain variable image thresholds, to compute measures of texture, and to obtain the skeleton of an object.

## B  Frequency-Domain Methods

The term *frequency domain* refers to an aggregate of complex pixels resulting from taking the Fourier transform of an image. The concept of "frequency" is often used in interpreting the Fourier transform and arises from the fact that this particular transform is composed of complex sinusoids. Due to extensive processing requirements, frequency-domain methods are not nearly as widely used as spatial-domain techniques. However, the Fourier transform does play an important role in areas such as the analysis of object motion and object description. In addition, many spatial techniques for enhancement and restoration are founded on concepts whose origins can be traced to a Fourier transform formulation. The material in this section will serve as an introduction to these concepts. A more extensive treatment of the Fourier transform and its properties may be found in Refs. 1 and 2.

Consider a function of one variable, $f(x)$, for $x = 0, 1, 2, \ldots, N-1$. The forward Fourier transform of $f(x)$ is defined as

$$F(u) = \frac{1}{N} \sum_{x=0}^{N-1} f(x) \exp\left(\frac{-j2\pi ux}{N}\right) \qquad (4)$$

for $u = 0, 1, 2, \ldots, N - 1$. In this equation $j = \sqrt{-1}$ and $u$ is the so-called *frequency variable*. The inverse Fourier transform of $F(u)$ yields $f(x)$ back, and is defined as

$$f(x) = \sum_{u=0}^{N-1} F(u) \exp\left(\frac{j2\pi ux}{N}\right) \tag{5}$$

for $x = 0, 1, 2, \ldots, N - 1$. The validity of these expressions, called the *Fourier transform pair*, is easily verified by substituting Eq. (4) for $F(u)$ in Eq. (5), or vice versa. In either case we would get an identity.

A direct implementation of Eq. (4) for $u = 0, 1, 2, \ldots, N - 1$ would require on the order of $N^2$ additions and multiplications. Use of a fast Fourier transform (FFT) algorithm significantly reduces this number to $N \log_2 N$. Similar comments apply to Eq. (5) for $x = 0, 1, 2, \ldots, N - 1$. A number of FFT algorithms are readily available in a variety of computer languages.

The two-dimensional Fourier transform pair of an $N \times N$ image is defined as

$$F(u, v) = \frac{1}{N} \sum_{x=0}^{N-1} \sum_{y=0}^{N-1} f(x, y) \exp\left[\frac{-j2\pi(ux + vy)}{N}\right] \tag{6}$$

for $u, v = 0, 1, 2, \ldots, N - 1$ and

$$f(x, y) = \frac{1}{N} \sum_{u=0}^{N-1} \sum_{v=0}^{N-1} F(u, v) \exp\left[\frac{j2\pi(ux + vy)}{N}\right] \tag{7}$$

for $x, y = 0, 1, 2, \ldots, N - 1$. It is possible to show through some manipulation that each of these equations can be expressed as separate one-dimensional summations of the form shown in Eq. (4). This leads to a straightforward procedure for computing the two-dimensional Fourier transform using only a one-dimensional FFT algorithm. We first compute and save the transform of each row of $f(x, y)$, thus producing a two-dimensional array of intermediate results. These results are multiplied by $N$ and the one-dimensional transform of each column is computed. The final result is $F(u, v)$. Similar comments apply for computing $f(x, y)$ given $F(u, v)$. The order of computation from a row–column approach can be reversed to a column–row format without affecting the final result.

## ENHANCEMENT IN THE SPATIAL DOMAIN    II

The following techniques are illustrative of the principal methods used for enhancing an image by spatial-domain techniques.

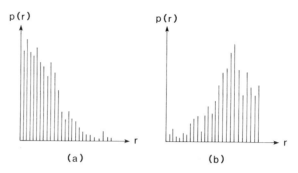

Fig. 4. Histogram of (a) a dark image and (b) a light image.

## A  Histogram Equalization

The histogram of intensities in an image gives a global description of the general appearance of the image. For example, the histogram shown in Fig. 4a would correspond to an image with generally dark characteristics, while the opposite would be true of an image with the histogram shown in Fig. 4b.

Let the variables $r_1, r_2, \ldots, r_L$ denote the discrete intensities in a given image. The $j$th value of the histogram is then given by

$$p_r(r_j) = n_j/n \tag{8}$$

where $n_j$ is the number of pixels with intensity $r_j$ and $n$ is the number of pixels in the image. The histogram equalization procedure is a mappng (transformation) function of the form

$$s_k = T(r_k) = \sum_{j=1}^{k} p_r(r_j) \tag{9}$$

for $k = 1, 2, \ldots, L$. In other words, every pixel in the original image having

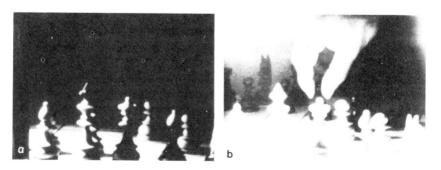

Fig. 5. (a) Original image and (b) result after histogram equalization. (From Woods and Gonzalez [3]. Copyright © 1981 IEEE.)

value $r_k$ is transformed in intensity to a value $s_k$ using the transformation function $T(r_k)$ given in Eq. (9). The objective of this transformation is to produce a histogram $p_s(s_j)$, $j = 1, 2, \ldots, L$ that is more spread out than the original histogram in order to take advantage of the full range of intensity levels. In theory, this histogram should be flat (i.e., uniform), but this is only achievable in the ideal case involving continuous rather than discrete intensities [3]. An example of typical results achievable by histogram equalization is shown in Fig. 5.

### Histogram Specification   B

Although histogram equalization is quite useful, it is sometimes desirable to be able to map the intensities of an image so that their histogram will approximate a specified shape (e.g., Gaussian). This technique, known as *histogram specification*, reduces to histogram equalization when the specified shape is a uniform histogram [3].

Let $p_z(z_j)$, $j = 1, 2, \ldots, L$, be the specified histogram. The histogram specification technique then consists of the following steps.

(1)   Histogram equalize the levels of the original image using Eq. (9). Let the resulting levels be denoted by $s_k$, $k = 1, 2, \ldots, L$.

(2)   Obtain a transformation function of the form

$$v_k = G(z_k) = \sum_{j=1}^{k} p_z(z_j) \qquad (10)$$

using the specified histogram.

(3)   Apply the inverse transformation function

$$z_k = G^{-1}(s_k) \qquad (11)$$

to the levels of the histogram-equalized image obtained in Step 1. The levels $z_k$, $1, 2, \ldots, L$, correspond to the enhanced image whose histogram approximates the desired shape.

As in the case of histogram equalization, the above procedure is exact only when we are dealing with continuous intensities [1, 3].

Figure 6 shows the advantage of histogram specification over histogram equalization. The image on the top left shows the original image and the image on the top right is the result of histogram equalization. In this case equalizing the histogram resulted in no visible improvement, because the original histogram already spanned the entire intensity scale. An improved image (bottom) was obtained by specifying a histogram of triangular shape, which compressed the intensity distribution toward the mid-range of the intensity scales.

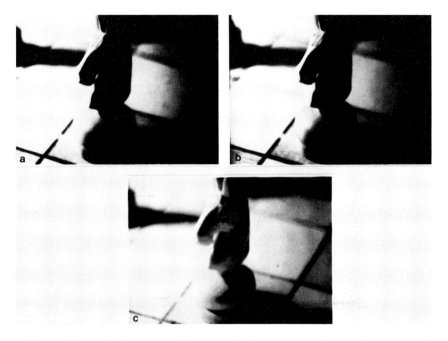

**Fig. 6.** (a) The original image and (b) the result of histogram equalization. The image in (c) was obtained by histogram specification. (From Wood and Gonzalez [3]. Copyright © 1981 IEEE.)

## C   Local Enhancement

The methods discussed in the previous two sections are global in the sense that pixels are modified by a transformation function that is based on the intensity distribution over an entire image. While this global approach is suitable for overall enhancement, it is often necessary to enhance details over small areas. Since the number of pixels in these areas may have negligible influence on the computation of a global transformation, the use of this type of transformation will not necessarily guarantee the desired local enhancement. The solution is to devise transformation functions that are based on the intensity distribution, or other properties, in the neighborhood of every pixel in a given image.

The histogram processing techniques developed in the last two sections are easily adaptable to local enhancement. The procedure is to define an $n \times m$ neighborhood and move the center of this area from pixel to pixel. At each location, we compute the histogram of the $n \times m$ points in the neighborhood and obtain either a histogram-equalization or histogram-specification transformation function. This function is finally used to map the intensity of the pixel centered in the neighborhood. The center of the $n \times m$ region is then moved to an adjacent pixel location and the procedure is repeated. Since only one new row or column of the neighborhood changes during pixel-to-pixel translation of the region, it is possible to update the histogram obtained in the previous location with the new data introduced at each motion step. This approach has obvious advantages over repeatedly computing the histogram over all $n \times m$ pixels every time the region is moved one pixel location. Another approach often used to reduce computation is to employ nonoverlapping regions, but this often produces an undesirable checkerboard effect.

Instead of using histograms, one could base local enhancement on other properties of the pixel intensities in a neighborhood. The intensity mean and variance (or standard deviation) are two such properties which are frequently used because of their relevance to the appearance of an image. That is, the mean is a measure of average brightness and the variance is a measure of contrast.

A typical local transformation based on these concepts maps the intensity of an input image $f(x, y)$ into a new image $g(x, y)$ by performing the following transformation at each pixel location $(x, y)$:

$$g(x, y) = A(x, y)[f(x, y) - m(x, y)] + m(x, y) \qquad (12)$$

where

$$A(x, y) = c \frac{M}{\sigma(x, y)}, \qquad 0 < c < 1 \qquad (13)$$

In this formulation $m(x, y)$ and $\sigma(x, y)$ are the intensity mean and standard deviation computed in a neighborhood centered at $(x, y)$, $M$ is the global mean of $f(x, y)$, and $c$ is a constant in the range indicated above.

It is important to note that $A$, $m$, and $\sigma$ are variable quantities that depend on a predefined neighborhood of $(x, y)$. Application of the local gain factor $A(x, y)$ to the difference between $f(x, y)$ and the local mean amplifies local variations. Since $A(x, y)$ is inversely proportional to the standard deviation of the intensity, areas with low contrast receive larger gain. The mean is added back in Eq. (12) to restore the average intensity level of the image in the local region. In practice, it is often desirable to add back a fraction of the local mean and to restrict the variations of $A(x, y)$ between two limits ($A_{min}$, $A_{max}$) in order to balance out large excusions of intensity in isolated regions.

The preceding enhancement approach has been implemented in hardware by Narendra and Fitch [4] and has the capability of processing images in real time (i.e., at 30 image frames/sec). An example of the capabilities of the technique using a local region on the order of $15 \times 15$ pixels is shown in Fig. 7. Note the enhancement of detail at the boundary between two regions of different overall intensities and the rendition of intensity details in each of the regions.

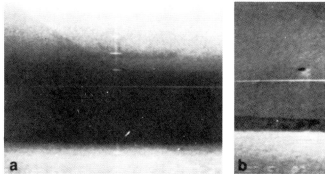

**Fig. 7.** Images (a) before and (b) after local enhancement. (From Narendra and Fitch [4]. Copyright © 1981 IEEE.)

## D  Smoothing

Smoothing operations are used for reducing noise and other spurious effects that may be present in an image as a result of sampling, quantization, transmission, or disturbances in the environment during image acquisition.

Neighborhood averaging is a straightforward spatial-domain technique for image smoothing. Given an image $f(x, y)$, the procedure is to generate a smoothed image $g(x, y)$ whose intensity at every point $(x, y)$ is obtained by averaging the intensity values of the pixels of $f$ contained in a predefined neighborhood of $(x, y)$. In other words, the smoothed image is obtained by using the relation

$$g(x, y) = \frac{1}{N} \sum_{(n, m) \varepsilon S} f(n, m) \qquad (14)$$

for all $x$ and $y$ in $f(x, y)$. $S$ is the set of coordinates of points in the neighborhood of $(x, y)$, including $(x, y)$ itself, and $N$ is the total number of points in the neighborhood. If a $3 \times 3$ neighborhood is used, we note by comparing Eqs. (14) and (3) that the former equation is a special case of the latter with $w_i = 1/9$. Of course, we are not limited to square neighborhoods in Eq. (14).

One of the principal difficulties of the method discussed above is that it blurs edges and other sharp details. This blurring can often be reduced significantly by the use of so-called *median filters*, in which we replace the intensity of each pixel by the median of the intensities in a predefined neighborhood of that pixel instead of by the average.

The median $M$ of a set of values is such that half of the values in the set are less than $M$ and half of the values are greater than $M$. In order to perform median filtering in a neighborhood of a pixel, we first sort the values of the pixel and its neighbors, determine the median, and assign this value to the pixel. For example, in a $3 \times 3$ neighborhood the median is the fifth largest value, in a $5 \times 5$ neighborhood it is the thirteenth largest value, and so on. When several values in a neighborhood are the same, we group all equal values as follows. Suppose that a $3 \times 3$ neighborhood has values (10, 20, 20, 15, 20, 20, 20, 25, 100). These values are sorted as (10, 15, 20, 20, 20, 20, 20, 25, 100), which results in a median of 20. The principal function of median filtering is to force points with very distinct intensities to be more like their neighbors, thus actually eliminating intensity spikes that appear isolated in the area of the filter mask.

Figure 8a shows an image with approximately 20% of the pixels corrupted by "impulse noise." The result of a $5 \times 5$ median filter is shown in Fig. 8b. The three bright dots remaining in Fig. 8b resulted from a large concentration of noise at those points, thus biasing the median calculation. Two or more passes with a median filter would eliminate these points.

### Sharpening   E

Sharpening is achieved by using one or more masks to approximate a derivative operation. The principal approach is to use the magnitude of the gradient at each pixel location:

$$G(x, y) = \sqrt{G_x^2 + G_y^2} \qquad (15)$$

where $G_x$ and $G_y$ are digital derivative operators defined as

$$G_x = [f(x + 1, y - 1) + 2f(x + 1, y) + f(x + 1, y + 1)]$$
$$- [f(x - 1, y - 1) + 2f(x - 1, y) + f(x - 1, y + 1)] \quad (16a)$$

and

$$G_y = [f(x + 1, y - 1) + 2f(x, y + 1) + f(x + 1, y + 1)]$$
$$- [f(x - 1, y - 1) + 2f(x, y - 1) + f(x - 1, y + 1)] \quad (16b)$$

The vertical derivative $G_x$ of $f(x, y)$ at any point $(x, y)$ can be computed by using the mask shown in Fig. 9a. Similarly, $G_y$ is computed using the mask shown in 9b. These two masks are commonly referred to as the Sobel operators. Figure 10 shows the result of a typical derivative operation. In general, gradient operations enhance edge detail while decreasing the intensity of smoothly varying backgrounds.

Another important derivative operation is the Laplacian, which is a second-derivative function. In digital form, the Laplacian at any point $(x, y)$ is given by

$$L(x, y) = [f(x + 1, y) + f(x - 1, y) + f(x, y + 1) + f(x, y - 1)$$
$$- 4 f(x, y)] \qquad (17)$$

and can be implemented by using the mask shown in Fig. 11.

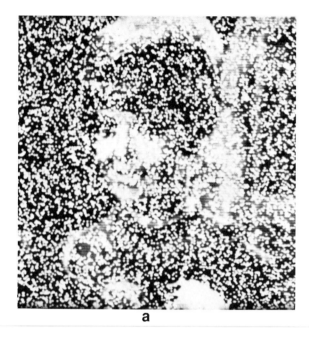

a

b

**Fig. 8.** (a) Image corrupted by impulse noise. (b) Result of 5 × 5 median filtering. (Courtesy of Martin Connor, Texas Instruments, Inc., Lewisville, Texas.)

| -1 | -2 | -1 |
|---|---|---|
| 0 | 0 | 0 |
| 1 | 2 | 1 |

(a)

| -1 | 0 | 1 |
|---|---|---|
| -2 | 0 | 2 |
| -1 | 0 | 1 |

(b)

**Fig. 9.** (a) Mask used to compute $G_x$. (b) Mask used to compute $G_y$.

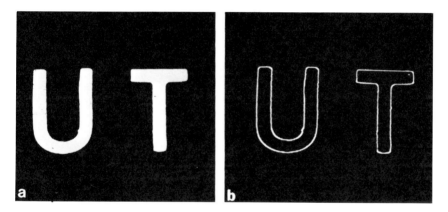

**Fig. 10.** (a) Original and (b) gradient image. (From Gonzalez and Wintz [1] ©1977, Addison—Wesley, Reading, Massachusetts. Reprinted with permission.)

| 0 | 1 | 0 |
|---|---|---|
| 1 | -4 | 1 |
| 0 | 1 | 0 |

**Fig. 11.** Mask used to compute the Laplacian.

The principal difference in terms of enhancement between the gradient and the Laplacian is that the gradient, being a first derivative, responds to an intensity transition and is thus used for edge detection. The Laplacian, on the other hand, is a second derivative and it is useful for determining whether a pixel lies on the dark or light side of an edge.

## III  ENHANCEMENT IN THE FREQUENCY DOMAIN

The basic approach for enhancing a digital image $f(x, y)$ via frequency-domain techniques is (1) to compute the FFT of $f(x, y)$, (2) multiply the result by a "filter" function $H(u, v)$, and (3) take the inverse FFT. In equation form,

$$G(u, v) = H(u, v)F(u, v) \tag{18}$$

The enhanced image $g(x, y)$ is given by the inverse FFT of $G(u, v)$. The nature of the enhancement lies in the choice of the filter function $H(u, v)$. The three principal uses of frequency-domain methods for image enhancement are (1) smoothing, (2) sharpening, and (3) contrast manipulation. These areas are discussed in the following.

### A  Smoothing

Image smoothing is achieved by selecting a low-pass filter which attenuates the high frequencies of $F(u, v)$. Since edge and other sharp intensity transitions (such as noise) are characterized by high frequencies, the effect of a low-pass filter is to smooth (blur) an image. One of the most popular low-pass filters is the Butterworth filter of order $n$, given by

$$H(u, v) = \frac{1}{1 + [D(u, v)/D_0]^{2n}} \tag{19}$$

where $D(u, v)$ is the distance from the origin of the frequency plane and $D_0$ is the half-power point of the filter (i.e., the value where $H(u, v) = \frac{1}{2}$). When using the FFT, a preprocessing step which multiplies $f(x, y)$ by $(-1)^{x+y}$ shifts the origin to the center of the plane. This facilitates the use of a symmetric filter such as the one given in Eq. (19).

### B  Sharpening

Sharpening is achieved by using a high-pass filter whose function is to attenuate low frequencies (background information). The result is to proportionately enhance edges and other sharp intensity transitions in an image. The Butterworth high-pass filter of order $n$ is one of the most popular filters for this purpose. It is given by

$$H(u, v) = \frac{1}{1 + [D_0/D(u, v)]^{2n}} \qquad (20)$$

As in the case of a low-pass filtering operation, use of this symmetric filter requires that the origin of $F(u, v)$ be shifted to the center of the frequency plane.

### Contrast Manipulation   C

Contrast manipulation is a key tool for image enhancement. This type of operation can be achieved in the frequency domain by the use of so-called *homomorphic filtering* techniques [5]. Basically, the approach is to model the image formation process as the product of an illumination and a reflectance component:

$$f(x, y) = i(x, y)r(x, y) \qquad (21)$$

Illumination is generally of a uniform nature and is thus composed of relatively smooth intensity variations, which yield low-frequency components in the Fourier transform. The nature of reflectance, on the other hand, is determined by the characteristics of an image and will typically have sharp transitions in intensity as a result of edges in the image. These are associated with high-frequency components in the Fourier transform. The basic idea behind homomorphic filtering is to operate separately on the frequency components of illumination and reflectance. However, $i(x, y)$ and $r(x, y)$ appear as a product in the spatial domain. Since the Fourier transform of a product of two functions is not the product of their individual transforms, the approach is to form a new image

$$z(x, y) = \ln f(x, y) = \ln i(x, y) + \ln r(x, y) \qquad (22)$$

Then, since the Fourier transform is distributive over summation, taking the transform of $z(x, y)$ is equivalent to obtaining the transform of $\ln i(x, y)$ and $\ln r(x, y)$ and summing the results. This approach provides a measure of separation between the low- and high-frequency components. Based on the foregoing discussion, we may summarize the homomorphic filtering process of an image $f(x, y)$ as follows:

(1)   Let $z(x, y) = \ln f(x, y)$.
(2)   Obtain the FFT of $z(x, y)$.
(3)   Apply a filter $H(u, v)$ to the result $S(u, v) = H(u, v)Z(u, v)$.
(4)   Obtain the inverse FFT to yield $s(x, y)$.
(5)   Let $g(x, y) = \exp[s(x, y)]$. This "reverses" the logarithm operation. The image $g(x, y)$ is the enhanced result.

**Fig. 12.** (a) Before and (b) after by homomorphic filtering. (From Stockman [5]. Copyright © 1972 IEEE.)

The key to this method is the choice of $H(u, v)$. As an example, the details (reflectance) of the image shown in Fig. 12a are obscured as a result of too much illumination on the front walls of the building. Using the filter function shown in Fig. 13 with $\gamma_L = 0.5$ and $\gamma_H = 2.0$ yielded the image shown in Fig. 12b. Note the details of the piping inside the room. In this case, enhancing the values of the high frequencies (associated with reflectance components) at the expense of the low frequencies (associated with illumination) vividly enhanced details hardly visible in the original image.

## IV  RESTORATION

As in image enhancement, the ultimate goal of restoration techniques is to improve a given image in some sense. Restoration is a process that attempts

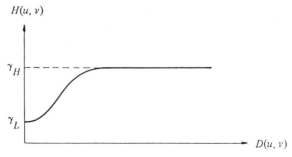

**Fig. 13.** Cross section of a homomorphic filter. (From Stockman [5]. Copyright © 1972 IEEE.)

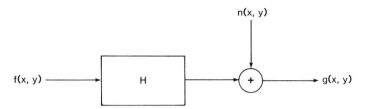

**Fig. 14.** Model for restoration.(From Gonzalez and Wintz [1]©1977, Addison—Wesley, Reading, Massachusetts. Reprinted with permission.)

to recover an image that has been degraded by using some *a priori* knowledge of the degradation phenomenon. Enhancement techniques, on the other hand, are basically heuristic procedures that are designed to manipulate an image in order to take advantage of the psychophysical aspects of the human visual system.

### A Basic Model for Restoration   A

As shown in Fig. 14, the degradation process may be modeled as an operator (system) $H$ which, together with an additive noise term $n(x, y)$, operates on an input image $f(x, y)$ to produce a degraded image $g(x, y)$. In equation form,

$$g(x, y) = Hf(x, y) + n(x, y) \qquad (23)$$

If $H$ is a linear position-invariant operator, it can be shown [1, 6] that Eq. (23) leads to the convolution integral

$$g(x, y) = \int_{-\infty}^{\infty} \int f(\alpha, \beta)h(x - \alpha, y - \beta) \, d\alpha \, d\beta + n(x, y) \qquad (24)$$

where $h$ is the impulse response of the operator $H$ and $\alpha$, $\beta$ are dummy variables of integration.

Based on the convolution theorem, the frequency-domain representation of Eq. (24) becomes

$$G(u, v) = H(u, v)F(u, v) + N(u, v) \qquad (25)$$

where $H(u, v)$ is the Fourier transform of $h(x, y)$ and $N(u, v)$ the transform of $n(x, y)$. Given $G$ and some knowledge about $H$ and $N$, the objective of linear restoration techniques is to recover $F$ [and thus $f(x, y)$ via the inverse Fourier transform].

## B   Restoration Filters

The most obvious way to recover $F$ from Eq. (25) is to perform an *inverse filtering process*:

$$F(u, v) = \frac{G(u, v)}{H(u, v)} - \frac{N(u, v)}{H(u, v)} \tag{26}$$

There are two major problems with this approach. First, $n(x, y)$ is seldom known well enough to obtain $N(u, v)$. Second, $H(u, v)$ often vanishes or becomes very small for specific values of $(u, v)$. This is true even for analytical models of a degradation process, such as image blurring caused by uniform linear motion between a scene and the imaging device [1].

Most well-known image restoration filters are formulations that attempt to circumvent the problems just mentioned. Perhaps the most famous of these is the Wiener filter, which yields a least-square approximation to $F(u, v)$:

$$\hat{F}(u, v) = \left[ \frac{H^*(u, v)}{|H(u, v)|^2 + [S_n(u, v)/S_f(u, v)]} \right] G(u, v) \tag{27}$$

where $H^*(u, v)$ is the complex conjugate of $H(u, v)$, $|H(u, v)|^2 = H^*(u, v)H(u, v)$, and $S_n(u, v)$ and $S_f(u, v)$ are the spectral densities of the image and noise components. When $S_n$ and $S_f$ are not known, a procedure often

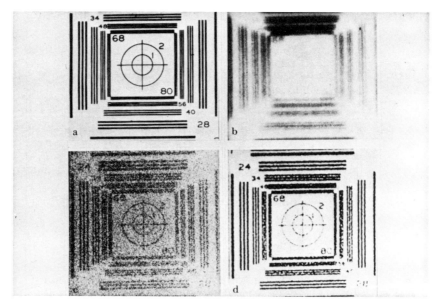

**Fig. 15.** Example of restoration. See text for discussion of figure parts (a), (b), (c), and (d). (From Hunt [7]. Copyright © 1973 IEEE.)

used is to let their ratio equal a constant, which can be varied to obtain approximate restoration results.

Another popular restoration filter is the constrained least-squares filter:

$$F(u, v) = \left[ \frac{H^*(u, v)}{|H(u, v)|^2 + \gamma |P(u, v)|^2} \right] G(u, v) \qquad (28)$$

where $P(u, v)$ is the Fourier transform of the Laplacian operator, and $\gamma$ is a parameter computed iteratively [7]. Figure 15 shows typical results obtainable with this filter. Figure 15a is the original image and Fig. 15b is the same image corrupted by a blurring function and additive Gaussian noise. Figure 15c is the result obtained by inverse filtering, and Fig. 15d the result obtained using Eq. (28). Note how the noise predominates in Fig. 15c as a result of dividing $N(u, v)$ by small values of $H(u, v)$.

### Interactive Restoration  C

Thus far, attention has been focused on analytical approaches to restoration. In many applications, it is practical to take advantage of human intuition and experience to restore images in an interactive mode. One of the simplest cases of image corruption that lends itself well to this approach is the occurrence of periodic interference (often called *coherent noise*) superimposed on an image. The periodic components of noise appear as "spikes" in the

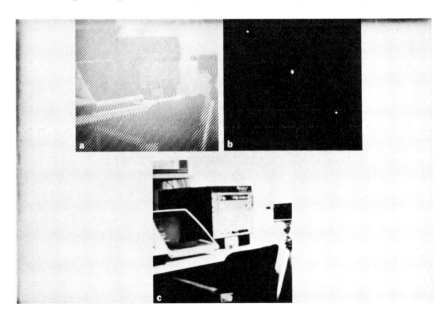

Fig. 16. Example of interactive restoration. See text for discussion of figure parts (a), (b), and (c). (From Gonzalez and Wintz [1] ©1977, Addison—Wesley, Reading, Massachusetts. Reprinted with permission.)

Fourier spectrum, and the approach is to eliminate these components from the Fourier transform. The inverse transform would then yield an image which is essentially free of the spatial noise component. This approach is illustrated in Fig. 16. Figure 16a shows an image corrupted by sinusoidal noise. The noise has the two spikes clearly visible in the spectrum shown in Fig. 16b. Elimination of the spikes followed by the inverse Fourier transform yielded the image shown in Fig. 16c.

## V   A LINK BETWEEN THE SPATIAL AND FREQUENCY DOMAINS

Although enhancement and restoration methods are generally easily formulated in the frequency domain, it is often of interest from a computational point of view to carry out an approximate implementation in the spatial domain using small convolution masks. In this section, a procedure is given for generating these masks from an enhancement or restoration filter specified in the frequency domain [8]. Let the filter be denoted by $H(u, v)$ and the mask by $r(x, y)$, with Fourier transform $R(u, v)$:

$$R(u, v) = \frac{1}{N} \sum_{u=0}^{N-1} \sum_{v=0}^{N-1} r(x, y) \exp\left[\frac{-j2\pi(ux + uy)}{N}\right] \tag{29}$$

The error between $H(u, v)$ and $R(u, v)$ may be expressed as

$$e^2 = \sum_{u=0}^{N-1} \sum_{v=0}^{N-1} |R(u, v) - H(u, v)|^2 \tag{30}$$

where $|\cdot|$ designates the complex magnitude.

If $r(x, y)$ is precisely the inverse of $H(u, v)$, then the error is zero. In other words, using a spatial convolution mask generated from the inverse transform of the filter should be zero based on the convolution theorem. Suppose, however, that $r(x, y)$ is only $n \times n$ with $n < N$. Equation (29) would then be expressed as

$$R(u, v) = \frac{1}{N} \sum_{x=0}^{n-1} \sum_{y=0}^{n-1} r(x, y) \exp\left[\frac{-j2\pi(ux + vy)}{N}\right] \tag{31}$$

and the objective is to select the coefficients of $r(x, y)$ which will give an $R(u, v)$ that minimizes Eq. (30).

Equation (31) can be expressed in the matrix form

$$\mathbf{R} = \mathbf{Cr} \tag{32}$$

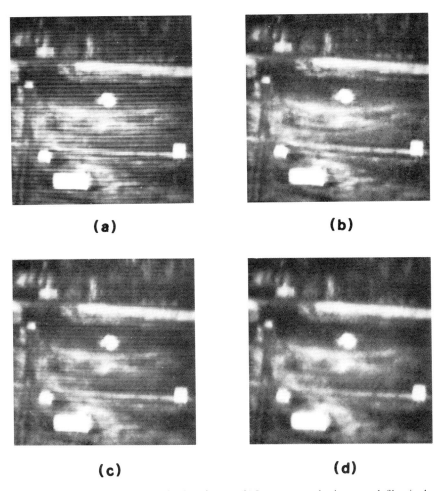

**Fig. 17.** (a) Infrared image showing interference. (b) Image restored using a notch filter in the frequency domain. (c) Image restored using a 9 × 9 convolution mask. (d) Result of applying the mask a second time.

where $\mathbf{R}$ is a column vector of order $N^2$, $\mathbf{r}$ a column vector of order $n^2$, and $\mathbf{C}$ an $N^2 \times n^2$ matrix of exponential terms. Using this notation, Eq. (30) becomes

$$e^2 = (\mathbf{R} - \mathbf{H})^*(\mathbf{R} - \mathbf{H}) = \|\mathbf{R} - \mathbf{H}\|^2 = \|\mathbf{Cr} - \mathbf{H}\|^2 \qquad (33)$$

where "*" is the conjugate transpose, $\| \cdot \|$ is the complex Euclidean norm, and $\mathbf{H}$ is a vector formed from the elements of $H(u, v)$. The minimum of Eq. (33) with respect to $\mathbf{r}$ is given by taking the derivative and setting it to zero:

$$\mathbf{r} = (\mathbf{C}^*\mathbf{C})^{-1}\mathbf{C}^*\mathbf{H} \qquad (34)$$

Thus, the coefficients of **r** which minimize the error function depend on the elements of matrix **C** and the elements of vector **H**, which was formed from the elements of the filter function $H(u, v)$.

As an illustration, Fig. 17a shows an infrared image of a set of military targets in a field. The image is corrupted by nearly periodic scanner interference visible as a "ripple" effect in the vertical direction. Because of its periodic nature, the interference produces bursts of concentrated energy in the vertical axis of the Fourier spectrum of the image, as shown in Fig. 18a.

A simple approach for reducing the effect of the interference is to use a notch filter, $H(u, v)$, which attenuates the values of the Fourier transform in the vertical axis and multiplies all other values of the transform by 1. Such a filter is shown in Fig. 18b superimposed on the spectrum, where the dark bands are the attenuated regions.

The result of using the notch filter and taking the inverse Fourier transform is shown in Fig. 17b. It is noted that, for all practical purposes, the interference was eliminated from the image. The image shown in Fig. 17c was obtained by applying a 9 × 9 convolution mask to the original, corrupted image. The coefficients of this mask were generated from the notch filter using Eq. (34). Since this small mask is only an approximation to the Fourier filtering process, some vertical lines are still visible in the processed image. A second pass of the mask further reduced the interference (at the cost of some noticeable blurring), as shown in Fig. 18d.

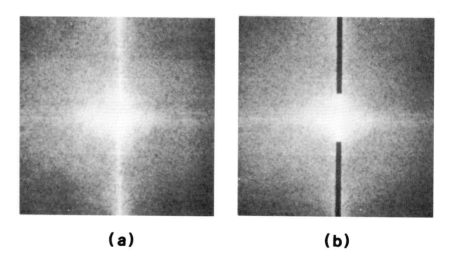

**(a)**                                    **(b)**

**Fig. 18.** (a) Fourier spectrum of the image in Fig. 17a. (b) Notch filter superimposed on the spectrum.

## REFERENCES

1. R. C. Gonzalez and P. Wintz, "Digital Image Processing." Addison-Wesley, Reading, Massachusetts, 1977.
2. A. Rosenfeld and A. C. Kak, "Digital Picture Processing." Academic Press, New York, 1982.
3. R. E. Woods and R. C. Gonzalez, Real-time digital image enhancement, *Proc. IEEE* **69**, No. 5, 643-654 (1981).
4. P. M. Narendra and R. C. Fitch, Real-time adaptive contrast enhancement, *IEEE Trans. Pattern Anal. Mach. Intell.* **PAMI-3**, No. 6, 655-661 (1981).
5. T. G. Stockman, Image processing in the context of a visual model, *Proc. IEEE* **60**, No. 7, 828-842 (1972).
6. H. C. Andrews and B. R. Hunt, "Digital Image Restoration." Prentice-Hall, Englewood Cliffs, New Jersey, 1977.
7. B. R. Hunt, The application of constrained least squares estimation to image restoration by digital computer, *IEEE Trans. Comput.* **C-22**, No. 9, 805-812 (1973).
8. E. R. Meyer and R. C. Gonzalez, Spatial image processing masks from frequency domain specifications, *Proc. SEG/USN Shear Waves and Pattern Recognition Symposium* 237-247 (1983).

# Chapter **9**

# Image Segmentation

R. NEVATIA

Intelligent Systems Group
University of Southern California
Departments of Electrical Engineering
and Computer Science
Los Angeles, California

## INTRODUCTION   I

The objective of *scene* segmentation is to separate the components of an image into subsets that correspond to the physical objects in the scene. The segmented components are then used by higher-level processes for interpretation and recognition.

The major difficulty in scene segmentation is due to the fact that we are usually interested in finding the boundaries of physical objects in a three-dimensional scene, but we typically only have monocular two-dimensional

215

image information, and hence we can only achieve *image* segmentation. The image segmentation methods assume that the objects have smooth homogeneous surfaces that correspond to regions of constant or smoothly varying intensity in the image and that the intensity changes abruptly at the boundaries. These assumptions are mostly, but not always, valid. There may be physical boundaries between similar surfaces that do not appear as image boundaries and image boundaries, such as surface markings, that do not correspond to physical boundaries. Surface texture and noise cause additional problems.

There exist two major approaches to image segmentation—edge based and region based. In edge-based methods, the local discontinuities are detected first and then connected to form longer, hopefully complete, boundaries. In region methods, areas of image with homogeneous properties are found, which in turn give the boundaries. The two methods are complementary and one may be preferred over the other for some applications. The two methods can also be combined to a certain extent. Image segmentation results can often be improved by a feedback method. Use of range data avoids some of the problems outlined above.

## II  EDGE AND CURVE DETECTION

The assumption for edge detection is that at the edge the intensity changes in a discontinuous way (usually as a step function, but some methods will handle other types of edges also). In two-dimensions, the edges have a direction as well as a magnitude, and the intensity profile is assumed to be more or less uniform along the edge. Figure 1 shows an ideal edge in a circular neighborhood. The following section describes various methods of edge detection.

## A  Edge Detection

## 1  Gradient Method

The simplest method is to compute a gradient of the image intensities; an edge is said to be present when the magnitude of the gradient exceeds a certain threshold. Many methods of approximating the gradient in a digital domain have been developed, two of the more common being the Roberts and Sobel methods. Figure 2 shows the intensity values in a $3 \times 3$ neighborhood. In Roberts' method, the gradient $R(i, j)$ at $(i, j)$ is computed by

$$R(i, j) = \sqrt{(a_4 - a_8)^2 + (a_7 - a_5)^2} \tag{1}$$

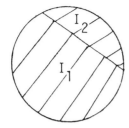

**Fig. 1.** An ideal edge.

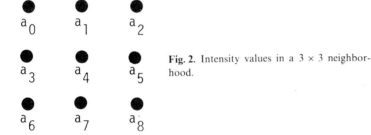

**Fig. 2.** Intensity values in a 3 × 3 neighborhood.

The direction of the gradient is given by

$$\alpha = -\frac{\pi}{4} + \tan^{-1}\left(\frac{a_7 - a_5}{a_4 - a_8}\right) \tag{2}$$

In Sobel's method, the gradient is given by the components $S_x$ and $S_y$ in the $x$ and $y$ directions, defined as

$$S_x = (a_2 + 2a_5 + a_8) - (a_0 + 2a_3 + a_6) \tag{3}$$

$$S_y = (a_6 + 2a_7 + a_8) - (a_0 + 2a_1 + a_2) \tag{4}$$

The Roberts and Sobel edge detectors are often used as "cheap and dirty" methods due to their simplicity and low computation costs, and they perform reasonably well in scenes of low noise and texture.

### Surface Fitting  2

In this class of methods, the intensity profile is approximated by an analytical function, which is then used to compute the derivatives or the best fit with an ideal edge. Two of the more prominent methods are the following.

(a) *Hueckel operator.* In this method, the intensity surface is approximated by expansion into the first nine coefficients of a radial Fourier series. Similar coefficients are computed for a parameterized ideal edge, and the

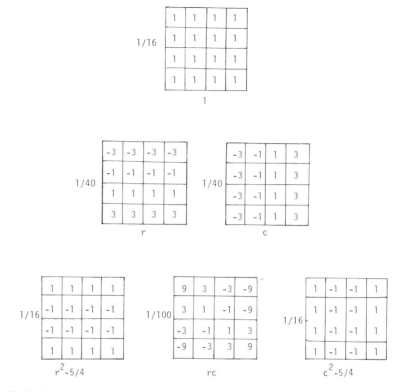

**Fig. 3.** Masks used to compute coefficients of discrete polynomials up to order two on a 4 × 4 mask.

parameters of the edge giving the best fit are determined. The computation is largely analytical, but the mathematics of the fit are rather complex and may be found in Ref. 1. Detection of an edge requires the magnitudes to exceed a threshold which is dependent on the degree of fit between an ideal edge and the approximated intensity profile. This operator was popular in the 1970s, but deeper analysis has found serious deficiencies due to the Fourier approximation [2].

(b) *Facet model.* Haralick has recently developed another method of surface fitting [3]. In this method the image intensity values in a neighborhood are approximated by a two-dimensional discrete orthogonal polynomial set. We must first choose a window size over which the polynomial fit is to be computed and then the highest order of the polynomials to be used. These define a set of base orthogonal polynomials. The approximated intensity function can then be computed as a linear combination of the discrete polynomials in the base set. Figure 3 shows a set of base polynomials of up to quadratic order over a 4 × 4 window. To compute the weight of each polynomial, we simply multiply the given masks with the image intensity

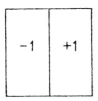

Fig. 4. Vertical edge mask.

functions. (Details of computing polynomials of any size and order may be found in Ref. 3).

Once the approximation has been computed, we have an analytical function for the image and the derivatives can be computed analytically. Haralick chooses to compute second-order directional derivatives; here an edge in the image results in a "zero crossing" of the second derivative (similar to the method described in Section II.A.4 later). The initial results of this method look good, but it has not been tested as extensively as other methods described in this chapter.

### Template Matching     3

In this approach, an ideal edge "mask" or "template" is convolved with the image; a high output can be expected where the image is like the mask. An ideal mask for a vertical step edge is shown in Fig. 4. To detect edges in any direction, a number of masks of difference orientation are used. For a step at any arbitrary angle, each pixel is assigned the difference between the dark and the light areas in a continuous representation of the step; thus, the resulting mask may not be binary (Fig. 5 shows 5 × 5 masks in six directions from Ref. 4). The mask giving the highest output at a pixel gives the magnitude and the direction of the potential edge at that pixel [4].

Note that this method will give high output at the edge as well as at its neighbors. We can simply pick the peak of the outputs (also called "nonmaxima suppression"). The output at neighbors can also be used to detect edges with more confidence—Nevatia and Babu require that for a pixel to have an edge, its neighbors normal to the direction of the edge must have orientations similar to that of the central pixel [4].

Choice of the size of the mask is important for such operators. A larger mask averages more noise and hence can detect lower contrast edges, but at the cost of lower precision in the position of the edge and higher computation cost. Also, a larger mask output may be confused by more than one edge in the window. An optimal size of the mask may be determined automatically by using different sizes and choosing the one that gives the highest output (the output will increase with mask size until a second edge is contained within the same mask).

| -100 | -100 | 0 | 100 | 100 |
|---|---|---|---|---|
| -100 | -100 | 0 | 100 | 100 |
| -100 | -100 | 0 | 100 | 100 |
| -100 | -100 | 0 | 100 | 100 |
| -100 | -100 | 0 | 100 | 100 |

(a) 0°

| -100 | 32 | 100 | 100 | 100 |
|---|---|---|---|---|
| -100 | -78 | 92 | 100 | 100 |
| -100 | -100 | 0 | 100 | 100 |
| -100 | -100 | -92 | 78 | 100 |
| -100 | -100 | -100 | -32 | 100 |

(b) 30°

| 100 | 100 | 100 | 100 | 100 |
|---|---|---|---|---|
| -32 | 78 | 100 | 100 | 100 |
| -100 | -92 | 0 | 92 | 100 |
| -100 | -100 | -100 | -78 | 32 |
| -100 | -100 | -100 | -100 | -100 |

(c) 60°

| 100 | 100 | 100 | 100 | 100 |
|---|---|---|---|---|
| 100 | 100 | 100 | 100 | 100 |
| 0 | 0 | 0 | 0 | 0 |
| -100 | -100 | -100 | -100 | -100 |
| -100 | -100 | -100 | -100 | -100 |

(d) 90°

| -100 | 100 | 100 | 100 | 100 |
|---|---|---|---|---|
| -100 | 100 | 100 | 78 | -32 |
| -100 | 92 | 0 | -92 | -100 |
| 32 | -78 | -100 | -100 | -100 |
| -100 | -100 | -100 | -100 | -100 |

(e) 120°

| 100 | 100 | 100 | 32 | -100 |
|---|---|---|---|---|
| 100 | 100 | 92 | -78 | -100 |
| 100 | 100 | 0 | -100 | -100 |
| 100 | 78 | -92 | -100 | -100 |
| 100 | -32 | -100 | -100 | -100 |

(f) 150°

**Fig. 5.** Masks in six directions for a 5 × 5 neighborhood.

## 4   Second-Derivative Methods

The methods described above essentially detect edges by computing the first derivative and suffer from the disadvantage that they respond erratically on a ramp intensity profile. A ramp profile is common for a slant surface illuminated by a single source of light. Use of second-derivative methods eliminates this difficulty. For a step edge, the second derivative is zero at the edge but has a positive and a negative peak on either side. Thus, edge detection is by locating zero crossings.

Marr and Hildreth [5] have suggested that the appropriate operator to use is a Laplacian–Gaussian defined as

$$\nabla^2 G(x, y) = -\frac{1}{2\pi\sigma^4}\left(2 - \frac{x^2 + y^2}{\sigma^2}\right)\exp -\left(\frac{x^2 + y^2}{2\sigma^2}\right) \qquad (5)$$

This operator is shown schematically in Fig. 6. The Gaussian serves as a smoothing function and the Laplacian gives a nondirectional derivative. Marr and Hildreth argue that this is a good model of the processing in the human visual system. They suggest use of four mask sizes, corresponding to different values of $\sigma$. A prominent edge will be seen with all masks; the details will be seen only with the smaller masks. The output of the four masks can be used separately with the results combined at a higher level or we could require concurrence of edges in two or more mask sizes.

The Laplacian–Gaussian masks can become rather large (say, 25 × 25 pixels) and hence computationally expensive. This operator can be approxi-

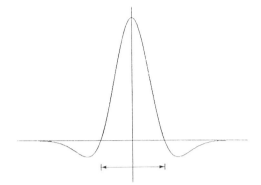

**Fig. 6.** A Laplacian–Gaussian mask.

mated by taking differences of Gaussian (DOG) instead:

$$\text{DOG}(\sigma_e, \sigma_i) = \left[ \frac{1}{\sqrt{2\pi}\sigma_e} \exp\left( -\frac{x^2}{2\sigma_e^2} \right) \right] - \left[ \frac{1}{\sqrt{2\pi}\sigma_i} \exp\left( -\frac{x^2}{2\sigma_i^2} \right) \right] \quad (6)$$

Marr and Hildreth suggest that a ratio of 1.6 for $\sigma_i/\sigma_e$ seems to achieve the best approximation.

### Use of Color    5

The color attribute of a pixel is a three-dimensional entity; many representations are possible, such as the "red," "green," and "blue" components of a sensor signal or the "intensity," "hue," and "saturation" attributes. To detect edges in color, we can detect edges in the three components separately and analyze the three sets of edges separately or require concurrence of two or more. Experience seems to indicate that color edges are highly correlated with intensity edges, and hence the extra computation for color edge detection may not be cost-effective in general cases [6].

### Thresholding and Thinning    6

Most of the edge detectors require a "threshold" to decide the presence of an edge or not. This threshold is usually determined by "trial and error" and hopefully applies to other similar images. If the noise parameters are known, a threshold can be picked by analysis of the expected contribution to noise.

Most edge detectors also produce a "thick" edge, since the detectors respond at and near an edge. The edges can be thinned by using nonmaxima suppression (discussed earlier) or simply by eliminating the "outside" edge, one layer at a time. The more effective methods use the direction of the edge as well and thin only in the direction normal to the edge (as in the Nevatia–Babu edge detector described above).

## 7   *Some Results*

The results of edge and line detection are seldom perfect. Of course, the edge detector design itself could be improved, but several of the factors come from the image itself, such as poor contrast, noise and surface texture. It is difficult to evaluate the various edge detectors, either analytically or empirically, for other than simple models of an ideal step edge with additive noise (even here, the nonlinearities of edge detection make analysis difficult). To give the reader some of the types of results that can be expected, we give the results of using the Nevatia–Babu edge detector [4] on an aerial image. Figure 7a shows the image, Fig. 7b shows the edges (after thinning), and Fig. 7c shows a piecewise linear approximation. Results obtained by using other edge detectors may be a little different, but the salient points are likely to be similar. The major features are extracted rather well, but some of the detail may have been lost. Also, the lines are fragmented and require some intelligent higher-level processing to group them into meaningful objects.

## B   Line Detection

The result of edge detection is to produce a binary image indicating where the edges are or a list of the edges, possibly with attached descriptions such as direction and contrast. To get boundaries, a further step of "linking" or grouping of the edges that correspond to a single boundary is required. Note that it is relatively easy to fit piecewise lines (or polynomials) once the groups or chains are obtained.

## 1   *Line Linking*

A simple linking method is to connect each edge point to one of its neighbors. In cases of multiple choice, the selection is made on similarities of edge properties such as orientation and direction, or alternatives are explored to see which paths give more desired longer chains (e.g., see Ref. 4).

In general, the problem may be viewed as that of finding low-cost paths in a graph. The nodes of the graph are given by the edges, and the arcs between them have a user-defined cost that is a function of the distance and similarity of edge properties. Some implementations may be found in Refs. 7 and 8.

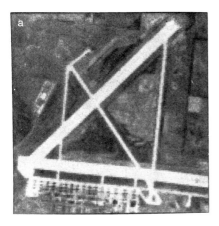
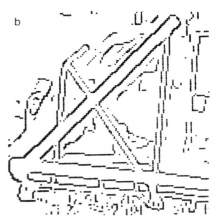

**Fig. 7.** An example of edge detection (using the Nevatia–Babu method). (a) Image (b) edges, and (c) lines.

Such techniques are efficient only if the start and end points are known or if the search can be constrained in some other way.

### Grouping by Using Hough Transforms 2

In this method, the edges are transformed to another space, called the Hough space, with the property that the desired groups of edges cluster in the transform space. Suppose that we wish to detect edges lying on a straight line. The general equation of a straight line can be written as

$$x \cos \theta + y \sin \theta = r \qquad (7)$$

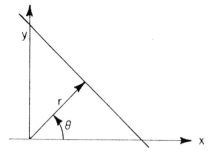

**Fig. 8.** Polar representation of a line.

where $\theta$ is the angle that a normal to the line makes with the $x$ axis and $r$ is the length of this normal (see Fig. 8). Any edge points $(x_i, y_i)$ on this line must satisfy

$$x_i \cos \theta + y_i \sin \theta = r \tag{8}$$

Equation (8) can be interpreted as a sinusoidal curve in $(r, \theta)$ space (see Fig. 9) and viewed as the Hough transform of the point $(x_i, y_i)$ into the $(r, \theta)$ space. Any point on the transform curve corresponds to a line constrained to go through the point $(x_i, y_i)$. If a number of points are collinear in the $(x, y)$ space, their Hough transform curves must intersect in the same point in the $(r, \theta)$ space. For a digital implementation, we must quantize the $(r, \theta)$ space. Each edge point $(x_i, y_i)$ then contributes a count to the cells given by Eq. (8), and the cells with high counts give the desired lines. The method can be generalized to curves of arbitrary shape, but with an increase in the dimensionality of the transform space [9].

## III  REGION SEGMENTATION

In region segmentation, we find a connected set of pixels that share a common property (such as intensity or color) and hence hopefully corresponds to a physical object or surface.

## A  Thresholding

The simplest technique of region segmentation is by thresholding. All pixels that are in a certain range of some image property, say, intensity, are taken to belong to one group. Connected regions in this set give us the desired segmentation. This method is suited for scenes containing homogeneous objects against high-contrast uniform backgrounds (such as characters on a

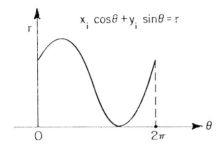

$$x_i \cos\theta + y_i \sin\theta = r$$

**Fig. 9.** Hough transform of a point.

printed page). The threshold may be selected by experience with a set of selected, typical images or from other *a priori* knowledge. Alternatively, a histogram of intensity values may be constructed. If the histogram has clear peaks, these peaks give the thresholds for the corresponding regions.

Many methods have been suggested for "smoothing" a histogram to give pronounced peaks. A technique called the "superspike" works based on iterative local averaging. Each pixel is averaged with those of its neighbors that satisfy the following criteria, based on the image's histogram.

(a)   The neighbor is more probable than the pixel, that is, its gray level has a higher value in the histogram.

(b)   The histogram has no concavity between the gray levels of the pixel and the neighbor (as would be the case if they belonged to two different peaks, or to a peak and shoulder).

The superspike method has been tested on infrared images of targets and appears to work well there [10].

Another method of choosing a threshold is by trying various threshold values and choosing the value that gives borders that are maximally coincident with points of maximum gradient (i.e., edges) in the image. This is known as the method of "superslice." [11]

**Recursive Segmentation**   **B**

In the histogram method for peak selection, the contributions of a small region may be masked by other larger regions. One solution is to apply thresholding recursively in the following way: the thresholded regions are considered as new images and the process of histogramming, peak selection, and thresholding is repeated until no new peaks can be found or regions become too small. An effective implementation of this method is described in Ref. 12. This method uses intensity and color information for threshold selection; the most "prominent" peak is selected at each iteration. Figure 10 shows an image with superposed boundaries of regions found in it. (Color

**Fig. 10.** An image and boundaries of regions found in it (using the Ohlander–Price–Reddy method [12]. (Courtesy Dr. K. Price.)

information was used in segmentation, although only a gray-level image is shown here.) Note that the method is quite successful in segmenting textured regions such as the grass lawn and the trees on both sides of the house.

## C   Region Growing

In this approach, we start with small "atomic" regions (say, the regions with uniform or nearly uniform pixel properties). Neighboring regions are then merged based on their relative properties, such as whether one region largely includes the other or the merged region has a more "regular shape." Let $L$ be the length of the common boundary between two regions of perimeter lengths $P_1$ and $P_2$; they may be merged if $L/P_1$ or $L/P_2$ exceeds a threshold [13]. The process is repeated until no new regions are formed. Region-growing methods typically result in a highly fragmented segmentation. To get larger regions, the merging process may be guided "semantically," that is, by using *a priori* properties of the image, such as adjacency relations between regions of various properties. An implementation is described in Ref. 14. A detailed survey of region-growing methods may be found in Ref. 15.

## Split and Merge Methods   D

In split and merge methods, both region-splitting and merging processes may take place. A tree maintains the information about the relationships of the regions (such as adjacency and parent-child relations) at any given stage of processing. A region is examined as a candidate for splitting or for merging based on some predefined criteria. The process switches from merging to splitting if no new regions can be merged and vice versa. An implementation is described in Ref. 16.

## Classification and Clustering   E

In clustering methods, the pixels are clustered in a feature space based on their properties; the clusters are not required to be spatially contiguous. Such methods are more effective when the number of clusters is known *a priori* [17].

Another method for segmentation is simply by classification of the individual pixels. Such methods can work only when the scene is simple enough (or constrained enough) that such classification is possible. The classification need not be in terms of object names, but could be between "dark" and "bright" areas, or between "object" and "background" pixels. Relaxation labeling methods are commonly used in this approach [18].

## Problems of Texture Segmentation   F

Presence of texture causes difficulty for both the edge- and region-based methods. Essentially, our hypothesis that the objects consist of relatively homogeneous surfaces is violated, and not all intensity changes now correspond to object boundaries. In edge-detection methods, we will get many edges corresponding to texture that must be differentiated from object boundaries; in region methods, we will get many small regions that correspond to texture.

We can consider the problem of separating texture and object boundaries to be a higher-level grouping problem, rather than a segmentation problem. One approach to solving this problem at the segmentation level itself is by characterizing each pixel by not only its individual properties but also by "texture properties" of its neighborhood. (Texture analysis is described in chapter 11; here we can assume that the description consists of a vector of members.) Texture properties can be used in a manner analogous to those of intensity. For edge detection, we must generalize to choosing among edges in more than one attribute. For region segmentation, we now have more than one property from which to choose threshold parameters.

One difficulty with the above approach is that texture properties are neighborhood properties and it is assumed that these properties are constant over the neighborhood of computation. This assumption is violated near the boundaries. Thus, texture segmentation gives poorly localized boundaries, the potential error being up to the size of the neighborhood used to compute texture measures. The localization of boundaries can be improved some if a model can be constructed for the regions on two sides (e.g., see Ref. 19).

## IV  PLANNING AND FEEDBACK

For complex scenes, the results of a segmentation process can be expected to be imperfect. Some segments of the boundary are likely to be missed due to poor contrast or other reasons. Some of these missing segments can be obtained in a variety of ways.

(1)  A more sensitive segmentation operator can be applied at the suspected places of missing information. The hypothesis of missing information may come from *a priori* knowledge of scene characteristics or from partial interpretation of the scene—implementation of these methods has been rather *ad hoc*. In a well-known system [20], Shirai devised a number of methods of predicting missing lines in scenes of polyhedral objects, such as interior lines of vertices. Further, the orientations of the lines were predicted to be parallel to other existing lines, relying on the regularity of polyhedral scenes.

(2)  Small gaps can be bridged simply by extrapolation or by examining the gaps and deciding on their probability of being edge points or not (the basic approach is to close gaps, unless evidence to the contrary is present). Note that some boundaries we see in images are "subjective" or inferred and do not correspond to any signal discontinuities.

A major difficulty in segmentation for large images is the amount of required computation. In many cases, the needed computation can be reduced by processing the images hierarchically. Images of successively lower resolution are formed by averaging the gray values of neighboring pixels in the higher-resolution images (reduction by a factor of two in each direction is commonly used). The various images can be considerd to form a "pyramid." Segmentation starts at a high level (i.e., low resolution) in this pyramid, and the features detected at the higher level are used to guide the segmentation at the next lower level. Thus, we need only look for edges in a small neighborhood of edges found at the next higher level. Similarly, regions found at high levels can be treated as subimages for further segmentation at the lower levels. In many cases, the higher levels will also eliminate texture found at the lower levels, and many segmentation errors may be avoided. However, it is also possible that many small features will also be eliminated and *not* rediscovered at the lower levels (e.g., a thin road is likely to be missed, even if it is very long).

## SEGMENTATION USING RANGE DATA    V

In many applications, range or distance to the points on the visible surface, and hence their three-dimensional positions (sometimes known as $2\frac{1}{2}$-dimensional data), are known. Such data may be derived from an active laser range finder analysis of a stereo pair of images, or a variety of other methods. Segmentation using range data avoids many difficulties of intensity-based segmentation, since the discontinuities in range data correspond directly to surface discontinuities on the object. Range segmentation methods can be grouped in two classes as before—those that use edge and boundary detection and those that use regionlike methods. We will use the term "range image" to refer to an image in which the value at each pixel contains the distance to the point on the surface casting the image at that pixel rather than its intensity.

### Range Boundary Detection    A

We can distinguish between two types of range boundaries:

(a) *Jump boundaries*—here the range values jump abruptly; they correspond to extremal object boundaries

(b) *Slope boundaries*—here the direction of the local surface normal changes abruptly; they correspond to "folds" or intersections of surfaces.

Jump boundaries in a range image are like ordinary intensity step boundaries and can be detected by one of the methods described earlier. Since range images tend to be less noisy and the desired jumps are sharper, a simple comparison of range values with the neighbors may suffice.

Slope boundaries can be detected by using second-derivative operators (e.g., the Laplacian–Gaussian operator described earlier). However, a slope edge will be detected as a maxima of the operator's response rather than a zero crossing, as for a jump boundary. Since the zero crossings of a jump boundary also give two maxima, we need to distinguish between the two types of edges. This can be done by checking for a positive and negative maxima in one case and only one maxima in the other and/or by changing the scale of the operator. In the case of jump boundaries, the zero crossing remains stationary with scale and the maxima move. In the case of slope boundaries, the maxima remain stationary.

Some results of applying edge-detection methods to range data are described in Ref. 21.

## B  Range Region Segmentation

### 1  Detection of Planar Surfaces

For many cases, planar surfaces are important and rather easy to detect. Note that we cannot just fit planes to the entire set of points but must first group points into sets belonging to one plane each.

Points belonging to planes can be detected by generalizing the Hough methods of detecting lines described earlier. A point constrains a family of planes that pass through it; this family can be described by a surface in the Hough space. Surfaces corresponding to the points belonging to the same plane will intersect at the same point in the Hough space. However, the dimensionality of this Hough space is now higher than for line detection, and hence detection is more expensive computationally.

Some specific planes can be detected more easily. The easiest to detect are horizontal planes since the only unknown is the height $z$. If a histogram of the $z$ values of the points on the surface is formed, the horizontal planes should give pronounced peaks. The method can be applied to a plane of any *known* orientation by transforming the coordinates so that the desires plane is horizontal.

Detection of vertical planes involves an extra degree of freedom. Here, we can project the three-dimensional points on the $x$–$y$ plane and detect straight lines among the projected points (by one of the line-detection methods described earlier). These lines should correspond to vertical planes.

Some experiments with the detection of planes using these methods are described in Refs. 22 and 23.

### 2  Region Growing

These methods work analogously to the intensity region-growing methods. Atomic regions consist of local planar faces. Adjacent regions are merged based on their properties, such as differences in local surface normals. Larger regions can be fit by quadratic surfaces, and merging continues so long as the merged regions remain quadratic. An implementation using this approach is given in Ref. 24.

## REFERENCES

1.  M. H. Hueckel, A local visual edge operator which recognizes edges and lines, *J. ACM* **20**, 634–647 (1973).
2.  I. Abdou, Quantitative methods of edge detection, Unpublished Ph.D. dissertation, Univ. of Southern California, Los Angeles, July 1978.
3.  R. M. Haralick, Digital step edge from zero crossing of second directional derivatives, *IEEE Trans Pattern Analysis Machine Intelligence* **6**, No. 1, 58–68 (1984).
4.  R. Nevatia and K. R. Babu, Linear feature extraction and description, *Computer Graphics Image Processing* **13**, 257–269 (1980).
5.  D. Marr and E. Hildreth, Theory of edge detection, *Proc. Royal Society London* **B207**, 187–217 (1980).
6.  R. Nevatia, A color edge detector and its use in scene segmentation, *IEEE Trans. Systems, Man, Cybernetics* **7**(11), 820–826 (1977).
7.  A. Martelli, An application of heuristic search methods to edge and contour detection, *Commun. ACM*, 73–83 (1976).
8.  U. Ramer, The transformation of photographic images into stock arrays, *Computer Graphics Image Processing* **22**, 363–374 (1975).
9.  D. H. Ballard, Generalizing the Hough transform to detect arbitrary shapes, *Pattern Recognition* **13**, No. 2, 111–122 (1981).
10. K. A. Narayana and A. Rosenfeld, Image smoothing by local use of global information, *IEEE Trans. Systems, Man, Cybernetics* **11**, 826–831 (1981).
11. D. I. Milgram, Region extraction using convergent evidence, *Computer Graphics Image Processing* **11**, 1–12 (1979).
12. R. Ohlander, K. Price and R. Reddy, Picture segmentation by a recursive region splitting method, *Computer Graphics Image Processing* **8**, 313–333 (1978).
13. C. R. Brice and C. L. Fennema, Scene analysis using regions, *Artificial Intelligence* **1**, 205–226 (Fall 1970).
14. J. A. Feldman and Y. Yakimovsky, Decision theory and artificial intelligence: I. A. semantics based region analyzer, *Artificial Intelligence* **5**, 349–371 (1974).
15. S. W. Zucker, Region growing: childhood and adolescence, *Computer Graphics Image Processing* **5**, 382–399 (1976).
16. S. L. Horowitz and T. Pavlidis, A graph-theoretic approach to picture processing, *Computer Graphics Image Processing* **7**, 282–291 (1978).
17. G. Coleman and H. C. Andrews, Image segmentation and clustering, *Proc. IEEE*, 773–785 (1979).
18. R. C. Smith and A. Rosenfeld, Threshold using relaxation, *IEEE Trans. Pattern Analysis Machine Intelligence* **3**, 598–605 (1981).
19. L. S. Davis and A. Mitchie, Edge detection in textures, *Computer Graphics Image Processing* **12**, 25–39 (1980).
20. Y. Shirai, Analyzing intensity arrays using knowledge about scenes, *in* "The Psychology of Computer Vision" (P. H. Winston, ed.), pp. 93–114, McGraw-Hill, New York, 1975.
21. S. Inokuchi and R. Nevatia, boundary detection in range pictures, *Proc. 5th Intl. Conference Pattern Recognition, Miami, Florida, Nov. 1980*, pp. 1301–1303 (1980).
22. D. Nitzan, A. E. Brain and R. O. Duda, The measurement and use of registered reflectance and range data in analysis. *Proc. IEEE* **65**, 206–220 (1977).
23. R. O. Duda, D. Nitzan and P. Barrett, Use of range and reflectance data to find planar surface regions, *IEEE Trans. Pattern Analysis and Machine Intelligence* **1** (3), 259–271 (1979).
24. M. Oshima and Y. Shirai, A scene description method using three-dimensional information *Pattern Recognition* **11**, 9–17 (1979).

# Chapter **10**

# Two-Dimensional Shape Representation

LARRY S. DAVIS

Computer Vision Laboratory
University of Maryland
College Park, Maryland

## INTRODUCTION   I

This chapter contains an overview of research on representations for two-dimensional shapes. Such representations support applications in fields as diverse as robotics, reconnaissance, cartography, and architectural design. For example, in robotics, the appearance of an object in an image can be modeled using appropriate two-dimensional shape representations, and then instances of such objects can be recognized and quantitatively inspected by comparing their actual appearance in a specific image with their expected appearance as determined by the model.

Representations can be based on a description of the *boundaries* of the shape or of the *regions* comprising the shape. Representations can be *structural* in the sense that the shape (i.e., its boundaries or areas) is broken into pieces and properties of the pieces are encoded, or they can be *global*, in which case properties of the entire shape are encoded. Finally,

233

representations can be *monolithic* or *hierarchical*. Hierarchical representations ordinarily involve describing the shape at multiple, discrete scales, while monolithic representations explicitly encode only properties at a single scale.

This chapter will not discuss global shape representations, which are adequately described in textbooks such as that of Rosenfeld and Kak [1] and which are ordinarily only useful in situations where a shape is completely visible in a sensor's field of view and can be reliably segmented from an image. It is often the case that parts of an object are occluded by other objects in the field of view and that the segmentation produced by low-level vision operations contains errors. We therefore restrict our attention to structural models, considering boundary-based representations in Section II and region-based representations in Section III.

## II   BOUNDARY-BASED SHAPE REPRESENTATIONS

Boundary-based shape representations involve *segmenting* the shape boundaries into simple pieces and then constructing descriptions of both the individual pieces and the relationships between pieces. The segmentation can be computed by algorithms similar to edge-detection and region-growing algorithms that are used to segment two-dimensional images. The analog of edge detection is *corner detection* and is described in Section II.A. The analog of region growing is *piecewise approximation* and is described in Section II.B. Section II.C discusses hierarchical representations based on both corner detection and piecewise approximation.

## A   Corner Detection

A curve in a digital picture can be represented by a sequence of points $\{(x_i, y_i)\}$ or, more compactly, by its *chain code*. The chain code is a slope intrinsic representation for the curve. Given any pair of consecutive points on the curve, $(x_i, y_i)$, $(x_{i+1}, y_{i+1})$, there are only eight possible locations for $(x_{i+1}, y_{i+1})$ relative to $(x_i, y_i)$, so that the curve can be represented by a sequence of direction changes (or *chainlets*). Figure 1 contains a simple digital curve (Fig. 1a) and its chain-coded representation (Fig. 1b). The chain code is a compact representation for a digital curve, and many of the algorithms for corner detection and piecewise approximation described later can be applied directly to the chain code. For simplicity, however, we describe those algorithms in terms of the absolute positions of points along the contour. For a survey of algorithms that operate directly on the chain code, see Freeman [2].

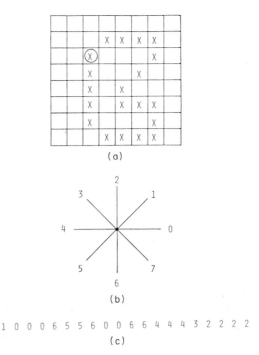

(a)

(b)

1 0 0 0 6 5 5 6 0 0 6 6 4 4 4 3 2 2 2 2

(c)

**Fig. 1.** Chain-code representation of a digital curve. (a) Digital curve—circled pixel is the starting point; (b) chain-code direction; (c) chain code for curve in (a).

Intuitively, corner points on a contour correspond to points of high curvature, so that the detection of corners first requires that we be able to compute an estimate of the curvature at points on the contour. A large number of techniques have been proposed for computing the curvature of digital curves. We will briefly describe a representative sample.

(1) A curve (ordinarily a biquadratic or a bicubic) can be fit to neighborhoods of points along the curve. The curvature of points along the original contour can then be estimated by the curvature of nearby points on the fitted curve (note that the fitted curve will not necessarily pass through any given contour point, especially if large neighborhoods of the contour are used to determine the curve). As a very simple example, a circle can be fit to neighborhoods of three or five points of the contour, and then the curvature of the circle can be used as an estimate of the curvature for the center point of the neighborhood.

(2) Lines can be fit to neighborhoods of the contour, and the curvature at any point on the contour can be computed from the difference of slopes of the lines fit to the two neighborhoods that meet at that point. One simple version of this approach is the so-called *k-curvature algorithm*. Here, for each point

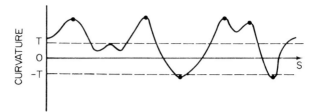

**Fig. 2.** Process of nonmaxima suppression. The curvature is thresholded absolutely at $T$ and positive maxima and negative minima are detected.

$(x_i, y_i)$ along the contour, we determine the unit vectors in the directions of the vectors joining $(x_i, y_i)$ to $(x_{i+k}, y_{i+k})$ and to $(x_{i-k}, y_{i-k})$ and take the dot product of those two unit vectors as an estimate of the curvature at the contour point. This algorithm was originally described by Rosenfeld and Johnston [3]; improvements were discussed by Rosenfeld and Weszka [4].

Once some measure of curvature has been estimated for all contour points, some selection criteria must be applied to those points to choose finally a set of corner points. Ordinarily, a two-stage procedure is applied to choose those corner points. First, some threshold is applied to the curvature estimates. This eliminates contour points whose curvature is absolutely too low to be considered as corner points. Second, a process of *nonmaxima supression* is applied to the remaining contour points to eliminate any points whose curvature estimates are not local maxima in a sufficiently large neighborhood of the contour. This second step is necessary because the curvature estimation algorithms all smooth the original contour to some extent and so tend to compute high curvature estimates not only at corner points but also in the neighborhood of corner points. See Fig. 2 for an illustration of the entire process.

## B   Piecewise Approximation

Piecewise approximation algorithms are analogous to region-based algorithms for two-dimensional images. Their goal is to segment the original contour into a small number of intervals that can be adequately represented by some simple model (e.g., a straight line). Piecewise approximation algorithms can be based on interval merging, interval splitting, or a combination of merging and splitting. The discussion that follows is illustrated using piecewise linear approximations; however, it is possible to construct higher-order approximations. The reader is referred to the excellent text by Pavlidis [5] for a comprehensive discussion of piecewise approximation algorithms and their relationship to computer vision and pattern recognition.

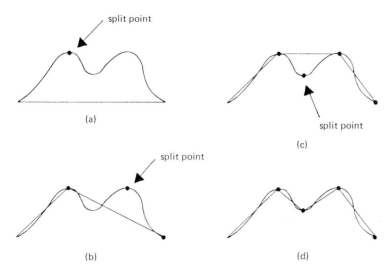

**Fig. 3.** Four stages of a splitting algorithm applied to a smooth curve.

Interval merging operates by first decomposing the contour into suffi-ciently small intervals and then iteratively applying a merging strategy to those intervals to construct larger intervals until further mergings would result in intervals not well fit by the model. The merging strategy can be either sequential, in which case a single initial interval is chosen as the "seed" for a segment and adjacent intervals are added to it as long as the goodness of fit is acceptable, or the strategy can be parallel, in which case all intervals are simultaneously compared against all adjacent intervals and a large subset of the possible merges are computed.

Interval splitting starts by first fitting a single curve to the entire contour. If the goodness of fit of that curve is sufficiently good, then the algorithm would terminate. Otherwise, the curve is split into pieces, and the fitting and testing process is applied recursively to each piece. Figure 3 contains a simple example of linear approximation by curve splitting base on an algorithm described by Ramer [6]. Here, a contour interval that is not well fit is split at the point of maximum departure from the approximating line.

Neither splitting nor merging by themselves is sufficient, however. Merging schemes are often inaccurate in the placement of boundaries between successive intervals. Consider, for example, interval merging using a sequen-tial merging strategy applied to a noiseless polygon. If any error is tolerated in the fit of a line to an interval, then the merging process will grow past a corner of the polygon until the error increases past threshold. Splitting schemes often lead to adjacent intervals that could be merged into longer intervals and still be adequately fit. An example is provided in Fig. 4. Therefore, it is desirable to employ a piecewise approximation algorithm that

**Fig. 4.** Splitting alone can lead to oversegmented curves: (a) original curve; (b) segments after two iterations of splitting—segments $b$ and $c$ should be merged.

employs a combined merging and splitting strategy. The reader is referred, again, to Pavlidis [5] for a detailed discussion of such algorithms.

## C    Hierarchical Boundary-Based Representations

Hierarchical representations are ordinarily more robust than monolithic representations and can be operated on more efficiently than monolithic representations. The hierarchy can be based on a variety of criteria; the most commonly used are goodness of fit, scale, and abstraction. We will illustrate each of these in the remainder of this section.

Ballard [7] introduced a hierarchical data structure called a *strip tree* as a representation for contours in cartographic applications. Each node in a strip tree represents an approximation by a single curve to a segment of the contour. This approximation is described by a *strip segment* (see Fig. 5). Here $x_b$ and $x_e$ correspond to the locations of the beginning and ending points of the contour segment represented by this strip segment. The orientation of the rectangle is determined by the slope of the line joining $x_b$ to $x_e$, and the width of the rectangle is chosen as small as possible so that it entirely includes the contour segment.

Each node in the strip tree has two sons. The contour segment represented at the father is partitioned into two pieces, and each son represents an approximation to one of those pieces. Figure 6 illustrates a curve and its corresponding strip tree.

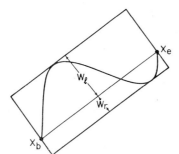

**Fig. 5.** Strip segment from $X_b$ to $X_e$. Here $W = W_l + W_r$ is the width of the segment.

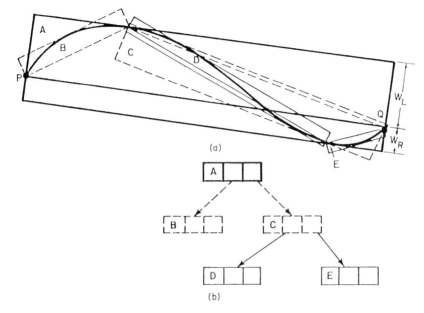

**Fig. 6.** Strip tree representation: (a) a curve and its decomposition into strips; (b) strip tree corresponding to (a). (From Samet [16].)

Ballard describes many algorithms that operate on the strip tree representation of contours. These include algorithms for deciding if two contours intersect, for deciding if a point is interior to a closed contour, and for computing the union of two strip trees.

Brady [8] describes a hierarchical shape representation based on a scale-space [9] analysis of the shape. Ideal models for shape primitives (corners, ends, bumps, and inflections) are developed by using a slope-intrinsic representation of the shape. For example, a model for a corner between two smooth curves is

$$f(s) = \begin{cases} \kappa_1 s + c & \text{if } s < 0 \\ \kappa_2 s + c + \phi & \text{if } s > 0 \end{cases}$$

where $\kappa_1$ and $\kappa_2$ are the curvatures of the two curves and $\phi$ is the angular discontinuity at the point where the two curves meet.

Next, the analytical form for the derivatives of the ideal model, as a function of scale, are determined. If the scale is determined by smoothing the slope-intrinsic representation of the ideal shape primitive with a Gaussian of specific width, then for the corner model illustrated earlier and for the special case of $\kappa_1 = \kappa_2$, Brady shows that

$$(G_\sigma * f)''(s) = \frac{1}{\sqrt{2\pi}\sigma} \frac{-\phi \exp(-s^2/2\sigma^2)}{\sigma^2}$$

Finally, one develops a program to detect instances of the ideal shape features in actual contours based on observations of the properties of this function with respect to position and scale. For example, Brady points out that an ideal corner has the following properties.

(a)  Function has a zero-crossing at $s = 0$.
(b)  Distance between peaks is $d = 2\sigma$.
(c)  Height of the peaks is $h = |\phi|/\sigma^2\sqrt{2\pi e}$.

Brady [8] contains similar analyses for shape primitives, including ends, cranks, bumps, and inflections.

Finally, one can develop a hierarchical shape representation based on levels of abstraction, that is, elements of the representation at low levels would correspond to small, geometrically primitive pieces of the shape, while elements at higher levels would correspond to larger, geometrically more complicated pieces of the shape.

Such a representation is ordinarily expressed using a grammatical framework. Fu [10] contains a comprehensive discussion of the design and application of a variety of shape grammars to shape recognition and analysis problems.

In order to illustrate the potential complexity of such grammars, we describe the stratified context-free shape grammars used by Davis and Henderson [11].

A stratified, context-free shape grammar is a 4-tuple $(T, N, P, S)$, where

(a)  $T$ is the set of terminal symbols,
(b)  $N$ is the set of nonterminal symbols,
(c)  $P$ is the set of productions, or rules, and
(d)  $S$ is the set of start symbols.

We will let $V = N \cup T$ be the set of vocabulary symbols. Associated with every symbol $v \in V$ is a level number, $\ln(v)$. A terminal symbol has level number 0. Each nonterminal symbol has a level number from 1 to $n$ associated with it. A start symbol has level $n$, and for any rule

$$v := v_1 v_2 \cdots v_r$$

if $\ln(v) = k$, then $\ln(v_i) = k - 1$, $i = 1, \ldots, r$. Vocabulary symbols themselves have nontrivial structure since they represent geometric entities. A vocabulary symbol has

(a)  a unique name by which the symbol is identified,
(b)  a set of *attachment points* which are used to join this symbol with other symbols to create more complex geometric entities, and
(c)  a set of *semantic constraints* which describe geometric properties of the symbol, such as its length, principle axis, etc.

```
<engine>{e1,e2}[a,span] :=
        <engine side>{e1´,e2´}[a´]
    +<engine front>{e1´´,e2´´}[a´´]
    +<engine side>{e1´´´,e2´´´}[a´´´]
```

$A$     : [Join(e1´ or e2´,e1´´) and Join(e1´´´ or e2´´´,e2´´)
        or Join(e1´´´ or e2´´´,e1´´) and Join(e1´ or e2´,e2´´)]

$C$     : [Parallel(a´,a´´´) and Length(a´) = Length(a´´´)
        and Perpendicular(a´,a´´)
        and Parallel(a´´,Vector(Midpt(a´),Midpt(a´´´)))]

$G_a$   : [Set(e1,Unjoined(e1´,e2´)) and
        Set(e2,Unjoined(e1´´´,e2´´´)) or
        Set(e1,Unjoined(e1´´´,e2´´´)) and
        Set(e2,Unjoined(e1´,e2´))]

$G_s$   : [a :=(a´+a´´´)/2 and span :=a´´].

**Fig. 7.** Production for an airplane engine. (From Davis and Henderson [11]. © 1981 IEEE.)

Finally, associated with each production $v := v_1 v_2 \cdots v_r$ of the grammar are

(a)   conditions specifying how the attachment points of the $v_i$ must be connected in order for the production to apply,

(b)   constraints on the geometric properties of the $v_i$,

(c)   rules for generating the attachment points of $V$ if the rule is applicable, and

(d)   rules for generating the semantic constraints on the geometric properties of $v$.

Figure 7 contains one production from the general grammar for airplanes used in Davis and Henderson [11].

## AREA-BASED SHAPE REPRESENTATIONS   III

Area-based shape representations involve decomposing the interior of a shape into simple subshapes and describing the properties of the individual pieces and relationships between the pieces. The decomposition can be either a partition or a covering. We discuss these two possibilities in the following two subsections.

## A   Partitions

A complex region can be partitioned into pieces of fixed shape (e.g., circles or squares) or pieces having simple shapes (e.g., convex pieces, star-shaped pieces, symmetric pieces). We first discuss pieces of fixed shape.

O'Rourke and Badler [12] describe an algorithm for covering a three-dimensional volume with spheres. This algorithm can be easily modified to cover a two-dimensional region with circles. Asano and Asano [13] describe an algorithm that computes the minimum partition of a polygon into trapezoids, and Ferrari et al. [14] present an algorithm for computing the minimal rectangular decomposition of a rectangular blob.

There has been significant interest, recently, in *quadtree* representations of two-dimensional shape. A quadtree represents a partition of a shape into maximal blocks of size $2^i \times 2^i$. Since the quadtree is developed from a binary image representation of the shape, the exact structure of the quadtree depends on the position and orientation of the shape in the array. This makes quadtrees difficult to use for shape recognition. Grotsky [15] presents an algorithm for determining the optimal placement of a region for constructing its quadtree; the optimality criteria are the number of nodes in the quadtree.

Figure 8, from Samet [16], shows a region, a binary array containing the region, the block decomposition of the region, and the quadtree representation of the blocks.

The important computational advantage of quadtrees is that most operations on shapes represented as quadtrees have complexity depending on the number of blocks in the quadtree and not on the number of pixels in the binary representation of the region. Efficient algorithms exist for computing the intersection, union, set difference, distance transform, genus, etc., of shapes from their quadtree representation. (See Samet [16] for an extensive discussion.) Samet [16] also presents an algorithm for constructing a quadtree from a binary array. Dyer [17] discusses converting between chain code and quadtree, while Hunter and Steiglitz [18] contain an algorithm for converting between a polygon and a quadtree.

It is also possible to partition a shape into convex pieces. Pavlidis [5] describes several algorithms that compute such convex decompositions. Partitions into convex subshapes have not yet turned out to have significant practical importance.

## B   Coverings

The symmetric or medial axis transform (Blum [19]) is a covering of a shape by a set of maximal disks that touch at least two points on the

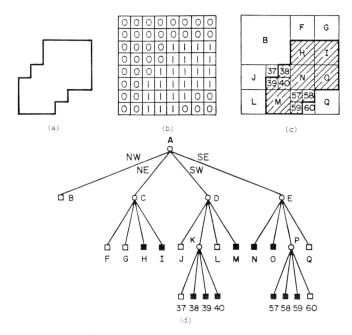

**Fig. 8.** (a) Region, (b) its binary array, (c) its maximal blocks (blocks in the image are shaded), and (d) the corresponding quadtree. (From Samet [16].)

boundary of the shape. The shape can, in principle, be reconstructed from the loci of the disk centers and knowledge of the disk radii.

Montanari [20] presents an algorithm for explicitly constructing the medial axis of a polygon. The loci of the disk centers, in this case, form straight line segments and parabolic arcs.

Chapter 11.2.1 of Rosenfeld [1] contains an algorithm for computing an approximation to the medial axis for a digital shape (i.e., a binary array). This algorithm is very efficient since it requires only two passes over the entire image. However, the digital medial axis produced is not ordinarily connected. Arcelli *et al.* [21] present an algorithm for computing a connected medial axis for a digital shape.

Blum originally proposed the medial axis as a model for describing biological growth and form. Attempts have been made to develop methods for shape recognition based on the medial axis transform. However, the medial axis transform is extremely sensitive to even small changes in the shape, and so much efforts have not been very successful.

It is also possible to decompose a shape into star-shaped regions. A region is star shaped if it contains a point that can "see" all other points in the region (i.e., the line segment joining that point and any other point in the shape is entirely contained in the shape). Shapiro and Haralick [22] describe a graph theoretic clustering algorithm for decomposing a digital shape into (nearly) star-shaped regions. Avis [23] contains an algorithm for decomposing a polygon into star-shaped regions. O'Rourke [24] shows that decomposition of a polygon into a *minimal* number of star-shaped regions is NP-hard. O'Rourke [24] also describes other NP-hard polygon decomposition problems.

## IV  CONCLUSIONS

While the previous two sections discussed algorithms which constructed either boundary-based or region-based shape representations, there have been several recent attempts to develop shape representations which combine both region-based and boundary-based descriptions. Brady [25] describes an approach to region decomposition based on what he refers to as *smooth local symmetries* and discusses how this could be combined with a hierarchical boundary representation (the curvature primal sketch discussed in Section II.C). Mumford and Latto [26] discuss an interesting proposal for an integrated region–boundary shape representation.

This overview has not discussed two important and interrelated problems—shape recognition and shape databases. There has been a significant amount of research on shape recognition, but the important problem of organizing large numbers of shape representations into a single database that supports partial shape matching without exhaustive search and comparison has not received adequate attention.

## REFERENCES

1. A. Rosenfeld and A. Kak, "Digital Picture Processing," 2nd Ed. Academic Press, New York, 1982.
2. H. Freeman, Computer processing of line drawing images, *Computer Surveys* **6**, 57–97 (1974).
3. A. Rosenfeld and E. Johnston, Angle detection on digital curves, *IEEE Trans. Computers* **22**, 875–878 (1973).
4. A. Rosenfeld and J. S. Weszka, An improved method of angle detection on digital curves, *IEEE Trans. Computer* **24**, 940–941 (1975).
5. T. Pavlidis, "Structural Pattern Recognition." Springer Publ., New York, 1977.
6. U. Ramer, An iterative procedure for the polygonal approximation of plane curves, *Computer Graphics Image Processing* **1**, 244–256 (1972).
7. D. H. Ballard, Strip trees: a hierarchical representation for curves, *Commun. ACM* **24**, 310–321 (1981).
8. H. Asada and M. Brady, The curvature primal sketch, *Proc. Workshop Computer Vision, Annapolis, Maryland*, 8–17 April 1984 (1984).
9. A. Witkin, Scale space filtering, *Proc. 7th Intl. Joint Conf. Aritifical Intelligence*, 1983, pp. 1010–1021 (1983).

10. K. S. Fu, Introduction to syntactic pattern recognition, *in* "Syntactic Pattern Recognition Applications," (K. S. Fu, ed.), pp. 1–31. Springer, Berlin, 1977.
11. L. S. Davis and T. C. Henderson, Hierarchical constraint processes for shape analysis, *IEEE Trans. Pattern Analysis Machine Intelligence* **3**, 265–277 (1981).
12. J. O'Rourke and N. Badler, Decomposition of three-dimensional objects into spheres, *IEEE Trans. Pattern Analysis Machine Intelligence* **1**, 295–305 (1979).
13. T. Asano and T. Asano, Minimum partition of polygon regions into trapezoids, Symposium on Foundations Computer Science, *1983*, pp. 233–241 (1983).
14. L. Ferrari, P. V. Sankar, and J. Sklansky, Minimal rectangular partition of digitized blobs, *Proc. 5th Intl. Conf. Pattern Recognition, 1980*, pp. 1040–1043 (1980).
15. W. I. Grotsky and R. Jain, Optimal quadtrees for image segments, *IEEE Trans Pattern Analysis Machine Intelligence* **5**, 77–83 (1983).
16. H. Samet, The quadtree and related hierarchical data structures, *ACM Computing Surveys* **16**, 187–260 (1984).
17. C. R. Dyer, A Rosenfeld, and H. Samet, Region representation: boundary codes from quadtrees, *Commun. ACM* **23**, 171–179 (1980).
18. G. M. Hunter and K. Steiglitz, Operations on images using quadtrees, *IEEE Trans. Pattern Analysis Machine Intelligence* **1**, 145–153 (1979).
19. H. Blum, A transformation for extracting new descriptors of shape, *in* "Models for the Perception of Speech and Visual Form," (W. Wathen-Dunn, ed.), pp. 362–380. M.I.T. Press, Cambridge, Massachusetts, 1967.
20. U. Montanari, Continuous skeletons from digitized images, *J. Assoc. Computing Mach.* **4**, 534–549 (1969).
21. C. Arcelli, L. P. Cordella, and S. Levialdi, From local maxima to connected skeletons, *IEEE Trans. Pattern Analysis Machine Intelligence* **3**, 134–143 (1981).
22. L. G. Shapiro and R. M. Haralick, Decomposition of two-dimensional shapes by graph theoretic clustering, *IEEE Trans. Pattern Analysis Machine Intelligence* **1**, 10–20 (1979).
23. D. Avis and G. T. Toussaint, An efficient algorithm for decomposing a polygon into star shaped polygons, *Pattern Recognition* **13**, 395–398 (1981).
24. J. O'Rourke and K. J. Supowit, Some NP-hard polygon decomposition problems, *IEEE Trans. Information Theory* **29**, 181–190 (1983).
25. M. Brady, Smoothed local Symmetries and local frame propagation, *Proc. Pattern Recognition Image Processing, 1982*, pp. 629–633 (1982).
26. A. Latto, D. Mumford, and J. Shah, The representation of shape, *Proc. Workshop on Computer Vision: Representation and Control, 1984*, pp. 183–191 (1984).

# Chapter **11**

# Statistical Image Texture Analysis

ROBERT M. HARALICK

Machine Vision International
Ann Arbor, Michigan

INTRODUCTION **I**

The advent of automatic image analysis resulted in two fundamentally different approaches to texture analysis: the statistical approach and the structural approach. The statistical approach generates parameters to characterize the stochastic properties of the spatial distribution of gray levels in an image. The structural approach analyzes visual scenes in terms of the organization and relationships among its substructures. In this chapter we present a survey of the representative literature regarding statistical texture analysis. However, we do include references to structural techniques for completeness. Thorough reviews of texture models and approaches have been presented by Haralick [1] and Ahuja and Rosenfeld [2].

247

**HANDBOOK OF PATTERN RECOGNITION
AND IMAGE PROCESSING**

Ehrich and Foith [3] summarize the main issues in texture analysis. These issues are listed in the general historical order that researchers have been concerned with them.

(1)   Given a textured region, determine to which of a finite number of classes does the region belong.
(2)   Given a textured region, determine a description or model for it.
(3)   Given an image having many textured areas, determine the boundaries between the differently textured regions.

Issue (1) has to do with the pattern recognition task of texture feature extraction. Issue (2) has to do with generative models of texture. Issue (3) has to do with using what we know about issues (1) and (2) in order to perform a texture segmentation of an image. In the remainder of this section we provide a brief historical elaboration of issues (1) and (2).

Early work in image texture analysis sought to discover useful features that had some relationship to the fineness and coarseness, contrast, directionality, roughness, and regularity of image texture. Tamuro, Mori, and Yamawaki [4] discuss the relationship of such descriptive measures to human visual perception. Typically, an image known to be texturally homogeneous was analyzed, and the problem was to measure textural features by which the image could be classified. For example, using microscopic imagery, discrimination between eosinophils and large lymphocytes was accomplished by using a texture feature for cytoplasm and a shape feature of the cell nucleus [5]. By using aerial imagery, discrimination of areas having natural vegetation and trees from areas having man-made objects, buildings, and roads [6] was accomplished using textural features. These statistical textural feature approaches included use of the autocorrelation function, the spectral power density function, edgeness per unit area, spatial gray-tone co-occurrence probabilities, gray-tone run-length distributions, relative extrema spatial distributions, and mathematical morphology.

Later approaches to image texture analysis sought a deeper understanding of what image texture is by the use of a generative image model. Given a generative model and the values of its parameters, it is possible to synthesize homogeneous image texture examples associated with the model and the given value of its parameters. This association provides a theoretical and visual means of understanding the texture. Image texture analysis then amounts to verification and estimation. First, it must be verified that a given image texture sample is consistent with or fits the model. Then the values of the model parameters must be estimated on the basis of the observed sample. Autoregressive moving-average time-series models (extended to two dimensions), Markov random fields, and mosaic models are examples of some of the model-based techniques.

In Section II we give a brief illustration of texture examples. Section III is the body of the paper and reviews and classifies the published literature on statistical texture analysis.

## TEXTURE EXAMPLES    II

To motivate our discussion of image texture, we illustrate how texture manifests itself on aerial imagery. We will see from these examples that spatial environments can be understood as being spatial distributions of various area-extensive objects having characteristic size and reflectance or emissive qualities and that the spatial organization and relationships of the area-extensive objects appear as gray-tone spatial distributions on imagery taken of the environment.

Figure 2, taken from Lewis [9], illustrates how texture relates to geomorphology. Here, we examine some plains, low hills, high hills, and mountains in the Panama and Columbia area as seen on some Westinghouse AN/APQ97 $K$-band radar imagery.

The plains have apparent relief of 0–50 m, the hills have apparent relief of 50–350 m, and the mountains have apparent relief of more than 350 m. The low hills have little dissection and are generally smooth, convex surfaces, whereas the high hills are highly dissected and have prominent ridge crests.

The mountain texture is distinguishable from the hill texture on the basis of the extent of radar shadowing (black tonal areas). The mountains have shadowing over more than half the area and the hills have shadowing over less than half the area. The hills can be subdivided from low to high on the basis of the abruptness of tonal change from terrain front slope to terrain back slope.

Figure 2, taken from McDonald [7], illustrates how texture relates to geology. Here, we examine some igneous and sedimentary rocks in Panama as seen on some Westinghouse AN/APQ97 $K$-band radar imagery. Figures 2i,k,l show a fine-textured drainage pattern, which is indicative of nonresistant, fine-grained sedimentary rocks. The coarser texture of Figure 2h, left and diagonal, is indicative of coarse-grained sediments. A massive texture with rugged and peaked divides (Figs. 2a,b,c,d,e) is indicative of igneous rocks. When erosion has nearly base leveled an area, the texture takes on the hummocky appearance of Fig. 2c.

Figure 3, taken from Haralick and Anderson [8], illustrates how texture relates to land use categories. Here, we examine five land use categories as they appear on panchromatic aerial photography. Notice how the texture of the wooded area is coarser and more definite than the scrub area. The swamps and marsh generate finer textures than those generated from wood

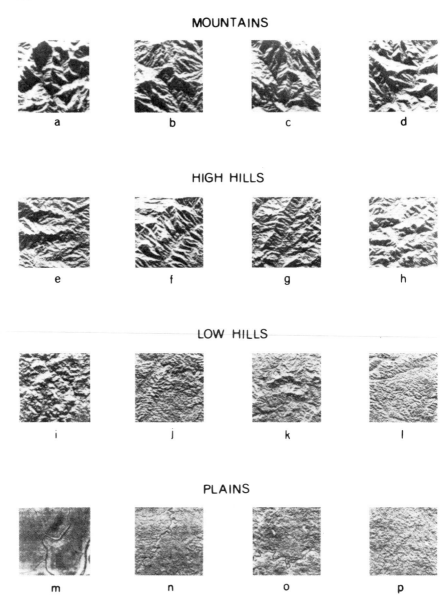

**Fig. 1.** K-band radar imaging illustrating how texture relates to geomorphology. (From Lewis [9].)

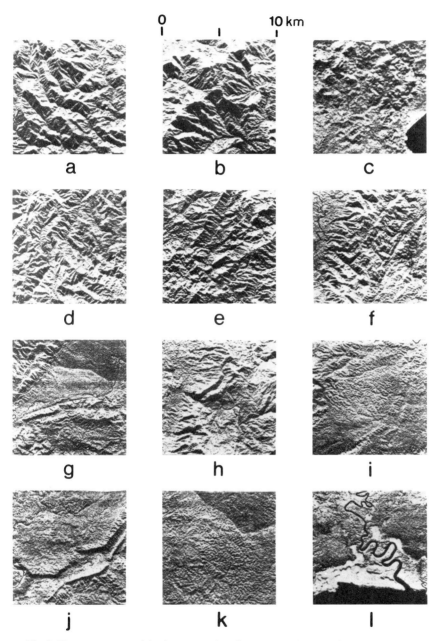

**Fig. 2.** Textures generated by igneous and sedimentary rocks on *K*-band radar imagery. (From McDonald [7].)

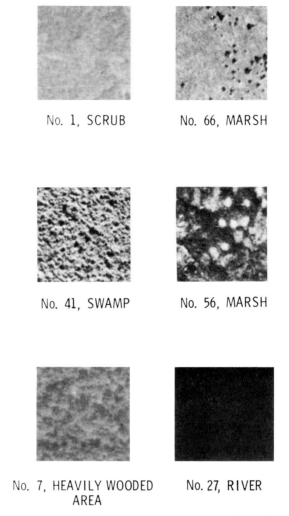

No. 1, SCRUB                    No. 66, MARSH

No. 41, SWAMP                   No. 56, MARSH

No. 7, HEAVILY WOODED           No. 27, RIVER
AREA

**Fig. 3.** Natural–environmental scenes illustrating how texture relates to land use categories in panchromatic aerial photography. No. 1, ETL No. 815-N2; No. 66, ETL No. 43-T3B; No. 41, ETL No. 43-TB; No. 56, ETl No. 53-T3A; No. 7, ETL No. 697-N1A; No. 27, ETL No. 88-R. (From Haralick and Anderson [8].)

or scrub areas. The swamp texture is finer and shows more gradual gray-tone change than the marsh-generated textures.

Figures 4–6 illustrate how the same environment can generate a variety of textures within the same texture type. Figure 4 shows five environments where the vegetation both increases in size and disperses. Figure 5, taken in the Pisgah Crater area, shows five environments where the vegetation

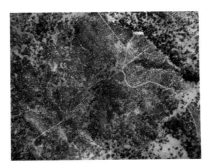

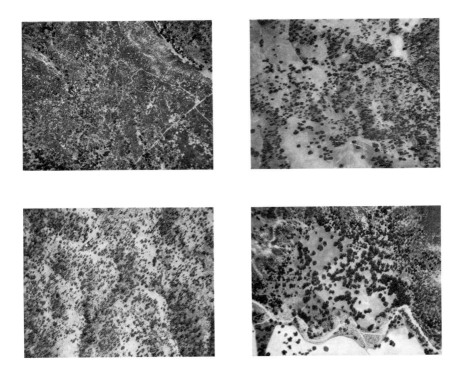

**Fig. 4.** Illustration of how the size and spacing of vegetation can cause texture to change from fine to coarse.

increases in size, probably due to greater available soil moisture. Figure 6, taken in the Pisgah Crater area, shows five environments of lava beds having increasingly distinct contrast.

In these examples it is clear that texture relates to land types and classification. Furthermore, any one land use type may generate a range of textures in the same texture grade on a scale of strong to weak, fine to coarse, etc.

**Fig. 5.** Negative images illustrating how the same kind of lava can have a different texture.

## III   STATISTICAL TEXTURE FEATURES

In this section we survey the following techniques of statistical textural measures: autocorrelation, orthogonal transforms, gray-tone co-occurrence, mathematical morphology, gradient analysis, relative extrema density, three-dimensional shape from texture, discrete Markov random fields, random mosaic models, and texture segmentation. In addition, we give a brief discussion of synthetic-texture image generation.

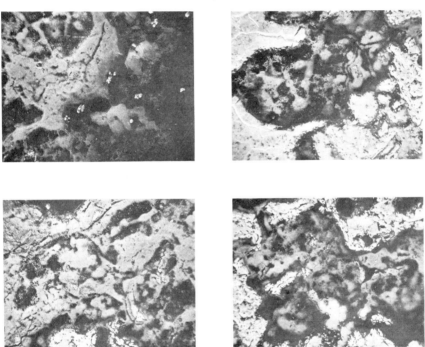

**Fig. 6.** Negative images illustrating how lava can have different textures.

### The Autocorrelation Function and Texture    **A**

From one point of view, texture relates to the spatial size of the tonal primitives on an image. Tonal primitives of larger size are indicative of coarser textures; tonal primitives of smaller size are indicative of finer textures. The autocorrelation function is a feature which tells about the size of the tonal primitives.

We describe the autocorrelation function with the help of a thought experiment. Consider two image transparencies which are exact copies of one another. Overlay one transparency on top of the other, and with a uniform source of light, measure the average light transmitted through the double transparency. Now translate one transparency relative to the other and measure only the average light transmitted through the portion of the image where one transparency overlaps the other. A graph of these measurements as a function of the $(x, y)$ translated positions and normalized with respect to the $(0, 0)$ translation depicts the two-dimensional autocorrelation function of the image transparency.

Let $I(u, v)$ denote the transmission of an image transparency at position $(u, v)$. We assume that outside some bounded rectangular region $0 \leq u \leq L_x$ and $0 \leq v \leq L_y$ the image transmission is zero. Let $(x, y)$ denote the 0 translation. The autocorrelation function $\rho$ for the image transparency $I$ is formally defined by

$$\rho(x, y) = \frac{\dfrac{1}{(L_x - |x|)(L_y - |y|)} \displaystyle\int\!\!\int_{-\infty}^{\infty} I(u, v)I(u + x, v + y)\, du\, dv}{\dfrac{1}{L_x L_y} \displaystyle\int\!\!\int_{-\infty}^{\infty} I^2(u, v)\, du\, dv}$$

where $|x| < L_x$ and $|y| < L_y$. Here we are assuming the image has mean 0.

If the tonal primitives on the image are relatively large, then the autocorrelation will drop off slowly with distance. If the tonal primitives are small, then the autocorrelation will drop off quickly with distance. To the extent that the tonal primitives are spatially periodic, the autocorrelation function will drop off and rise again in a periodic manner. The relationship between the autocorrelation function and the power spectral density function is well known: they are Fourier transforms of one another [10].

The tonal primitive in the autocorrelation model is the gray tone. The spatial organization is characterized by the correlation coefficient, which is a measure of the linear dependence one pixel has on another pixel displaced from it by the vector $(x, y)$.

An experiment was carried out by Kaizer [11] to see if the autocorrelation function had any relationship to the texture that photointerpreters see in images. He used a series of seven aerial photographs of an Arctic region and determined the autocorrelation function of the images with a spatial correlator that worked in a manner similar to the one envisioned in our thought experiment. Kaizer assumed the autocorrelation function was circularly symmetric and computed it only as a function of radial distance. Then, for each image, he found the distance $d$ such that the autocorrelation function $\rho$ at $d$ took the value $1/e$ (i.e., $\rho(d) = 1/e$).

Kaizer then asked 20 subjects to rank the 7 images on a scale from fine detail to coarse detail. He correlated the rankings with the distances corresponding to the $(1/e)$th value of the autocorrelation function. He found a correlation coefficient of 0.99. This established that, at least for his data set, the autocorrelation function and the subjects were measuring the same kind of textural features.

Kaizer noticed, however, that even though there was a high degree of correlation between $\rho^{-1}(1/e)$ and subject rankings, some subjects put first what $\rho^{-1}(1/e)$ put fifth. Upon further investigation, he discovered that a relatively flat background (indicative of high frequency or fine texture) can be interpreted as a fine-textured or coarse-textured area. This phenomena is not unusual and actually points out a fundamental characteristic of texture: it cannot be analyzed without a reference frame of tonal primitive being stated or implied. For any smooth gray-tone surface, there exists a scale such that when the surface is examined, it has no texture. Then, as resolution increases, it takes on a fine texture and then a coarse texture. In Kaizer's situation, the resolution of his spatial correlator was not good enough to pick up the fine texture which some of his subjects did in an area that had a weak but fine texture.

## Orthogonal Transformations    B

Spatial frequency characteristics of two-dimensional images can be expressed by the autocorrelation function or by the power spectra of those images. Both may be calculated digitally and/or implemented in a real-time optical system.

Lendaris and Stanley [12, 13] used optical techniques to perform texture analysis on a database of low-altitude photographs. They illuminated small circular sections of those images and used the Fraunhoffer diffraction pattern to generate features for identifying photographic regions. The major discriminations of concern to these investigators were those of man-made roads, intersections of roads, buildings, and orchards.

Feature vectors extracted from these diffraction patterns consisted of 40 components. Twenty of the components were mean energy levels in concentric annular rings of the diffraction pattern, and the other 20 components were mean energy levels in $9°$ wedges of the diffraction pattern. Greater than $90\%$ classification accuracy was reported using this technique.

Cutrona, Leith, Palermo, and Porcello [14] present a review of optical processing methods for computing the Fourier transform. Goodman [15], Preston [16], and Shulman [17] also present comprehensive reviews of Fourier optics in their books. Swanlund [18] discusses the hardware specifications for a system using optical techniques to perform texture analysis.

Gramenopoulos [19] used a digital Fourier transform technique to analyze aerial images. He examined subimages of $32 \times 32$ pixels and determined that for a LANDSAT image over Phoenix, spatial frequencies between 3.5 and 5.9 cycles/km contained most of the information required to discriminate among terrain types. An overall classification accuracy of 87 % was achieved using image categories of clouds, water, desert, farms, mountain, urban, river bed, and cloud shadows. Horning and Smith [20] used a similar approach to interpret aerial multispectral scanner imagery.

Bajscy [21] and Bajscy and Lieberman [22, 23] computed the two-dimensional power spectra of a matrix of square image windows. They expressed the power spectrum in a polar coordinate system of radius versus angle. They determined that directional textures tend to have peaks in the power spectrum along a line orthogonal to the direction of the texture. Bloblike textures tend to have peaks in the power spectrum at radii associated with the sizes of the blobs. This work also shows that texture gradients can be measured by determining the trends of relative maxima of radii and angles as a function of the position of the image window whose power spectrum is being analyzed. For example, as the power peaks along the radial direction tend to shift toward larger values, the image surface becomes more finely textured.

In general, features based on Fourier power spectra have been shown to perform more poorly than features based on second-order gray-level co-occurrence statistics [24] or those based on first-order statistics of spatial gray-level differences [25, 26]. The presence of aperture effects has been hypothesized to account for part of the unfavorable performance by Fourier features compared to space-domain gray-level statistics [27], although experimental results indicate that this effect, if present, is minimal. However, D'Astous and Jernigan [28] argue that the reason for the poorer performance is that earlier studies using the Fourier transform features used summed spectral energies within band- or wedge-shaped regions in the power spectrum. They argue that additional discriminating information can be obtained from the power spectrum in terms of characteristics such as regularity, directionality, linearity, and coarseness. The degree of regularity can be measured by the relative strength of the highest non-dc peak in the power spectrum. Other peak features include the Laplacian at the peak, the number of adjacent neighbors of the peak containing at least 50 % of the energy in the peak, the distance of the peak from the origin, and the polar angle of the peak. In the comparative experiment reported by D'Astous and Jernigan, the peak features yielded uniformly greater interclass difference than the co-occurrence features, and the co-occurrence features yielded uniformly greater interclass distances than the summed Fourier energy features.

Pentland [29] computed the discrete Fourier transform for each block of $8 \times 8$ pixels of an image and determined the power spectrum. He then used a linear regression technique on the log of the power spectrum as a function of frequency to estimate the fractal dimension $D$. For gray-tone intensity surfaces of textured scenes which satisfy the fractal model [30], the power spectrum satisfies

$$P(f) = Cf^{-1(2D+1)}$$

Pentland reported a classification accuracy of 84.4% on a texture mosaic using fractal dimensions computed in two orthogonal directions.

Transforms other than the Fourier transform can be used for texture analysis. Kirvida [31] compared the fast Fourier, Hadamard, and Slant transforms for textural features on aerial images of Minnesota. Five classes (hardwood trees, conifers, open space, city, and water) were studied using $8 \times 8$ subimages. A 74% correct classification rate was obtained using only spectral information. This rate increased to 98.5% when textural information was also included in the analysis. These researchers reported no significant difference in the classification accuracy as a function of which transform was employed.

The simplest orthogonal transform that can be locally applied is the identity transformation. Lowitz [32, 33] and Carlotto [34] suggest using the local histogram for textural feature extraction. Lowitz uses window sizes as large as $16 \times 16$. Corlotto uses window sizes as large as $33 \times 33$.

## Gray-Tone Co-Occurrence    C

Textural features can also be calculated from a gray-level spatial co-occurrence matrix. The co-occurrence $(Pi, j)$ of gray tones $i$ and $j$ for an image $I$ is defined as the number of pairs of resolution cells (pixels) having gray levels $i$ and $j$, respectively, and which are in a fixed spatial relationship, such as a fixed distance apart or a fixed distance and a fixed angle. The co-occurrence matrix can be normalized by dividing each entry by the sum of all of the entries in the matrix. Conditional probability matrices can also be used for textural feature extraction, with the advantage that these matrices are not affected by changes in the gray-level histogram of an image, only by changes in the topological relationships of gray levels within the image.

Formally, let $S$ be the set of all pairs of pixels in the given spatial relation. Then

$$P(m, n) = |\{((i, j), (k, l)) \in S \mid I(i, j) = m \text{ and } I(k, l) = n\}|$$

Zucker [35] suggested using a distance $d$ for the spatial relationship which maximizes a chi-square statistic of $P$. Julesz [36] was the first to use co-occurrence statistics in visual human texture discrimination experiments. Zobrist and Thompson [37] used co-occurrence statistics in a Gestalt grouping experiment. Darling and Joseph [38] used statistics obtained from nearest-neighbor gray-level transition probability matrices to measure textures using spatial intensity dependence in satellite images taken of clouds. Deutsch and Belknap [39] used a variant of co-occurrence matrices to describe image texture. Bartels and Wied [40], Bartels et al. [41], and Wied et al. [42] used one-dimensional co-occurrence statistics for the analysis of

cervical cells. Rosenfeld and Troy [43], Haralick [44], and Haralick *et al.*
[24] suggested the use of spatial co-occurrence for arbitrary distances and
directions. Galloway [45] used gray-level run-length statistics to measure
texture. These statistics are computable from co-occurrence assuming that
the image is generated by a Markov process. Chen and Pavlidis [46] used the
co-occurrence matrix in conjunction with a split-and-merge algorithm to
segment an image at textural boundaries. Tou and Chang [47] used statistics
from the co-occurrence matrix, followed by a principal components eigenvector dimensionality reduction scheme, to reduce the dimensionality of the
classification problem.

Statistics that Haralick *et al.* [24] compute from such co-occurrence
matrices of equal-probability quantized images (see also Conners and
Harlow [48]) have been used to analyze textures in satellite images [49]. An
89% classification accuracy was obtained. Additional applications of this
technique include the analysis of microscopic images [6], pulmonary radiographs [50], and cervical cell, leukocyte, and lymph node tissue section
images [51, 52].

Commonly used statistics of the co-occurrence probabilities include energy, entropy, contrast, correlation, and homogeneity. They are defined as

$$\text{Energy} \qquad \sum_i \sum_j P(i,j)^2$$

$$\text{Entropy} \qquad \sum_i \sum_j P(i,j) \log P(i,j)$$

$$\text{Contrast} \qquad \sum_i \sum_j (i-j)^2 P(i,j)$$

$$\text{Correlation} \qquad \sum_i \sum_j (i-u_x)(j-u_y)P(i,j) \Big/ \sigma_x \sigma_y$$

$$\text{Homogeneity} \qquad \sum_i \sum_j \frac{P(i,j)}{1+|i-j|}$$

Vickers and Modestino [53] argue that using features of the co-occurrence
matrix in a classification situation is surely suboptimal and that better results
would be obtained by using the co-occurrence matrix directly in a maximum-
likelihood classifier. They report better than 95% correct identification
accuracy in distinguishing between tree bark, calf leather, wool, beach sand,
pigskin, plastic bubbles, herringbone weave, raffia, and wood grain textures.

Bacus and Gose [5] used a gray-tone difference variant of the co-
occurrence matrix to help distinguish between eosimophils and lymphocytes.
They used the probability of a given contrast occurring in a given spatial
relationship as a textural feature. This gray-tone difference probability can be
defined in terms of the co-occurrence probabilities by

$$P(d) = \sum_i \sum_j P(i,j), \qquad |i-j| = d$$

For a coarse texture, the probability of a small contrast $d$ will be much higher than the probability of a small contrast for a fine texture. Bacus and Gose used statistics of the differences between a pixel on a red image and a displaced pixel on a blue image. Rosenfeld *et al.* [54] also suggest using multispectral difference probabilities. Haralick and Shanmugam [24] used multispectral co-occurrence probabilities.

Weszka *et al.* [25] used the contrast, energy, entropy, and mean of $P(d)$ as texture measures and report that they do about as well as the co-occurrence probabilities. Sun and Wee [55] suggested a variant of the gray-level difference distribution. They fix a distance $d$ and a contrast $c$ and determine the number of pixels each having gray tone $g$ and each having $n$ neighbors that are within distance $d$ and within contrast $c$. That is,

$$P(g, n) = \#\{(i, j) | I(i, j) = g \text{ and } \#\{(k, l) | \rho((i, j), (k, l)) \le d$$

$$\text{and } |I(i, j) - I(k, l)| \le c\} = n\}$$

From $P(g, n)$ they compute a variety of features, such as entropy and energy. They report an $85\%$ classification accuracy on distinguishing between textures of three different geological terrain types on Landsat imagery. Wechsler and Kidode [56] and Wechsler and Citron [57] used the gray-tone difference probabilities to define a random-walk model for texture. See DeSouza [58] and Percus [59] for some comments about the random-walk model.

Haralick [60] illustrated a way to use co-occurrence matrices to generate an image in which the value at each resolution cell is a measure of the texture in the resolution cell's neighborhood. All of these studies produced reasonable results on different textures. Conners and Harlow [61, 26] concluded that this spatial gray-level dependence technique is more powerful than spatial frequency (power spectra), gray-level difference (gradient), and gray-level run-length methods [45] of texture quantitation.

Dyer *et al.* [62] and Davis *et al.* [63] computed co-occurrence features for local properties such as edge strength maxima and edge direction relationships. They suggested computing gray-tone co-occurrence only involving those pixels near edges. Zucker and Kant [64] also suggested using generalized co-occurrence statistics. Terzopoulos and Zucker [65] reported a $13\%$ increase in accuracy when combining gray-tone co-occurrence features with edge co-occurrence features in the diagnosis of osteogenesis imperfecta from images of fibroblast cultures.

Davis [66] computed co-occurrence probabilities for spatial relationships parameterized by angular orientation. He defined the polarogram to be a statistic of these co-occurrence probabilities as a function of the angular orientation. See also Chetverikov [67]. Chetverikov [68] used co-occurrence statistics as a function of displacement to determine texture regularity.

**D  Mathematical Morphology**

Mathematical morphology is the study of shape. For texture analysis, the shapes analyzed are the shapes of the tonal primitives. The morphological approach to the texture analysis of binary images was proposed by Matheron [69] and Serra and Verchery [70]. This approach requires the definition of a structuring element (i.e., a set of pixels constituting a specific shape, such as a line, a disk, or a square) and the generation of binary images, which result from the translation of the structuring element through the image and the erosion of the image by the structuring element. The textural features can be obtained from the new binary images by counting the number of pixels having the value 1. This mathematical morphology approach of Serra and Matheron is the basis of the Leitz Texture Analyser (TAS) [71–73] and the Cyto Computer [74]. A broad spectrum of applications has been found for this quantitative analysis of microstructures method in materials science and biology.

Watson [75] summarizes this approach to texture analysis. Let $H$, a subset of resolution cells, be the structuring element. We define the translate of $H$ by row–column coordinates $(r, c)$ as $H(r, c)$, where

$$H(r, c) = \{(i, j) \mid \text{for some } (r', c') \in H, i = r + r', j = c + c'\}$$

Then the erosion of $F$ by the structuring element $H$, written $F \ominus H$, is defined as

$$F \ominus H = \{(m, n) \mid H(m, n) \subseteq F\}$$

The eroded image $J$ obtained by eroding $F$ with structuring element $H$ is a binary image where pixels take the value 1 for all resolutions cells in $F \ominus H$. Textural properties can be obtained from the erosion process by appropriately parameterizing the structuring element ($H$) and determining the number of elements of the erosion as a function of the parameter's value.

For example, a two-pixel structuring element can be parameterized by fixing a row distance and column distance between two pixels. The normalized area of the erosion as a function of row and column distance is the autocorrelation function of the binary image. Another one-parameter structuring element is a disk. Another is a one-pixel width annulus. The parameter in both cases is the radius. The area of the eroded image as a function of the parameter provides a statistical description of the shape distribution of the image.

The dual operation to erosion is dilation. The dilation of $F$ by structuring element $H$, written $F \oplus H$, is defined by

$$F \oplus H = \{(m, n) \mid \text{for some } (i, j) \in F \text{ and } (r, s) \in H, \quad m = i + r \text{ and } n = j + s\}$$

Compositions of erosions and dilations determine two other important morphological operations which are idempotent and are duals of one another: openings and closings. The opening of $F$ by $H$ is defined by $(F \ominus H) \oplus H$. The closing of $F$ by $H$ is defined by $(F \oplus H) \ominus H$.

The number of binary 1 pixels of the opening as a function of the size parameter of the structuring element can determine the size distribution of the grains in an image. We just take $H_d$ to be a line-structuring element of length $d$ or a disk-structuring element of diameter $d$. We can then define the granularity of the image $F$ by

$$G(d) = 1 - \frac{|(F \ominus H_d) \oplus H_d|}{|F|}$$

where $|F|$ means the number of elements in $F$. $G(d)$ measures the properties of grain pixels which cannot be contained in some translated structuring element of size $d$ which is entirely contained in the grain and which contains the given pixel. Thus, it measures the proportion of pixels participating in grains having a size smaller than $d$.

Sternberg [76] has extended the morphological definition of erosion to gray-tone images. The erosion of gray-tone image $I$ by gray-tone structuring element $H$ produces a gray-tone image $J$ which is defined by

$$J(r, c) = \min_{(i, j)}\{I(r + i, c + j) - H(i, j)\} = (I \ominus H)(r, c)$$

The dilation of gray-tone image $I$ by gray-tone structuring element $H$ produces a gray-tone image $J$ which is defined by

$$J(r, c) = \max_{(i, j)}\{I(r - i, c - j) + H(i, j)\} = (I \oplus H)(r, c)$$

The gray-tone opening is defined as a gray-tone erosion followed by a gray-tone dilation. The gray-tone closing is defined as a gray-tone dilation followed by a gray-tone erosion. Commonly used gray-tone structuring elements include rods, disks, cones, paraboloids, and hemispheres.

Peleg et al. [77] use gray-tone erosion and dilation to determine the fractal surface of the gray-tone intensity surface of a textural scene. They define the scale $k$ volume of the blanket around a gray-tone intensity surface $I$ to be

$$V(k) = \sum_{(r, c)} (I \oplus H^k)(r, c) - (I \ominus H^k)(r, c)$$

where $H^k$ is the dilation of $H$ with itself $k$ times and $H$ is defined over the five-pixel cross neighborhood, taking the value of 1 for the center pixel and 0 elsewhere. The fractal surface area $A$ at scale $k$ is then defined by

$$A(k) = [V(k) - V(k - 1)]/2$$

The fractal signature $S$ at scale $k$ is then defined by

$$S(k) = \frac{d}{d \log k} \log A(k) = \frac{k A'(k)}{A(k)}$$

They compare the similarity between textures by the weighted distance $D$ between their fractal signatures:

$$D = \sum_k (S_1(k) - S_2(k))^2 \log\left[\frac{k + (1/2)}{k - (1/2)}\right]$$

Werman and Peleg [78] give a fuzzy set generalization to the morphological operators. Meyer [79] and Lipkin and Lipkin [80] have demonstrated the capability of morphological textural parameters in biomedical image analysis. Theoretical properties of the erosion operator as well as other operators are presented by Matheron [81], Serra [82, 83], and Lantuejoul [84]. The importance of this approach to texture analysis is that properties obtained by the application of operators in mathematical morphology can be related to physical three-dimensional shape properties of the materials imaged.

## E   Gradient Analysis

Rosenfeld and Troy [43] and Rosenfeld and Thurston [85] regard texture in terms of the amount of "edge" per unit image area. An edge can be detected by a variety of local mathematical operators which essentially measure some property related to the gradient of the image intensity function. Rosenfeld and Thurston use the Roberts gradient and then compute, as a measure of texture for any image window, the average value of the Roberts gradient taken over all of the pixels in the window. Sutton and Hall [86] extend this concept by measuring the gradient as a function of the distance between pixels. An 80% classification accuracy was achieved by applying this textural measure in a pulmonary disease identification experiment.

Related approaches include Triendl [87], who smoothed the image using $3 \times 3$ neighborhood, then applied a $3 \times 3$ digital Laplacian operator, and finally smoothed the image with an $11 \times 11$ window. The resulting texture parameters obtained from the frequency-filtered image can be used as a discriminatory textural feature. Hsu [88] determines edgeness by computing variance-like measures for the intensities in a neighborhood of pixels. He suggested as a textural feature the deviation of the intensities in a pixel's neighborhood from both the intensity of the central pixel and from the average intensity of the neighborhood. The histogram of a gradient image was used to generate texture properties of the nuclei of leukocytes by Landeweerd and Gelsema [89]. Rosenfeld [90] generated an image whose intensity is proportional to the edge per unit area of the original image. This transformed image is then further processed by gradient transformations prior to textural feature extraction. Harris and Barrett [91] used vector dispersion as a feature to identify cloud types. They reported a 72% identification accuracy. Lu *et al* [92] used a 2 × 2 operator which estimates the second mixed partial derivative to make the resulting image be stationary, and they then used a first-order autoregressive moving-average model to describe the texture of the filtered image. Carlotto [34] computed the gradient and gradient angle at each pixel and used the histograms of these for textural features. Shen and Wong [93] similarly used the local gradient and gradient angle histogram for a variety of window sizes.

## Relative Extrema Density    F

Rosenfeld and Troy [43] suggested the number of extrema per unit area for a texture measure. They defined extrema in a purely local manner, allowing plateaus to be considered as extrema. Ledley [94] and Rotolo [95] also suggested computing the number of extrema per unit area as a texture measure. They, as well as Mitchell *et al.* [96], suggested operating on a smoothed image to eliminate extrema due to noise. (See also Carlton and Mitchell [97] and Ehrich and Foith [3, 98].

One problem with simply counting all extrema in the same extrema plateau as extrema is that extrema per unit area is not sensitive to the difference between a region having a few large plateaus of extrema and many single-pixel extrema. The solution to this problem is to only count an extrema plateau once. This can be achieved by locating some central pixel in the extrema plateau and marking it as the extrema associated with the plateau. Another way of achieving this is to associate a value $1/N$ for every extrema in an $N$-pixel extrema plateau.

In the one-dimensional case, there are two properties that can be associated with every extrema: its height and its width. The height of a maximum can be defined as the difference between the value of the maxima and the highest adjacent minimum. The height (depth) of a minimum can be defined as the difference between the value of the minimum and the lowest adjacent maximum. The width of a maximum is the distance between its two adjacent minima. The width of a minimum is the distance between its two adjacent maxima. Osmon and Saukar [99] use the mean and standard deviation of the spacing between relative extrema to characterize the surface texture of materials.

Two-dimensional extrema are more complicated than one-dimensional extrema. One way of finding extrema in the full two-dimensional sense is by the iterated use of some recursive neighborhood operators propagating extrema values in an appropriate way. Maximally connected areas of relative extrema may be areas of single pixels or may be plateaus of many pixels. We can mark each pixel in a relative extrema region of size $N$ with the value $h$, indicating that it is part of a relative extrema having height $h$, or mark it with the value $h/N$, indicating its contribution to the relative extrema area. Alternatively, we can mark the most centrally located pixel in the relative extrema region with the value $h$. Pixels not marked can be given the value 0. Then for any specified window centered on a given pixel, we can add up the values of all pixels in the window. This sum divided by the window size is the average height of extrema in the area. Alternatively, we could set $h$ to 1 and the sum would be the number of relative extrema per unit area to be associated with the given pixel.

Going beyond the simple counting of relative extrema, we can associate properties to each relative extremum. For example, given a relative maximum, we can determine the set of all pixels reachable only by the given relative maximum and not by any other relative maxima by monotonically decreasing paths. This set of reachable pixels is a connected region and forms a mountain. Its border pixels may be relative minima or saddle pixels.

The relative height of the mountain is the difference between its relative maximum and the highest of its extractor border pixels. its size is the number of pixels which constitute it. Its shape can be characterized by features such as elongation, circularity, and symmetric axis. Elongation can be defined as the ratio of the larger to smaller eigenvalue of the $2 \times 2$ second-moment matrix obtained from the coordinates of the border pixels [100, 101]. Circularity can be defined as the ratio of the standard deviation to the mean of the radii from the center of the region to its border [60]. The symmetric axis feature can be determined by thinning the region down to its skeleton and counting the number of pixels in the skeleton. For regions that are elongated, it may be important to measure the direction of the elongation or the direction of the symmetric axis.

## G  Shape from Texture

Image texture gradients on oblique photography can be used to estimate the surface orientation of the observed three-dimensional object. The first work of this kind was done by Carel et al. [102] and Charton and Ferris [103]. They did a conceptual design of a system called VISILOG, which could direct a freely moving vehicle through an undetermined environment. One important kind of guidance information needed by such a vehicle is the surface orientation of the surface over which the vehicle is moving. The basis of the design was an analysis that related surface slant to the texture gradient in the perspective projection image. Assumptions were that a stochastically regular surface is observed through a perspective projection and the number of texture elements could be measured along two parallel line segments perpendicular to the view direction and two parallel line segments parallel to the view direction. They measured the number of texture elements in a line by measuring the number of changes in brightness along the line. The number of changes in brightness is the number of relative extrema.

Witkin [104], apparently unaware of the earlier work, derived equations for the slant and tilt angle of a planar surface under orthographic projection by measuring the distribution of tangent direction of zero-crossing contours. Witkin divided the tangent angle interval $[0, \pi]$ into $n$ equal intervals, the $i$th interval being $[(i-1)\pi/n, i\pi/n]$ $(i = 1, \ldots, n)$, and measured the number $k(i)$ of tangent directions that fall in the $i$th interval. The slant angle $s$ and the tilt angle $t$ of the observed surface is estimated to be that pair of values maximizing the a posteriori probability of $(s, t)$ given the observed $k(i)$, $i = 1, \ldots, n$. Davis et al. [105] indicated some mistakes in the Witkin paper and give the joint a posteriori probability of $(s, t)$ as proportional to

$$P(s, t/k(i), \ldots, k(n)) = \alpha \sin s \cos^n s / \prod_{i=1}^{n} \left\{ 1 - \sin^2 s \sin^2 \left[ \frac{(2i-1)\pi}{2n} - t \right] \right\}$$

They also gave a modified version of the two-dimensional Newton method for determining the $(s, t)$ achieving the maximization.

Other work that relates to surface orientation recovery from texture includes that of Kender [106], who described an aggregation Hough-related transform that groups together edge directions associated with the same vanishing point. An edge direction $E = (E_x, E_y)$ at position $P = (P_x, P_y)$ has coordinates $T = (T_x, T_y)$ in the transformed space where

$$T = \frac{\mathbf{E} \cdot \mathbf{P}}{\mathbf{E} \cdot \mathbf{E}} \, E$$

### Discrete Markov Random Fields   H

The Markov random-field model for texture assumes that the texture field is stochastic, stationary, and satisfies a conditional independence assumption. Let $\mathbf{R} \times \mathbf{C}$ be the spatial domain of an image, and for any $(r, c) \in \mathbf{R} \times \mathbf{C}$ let $N(r, c)$ denote the neighbors of $(r, c)$. Because the field is stationary, $(a, b) \in N(r, c)$ if and only if $(a + i, c + j) \in N(r + i, c + j)$. This means that the spatial neighborhood configuration is the same all over the image. There is an obvious difficulty with this condition holding at pixels near the image boundary. The usual way of handling the problem theoretically is to assume the image is wrapped around a torus. In this case, the canonical spatial neighborhood can be given as $N(0, 0)$.

The conditional independence assumption is that the conditional probability of the pixel given all the remaining pixels in the image is equal to the conditional probability of the pixel given just the pixels in its neighborhood. That is,

$$P(I(r, c)|I(i, j): (i, j) \in \mathbf{R} \times \mathbf{C}, (i, j) \neq (r, c))$$
$$= P(I(r, c)|I(i, j): (i, j) \in N(r, c))$$

Markov mesh models were first introduced into the pattern recognition community by Chow [107] and then Abend, et al. [108]. One important issue is how to compute the joint probability function $P(I(r, c): (r, c) \in \mathbf{R} \times \mathbf{C})$. Hassner and Sklansky [109] note that this can be done by identifying the conditional probability assumption with Gibbs ensembles, which are studied in statistical mechanics. Woods [110] showed that when the distributions are Gaussian, the discrete Gauss–Markov field can be written as an equation in which each pixel's value is a linear combination of the values in its neighborhood plus a correlated noise term. That is,

$$I(r, c) = \sum_{(i, j) \in N(0, 0)} I(r - i, c - j)h(i, j) + u(r, c)$$

where the coefficients of the linear combination are given by the function $h$ and $\{u(r, c)|(r, c) \subset \mathbf{R} \times \mathbf{C}\}$ represent a joint set of possible correlated Gaussian random variables. This equation has a lot of similarity to the autoregressive moving-average time-series models of Box and Jenkins [111]. Here the relationship would be expressed by

$$I(r, c) = \sum_{(i, j) \in N(0, 0)} I(r - i, c - j)h(i, j) + \sum_{(i, j) \in N(0, 0)} u(r - i, c - j)k(i, j)$$

where $N(0, 0)$ represents a domain which contains only pixels occurring after $(0, 0)$ in the usual top-down raster scan order of an image. Hence, each term in the summation $I(r - i, c - j)$ contains only pixels occurring before pixel $(i, j)$ in the raster scan order. The first summation is called the autoregressive term and the second term is called the moving-average term. When $N(0, 0)$ contains pixels occurring before and after $(0, 0)$ in the raster scan order, the model is called a simultaneous autoregressive model.

It is apparent that the discrete Markov random-field model is a generalization of time-series autoregressive moving-average models, which were initially explored for image texture analysis by McCormick and Jayaramamurthy [112], Tou and Chang [113], Tou et al. [114], and Deguchi and Morishita [115]. Related papers include Delp et al. [116], Tou [117], Chen [118], Faugeras [119], Therrien [120], and Jau et al. [121]. Issues concerning the estimation of $h$ from texture samples can be found in Kashyap and Challappa [122]. DeSouza [123] develops a chi-square test to discriminate microtextures described by autoregressive models.

Pratt [124], Pratt et al. [125], and Faugeras and Pratt [126] consider only the autoregressive term with independent noise and rewrite the autoregressive equation as

$$I(r, c) - \sum_{(i, j) \in N(0, 0)} I(r - i, c - j)h(i, j) = u(r, c)$$

Here, $\{u(r, c)|(r, c) \in \mathbf{R} \times \mathbf{C}\}$ represents independent random variables, not necessarily Gaussian. The left-hand side represents a convolution which decorrelates the image. Faugeras and Pratt characterize the texture by the mean, variance, skewness, and kurtosis of the decorrelated image, which is obtained either by estimating $h$ or by using a given gradient- or Laplacian-like operator to perform the decorrelation.

Another related approach is the texture energy transform approach described by Laws [127]. Laws applied a variety of linear operators on an image. Each operator had a small neighborhood for its domain. The squared operator outputs were then averaged with an equally weighted running-average window having a larger spatial domain than the original operators. The resulting values constituted the textural feature vector at each pixel. In the comparative experiment Laws performed, the co-occurrence features yielded an identification accuracy of 72%. The texture energy transform approach yielded an identification accuracy of 87%. Unser [128] noted that one could use a discrete orthogonal transform such as the discrete sine or discrete cosine transforms applied locally to each pixel's neighborhood instead of using the ad hoc linear operators of Laws. He indicated a classification accuracy above 96% with the discrete sine transform in distinguishing between textures of paper, grass, sand, and raffia. Ikonomopoulos and Unser [129] suggested local directional filters. Jernigan and D'Astous [130] computed a fast Fourier transform on windows and then used the entropy in different-sized regions for the normalized power spectrum for textural features.

## Random Mosaic Models  |

The random mosaic models are constructed in two steps. The first step provides a means of tessellating a plane into cells, and the second step assigns a property value to each cell. In the Poisson line model [131], the plane is tessellated by a random set of lines. Each cell is then a connected region whose boundary consists of line segments from the lines in the random set. In the occupancy model [132], a tesselation is produced by a random process which plants points in the plane. Each point determines a cell which consists of all points in the plane closest to the given planted point. In the Delauney model, a line segment is drawn between each pair of planted points whose corresponding cells in the occupancy model share a common border segment.

Schachter *et al.* [133] and Schachter and Ahuja [134] derived the statistical properties for these random mosaic models. Ahuja, *et al.* [135] compared properties of synthetically generated textures with their theoretical values. Schachter [136] summarized how texture characteristics are related to the texture's variogram and correlation function. Modestino *et al.* [137, 138] computed the power spectral density function for a plane tesselated by a random line process and in which the gray levels of one cell have a Markov dependence on the gray levels of the cells around them. They gave a maximum-likelihood texture discriminant for this mosaic model and illustrated its use on some sample images. Therrien [139] used an autoregressive model for each cell and, like Modestino *et al.* [137, 138], superimposed a Markov random field to describe transitions between cells. Other models include the Johnson–Mehl model [140] and the bombing model [141].

## J   Texture Segmentation

Most work in image texture analysis has been devoted to texture feature analysis of an entire image. However, it is apparent that an image is not necessarily homogeneously textured. An important image processing operation, therefore, is the segmentation of an image into regions, each of which are homogeneously textured. The constraint is that each pair of adjacent regions is differently textured. Bajcsy [142] was one of the first researchers to do texture segmentations for outdoor scenes. Her algorithm merged together small, nearly connected regions having similar local texture or color descriptors. For texture descriptors she used Fourier transform features. The descriptors for each region included an indication of whether the texture is isotropic or directional, the size of the texture element, and the separation between texture elements. If the texture was considered directional, then the description included the orientation.

Chen and Pavlidis [46] used the split-and-merge algorithm on the co-occurrence matrix of regions as the basis for merging. Let the four $2^{N-1} \times 2^{N-1}$ windows in a $2^N \times 2^N$ window have $C^{\text{NE}}$, $C^{\text{NW}}$, $C^{\text{SE}}$, and $C^{\text{SW}}$ for their respective co-occurrence matrices. Then, with only little error, the co-occurrence matrix $C$ of the $2^N \times 2^N$ window can be computed by

$$C(i, j) = \tfrac{1}{4}[C^{\text{NE}}(i, j) + C^{\text{NW}}(i, j) + C^{\text{SE}}(i, j), C^{\text{SW}}(i, j)]$$

Experiments done by Hong *et al.* [143] indicate that the error of this computation is minimal. The $2^N \times 2^N$ window is declared to be uniformly textured if, for the user specified threshold $T$,

$$\sum_{(i, j)} \max\{C^{\text{NE}}(i, j), C^{\text{NW}}(i, j), C^{\text{SE}}(i, j), C^{\text{SW}}(i, j)\}$$

$$- \min\{C^{\text{NE}}(i, j), C^{\text{NW}}(i, j), C^{\text{SE}}(i, j), C^{\text{SW}}(i, j)\} < T$$

Using this criteria Chen and Pavlidis begin the merging process using $16 \times 16$ windows. Any $16 \times 16$ window not merged is split into four $8 \times 8$ windows. The splitting continues until the window size is $4 \times 4$. The gray tones of the images were quantized to eight levels. Chen and Pavlidis [144] used a similar split-and-merge algorithm, with the correlation coefficients between vertically adjacent and horizontally adjacent pixels as the feature vectors. Modestino *et al.* [138] used a Poisson line process to partition the plane and assign gray levels to each region by a Gauss–Markov model using adjacent regions. They developed a maximum-likelihood estimator for the parameters of the process and show segmentation results on artificially generated images having three different texture types.

Connors, *et al.* [145] use six features from the co-occurrence matrix to segment an aerial urban scene into nine classes: residential, commercial/industrial, mobile home, water, dry land, runway/taxiway, aircraft parking, multilane highway, and vehicle parking. Their work is important because it combined the splitting idea of Chen and Pavlidis into a classification setting. Any window whose likelihood ratio for its highest likelihood class against any other class is too low is considered a boundary region and split. Any window whose likelihood ratio for its highest likelihood class against each other class is high enough is considered to be uniformly textured and assigned to the highest likelihood class.

Kashyap and Khotanzad [146] used a simultaneous autoregressive and circular autoregressive model for each $3 \times 3$ neighborhood of an image. Here each neighborhood produced a feature vector associated with the model. The set of feature vectors generated from the image was clustered and each pixel was labeled with the cluster label of the feature vector associated with its $3 \times 3$ neighborhood. Pixels associated with outlier feature vectors are given the cluster label of the majority of its labeled neighbors. Therrien [139] used an autoregressive model for each textured region and superimposed a Markov random field to describe the transitions of one region to another. He used maximum likelihood and maximum a posteriori estimation techniques to achieve a high-quality segmentation of aerial imagery.

### Synthetic-Texture Image Generation    K

There have been a variety of approaches to the generation of synthetic-texture images. Rather than giving a detailed description of each, we just provide a brief guide to some of the representative papers in the literature. McCormick and Jayaramamurthy [112] used a time-series model for texture synthesis, as do Tou *et al.* [114]. Yokoyama and Haralick [147] used a structured growth model to synthesize a more complex image texture. Pratt *et al.* [125, 148] developed a set of techniques for generating textures with identical means, variances, and autocorrelation functions but different higher-order moments. Gagalowicz [149] gave a technique for generating binary texture fields with prescribed second-order statistics. Chellappa and Kashyap [150] described a technique for the generation of images having a given Gauss–Markov random field.

Yokoyama and Haralick [151] described a technique that uses a Markov chain method. Schachter [152] used a long, crested wave model. Monne *et al.* [153] used an interlaced vertical and horizontal Markov chain method to generate a texture image. Garber and Sawchuk [154] used a best fit model instead of the *N*th-order transition probabilities to make good simulations of texture without exceeding computer memory limits on storing *n*th-order probability functions. Schmitt *et al.* [155] added vector quantization to the bidimensional Markov technique of Monne *et al.* [153] to improve the appearance of the texture image. Gagalowicz [156] described a texture synthesis technique that produces textures as they would appear on perspective projection images of three-dimensional surfaces. Ma and Gagalowicz [157] described a technique to synthesize artificial textures in parallel from a compressed data set and retain good visual similarity to natural textures.

## REFERENCES

1. R. M. Haralick, Statistical and structural approaches to texture, *Proc. IEEE* **67**(5) 786–804 (May 1979).
2. N. Ahuja and A. Rosenfeld, Mosaic models for textures, *IEEE Transactions on Pattern Analysis and Machine Intelligence* **PAMI-3** (1) 1–11 (1981).
3. R. Ehrich and J. Foith, Topology and semantics of intensity arrays, *in* "Computer Vision" (Hanson and Riseman, eds.). Academic Press, New York, 1978.
4. H. Tamura, S. Mori and T. Yamawaki, Textural features corresponding to Visual Perception, *IEEE Transactions on Systems, Man, and Cybernetics* **SMC-8** (6), 460–473 (1978).
5. J. Bacus and E. Gose, Leukocyte pattern recognition, *IEEE Transactions on Systems, Man, and Cybernetics* **SMC-2** (4), 513–526 (1972).
6. R. M. Haralick and K. Shanmugam, Combined spectral and spatial processing of ERTS imagery data, *Proc. 2nd Symp. Significant Results Obtained from Earth Resources Technology Satellite-1, NASA SP-327, NASA Goddard Space Flight Center, Greenbelt, Maryland, Mar. 5–9, 1973*, pp. 1219–1228 (1973).
7. H. C. McDonald, Geologic evaluation of radar imagery from Darien province Panama, *CRES Technical Report* **133-6**, University of Kansas Center for Research, Inc., Lawrence, Kansas (1970).
8. R. M. Haralick and D. E. Anderson, Texture–tone study with application to digitized imagery, *CRES Technical Report* **182-2**, University of Kansas Center for Research, Inc., Lawrence, Kansas (November 1971).
9. A. J. Lewis, Geomorphic evaluation of radar imaging of southeastern Panama and northwestern Columbia, *CRES Technical Report* **133-18**, University of Kansas Center for Research, Inc., Lawrence, Kansas (February 1971).
10. A. M. Yaglom, "Theory of Stationary Random Functions." Prentice-Hall, Englewood Cliffs, New Jersey, 1962.
11. H. Kaizer, A quantification of textures on aerial photographs, *Tech Note* **121**, AD 69484, Boston University Research Laboratories, Boston University, Boston, Massachusetts, 1955.

12. G. Lendaris and G. Stanley, Diffraction pattern sampling for automatic pattern recognition, *SPIE Pattern Recognition Studies Seminar Proc., June 9–10, 1969*, pp. 127–154 (1969).

13. G. Lendaris and G. Stanley, Diffraction pattern samplings for automatic pattern recognition, *Proceedings of the IEEE* **58**, 198–216 (1970).

14. L. J. Cutrona, E. N. Leith, C. J. Palermo, and L. J. Porcello, Optical data processing and filtering systems, *IRE Transactions on Information Theory* **15** (6), 386–400 (1969).

15. J. W. Goodman, "Introduction to Fourier Optics." McGraw-Hill, New York, 1968.

16. K. Preston, "Coherent Optical Computers." McGraw-Hill, New York, 1972.

17. A. R. Shulman, "Optical Data Processing." Wiley, New York, 1970.

18. G. D. Swanlund, Design requirements for texture measurements, *Proc. Two Dimensional Digital Signal Processing Conf., Oct. 1971* (1971).

19. N. Gramenopoulas, Terrain type recognition using ERTS-1 MSS images, *Rec. Symp. Significant Results Obtained from the Earth Res. Technol. Satellite, NASA SP-327, Mar. 1973*, pp. 1229–1241.

20. R. J. Horning and J. A. Smith, Application of Fourier analysis to multispectral/spatial recognition, *Management and Utilization of Remote Sensing Data ASP Symposium, Sioux Falls, South Dakota, Oct. 1973* (1973).

21. R. Bajcsy, Computer identification of visual surfaces *Computer Graphics and Image Processing* **2**, 118–130 (1973).

22. R. Bajcsy and L. Lieberman, Computer description of real outdoor scenes, *Proc. 2nd Intl. Joint Conf. on Pattern Recognition, Copenhagen, Denmark, Aug. 1974*, pp. 174–179 (1974).

23. R. Bajcsy and L. Lieberman, Texture gradient as a depth cue, *Computer Graphics Image Processing* **5**, No. 1, 52–67 (1976).

24. R. M. Haralick, K. Shanmugam, and I. Dinstein, Textural features for image classification, *IEEE Transactions on Systems, Man, and Cybernetics* **SMC-3**, 610–621 (1973).

25. J. Weszka, C. Dyer, and A. Rosenfeld, A comparative study of texture measures for terrain classification, *IEEE Transactions on Systems, Man, and Cybernetics* **SMC-6** (4), 269–285 (1976).

26. R. W. Conners and C. A. Harlow, A theoretical comparison of texture algorithms, *IEEE Transactions on Pattern Analysis and Machine Intelligence* **PAMI-2** (3), 204–222 (1980).

27. C. Dyer and A. Rosenfeld, Fourier texture features: suppression of aperture effects, *IEEE Transaction on Systems, Man, and Cybernetics* **SMC-6**, 703–705 (1976).

28. F. D'Astous and M. E. Jernigan, Texture discriminant based on detailed measures of the power spectrum, *7th Intl. Conference on Pattern Recognition, Montreal, July 30–Aug. 2, 1984*, pp. 83–86 (1984).

29. A. P. Pentland, Fractal-based description of natural scenes, *IEEE Transactions on Pattern Analysis and Machine Intelligence* **PAMI-6** (6), 661–675 (1984).

30. B. B. Mandelbrot, "The Fractal Geometry of Nature" Freeman, San Francisco, California, 1982.

31. L. Kirvida, Texture measurements for the automatic classification of imagery, *IEEE Transactions on Electromagnetic Compatibility* **18**, 38–42 (1976).

32. G. E. Lowitz, Can a local histogram really map texture information? *6th Intl. Conference on Pattern Recognition, Munich, Germany, Oct. 19–22, 1982*, pp. 293–297 (1982).

33. G. E. Lowitz, Can a local histogram really map texture information?, *Pattern Recognition* **16**, No. 2, 141–147 (1983).

34. M. J. Carlotto, Texture classification based on hypothesis testing approach, *7th Intl. Conference on Pattern Recognition, July 30–Aug. 2, 1984*, pp. 93–96 (1984).

35. S. W. Zucker, Finding structure in co-occurrence matrices for texture analysis, *Computer Graphics and Image Processing* **12**, 286–308 (1980).

36. B. Julesz, Visual pattern discrimination, *IRE Transactions on Information Theory* **8** (2), 84–92 (1962).

37. A. L. Zobrist and W. B. Thompson, Building a distance function in Gestalt grouping, *IEEE Transaction on Computers* **C-4** (7), 718–728 (1975).
38. E. M. Darling and R. D. Joseph, Pattern recognition from satellite altitudes, *IEEE Transactions on Systems, Man, and Cybernetics* **SMC-4**, 38–47 (1968).
39. W. S. Deutsch and N. J. Belknap, Texture descriptors using neighborhood information, *Computer Graphics and Image Processing* **1**, 145–168 (1972).
40. P. H. Bartels and G. L. Wied, Extraction and evaluation of information from digitized cell images, "Mammalian Cells: Probes and Problems," U.S. Technical Information Center, Springfield, Virginia, 1975.
41. P. Bartels, G. Bahr, and G. Weid, Cell recognition from line scan transition probability profiles, *Acta Cytol* **13**, 210–217 (1969).
42. G. Weid, G. Bahr, and P. Bartels, Automatic analysis of cell images, *in* "Automated Cell Identification and Cell Sorting" (Weid and Bahr, eds.), pp. 195–360. Academic Press, New York, 1970.
43. A. Rosenfeld and E. Troy, Visual texture analysis, *Tech. Rep.* **70-116**, University of Maryland, College Park, Maryland, (June 1970). [Also in *Conference Record for Symposium on Feature Extraction and Selection in Pattern Recognition, Argonne, Illinois.* (IEEE Publication 70C-51C) *Oct. 1970*, pp. 115–124 (1970).]
44. R. M. Haralick, A texture–context feature extraction algorithm for remotely sensed imagery, *Proc. 1971 IEEE Decision and Control Conf., Gainesville, Florida, Dec. 15–17, 1971*, pp. 650–657 (1971).
45. M. M. Galloway, Texture analysis using gray level run lengths, *Comput. Graphic Image Process* **4**, 172–179 (1975).
46. P. C. Chen and T. Pavlidis, Segmentation by texture using a co-occurrence matrix and a split-and-merge algorithm, *Tech. Rep.* **237**, Princeton University, Princeton, New Jersey, (January, 1978).
47. J. T. Tou and Y. S. Chang, Picture understanding by machine via textural feature extraction, *Proc. 1977 IEEE Conf. on Pattern Recognition and Image Processing, Troy, New York, June 1977* (1977).
48. R. W. Conners and C. A. Harlow, Equal probability quantizing and texture analysis of radiographic images, *Computer Graphics and Image Processing*, **8**, 447–463 (1978).
49. R. M. Haralick and K. Shanmugam, Combined spectral and spatial processing of ERTS imagery data, *J. remote Sensing Environment* **3**, 3–13 (1974).
50. Y. P. Chien and K. S. Fu, Recognition of X-ray picture patterns, *IEEE Transactions on Systems, Man, and Cybernetics* **SMC-4** (2), 145–156 (1974).
51. N. J. Pressman, N. J. Markovian analysis of cervical cell images, *Journal of Histochem. Cytochem.* **24**, No. 1, 138–144 (1976).
52. N. J. Pressman, Optical texture analysis for automated cytology and histology: A Markovian approach, Unpublished dissertation, Lawrence Livermore Laboratory Report UCRL-52155, Livermore, California (1976).
53. A. L. Vickers and J. W. Modestino, A maximum likelihood approach to texture classification, *IEEE Transactions on Pattern Analysis and Machine Intelligence* **PAMI-4** (1), (1982).
54. A. Rosenfeld, C. Wang, and A. Y. Wu, Multispectral texture, *IEEE Transactions on Systems, Man, and Cybernetics* **SMC-12** (1), 79–84 (1982).
55. C. Sun and W. G. Wee, neighboring gray level dependence matrix for texture classification, *Computer Vision, Graphics, and Image Processing* **23**, 341–352 (1983).
56. H. Wechsler and M. Kidode, A random walk procedure for texture discrimination, *IEEE Transactions on Pattern Analysis and Machine Intelligence* **PAMI-1** (3), 272–280 (1979).
57. H. Wechsler and T. Citron, Feature extraction for texture classification, *Pattern Recognition* **12**, 301–311 (1980).
58. P. DeSouza, P. A note on a random walk model for texture analysis, *Pattern Recognition* **16**, No. 2, 219–283 (1983).

59. J. K. Percus, On the Wechsler–DeSouza discussion, *Pattern Recognition* **16**, No. 2, 269–270 (1983).
60. R. M. Haralick, A textural transform for images, *Proc. IEEE Conf. Computer Graphics, Pattern Recognition, and Data Structure, Beverly Hills, May 14–15, 1975* (1975).
61. R. W. Conners and C. A. Harlow, Some theoretical considerations concerning texture analysis of radiographic images, *Proc. 1976 IEEE Conf. on Decision and Control* (1976).
62. C. R. Dyer, T. Hong, and A. Rosenfeld, Texture classification using gray level cooccurrence based on edge maxima, *IEEE Transactions on Systems, Man, and Cybernetics* **SMC-10** (3), 158–163 (1980).
63. L. S. Davis, M. Clearman, and J. K. Aggarwal, An empirical evaluation of generalized cooccurrence matrices, *IEEE Transactions on Pattern Analysis and Machine Intelligence* **PAMI-3** (2), 214–221 (1981).
64. S. W. Zucker and K. Kant, Multiple-level representations for texture discrimination, *Pattern Recognition and Image Processing Conference, Dallas, Texas, Aug. 3–5, 1981*, pp. 609–614 (1981).
65. D. Terzopoulos and S. W. Zucker, Detection of osteogenesis imperfecta by automated texture analysis, *Computer Graphics and Image Processing* **20**, 229–243 (1982).
66. L. S. Davis, Polarograms: a new tool for image texture analysis, *Pattern Recognition* **13**, No. 3, 219–233 (1981).
67. D. Chetverikov, Textural anisotrophy features for texture analysis, *Pattern Recognition and Image Processing Conference, Dallas, Texas, Aug. 3–5, 1981*, pp. 583–588 (1981).
68. D. Chetverikov, Measuring the degree of texture regularity, *7th International Conference on Pattern Recognition*, Montreal, Canada, 80–82 (July 30–August 2 1984).
69. G. Matheron, "Elements Pour Une Theorie das Milieux Poreux." Masson, Paris, 1967.
70. J. Serra and G. Verchary, Mathematical morphology applied to fibre composite materials, *Film Sci. Tech.* **6**, 141–158 (1973).
71. W. Muller and W. Hunn, Texture analyzer system, *Industrial Research*, 49–54 (1974).
72. W. Muller, The Leitz texture analyzes systems, *Leitz Sci. Tech. Inform.*, Suppl. 1, No. 4, 101–136, Wetzlar, Germany (April 1974).
73. J. Serra, Theoretical bases of the Leitz texture analysis system, *Leitz Sci. Tech. Inform.* Suppl. 1, No. 4, 125–136 Wetzlar, Germany, (April 1974).
74. S. Sternberg, Parallel architectures for image processing, *Proceedings of COMPSAC, 1979* (1979).
75. G. S. Watson, *Geological Society of America Memoir* **142**, 367–391 (1975).
76. S. Sternberg, Biomedical image processing, *Computer* **16** No. 1, 22–34 (1983).
77. S. Peleg, J. Naor, R. Hartley, and D. Avnir, Multiple resolution texture analysis and classification, *IEEE Transactions on Pattern Analysis and Machine Intelligence* **PAMI-6** (4) (1984).
78. M. Werman and S. Peleg, Multiresolution texture signatures using min–max operators, *7th Intl. Conference on Pattern Recognition, Montreal, July 30–Aug. 2*, 1984, pp. 97–99 (1984).
79. F. Meyer, Iterative image transformations for an automatic screening of cervical smears, *J. Histochem. Cytochem.* **27**(1), 128–135 (1979).
80. Lipkin and Lipkin (1974).
81. G. Matheron, "Random Sets and Integral Geometry." Wiley, New York, 1975.
82. J. Serra, One, two, three , . . . , infinity, *in* "Quantitative Analysis of Microstructures in Materials Science, Biology, and Medicine" (J. L. Chernant, ed.), Riederer-Verlag, Stuttgart, Germany, pp. 9–24.
83. J. Serra, "Image Analysis and Mathematical Morphology." Academic Press, New York, 1982.
84. C. Lantuejoul, Grain dependence test in a polycrystalline ceramic, *in* "Quantitative Analysis of Microstructures in Materials Science, Biology, and Medicine" (J. L. Chernant, ed.), pp. 40–50. Riederer-Verlag, Stuttgart, 1978.

85. A. Rosenfeld and M. Thurston, Edge and curve detection for visual scene analysis, *IEEE Transactions on Computers* **C-20** (5), 562–569 (1971).

86. R. Sutton and E. Hall, Texture measures for automatic classification of pulmonary disease, *IEEE Transactions on Computers* **C-21**, No. 1, 667–676 (1972).

87. E. E. Triendl, Automatic terrain mapping by texture recognition, *Proceedings of the 8th Intl. Symposium on Remote Sensing of Environment*, Environmental Research Institute of Michigan, Ann Arbor, Michigan (October 1972).

88. S. Hsu, A texture-tone analysis for automated landuse mapping with panchromatic images, *Proc. Am. Soc. Photogrammetry*, 203–215 (March 1977).

89. G. H. Landerweerd and E. S. Gelsema, The use of nuclear texture parameters in the automatic analysis of leukocytes, *Pattern Recognition* **10**, 57–61 (1978).

90. A. Rosenfeld, A note on automatic detection of texture gradients, *IEEE Transactions on Computers* **C-23** (10), 998–991 (1975).

91. R. Harris and E. C. Barrett, Toward an objective nephanalysis *Journal of Applied Meteorology* **17**, 1258–1266 (1978).

92. D. Lu, J. T. Tou, and T. Gu, A simplified procedure for statistical feature extraction in texture processing, *IEEE Pattern Recognition and Image Processing Conference, Dallas Texas, August 3–5, 1981*, pp. 589–592 (1981).

93. H. C. Shen and A. K. Wong, Generalized texture representation and metric, *Computer Vision Graphics and Image Processing* **23**, 187–206 (1983).

94. R. S. Ledley, Texture problems in biomedical pattern recognition, *Proceedings of the 1972 IEEE Conf. on Decision and Control and the 11th Symposium on Adaptive Processes, New Orleans, Louisiana, Dec. 1972* (1972).

95. L. S. Rotolo, Automatic texture analysis for the diagnosis of pneumoconiosis, *26th ACEMB, Minneapolis, Minnesota, Sept. 30–Oct. 4, 1973*, p. 32 (1973).

96. O. Mitchell, C. Myers, and W. Boyne, A max–min measure for image texture analysis, *IEEE Transactions on Computers* **C-25**, 408–414 (1977).

97. S. G. Carlton and O. Mitchell, Image segmentation using texture and grey level, *Pattern Recognition and Image Processing Conference, Troy, New York, June, 1977*, pp. 387–391 (1977).

98. R. Ehrich and J. P. Foith, Representation of random waveforms by relational trees, *IEEE Transactions on Computers* **C-25**, 725–736 (1976).

99. M. O. M. Osman and T. S. Saukar, The measurement of surface texture by means of random function technique, ISA ASI 75262, American Institute of Aeronautics and Astronautics Technical Information Service A 76-14546, pp. 355–360 (1975).

100. R. Bachi, Geostatistical analysis of territories, *Proc. 39th Session—Bulletin of the Intl. Statistical Inst., Vienna, Austria, 1973*, (1973).

101. Y. S. Frolov, Measuring the shape of geographical phenomena: a history of the issue, *Sov. Geog.: Rev. Transl.* **16**, (10), 676–687 (1975).

102. W. Carel, W. Purdy, and R. Lulow, The VISILOG: A bionic approach to visual space perception and orientation, *Proceedings 1961 National Aerospace Electronics Conference (NAECON), Dayton, Ohio, May 8–10, 1961*, pp. 295–300 (1961).

103. P. W. Charton and E. E. Ferris, "The VISILOG: A synthetic eye," General Electric Company Technical report Al-TDR-64-185, DDC No. AD611539, January, 1965.

104. A. P. Witkin, Recovering surface shape and orientation from texture, *Artificial Intelligence* **17**, 17–45 (1981).

105. L. S. Davis, L. Janos, and S. Dunn, Efficient recovery of shape from texture, *IEEE Transactions on Pattern Analysis and machine Intelligence* **PAMI-5** (5), 485–492 (1983).

106. J. R. Kender, Shape from texture: An aggregation transform that maps a class of textures into surface orientation, *Int. Joint Conference on Artificial Intelligence, Tokyo, Japan, Aug. 20–23, 1979*, pp. 475–480 (1979).

107. C. K. Chow, A recognition method using neighbor dependence, *IRE Transactions on Electronic Computers* **11**, 683–690 (1962).

108. K. Abend, T. J. Harley, and L. N. Kanal, Classification of binary random patterns, *IEEE Transactions on Information Theory* **IT-11** (4) 538–544 (1965).

109. M. Hassner and J. Sklansky, The use of Markov random fields as models of texture, *Computer Graphics and Image Processing* **12**, 357–370 (1980).

110. J. W. Woods, Two-dimensional discrete Markovian fields, *IEEE Transactions on Information Theory* **IT-18**, 232–240 (1972).

111. J. E. Box and G. M. Jenkins, "Time Series Analysis" Holden-Day, San Francisco, California, 1970.

112. B. H. McCormick and S. N. Jayaramamurthy, Time series model for texture synthesis, *Int. J. Comput. Inform. Sci.* **3** (4) 329–343 (1974).

113. J. T. Tou and Y. S. Chang, An approach to texture pattern analysis and recognition, *Proc. 1976 IEEE Conf. on Decision and Control, 1976* (1976).

114. J. T. Tou, D. B. Kao, and Y. S. Chang, Pictorial texture analysis and synthesis, *3rd Intl. Joint Conf. on Pattern Recognition, Coronado, California, Nov. 1976*, pp. 590–590e (1976).

115. K. Deguchi and I. Morishita, Texture characterization and texture-based image partitioning using two-dimensional linear estimation techniques, *IEEE Transactions on Computers* **27**, No. 8, 739–745 (1978).

116. E. J. Delp, R. L. Kashyap, and O. R. Mitchell, Image data compression using autoregressive time series models *Pattern Recognition* **11**, 313–323 (1979).

117. J. T. Tou, Pictorial feature extraction and recognition via image modeling, *Computer Graphics and Image Processing* **12**, 376–406 (1980).

118. C. H. Chen, On two-dimensional ARMA models for image analysis, *5th Intl. Conference on Pattern Recognition, Miami, Florida, Dec. 1–4, 1980*, pp. 1129–1131 (1980).

119. O. D. Faugeras, Autoregressive modeling with conditional expectation or texture synthesis, *5th Intl. Conference on Pattern Recognition, Miami, Florida, Dec. 1–4, 1980*, pp. 792–794 (1980).

120. C. W. Therrien, Linear filtering models for texture classification and segmentation, *5th Intl. Conference on Pattern Recognition, Miami, Florida, Dec. 1–4, 1980*, pp. 1132–1135 (1980).

121. Y. C. Jau, R. T. Chin, and J. A. Weinman, Time series modeling for texture analysis and synthesis with application to cloud field morphology study, *7th Intl. Conference on Pattern Recognition, Montreal, Aug. 1984*, pp. 1219–1221 (1984).

122. R. L. Kashyap and R. Chellappa, Decision rules for choice of neighbors in random field models of images, *Computer Graphics and Image Processing* **15**, 301–318 (1981).

123. P. DeSouza, Texture recognition via autoregression, *Pattern Recognition* **15**, No. 6, 471–475 (1982).

124. W. K. Pratt, Image feature extraction, "Digital Image Processing," pp. 471–513, Wiley (Interscience), New York, 1978.

125. W. K. Pratt, O. D. Faugeras, and A. Gagalowicz, Visual discrimination of stochastic texture fields, *IEEE Transactions on Systems, Man, and Cybernetics* **SMC-8** (11), 796–804 (1978).

126. O. D. Faugeras and W. K. Pratt, Decorrelation methods of texture feature extraction, *IEEE Transactions on Pattern Analysis and Machine Intelligence* **PAMI-2** (4), 323–332 (1980).

127. K. Laws, Textured image segmentation, USCIPI Report 940, Image Processing Institute, University of Southern California (January 1980).

128. M. Unser, Local linear transforms for texture analysis, *7th Intl. Conference on Pattern Recognition, Montreal, July 30–Aug. 2, 1984*, pp. 1206–1208 (1984).

129. A. Ikonomopoulos and M. Unser, A directional filtering approach to texture discrimination, *7th Intl. Conference on Pattern Recognition, July 30–Aug. 2, 1984*, pp. 87–89 (1983).

130. M. E. Jernigan and F. D'Astous, Entropy-based texture analysis in the spatial frequency domain *IEEE Transactions on Pattern Analysis and machine Intelligence* **PAMI-6**, No. 2, 237–243 (March 1984).

131.  R. Miles, Random polygons determined by random lines in the plane, *Proc. National Academy of Sciences U.S.A.* **52**, 901–907, 1157–1160 (1969).

132.  R. Miles, On the homogeneous planar Poisson point-process, *Math. Biosciences* **6**, 85–127 (1970).

133.  B. J. Schachter, A. Rosenfeld, and L. S. Davis, Random mosaic models for textures, *IEEE Transactions on Systems, Man, and Cybernetics* **SMC-8** (9), 694–702 (1978).

134.  B. Schachter and N. Ahuja, Random pattern generation process, *Computer Graphics and Image Processing* **10**, 95–114 (1979).

135.  N. Ahuja, T. Dubitzki, and A. Rosenfeld, Some experiments with mosaic models for images, *IEEE Transactions on Systems, Man, and Cybernetics* **SMC-10** (11), 744–749 (1980).

136.  B. Schachter, Long crested wave models, *Computer Graphics and Image Processing* **12**, 187–201 (1980).

137.  J. W. Modestino, R. W. Fries, and A. L. Vickers, Stochastic image models generated by random tessellations of the plane, *Computer Graphics and Image Processing* **12**, 74–98 (1980).

138.  J. W. Modestino, R. W. Fries, and A. L. Vickers, Texture discrimination based upon an assumed stochastic texture model, *IEEE Transactions on Pattern Analysis and Machine Intelligence* **PAMI-3** (5) 557–580 (1981).

139.  C. W. Therrien, An estimation-theoretic approach to terrain image segmentation, *Computer Vision, Graphics and Image Processing* **22**, 313–326 (1983).

140.  E. Gilbert, Random subdivisions of space into crystals, *Annals Math. Stat.* **33**, 958–972 (1962).

141.  P. Switzer, Reconstructing patterns for sample data, *Annals Math. Stat.* **38**, 138–154 (1967).

142.  R. Bajcsy, Computer description of textured surfaces, *3rd Intl. Joint Conf. on Artificial Intelligence, Stanford, California, Aug. 20–23, 1973*, pp. 572–578 (1973).

143.  T. Hong, A. Wu, and A. Rosenfeld, Feature value smoothing as an aid in texture analysis, *IEEE Transactions on Systems, Man, and Cybernetics* **SMC-10**, No. 8, 519–524 (August 1980).

144.  P. C. Chen and T. Pavlidis, Segmentation by texture using correlation *IEEE Transactions on Pattern Analysis and Machine Intelligence* **PAMI-5** (1), 64–69 (1983).

145.  R. W. Conners, Trivedi, and C. A. Harlow, (1984).

146.  R. L. Kashyap and A. Khotanzad, A stochastic model based technique for texture segmentation *7th int. Conference on Pattern Recognition, Montreal, July 30–Aug. 2, 1984*, pp. 1202–1205 (1984).

147.  Yokoyama and Haralick, Texture synthesis using a growth model, *Computer Graphics and Image Processing* **8**, 369–381 (1978).

148.  W. K. Pratt, O. D. Faugeras, and A. Gagalowicz, Applications of stochastic texture field models to image processing, *Proceedings of the IEEE* **69** (5), 542–551 (1981).

149.  A. Gagalowicz, A new method for texture fields synthesis: some applications to the study of human vision, *IEEE Transactions on Pattern Analysis and Machine Intelligence* **PAMI-3** (5), 520–533 (1981).

150.  R. Chellappa and R. L. Kashyap, Synthetic generation and estimation in random field models of images, *Proceedings of the 1981 Pattern Recognition and Image Processing Conference, Dallas, Texas, Aug. 3–5*, pp. 577–582 (1981).

151.  Yokoyama and Haralick, Texture pattern image generation by regular Markov chains, *Pattern Recognition* **11**, 225–254 (1979).

152.  B. Schachter, Model based texture measures, *IEEE Transactions on Pattern Analysis and Machine Intelligence* **PAMI-2** (2), 169–171 (1980).

153.  J. Monne, F. Schmitt, and C. Massaloux, Bidimensional texture synthesis by Markov chains, *Computer Graphics and Image Processing* **17**, 1–23 (1981).

154. D. Garber and A. A. Sawchuk, Texture simulation using a best fit model, *Pattern Recognition and Image Processing Conference, Dallas, Texas, Aug. 3–5, 1981*, pp. 603–608.
155. F. Schmitt, M. Goldberg, N. Ngwa-Ndifor, and P. Baucher, Texture representation and synthesis, *7th Intl. Conference on Pattern Recognition, Montreal, July 30–Aug. 2, 1984*, pp. 1222–1225 (1984).
156. A. Gagalowicz, Synthesis of natural textures on 3-D surfaces, *7th Intl. Conference on Pattern Recognition, Montreal, July 30–Aug. 2, 1984*, pp. 1209–1212 (1984).
157. Ma. S. and A. Gagalowicz, A parallel method for natural texture synthesis, *7th Intl. Conference on Pattern Recognition, Montreal, July 30–Aug. 2, 1984*, pp. 90–92 (1984).

# Chapter **12**

# Image Models

R. L. KASHYAP*

School of Electrical Engineering
Purdue University
West Lafayette, Indiana

* Partially supported by the Office of Naval Research under grant N00014-82K-0360.

281

# I  INTRODUCTION†

Image modeling refers to the development of representations for explaining the intensity distribution in a given image. There are various types of models, the models of each type being appropriate for one family of applications. Each model captures only some important aspects about the intensity distribution, and no single model can capture *all* the important aspects of the data. We will give a brief response to the perennial question, Why do we need image models? The models are useful in tasks such as edge detection, segmentation, texture recognition, synthesis of texture, texture boundary recognition, etc. For every basic image processing task like edge detection and segmentation, there is a plethora of algorithms usually derived on an ad hoc basis, often based on intuition. Each algorithm does assume a specific model of image, even though the model may not be explicitly stated. The performance of these algorithms can be compared theoretically when we recognize the underlying image models and discuss the validity of the built-in assumptions. It is as important to understand why certain algorithms fail as to appreciate the "success" of the successful algorithms. For instance, some popular image segmentation algorithms determine the segments by thresholding the image intensity. This procedure can work well only when there is a single object against a homogeneous background, the lighting conditions are good, and the noise is low. It cannot work well if the noise is substantial or if the scene is more complex. A careful analysis indicates the need for more accurate models for the intensity distribution.

A common misunderstanding regarding image modeling [1] is that the intensity is assumed to be constant over a homogeneous region with noise superposed. This statement is true only for very simple models. As a matter of fact, image modeling gives a quantitative answer to the question, What is a homogeneous scene? For example, if we have two photographs of the same beach having only sand, each image having completely different intensities, it is interesting to develop models for the two images that give invariant parameters uniquely associated with sand. Similarly, if we have a natural scene of a bay having both water and land, we have to inquire into models and algorithms that give the water–land boundary only without the micro-edges characteristic of a land scene or water scene. Such complex scenes need more complex models discussed later.

Many of the successful models are stochastic, and an often-heard quip is

---

† Notation: $r, c, i, j$: scalar integers. $s, t$: two-dimensional vectors with integer components specifying grid points. $y(s), y(r, c)$: intensity at the pixel $s = (r, c)$; $r$ stands for row component; $c$ stands for column component. $\lambda_1, \lambda_2$: frequency variables. $w(\cdot)$: independent random sequence. $\alpha, \beta, \gamma, \theta_i$: scalar coefficients. $\Omega$: a finite $M \times M$ grid $\{(r, c): 0 \leq r, c \leq M - 1\}$. $N$: a finite set of vectors $(r, c), (r, c) \neq (0, 0)$. $z = (z_1, z_2), z_1 = \exp(\sqrt{-1}\lambda_1), z_2 = \exp(\sqrt{-1}\lambda_2). A(z) = A(z_1, z_2)$: a scalar polynomial in $z_1$ and $z_2$.

that one cannot model a real-life scene by random numbers, a latter-day version of the saying "God does not play with dice." It is clearly inappropriate to call these models pure chance models—the pixel intensities of a realistic image cannot be represented by a sequence of independent random variables. A more appropriate terminology is "constrained chance models" [2]. The model will include all the relevant available structural information, and only those variables over which we do not have any information will be modeled by a sequence of independent random variables.

It was said earlier that different types of applications need different types of models. The methodology contains four steps. The first step is the recognition of the type of model appropriate to the given application, taking into account the inevitability of noise. The second step is the choice of a criterion for estimating the parameters in the model using the given image. The third step is the development of a decision rule for the given task, such as edge detection or texture boundary detection. The last step is a quantitative and qualitative analysis of the performance of the decision rule to do the given task.

It is well known that a given intensity distribution is caused by a variety of factors, such as lighting, shape of the surface, reflectance of the surface, shadows, etc. The model under discussion cannot take into account specific factors like reflectance. It is hoped that additional information can be incorporated into these models.

## REGION AND TEXTURE MODELS     II

A discrete two-dimensional image intensity function $y(r, c)$ can be viewed as a surface in three dimensions, where $r$ and $c$ assume only integral values, $r$ is the row number, and $c$ is the column number. Our intention is to develop various possible models for describing such surfaces. No image is smooth enough to be described by a purely deterministic model. Any realistic model is made up of a structural part which incorporates all the known information about the image and a pure noise part to account for those aspects of the image over which no knowledge is available. There are several types of models, each type of model being suitable for a specific class of images and a specific class of applications. Depending on the type of image and application, an appropriate image model has to be chosen. Before fitting a model to a given image, it is usually assumed that the image is homogeneous. A loose definition of homogeneity is that there exists a model such that it is valid over the entire image.

Models can be broadly divided into two groups, namely, descriptive and generative models. A descriptive model for an image summarizes the intensity distribution into a finite number of statistics. An example is the cooccurrence matrix [3] used in texture analysis. The generative model, on the other hand, allows one to synthesize an image obeying the given model by using the model description and a set of random numbers. We will restrict ourselves to generative models since they can be used for a variety of applications.

We can further divide the generative models into two classes. In the first class, the observed intensity function $y(r, c)$ is assumed to be the sum of a deterministic function $f(r, c)$ in $(r, c)$—usually polynomial or sinusoid—and an additive noise. In the second class, the image intensity function is generated as the output of a transfer function model whose input is a sequence of independent random variables. The transfer function represents the known structural information on the image surface; the independent random sequence accounts for the unknown part. Note that the neighboring pixels are highly correlated, unlike in the earlier case, and the transfer function accounts for the covariance. There are other types of models, such as mosaic models [4, 5].

## A  Facet Model and Its Variants

In the facet model, the observed intensity function $y(r, c)$ is the sum of a determinisitic function–polynomial in $(r, c)$ and an additive noise:

$$y(r, c) = \alpha r + \beta c + \gamma + w(r, c)$$

Higher-order terms such as $r^2$, $rc$, etc., can be introduced with appropriate coefficients. The sequence $\{w(r, c)\}$ is independent and has zero mean and variance $\rho$. The parameters $\alpha$, $\beta$ $\gamma$ can be estimated by fitting the model to a given image $\{y(r, c), (r, c) \in \Omega\}$ via a least squares approach, where $\Omega$ is the finite grid $\{0 \leq r, c \leq M - 1\}$.

Let

$$x(r, c) = \begin{bmatrix} r \\ c \\ 1 \end{bmatrix}, \qquad \theta = \begin{bmatrix} \alpha \\ \beta \\ \gamma \end{bmatrix}$$

$\hat{\theta}$ is the least squares estimate of $\theta$, and we have

$$\hat{\theta} = \left( \sum_{\Omega} x(r, c) x^{T}(r, c) \right)^{-1} \sum_{\Omega} x(r, c) y(r, c)$$

Consider the residuals $\hat{w}$:

$$\hat{w}(r, c) = y(r, c) - (\hat{\theta})^{T} x(r, c)$$

If the model is adequate for the given image, the sequence $\{\hat{w}(r, c), (r, c) \in \Omega\}$ should behave like a set of independent random variables. We can use standard tests [6] to find whether the residual sequence $\{\hat{w}(r, c), (r, c) \in \Omega\}$

can be regarded as white. This procedure is one of several methods available for testing the adequacy of a model for respresenting a given image.

Longuet-Higgins [7] has suggested using two-dimensional sinusoids for representing the deterministic part:

$$y(r, c) = \alpha_1 \cos(\lambda_1 r + \cos \lambda_2 c + \gamma_1) + w(r, c)$$

The parameters $\alpha_1, \lambda_1, \lambda_2,$ and $\gamma_1$ can be estimated from the given image using the least squares criterion. The criterion function is not a quadratic function of the unknown parameters, namely, $\alpha_1, \lambda_1, \lambda_2, \gamma_1$, so an explicit expression for the estimate is not available. The estimates have to be obtained by using an iterative minimization approach. Other relevent work is found in Refs. 4 and 8.

### Spatial Autoregressive Models    B

In the spatial interaction models, the pixel intensity $y(s)$ is a linear combination of the intensities of the pixels located in a small neighborhood around $s$ plus an additive noise. The noise sequence can be independent or otherwise yielding various types of spatial interaction models. The literature on this topic is extensive.

In the spatial autoregressive model [9, 10], the additive noise sequence, say, $w(\cdot)$, is independent with a common Gaussian density, say, $N(0, \rho)$. Thus the spatial autoregressive model can be described as follows:

$$y(r, c) = \sum_{i, j \in N} \theta_{i, j} y(r + i, c + j) + w(r, c)$$

or

$$y(s) = \sum_{t \in N} \theta_t y(s + t) + w(s) \tag{1}$$

Note that both $s$ and $t$ are two-dimensional vectors with integer components. The so-called neighbor set $N$ is a set of grid points excluding $(0, 0)$. The model is labeled causal or noncausal depending on the choice of $N$. For a causal neighborhood, $N$ is a subset of the quarter plane $\{(i, j), i < 0, j < 0\}$. The model equation can be rewritten as shown below using the operators $z_1$ and $z_2$. $z_1$ and $z_2$ are unit lead operators in the row or $r$ direction and column or $c$ direction, respectively:

$$z_1 y(r, c) \triangleq y(r + 1, c), \qquad z_2 y(r, c) \triangleq y(r, c + 1)$$

$$A(z)y(s) = w(s), \qquad\qquad z = (z_1, z_2)$$

$$A(z) = 1 - \sum_{(i, j) \in N} \theta_{ij} z_1^i z_2^j$$

If $N$ is noncausal, a necessary condition for the stationarity of the process $y(\cdot)$ is given as

$$A(z_1, z_2) \neq 0 \quad \text{for} \quad |z_1| = 1 \quad \text{and} \quad |z_2| = 1 \tag{2}$$

There is a fundamental difference between the facet model and the spatial autoregressive model. Let

$$R_{i,j} = \text{cov}[y(r, c), y(r + i, c + j)]$$
$$= E[(y(r, c) - E(y(r, c)))(y(r + i, c + j) - E(y(r + i, c + j)))]$$

In the facet model, $R_{ij} = 0 \; \forall (i, j) \neq (0, 0)$. In the spatial autoregressive model in (1) the function $R_{i,j}$ is nonzero for all $i$, $j$ and decreases to zero asymptotically.

The covariance function can be evaluated from the corresponding spectral density of $y$ labeled $S(z_1, z_2)$, $z_1 = \exp(\sqrt{-1}\lambda_1)$, $z_2 = \exp(\sqrt{-1}\lambda_2)$, $\lambda_1$, $\lambda_2$ being the frequency variables in the $r$ and $c$ directions:

$$S(z_1, z_2) = \rho/A(z_1, z_2)A(z_1^{-1}, z_2^{-1}) \tag{3}$$

One interesting property of the process $y(\cdot)$ is its weak Markov property, stated as

$$E[y(s)|\text{all } y(t), t \neq s] = E[y(s)|\text{only } y(t), t \in N_1]$$

where $N_1$ is a finite superset of $N$. To fit a model to the given image, we need a method for determining the set $N$ and the estimates of parameters $\theta_s$, $s \in N$, and $\rho$. Let us concentrate on the estimation of $\theta_s$ given $N$. The simplest method is to estimate the parameters via the least squares approach, similar to that used in the facet model. Even though the computation of the estimate is easy, the quality of the estimate is known to be poor [11]. Specifically, the mean square error between the estimate and true value will not tend to zero even when the number of intensity observations tends to infinity. Hence we need a more sophisticated scheme like the maximum likelihood. However, with the Gaussian assumption, the expression of the joint probability density of the $M^2$ pixel intensities $\{y(r, c), 0 \leq r, c \leq M - 1\}$ of the given image is complicated. To simplify the procedure, we will replace the model in (1) by its toroidal approximation given below, which is valid only for $s \in \Omega$:

$$y(s) = \sum \theta_t y(s \oplus t) + w(s), \quad s \in \Omega \tag{4}$$

where $s \oplus t$ stands for sum modulo $M$ in both components. The error introduced by the approximation has been investigated in Ref. 12, and it is negligible for even relatively small $M$ like $M = 32$. Let $\{Y_r, r \in \Omega\}$ be a discrete

Fourier transform of $\{y(s), s \in \Omega\}$. One can easily show that the joint probability density of $\{Y_r\}$ is

$$P(Y_{0,0}, Y_{01}, \ldots, Y_{M-1, M-1}) = \frac{1}{(2\pi)^{M^2/2}} \prod_{t \in \Omega} S_t^{-1/2} \exp\left[-\left(\frac{1}{2}\right) \frac{Y_t Y_t^*}{S_t M^2}\right]$$

$$S_t = S_{i,j} = S\left[z_1 = \exp\left(\sqrt{-1} \frac{2\pi i}{M}\right), z_2 = \exp\left(\sqrt{-1} \frac{2\pi j}{M}\right)\right]$$

The spectral density $S(\cdot)$ is defined in (3). An algorithm is given in Ref. 13 for maximizing the expression with respect to the unknowns $\theta_t$ and $\rho$. The maximum-likelihood estimates possess excellent asymptotic behavior.

The choice of an appropriate neighbor set $N$ is also important. Often the unsatisfactory performance of the model noticed in some applications can be traced to the inappropriate choice of $N$. The method is to consider several neighbor sets, say, $N_1, N_2, N_3$, etc., fit the corresponding models to the given data, and compare them based on an appropriate statistic. The most widely used criterion is Akaike's information criterion (AIC) [14]. Akaike's criterion is to choose the neighbor set which gives the least value for AIC, where AIC = $-2$ log(maximum likelihood) + $2\alpha$, $\alpha$ being the number of parameters to be estimated. This criterion is not consistent for autoregressive [14] processes and tends to prefer models with larger neighbor sets. The Bayesian approach gives a transitive, parsimonious, and weakly consistent rule. In the Bayes approach (9.15] one calculates the following test statistics and choose the model having the least value of $B$:

$$B = -2 \log(\text{maximum likelihood}) + \alpha \log M^2$$

where $M^2$ is the number of data points used in the maximum-likelihood estimation of parameters. The utility of this rule for image processing is discussed in Refs. 13 and 16.

## Spatial Markov and ARMA Models    C

In the spatial Markov model [17, 18], the image intensity is regarded as the output of an all-pole transfer function whose input is a *colored* noise. Specifically,

$$y(s) = \sum_{t \in N} \theta_t \, y(s + t) + e(s)$$

where $N$ is symmetric, that is, if $(r, c) \in N$, $(-r, -c) \in N$, $\theta_{r,c} = \theta_{-r, -c}$, and the input sequence $e(\cdot)$ is Gaussian, correlated with the finite memory and spectral density $S_e$.

$$S_e(z) = \beta A(z)$$

where

$$A(z_1, z_2) = 1 - \sum_{(r,c) \in N} \theta_{r,c} z_1^r z_2^c$$

For stationarity of $y(\cdot)$, $A(\cdot)$ should obey the following condition:

$$A(z_1, z_2) > 0 \qquad \forall |z_1| = 1 \quad \text{and} \quad |z_2| = 1$$

The name Markov comes in because of the following property:

$$E[y(s)| \text{ all } y(t), t \neq s] = \sum_{t \in N} \theta_t y(s + t)$$

that is, the conditional expectation of $y(s)$ depends only on the intensities of the neighboring pixels. The spectral density of $y$ is $\beta/A(z)$. The importance of this class of models comes from the fact that it subsumes the class of the spatial autoregressive models. Specifically, for every autoregressive model there is an equivalent Markov model, but not vice versa. For example, a Markov model with $N = \{(1,0), (-1,0), (0,1), (0,-1)\}$ does not have an equivalent autoregressive model having the same spectral density.

The parameter estimation can be done via the likelihood approach and toroidal assumption. The details are in Ref. 19.

The most general model in the spatial interaction family [10] is the autoregressive moving-average (ARMA) model. Its definition is different from the corresponding one-dimensional definition. Such a model can represent any stationary process whose spectral density is the ratio of two positive linear combinations of sinusoids. However, unlike the one dimensional case, it has no Markov property.

## D  Fractional Models and Fractals

A common property of all spatial autoregressive and Markov models is that they have very little power at low frequencies, and hence they are not good for modeling processes with relatively long periodicities. Mandelbrot [20] has argued that many processes in nature possess the property that the correlation between widely separated events, separated either in time or space, is significant, indicating the presence of significant, relatively long time constants. Mandelbrot suggested that their frequency behavior for small frequencies can be modeled by a spectral density which behaves like $\lambda^{-2d}$, where $\lambda$ is the frequency variable and $d > 0$, so that the process has infinite power at zero frequency. Mandelbrot and Van Ness [21] have surveyed the theoretical developments of such processes in continuous time, and the name *fractals* has been given to such processes. Hosking [22] argued that the fractal models explain the low-frequency behavior well but cannot explain the high-frequency behavior and suggested an approach in discrete time which accounts both for long- and short-term effects. We will give below a two-dimensional version of the Hoskins model suggested by Lapsa [23, 24]:

$$A(z_1, z_2)y(r, c) = (1 - z_1^{-1})^{-d_1}(1 - z_2^{-1})^{-d_2}w(r, c)$$

where $d_1, d_2 > 0$ and $(1 - z_1^{-1})^{-d_1}$ should be interpreted as the corresponding infinite series. $A(z_1, z_2)$ is the polynomial defined earlier and $w(r, c)$ is an independent sequence. Surprisingly, the process $y(\cdot)$ is stationary with spectral density

$$S(z_1, z_2) = \frac{\rho}{|A(z_1, z_2)|^2} (\sin \lambda_1)^{-2d_1}(\sin \lambda_2)^{-2d_2}$$

As $\lambda_1$ tends to zero, $(\sin \lambda_1)^{-2d_1}$ behaves like $\lambda_1^{-2d}$, yielding the fractal behavior.

Lapsa [24] and Pentland [2] have successfully used the fractal models for a variety of applications in image processing. One of the important advantages of the fractional model is that the parameter $d$ is scale invariant, that is, if a $2M \times 2M$ image is reduced to an $M \times M$ image by reducing a $2 \times 2$ window into a single pixel, the corresponding estimates of $d$ of the 2 images are close. This statement is not true for the parameters of other spatial interaction models in general.

## EDGE DETECTION   III

The availability of image intensity models offers interesting insights about the performance of various algorithms for detecting edges in an image. Every algorithm designed for edge detection is based on some model of the image, sometimes explicitly stated and sometimes not. The performance of the algorithms can be evaluated quantitatively only be examining their underlying assumptions. There are basically two types of assumptions. The first type of assumption deals with the nature of transition in image intensities at the edge. The second type of assumption deals with the description of intensities on either side of the edge. Commonly, the transition in the intensities is described by a step function and the image intensities on either side of the edge are assumed to be constants. Clearly, both of these assumptions are highly unrealistic. The performance of the edge-detection algorithms can be considerably improved by basing the algorithms on more realistic assumptions. We will consider some representative algorithms.

### Hueckel Operator   A

Hueckel [25] assumed that the edge transition is a step function, the edge location itself is described by a straight line, $\alpha r + \beta c = p$, and the image intensities on either side of the edge are constants, $b$ and $b + d$, respectively,

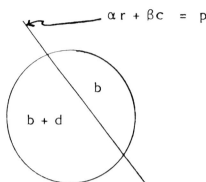

$$\alpha r + \beta c = p$$

Fig. 1. Hueckel's ideal edge.

as shown in Fig. 1. The ideal image intensity function $F$ is described as

$$F(r, c, \alpha, \beta, p, b, d) = b \qquad \text{if} \quad \alpha r + \beta c \le p$$
$$= b + d \qquad \text{otherwise}$$

If the actual image intensity function is $y(r, c)$, the quantities $\alpha$, $\beta$, $p$, $b$, and $d$ are obtained by minimizing the following quadratic function:

$$J(\alpha, \beta, p, b, d) = \int_D (y(r, c) - F(r, c, \alpha, \beta, p, b, d))^2 \, dr \, dc$$

The minimization is accomplished in polar coordinate Fourier space by expanding $F$ in terms of basis functions and limiting the number of terms in it.

## B  Gaussian–Laplacian Operators

Shanmugam *et al.* [26] posed the edge-detection procedure as one of finding a filter whose input is the raw image and whose output after appropriate thresholding yields the location of all the edges in the image. The problem is finding the transfer function of the filter. They also assume that the image transition in an edge is a step function, but they do not assume that the edges are straight lines. The filter produced by Shanmugam *et al.* is optimum in the sense that it maximizes the energy near the vicinity of the edge. The optimization is carried out in the *frequency domain*. In one dimension the filter transfer function has the following form:

$$H_0(\lambda) = k_1 \lambda^2 \exp(-k_2 \lambda^2), \qquad |\lambda| < \alpha$$
$$= 0, \qquad\qquad\qquad \text{elsewhere}$$

In two dimensions, the term $\lambda^2$ is replaced by $\lambda_1^2 + \lambda_2^2$, the sum of the squares of the two frequencies. The above operator $H_0$ is commonly referred to as a Laplacian on Gaussian operator because $\lambda_1^2 + \lambda_2^2$ is the transform of a two-dimensional Laplacian. Jernigan and Wardell [27] showed that $H_0(\lambda)$

can be approximated by a difference of Gaussians (DOG)

$$H_1(\lambda) = \exp[-k_2\lambda^2] - \exp[-(k_1 + k_2)\lambda^2]$$

The DOG model was first suggested by Wilson and Bergen [28] based on analysis of human vision. Marr and Hildreth [29] also proposed the Laplacian on Gaussian model based on intuitive considerations.

**Window Operators   C**

An intuitive idea to locate a pixel which may possibly lie on an edge is to compute an average gradient of the intensities around the pixel and threshold it. There are several ways of computing the average gradient suggested by Roberts, Prewitt, and Sobel. All of them compute gradients in two ortho-gonal directions and sum their squares. If we label the eight intensities around the central pixel as $A_0$ through $A_7$ as indicated, then the three suggested gradient averages are $R$ (Roberts), $P$ (Prewitt), and $S$ (Sobel):

$$
\begin{array}{ccc}
A_0 & A_1 & A_2 \\
A_7 & \cdot & A_3 \\
A_6 & A_5 & A_4
\end{array}
$$

$$R = (A_0 - A_4)^2 + (A_2 - A_8)^2$$

$$P = (A_2 + A_3 + A_4 - A_0 - A_7 - A_6)^2$$
$$\quad + (A_0 + A_1 + A_2 - A_6 - A_5 - A_4)^2$$

$$S = (A_2 + 2A_3 + A_4 - A_0 - 2A_7 - A_6)^2$$
$$\quad + (A_0 + 2A_1 + A_2 - A_6 - 2A_5 - A_4)^2$$

However, a quantitative comparison of these windows cannot be done without an explicit model for the image around an edge. Nasburg [30] suggests that a realistic intensity model for an edge is a ramp function. Let the ramp have slope $H$ per pixel and let it be oriented at an angle $\theta$ with the row axis. It is also assumed that the observed intensity is a sum of the ideal intensity and an additive noise which is zero mean, white, and Gaussian $N(0, \rho)$. Let the quantities $A_i$ mentioned earlier stand for the actual or observed intensities. Let $w_i$, 0, ..., 7, stand for the noise terms. Then the differences in the noise intensities needed for computing the statistics $R$, $P$, and $S$ can be expressed in terms of $H$, $\theta$, and $w_i$. For instance,

$$A_3 - A_7 = H \cos\theta + w_3 - w_7$$

$$A_4 - A_6 = H \sin\theta + w_4 - w_6$$

$$A_2 - A_6 = \sqrt{2}H \cos(\theta + 45°) + w_2 - w_6, \quad \text{etc.}$$

The criterion for comparing the various windows suggested by Nasburg [30] is the variance of the output, after normalizing all the windows by multiplying by a constant so that the expected values of $R$, $S$, and $P$ equal 1 when $H = 1$. The expressions for the normalized variances are

$$V[R] = E[(R - E(R))^2] = 4H^2\rho + 4\rho^4$$

$$V[S] = 3H^2\rho + 2.25\rho^2$$

$$V[P] = 2.66H^2\rho + 1.77\rho^2$$

Clearly, the window due to Prewitt has the least variance. This result has been confirmed by the simulation results of Abdou and Pratt [31], who showed the superiority of the Prewitt operator over those of Hueckel and Roberts.

## D   Facet Model

In Haralick's facet model [32], the observed intensity function is a sum of a parameterized ideal intensity function and an additive noise. The ideal intensity function is represented by a cubic function in the two variables $r$ and $c$:

$$f(r, c) = \sum_{i=0}^{3} \sum_{j=0}^{3} r^i c^j \alpha_{ij}, \qquad |i + j| \leq 3$$

The coefficients $\alpha_{ij}$ can be estimated from the given image by the least squares approach. The knowledge of the surface $f(r, c)$ allows us to evaluate the gradient of intensity at any point more accurately than before. Specifically, according to Zunaiga and Haralick [33], a pixel $(r_0, c_0)$ is classified as an edge pixel if its first directional derivative $f'_\theta(r_0, c_0)$ is nonzero and its second derivative $f''_\theta(r_0, c_0)$ equals zero, where $\theta$ is the gradient angle at $(r_0, c_0)$, that is,

$$\theta = (\tan^{-1}(\partial f / \partial r)) / \tan^{-1}(\partial f / \partial c)\Big|_{r_0, c_0}$$

Zunaiga and Haralick claim that their procedure locates edges and corners in noisy aerial images with greater precision than other methods.

## E   Nonparametric Methods

All the models used earlier are parametric models. In addition, even when the presence of noise is accepted, its density is implicitly assumed to be Gaussian in view of the fact that the least squares approach is used for parameter estimation. The use of decision rules based on nonparametric statistics is interesting because no specific assumption, implicit or explicit, is made on the distribution of the noise variables. Bovik *et al.* [34] have used nonparametric methods for edge detection. The intensity transition caused by an edge is assumed to be a step function, the edge direction being vertical, but no assumption is made on the additive noise. Two different decision rules are proposed based on the Wilcoxon and median rank statistics. One first detects all the vertical edges, then all the horizontal edges, and the results are integrated.

There are other statistical model-based approaches for edge detection given in Refs. 35–37.

## IMAGE SEGMENTATION VIA MODELING  IV

The intuitive idea behind image segmentation is to divide the image into segments such that each segment is homogeneous in some sense and two neighboring segments differ from one another in the same sense. Traditionally, a segment is considered as homogeneous if all the pixels in it have at least approximately the same brightness. Such a definition of homogeneity is too narrow, and the resuts of algorithms based on this definition are not often meaningful. Some workers have suggested normalizing the image before segmenting, but this modification is also not successful. This state of affairs has lead some workers [38] to call image segmentation a not well-posed problem. Clearly, there is a need for a quantitative definition of homogeneity, and the definition should be testable without appealing to thresholds chosen in an *ad hoc* manner. It is clear that there are several possible definitions of homogeneity which are appropriate under different conditions.

Let us consider scenes having several objects against a background, a common paradigm in computer vision. We will assume that the actual image intensity of a homogeneous part is described by a deterministic constant slope function plus additive noise:

$$y(r, c) = \alpha_1 r + \beta_1 c + \gamma_1 + w(r, c)$$

The given image is divided into a number of nonoverlapping windows or segments. Two neighboring segments of the same size will be considered, and a test is developed to determine whether the two segments should be regarded as distinct or whether they should be merged into a single segment. The test can be applied recursively to all pairs of segments until the final segmentation is achieved.

Let us consider the details when the underlying segments obey facet models in which the observed image function is a sum of a linear function and an additive noise. Consider two neighboring $(2m + 1) \times (2m + 1)$ segments in which the observed intensities are $[y_{ij}^1, i, j = 0, \pm 1, \pm 2, \ldots \pm m]$ and $[y_{ij}^2, i, j = 0, \pm 1, \ldots, \pm m]$, respectively. Let the observed image intensity of segment 1 obey the model in (5) and the corresponding quantities of segment 2 obey the model in (6):

$$y_{ij}^1 = \alpha_1 i + \beta_1 j + \gamma_1 + \omega_{ij}^1 \tag{5}$$

$$y_{ij}^2 = \alpha_2 i + \beta_2 j + \gamma_2 + \omega_{ij}^2 \tag{6}$$

where $\{\omega_{ij}^k\}$ are sequences of independent random variables with a common density $N(0, \rho^k)$. Let the coordinates of the center of segment 1 with respect to the center of segment 2 be $(\Delta i, \Delta j)$, $\Delta i$ being displacement in the row direction and $\Delta j$ that in the column direction.

Then the conditions on the parameters so that the two segments are parts of the same sloped surface are given as

$$\alpha_1 - \alpha_2 = 0 \tag{7}$$

$$\beta_1 - \beta_2 = 0 \tag{8}$$

$$(\alpha_1 + \alpha_2)\, \Delta i/2 + (\beta_1 + \beta_2)\, \Delta j/2 + \gamma_1 - \gamma_2 = 0 \tag{9}$$

Condition (9) implies the continuity of the image intensity at the boundary between the two segments. We need to develop a test to check whether the conditions (7)–(9) are true. Let $\hat{\alpha}_1$, $\hat{\beta}_1$, and $\hat{\gamma}_1$ be the least squares estimates of $\alpha_1, \beta_1$, and $\gamma_1$ obtained by fitting (5) to segment 1. Similarly, $\hat{\alpha}_2, \hat{\beta}_2$, and $\hat{\gamma}_2$ for segment 2. We then have

$$\hat{\alpha}_k, \hat{\beta}_k, \text{ and } \hat{\gamma}_k = \text{value of } \alpha_k, d_k, \gamma_k \text{ minimizing } \sum_{(i,\,j)\,\in\,\Omega_1} (y_{ij}^k - \alpha_k i - \beta_k j - \gamma_k)^2$$

$$\Omega_1 = \{(i, j), i, j = 0, \pm 1, \ldots, \pm m\}$$

The corresponding mean square of the residuals is

$$\varepsilon_k^2 = \sum_{i,\,j\,\in\,\Omega} (y_{ij}^k - \hat{\alpha}_k i - \hat{\beta}_k j - \hat{\gamma}_k)^2$$

Testing the validity of the conditions (7)–(9) by replacing the unknowns by their estimates is futile because $\hat{\alpha}_1 \neq \hat{\alpha}_2$ is always true. Based on statistical reasoning we will choose a single statistic to test the validity of conditions (7–9). The test statistic is [32]

$$d = \left\{ \frac{1}{2}(\hat{\alpha}_1 - \hat{\alpha}_2)^2 \sum_{i,\,j} i^2 + \frac{1}{2}(\hat{\beta}_1 - \hat{\beta}_2)^2 \sum_{i,\,j} j^2 \right.$$

$$\left. + \frac{(\hat{\alpha}_1 + \hat{\alpha}_2)(\Delta i/2) + (\hat{\beta}_1 + \hat{\beta}_2)(\Delta j/2) + (\hat{\gamma}_1 - \hat{\gamma}_2)}{2[(\Delta_i/2)^2 \sum_{i,\,j} i^2 + (\Delta j/2)^2 \sum_{i,\,j} j^2 + 1/\sum_{i,\,j} 1]} \right\} \frac{\{2\Sigma_{i,\,j} 1 - 6\}}{(\varepsilon_1^2 + \varepsilon_2^2)3}$$

The summation $i, j$ is over the lattice $\Omega_1$.

If the hypothesis of homogenity is true, $d$ obeys an $F$ distribution $F(3, 2 \Sigma_{i,j} 1 - 6)$. A significance level is chosen, say, $\alpha$ percent, and the threshold $\delta_\alpha$ is read from the tabulated values of the $F$ function, which is indexed by the two parameters $(3, 2 \Sigma_{i,j} 1 - 6)$. If $d \leq \delta_\alpha$, the hypothesis of homogenity of the two segments is accepted; otherwise, the hypothesis of homogeneity is rejected. The significance level is related to the probability of error that the above test will reject the hypothesis when it is true. For example, if $m = 1$, then $\Sigma_{i,j} 1 = 9$, since there are 9 pixels in each window. The corresponding $F$ distribution is $F(3, 12)$. For $\alpha = 1\%$, the threshold is 5.95. For segmentating the entire image, the test given above is repeated for every pair of neighboring $3 \times 3$ windows and repeating recursively.

We have illustrated the procedure using the facet model. We can use any signal-plus-noise model or a pure-noise model, as suggested by Chen and Pavlidis [39].

SYNTHESIS OF IMAGES   V

One interesting test for the validity of a generative model to a given image is to synthesize an image obeying the given generative model and compare the synthesized image with the original image for visual similarity. This test should be particularly interesting for textures such as leather, sand, grass, etc., where the intensity distribution is complex. A high degree of resemblance indicates the validity of the model. The similarity also indicates that the image model can be used as a tool for image data compression.

Let us first consider the spatial autoregressive model

$$y(s) = \sum_{t \in N} \theta_t y(s + t) + \sqrt{\beta}\, w(s) \tag{10}$$

where $w(s)$ is a sequence of independent variables and $N$ is arbitrary. There are two approaches for synthesizing an $M \times M$ image obeying (10). In the first approach, we can find the probability density of the $M^2$ pixels, namely, $p(y(r, c), (r, c) \in \Omega)$, obeying for Eq. (10) in terms of $\beta$, $\theta_t$ and the density of $w(\cdot)$. A Monte Carlo procedure can be used to synthesize an $M \times M$ image from the density [40]. This procedure appears to be computationally very expensive.

An alternative procedure is given which needs fewer computations. The procedure is based on approximating the model by its toroidal version:

$$y(s) = \sum \theta_t y(s \oplus t) + \sqrt{\beta}\, w(s), \qquad s \in \Omega$$

Let $\{Y_t\}$ and $\{W_t\}$ be two-dimensional discrete Fourier transforms (DFTs) of the finite sequences $\{y(\cdot)\}$ and $\{w(\cdot)\}$.

Let

$$A_t = A_{i,j} = A(z_1 = \exp(i2\pi\sqrt{-1}/M), z_2 = \exp(i2\pi\sqrt{-1}/M))$$

where

$$A(z) = 1 - \sum_{t \in N} \theta_t z^t$$

Then the dynamical equation given above for $y(\cdot)$ leads to the following equation

$$Y_t = \sqrt{\beta} W_t/A_t, \qquad t \in \Omega \tag{11}$$

Thus there are two steps in the synthesis: (1) generate a finite set of independent random variables $\{w(t), t \in \Omega\}$ and its DFT $\{W_t\}$; (2) compute $\{Y_t\}$ from (11). Its inverse DFT is the required image $\{y_t\}$.

Next let us consider the problem of synthesizing an image to resemble another image. For determining the appropriate model we need the neighbor

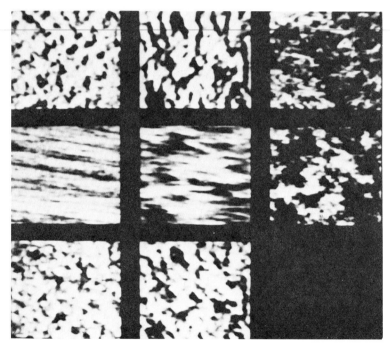

**Fig. 2.** Results of fitting NCAR models to other textures. All the synthetic textures were generated using $N = [(i,j)(i) + |j| \leq 3, (i,j), i,j = \pm 2]$ and histogram-matched residuals. (1, 1) and (1, 2), original and synthetic paper; (1, 3) and (2, 3), original and synthetic grass; (2, 1) and (2, 2), original and synthetic wood; (3, 1) and (3, 2), original and synthetic sand. (From Chellappa and Kashyap [12].

set $N$, the coefficients $\theta_s$, $s \in N$, and the probability density of the random variables $w(\cdot)$ for generating the input variables. Using the given image, we can estimate $N$ and $\theta_s$ by methods mentioned in Section II. As a first step, the density of $w(\cdot)$ can be taken to be Gaussian, $N(0, \hat{\rho})$. A better choice of the density is obtained by the histogram of the residuals $\hat{w}(\cdot)$ obtained from the fitted model and the image:

$$\hat{w}(s) = y(s) - \sum_{t \in N} \hat{\theta}_t y(s \oplus t)$$

Some further details are given in Ref. 41 for synthesizing images to resemble some actual textures from which the examples displayed in Fig. 2 are taken. The similarity between the original images and their synthesized counterparts in Fig. 2 is striking. Some other methods of synthesizing images can be found in Refs. 4, 23, 24, and 42–46.

## VI  CLASSIFICATION OF TEXTURES

Texture classification has been the focus of interest for the last 20 years. Briefly stated, there is a finite number of classes, say, $n$. A number of so-called training images belonging to each class is available. Based on the information extracted from these sets, a rule is designed which classifies a given test image of unknown class to one of the $n$ classes. The key step in any classification problem is the choice of a set of features which reduces the dimension of data to a computationally reasonable amount while preserving much of the classifying information present in the actual data.

A number of approaches to the texture analysis and classification problem have been developed over the years. Some of the methods presented in the literature address the classification problem under the assumption that the test sample from an unknown texture possesses the same orientation as the training samples. The aim here is to develop features and classify textures when the orientation of the test sample is *arbitrary*, that is, when the accuracy of classification is not affected by the rotation of the test texture.

Bajcsy [47] and Weszka et al. [48] suggested statistical features derived from a Fourier power spectrum of the image. These features are not rotation invariant. Haralick et al. [3] defined textural features derived from the gray-level co-occurrence matrix (GLCM), which is essentially the discrete joint probability densities of co-occurring gray-levels. Davis et al. [49] generalized the co-occurrence idea to include the spatial interdependence of sets of local features and not necessarily the gray-levels. They defined their features on the entries of another matrix called the generalized co-occurrence matrix (GCM). Zucker and Terzopoulos [50] present a statistical approach for relating the structure in an image pattern to the co-occurrence matrix. An experimental

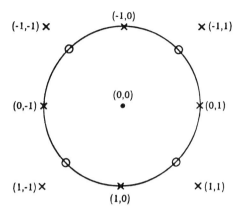

**Fig. 3.** Circular neighbor set $N_c$: ●, ×, original grid points; ○, interpolated pixels.

study by Weszka *et al.* [48] revealed the superiority of the spatial gray-level dependence method (GLDM) to gray-level run length and power spectrum methods when the orientation of the test image is *known*.

There are a number of difficulties associated with utilizing the GLCM or GCM for feature extraction and texture classification purposes. Both matrices are *rotation variant*. In an attempt to make the features derived from the GLCM rotation invariant, Haralick suggested calculating 45°, 90°, and 135° and taking their average as a rotation-invariant feature. This method works as long as the texture under study is rotated by an angle that is a multiple of 45°, but in general will not yield a good result if the angle is far from a multiple of 45° (e.g., 30°). The features derived from the GLCM are also not very useful in discriminating between macrotextures [49]. The rotation invariancy of features has also been studied via polagrams [51] and anisotropy indicatrixes [52]. Rotational invariant structural features were used in [59].

A feature set obtained by fitting simultaneous autoregressive (SAR) models to the image is given in Ref. 53. The set of parameters of the model was taken as the feature set and classification experiments with nine different textures were carried out. The disadvantage of this method is its rotation variancy. This model will be modified so as to yield rotation *invariancy*. The modified model is called the circular autoregressive model [53], described below:

$$y(s) = \alpha \sum_{t \in N_{1c}} y(s \oplus t) + \sqrt{\beta}\omega(s), \qquad s = (r, c), \qquad t = (r_1, c_1) \quad (12)$$

where $\oplus$ means addition modulo $M$. The circular neighbor set $N_{1c}$ consists of eight symmetrical pixels, all of which are located on a circle in the image plane centered at $s$ with unit radius. The set $N_{1c}$ is illustrated in Fig. 3.

In (12), $w(s)$ is an independent sequence with zero mean and unit variance. The parameters of the model are $\alpha$ and $\beta$. Four members of $N_{1c}$ correspond to grid points and therefore their intensity values are available. The other four diagonal members do not fall on the grid points and their intensities should be interpolated. Let $t = (t_1, t_2)$ be one such pixel. Take $s^{(i)}, i = 1, 2, 3, 4$, as the coordinates of the four nearest grid points surrounding $t$. The function $y(t)$ is assumed to be a linear combination of $\{y(s^{(i)}), i = 1, 2, 3, 4\}$ weighted by normalized inverse Euclidean distance between $t$ and $s^{(i)}$:

$$y(t) = \left(1 \,\middle/\, \sum_{i=1}^{4} d_i\right)\left(\sum_{i=1}^{4} d_i y(s^{(i)})\right), \qquad d_i = \frac{1}{\|t - s^{(i)}\|}, \qquad i = 1, 2, 3, 4 \quad (13)$$

The interpolated intensities of the pixels of $N_{1c}$ can be expanded in terms of the intensities of their four neighbor grid points. Then the model of Eq. (13) could be rewritten as

$$y(s) = \alpha f(s) + \sqrt{\beta}\,\omega(s), \qquad f(s) = \sum_{t \in N_{2c}} g_t y(s \oplus t), \qquad s \in \Omega \quad (14)$$

where $N_{2c}$ is a neighbor set containing nine grid points,

$$N_{2c} = \{(-1, -1), (-1, 0), (-1, 1), (0, -1), (0, 0), (0, 1), (1, -1), (1, 0), (1, 1)\}$$

$$g \text{ matrix:} \quad \begin{bmatrix} 0.005 & 1.4336 & 0.4005 \\ 1.4336 & 0.6636 & 1.4336 \\ 0.4005 & 1.4336 & 0.4005 \end{bmatrix}$$

The parameter vector of the model in (14) is estimated by the least squares technique. Let $\hat{\alpha}$ and $\hat{\beta}$ be least squares estimates of $\alpha$ and $\beta$:

$$\hat{\alpha} = \sum_{s \in \Omega} y(s) f(s) \sum_{s \in \Omega} f^2(s), \qquad \hat{\beta} = \frac{1}{M^2} \sum_{s \in \Omega} [y(s) - \hat{\alpha} f(s)]^2$$

*Rotation-Invariant Features.* As given above $\hat{\alpha}$ and $\hat{\beta}$ are natural candidates for rotation-invariant features. Other rotation-invariant features can be generated from other autoregressive models also. Consider the autoregressive model with neighbor set $N$ made of four nearest neighbors. The function $\rho^*$, which is the corresponding maximum-likelihood estimate of $\rho$, the input noise variance, is also approximately rotational invariant. Another useful feature, a measure of the directionability of a texture, can be generated as follows. We fit two different autoregressive models with neighbor sets $N_1$ and $N_2$, respectively:

$$N_1 = \{(1, 0), (-1, 0), (0, 1), (0, -1)\}$$

$$N_2 = \{(1, 1), (1, -1), (-1, 1), (-1, -1)\}$$

Let $\theta_s = \theta_{-s}$. Consider the feature

$$\xi = \max(|\theta_{1,0}^* - \theta_{0,1}^*|, |\theta_{1,1}^* - \theta_{1,-1}^*|)$$

where $\theta_{1,0}^*$ and $\theta_{0,1}^*$ are parameter estimates derived from first model; $\theta_{1,1}^*$

**Fig. 4.** Zero degree, 64 × 64 windows of textures. Row-by-row from top left to right: calf leather, wool, sand, pig skin, plastic bubbles, herringbone weave, raffia, wood, grass, straw, brick wall, and bark of tree. (From Brodatz [54].)

and $\theta^*_{1, -1}$ are derived from the second model. The term $\xi$ is a measure of the texture variability in two orthogonal directions. A texture like wood having directionality will have a relatively large value of $\xi$.

An experimental study was conducted to evaluate the efficiency of the above feature set. Nine different textures, (a) Calf leather (D24), (b) wool (D19), (c) beach sand (D29), (d) pig skin (D92), (e) plastic bubbles (D112), (f) herringbone weave (D17), (g) raffia (D84), (h) wood grain (D68), and (i) grass (D9), were chosen from the photo album by Brodatz [54]. Seven rotated 256 × 256 digitized images with relative angles of rotation 0°, 30°, 60°, 90°,

TABLE I

Sample Means and Standard Deviations (SD) of Features of Raffia Texture[a]

| Rotation angle (deg) | $\hat{\alpha}_1$ | | $\hat{\beta}_1$ | | $\rho^*$ | | $\varsigma$ | |
|---|---|---|---|---|---|---|---|---|
| | Mean | SD | Mean | SD | Mean | SD | Mean | SD |
| 0 | 0.1750 | 0.0050 | 0.3465 | 0.0106 | 0.3599 | 0.0086 | 0.0965 | 0.0144 |
| 30 | 0.1717 | 0.0039 | 0.3804 | 0.0038 | 0.4920 | 0.0070 | 0.0521 | 0.0313 |
| 60 | 0.1701 | 0.0045 | 0.3705 | 0.0098 | 0.4461 | 0.0125 | 0.0963 | 0.0192 |
| 90 | 0.1737 | 0.0057 | 0.3388 | 0.0206 | 0.3517 | 0.0203 | 0.1040 | 0.0102 |
| 120 | 0.1693 | 0.0027 | 0.3753 | 0.0145 | 0.4801 | 0.0223 | 0.0586 | 0.0277 |
| 150 | 0.1701 | 0.0070 | 0.3723 | 0.0154 | 0.4508 | 0.0215 | 0.1001 | 0.0089 |
| 200 | 0.1709 | 0.0073 | 0.3601 | 0.0106 | 0.4276 | 0.0140 | 0.0634 | 0.0313 |

[a] Fourteen unidirectional $64 \times 64$ samples per angle.

$120°$, $150°$, and $200°$ were taken from each texture (total of 63). The gray-scale value range was between 0 and 255. The nine textures are shown in Fig. 4. Each $256 \times 256$ image is segmented into $64 \times 64$ images. Eight of them are used for training and the remaining eight for testing. Therefore 56 training and 56 test samples from each texture class are available.

Table I shows the rotational invariancy of the four features $\alpha$, $\beta$, $\rho$, and $\xi$ of

TABLE II

Sample Means and Standard Deviations (SD) of Training Features Utilized in Classification[a]

| Texture | $\hat{\alpha}_1$ | | $\hat{\beta}_1$ | | $\rho^*$ | | $\varsigma$ | |
|---|---|---|---|---|---|---|---|---|
| | Mean | SD | Mean | SD | Mean | SD | Mean | SD |
| Calf leather | 0.1553 | 0.0049 | 0.5595 | 0.0420 | 0.6401 | 0.0705 | 0.2000 | 0.0256 |
| Wool | 0.1447 | 0.0023 | 0.2149 | 0.0124 | 0.2444 | 0.0175 | 0.0521 | 0.0143 |
| Sand | 0.1563 | 0.0023 | 0.4076 | 0.0166 | 0.4903 | 0.0266 | 0.0586 | 0.0201 |
| Pig skin | 0.1553 | 0.0016 | 0.3211 | 0.0145 | 0.3818 | 0.0196 | 0.0626 | 0.0223 |
| Plastic bubbles | 0.1445 | 0.0016 | 0.2069 | 0.0104 | 0.2312 | 0.0170 | 0.0453 | 0.0162 |
| Herringbone | 0.1763 | 0.0099 | 0.6951 | 0.0311 | 0.8342 | 0.0290 | 0.0251 | 0.0097 |
| Raffia | 0.1718 | 0.0055 | 0.3656 | 0.0208 | 0.4328 | 0.0566 | 0.0802 | 0.0297 |
| Wood | 0.1474 | 0.0054 | 0.3530 | 0.0395 | 0.2030 | 0.1190 | 0.4984 | 0.0263 |
| Grass | 0.1475 | 0.0034 | 0.4710 | 0.0179 | 0.5710 | 0.0226 | 0.0753 | 0.0135 |
| Straw | 0.1407 | 0.0057 | 0.3675 | 0.0696 | 0.3171 | 0.1740 | 0.3743 | 0.0771 |
| Brick | 0.1451 | 0.0027 | 0.2258 | 0.0308 | 0.2349 | 0.0589 | 0.2511 | 0.0539 |
| Tree | 0.1154 | 0.0008 | 0.2236 | 0.0200 | 0.2521 | 0.0287 | 0.0908 | 0.0217 |

[a] Fourteen differently oriented $64 \times 64$ samples per class.

the raffia texture. The means and standard deviations of the four features for the nine textures are given in Table II. It was claimed before that $\beta$ is a measure of nonisotropy of the texture, or better to say that $1 - \beta$ is a measure of isotropy. This could be confirmed by looking at Table II. $\beta$ has small values for textures like plastic bubbles, raffia, and wool. These textures, although not completely isotropic, exhibit a rather similar correlation structure in different directions. On the other hand, nonisotropic textures like grass, calf leather, and wood grain show large values of $\beta$. It is also noticed that textures like calf leather, grass, and sand possess high values of $\rho^*$, as expected. The directionality feature $\xi$ is high only for wood grain and calf leather, the textures displaying directionality.

A classification experiment was performed using the minimum distance rule and the four features and nine textures in Fig. 4. Out of 504 test samples, only 23 were erroneously classified, yielding a correct recognition accuracy of 95.44%. Most of the error occurred between pig skin texture and sand texture. The use of another feature to distinguish between them could further enhance the recognition accuracy.

## VII  TEXTURE BOUNDARY RECOGNITION AND SEGMENTATION

Consider a photograph of a natural scene such as a bay having both land and water. If we need to segment the scene so as to identify the land and water segments, by finding their boundaries, traditional methods of edge detection are not successful. The water scene is itself a homogeneous texture having many micro edges in it; similarly the land scene. The traditional edge-location methods applied to the entire scene cannot distinguish between the micro edges within each texture and the boundary between the textures. One reason for their failure is their inability to properly characterize a texture. As mentioned earlier, two different $64 \times 64$ slices of a cork texture may have entirely different image intensity distributions, yet it is easy to visually recognize that they belong to the same texture. In other words, we have to investigate the features common to both of the slices. It is precisely here that the texture modeling is successful. If we fit an appropriate model to both slices of the same texture, the corresponding parameter estimates are numerically close to one another. Similarly, the parameter estimates of the models fitted to slices of different textures will be significantly different. This difference in parameter estimates can be used to locate the segment boundaries.

For instance, consider a relatively simple scene such as a bay involving only two textures, namely, land and water. Let the boundary between the two textures be arbitrary and not limited to any linearity restriction. The model considered by Pentland [2] to segment the scene is the fractal model considered earlier involving one parameter $d$. Let the entire image be divided into $8 \times 8$ slices. The fractal model is fitted to each slice, and the parameter $d$ is estimated from each slice. If a histogram of all $d$ estimates is plotted, it has two sharp peaks widely differing from one another with a valley in between. Choose the value of $d$, say $d_0$, corresponding to the valley. Then assign every slice of the image with its estimate of $d$ greater than $d_0$ to one texture and the remainder to the other texture. Pentland [2] claims that this simple procedure locates the land–water boundary very well, much better than all the current methods of image segmentation and edge detection.

It is appropriate to distinguish between the texture boundary recognition and texture classification problems discussed earlier. The texture classification belongs to the class of *supervised* classification problems because we know the number of classes and the training patterns of each class. In the texture boundary problem, we do not know the number of different textures in the scene and their types. If we know in advance the types of all the textures in the scene, then we can use the paradigm of texture classification mentioned earlier to find the boundary, that is, divide the scene into various slices, fit a model to each slice, and assign the slice to that class depending on the proximity of the feature set of that slice to the ideal feature sets of the various classes. However, we are concerned with a much harder problem in which we do not know the number of different textures in the scene and the types of textures. In this case we can fit an appropriate model having $n$ undetermined parameters to each slice and plot the estimated parameter vector $\phi$ in an $n$-dimensional space. The number of distinct clusters in the $n$-dimensional space should indicate the number of dominant textures in the scene, and the texture boundaries can be determined by assigning each slice to the cluster closest to its feature point in the $n$-dimensional feature space. This approach has been used with some success by Kashyap and Khotanzand [55]. This approach involves the use of clustering algorithms, which can be a drawback computationally.

To overcome these problems, one approach is to divide the image into strips and test whether each strip has one texture or two textures. If we decide that there is more than one texture, the boundary or boundaries are also determined. Then, joining the boundaries given by the various strips gives us the required overall boundary between various textures in the scene, after appropriate smoothing. Specifically, consider an $R \times C$ slice of an image described by an array of pixel intensities $\{y(r, c), r = 1, \ldots, R, c = 1, \ldots, C\}$. Let the image be made up of two textures, as shown in Fig. 5 with $\bigcirc$ indicating one texture and $\square$ indicating the other, the boundary being vertical, located at column $n^0$. (Later we will relax the assumption about the boundary being vertical.) The value of $n^0$ is unknown. Using only the information in the slice, we will estimate $n^0$, the edge column number. Let the texture on the left side of the column $n^0$ obey the following autoregressive

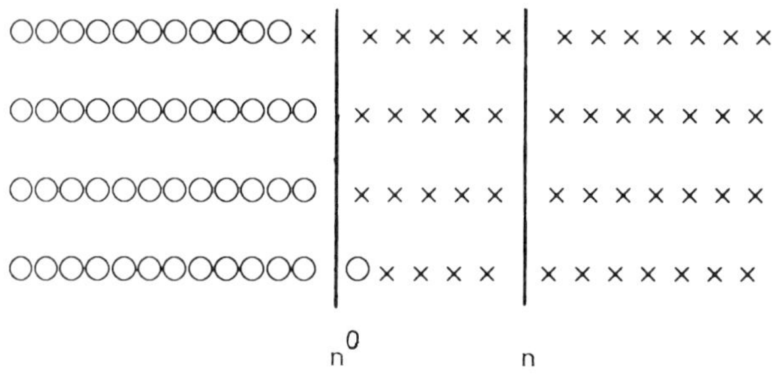

**Fig. 5.** Boundary model of texture.

model in (15) and the texture on the right side obey the model in (16):

$$y(s) = (\theta^{(1)})^{\mathrm{T}}x(s) + (\rho^1)^{1/2}w(s), \tag{15}$$

$$y(s) = (\theta^{(2)})^{\mathrm{T}}x(s) + (\rho^2)^{1/2}w(s), \tag{16}$$

where

$$\theta^{(k)} = \mathrm{col}[\theta_0^k, \theta_s^k, s \in N], \qquad k = 1, 2$$

$$x(s) = \mathrm{col}[1, y(s+t), t \in N], \qquad (\theta^{(k)})^{\mathrm{T}}x(s) - \sum_{t \in N} \theta_t^k y(s+t) + \theta_0^k$$

and $N$ is an appropriate set of neighbors around $(0,0)$. In our case, $N = \{(-1,1), (-1,-1), (-1,0), (0,-1)\}$. The function $w(\cdot)$ is a two-dimensional normal $(0,1)$ sequence. The values of $\theta^{(k)}$, $\rho^{(k)}$, $(k = 1,2)$ are unknown, and $\phi^{(k)} = \{\theta^k, \rho^k\}, (k = 1, 2)$. Let $n$ be our *guess* (or estimate) of $n^0$. Let $\Omega_{1,n}$ be the set of pixels to the left of the column $n$ and $\Omega_{2,n}$ be the set of pixels to the right of column $n$. Let $y_n^{(k)} = \{y(s): s \in \Omega_{k,n}\}$, $k = 1, 2$. Let $\mathbf{y} = \mathbf{y}_n^{(1)} \cup \mathbf{y}_n^{(2)}$ be the entire image array. Let us obtain an expression for the joint probability density of the entire image given that $n$ is the *true edge*, namely, $p(\mathbf{y}|n)$ or $p(\mathbf{y}_n^{(n)}, \mathbf{y}_n^{(2)}|n)$. Note that $p(\cdot)$ involves only the image $\mathbf{y}$ and nothing else. The required best estimate $\hat{n}$ of $n^0$ is obtained by maximize $p(\mathbf{y}|n)$ with respect to $n$. Given below is $J(n)$, an approximate expression to $\log p(\mathbf{y}|n)$. (the details of the derivation are given in Ref. 56):

$$J(n) = \sum_{k=1,2} \{-(N_k - m - 2)\ln \hat{\rho}^k\} - (m+1)\ln(N_k) + \ln \det\left(\frac{G^{(k)}}{N}\right)$$

where $N_k$ is the number of members in $\Omega_{k,n}$, $k = 1, 2$, and

$$\hat{\rho}^k = \frac{1}{N_k} \sum_{s \in \Omega_{k,n}} (y(s) - (\hat{\theta}^k)^{\mathrm{T}}x(s))^2$$

$$G^{(k)} = \left(\sum_{s \in \Omega_{k,n}} x(s)x^{\mathrm{T}}(s)\right)^{-1}, \qquad \hat{\theta}^k = G^{(k)} \sum_{s \in \Omega_{k,n}} y(s)x(s)$$

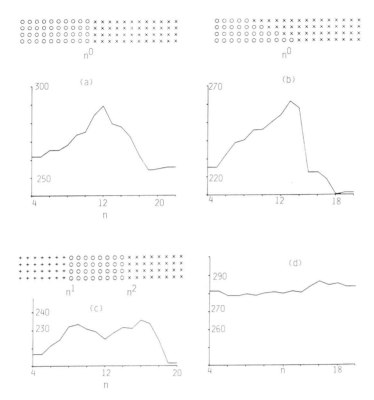

**Fig. 6.** The 4 × 20 image window and the corresponding graph of $J_2(n)$ vs. $n$ for 4 different cases. (a) Window with a vertical edge; (b) window with a slanted edge; (c) window with 2 edges; (d) window with no edge, hence window is not displayed.

*The Likelihood Boundary Detection Principle.* The most likely estimate of the column number of the boundary is the value of $n$ which maximizes $J(n)$. If a window has one edge, whether vertical or slanted, the graph of $J(n)$ versus $n$ has one dominant peak, as indicated in Figs. 6a,b. If the window has two edges, then the graph of $J(n)$ versus $n$ indicates two distinct peaks, as in Fig. 6c. Thus we can detect both the edges in the image, even though the theoretical development used a very restrictive assumption of only one edge in an image.

Consider an image which has *no* edge. The graph $J(n)$ versus $n$ in that case is given in Fig. 6d. Note that the graph is relatively flat. For judging the flatness of the $J(n)$ graph, we use the following criterion. Let the image window be of size 4 × 24, as in our experiments. Let $h = |\max J(\cdot) - (\frac{1}{2})(J(5) + J(19))|$. If the value of $n$ that maximizes $J$ is within $a$ pixels of either end of the window, or if the ratio of the measure $h$ to the standard deviation of $J$ is less than $b$, then there is no edge in the window. The values of $a$ and $b$ are chosen to give good results. The values used here were $a = 6$ and $b = 2$.

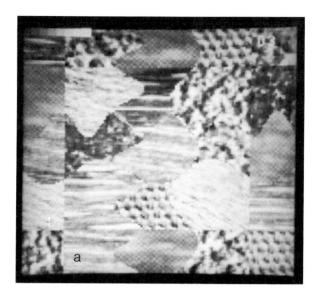

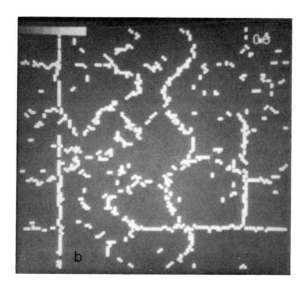

**Fig. 7.** (a) An image constructed from several textures in Ref. 54. (b) The superposition of the "very likely" vertical boundaries and "very likely" horizontal boundaries for the image in (a). (From Brodatz [54].)

*Experimental Results and Discussion.* Various types of test images were constructed from natural textures taken from the Brodatz album [54] with the number of edges ranging from zero to two. Five different experiments were performed using the test images described below, and the results are in Ref. 56.

(1)   1000 4 × 24 images having exactly one vertical edge
(2)   1000 4 × 24 images having one slanted edge
(3)   1000 4 × 24 images windows with exactly two vertical edges
(4)   400 4 × 24 images with no edge
(5)   An 128 × 128 image made of *several* textures so that the edges cover all directions given in Fig. 7a.

Summarizing the results of experiments (1) through (4), the scheme is very good at detecting an edge that is between columns 6 and 18 of the window and is closer to being vertical than horizontal. If the true edge is any closer to one end of the window or if it is too near to being horizontal, then the scheme is not likely to detect the edge. For windows with no actual edge, an edge will be detected about $\frac{1}{4}$ of the time. If we had increased the size of the window, the rate of false edge detection would have gone down at the expense of higher computing cost. Thus if an edge does exist, the scheme usually finds it.

Next, consider the composite structure given in (5). It is divided into horizontal strips and the boundary columns are detected. Next the image is divided into vertical strips and the boundary rows are detected. The two types of information are merged as indicated is Fig. 7.

## OTHER APPLICATIONS   VIII

We have considered only some important models and some of their applications. Image models have also been used with much success in spectral estimation [19, 57], restoration of images degraded by blur and additive noise [16, 57, 58], image coding [42, 57], and image registration [24]. There are also many other types of image models, such as mosaic models, for which Refs. 4 and 5 are good starting points.

## REFERENCES

1. J. M. Tanenbaum, M. A. Fischler, and H. G. Barrow, Scene modelling: A structural basis for image description, *in* "Image Modelling," (A. Rosenfeld, ed.), Academic Press, New York, 1981.
2. A. Pentland, Fractal based description of natural scenes, *IEEE Computer Soc. Conf. CVPR*, (June 1983).
3. R. M. Haralick, K. Shanmugam, and I. Dinstein, Textural features for image classification, *IEEE Trans. Syst., Man, Cybern.* **SMC-3**, No. 6, 610-621, (1973).

4. N. Ahuja and B. J. Schacter, "Pattern Models." Wiley, New York, 1983.

5. A. Rosenfeld (ed.), "Image Modelling." Academic Press, New York, 1981.

6. R. L. Kashyap and A. R. Rao, "Stochastic Dynamic Models from Empirical Data." Academic Press, New York, 1976.

7. M. S. Longuet-Higgins, Statistical properties of an isotropic random surface, *Philos. Trans. R. Soc. London Ser. A* **250**, 157–171 (October 1957).

8. D. P. Panda, Statistical properties of thresholded images, *Computer Graphics and Image Processing*, 334–354 (1978).

9. R. L. Kashyap, A Bayesian comparison of different classes of models using empirical data, *IEEE Trans. Automat. Contr.* **AC-22**, 715–727 (1977).

10. R. L. Kashyap, Characterization and estimation in 2-D ARMA models for images, *IEEE Trans. Information Theory* (1984).

11. P. Whittle, On the stationary processes on the plane, *Biometrika* **41**, 434–449 (1954).

12. R. Chellappa, Stochastic models in image analysis and processing, Unpublished Ph.D. thesis, Purdue University, West Layfayette, Indiana, August 1981.

13. R. L. Kashyap and R. Chellappa, Estimation and choice of neighbors in spatial interaction models of images, *IEEE Trans. Information Theory* **IT-29**, 60–72 (1983).

14. R. L. Kashyap, Inconsistency of the AIC rule for estimating the order of autoregressive models, *IEEE Trans. Automat. Conrl.* **AC-25**, 996–998 (1980).

15. R. L. Kashyap, R. Chellappa, and N. Ahuja, Decision rules for the choice of neighbors in random field models of images, *Computer Graphics and Image Processing* **15**, 310–318 (1981).

16. R. Chellappa and R. L. Kashyap, Digital image restoration using spatial interaction models, *IEEE Trans. Acoust., Speech Signal Proc.*, 461–472. (1982).

17. R. L. Kashyap, Analysis and synthesis of image patterns by spatial interaction models, *in* "Progress in Pattern Recognition" (Kanal and Rosenfeld, eds.), Vol. I, North-Holland Publ., Amsterdam, 1981.

18. J. W. Woods, Two-dimensional discrete Markovian fields *IEEE Trans. Inform. Theory* **IT-18**, 232–240 (1972).

19. R. Chellappa, H. Y. Hu, and S. U. Kung, On two dimensional Markov spectral estimation, *IEEE Trans. ASSP* **ASSP-31**, 836–841 (1983).

20. B. Mandelbrot, "Fractals-form, Chance and Dimension." Freeman, San Francisco, California, 1977.

21. B. Mandelbrot and J. W. Van Ness, Fractional Brownian motions, fractional noises and applications, *SIAM Rev.* **10**, No. 4 (1968).

22. J. R. M. Hosking, Fractional differencing, *Biometrika* 68, 165–176 (1981).

23. R. L. Kashyap and P. M. Lapsa, Long correlation models for random fields, *Proc. IEEE Computer Soc. Conf. PRIP, Las Vegas, Nevada, 1982* (1982).

24. P. M. Lapsa "New models and techniques for synthesis, estimation and segmentation of random fields," Unpublished Ph.D. thesis, Purdue University, West Layfayette, Indiana, 1982.

25. M. H. Hueckel, A local visual operator which recognizes edges and lines, *J. Assoc. Comput. Mach.* **20**, 634–647 (1973).

26. K. S. Shanmugam, F. M. Dickey, and J. A. Green, An optimal frequency domain filter for edge detection in digital pictures, *IEEE Trans. Pattern Anal. Mach. Intelligence* **PAMI-1,** No. 1, 37–49 (1979).

27. M. E. Jernigan and R. W. Wardell, Does the eye contain optimal edge detection mechanisms, *IEEE Trans. SMC* **SMC-11**, No. 6, 441–444 (1981).

28. H. R. Wilson and J. R. Bergen, A four mechanism model for threshold spatial vision, *Vision Res.* **19**, 19–32 (1979).

29. D. Marr and E. Hildreth, Theory of edge detection, *Proc. R. Soc. London B* **207**, 187–217 (1980).

30. R. Nasburg and M. Lineberry, "Noise effects of edge operators."

31. I. E. Abdou and W. K. Pratt, Quantitative design and evolution of enhancement/thresholding edge detectors, *Proc. IEEE* **67**, No. 5, 756–763 (1979).

32. R. M. Haralick, Edge and region analysis for digital image data, *in* "Image Modelling," (A. Rosenfeld, ed.), Academic Press, New York, 1981.

33. O. Zunaiga and R. M. Haralick, Corner detection using the facet model, *IEEE Computer Soc. Conf. Computer Vision Pattern Recognition, Washington, D. C., June, 1983* (1983).

34. C. Bovik, T. S. Huang, and D. C. Munson, Jr., Nonparametric edge detection with an assumption on minimum edge height, *IEEE Computer Soc. Conf. CVPR*, (1983).

35. D. B. Cooper, H. Elliott, F. Cohen, L. Reiss, and P. Symosek, Stochastic boundary estimation and object recognition, *in* "Image Modelling" (A. Rosenfeld, ed.). Academic Press, New York, 1981.

36. L. S. Davis and A. Mitiche, Edge detection in textures, *Computer Graphics and Image Processing* **12**, (1980).

37. R. Nevatia and K. R. Babu, Linear feature extraction, *Proc. 1978 Image Understanding Workshop, Pittsburgh, Pennsylvania, 1978*; *in* "Science Applications" (L. S. Baumann, ed.). (1978).

38. M. Brady, Computational approaches to image understanding, *ACM Computing Surveys* **14**, No. 1, 3–72 (1982).

39. P. C. Chen and T. Pavlidis, Image segmentation as an estimation problem, *in* "Image Modelling" (A. Rosenfeld, ed.), Academic Press, New York, 1981.

40. G. R. Cross and A. K. Jain, Markov random field texture models, *IEEE Trans. Pattern Anal. Mach. Intel.* **PAMI-5**, 25–40 (1983).

41. R. Chellappa and R. L. Kashyap, Synthetic generation and estimation in random field models of images, *Proc IEEE Computer Society Conf. Pattern Recognition Image Processing, Dallas, Texas, August 1981* pp. 577–582 (1981).

42. E. J. Delp, R. L. Kashyap, and O. R. Mitchell, Image data compression using autoregressive time series models, *Pattern Recognition* **11**, 313–323 (1979).

43. A. Fournier, D. Fussell, and L. Carpenter, Computer Rendering of Stochastic Models, *Commun. ACM* **25**, 371–384 (1982).

44. A. Gagalowicz, A new method for texture fields synthesis: Some applications to the study of human vision, *IEEE Trans. Patt. Anal. Machine Intell.* **PAMI-3**, 520–533 (1981).

45. D. D. Garber and A. A. Sawchuk, Computational models for texture analysis and synthesis, *Proc. Image Understanding Workshop, April 1981*, pp. 69–88 (1981).

46. B, H. McCormick and S. N. Jayaramamurthy, Time series models for texture synthesis, *Intl. J. Comput. Inform. Sci.* **4**, 329–343 (December 1974).

47. R. Bajcsy, Computer description of textured surfaces, *Proc. 3rd Int. Joint Conf. Int.*, 572–579 (August 1973).

48. J. S. Weszka, C. R. Dyer, and A. Rosenfeld, A comparative study of texture measures for terrain classification, *IEEE Trans. Syst., Man, Cybern.* **SMC-6**, No. 4, 269–285 (1976).

49. L. S. Davis, M. Clearman, and J. K. Aggrawal, An empirical evaluation of generalized co-occurrence matrices, *IEEE Trans. Pattern Anal. Machine Intel.* **PAMI-3**, No. 2, 214–221 (1981).

50. S. W. Zucker and D. Terzopoulos, Finding structure in co-occurrence matrices for texture analysis, *in* "Image Modelling," (A. Rosenfeld, ed.) Academic Press, New York, 1981.

51. L. S. Davis, Polograms: A new tool for image texture analysis, *Pattern Recognition* **13**, No. 3, 219–223 (1981).

52. D. Chetverikov, Experiments in the rotation-invariant texture discrimination using anisotropy features, *Proc. 6th Intl. Conf. Pattern Recognition, Munich, Germany, October 1982*, pp. 1071–1073, (1982).

53. R. L. Kashyap and A. Khotanzad, Rotation invariant texture classification using circular random field modes, *IEEE Computer Society Conf. Computer Vision Pattern Recognition, June 19–23, Washington, D.C.* (1983).

54. P. Brodatz, "Textures: A Photographic Album for Artists and Designers." Dover, Toronto, 1966.
55. R. L. Kashyap and A. Khotanzad, A stochastic model based technique for texture segmentation, *Proc. 7th Intl. Conf. Pattern Recognition, July 1984.* (1984).
56. R. L. Kashyap and R. D. Bauer, A statistical model based approach to edge detection in textures, *Proceedings of 21st Allerton Conference on Communication, Control and Computers* (1983).
57. A. K. Jain, Advances in mathematical models for image processing, *Proc. IEEE* **69**, 512–528 (1981).
58. J. W. Modestino and R. W. Fries, Edge detection in noisy images using recursive digital filtering, *Computer Graphics Image Processing* **6**, 409–433 (1977).
59. F. M. Vilnrotter, Structural analysis of natural textures, Unpublished Ph.D. dissertation, TR No. USCISG 100, USCIPI 1040, Departments of Electrical Engineering and Computer Science, University of Southern California, Los Angeles, California, September 1981.

# Chapter **13**

# A Computational Analysis of Time-Varying Images

AMAR MITICHE*
and
J. K. AGGARWAL

Laboratory for Image and Signal Analysis
College of Engineering
The University of Texas at Austin
Austin, Texas

## INTRODUCTION: THE IMPORTANCE OF MOTION    I

Psychologists have long asserted the role and significance of motion in the perception of space. The cue of motion is commonly used by the animal

* Present address: Institut National de la Recherche Scientifique, Université du Québec, Verdun, Québec, Canada.

311

visual system, and the survival of some species such as frogs, pit vipers, and boid snakes indeed depends on it. Gibson demonstrated this important use of motion by the human visual system in an experiment at Cornell University [1]. Two translucent plastic sheets containing similar random spot patterns were placed vertically and lighted from one side while being viewed through a screen on the other side. Observers could not segregate the patterns on the plastic sheets when these were stationary, but they could see two planes at different distances, thus segmenting the scene, when the plastic sheets were moved in a direction parallel to the screen. The discrimination of regions in space on the basis of motion has also been demonstrated in Ullman's experimental setup [2] of rotating cylinders, which is similar to the setup of Gibson.

Machines can also record data over time, and temporal integration of these data can reveal a wealth of otherwise unavailable information. For instance, one can detect and measure change and motion from a time-ordered sequence of images. Motion and change in images can then be related to structure and motion of objects in space. For example, one can determine the position of a number of points in space from the observation of these points in two distinct images. Moreover, one can recover the relative position of the viewpoints from which the images are obtained.

In computer vision, motion in images is recovered from a time-ordered sequence of image. This motion is described, basically, either in terms of *image positions* recorded from different views of an observed scene or in terms of *optical flow*. Specifically, optical flow is the field of two-dimensional velocities on the "retinal" surface (optical velocities), these two-dimensional velocities being the projection of the three-dimensional velocities of points moving in space. It is possible to relate analytically either of these observables to structure and motion in space. Also, the Gestalt law of common fate can be translated into a computational process that groups visually distinct regions having similar velocities. In many instances, such a segmentation of the observed environment would not be achieved without the use of motion, just as demonstrated in the psychophysical experiment of Gibson. The assumption here is that regions in images with similar optical velocities correspond to the same object in the scene being viewed.

Dynamic scene analysis, the analysis of time-varying imagery, and image sequence processing all refer to the young field concerned with the processing of sequences or collections of images with the objective of collecting information from the set as a whole that may not be obtained from any one image by itself. This research area of computer vision and computer graphics is relatively new. However, the applications are extensive and the issues are fundamental. The applications for analysis of sequences or collections of images cover a broad range of fields including medicine, autonomous navigation, tomography, communications and television, dancing and choreography, meteorology, and animation. Motivation for this interest becomes evident if one examines any of these endeavors in detail. For example, the automatic analysis of scintigraphic image sequences of the human heart is used to assess motility of the heart and is finding application in diagnosis and supervision of patients after heart surgeries. For sequences of television images, one is able to reduce the bandwidth necessary for the transmission of television signals through motion estimation and compensation. The reduction in the necessary bandwidth may enable the transmission of certain classes of television images on existing low-bandwidth channels. The process-ing of sequences of images for the recognition and the tracking of targets is of immense interest to the department of defense of every country. The computation, characterization, and understanding of human motion in contexts of dancing and athletics is another field of endeavor receiving much attention. In meteorology, the satellite imagery provides opportunity for interpretation and prediction of atmospheric processes through estimation of shape and motion parameters of atmospheric disturbances. Robotics is also a discipline in which three-dimensional vision in general and motion in particular is of significant importance. Indeed, robotics tasks in industrial and manufacturing domains often necessitate control of the visual space, typically for inspection and for locating and tracking mobile objects. Three-dimensional analysis capabilities are needed in many other applications for locating and tracking mobile objects, as in surveillance, guidance, and traffic monitoring. The preceding examples are indicative of the broad interest in motion, time-varying imagery, and dynamic scene analysis.

This broad interest has been evident since the first workshop in Philadelphia [3]. The workshop was expected to be a meeting of a relatively small number of specialists, but it turned into a full-scale conference. Since then, several additional meetings and special issues have contributed to the exchange of ideas and the dissemination of results. In addition, there are several sessions on motion and related issues at meetings such as the IEEE Computer Society Pattern Recognition and Image Processing Conference (now known as the Computer Vision and Pattern Recognition Conference). The list of workshops and special issues devoted exclusively to motion and time-varying imagery includes three special issues [4–6], a book [7], a NATO Advanced Study Institute [8], an ACM workshop [9], a European meeting on time-varying imagery [10], and a host of survey papers [11–13]. The list is incomplete at best. A better guage of the breadth and depth of interest is provided by the table of contents of the book published to document the proceedings of the NATO-ASI [14].

In this chapter we are concerned with a particular problem in dynamic scene analysis: determining three-dimensional structure and motion of objects in space from images. We are specifically interested in the mathematical relationships between image variables (image position and optical velocity) and space variables (position and motion in space). For each image variable, we will present a computational analysis for the perception of space based on the principle of *conservation of distance* in rigid objects.

The remainder of this chapter is organized as follows. In Section II, we review the literature on the subject of measurement of three-dimensional structure and motion from images. In Section III we describe how, in the case of image positions as input, the positions of points in space can be recovered from the observation of these points in two distinct images. We treat the general problem which also involves determining the relative displacement of the viewpoints (defined subsequently in terms of camera-centered coordinate systems) from which the images are taken. We also consider the special case of stereoscopic depth measurement when this relative displacement of viewpoints is known a priori. In Section IV, we are concerned with the perception of space from optical flow. Finally, Section V summarizes the chapter.

## II  REVIEW OF METHODS

The analysis of time-varying imagery is the processing of a time-ordered sequence of images. The ultimate goal is to assimilate information from the sequence as a whole that cannot be obtained from any one image by itself. The principal issues and ingredients of dynamic scene analysis are (a) dynamic scene segmentation, (b) the detection and analysis of occlusion, and (c) the extraction of three-dimensional information from images.

Dynamic scene segmentation consists of dividing images into parts that are changing and parts that are constant, or finding the moving part in each element of the sequence of images. Occlusion occurs when some objects interfere with the visual perception of other objects in the scene. The goal of occlusion analysis is to determine the environmental layout of objects. The extraction of three-dimensional information from images is performed by relating measures in images to measures in space (structure of motion of objects).

Early studies of sequences of images were motivated by the desire to analyze two-dimensional motion, for example, the satellite imagery of clouds. Several researchers also considered abstract models of two-dimensional motion using polygonal as well as curvilinear figures. The use of planar figures and parallel projection allowed these systems to ignore considerations of the third dimension. In contrast to the above purely two-dimensional works, certain researchers have considered scenes containing objects undergoing three-dimensional motion. The initial research, however, analyzed only the image plane motions, taking the two-dimensional approximation to be adequate. This emphasis on two-dimensional motion was a natural outgrowth of the research. Recovery of three-dimensional structure of objects and the parameters of motion are certainly more complex.

**Methods Based on the Use of Image Positions   A
Recorded from Different Viewpoints**

When only this perspective change is used, the problem is that of estimating object position and viewpoint displacement from the observation of a number of points on the object in two distinct images of the object. This problem has been (and still is) of importance in many existing and potential applications. Several authors have contributed answers to some important aspects of the problem.

Ullman [15], in an early paper, has shown that one can determine the exact model of a nonplanar structure of four points, up to a reflection, from three views of this structure; Ullman assumed parallel projection to model this imaging process. Badler [16] considered translating objects and assumed spherical projection in a task that consisted of predicting point positions in successive images of the objects.

The first formulation of the problem using central projection, which is the most realistic model for camera imaging, was that of Roach and Aggarwal [17]. They translated the projective constraints for 5 observed points in two views into a system of 18 nonlinear, transcendental equations in 18 unknowns. The approach was quite sensitive to noise and choice of initial guesses for the unknowns when solving the system of equations numerically using existing iterative algorithms. The method was reasonably accurate only when many more points were taken into account in order to provide a well-overdetermined set of equations.

Huang and co-workers [18-23] have addressed the problem from a slightly different perspective. The approach consisted basically of writing equations for each observed point that related image shifts (the difference in image coordinates of the projections of the point in the two views) and image positions (the coordinates of the projections of the point in the two views) to the relative depth of the point and the parameters of motion. The authors considered several cases, including restricted motion (small angle rotation), restricted geometric configuration of objects (planar patches), and the case of general structure and motion. In the case of small angle rotation, trigonometric simplifications led to a simplification of the problem which was then translated into a set of 10 nonlinear equations in 10 unknowns obtained from 5 observed points [18]. The authors have also considered combining the original equation with the gradient constraint which relates image shifts to spatial and temporal changes in image intensity. However, with this formulation, the problem became feasible only when one made simplifying assumptions on the geometric structure of the observed object. For instance, Huang and Tsai [18] proposed a formulation involving eight points on a planar patch. Without the use of an image intensity constraint, but still restricting the type of object surface to planar patches, Tsai and Huang [20] arrived at a form that necessitated the observation of four points in three views.

Tsai and Huang [22] and Longuet-Higgins [24] have considered the case of objects with curved surfaces and proposed an approach based directly and solely on the use of projective relations for eight points in general positions in space. Tsai and Huang as well as Longuet-Higgins were concerned with the problem of uniqueness of computed motion. Recently Longuet–Higgins [25] has shown formally which degenerate configurations defeat his eight-point algorithm.

Most of these approaches have derived equations which exploited directly projective relations for the observed points and which involved both the three-dimensional coordinates of the points and the parameters of motion. Then a typical counting argument dictated the number of points that had to be observed [26] in order to solve the relations. This generally led to a large set of complicated nonlinear equations or required the observation of a large number of points. To reduce complexity, either simplifying assumptions were introduced (e.g., parallel projection to model imaging, restricted motion such as pure translation or pure or small-angle rotation, known object geometry) or one relied on additional constraints such as the gradient intensity constraint [27]. Linear methods have also been considered when more points could be observed in the images.

In this chapter, we describe a method based on the principle of conservation of distance in rigid objects that is characterized by the following properties: (a) it treats the general case of structure and motion; (b) it separates totally the problem of estimating object position from that of determining motion parameters (this separation renders the first problem much simpler and the second an almost trivial one); (c) it is rather stable numerically; and (d) the solution is unique up to a global scale factor, a reflection in space, and a singular configuration.

## B  Methods Based on Optical Flow

In computer vision, optical flow has been used (a) as a primary cue to structure and motion of objects in space [28–35], (b) to segment scenes into moving and stationary objects from the perception of motion boundaries [36, 37], and (c) to predict future environmental layout [38 and references cited therein].

Most methods that use optical flow to recover structure and motion in space exploit projective relations and the decomposition of motion into a translational and a rotational component but do not incorporate the principal of conservation of distances in rigid objects. This is particularly the case with Nakayama and Loomis [30], Bruss and Horn [31], Lawton and

Rieger [32], Longuet-Higgins and Prazdny [33], and Prazdny [34]. In this chapter we relate object structure and motion in space to image positions and optical flow using (a) rigid-motion relations that characterize the movement of rigid objects in space, (b) the decomposition of motion in terms of translational and rotational components, and (c) projective relations that express the positional relationships between points and their projections on the image plane.

The computation of optical flow itself is a hard but a popular problem in computer vision. The several methods proposed to compute optical velocities fall into two broad classes: feature based and gradient based. Feature-based methods, in which matching is the main operation, generally provide a process that tracks characteristic brightness patterns from frame to frame in a time-ordered sequence of images.

Gradient-based techniques rely on an equation that relates optical velocities to spatial and temporal changes in the image:

$$\frac{\partial f}{\partial x} u + \frac{\partial f}{\partial y} v + \frac{\partial f}{\partial t} = 0 \tag{1}$$

where $f$ is the image function, $t$ is time, $\partial$ is the partial derivative operator, and $u$ and $v$ are the $x$ and $y$ components of optical velocity. A survey of gradient-based techniques can be found in Thompson and Barnard [35]. Both classes of techniques, feature based and gradient based, yield velocities that can be locally inconsistent because of noise and other errors. Therefore, smoothing is often necessary.

Equation (1) alone is, of course, not sufficient to determine the two unknowns $u$ and $v$. Various additional constraints have been proposed in the literature, such as the following.

(a)   Optical velocity is the one that best satisfies (1) in an appropriate neighborhood of a point under consideration. This approach is extensively used in motion-compensated video coding.

(b)   Optical flow is smooth (neighboring points have similar velocities).

(c)   Optical flow is constant over entire segments in the image.

(d)   Optical flow is the result of restricted motion (e.g., planar motion).

## PERCEPTION OF SPACE USING IMAGE POSITIONS   III
## FROM DIFFERENT VIEWPOINTS

In this section we treat the general case of recovering positions of points from two distinct views of these points and the relative displacement of the viewpoints from which the images were obtained. We also consider the special case of stereoscopic depth measurement when this relative displacement of viewpoints is known beforehand.

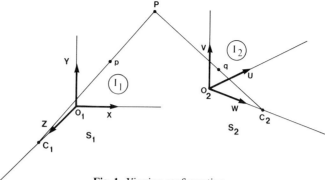

**Fig. 1.** Viewing configuration.

## A   Imaging Geometry: The Scalar Form of Projective Relations

Because the world is static, it is, of course, irrelevant whether we have two views from one camera at two distinct instants of time or one view from each of two cameras. Time does not play a direct role in the analysis. For ease in description we will assume two cameras, the configuration of which is shown in Fig. 1. Both cameras are represented by a central projection model modified not to invert images. The cameras will be called the first and second camera. The first and second cameras have, in this order, projection centers $C_1$ and $C_2$ and image planes $I_1$ and $I_2$. The first and second camera have coordinate systems $S_1 \equiv (O_1, X, Y, Z)$ and $S_2 \equiv (O_2, U, V, W)$, where $(O_1, X, Y)$ and $(O_2, U, V)$ are, in this order, the $I_1$ and $I_2$ image coordinate systems. The coordinates of $C_2$ in $S_1$ are $(0, 0, f_1)$ and the coordinates of $C_2$ in $S_2$ are $(0, 0, f_2)$, where $f_1$ and $f_2$ are positive real numbers. The principal axis of the cameras are aligned with the $Z$ axis and the $W$ axis.

A point $P_i$ in space, the coordinates of which are $(X_i, Y_i, Z_i)$ in $S_1$ and $(U_i, V_i, W_i)$ in $S_2$, is imaged on $p_i$ in $I_1$ and $q_i$ in $I_2$. Because $P_i$ is on line $C_i p_i$ (cf. Fig. 1), there exists $\lambda_i > 1$ such that

$$X_i = \lambda_i x_i, \qquad Y_i = \lambda_i y_i, \qquad Z_i = (1 - \lambda_i) f_1 \qquad (2)$$

where $(x_i, y_i)$ are the coordinates of $p_i$ in the $I_i$ image coordinate system. Similarly, $P_i$ is on line $C_2 q_i$, and if $(u_i, v_i)$ are the coordinates of $q_i$ in the $I_2$ coordinate system, then there exist $\gamma_i > 1$ such that

$$U_i = \gamma_i u_i, \qquad V_i = \gamma_i v_i, \qquad W_i = (1 - \gamma_i) f_2 \qquad (3)$$

This formulation will be used in subsequent analysis and referred to as the *scalar form* of projective relations.

The main idea in this method is the use of the principle of conservation of distances in rigid objects and rigid motion. This principle, which is the subject of a theorem in kinematics of solids [39], simple states an obvious fact: distances in a rigid configuration of points do not change during rigid motion. It was shown by Mitiche [28, 29] that this characterization of rigid motion can lead to powerful formulations of various structure and motion problems.

The distance between points $P_i$ and $P_j$ expressed in $S_1$ is therefore

$$d_{ij}^{S_1} = (X_i - X_j)^2 + (Y_i - Y_j)^2 + (Z_i - Z_j)^2$$

or, using the scalar form of projective relations developed earlier [Eqs. (2) and (3),

$$d_{ij}^{S_1} = (\lambda_i x_i - \lambda_j x_j)^2 + (\lambda_i y_i - \lambda_j y_j)^2 + (\lambda_i - \lambda_j)^2 f_1^2$$

Similarly, the distance between $P_i$ and $P_j$ expressed in $S_2$ is

$$d_{ij}^{S_2} = (\gamma_i u_i - \gamma_j u_j)^2 + (\gamma_i v_i - \gamma_j v_j)^2 + (\gamma_i - \gamma_j)^2 f_2^2$$

Now the principle of conservation of distance allows us to write (assuming, of course, identical units of measurement in $S_1$ and $S_2$)

$$d_{ij}^{S_1} = d_{ij}^{S_2}$$

or

$$(\lambda_i x_i - \lambda_j x_j)^2 + (\lambda_i y_i - \lambda_j y_j)^2 + (\lambda_i - \lambda_j)^2 f_1^2$$
$$= (\gamma_i u_i - \gamma_j u_j)^2 + (\gamma_i v_i - \gamma_j v_j)^2 + (\gamma_i - \gamma_j)^2 f_2^2 \qquad (4)$$

It may be seen that each point $P_i$ contributes two unknowns $\lambda_i$ and $\gamma_i$, and each pair of points $(P_i, P_j)$ gives one second-order equation [Eq. (4)]. Therefore, 5 points yield 10 equations in 10 unknowns. Note that (4) can be rewritten equivalently using a scale factor; this is a translation of the fact that the scale of the observed structure of points cannot be known. We can fix this scale by fixing the distance of a point from one of the cameras which amounts to fixing arbitrarily one of the variables. Therefore, we end up with a system of 10 equations in 9 unknowns. Note that each equation involves only four of the unknowns. Note also that the formulation so far does not involve the parameters of the displacement between the two cameras. Because these parameters do not appear in the equations and also because only some of the unknowns of position appear in each of them, the resulting system of equations can be solved quite efficiently using existing numerical iterative algorithms.

The following is an intuitive explanation of this method. Refer to Fig. 2. Call $B_1$ the bundle of projecting lines going through projection center $C_1$ and the five given image points in $I_1$; also call $B_2$ the bundle of projecting lines through $C_2$ and the corresponding five image points in $I_2$. What we really did when we solved the system of equations (4) was to determine five points $P_1, \ldots, P_5$, one on each line of bundle $B_1$, and five points $Q_1, \ldots, Q_5$, one on each line of bundle $B_2$, such that distances between points $\{P_i\}$, $i = 1, 5$, and distances between corresponding points $\{Q_i\}$, $i = 1, 5$, are the same. In the next section we will simply "register" these points to determine the relative position of the cameras.

Also, it may be noted that since distances between points define our structure only up to a reflection in space [40], the solution of system (4), which is based on these distances, will also be subject to this uncertainty. Moreover, it can be shown that all other cases where uniqueness cannot be ascertained are singular configuration of points in space [41].

The preceding analysis can be summarized as follows: the position of a rigid structure of five points in space can be computed given the central projection of these points in two distinct images.

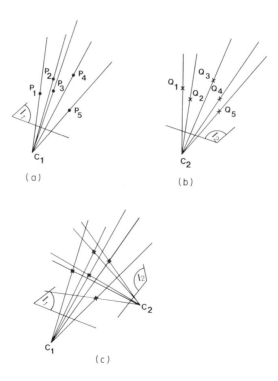

**Fig. 2.** (a) Five projected lines and points in the first view, (b) five projected lines and points in the second view, and (c) points registered.

**Estimation of Camera Relative Position and Orientation   C**

When the position of the points has been computed, determining the relative position of the cameras becomes a simple matter. Indeed, take four non-coplanar points (from the five observed points in space) and call $A_1$ and $A_2$ the matrices of homogeneous coordinates of these in $S_1$ and $S_2$, respectively. Then, if $M$ is the transformation matrix (in homogeneous coordinate form) that takes $S_1$ onto $S_2$, we have

$$A_2 = M_1 A_1 \qquad (5)$$

Since the four points are not coplanar, Eq. (5) can be solved for $M$.

Now if we decompose the motion into a rotation through angle $\theta$ about an axis through the origin the direction cosines of which are $n_1, n_2, n_3$, followed by a translation $(t_1, t_2, t_3)$, and if it is written as

$$M = \begin{bmatrix} a_1 & a_2 & a_3 & 0 \\ a_4 & a_5 & a_6 & 0 \\ a_7 & a_8 & a_9 & 0 \\ b_1 & b_2 & b_3 & 1 \end{bmatrix}$$

then one can show that (see [40] and [22] for details) that

$$t_1 = b_1, \qquad t_2 = b_2, \qquad t_3 = b_3$$

$$\cos \theta = \frac{a_1 + a_5 + a_9 - 1}{2}, \qquad \sin \theta = \frac{a_6 - a_8}{2n_1}$$

$$n_1 = \sqrt{\frac{a_1 - \cos \theta}{1 - \cos \theta}}, \qquad n_2 = \frac{a_2 + a_4}{2n_1(1 - \cos \theta)}, \qquad n_3 = \sqrt{1 - n_1^2 - n_2^2}$$

*Examples.* A large number of five-point sets were generated in a $1\,\text{m}^3$ space approximately $2\,\text{m}$ away from the cameras, and their image positions were moved randomly to simulate errors. These errors on image position are quite often on the order of one or two pixels, where a pixel is that of a $36 \times 36\,\text{mm}^2$ image window digitized $360 \times 360$. The equations were solved by least-squares analysis using a modification of the Levenberg–Marquandt algorithm. The plot of Fig. 3 shows the performance of the algorithm for computing the position of points in space. This plot represents relative error on distances between computed points versus cumulative frequency of the error measured as a fraction of unity. The few cases for which the error is large probably come from singular or near-singular configurations in space.

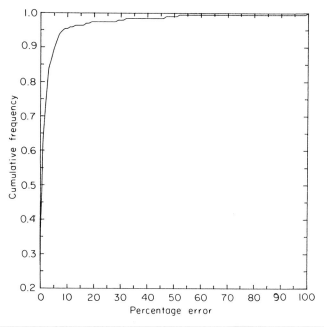

**Fig. 3.** Present error versus cumulative frequency of cases measured as a fraction of unity.

## D   Stereoscopic Depth Measurement

In this case, we know the relative displacement between the two views and the problem becomes that of triangulation [42]. Let the transform taking $S_1$ onto $S_2$ be decomposed into a rotation about an axis through the origin $O_1$ and a translation. Let the rotation be described by the matrix

$$\mathbf{R} = \begin{bmatrix} a_{11} & a_{12} & a_{13} \\ a_{21} & a_{22} & a_{23} \\ a_{31} & a_{32} & a_{33} \end{bmatrix}$$

and the translation by the vector $\mathbf{T} = (U_T, V_T, W_T)$.

Let $P$ be a point in space with coordinates $(X, Y, Z)$ in $S_1$ and $(U, V, W)$ in $S_2$ and let its projections on $I_1$ and $I_2$ be, respectively, $p$ with coordinates $(x, y)$ and $q$ with coordinates $(u, v)$. Using the $S_1$-onto-$S_2$ transform, we can write

$$(U, V, W) = (X, Y, Z) \cdot \mathbf{R} + \mathbf{T}$$

Using the scalar notation of Section II.A with scalars $\lambda$ and $\gamma$ we can rewrite this formula as

$$(\gamma u, \gamma v, (1 - \gamma)f_2) = (\lambda x, \lambda y, (1 - \lambda)f_1) \cdot \mathbf{R} + \mathbf{T}$$

or in expanded form,

$$a_{11}x\lambda + a_{21}y\lambda + a_{31}(1 - \lambda)f_1 + U_T = \gamma u$$
$$a_{12}x\lambda + a_{22}y\lambda + a_{32}(1 - \lambda)f_1 + V_T = \gamma v \qquad (6)$$
$$a_{13}x\lambda + a_{23}y\lambda + a_{33}(1 - \lambda)f_1 + W_T = (1 - \gamma)f_2$$

Two of these equations are used to solve for $\lambda$ and $\gamma$ and thus for the position of $P$ in space. The third equation should be satisfied by the pair $(\lambda, \gamma)$ computed from the other two equations. This provides a necessary condition for correspondence between image points $p$ and $q$. A geometric interpretation of this argument is as follows. Solving for $\lambda$ and $\gamma$ from two of the equations in (6) (say, the first two) means that we are determining a point $P_1$ on line $C_1 p$ and a point $P_2$ on line $C_2 q$ such that their first two coordinates in $S_2$ are equal. If the lines actually intersect and their analytic representation is exact, then the third equation, when satisfied by $\lambda$ and $\gamma$, expresses this fact. If the two lines do not intersect, then the absolute difference between the left- and right-hand side of the third equation measures the distance between $P_1$ and $P_2$, line $P_1 P_2$ being orthogonal to the plane of the first two coordinates in $S_2$. This distance can be used as an error measure when solving for the intersection of lines in practical cases.

A solution to two from the three equations in (6) does not exist when the projections of lines $C_1 p$ and $C_2 q$ on the plane of the coordinates in $S_2$ corresponding to the two equations are parallel. Also, note that an infinite number of pairs of points $P_1$ and $P_2$ exist that have the same two coordinates in $S_2$ when lines $C_1 p$ and $C_2 q$ have the same projection on the plane of these two coordinates. In such a case, one should switch to two other equations from (6).

*Example* (a) $S_2$ is obtained from $S_1$ by a translation $(\alpha, \beta, 0)$ in the $(X, Y)$ plane. In this case we have

$$\mathbf{R} = \begin{bmatrix} 1 & 0 & 0 \\ 0 & 1 & 0 \\ 0 & 0 & 1 \end{bmatrix}, \qquad \mathbf{T} = (-\alpha, -\beta, 0)$$

and (6) becomes

$$\lambda x = \gamma u + \alpha$$
$$\lambda y = \gamma v + \beta$$
$$(1 - \lambda)f_1 = (1 - \gamma)f_2$$

If $f_1 = f_2$ then

$$\lambda = \gamma = \alpha/(x - u) = \beta/(y - v)$$

(b) $S_2$ is obtained from $S_1$ by a rotation through angle $\phi$ about axis $O_1 Y$

followed by a translation $(\alpha, 0, 0)$ along $O_1 X$. Then

$$\mathbf{R} = \begin{bmatrix} \cos\phi & 0 & \sin\phi \\ 0 & 1 & 0 \\ -\sin\phi & 0 & \cos\phi \end{bmatrix} \qquad \text{and} \qquad \mathbf{T} = (-\alpha, 0, 0)$$

and one can arrive at

$$\lambda = \frac{(f\sin\phi - \alpha)v}{yu - v(x\cos\phi - f\sin\phi)}, \qquad \gamma = \lambda\frac{y}{v}$$

## IV  PERCEPTION OF SPACE FROM OPTICAL FLOW

In the following section we are concerned with the problem of recovering structure and motion from optical flow. Optical flow is the field of two-dimensional velocities on the projection surface of the images of points moving in space. Since we are using velocities, we will, for ease of analysis, treat time as a continuous variable. We will therefore consider instantaneous, continuous motion, in contrast to discrete, three-dimensional displacements, as in the preceding section. Although motion is understood here to be a relative concept, subsequent discussions apply to a mobile scene and stationary viewing system.

## A  Rigid Motion

To test for rigid motion we will again use the principle of conservation of distance in rigid objects. Since we are considering instantaneous motion, we express this principle in terms of time as a continuous variable. In this context, the principle of conservation of distance is the subject of a theorem in kinematics of solids. This theorem is a characterization of a rigid motion and states that a motion is that of a rigid object *if and only if* the distance between points of the body is invariant with time. A formal statement of the theorem can be found in Lelong-Ferrand and Arnaudies [39]. We recall it here and give a proof without mathematical formalism. For instance, when no confusion is possible, we will not make a distinction between a point in a body and the position it occupies in space at a given time. In particular, we will designate these by the same name. Also, for notational convenience, dependence of position on time is left implicit.

The theorem states that for a body $B$, defined by a discrete set of points $E$, a $C^1$ motion of $B$ is a rigid motion if and only if at each instant $t$ its field of

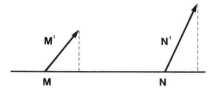

**Fig. 4.** Three-dimensional velocities of points on a rigid object are equiprojective.

three-dimensional velocities is equiprojective (see Figure 4), that is, it satisfies the following relation for each pair of points $(M, N)$:

$$(M' - N') \cdot \mathbf{MN} = 0$$

where $M'$ and $N'$ are the three-dimensional velocities of $M$ and $N$, respectively, $\mathbf{MN}$ is the vector with origin $M$ and endpoint $N$, and "·" designates the dot product. A $C^1$ motion is a motion such that the functions that represent positions of points as a function of time are of class $C^1$ (continuously differentiable). A velocity field of a motion at time $t$ is the field of velocities of points of $E$ at time $t$.

The proof is really trivial; let **OM** and **ON** be the vectors associated with points $M$ and $N$, respectively (vectors emanating from the origin with endpoints $M$ and $N$, respectively). The motion is rigid if and only if the distance between each pair of points in $E$ is invariant with time, that is, if and only if

$$(\forall t)(\forall M \in E) \quad (\forall N \in E) \quad \frac{d}{dt} \overline{\mathbf{MN}}^2 = 0$$

or, equivalently,

$$\left( \frac{d}{dt} \mathbf{OM} - \frac{d}{dt} \mathbf{ON} \right) \cdot \mathbf{MN} = 0$$

or simply

$$(M' - N') \cdot \mathbf{MN} = \bar{0}$$

which completes the proof.

### Rigid Motion and Optical Flow    **B**

The preceding theorem may be stated explicitly in terms of image positions and optical velocities. Let $P$ be any point in space with space coordinates $(X, Y, Z)$ and image coordinates $(x, y)$. Let $(u, v)$ designate the optical velocity of $P$. For ease of analysis and without loss of generality, we will modify our central projection model slightly by placing the origin at the projection center and setting the focal length to 1. The configuration is as in Fig. 5. We have

$$X = xZ, \qquad Y = yZ \tag{7}$$

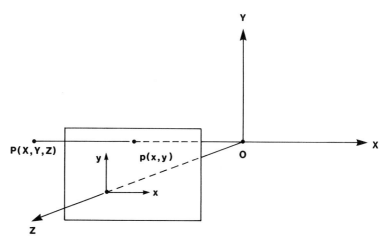

**Fig. 5.** Viewing configuration for optical flow computation.

Therefore, if $(X', Y', Z')$ is the three-dimensional velocity vector of $P$ (the time derivatives of the coordinates of $P$), then

$$X' = uZ + xZ', \qquad Y' = vZ + yZ' \tag{8}$$

Then, if we are given two points $P_1$ and $P_2$, the rigid motion constraint for these two points can be written as

$$(X_1' - X_2')(X_2 - X_1) + (Y_1' - Y_2')(Y_2 - Y_1) + (Z_1' - Z_2')(Z_2 - Z_1) = 0 \tag{9}$$

If we substitute (7) and (8) in (9), we can phrase the principle of conservation of distance in rigid objects as follows: for a body $B$ defined by a discrete set of points $E$, a $C^1$ motion of $B$ is a rigid motion if and only if

$(\forall t)(\forall P_1 \in E)(\forall P_2 \in E)$

$$aZ_1^2 + bZ_2^2 + cZ_1Z_2 + dZ_1Z_1' + eZ_1Z_2' + fZ_2Z_2' + eZ_2Z_1' = 0 \tag{10}$$

where

$$a = -u_1x_1 - v_1y_1$$

$$b = -u_2x_2 - v_2y_2$$

$$c = u_1x_2 + v_1y_2 + u_2x_1 + v_2y_1$$

$$d = -x_1^2 - y_1^2 - 1$$

$$e = x_1x_2 + y_1y_2 + 1$$

$$f = -x_2^2 - y_2^2 - 1$$

The rigid motion constraint in this form relates image positions and optical velocities explicitly to depth ($Z$ and $Z'$). Now we want to go one step further and use the fact that rigid motion can be expressed in terms of a rotation and a translation. If we designate the translational velocity of motion by $\mathbf{T} = (T_1, T_2, T_3)$ and the rotational velocity by $\mathbf{\Omega} = (\Omega_1, \Omega_2, \Omega_3)$, then the velocity $P' = (X', Y', Z')$ of point $P = (X, Y, Z)$ is, assuming moving points and a stationary viewing system,

$$P' = \mathbf{T} + \mathbf{\Omega} \times \mathbf{OP}$$

or, in expanded form,

$$X' = T_1 + \Omega_2 Z - \Omega_3 Y$$
$$Y' = T_2 + \Omega_3 X - \Omega_1 Z \tag{11}$$
$$Z' = T_3 + \Omega_1 Y - \Omega_2 X$$

We will be concerned with the third equation of (11), in which we will replace $X$ and $Y$ by their expression in (7), namely,

$$Z' = T_3 + \Omega_1 y Z - \Omega_2 x Z \tag{12}$$

Now, if we substitute (12) in (10), we obtain the following rigid-motion equation for points $P_1$ and $P_2$, in the unknowns $Z_1, Z_2, \Omega_1, \Omega_2$, and $T_3$:

$$(a - dx_1\Omega_2 + dy_1\Omega_1)Z_1^2 + (b - fx_2\Omega_2 + fy_2\Omega_1)Z_2^2$$
$$+ [c - e(x_1 + x_2)\Omega_2 + e(y_1 + y_2)\Omega_1]Z_1 Z_2$$
$$+ (d + e)T_3 Z_1 + (f + e)T_3 Z_2 = 0 \tag{13}$$

From the preceding analysis, we can readily make the following observations.

(1)   Since structure can be known only up to a scale factor, we can choose this factor arbitrarily and fix one point in space by setting its $Z$ coordinate arbitrarily. When we do so, and if we recall that motion parameters ($T$'s and $\Omega$'s) are global parameters and hence the same for all points belonging to the same rigid body, then a simple counting argument indicates that a set of four points yields six unknowns, $Z_2, Z_3, Z_4, T_3, \Omega_1, \Omega_2$, and provides six equations such as (13). Image positions and optical velocities are assumed known, and $Z_1$ is chosen arbitrarily.

(2)   When we solve for depth ($Z$ and $Z'$ or, equivalently, $Z$ and $T_3, \Omega_1, \Omega_2$), then structure is determined from (7) knowing $Z$, and image positions and three-dimensional motion are determined from (8) knowing $Z, Z'$, image positions, and optical velocities.

We summarize the analysis by the following proposition: the position and motion of a rigid structure of four points can be computed given the points' image positions and optical velocities under a central projection model.

**TABLE I**
**Coordinates of the Structure in Space**
**(Noise-Free Case)**

|        | $X$  | $Y$  | $Z$  |
|--------|------|------|------|
| $P_1$  | 0.3  | 0.3  | 1.5  |
| $P_2$  | 0.3  | 0.5  | 1.5  |
| $P_3$  | 0.5  | 0.3  | 1.5  |
| $P_4$  | 0.3  | 0.5  | 1.7  |

**TABLE II**
**Computed Parameters for Various Initial Approximations**
**(Noise-Free Case)[a]**

|          | $Z_2$ | $Z_3$ | $Z_4$ | $\Omega_1$ | $\Omega_2$ | $T_3$ |
|----------|-------|-------|-------|-----------|-----------|-------|
| Actual   | 1.5   | 1.5   | 1.7   | 0.        | 0.        | 1.0   |
| Initial  | 1.4   | 1.4   | 1.5   | 0.5       | 0.5       | 0.5   |
| Computed | 1.475 | 1.483 | 1.575 | −0.189    | 0.111     | 1.102 |
| Initial  | 1.4   | 1.4   | 1.6   | 0.5       | 0.5       | 0.5   |
| Computed | 1.519 | 1.511 | 1.799 | 0.046     | 0.027     | 0.979 |
| Initial  | 1.45  | 1.45  | 1.6   | 0.5       | 0.5       | 0.5   |
| Computed | 1.501 | 1.500 | 1.705 | 0.003     | 0.002     | 0.998 |

[a] The coordinates are measured in meters.

**TABLE III**
**Effect of Noisy Optical Velocities[a]**

|               | $Z_2$ | $Z_3$ | $Z_4$ | $\Omega_1$ | $\Omega_2$ | $T_3$ |
|---------------|-------|-------|-------|-----------|-----------|-------|
| Actual        | 1.5   | 1.5   | 1.7   | 0.        | 0.        | 1.0   |
| Initial       | 1.45  | 1.45  | 1.6   | 0.5       | 0.5       | 0.5   |
| Computed      |       |       |       |           |           |       |
| Noise = 0.01  | 1.480 | 1.505 | 1.660 | −0.044    | 0.005     | 1.037 |
| Noise = 0.02  | 1.470 | 1.518 | 1.677 | −0.040    | 0.014     | 1.050 |
| Noise = 0.05  | 1.434 | 1.509 | 1.579 | −0.236    | 0.025     | 1.162 |

[a] Noise measured as a fraction of the velocity randomly added or subtracted.

*Examples.* Tables I–IV contain results from experiments in which the
system of equations (13) is solved using the secant method as implemented in
the routine ZSCNT under the IMSL library. This method is iterative and
requires an initial guess for the unknowns. Although solutions are quite
accurate when the level of noise in the data is reasonable, they are sensitive
to higher perturbations of image positions and optical velocities. This seems

**TABLE IV**
**Effect of Noisy Image Positions[a]**

|  | $Z_2$ | $Z_3$ | $Z_4$ | $\Omega_1$ | $\Omega_2$ | $T_3$ |
|---|---|---|---|---|---|---|
| Actual | 1.5 | 1.5 | 1.7 | 0.0 | 0.0 | 1.0 |
| Initial | 1.45 | 1.45 | 1.6 | 0.5 | 0.5 | 0.5 |
| Computed |  |  |  |  |  |  |
|   Noise = 0.25 pixels | 1.495 | 1.497 | 1.678 | −0.015 | 0.0095 | 1.008 |
|   Noise = 0.5 pixels | 1.489 | 1.493 | 1.644 | −0.049 | 0.029 | 1.025 |
|   Noise = 1.0 pixels | 1.472 | 1.482 | 1.562 | −0.242 | 0.142 | 1.133 |

[a] Noise measured in pixels, where a pixel is that of a 36-mm film digitized 360 × 360.

to indicate that computational processes that rely on optical flow to recover structure and motion will be successful only if image variables can be measured with accuracy. Results in Tables I–IV are for a four-point structure receding in space at uniform speed. An object with such a motion would exhibit an optical flow field such as the one in Fig. 6. Similar results have been obtained for other motions.

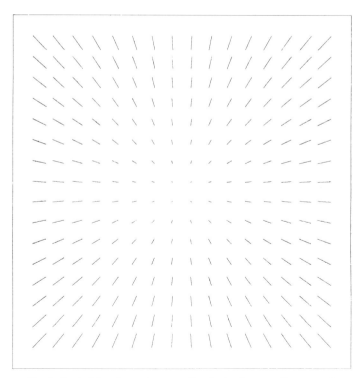

**Fig. 6.** Optical flow for a plane receding in depth at a uniform speed.

## V  SUMMARY

In this chapter we have described a computational approach to the perception of space. We have considered two inputs: image positions from different viewpoints and optical flow. In the case of image positions from different viewpoints, time did not play an explicit role because the world was assumed static and rigid. The problem was then defined as that of recovering the position of points in space from the observation of these points in two distinct images. The time at which these images were acquired was irrelevant to the problem. We presented a solution based on the principle of conservation of distances in rigid objects. This solution required the observation of at least five points in two images. The correspondence between these points in the two images was also assumed known. We also considered the problem of determining the relative position of the viewpoints. We have shown that this problem becomes an easy one to solve when the position of the points in space is known. When this relative position of the viewpoints is known beforehand, the problem is that of stereoscopic depth measurement, for which we have shown a solution based on the scalar form of projective relations which we have used throughout the chapter.

With optical flow, we used optical velocities in addition to image positions. We have described a formulation which allowed the computation of object position and motion in space from the observation of these image positions and optical velocities at four distinct points in image space. The formulation was also based on the principle of conservation of distance in rigid objects.

## REFERENCES

1. E. J. Gibson, J. J. Gibson, O. W. Smith, and H. Flock, Motion parallax as a determinant of perceived depth, *J. Exp. Psychol.* **58**, 40–51 (1959).
2. S. Ullman, "The Interpretation of Visual Motion." Cambridge, MIT Press, Massachusetts, 1979.
3. J. K. Aggarwal and N. I. Badler (eds.), Abstracts for the Workshop on Computer Analysis of Time-Varying Imagery, University of Pennsylvania, Moore School of Electrical Engineering, Philadelphia, Pennsylvania, April 1979.
4. J. K. Aggarwal and N. I. Badler (Guest eds.), Special issue on motion and time-varying imagery, *IEEE Trans. on Pattern Analysis and Machine Intelligence* **PAMI-2** (6) (1980).
5. W. E. Snyder (Guest ed.), Computer analysis of time-varying images, *IEEE Computer* **C-14** (8) (1981).
6. J. K. Aggarwal (Guest ed.), Motion and time varying imagery, *Computer Vision, Graphics and Image Processing* **21**, (1 and 2) (1983).
7. T. S. Huang, "Image Sequence Analysis." Springer-Verlag, New York, 1981.
8. NATO advanced study institute on image sequence processing and dynamic scene analysis, *Advance Abstracts of Invited and Contributory Papers, June 21–July 2, 1982, Braunlage, West Germany* (1982).
9. Siggraph/Siggart Interdisciplinary Workshop on Motion: Representation and Perception, Toronto, Canada, April 4–6, 1983.

10. European Conference on Time-Varying Imagery, Florence, Italy, 1982.
11. W. N. Martin and J. K. Aggarwal, Dynamic scene analysis: A survey, *Computer Graphics and Image Processing* **7**, 356–374 (1978).
12. H.-H. Nagel, Analysis techniques for image sequences, *Proc. IJCPR-78, Kyoto, Japan, November 1978, pp.* 186–211 (1978).
13. J. K. Aggarwal and W. N. Martin, Dynamic scene analysis, *in* "Image Sequence Processing and Dynamic Scene Analysis" (T. S. Huang, ed.), pp. 40–74. Springer-Verlag, New York, 1983.
14. T. S. Huang (ed.), Image sequence processing and dynamic scene analysis, *Proceedings of NATO Advanced Study Institute at Braunlage, West Germany*, Springer-Verlag, New York, 1983.
15. S. Ullman, The interpretation of structure from motion, *MIT Artificial Intelligence Laboratory, AI Memo* **476**, (October 1976).
16. N. Badler, Temporal scene analysis: Conceptual descriptions of object movements, Unpublished Ph.D dissertation, University of Toronto, Toronto, Ontario, Canada, TR80, 1975.
17. J. W. Roach and J. K. Aggarwal, Determining the movement of objects from a sequence of images, *IEEE Transactions on Pattern Analysis and Machine Intelligence* **PAMI-6**, 554–562 (1980).
18. T. S. Huang and R. Y. Tsai, Image sequence analysis: Motion estimation, *in* "Image Sequence Analysis" (T. S. Huang, ed.), Chapter 1.
19. R. Y. Tsai and T. S. Huang, Estimating three-dimensional motion parameters of a rigid planar patch, *Proceedings of the IEEE Conference on Pattern Recognition and Image Processing, Dallas, Texas pp.* 94–97 (1981).
20. R. Y. Tsai and T. S. Huang, Uniqueness and estimation of three-dimensional motion parameters of a rigid planar patch from three perspective views, *Proc. IEEE International Conference on Acoustics, Speech and Signal Processing, Paris, France pp.* 834–838 (1982).
21. J. Q. Fang and T. S. Huang, Solving three-dimensional small-rotation motion equations, *Proc. IEEE Conf. Computer Vision Pattern Recognition, Washington, D.C.* pp. 253–258 (1983).
22. R. Y. Tsai and T. S. Huang, Uniqueness and estimation of three-dimensional motion parameters of rigid objects with curved surfaces, *IEEE Transactions on Pattern Analysis and Machine Intelligence* **PAMI-6** (1), 13–26 (1984).
23. B. L. Yen and T. S. Huang, Determining 3-D motion/structure of a rigid body over 3 frames using straight line correspondences, *Proc. IEEE Conf. Computer Vision Pattern Recognition, Washington, D.C.* pp. 267–272 (1983).
24. H. C. Longuet-Higgins, A computer algorithm for reconstructing a scene from two projections, *Nature (London)* **293**, 133–135 (1981).
25. H. C. Longuet-Higgins, The reconstruction of a scene from two projections—configuration that defeat the 8 point algorithm, *Proc. 1st Conference on Artificial Intelligence Applications, Denver Colorado,* pp. 395–397 (1984).
26. A. Z. Meiri, On monocular perception of 3-D moving objects, *IEEE Transactions on Pattern Analysis and Machine Intelligence* **PAMI-2** (6) 582–583 (1980).
27. B. K. P. Horn and B. G. Schunk, Determining optical flow, *Artificial Intelligence* **17**, 185–203 (1983).
28. A. Mitiche, Computation of optical flow and rigid motion, *Proc. Workshop on Computer Vision: Representation and Control Annapolis, Maryland* 63–71 (1984).
29. A. Mitiche. On combining stereopsis and kineopsis for space perception, *Proc. 1st Conference on Artificial Intelligence Applications, Denver, Colorado* 156–160 (1984).
30. K. Nakayama and J. M. Loomis, Optical velocity patterns, velocity-sensitive neurons, and space perception: a hypothesis *Perception* **3**, 63–80 (1974).
31. A. R. Bruss and B. K. P. Horn, Passive navigation, *Computer Vision, Graphics, and Image Processing* **21**, 3–20 (1983).

32. D. T. Lawton and J. H. Rieger, The use of difference fields in processing sensor motion, *Proc. Image Understanding Workshop, Washington D.C.*, pp. 77–83 (1983).

33. H. C. Longuet-Higgins and K. Prazdny, The interpretation of a moving retinal image, *Proc. R. Soc. London Ser. B* **208**, 385–397 (1980).

34. K. Prazdny, On the information in optical flows, *Computer Vision, Graphics, and Image Processing* **22**, 239–259 (1983).

35. W. B. Thompson and S. T. Barnard, Lower-level estimation and interpretation of visual motion, *Computer* **14**, 20–28 (1981).

36. W. B. Thompson, Combining motion and contrast for segmentation, *IEEE Transactions on Pattern Analysis and Machine Intelligence* **PAMI-2**, 543–549 (1980).

37. J. L. Potter, Scene segmentation using motion information, *Computer Graphics and Image Processing* **6**, 558–581 (1972).

38. R. Paquin and E. Dubois, A spatio-temporal gradient method for estimating the displacement field in time-varying imagery, *Computer Vision, Graphics, and Image Processing*, 205–221 (1983).

39. J. Lelong-Ferrand and J. M. Arnaudies, "Cours de Mathématiques," Tome 3, 2nd Ed. Dunod Université, Paris, France, 1974.

40. A. Mitiche and P. Bouthemy, Tracking modelled structures using bionocular images, *Computer Vision, Graphics, and Image Processing*, in press.

41. A. Mitiche, S. Sieda, and J. K. Aggarwal, Determining position and displacement in space from two images, *Proc. Conf. Computer Vision and Pattern Recognition* (1985).

42. R. O. Duda and P. E. Hart, "Pattern Classification and Scene Analysis." Wiley, New York, 1973.

Chapter **14**

# Determining Three-Dimensional Motion and Structure from Two Perspective Views

THOMAS S. HUANG

Coordinated Science Laboratory
University of Illinois
Urbana, Illinois

HANDBOOK OF PATTERN RECOGNITION
AND IMAGE PROCESSING

# I  INTRODUCTION

Determining the relative motion between an observer and his environment is a major problem in computer vision. Its applications include mobile robot navigation and monitoring dynamic industrial processes. Motion estimation also has many applications in image processing. For example, in efficient coding using differential pulse code modulation (DPCM) in time, motion estimation and compensation can potentially improve the compression significantly. In reducing noise in image sequences by temporal filtering, registration of the object of interest from frame to frame is necessary to avoid blurring, and registration is, in essence, equivalent to motion estimation. The reader is referred to Huang [1, 2] for some of these applications.

In this chapter we present an approach to the determination of three-dimensional motion of a single, isolated rigid body from two time-sequential perspective views (image frames).

## A  Problem Statement

The basic geometry of the problem is sketched in Fig. 1. The object-space coordinates are denoted by lowercase letters, and the image-space coordinates are denoted by uppercase letters. Let the two views be taken at $t_1$ and $t_2$, respectively, and let $t_1 < t_2$. The coordinates at $t_2$ are primed, while the coordinates at $t_1$ are unprimed. Specifically, consider a particular physical point $p$ on the surface of a rigid body in the scene. Let $(x, y, z)$ be the object-space coordinates of $P$ at time $t_1$, $(x', y', z')$ the object-space coordinates of $P$ at time $t_2$, $(X, Y)$ the image-space coordinates of $P$ at time $t_1$, and $(X', Y')$ the image-space coordinates of $P$ at time $t_2$. We define

$$\Delta X \triangleq X' - X, \qquad \Delta Y \triangleq Y' - Y \tag{1}$$

as the image-space shifts (or displacements) of $P$ from $t_1$ to $t_2$.

It is well known from kinematics that the object coordinates of $P$ at time instants $t_1$ and $t_2$ are related by

$$\begin{bmatrix} x' \\ y' \\ z' \end{bmatrix} = R \begin{bmatrix} x \\ y \\ z \end{bmatrix} + \mathbf{T} = \begin{bmatrix} r_{11} & r_{12} & r_{13} \\ r_{21} & r_{22} & r_{23} \\ r_{31} & r_{32} & r_{33} \end{bmatrix} \begin{bmatrix} x \\ y \\ z \end{bmatrix} + \begin{bmatrix} \Delta x \\ \Delta y \\ \Delta z \end{bmatrix} \tag{2}$$

where $R$ represents a rotation and $\mathbf{T}$ a translation. To make the representation unique, we specify that the rotation is around an axis passing through the origin of our coordinate system. Let $\hat{n} = (n_1, n_2, n_3)$ be a unit vector along the axis of rotation, and let $\theta$ be the angle of rotation from $t_1$ to $t_2$. Then the elements of $R$ can be expressed in terms of $n_1$, $n_2$, $n_3$, and $\theta$. Remembering

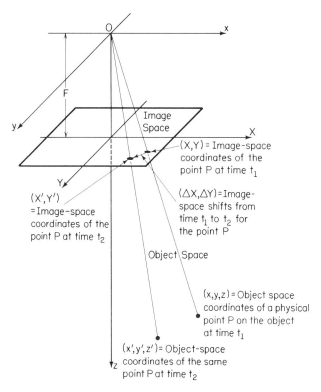

**Fig. 1.** Basic geometry for three-dimensional motion estimation.

that $n_1^2 + n_2^2 + n_3^2 = 1$, we see that there are six motion parameters that we have to determine: $n_1, n_2, \theta; \Delta x, \Delta y, \Delta z$. However, from the two perspective views, it is impossible to determine the magnitude of the translation. If the object were two times farther away from the image plane, twice as big, and translated at twice the speed, we would get exactly the same two image frames. We can therefore determine the translation to only within a scale factor.

To summarize, our problem is:

*Given*: two image frames at $t_1$ and $t_2$
*Find*: the motion parameters **T** (to within a scale factor) and $R$.

As we shall see later, the equations relating the motion parameters to the image-point coordinates inevitably involve the ranges ($z$-coordinates) of the object points. Therefore, in determining the motion parameters we also determine the ranges of the observed object points. It will be seen that the translation vector **T** and the object-point ranges can be determined to within a global positive scale factor. The value of this scale factor can be found if we know the magnitude of **T** or the absolute range of any observed object point.

## B  Rotation Matrix Representation

Before we outline an approach to solving the posed problem, we present a few comments on the rotation matrix $R$. In terms of $\hat{n} = (n_1, n_2, n_3)$ and $\theta$, $R$ can be written as

$$R = S + K \tag{3}$$

$$S = (\cos \theta)I + (1 - \cos \theta)\hat{n}\hat{n}^{t} \qquad \text{(symmetric)} \tag{4}$$

$$K = (\sin \theta)N \qquad \text{(skew symmetric)} \tag{5}$$

where $I$ is a $3 \times 3$ unit matrix,

$$N = \begin{bmatrix} 0 & -n_3 & n_2 \\ n_3 & 0 & -n_1 \\ -n_2 & n_1 & 0 \end{bmatrix} \tag{6}$$

$\hat{n}$ is considered as a $3 \times 1$ column matrix, and $\hat{n}^{t}$ is the transpose of $\hat{n}$. It is obvious that $\hat{n}$ and $\theta$ can be obtained easily from $R$. In fact,

$$\mathrm{Tr}(R) = r_{11} + r_{22} + r_{33} = 1 + 2 \cos \theta \tag{7}$$

and

$$\begin{bmatrix} r_{32} - r_{23} \\ r_{13} - r_{31} \\ r_{21} - r_{12} \end{bmatrix} = 2(\sin \theta)\hat{n} \tag{8}$$

## C  A Two-Stage Approach to Solving the Problem

We present a two-stage method for solving the problem posed in Section I.A. In the first stage, we find point correspondences in the two perspective views (images). By a point correspondence, we mean a pair of image coordinates $(X_i, Y_i)$, $(X'_i, Y'_i)$ that are images at $t_1$ and $t_2$, respectively, of the same physical point on the object. Then, in the second stage, we determine the motion parameters from these image coordinates by solving a set of equations. The main bulk of this chapter deals with the second stage. We will see that with eight or more point correspondences, a linear algorithm is available. When the number of point correspondences is seven, six, or five, nonlinear equations must be solved.

The structure of this chapter is as follows. In Section II, we describe very briefly the problem of finding point correspondences. In Section III, nonlinear basic equations relating the motion parameters, the image coordinates at $t_1$ and $t_2$, and the range of the observed point are presented. We then show in Section IV that if eight or more point correspondences are found, a linear algorithm is possible. The important degenerate case in which all observed points line on a plane in three dimensions is considered in Section V. In Section VI, the various algorithms are summarized in a flow chart which we can follow to solve the motion problem. Finally, in Section VII, we discuss the issue of numerical accuracy.

## FINDING POINT CORRESPONDENCES   **II**

In order to be able to find point correspondences, the images must contain points that are distinctive in some sense. For example, images of man-made objects often contain sharp corners, which are relatively easy to extract [3]. More generally, image points where the local gray-level variations (defined in some way) are maximum can be used [4].

In any case, we first extract in each of the two images a large number of points that are distinctive. We then try to match the two point patterns in the two images by using spatial structures of the patterns [5]. The matching will be successful only if the amount of rotation ($\theta$) is relativelsy small (so that the perspective distortion is small). For example, Fang and Huang [5] obtained good matching results if $\theta < 5°$. This restriction may be relaxed if we have some a priori information about the object [6].

## BASIC EQUATIONS FOR MOTION AND STRUCTURE   **III**
## FROM POINT CORRESPONDENCES

From Fig. 1, we have the following relationship between the image-space and the object-space cocordinates:

$$X = F\frac{x}{z}, \qquad Y = F\frac{y}{z} \qquad (9)$$

For simplicity, we shall assume throughout this chapter that $F = 1$. Before we consider the general case, we first look at two special cases: pure translation and pure rotation.

## A   Pure Translation

### 1   *Basic Equations*

Equation (2) becomes

$$\begin{bmatrix} x' \\ y' \\ z' \end{bmatrix} = \begin{bmatrix} x \\ y \\ z \end{bmatrix} + \mathbf{T} = \begin{bmatrix} x \\ y \\ z \end{bmatrix} + \begin{bmatrix} \Delta x \\ \Delta y \\ \Delta z \end{bmatrix} \tag{10}$$

From (9) and (10), we obtain the following basic equations:

$$X' = \frac{Xz + \Delta x}{z + \Delta z}$$
$$Y' = \frac{Yz + \Delta y}{z + \Delta z} \tag{11}$$

Alternatively,

$$\Delta X = \frac{\Delta x - X\,\Delta z}{z + \Delta z}$$
$$\Delta Y = \frac{\Delta y - Y\,\Delta z}{z + \Delta z} \tag{12}$$

whence

$$\Delta Y\,\Delta x - \Delta X\,\Delta y + (Y\,\Delta X - X\,\Delta Y)\,\Delta z = 0 \tag{13}$$

and, assuming $\Delta X \neq 0$ and $\Delta Y \neq 0$,

$$z' = \frac{\Delta x - X\,\Delta z}{\Delta X} = \frac{\Delta y - Y\,\Delta z}{\Delta Y} \tag{14}$$

$$z = \frac{\Delta x - X'\,\Delta z}{\Delta X} = \frac{\Delta y - Y'\,\Delta z}{\Delta Y} \tag{15}$$

### 2   *Solving for T*

Equation (13) is linear and homogeneous in the three unknowns $\Delta x$, $\Delta y$, and $\Delta z$. We need a minimum of two point correspondences to determine these unknowns to within a common scale factor. Assume the two point correspondences are $(X_i, Y_i)$, $(X'_i, Y'_i)$, $i = 1, 2$. Then, the matrix equation to solve is

$$D \begin{bmatrix} \Delta x \\ \Delta y \\ \Delta z \end{bmatrix} = 0 \tag{16}$$

where

$$D = \begin{bmatrix} \Delta Y_1 & -\Delta X_1 & (Y_1 \, \Delta X_1 - X_1 \, \Delta Y_1) \\ \Delta Y_2 & -\Delta X_2 & (Y_2 \, \Delta X_2 - X_2 \, \Delta Y_2) \end{bmatrix} \tag{17}$$

To solve the equation, we choose a $2 \times 2$ submatrix in $D$ which is nonsingular. (If more than one submatrix is nonsingular, we may want to pick the one with the smallest condition number.) If the $i$th column of $D$ is not in the chosen $2 \times 2$ matrix, we set the $i$th variable in (16) to 1 and solve for the other two variables. For example, if the third column of $D$ is not in the submatrix, then we set $\Delta z = 1$ in (16) and solve for $\Delta x$ and $\Delta y$. Call the solution thus obtained $\bar{T} = (\overline{\Delta x}, \overline{\Delta y}, \overline{\Delta z})$. It is then related to the true translation vector $\mathbf{T} = (\Delta x, \Delta y, \Delta z)$ by a scale factor:

$$\bar{T} = \alpha \mathbf{T} \tag{18}$$

However, $\alpha$ can be negative.

To find the sense of the translation vector, we use the conditions

$$z_i > 0, \qquad z'_i > 0 \tag{19}$$

From (14) and (15) we obtain,

$$\bar{z}' = \alpha z' = \frac{\overline{\Delta x} - X \, \overline{\Delta z}}{\overline{\Delta X}} = \frac{\overline{\Delta y} - Y \, \overline{\Delta z}}{\overline{\Delta Y}} \tag{20}$$

$$\bar{z} = \alpha z = \frac{\overline{\Delta x} - X' \, \overline{\Delta z}}{\overline{\Delta X}} = \frac{\overline{\Delta y} - Y' \, \overline{\Delta z}}{\overline{\Delta Y}} \tag{21}$$

If $\bar{T}$ makes $\bar{z}'$ and $z'$ positive, we know that $\alpha > 0$; if $\bar{z}'$ and $\bar{z}$ are negative, we change the signs of $\bar{T}$, $\bar{z}$, and $\bar{z}$ to obtain the final solution.

We note that, in practice, because of the noise in the image data, we would try to get more than two point correspondences and then either find a least-square solution or use a RANSAC-like procedure [7].

### A Graphical Interpretation   3

Assuming $\Delta X \neq 0$ and $\Delta z \neq 0$, then from (12),

$$\frac{\Delta Y}{\Delta X} = \frac{(\Delta y / \Delta z) - Y}{(\Delta x / \Delta z) - X} \tag{22}$$

which implies that in the image space, all straight lines joining correspondence point pairs $(X_i, Y_i)$, $(X'_i, Y'_i)$ intersect at one point $(\Delta x / \Delta y, \Delta y / \Delta z)$. This point is called the focus of expansion.

## B  Pure Rotation

Assume $\mathbf{T} = 0$, which means that the rigid body is rotating around an axis through the origin:

$$\begin{bmatrix} x' \\ y' \\ z' \end{bmatrix} = R \begin{bmatrix} x \\ y \\ z \end{bmatrix} \tag{23}$$

From (23) and (9),

$$X' = \frac{r_{11}X + r_{12}Y + r_{13}}{r_{31}X + r_{32}Y + r_{33}}$$

$$Y' = \frac{r_{21}X + r_{22}Y + r_{23}}{r_{31}X + r_{32}Y + r_{33}} \tag{24}$$

We observe that with four point correspondences we can solve a set of eight linear equations to determine the values of $r_{ij}$. However, it can be shown [8] that only two point correspondences are needed to determine $R$.

Note that since $z$ does not appear in (24), there is no way we can find it from the image data. Therefore, in the case of pure rotation (around an axis through the origin), we cannot determine the relative ranges of observed object points. We will come back to this point in Section V.C.3.

## C  General Three-Dimensional Motion

### 1  Basic Equations

The motion is described by (2). From (2) and (9) we obtain,

$$X' = \frac{(r_{11}X + r_{12}Y + r_{13})z + \Delta x}{(r_{31}X + r_{32}Y + r_{33})z + \Delta z}$$

$$Y' = \frac{(r_{21}X + r_{22}Y + r_{23})z + \Delta y}{(r_{31}X + r_{32}Y + r_{33})z + \Delta z} \tag{25}$$

where $r_{ij}$ values can be expressed in terms of $n_1, n_2, n_3$, and $\theta$ from (3)–(6). Eliminating $z$ from (25), we obtain

$$(\Delta x - X' \Delta z)[y'(r_{31}X + r_{32}Y + r_{33}) - (r_{21}X + r_{22}Y + r_{23})]$$
$$= (\Delta y - Y' \Delta z)[X'(r_{31}X + r_{32}Y + r_{33}) - (r_{11}X + r_{12}Y + r_{13})] \tag{26}$$

Also,

$$
\begin{aligned}
z &= \frac{\Delta x - X' \Delta z}{X'(r_{31}X + r_{32}Y + r_{33}) - (r_{11}X + r_{12}Y + r_{13})} \\
&= \frac{\Delta y - Y' \Delta z}{Y'(r_{31}X + r_{32}Y + r_{33}) - (r_{21}X + r_{22}Y + r_{23})}
\end{aligned}
\tag{27}
$$

### Solving for R, T   2

Equation (26) is nonlinear in the six unknowns $\Delta x, \Delta y, \Delta z; n_1, n_2, \theta$. Also, it is homogeneous in $\Delta x, \Delta y, \Delta z$. Therefore, as mentioned earlier, we can only hope to find $\mathbf{T}$ to within a scale factor. After we have found $\mathbf{T}$ (to within a scale factor) and $R$, we can find $z_i$ for each observed point to within the same scale factor by using (27).

To fix ideas, let us say we want to find the unit translation vector

$$
\hat{T} = (\Delta \hat{x}, \Delta \hat{y}, \Delta \hat{z}) \triangleq (\Delta x^2 + \Delta y^2 + \Delta z^2)^{-1/2} \mathbf{T}
\tag{28}
$$

Then, (26) can be considered as a nonlinear equation in the five unknowns $\Delta \hat{x}, \Delta \hat{y}; n_1, n_2, \theta$. Thus, with five point correspondences, we will have five equations with five unknowns. Well-known iterative techniques can then be used to find solutions. In practice, because of noise in the image data, we try to find more than five point correspondences and seek a least-squares solution.

We note in passing that alternative nonlinear methods have been proposed by Mitche and Aggawal [9] and Roach and Aggawal [10].

### Disadvantages of Solving Nonlinear Equations   3

To find a least-squares solution of a small set of nonlinear equations (26) using iterative methods is not computationally expensive. However, unless we have a good initial guess solution, the iteration may not converge, or it may converge to a local but not global minimum. Furthermore, with nonlinear equations it is very difficult to analyze the question of solution uniqueness.

In fact, it is an open theoretical question: What is the minimum number of point correspondences that will ensure a unique solution for the five motion parameters $\Delta \hat{x}, \Delta \hat{y}; n_1, n_2, \theta$? With five point correspondences, the number of equations becomes equal to the number of unknowns. However, since the equations are nonlinear, we would expect that the solution is generally not unique. This has indeed been verified by extensive computer simulations in which global searches were made. The results of such simulations indicated that with five point correspondences, we generally have more than one (but a finite number of) solutions; with six or more point correspondences, the solution is generally unique. Note that in the case of five point correspondences, even though the solution may not be unique, if we start the iteration at a guess solution that is close to the true solution, then we will most likely converge to it.

The conclusion is, then, that the approach of solving nonlinear equations is viable, if we have a good initial guess solution. Otherwise, a better alternative is described in the next section, where we see a linear algorithm that requires eight or more point correspondences.

## IV  A LINEAR ALGORITHM

It turns out that by introducing appropriate intermediate variables (which are functions of the motion parameters), Eq. (26) becomes linear [11, 12].

### A  A Two-Step Linear Algorithm

If we define

$$E = \begin{bmatrix} e_1 & e_2 & e_3 \\ e_4 & e_5 & e_6 \\ e_7 & e_8 & e_9 \end{bmatrix} = GR \qquad (29)$$

where

$$G = \begin{bmatrix} 0 & -\Delta \hat{z} & \Delta \hat{y} \\ \Delta \hat{z} & 0 & -\Delta \hat{x} \\ -\Delta \hat{y} & \Delta \hat{x} & 0 \end{bmatrix} \quad \text{(skew symmetric)} \qquad (30)$$

$\hat{T} = (\Delta \hat{x}, \Delta \hat{y}, \Delta \hat{z})$ is the unit translation vector defined in (28), and $R$ is the orthonormal rotation matrix, then (26) becomes

$$[X' \quad Y' \quad 1] \quad E \begin{bmatrix} X \\ Y \\ 1 \end{bmatrix} = 0 \qquad (31)$$

which is linear and homogeneous in the nine new unknowns $e_1, e_2, \ldots, e_9$. The two-step linear algorithm is then:

*Step 1*: from eight or more point correspondences, determine $E$ to within a scale factor $k$.

*Step 2*: decompose $kE$ to obtain $R$ and $\hat{T}$.

### Finding $kE$   B

Given eight point correspondences $(X_i, Y_i)$, $(X'_i, Y'_i)$; $i = 1, 2, \ldots, 8$, we have from (31),

$$
B \begin{bmatrix} e_1 \\ e_2 \\ \vdots \\ e_9 \end{bmatrix} = \begin{bmatrix} X'_1 X_1 & X'_1 Y_1 & X'_1 & Y'_1 X_1 & Y'_1 Y_1 & Y'_1 & X_1 & Y_1 & 1 \\ & \vdots & & & & & & & \\ X'_8 X_8 & X'_8 Y_8 & & & \cdots & & X_8 & Y_8 & 1 \end{bmatrix} \begin{bmatrix} e_1 \\ e_2 \\ \vdots \\ e_9 \end{bmatrix} = 0
$$

$$(32)$$

To find the value of $e_i$ to within a scale factor, we proceed as follows. We choose from $B$ a nonsingular $8 \times 8$ submatrix. (If there are more than one nonsingular $8 \times 8$ submatrices, we may want to pick the one with the smallest condition number.) Let the $i$th column of $B$ be missing from the chosen submatrix. Then, we set $e_i$ to 1 in (32) and solve for the remaining values of $e_j$.

Again, in practice, because of image noise, we try to obtain more than eight point correspondences and then either find a least-squares solution or use a RANSAC-like procedure.

### Rank of the Coefficient Matrix $B$   C

We can find the values of $e_i$ uniquely except for a scale factor if and only if the rank of the coefficient matrix $B$ in (32) is 8. The question of when the rank of $B$ is 8 has been answered by Longuet-Higgins [13] and Zhuang and Haralick [14]. To put the result succinctly: Rank($B$) < 8 if and only if either $T = 0$ or the surface assumption is violated. The surface assumption can be stated more easily if we assume that the object is stationary and the camera is moving. Let the origin of the camera system be 0 and 0' at $t_1$ and $t_2$, respectively. Then we say that the surface assumption holds if and only if the three-dimensional points corresponding to the image points we used in (32) do not lie on a quadratic surface passing through 0 and 0'.

It is important to realize that if Rank($B$) < 8, it does not necessarily mean that the five motion parameters cannot be determined uniquely, even though the linear algorithms breaks down. Thus, if we find Rank($B$) < 8, we can try two things: (i) determine whether $T = 0$, and if it is, find $R$; (ii) use the nonlinear approach of Section III.C to find $(R, \hat{T})$. One way of carrying out (i) is decribed in Section V.C.3, where we discuss the important special case in which all the three-dimensional points we observe lie on a plane.

**D   Decomposition of *kE* to Obtain (*R*, $\hat{T}$)**

Assume that $\text{Rank}(B) = 8$, and that we have solved (32) to obtain

$$E' = \begin{bmatrix} e_1 & e_2 & e_3 \\ e_4 & e_5 & e_6 \\ e_7 & e_8 & e_9 \end{bmatrix} = [e_1', \ e_2', \ e_3'] = kE \qquad (33)$$

where $k$ is a scale factor, $E$ is as defined in (29), and $e_1'$, $e_2'$, $e_3'$ denote the three columns of the $E'$ matrix. The next step is to find $(R, \hat{T})$ from $E'$. Several methods to achieve this end have been proposed [11, 12, 14, 15]. We shall follow Yen and Huang [15]. As we shall see, with the help of a point correspondence, we can find $(R, \hat{T})$ uniquely from $E'$.

We first observe that the matrix $E$ defined in (29) can be written in the following alternative form:

$$E = [\hat{T} \times \hat{c}_1, \hat{T} \times \hat{c}_2, \hat{T} \times \hat{c}_3] \qquad (34)$$

where $\hat{T}$ is the unit translation vector defined in Eq. (28) and $\hat{c}_1, \hat{c}_2, \hat{c}_3$ are the three columns of the rotation matrix

$$R = [\hat{c}_1, \hat{c}_2, \hat{c}_3] \qquad (35)$$

Note that in (34), $\hat{T}, \hat{c}_1 \hat{c}_2$, and $\hat{c}_3$ are considered as vectors and $\times$ denotes the cross product.

**1   Finding $\hat{T}$**

From (33) and (34),

$$E' = [e_1', e_2', e_3'] = [k\hat{T} \times \hat{c}_1, k\hat{T} \times \hat{c}_2, k\hat{T} \times \hat{c}_3] \qquad (36)$$

Note that each column of $E'$ is a vector orthogonal to $\hat{T}$. Therefore, the direction of $\hat{T}$ (to within a sign) can be obtained by taking the cross product of two of the three columns of $E'$:

$$\hat{T} = \pm \frac{e_i' \times e_j'}{\|e_i' \times e_j'\|} \qquad i \neq j \qquad (37)$$

where $\|\cdot\|$ denotes the $L_2$ norm of a vector. In fact,

$$\begin{aligned} e_1' \times e_2' &= k^2 \hat{T}(\hat{T} \cdot \hat{c}_3) \\ e_2' \times e_3' &= k^2 \hat{T}(\hat{T} \cdot \hat{c}_1) \\ e_3' \times e_1' &= k^2 \hat{T}(\hat{T} \cdot \hat{c}_2) \end{aligned} \qquad (38)$$

where $\times$ and $\cdot$ denote the cross and the dot products, respectively.

It can also be shown that

$$k^2 = \tfrac{1}{2}(e'_1 \cdot e'_1 + e'_2 \cdot e'_2 + e'_3 \cdot e'_3) \tag{39}$$

Thus, $k$ is determined to within a sign. In what follows we denote the two solutions of $\hat{T}$ by $\hat{T}_0$ and $-\hat{T}_0$ and the two solutions of $k$ by $k_0$ and $-k_0$.

### Finding R    2

It is well known in vector analysis that we can find an unknown vector if we know its dot and cross products with a known vector. Now, from (36),

$$\hat{T} \times \hat{c}_1 = \frac{1}{k} e'_1 \tag{40}$$

and from (38)

$$\hat{T} \cdot \hat{c}_1 = \frac{1}{k^2} \hat{T} \cdot (e'_2 \times e'_3) \tag{41}$$

Thus,

$$\hat{c}_1 = (\hat{T} \times \hat{c}_1) \times \hat{T} + (\hat{T} \cdot \hat{c}_1)\hat{T}$$

$$= \frac{1}{k}(e'_1 \times \hat{T}) + \frac{1}{k^2}[\hat{T} \cdot (e'_2 \times e'_3)]\hat{T}$$

and similarly,

$$\hat{c}_2 - \frac{1}{k}(e'_2 \times \hat{T}) + \frac{1}{k^2}[\hat{T} \cdot (e'_3 \times e'_1)]\hat{T}$$

$$\hspace{8cm}(42)$$

$$\hat{c}_3 = \frac{1}{k}(e'_3 \times \hat{T}) + \frac{1}{k^2}[\hat{T} \cdot (e'_1 \times e'_2)]\hat{T}$$

Since $\hat{T}$ and $k$ were determined only to within a sign, there are two solutions to $R = [\hat{c}_1, \hat{c}_2, \hat{c}_3]$, one corresponding to $(\hat{T}_0, k_0)$ and $(-\hat{T}_0, -k_0)$, and the other to $(\hat{T}_0, -k_0)$ and $(-\hat{T}_0, k_0)$. We call the first solution $R^a$ and the second solution $R^b$.

To summarize, at this stage we have obtained four solutions for $(R, \hat{T})$: $(R^a, \hat{T}_0)$, $(R^a, -\hat{T}_0)$, $(R^b, \hat{T}_0)$, and $(R^b, -\hat{T}_0)$. We next demonstrate that with the help of one point correspondence we can pick out from these four solutions the true one.

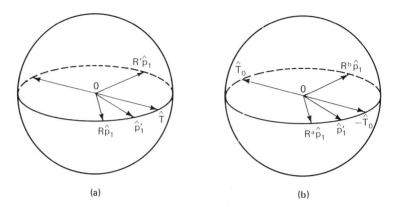

**Fig. 2.** (a) Geometrical constraint that determines a unique solution for $(R, \hat{T})$. (b) Example in which the true solution is determined to be $(R^a, -\hat{T}_0)$.

## 3    Determine $(R, \hat{T})$ Uniquely

We take a point correspondence, say, $(X_1, Y_1)$, $(X'_1, Y'_1)$, and define the unit vectors

$$\hat{p}_1 = (X_1^2 + Y_1^2 + 1)^{-1/2}(X_1, Y_1, 1)$$

$$\hat{p}'_1 = (X'^2_1 + Y'^2_1 + 1)^{-1/2}(X'_1, Y'_1, 1)$$

(43)

Note that $\hat{p}'_1$ and $\hat{p}_1$ are the projections (at $t_1$ and $t_2$, respectively) of the three-dimensional point $P_1$ onto a unit sphere centered at the origin 0 in Fig. 1. Yen and Huang [15] have shown that if $(R, \hat{T})$ is the true solution, then the three points $R\hat{p}_1, \hat{p}'_1, \hat{T}$ on the unit sphere (note that in $R\hat{p}_1$, we have considered $\hat{p}_1$ as a column matrix) lie on a great circle and the arc $\overset{\frown}{R\hat{p}_1, \hat{p}_1, \hat{T}}$ is smaller than 180°. Furthermore, if $R'$ is the other (false) solution that we have obtained from (42), then the point $R'\hat{p}_1$ lies on the same great circle at a position symmetrical to $R\hat{p}_1$ with respect to $\hat{T}$. This situation is illustrated in Fig. 2a.

This geometrical constraint can be used to pick out the true solution from the four solutions we obtained at the end of Section IV.D.2. We first calculate $R^a\hat{p}_1$ and $R^b\hat{p}_1$ and find out which of the two lies to the same side of $\hat{T}_0$ as $\hat{p}'_1$. For example, if the situation is as shown in Fig. 2b, then we know that $R^a$ is the true solution for the rotation matrix. Computationally, this can be done, for example, as follows. Let

$$S = \hat{T}_0 \times (\hat{p}'_1 \times \hat{T}_0)$$

(44)

Then we choose between $R^a$ and $R^b$ the one that satisfies

$$R\hat{p}_1 \cdot S > 0 \tag{45}$$

The next step is to choose from $\hat{T}_0$ and $-\hat{T}_0$ the true $\hat{T}$. This can again be done easily using the geometrical constraint. For example, if the situation is as shown in Fig. 2b, then we will pick $-\hat{T}_0$ because the arc $\widehat{R^a\hat{p}_1, \hat{p}'_1, \hat{T}_0}$ is larger than $180°$. Computationally, this can be done, for example, as follows. We pick between $\hat{T}_0$ and $-\hat{T}_0$ the one that satisfies

$$(\hat{p}'_1 - R^a\hat{p}_1) \cdot \hat{T} > 0 \tag{46}$$

This completes our linear algorithm for determining the motion parameters of a rigid body from two perspective views.

Once we have found $(R, \hat{T})$, the relative ranges of the observed object points can be obtained from (27).

## PLANAR PATCH CASE V

In many applications, the points we observe may all lie on a rigid planar patch in three dimensions. This clearly violates the surface assumption stated in Section IV.C, and therefore the linear algorithm of Section IV breaks down. We can go back to use the nonlinear algorithm of Section III.C. However, it turns out that a more computationally efficient, and in fact linear, algorithm exists for the planar patch case [16–18]. This linear algorithm also throws light on the uniqueness question for the planar case. We now describe this algorithm.

### A Two-Step Linear Algorithm for Planar Patches A

Let the three-dimensional points we observe all lie on a plane whose equation at $t_1$ is

$$ax + by + cz = 1$$

or

$$[a, b, c] \begin{bmatrix} x \\ y \\ z \end{bmatrix} = 1 \tag{47}$$

Later, we use the notation

$$g = [a, b, c]^t$$

(the superscript t denotes transposition). Then, we have from (2) and (47),

$$\begin{bmatrix} x' \\ y' \\ z' \end{bmatrix} = R \begin{bmatrix} x \\ y \\ z \end{bmatrix} + \mathbf{T} = R \begin{bmatrix} x \\ y \\ z \end{bmatrix} + \mathbf{T}[a, b, c] \begin{bmatrix} x \\ y \\ z \end{bmatrix}$$

$$= (R + \mathbf{T}[a, b, c]) \begin{bmatrix} x \\ y \\ z \end{bmatrix} \tag{48}$$

or

$$\begin{bmatrix} x' \\ y' \\ z' \end{bmatrix} = A \begin{bmatrix} x \\ y \\ z \end{bmatrix} \tag{49}$$

where

$$A = \begin{bmatrix} a_1 & a_2 & a_3 \\ a_4 & a_5 & a_6 \\ a_7 & a_8 & a_9 \end{bmatrix} = R + \begin{bmatrix} \Delta x \\ \Delta y \\ \Delta z \end{bmatrix} [a, b, c] = R + \mathbf{T} g^t \tag{50}$$

From (9) and (49) we obtain,

$$X' = \frac{a_1 X + a_2 Y + a_3}{a_7 X + a_8 Y + a_9}$$

$$Y' = \frac{a_4 X + a_5 Y + a_6}{a_7 X + a_8 Y + a_9} \tag{51}$$

Some other useful formulas are, from (47),

$$1/z = aX + bY + c \tag{52}$$

and from (49),

$$z'/z = a_7 X + a_8 Y + a_9 \tag{53}$$

Our two-step linear algorithm is a follows.

*Step 1*: from four or more point correspondences, we solve a set of linear homogeneous equations (51) to find $A$ to within a scale factor.

*Step 2*: from A, we determine $R$, $w\mathbf{T}$, and $(1/w)g$, where $w$ is a positive scale factor.

Given four point correspondences $(X_i, Y_i)$, $(X'_i, Y'_i)$, $i = 1, 2, 3, 4$, we obtain from (51),

$$
H \begin{bmatrix} a_1 \\ a_2 \\ \vdots \\ a_9 \end{bmatrix} = \begin{bmatrix} X_1 & Y_1 & 1 & 0 & 0 & 0 & -X_1 X'_1 & -Y_1 X'_1 & -X'_1 \\ 0 & 0 & 0 & X_1 & Y_1 & 1 & -X_1 Y'_1 & -Y_1 Y'_1 & -Y'_1 \\ \vdots & & & & & & & & \vdots \\ X_4 & Y_4 & 1 & 0 & 0 & 0 & -X_4 X'_4 & -Y_4 X'_4 & -X'_4 \\ 0 & 0 & 0 & X_4 & Y_4 & 1 & -X_4 Y'_4 & -Y_4 Y'_4 & -Y'_4 \end{bmatrix} \begin{bmatrix} a_1 \\ a_2 \\ \vdots \\ a_9 \end{bmatrix} = 0
$$

(54)

We can show that the rank of the coefficient matrix $H$ is eight, if and only if no three of the four observed points are colinear in three dimensions. We can then solve (54) to obtain $A$ to within a scale factor. The procedure for solving (54) is similar to that for solving (32) in Section IV.B.

Let us call the solution we obtain

$$
A' = \begin{bmatrix} a'_1 & a'_2 & a'_3 \\ a'_4 & a'_5 & a'_6 \\ a'_7 & a'_8 & a'_9 \end{bmatrix} = \gamma A
$$

(55)

We can make the constant $\gamma$ positive by demanding that

$$
z'_i / z_i = a'_7 X_i + a'_8 Y_i + a'_9 > 0
$$

(56)

for any and all image points $(X_i, Y_i)$. (For our imaging setup shown in Fig. 1, the object is in front of the image plane both at $t_1$ and $t_2$. Therefore, $z_i > 0$ and $z'_i > 0$.) If $a'_7 X_i + a'_8 Y_i + a'_9 < 0$, we replace $A'$ by $-A'$.

Assume that we have solved (54) to obtain $A' = \gamma A$, where $\gamma$ is an unknown positive scale factor. We describe a procedure for finding $R$, $\mathbf{T}$, and $g$ from $A'$. The reader is referred to Tsai *et al.* [17] for derivations. We first find a singular-value decomposition of $A'$:

$$
A' = U \begin{bmatrix} \lambda_1 & 0 & 0 \\ 0 & \lambda_2 & 0 \\ 0 & 0 & \lambda_3 \end{bmatrix} V^t
$$

(57)

where $U$ and $V$ are $3 \times 3$ orthonormal matrices and $\lambda_1 \geq \lambda_2 \geq \lambda_3 \geq 0$. We have used a superscript t to denote matrix transposition. There are then three different cases.

*Case* 1. If the singular values $\lambda_1, \lambda_2, \lambda_3$ are all distinct, with $\lambda_1 > \lambda_2 > \lambda_3$, then there are two solutions to the motion parameters:

$$R = U \begin{bmatrix} \alpha & 0 & \beta \\ 0 & 1 & 0 \\ -s\beta & 0 & s\alpha \end{bmatrix} V^t \tag{58}$$

$$\mathbf{T} = \begin{bmatrix} \Delta x \\ \Delta y \\ \Delta z \end{bmatrix} = w\left\{ -\beta U_1 + \left(\frac{\lambda_3}{\lambda_2} - s\alpha\right) U_3 \right\} \tag{59}$$

$$g = \begin{bmatrix} a \\ b \\ c \end{bmatrix} = \frac{1}{w}(\delta V_1 + V_3) \tag{60}$$

where

$$\delta = \pm \left(\frac{\lambda_1^2 - \lambda_2^2}{\lambda_2^2 - \lambda_3^2}\right)^{1/2} \tag{61}$$

$$\alpha = \frac{\lambda_1 + s\lambda_3 \delta^2}{\lambda_2(1 + \delta^2)} \tag{62}$$

$$\beta = \frac{1}{\delta}\left(\alpha - \frac{\lambda_1}{\lambda_2}\right) \tag{63}$$

$$s = \det(U)\det(V) \tag{64}$$

and $w$ is an arbitrary real constant. We have used $U_i$ and $V_j$ to denote the $i$th column of $U$ and the $j$th column of $V$, respectively. In this case, the motion can be decomposed into rotation around an axis through the origin, followed by a translation along a direction different from the normal direction of the plane at $t_1$.

The senses of $\mathbf{T}$ and $g$ can be determined as follows. Let us rewrite (59) and (60) as

$$\mathbf{T} = w \begin{bmatrix} \Delta x' \\ \Delta y' \\ \Delta z' \end{bmatrix} = wT' \tag{65}$$

$$g = \frac{1}{w} \begin{bmatrix} a' \\ b' \\ c' \end{bmatrix} = \frac{1}{w}g' \tag{66}$$

Then our imaging geometry (Fig. 1) demands that

$$1/z_i = aX_i + bY_i + c = w(a'X_i + b'Y_i + c') > 0 \tag{67}$$

for all image points $(X_i, Y_i)$.

Thus, if $(a'X_i + b'Y_i + c') > 0$, then we know that $w$ is positive. If

$(a'X_i + b'Y_i + c') < 0$, we will replace $g'$ and $T'$ by $-g'$ and $-T'$ and use a positive scale factor.

Furthermore, if for one of the two solutions, the sign of $(a'X_i + b'Y_i + c')$ is not the same for all image points, then this solution can be ruled out.

*Case* 2. If the multiplicity of the singular values is two, for example, $\lambda_1 = \lambda_2 \neq \lambda_3$, then the solution for the motion parameters is unique:

$$R = \frac{1}{\lambda_1} A' - \left(\frac{\lambda_3}{\lambda_1} - s\right) U_3 V_3^t \tag{68}$$

$$\mathbf{T} = \begin{bmatrix} \Delta x \\ \Delta y \\ \Delta z \end{bmatrix} = w\left(\frac{\lambda_3}{\lambda_1} - s\right) \tag{69}$$

$$g = \begin{bmatrix} a \\ b \\ c \end{bmatrix} = \frac{1}{w} V_3 \tag{70}$$

where

$$s = \det(U)\det(V) \tag{71}$$

and $w$ is an arbitrary real constant. In this case, the motion can be decomposed into a rotation around an axis through the origin, followed by a translation along the normal direction of the plane at $t_1$.

The senses of $\mathbf{T}$ and $g$ can again be fixed as in Case 1.

*Case* 3. If the multiplicity of the singular values is three, $\lambda_1 = \lambda_2 = \lambda_3$, then the motion is a pure rotation around an axis through the origin, and $R$ is uniquely determined by

$$R = (1/\lambda_1)A' \tag{72}$$

However, $\mathbf{T}$ and $g$ cannot be determined at all.

Recall that in Section III.B we stated that in the case of pure rotation around an axis through the origin, it is impossible to get any range information. Therefore, it does not matter whether the three-dimensional points are on a plane or not. In fact, (24) of Section III.B has the same form as (51) for the planar case in Section V.B. The conclusion is that the case of pure rotation around an axis through the origin can be handled by the planar patch algorithm irrespective of the actual three-dimensional configuration.

**Testing for Planar Configuration   D**

Given $N$ ($>4$) point correspondences $(X_i, Y_i), (X_i', Y_i'); i = 1, 2, \ldots, N$, we can determine whether the $N$ three-dimensional points lie on a plane as

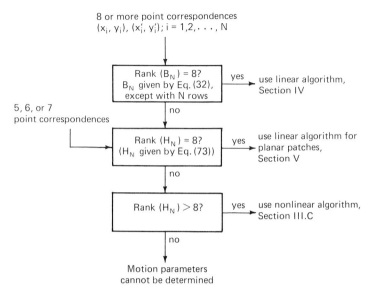

**Fig. 3.** Flowchart for motion determination from two perspective views.

follows. Define the $2N \times 9$ matrix

$$
H_N = \begin{bmatrix}
X_1 & Y_1 & 1 & 0 & 0 & 0 & -X_1 X_1' & -Y_1 X_1' & -X_1' \\
0 & 0 & 0 & X_1 & Y_1 & 1 & -X_1 Y_1' & -Y_1 Y_1' & -Y_1' \\
\vdots & & & & & & & & \\
X_N & Y_N & 1 & 0 & 0 & 0 & -X_N X_N' & -Y_N X_N' & -X_N' \\
0 & 0 & 0 & X_N & Y_N & 1 & -X_N Y_N' & -Y_N Y_N' & -Y_N'
\end{bmatrix}
\tag{73}
$$

Then the $N$ three-dimensional points lie on a plane if and only if $\text{Rank}(H_N)$ $\le 8$.

## VI  SUMMARY OF ALGORITHMS

In Fig. 3 we show a flowchart which we can follow to determine the motion parameters of a rigid body from point correspondences. If we have eight or more point correspondences, we should try to use the linear algorithm of Section IV. This is possible if the rank of $B_N$ is 8. Here $B_N$ is the same as $B$ in (32) except that it has $N$ rows instead of 8 rows.

If the rank of $B_N$ is less than 8, then either we have a pure rotation case or the surface assumption is violated. However, from the image data, we cannot easily test whether the surface assumption is violated except for the special case of a planar configuration, which includes the pure rotation situation. If the rank of $H_N$, given by (73), is 8, then we know that either all the three-dimensional points lie on a plane or the motion is a pure rotation around an axis through the origin. The linear algorithm of Section V can be used. If Rank($H_N$) > 8, then the three-dimensional points do not lie on a plane, and we can try to use the nonlinear algorithm of Section III.C. Finally, if Rank ($H_N$) < 8, then we do not have enough information to determine the motion parameters.

## DISCUSSION VII

The reader should be warned that computer simulations and experiments with real images [5, 19] have indicated that in order to estimate motion parameters reasonably accurately (around 10 % error, say) from two perspective views, the image resolution must be quite high (typically $1000 \times 1000$ picture elements, assuming image-point features can be measured to within one picture element). Theoretical studies or even systematic simulation studies on how the estimation errors depend on various factors are yet to be made.

However, from past work the following tentative conclusions can be drawn. The two most important factors that affect estimation accuracy are probably (i) the sizes of the total image-space shift and its components due to rotation and translation, respectively, at each image point used in the algorithm; and (ii) the distances between the image points used. Typically, in order to achieve an estimation error of about 10 %, the sizes of the image-space shifts (the total as well as the components due to rotation and translation, respectively) of most image points used in the algorithm should be larger than about 10 picture elements; furthermore, the distance between two image points (in the same image frame) used in the algorithm should be larger than about 100 picture elements for most image-point pairs. This is assuming that the position of an image-point feature can be measured to within a picture element.

### ACKNOWLEDGEMENT

The preparation of this paper was supported by National Science Foundation Grant No. ECS-83-19509. The author would like to thank H. C. Longuet-Higgins and X. Zhuang for some very illuminating discussions.

### REFERENCES

1. T. S. Huang (ed.), "Image Sequence Analysis." Springer-Verlag, Berlin and New York, 1981.
2. T. S. Huang (ed.), "Image Sequence Processing and Dynamic Scene Analysis." Springer-Verlag, Berlin and New York, 1983.

3. J. Q. Fang and T. S. Huang, A corner finding algorithm for image analysis and registration, *Proc. AAAI-82, Pittsburgh, Pennsylvania, August 18–20, 1982*, pp. 46–49 (1982).

4. H. P. Moravec, Obstacle avoidance and navigation in the real world by a seeing robot rover, Unpublished Ph.D. dissertation, Stanford Univ., Stanford, California, 1980.

5. J. Q. Fang and T. S. Huang, Some experiments on estimating the 3-D motion parameters of a rigid body from two consecutive image frames, *IEEE Trans. on Pattern Analysis and Machine Intelligence* **PAMI-6** (5), 547–554 (1984).

6. W. K. Gu, J. Y. Yang, and T. S. Huang, Matching perspective views of a 3-D object using composite circuits, *Proc. 7th ICPR, July–August 1984* (1984).

7. M. A. Fischler and R. C. Bolles, Random samples consensus: A paradigm for model fitting with applications to image analysis and automated cartography, *Comm. ACM* **24** (6), (June 1981).

8. B. L. Yen and T. S. Huang, Determining 3-D motion and structure of a rigid body using the spherical projection, *Computer Vision, Graphics, and Image Processing* **21**, 21–32 (1983).

9. A. Mitiche and J. K. Aggawal, A computational analysis of time-varying images, *in* "Handbook of Pattern Recognition and Image Processing" (T. Y. Young and K. S. Fu, eds.), Academic Press, New York, 1986.

10. J. W. Roach and J. K. Aggawal, Dertermining the movement of objects from a sequence of images, *IEEE Trans. on Pattern Analysis and Machine Intelligence* **PAMI-6**, 554–562 (1980).

11. H. C. Longuet-Higgins, A computer program for reconstructing a scene from two projections, *Nature (London)* **293**, 133–135 (1981).

12. R. Y. Tsai and T. S. Huang, Uniqueness and estimation of 3-D motion parameters of rigid bodies with curved surfaces, *IEEE Trans. on Pattern Analysis and Machine Intelligence* **PAMI-6** (1), 13–27 (1984).

13. H. C. Longuet-Higgins, The reconstruction of a scene from two projections—configurations that defeat the 8-point algorithm, *Proc. 1st Conf. Artificial Intelligence Applications, Dec. 5–7, 1984, Denver, Colorado*, 395–397 (1984).

14. X. Zhuang and R. M. Haralick, Two view motion analysis, *Proc. ICASSP, March 1985, Tampa, Florida* (1985).

15. B. L. Yen and T. S. Huang, Determining 3-D motion parameters of a rigid body: A vector-geometric approach, *Proc. ACM Workshop on Motion, April 1983, Toronto, Canada* (1983).

16. R. Y. Tsai and T. S. Huang, Estimating 3-D motion parameters of a rigid planar patch, *IEEE Trans. ASSP* **29** (6), 1147–1152 (1981).

17. R. Y. Tsai, T. S. Huang, and W. L. Zhu, Estimating 3-D motion parameters of a rigid planar patch, II: Singular value decomposition, *IEEE Trans. ASSP* **30** (4), 525–534 (1982); Correction, **ASSP-31** (2), 514 (1983).

18. R. Y. Tsai and T. S. Huang, Estimating 3-D motion parameters of a rigid planar patch, III: Finite point correspondences and the three-view problem, *IEEE Trans. ASSP* **32** (2), 213–220 (1984).

19. J. Q. Fang and T. S. Huang, Solving 3-D small-rotation motion equations, *Computer Vision, Graphics, and Image Processing* **26**, 183–206 (1984).

Chapter **15**

# Computer Vision

AZRIEL ROSENFELD

Center for Automation Research
University of Maryland
College Park, Maryland

## COMPUTER VISION PARADIGM   I

The general goal of the computer vision process is to construct descriptions of a scene based on information extracted from images of that scene. In this section we describe the basic steps in this process, with emphasis on the case in which the scene is fundamentally three-dimensional, involving substantial surface relief and object occlusion.

We first briefly review the two-dimensional case. Many types of scenes are essentially two-dimensional; documents are an obvious example, but two-dimensional treatment is often quite adequate in applications such as remote sensing (flat terrain seen from very high altitudes), radiology (where the image is a shadow of the object), or microscopy (where the image is a cross section of the object). In such situations, the computer vision process becomes essentially a two-dimensional process of image description and generally proceeds as follows. We extract "features" such as edges from the

HANDBOOK OF PATTERN RECOGNITION
AND IMAGE PROCESSING

image, or segment the image into regions, thus obtaining a map-like representation consisting of image features labeled with their property values. Grouping processes may then be used to obtain improved maps from the initial one. The maps may be represented by abstract relational structures in which, for example, nodes represent regions, labeled with various property values (color, texture, shape, etc.), and arcs represent relationships among regions. Finally, these structures are matched against stored models, which are generalized relational structures representing classes of maps that correspond to general types of images. Successful matches yield identifications for the image parts and a structural description of the image in terms of known entities.

The situation is more complex for three-dimensional scenes, such as those arising in many robot vision applications. Here the regions in the image arise from visible surfaces in the scene, and a key step in the analysis is to infer the surface orientation at each image point. Clues to surface orientation can be derived directly from shading (i.e., gray-level variation) in the image. Alternatively, two-dimensional segmentation and feature extraction techniques can first be applied to the image to extract such features as surface contours and texture primitives, and surface orientation clues can then be derived from contour shapes or from textural variations. Using the surface orientation map, feature extraction and segmentation techniques can once again be applied to yield a segmentation into (visible parts of) bodies or objects, and these can in turn be represented by a relational structure. Finally, the structure can be matched against models to yield an interpretation of the scene in terms of known objects. Note that the matching process is more difficult in the three-dimensional case since the image only shows one side of each object and objects may partially occlude one another.

Our computer vision paradigm is simplified in a number of respects. We have treated model matching as a simple, one-step process, but in fact models are often quite complex and may be best handled hierarchically, with parts composed of subparts, etc. We have treated the entire process of scene description as a simple sequence of steps; but in fact, it may be quite difficult to decide what to do at a given stage and how to use knowledge gained at a given stage to determine what processing to perform at subsequent stages.

In the following sections we discuss some of the problems that are particularly relevant to three-dimensional computer vision. We emphasize the problems of inferring three-dimensional information about the scene and of defining and matching models of three-dimensional objects.

## II  SURFACE ORIENTATION ESTIMATION

In this section we describe various methods of inferring the three-dimensional shape of a surface (i.e., its orientation as a function of position) from information in a single image. These methods are known collectively as "shape from $x$" methods, where $x$ represents the property of the image from which the surface orientation information is inferred.

### Shape from Shading   A

The reflectivity of a surface, that is, the fraction of an incident ray of light (of a given wavelength) that emerges from a given point $P$ in a given direction, depends on the angles that the incident ray $i$ and the emergent ray $e$ make with the normal $n$ to the surface at $P$. In many cases, we can express this dependency in terms of a reflectance function of the form $r(\theta_i, \theta_e)$, where $\theta_i, \theta_e$ are the angles that $i$ and $e$ make with $n$, respectively. For perfectly *specular* reflection, we have $r = 1$ if $\theta_i = \theta_e$ and $i$ and $e$ are both coplanar with $n$, and $r = 0$ otherwise. At the other extreme, for perfectly *diffuse* or Lambertian reflection, $r$ depends only on $\theta_i$ and not on $\theta_e$, and we have $r = \rho \cos \theta_i$, where $0 \leq \rho \leq 1$ is a constant.

Suppose the surface is illuminated by a small ("point") light source in a known position. If the source and observer are not too close to the surface, the directions $\theta_i$ and $\theta_o$ to the source and observer, respectively, are essentially the same for two neighboring surface points $P$ and $P'$. The brightnesses of the surface at $P$ and $P'$ are given by the intensities of the emergent rays from these points. Thus, the change in brightness from $P$ to $P'$ gives us a constraint on how the surface normal has rotated as we move from $P$ to $P'$.

For smooth surfaces, iterative methods can be used to derive surface orientation information from these constraints, with the aid of boundary conditions that specify the orientations of the normals at some points of the surface. For example, at an occluding contour on a smooth surface, the direction $\theta_o$ to the observer must be tangential to the surface, so that the surface normal lies in the plane perpendicular to $\theta_o$ and is orthogonal to the occluding edge; thus, occluding contours are one possible source of the needed boundary conditions.

Figure 1 illustrates how surface orientation (i.e., three-dimensional shape) can be derived from brightness variations (shading) using this method. The input image is shown in Fig. 1a. An iterative method was used to estimate surface orientation subject to the boundary conditions derived from the occluding edge. Figure 1b shows the sampled array of surface normals (displayed as line segments of unit length projected onto the image plane) obtained in this way at various stages of the iteration process.

Another way of obtaining surface orientation from brightness information is to illuminate the surface successively from two or more directions. The change in brightness at a given point $P$ under this change in illumination gives us information about the orientation of the surface normal $n$ at $P$

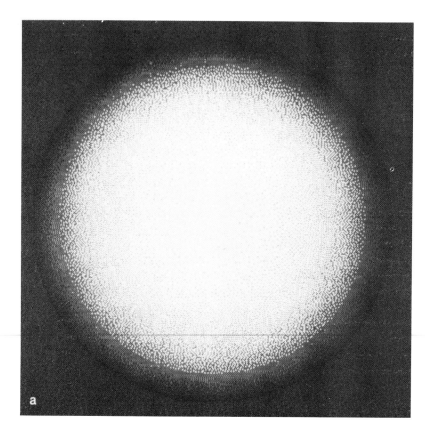

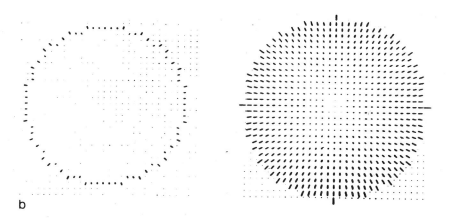

**Fig. 1.** Shape from shading. (a) Input image. (b) Array of estimated surface normals: (left) initial and (right) after 30 iterations. (From Ikeuchi and Horn [1].)

relative to these directions, and this allows us to determine $n$. For further details on this *photometric stereo* method, and on the topic of shape from shading in general, see Ikeuchi and Horn [1] and Woodham [2]. Much of this work has assumed diffuse reflectance and needs to be extended to reflectance functions that have strong specular components; in such cases the shapes and positions of highlights may provide additional information.

## Shape from Edges or Surface Contours   B

An edge (i.e., an abrupt brightness change) in an image can have several possible causes in the original scene. It might be due to an abrupt change in illumination, that is, it might be the edge of a shadow. Alternatively, it might be due to a change in reflectivity (i.e., in surface material) or to a change in range (i.e., an occluding edge at which one surface is partially visible behind another). It would be useful to distinguish these types of edges from one another; for example, as we saw earlier, occluding edges of smooth surfaces provide useful boundary conditions for solving the shape-from-shading problem. Ideally, it should be possible to distinguish between the various types of edges by careful analysis of the brightness variations in their vicinities, for example, a shadow edge might not be very sharp, a convex orientation edge might have a highlight on it, and so on. For further discussion of this topic see Binford [3]. Edges belonging to the same object may also be recognizable by virtue of having similar patterns of brightness variations [4].

The two-dimensional shapes of edges also provide important information about three-dimensional surface shape [5], as illustrated in Fig. 2. Here a line drawing of a set of occluding edges conveys strong clues about the three-dimensional shapes of the surfaces. If we make suitable assumptions about the nature of the surface, its shape can in fact be determined from the two-dimensional shape of the occluding edge. For example, we might assume that the actual occluding edge is the most nearly planar and most uniformly curved space curve that could give rise to the observed edge in the image. We might further assume that the surface has the least possible curvature of all surfaces containing this space curve (i.e., it is a "soap film" surface) or is as uniformly curved as possible.

The two-dimensional shapes of surface contours (i.e., curves that lie on the surface) also provide strong clues to surface shape [6], as illustrated in Fig. 3. Here the key assumptions seem to involve stipulating that the principal normal to the curve not lie in the plane of the surface and that the curve not be of least possible curvature. Early work on shape from shape developed methods of inferring the nature of edges in a scene (e.g., convex, concave, or occluding) from the shapes of the junctions at which the edges meet as seen in the image.

**Fig. 2.** Example showing how a drawing of a small set of edges (primarily occluding edges) strongly conveys three-dimensional information about surfaces. (From Barrow and Tenenbaum [5].)

## C   Shape from Two-Dimensional Shape and from Texture

Various global types of assumptions can also be used to deduce three-dimensional shape from two-dimensional shape (i.e., from shape in the image). For example [4], suppose that the observed two-dimensional shape has *skewed symmetry*, that is, it has a family of parallel chords whose midpoints are collinear (but not necessarily on a line perpendicular to the

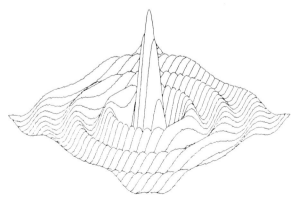

**Fig. 3.** Example showing how surface contours convey a strong impression of three-dimensional surface shape. (From Stevens [6].)

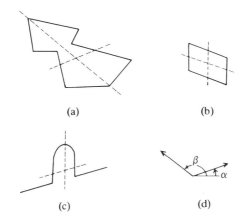

Fig. 4. Examples of skew symmetry. (From Kanade [4].)

chords), as shown in Fig. 4. It may be plausible to assume that this arises from a perspective view of a symmetric shape. As another example, it may be plausible that parallel lines in the two-dimensional image arise from parallel lines in space. In general, if an observed two-dimensional shape could have arisen from a more symmetrical shape by a three-dimensional rotation (e.g., an ellipse could be the image of a tilted circle), one might assume that this is actually the case.

An analogous argument can be used to deduce three-dimensional surface orientation from anisotropies in the texture of a region in the image [7]. If we assume that the surface texture is actually isotropic, the orientations of microedges in the texture should be uniformly distributed (and similarly, the spacings between facing pairs of edges should be independent of orientation). If the observed distribution is nonuniform in such a way that the nonuniformity could have arisen from three-dimensional rotation of an isotropically textured surface, we can assume that the surface is actually oriented in that way. (We do not really have to assume that the texture is isotropic, but only that its nonisotropy does not mimic the effects of three-dimensional rotation.) This method of deriving surface orientation from textural anisotropy is illustrated in Fig. 5. This work needs to be extended to make use of a variety of types of texture descriptors, for example, edge- or primitive-based as well as pixel-based descriptors; the richer the descriptors, the more likely the inference is to be reliable.

## RANGE ESTIMATION   III

If a high-resolution range sensor is available, the shapes of the visible surfaces in a scene can be obtained directly by constructing a range map. In

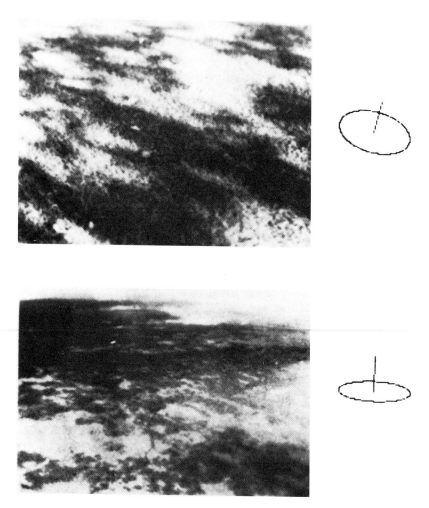

**Fig. 5.** Surface orientation estimation from texture anisotropy. The ellipse is the projection of a circle lying on a surface having the estimated orientation. (From Witkin [7].)

this section we assume that range information is not directly available. In its absence, range can be inferred from stereopairs by measuring stereo parallax, or relative range can be inferred from image sequences obtained from a moving sensor by analyzing the motions of corresponding pixels from frame to frame (optical flow).

Stereomapping is based on identifying corresponding points in the two images using image matching techniques. It is well known that matching performance is improved if we match features such as edges rather than intensity values. One approach to automatic stereomapping [8] is based on applying a set of edge operators, having a range of sizes, to the image;

matching the edges produced by the coarsest operator to yield a rough correspondence between the images; and then refining this correspondence by using successively finer edges. Edge-based approaches may still yield ambiguous results in heavily textured regions where edges are closely spaced. The ambiguity can be reduced by using intensity matching as a check or by classifying the edges into types (e.g., discontinuities in illumination, range, or orientation) and requiring that corresponding edges be of the same type. In general, matching should be based on feature descriptions, rather than on raw feature response values. Work is needed on the development of matching methods based on other feature types, and particularly on features derived from surface orientation maps, for example, matching of surface patches. Matching yields a set of range values at the positions of features; methods have been developed for fitting smooth range surfaces to these values. For wide-angle stereo, where there is significant perspective distortion, derivation of a camera model and rectification of the images prior to matching are very desirable.

When a static scene is viewed by a moving sensor, yielding a succession of images, the relative displacements of pixels from one image to the next are known as *optical flow*. If these displacements could be computed accurately, it would be possible in principle to infer the motion of the sensor relative to the scene and the relative distances of the scene points from the sensor (but note that there is an inherent speed–range ambiguity). The problems of computing optical flow from image sequences and inferring scene structure from the flow field are treated in other chapters in this volume.

## OBJECT REPRESENTATION  IV

The algorithms used to measure properties of image or scene parts depend on the data structures used to represent the parts. In this section we review the basic types of representations, both two- and three-dimensional, that are commonly used in computer vision.

Digital images are two-dimensional arrays in which each pixel value gives the intensity (in one or more spectral bands) of the radiation received by the sensor from the scene in a given direction. Other viewer-centered representations of the scene are also conveniently represented in array form, with the value of a pixel representing illumination, reflectivity, range, or components of surface slant at the scene point located along a given direction. Various types of image transforms, as well as symbolic "overlay" images defining the locations of features (contours, curves, etc.) or regions, are other examples of two-dimensional arrays that are often used in image processing.

Features and regions in any image can also be represented in other ways which are usually more compact than the overlay array representation and which also may make it easier to extract various types of information about their shapes. The following representations are all two-dimensional and are appropriate only if three-dimensional information is not known. One classical approach is to represent regions by border codes, defining the sequence of moves from neighbor to neighbor that must be made in order to circumnavigate the border; curves can also be represented by such move sequences (chain codes). Another standard way of representing regions is as unions of maximal "blocks" contained in them, for example, maximal "runs" of region points on each row of the image or maximal upright squares contained in the region. The set of run lengths on each row, or the set of centers and radii of the squares (known as the medial axis), completely determines the region. The square centers tend to lie on a set of arcs or curves that constitute the "skeleton" of the region; if we specify each such arc by a chain code and also specify a radius function along the arc, we have a representation of the region as a union of generalized ribbons (see the end of this section).

There has been recent interest in the use of hierarchically structured representations that incorporate both coarse and fine information about a region or feature. One often-used hierarchical maximum-block representation is based on recursive subdivision into quadrants, where the blocks can be represented by the nodes of a degree-four tree (a quadtree) [9]. Hierarchical border or curve representations can be defined based on recursive polygonal approximation, with the segments represented by the nodes of a strip tree [10] or based on quadrant subdivision [11].

At a higher level of abstraction, a segmented image is often represented by a graph in which the nodes correspond to regions (or parts of surfaces, if three-dimensional information is available) or features, labeled with property names or values, and the arcs are labeled with relation values or names. A problem with this type of representation is that it does not preserve the details of region geometry and so can only provide simplified information about geometrical properties and relations, many of which have no simple characterizations. An ideal representation should provide information at multiple resolution so that both gross geometry and important local features are easily available, together with the topological and locational constraints on the positions of the features, where these constraints may have varying degrees of fuzziness. It should also be easy to modify the representation to reflect the effects of three-dimensional geometrical transformations so that representations of objects viewed from different positions can be easily compared.

Representations of surfaces and objects, that is, $2\frac{1}{2}$-dimensional and three-dimensional scene representations, are also an important area of study. The visible surfaces in a scene can be represented by an array of slope vectors; the histogram of these vectors is known as the *gradient space* map. The range to each point in the scene is another important type of viewer-centered array representation.

In order to identify the objects in a scene, it is desirable to relate the viewer-centered representations of the visible surfaces to object-centered representations that describe the objects on a three-dimensional level. A variety of object representations can be defined, generalizing the representations of two-dimensional regions described earlier. An object can be represented by a series of slices, and a two-dimensional representation can be used for each slice. Alternatively, an object can be represented as a union of maximal blocks, for example, by an octree (based on recursive subdivision of space into octants) or by a three-dimensional medial axis. If this axis is approximated by a set of space curves, each represented by a three-dimensional chain code, and we also specify a radius function along each curve, we have a representation of the object as a union of generalized cylinders or generalized cones. Such representations can themselves be hierarchical, based on a succession of increasingly refined approximations to the object (body; head, trunk, arms, and legs; arm joints and hand; hand parts and fingers; and finger joints) [12].

## MODEL MATCHING   V

A "literal" description of an image or scene can be given in the form of a relational structure in which the nodes correspond to features, regions, or objects, labeled by lists of their property values (shape, texture, color, etc.). However, this type of semantics-free description is usually not what is wanted; rather, we want a description in terms of a known configuration of known objects. This requires "recognizing" the objects by comparing their descriptions to stored models, which are generalized descriptions defining object classes.

Even in two dimensions, such models are often very difficult to formulate, since the constraints on the allowable property values and relationships are hard to define. In three dimensions, the problem is rendered even more difficult by the fact that only one side of an object can be visible in an image; the image description is two-dimensional, while the stored object models are presumably three-dimensional, object-centered representations.

The most extensive work on recognition of three-dimensional objects from images is embodied in the ACRONYM system [13]. This system incorporates methods of predicting the two-dimensional appearance (shape, shading, etc.) of a given object in an image taken from a given point of view. Conversely, it provides means of defining constraints on the three-dimensional properties of the object that could give rise to a given image and for manipulating sets of such constraints. These capabilities are incorporated in a prediction–verification process that uses the image to make predictions about the object and verifies that the image could in fact have arisen from an object that satisfies the resulting set of constraints. Thus far, ACRONYM has been implemented only in restricted domains, but it is based on very general principles and should be widely extendable.

It is often appropriate to model regions or objects hierarchically, that is, as composed of parts arranged in particular ways, where the parts themselves are arrangements of subparts, and so on. There is an analogy between this type of hierarchical representation and the use of grammars to define languages; here a sentence is composed of clauses which are in turn composed of phrases, etc. Based on this observation, the process of recognizing an object as belonging to a given hierarchically defined class of objects is analogous to the process of recognizing a well-formed sentence as belonging to a given language, by *parsing* it with respect to a grammar for that language. This syntactic approach to object (or pattern) recognition has been extensively studied [14]. It has been used successfully for recognition of two-dimensional shapes, patterns, and textures, but it is less appropriate for three-dimensional object recognition, since it is not obvious how to incorporate in it mechanisms for relating two-dimensional images to three-dimensional objects.

Many difficult problems are associated with the model-matching task. It is not trivial to define models for given classes of patterns or objects. (In the case of syntactic models, the problem of inferring them from sets of examples is known as *grammatical inference*. The inference of relational structure models from examples is treated by Winston [15].) Given a large set of models, it is not obvious how to determine the right one(s) with which to compare a given object; this is known as the *indexing problem*. Even if the correct model is known, comparing it with the descriptions of a given object may involve combinatorial search. (Here, however, relaxation or constraint satisfaction methods can often be used to reduce the search space.) The best approach is to use the model(s) to control the computer vision process and to design this process in such a way that most of the possible models are eliminated at early stages of the analysis. Unfortunately, there exists as yet no general theory of how to design computer vision processes based on given sets of models; the control structures used have been designed largely on heuristic grounds.

## VI   CONCLUDING REMARKS

We have seen that computer vision involves, in general, many different processes that incorporate many different types of information about the class of scenes being analyzed. There is no general theory of control in computer vision; in other words, there are no general principles that specify how these processes should interact in carrying out a given task. In particular, when a number of methods exist for performing a given task, for example, feature detection or inference of surface orientation, it would usually be desirable to implement several of the methods in order to obtain a consensus. However, there is no general theory of how to combine evidence from multiple sources.

Most of the successful applications of computer vision have involved relatively simple domains and have been primarily two-dimensional. For example, in robot vision, systems that recognize parts on a belt (well illuminated, nonoverlapping, in specific three-dimensional orientations) are not hard to build, but systems that recognize parts in a bin (shadowed, overlapping, arbitrarily oriented) are still a research issue. Techniques exist that will in principle handle such complex situations, but they need to be refined and extensively tested before they can be used in practice.

The discussion of the computer vision process in this chapter has been quite general purpose, without emphasis on particular domains of application. It is also possible to build specialist or expert systems tailored to a specific domain which make use of methods especially designed for that domain. From a practical standpoint, successful applications of computer vision are likely to be of this specialized nature. It is the general approach, however, that makes computer vision at least potentially a science and will continue to provide a theoretical background for the design of application-oriented systems.

This chapter has touched on some of the basic techniques of computer vision but has not been able to treat the subject in detail. Further information on the topics treated in this chapter, and on other aspects of computer vision, can be found in recent books on the subject [16–18].

## ACKNOWLEDGEMENT

The help of Janet Salzman in preparing this chapter is gratefully acknowledged.

## REFERENCES

1. K. Ikeuchi and B. K. P. Horn, Numerical shape from shading and occluding boundaries, *Artificial Intelligence* **17**, 141–184 (1981).
2. R. J. Woodham, Analyzing images of curved surfaces, *Artificial Intelligence* **17**, 117–140 (1981).
3. T. O. Binford, Inferring surfaces from images, *Artificial Intelligence* **17**, 205–244 (1981).
4. T. Kanade, Recovery of the three-dimensional shape of an object from a single view, *Artificial Intelligence* **17**, 409–460 (1981).
5. H. R. Barrow and J. M. Tenenbaum, Interpreting line drawings as three-dimensional surfaces, *Artificial Intelligence* **17**, 75–116 (1981).
6. K. A. Stevens, The visual interpretation of surface contours, *Artificial Intelligence* **17**, 47–73 (1981).
7. A. P. Witkin, Recovering surface shape and orientation from texture, *Artificial Intelligence* **17**, 17–45 (1981).

8. W. E. L. Grimson, "From Images to Surfaces: A Computational Study of the Human Early Visual System." MIT Press, Cambridge, Massachusetts, 1981.
9. H. Samet and A. Rosenfeld, Quadtree representation of binary images, *Proc. 5th Intl. Conf. Pattern Recognition, 1980*, pp. 815–818 (1980).
10. D. Ballard, Strip trees: a hierarchical representation for curves, *Comm. ACM* **24**, 319–321 (1981).
11. M. Shneier, Two hierarchical linear feature representations: edge pyramids and edge quadtrees, *Computer Graphics Image Processing* **17**, 211–224 (1981).
12. H. K. Nishihara, Intensity, visible-surface, and volumetric representations, *Artificial Intelligence* **17**, 265–284 (1981).
13. R. A. Brooks, Symbolic reasoning among 3-D models and 2-D images, *Artificial Intelligence* **17**, 285–348 (1981).
14. K. S. Fu, "Syntactic Pattern Recognition and Applications." Prentice-Hall, Englewood Cliffs, New Jersey, 1982.
15. P. H. Winston, Learning structural descriptions from examples, *in* "The Psychology of Computer Vision," (P. H. Winston, ed.), pp. 157–209. McGraw-Hill, New York, 1975.
16. D. Ballard and C. Brown, "Computer Vision." Prentice-Hall, Englewood Cliffs, New Jersey, 1982.
17. R. Nevatia, "Machine Perception." Prentice-Hall, Englewood Cliffs, New Jersey, 1982.
18. D. Marr, "Vision." Freeman, San Francisco, California, 1982.

Part **III**

# Systems and Architectures

Chapter **16**

# Image Database Systems

SHI-KUO CHANG

Information Systems Laboratory
Illinois Institute of Technology
Chicago, Illinois

## IMAGE INFORMATION SYSTEMS I

Images are natural means for man–machine communication. An *image information system* (IIS) is the software system to control and manage the image input device, image processor, image output device, image storage

371

system, and image communication interface in order to provide a collection of image data for easy access by a large number of users. An *image database* (IDB) or a *pictorial database* (PDB) is a collection of shareable image data encoded in various formats. The image database is the core of an image information system.

Advances in image information systems are technology driven. New hardware devices include the following.

(1) *Image input device.* High-resolution scanners, with resolution of several hundred to a couple of thousand lines per inch are now available [1].

(2) *Image processor.* Stand-alone image processors incorporating micro-processors and array processors can be interfaced with most mini- and microcomputers. Their processing functions include pixel-by-pixel process-ing, spatial convolution, zoom, rotation, floating-point vector–matrix pro-cessing, smoothing, image enhancement, etc. The availability of image processors implies that many image processing and signal processing func-tions previously requiring large CPU time can now be off-loaded to these processors and computed efficiently. Highly parallel systems can also be configured to further improve processing speed [2].

(3) *Image output device.* High-resolution color graphics raster displays, typically with display resolutions of up to $1024 \times 1024$ pixels and multiple colors, offer high-quality image and graphics output.

(4) *Image storage system.* In addition to the traditional mass storage systems, there is renewed interest in using microfiche for storage–retrieval of large quantities of images. A minicomputer stores the microfilm address and key descriptors and controls the retrieval of specific document images. Such an electronic filing system can be used to create and maintain an image database [3]. The video-disk technology offers another means of creating and maintaining nonerasable image databases [4].

In addition to these hardware components/systems, the recent advances in data communications, especially broadband local area networks, provide the means to interconnect many workstations for *multimedia communication,* including voice, data, and image.

These technological advances stimulate the design of advanced image information systems. From the software viewpoint, system-wide compatible software modules must be designed for image input, image editing, image processing, image storage, image retrieval, image output, and image com-munication.

## II NEEDS FOR IMAGE INFORMATION SYSTEMS

Image information systems are needed as subsystems for advanced infor-mation systems in many application areas and as *stand-alone systems,* depending on the needs and practical applications.

### Fifth-Generation Computer Systems (Knowledge-Based Systems)    A

The proposed fifth-generation computer systems [5] will be knowledge information processing systems that can offer advanced functions expected to be required in the 1990s, thus overcoming technical restrictions inherent to conventional computers. In these systems, machine intelligence will be greatly improved and the man-machine interface will become closer to the human system. The intelligent user interface functions include the capabilities of understanding speech, image, and natural language. For many new applications, an intelligent user interface capable of image communication and image understanding is required.

### Office Automation Systems    B

The ability to handle documents and forms is required for almost all office automation (OA) systems. Certain fields in documents and forms, such as signature fields, photographs, and special symbols, also have a natural image representation [6]. Since documents often contain both text and graphics data, they are sometimes better treated as images (document images). Such document images need to be created, encoded, edited, stored, retrieved, and transmitted. Since office automation systems are distributed systems designed around local area networks, image communications and multimedia communications are emphasized in such systems.

### Computer-Aided Design Systems    C

Computer-aided design (CAD) is an important image database application area. Research projects are being undertaken at many research laboratories as well as universities [7]. Investigations on CAD/CAM database design, which is closely related to image database design, have also received increasing attention [8, 9].

### Image Understanding Systems    D

Image understanding (IU) systems are traditionally of interest to defense-related industries. More recently, we have seen the interests widen to include other industries, such as the aerospace and semiconductor industries. The combination of image understanding, knowledge base, and image information handling is needed in the design of sophisticated image understanding systems. The image information system is a useful tool, and an important subsystem, for such systems.

TABLE I
Needs for Image Information Systems

|  | Flexible user interface | Ability for image communication | Design tools for various applications |
|---|---|---|---|
| Fifth-generation computer systems | × |  | × |
| OA systems | × | × |  |
| CAD systems |  |  | × |
| IU systems |  |  | × |
| CIM systems | × | × |  |

## E   Computer-Integrated Manufacturing Systems

For computer vision systems in robotics and computer-aided manufacturing (CAM), an image information system is also needed as a subsystem. For example, in automated VLSI chip inspection, hundreds and thousands of mask patterns need to be stored in a pattern database (which is an image database), and the image observed by the electron microscope is analyzed with respect to these reference patterns for possible faults. Manufacturing automation also includes inventory control, warehouse management, and parts and materials input and output. In so-called computer-integrated manufacturing (CIM) systems, how to integrate many heterogeneous databases to form an integrated information repertoire becomes an important issue. Image databases are not only useful because of application requirements (for example, the VLSI pattern database cited earlier) but can also be used as tools in the description of other databases to be integrated (for example, in the design of CAD or CAM databases, or as a metadatabase in a knowledge-based system).

The needs for image information systems are summarized in Table I. In Table I, the primary emphasis for each application area is indicated with an × . It can be seen for integrated information systems such as OA and CIM systems that the emphasis is on flexible user interface and image communications. For other types of information systems, the emphasis is on image database and image information subsystems as design tools.

## III   REQUIREMENTS FOR IMAGE INFORMATION SYSTEMS

In order to compare the requirements of diversified image information systems, we first list the major features of an (idealized) image information system.

**TABLE II**
**Requirements for Image Information Systems**

|                                | Image input | Image editing | Image processing | Image storage | Image retrieval | Image output | Image communication |
|--------------------------------|-------------|---------------|------------------|---------------|-----------------|--------------|---------------------|
| Fifth-generation computer systems | Maybe    | —             | Some             | Yes           | Yes             | Yes          | Maybe               |
| OA systems                     | Maybe       | Maybe         | Some             | Yes           | Yes             | Yes          | Yes                 |
| CAD systems                    | Maybe       | Yes           | —                | Yes           | Yes             | Yes          | —                   |
| IU systems                     | Yes         | —             | Yes              | Maybe         | Maybe           | Yes          | —                   |
| CIM systems                    | Maybe       | —             | Some             | Yes           | Yes             | Yes          | Yes                 |

(1) *Image input*: the means of capturing or digitizing an optical image, which may be originally on paper, on film, or through a camera.

(2) *Image editing*: the means of changing the contents of a digitized image, as well as interactively or automatically creating a new image or destroying an old image.

(3) *Image processing*: the enhancement of an image, edge detection, texture analysis, segmentation and pattern recognition techniques, as well as algorithmic or optical means of image transformation.

(4) *Image storage*: the formatting, encoding and decoding, data structuring, and indexing of images for storage in a given storage medium.

(5) *Image retrieval*: the retrieval of images from the image database by indexing or by more flexible means of retrieval using similarity measures or some type of query language.

(6) *Image output*: how images are displayed and how hard- copies are obtained. Whether it is possible to obtain image montage and partial images.

(7) *Image communication*: how images can be transmitted to computers at another location or another workstation.

The requirements of various application areas are listed in Table II.

## IMAGE DATABASE DESIGN IV

Since the core of the image information system is the image database system, many researchers recently have concentrated on the problems of image database design—how to provide a unified approach for image data retrieval-manipulation, how to utilize spatial data structures to facilitate image database operations, and how to compress-decode image data. In addition, since many image information systems emphasize user-friendliness, the design of flexible user interfaces is also of great importance. Last but not least, the problems of image communications need be studied.

In what follows, we describe recent approaches in image database design, spatial data structures, image data compaction and encoding techniques, user interface design, and image communications. Interested readers are referred to two recent surveys containing valuable information on image database [10] and image query processing [11].

## A    The Relational Model

The relational model for image database systems was first proposed by Kunii [12]. A relational database scheme for describing complex images with color and texture is presented. Structure independence, modularity, associativity, and machine independence for complex image description are discussed.

To motivate the relational database approach for image data management, we will use a geographic information system as an example. Much data has been collected according to regional or geographic units for analysis. For example, the U.S. Census Bureau collects innumerable descriptive statistics about population and housing by various political units. Marketing companies collect market data by zip codes to determine in which areas to target their advertising campaign. Land use planning organization requires information on soil type for each land parcel. Storing data as attributes for each geographic unit lends itself to the development of a relational database. This database organization allows the user to algebraically manipulate the data in order to answer complex questions and to generate new information which could be converted to images. Several researchers have suggested the desirability of the relational database as the underlying structure for a geographic information system with cartographic output. The structural power of a relational database requires data aggregated by and associated with geographic units.

An image divided into frames is shown in Fig. 1a; the corresponding relations are shown in Fig. 1b. The process of converting an image (the map) into its relational representation (the d-map) is called *abstraction*; the inverse process of converting a relational representation into an image is called *materialization*.

## B    Image Algebra

At the Information Systems Laboratory at IIT, extensive results for integrated relational database design are presented, and the traditional relational algebra is found insufficient to manipulate these data, for example,

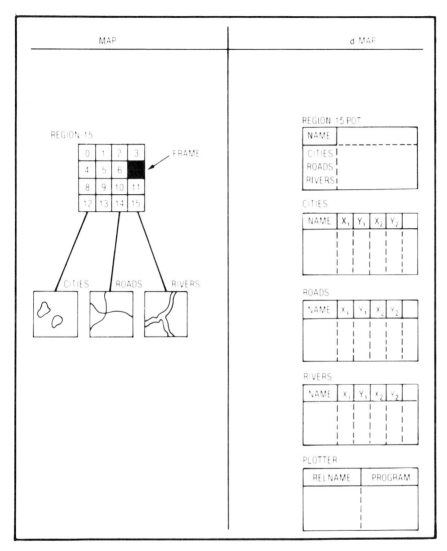

**Fig. 1.** Pictorial relational database and its materialization. (a) Map and (b) d-map. (From Chang and Kunii [13]. © 1981 IEEE.)

to *analyze spatial relationships* among various image objects [14, 15]. A set of picture operations, called *image algebra*, is designed to handle the spatial data for storage, retrieval, manipulation, and transformation [16]. An integrated image database management system is designed. This system combines a relational database management system, RAIN, with an image manipulation system to enable the user to perform various image information retrievals by

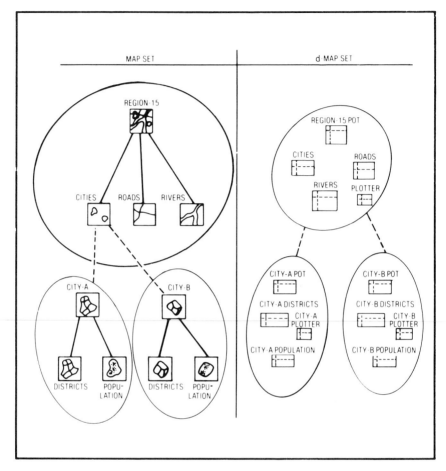

**Fig. 2.** Hierarchical structure of pictorial relational databases. (From Chang and Kunii [13]. © 1981 IEEE.)

using zooming, panning, and spatial relation analysis operations to manipulate the image database. This image database contains image data in two
forms: a relational table form and a raster image form. The user can specify
his image query in GRAIN language which is imbedded in the DIMAP
(distributed image management and projection) system. As shown in Fig. 2, a
hierarchically structured collection of image objects is organized in order to
allow logical zooming, which is used to navigate into the detailed description
or to browse through the image objects similar to the interested image. This
concept can be applied to the storage and manipulation of a large number of
images, some of which can be very complex. A query language is developed

for image information retrieval, which utilizes an *image database skeleton* as the knowledge model [17].

The work by Chang and Fu [18] also utilizes a relational database framework. Algorithms are provided to convert relational graphs into relations and vice versa, and a picture-query-by-example (PQBE) user interface is formulated. The data-flow diagram of their IMAID system is shown in Fig. 3. A more recent work by Roussopoulos [20] has extended the SQL query language to pictorial SQL (PSQL), which is supported by a new indexing technique based upon two-dimensional $B$-trees.

## SPATIAL DATA STRUCTURES     V

Generalized spatial data structures which can be used to represent spatial objects have been proposed by many researchers. We will survey a few interesting approaches.

Shapiro's structure [21] consists of a set of $N$-ary relations, often including an attribute-value table. The entries in the table and the objects on which the relations are defined may also be spatial data structures. In this approach, the description of spatial structure is emphasized. Retrieval processing is through the attributes of spatial data. A semantic table is set up for the spatial relation analysis in order to speed up the retrieval process. Database updating is somewhat complicated.

Sties [22] described an image information system in which an object is described in terms of shape, symbolic description, and relations with the other objects. Objects in an image can be retrieved in terms of symbolic description and/or object relationships. A multisensor image database system (MIDAS) which can perform image understanding and knowledge acquisition is described by McKeown. A hierarchical data structure is chosen primarily to store symbolic representations in the image database system. Images are stored hierarchically with different resolutions, which is called an *iconic data structure*. Partial image description is stored in a relational database which is used for performance evaluation purposes.

Klinger [23] has proposed a hierarchical data structure scheme for storing images by regular decomposition of images into adjacent quadrants with different resolutions. Each quadrant corresponds to a node in a tree called a $W$-tree. In keeping with the theories on database design, this image data structure facilitates accessibility of image data in storage, flexibility in image data storage, image data independence, redundancy reduction in multilevel structured data, and analysis of small portions of an image with efficiency. A further generalization of quadrant tree structure to iconic–symbolic tree

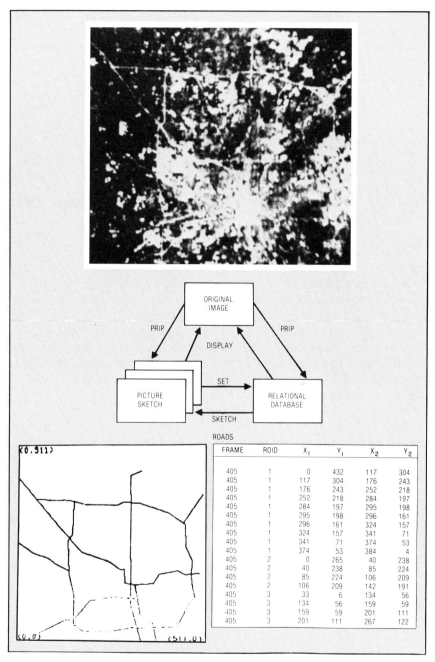

**Fig. 3.** Data-flow diagram of IMAID. (From Chang and Fu [19]. © 1981 IEEE.)

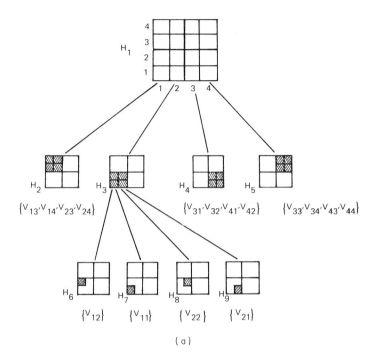

(a)

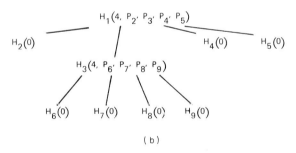

(b)

**Fig. 4.** Example of (a) a picture tree and (b) a query tree.

structure has been proposed by Tanimoto [24]. Algorithms for the construction of abstracted icons to serve as indexes for pictorial databases are described by Chang and Lin [25]. An example of a *picture tree*, which is a generalization of the quadrant tree and also incorporates the main concepts of the iconic–symbolic tree, is shown in Fig. 4a, and the corresponding query tree illustrating the picture indexing approach (the picture indexes are logical predicates used as indexes) is shown in Fig. 4b.

## VI  COMPACTION AND ENCODING OF IMAGE DATA

There are two commonly used formats in representing image information. Computer cartography, topography, and spatial analysis in the geographic information system have traditionally used a *vector format*. However, more and more image data are becoming available via new image capture devices which generate data in *raster format*, such as LANDSAT imagery and drum scanner output. Advanced technologies in computer graphics such as video frame buffer memories and improvements in CRT resolution have made feasible the increasing use of raster-scan displays as interactive graphics terminals. Algorithms and data structures for manipulating raster-formatted spatial data have also been explored. Recursive description and processing of hierarchically structured image data in a raster format is proposed, and its implementation is reported. The logical basis of raster-format processing is established. These recent advances have led to the development of image database systems capable of managing image data encoded in various formats.

## VII  USER INTERFACE DESIGN

In order to facilitate man–machine interaction, information retrieval requests, or queries, retrieval images from an image database can be specified in several ways. The simplest way is by means of an index or a key. A command language can be designed to retrieve images by keys from an image storage system. Many researchers have worked on *picture query languages* to specify user's queries. The GRAIN system described earlier is an example. For example, to retrieve the image containing major highways through Tokyo, the GRAIN query is [16, 17].

Sketch highway; through (cityname is 'Tokyo')

As another interesting approach to image query formulation, Chang and Fu [18] at Purdue University describe a relational database system which is interfaced with an image understanding system and the design of a flexible query language for image information retrieval based upon Zloof's query-by-example (QBE) approach [26]. An example is illustrated in Fig. 5. The importance of spatial operations is also emphasized as a clue to retrieving images from an image database.

*Sample query 1:* Print the names of roads that appear in the same frame as city Lafayette.

Initially, the system displays a blank table. The user, knowing that the answer to the query is in the RONAME and CINAME tables, enters RONAME and CINAME as the table names. The system responds by filling in the corresponding column names. Now the user can express the query by making entries in four positions on these two tables, as follows:

| CINAME | FRAME | CIID | NAME |
|--------|-------|------|------|
|        | 10    |      | LAFAYETTE |

| RONAME | FRAME | ROID | NAME |
|--------|-------|------|------|
|        | 10    |      | P.MAIN |

The P. stands for PRINT, an output operator. These two tables are connected by the common example 10. This query can also be formulated in predicate calculus, as follows:

$$\{x : \exists y \exists w \exists z((y,z,\text{LAFAYETTE})$$
$$\epsilon \text{ CINAME} \wedge (y,w,x) \epsilon \text{ RONAME})\}$$

More complicated queries can be made by establishing connections among rows of one table or among several tables.

**Fig. 5.** Example of a flexible query language for image information retrieval based on the QBE approach. (From Chang and Fu [19]. © 1981 IEEE.)

## IMAGE COMMUNICATIONS    VIII

Image communications is a new area of research of interest mainly to people working on office automation. However, it is expected that this area will receive increasing attention in the future.

A conceptual framework for multimedia messages is presented by the University of Toronto group [27]. In this framework, a message has a type, a set of attributes, a text part, an image part, a voice part, and an annotation part. The image part consists of an image type, a vector form (used to represent the picture as a collection of easy-to-store primitive objects like lines, polylines, and circles), a raster form (a set of pixels), a statistical part (used to store image statistics, such as histograms, etc.), and a text part. In other words, an image has an object form and a raster form. Multimedia messages are retrieved by specifying message content information instead of a unique message identifier. Image content addressability can be achieved by specifying conditions on the image text part and on the image statistical part as well as similarity relationships among image objects. The user can also enhance his retrieval capability by specifying conditions on the external presentation form of a message.

Diamond is a computer-based system developed at BBN Laboratories for creating, editing, transmitting, and printing multimedia documents [28], which are viewed to be the structured composition of objects of possibly different media types to be presented in a coordinated way. A diamond document is a collection of objects which may be represented either directly [e.g., text, images, graphics) or indirectly by means of icons on a two-dimensional surface, such as a display device or a piece of paper. The types of objects that may appear in a Diamond document include graphics (lines, geometric figures, text strings), images (maps, photographs, etc.), voices, spreadsheets and charts, and connections (lines with arrows to connect a point within one box to a point within another). For composition, editing, and viewing purposes, a Diamond document is organized as a set of nonoverlapping boxes, each of which can contain objects of a given type, plus connections relating points in one box to points in other boxes.

Although research on multimedia communications has just begun, it is important to note that images are regarded as objects so that they can be managed and manipulated by the image database system.

## IX  SOFTWARE DESIGN APPROACH

Based upon considerations of the requirements of image information systems, an approach of software design to achieve system integration will now be described.

## A  Software Portability and Modularity

Since image information systems need image processing software to do image analysis, image enhancement, data compression, etc., it is important to have general-purpose image processing software packages that can be transported easily to different computer systems. Recently, several portable image processing software packages have become available.

A standard image access protocol has been proposed by Haralick [29], and a transportable image processing package has been designed according to that protocol [30]. Another package, SPIDER, consists of over 400 FOR-

TRAN IV subroutines and is completely independent of I/O devices [31]. The specifications of SPIDER programs also regulate the style of comments in source programs. Such *self-descriptive program modules* can also be enforced to ensure system extendability. The general availability of such software packages makes the design of integrated image information systems easier.

Image communications will undoubtedly play an important role in next-generation image information systems. Standard image formats and standard image communication protocols are needed for image communication protocols are needed for image communications, either across the boundary of two systems or within the same system. *Self-descriptive data structures*, therefore, become an important concern. The least that can be done is to have a standard header format for image files. Standard image presentation and conversion protocols also need to be defined. Several image access protocols and standard formats have been proposed [29, 32]. A self-describing and self-documenting database system has been proposed by Roussopoulos and Mark [33], where the database dictionary is enhanced to provide complete documentation of the database. Such an approach could be extended to benefit image database design.

## Image Processing Language and Programming Environment    B

A recent survey of image processing languages shows most image processing languages are pixel oriented [34]. For image information systems, we need a unified image processing language and a programming environment supporting the language primitives for an image information system. The main characteristics of such a language are that it should be flexible and extendable. It should also allow the user to navigate through the image database using image icons.

As an example of a general-purpose image processing language, the image processing language IPL [35] consists of three subsets: the logical image processing language, the interactive image processing language, and the physical image processing language.

The user interacts with the image information system using the interactive image processing language. The logical image processing language is used to retrieve–manipulate logical images stored in the image database. The user can also employ the physical image processing language to process–manipulate physical images stored in the image store.

## Flexible User Interface    C

The user interface should be customized to local needs. Yet it should be capable of translating the local image manipulation commands into the unified image processing language. The user should be able to navigate in the image database with ease by manipulating user-defined icons, windows, and ports.

An image database generally has a complex hierarchical structure. Since at any given time the user will always focus his attention on a small portion of the image database, we could maintain a user workspace which is a temporary work area to store the current entities of interest. Thus, all data which are used for a specific application can normally be handled in a workspace by means of predefined metadata structures and user commands. A workspace can be saved, loaded, and deleted, and a new workspace can be created when needed. Communication between a workspace and a database or any external device can be made by associating data in the workspace with ports. Implementations of workspaces can easily be done in, for instance, LISP, APL, or FORTH, because these languages already support workspaces in their programming environment. However, it could be implemented in other programming languages as well.

## X  GENERALIZED ICONS FOR SYSTEM INTEGRATION

### A  Why Icons?

The concept of icons has been advanced by many researchers. Some proposed icons as part of the spatial data structure [24]. Some used icons as a navigational aid [36]. In the SDMS approach, icons have been used to give database objects a pictorial representation. In image communications, the definition of image messages also consists of the following dual forms: an object form and an image form. This duality is essential for the logical–physical representation of images. In an image information system, some software modules will be dealing with the physical image representation, some software modules will be dealing with the logical object representation, and others will be dealing with both. Thus, in order for the software modules to deal with images in a uniform way, a dual representation in terms of logical objects–physical images is necessary.

Moreover, an emerging trend in modern man–machine interface design is the use of icons or visual symbols in representing abstract objects [3]. As discussed by Chang et al. [35], we can distinguish four types of icons: object icons, command icons, window icons, and port icons. The icons appearing in the user interface of many modern personal computers are usually command icons, window icons, or port icons. What Chang et al. proposed is the notion of a generalized icon, which is an extension of the notion of an object icon discussed by Tanimoto [24]. In other words, in addition to representing commands, windows, or ports, which are specialized objects, generalized icons can represent any abstract object or object class.

Icons are objects with dual representations and multiple interpretations. An icon has, in general, two representations: a visual (or physical) representation by an image and an abstract (or logical) representation by a structure. For example, a command icon may have the visual representation of a mail drop. Its abstract representation could be a list of strings (COMMAND mail sender receiver message), denoting a command object, the command name, and three parameters. When invoked, its default interpretation is the execution of the mail command to send a message from the sender to the receiver.

A window icon may have the visual representation of a rectangular frame. Its abstract representation could be (WINDOW w12 x y 1x 1y), denoting a window object, the window name, and four parameters. When invoked, its default interpretation is the execution of a window command to superpose a window on the current image in the workspace.

A port icon may have the visual representation of a camera. Its abstract representation could be (PORT camera input), denoting a visual input device. When invoked, its default interpretation could be the opening or closing of the camera port. (The zooming port of SDMS, when invoked, will lead to the execution of a default display program.)

More generally, an object icon has a visual representation, called the *icon sketch*, and an abstract representation, called the *picture object*. The icon sketch could be a low-resolution raster image, a line drawing, a chain-coded sketch, or some predefined pictorial symbol (such as one of the available symbols on a keyboard). The picture object is specified by a list of (attribute-name, attribute value, evaluation-procedure) triples. It could also be a *virtual object* specified by a picture query or a rule [25], or a pointer to a rule query. When invoked, the default interpretation is to show the picture object in an external representation. However, the interpretation depends upon the amount of detail the user wishes to see and the format in which it is shown.

An icon is created by defining an icon type (i.e., a picture object or object class, a command, a window, a port) and an icon sketch. In other words, the icon can be regarded as the cross index relating the icon type and the icon sketch.

A simple example of icon construction will now be presented. An icon sketch corresponding to an image can be constructed by obtaining the half-tone (binary) image from the original image. The binary image, after size reduction, becomes the icon sketch. An example is illustrated in Fig. 6. In Fig. 6a, the original image is shown. Two types of half-tone image are shown

**Fig. 6.** (a) Original image. (b) Half-tone image of (a). (c) Another half-tone image of (a). (d) Icon sketch. (e) Another icon sketch.

in Figs. 6b and 6c. After size reduction, the icon sketches are shown in Figs. 6d and 6e. Icon sketches can also be constructed interactively. Line drawings can be created, and simple sketches can be combined to create more complex icon sketches.

## C   Image Database Design Using Icons

We are now ready to give a scenario for image database design using icons. Figure 7a shows an actual SEASAT image. By applying image processing and pattern recognition algorithms, certain shiplike objects in this image can be reduced to object icons. Some more complex objects, such as the shore

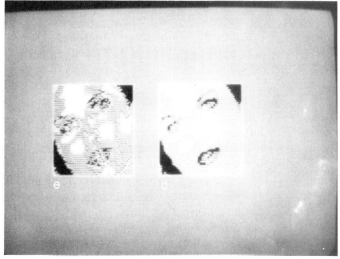

**Fig. 6.** (*Continued*)

area, can be reduced to virtual object icons. The icon sketch construction techniques described previously can be used to generate these icon sketches. The image now becomes an image consisting in part of the real image and in part of object icons. Figure 7b illustrates the result. Window icons are then created, as shown in Fig. 7c. These window icons, together with ports, define the image hierarchy, that is, the picture tree. The final result is illustrated in Fig. 7d.

This example shows that by constructing icons we can design the image database interactively. Conversely, the hierarchical structure then enables the user to navigate in the image database using logical zooming techniques [38].

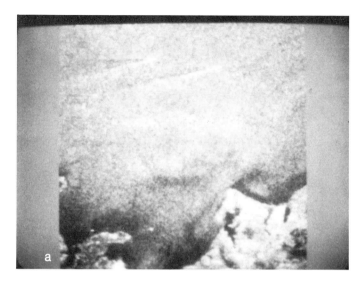

**Fig. 7.** (a) Original image. (b) Icons are identified. (c) Windows are added. (d) The picture tree.

Generalized icons thus serve several purposes.

(1)   An icon, or a (physical representation, logical representation) pair, becomes the unit of information exchange among various software modules. This representation can be made self-descriptive, so that the interface among software modules becomes straightforward.

(2)   The image processing language can be based on the manipulation of icons [35]. Moreover, as illustrated by the preceding example, the image database can be designed by constructing icons.

(3)   The user interface can be designed entirely around icons. Icons also serve as the unit for image communications.

With the concept of generalized icons, it becomes possible for various software modules to be interfaced in a uniform way.

## REFERENCES

1. G. Nagy, Optical scanners, *Computer*, (April 1983).
2. K. Hwang (ed.), *Special Issue on Computer Architectures for Image Processing, Computer* (January 1983).
3. Toshiba Corporation, "Toshiba Document Filing System: Specification Manual" (1982).
4. H. Tan, High density optical storage, *C&IT Report*, No. 9 (1982)
5. P. C. Treleaven and I. G. Lima, Japan's fifth-generation computer systems, *Computer* (August 1982).
6. A. Myers, Trends in office automation technology, *Technical Report RC9321, IBM Watson Research Center, Yorktown Heights, New York, April 1982.*
7. *IEEE Spectrum Special Issue on Data Driven Automation, Spectrum* (May 1983).

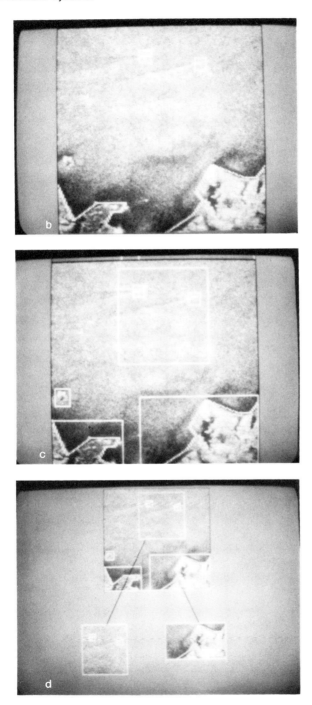

**Fig. 7.** (*Continued*)

8. J. C. Dorng and S. K. Chang, Design considerations for CAD/CAM databases, *Proceedings of International Computer Symposium, Taipei, Taiwan, Dec. 1984* 400–403 (1984).

9. Y. C. Lee and K. S. Fu, A CAD/CAM database management system and its query languages, *in* "Languages for Automation," (S. K. Chang, ed.), Plenum, New York, pp. 245–273 1985.

10. H. Tamura and Y. Naokazu, Image database systems: A survey, *International Journal of Pattern Recognition* **17**, (1), 29–43 (1984).

11. Y. C. Lee and K. S. Fu, Query languages for pictorial database system, *School of Electrical Engineering, Purdue University*, TR-EE-83-30, September 1983.

12. T. Kunii, S. Weyl, and J. M. Tenenbaum, A relational database schema for describing complex pictures with color and texture, *Proceedings of the 2nd International Joint Conference on Pattern Recognition, IEEE Computer Society, Aug. 1974*, pp. 310–316 (1974).

13. S. K. Chang and T. Kunii, Pictorial database systems, *IEEE Computer Magazine Special Issue on Pictorial Information Systems* (S. K. Chang, ed.), pp. 13–21 November 1981.

14. S. K. Chang, J. Reuss, and B. H. McCormick, An integrated relational database system for Pictures, *Proceedings of 1977 IEEE Workshop on Picture Data Description and Management, Chicago, Illinois, April 21–22*, pp. 142–149 (1977).

15. S. K. Chang, *et al.*, Design considerations of a pictorial database system, *International Journal on Policy Analysis and Information Systems* **1** (2), 49–70 (1978).

16. B. S. Lin and S. K. Chang, Picture algebra for interface with pictorial database systems, *Proceedings of COMPSAC 79, Nov. 6–8, 1979, Chicago*, pp. 525–530 (1979).

17. B. S. Lin and S. K. Chang, GRAIN—A pictorial database interface, *Proceedings of 1980 IEEE PDDM Workshop August 27–29, 1980*, pp. 83–88 (1980).

18. N. S. Chang and K. S. Fu, Query-by-pictorial-example, *Proceedings of COMPSAC 79, IEEE Computer Society*, 325–330 (1979),

19. N. S. Chang and K. S. Fu, Picture query languages for pictorial data-base systems, *IEEE Computer*, 23–33 (1981).

20. N. Roussopoulos and D. Leifker, An introduction to PSQL: A pictorial structure query language, *Proc. of IEEE Workshop on Visual Languages, Hiroshima, Japan, Dec. 1984* (1984).

21. L. G. Shapiro and R. M. Haralick, A spatial data structure, Technical Report #CS 79005-R, p. 35. Dept. of Computer Science, Virginia Polytechnic Institute and State Univ. (August 1979).

22. M. Sties, B. Sanyal, and K. Leist, Organization of object data for an image information system, *Proceedings of the 3rd International Joint Conference on Pattern Recognition, IEEE Computer Society, 1976*, pp. 863–869 (1976).

23. A. Klinger, M. L. Rhode, and V. T. To, Accessing image data, *International Journal on Policy Analysis and Information Systems* **1** (2), 171–189, Knowledge System Laboratory, UICC (1978).

24. S. L. Tanimoto, An iconic/symbolic data structuring scheme, *in Pattern Recognition and Artificial Intelligence* pp. 452–471, Academic Press, New York, 1976.

25. S. K. Chang and S. H. Liu, Indexing and abstraction techniques for pictorial databases, *IEEE Transactions on Pattern Analysis and Machine Intelligence*, 475–484 (1984).

26. M. M. Zloof, Query by example, *Proceedings of National Conference, AFIPS* **44**, 431–438 (1975).

27. D. Tsichritzis, *et al.* Multimedia office filing system, *Proceedings of VLDB*, (1983).

28. H. C. Forsdick, R. H. Thomas, G. G. Robertson, and V. M. Travers, Initial experience with multimedia documents in diamond, *Computer Message Service, Proc. IFIP 6.5 Working Conference, IFIP 1984*, pp. 97–112 (1984).

29. R. M. Haralick, Image access protocol for image processing software, *IEEE Trans. Software Engineering* **SE-3**, 190–192 (1977).

30. R. G. Hamlet and R. M. Haralick, Transportable 'package' software, *Software, Pract. Exp.* **10**, 1009–1027 (1980).

31. H. Tamura, *et al.*, Design and implementation of SPIDER—A transportable image processing software package, *Computer Vision, Graphics, and Image Processing* **23**, 273–294 (1983).

32. J. M. Evans, Jr., *et al.* (eds.), *Proceedings of Workshop on Standards for Image Pattern Recognition*, NBS Special Publication 500-8 (1977).
33. N. Roussopoulos and L. Mark, Self-describing and self-documenting database systems, *in* "Languages for Automation," (S. K. Chang, ed.), pp. 278–295, Plenum, New York, 1985.
34. K. Preston, Jr., Image processing software: A survey *in* "Progress in Pattern Recognition," (L. N. Kanal and A. Rosenfeld, eds.), pp. 123–148. North-Holland Publ. Amsterdam, 1981.
35. S. K. Chang, E. Jungert, S. Levialdi, G. Tortora, and T. Ichikawa, IPL—An image processing language and programming environment *Proceedings of IEEE Workshop on Languages for Automation, Nov. 9–11 1983, Illinois, Chicago*, pp. 78–84 (1983). [Improved version is available from the author upon request.]
36. F. C. Herot, Spatial management of data, *ACM Trans. on Database Systems* **5** (4) (1980).
37. G. Rohr, Understanding visual symbols, *Proceedings of IEEE Workshop on Visual Languages, Hiroshima, Japan, Dec. 9–11 1984* (1984).
38. S. K. Chang, B. S. Lin, and R. Walser, A generalized zooming technique for pictorial database systems, *Proceedings of National Computer Conference, June 1979*, pp. 147–156 (1979).

# Chapter **17**

# Cellular Logic Arrays for Image Processing

KENDALL PRESTON, Jr.

Department of Electrical and Computer Engineering
Carnegie-Melon University
Pittsburgh, Pennsylvania

**HANDBOOK OF PATTERN RECOGNITION
AND IMAGE PROCESSING**

## I    INTRODUCTION

Even in a handbook, a short historical background on the origins of cellular computer architecture is important. Such information is unobtainable elsewhere and forms the framework for what follows. In 1944, Herman Goldstine [1] introduced John von Neumann to the ENIAC (Electronic Numerical Integrator and Computer) then under construction at the University of Pennsylvania. Recognizing the importance of the ENIAC, the nation's first electronic computer, von Neumann formed a task force to study electronic computers and their applications. Among others, the task force included Howard Aiken (Harvard) and Norbert Wiener (MIT). Because von Neumann's interests also encompassed neural networks in the brain, introduced to him by McCulloch and Pitts [2], von Neumann included in the task force charter studies of the "communication and control aspects of the nervous system."

Subsequently, von Neumann's exposure to the ideas on automata of Post [3] and Turing [4] inspired him not only to design the first stored-program computer (EDVAC) but also to begin work on the design of systems that would be self-reproductive. Conversations with Ulam [5] convinced von Neumann to pursue such research by modeling self-reproductive systems using an array of "processing elements." von Neumann put his early ideas on this subject into writing by 1952 and by 1953 had introduced them in a series of lectures at Princeton University which were then summarized by Kemeny [6] in 1955. von Neumann's premature death in 1957 prevented completion of these formulative concepts, but, by that time, the idea of the cellular array computer or "cellular automaton" had been born. The next section gives a brief account of the events that followed.

## II    IMAGE PROCESSING

During von Neumann's era, Bronowski [7], at a meeting in 1951 of the National Coal Board of Great Britain, suggested that a television camera and electronic computer be combined "for the possibility of making a machine to replace the human observer." Following Bronowski's urging, Causley and Young [8] completed a computerized television microscope in the mid-1950s. Although there was no direct connection between this work and that of von Neumann, it is now recognized that the logic circuits used in this first computer system for image processing were essentially sequential mechanisms for emulating the action of a cellular array computer.

Shortly thereafter, Moore [9], at the U.S. National Bureau of Standards, coupled a scanner to the SEAC (Standards Electronic Analyzer and Computer) and studied the application of cellular array computing to images of metallurgical specimens. His work was accompanied by that of Kirsch [10]—a colleague at the National Bureau of Standards—and by that of Selfridge and Dinneen at the MIT Lincoln Laboratory [11]. The image processing operations performed by these workers became known as "cellular *logic* transforms" since their mathematics was based on Boolean logic.

By the late 1950s and early 1960s the work of these early investigators was augmented by Unger [12] at Bell Telephone Laboratories as well as Golay [13] and Preston [14] at the Perkin-Elmer Corporation. The latter constructed the first known dedicated cellular logic machine (CELLSCAN ). It was a reduction to practice of Golay's concept of a cellular array emulator in hardware. During this same era, work continued at MIT, where cellular logic arrays were emulated using general-purpose computers. Fredkin [(15] discovered self-reproducing constructs far simpler than the array of 29-state processing elements initially hypothecated by von Neumann. Banks [16], a student of Fredkin, proved the existence of a self-reproducing cellular automaton using four-state computing elements. Simultaneously, Schrandt and Ulam [17] pursued studies at Los Alamos on simple cellular arrays of two-state computing elements. Additional studies were carried out at the University of Pennsylvania and Fort Monmouth [18] and at the Polytechnic Institute of Brooklyn [19]. Surveys were written in Japan in a series of papers on the subject produced by Tojo [20, 21, 22]. By 1975, a conference on cellular automata was held by the Institute of Electrical and Electronics Engineers [23]. A second meeting took place in 1983 sponsored by the Department of Energy [24].

Besides these academic studies, work on hardware produced a series of machines built in many laboratories. Like CELLSCAN, they used the sequential performance of a single processing element to operate on the values of an array of numbers just as if these values resided in an array of processing elements. The principles demonstrated by these machines led to advances in the design and construction of commercially successful cellular array image analyzers. These principles were subsequently put to use in building full-array cellular automata, which had been economically impractical until the development of large-scale integrated (LSI) circuitry in the 1970s.

The first full-array systems to be proposed were the SOLOMON, conceived at Westinghouse [25], and the ILLIAC III, conceived at the University of Illinois [26]. Neither machine was ever completed. A small cellular array computer ($8 \times 8$), called ILLIAC IV, also conceived at the University of Illinois [27], was then built by Burroughs. This machine, costing tens of millions of dollars, was finally installed and used during the 1970s at the Ames Laboratory of the National Aeronautics and Space Administration. At more or less the same time, workers at University College London began work on a series of full-array cellular automata called CLIPs (Cellular Logic

Image Processors). The CLIP3—the third in this series—became operational in 1973 as a 12 × 16 array [28]. This was followed by the CLIP4 in 1980 [29]. This is a 96 × 96 cellular automaton composed of some 3,000,000 transistors integrated at 3000 per semiconductor chip. This machine, as well as the 64 × 64 distributed array processor (DAP) built by International Computers Ltd. [30] and the 128 × 128 massively parallel processor (MPP) of Goodyear Aerospace Corporation [31], represent the fruition of von Neumann's visionary work in the 1950s.

All of these full-array machines are limited in their array size in comparison with the growing interest in processing images 1024 × 1024 and larger. Economics is still a limitation. As array size has grown, expense has spiraled; for example, the development cost of the MPP was several million dollars. However, the advance in computing speed achieved by these cellular array computers over the past three decades has been nothing short of astounding. When computing speed is measured in the number of data points processed per unit time (often called picture point operations per unit time and measured in pixops per second), the achievements of these machines may be graphed as in Fig. 1. As can be seen, CELLSCAN handled a mere 4000 pixops/s. The MPP computes at the rate of a thousand billion. This growth in computing speed (approximately 30 decibels per decade) is overwhelming indeed.

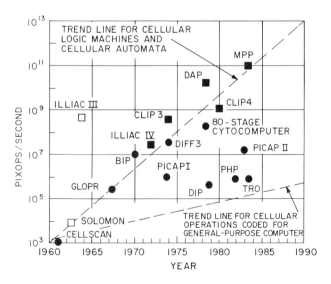

**Fig. 1.** Operational rate (pixops/sec) of cellular logic array computers constructed from 1960 to 1985. ●, subarray computers; □, full-array computers designed but not completed; ■, full-array computers fabricated and operational.

## CELLULAR LOGIC ARRAY ARCHITECTURES   III

Before proceeding with a detailed description of the architecture and applications of cellular array computers, we would do well to categorize the various architectures that have arisen. There are five major architectural types in the machines which have been constructed to date. Each architecture is comprised of one (or more) *primary store(s)* which contains the full image.

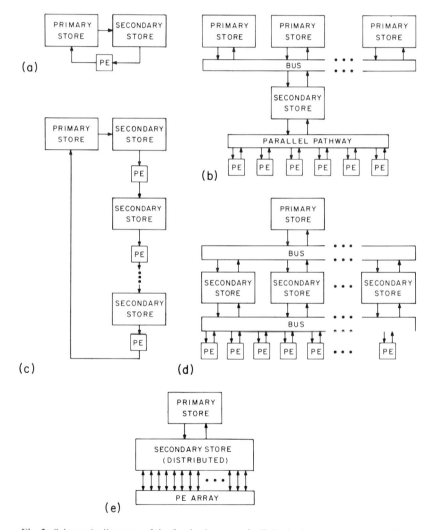

**Fig. 2.** Schematic diagrams of the five basic types of cellular logic array computers. (See text for details.)

The primary store(s) connects to one or more processing elements (PEs) via one (or more) *secondary store*(s) which holds some portion of the image. Transfer paths may be *binary*, moving one bit at a time, or *multilevel*, moving many bits in parallel.

CELLSCAN, and the machines which succeeded it both at Perkin-Elmer [32] and elsewhere [33, 34], used a single high-speed processing element which operated on the data contained in a 3 × 3 "subarray" which was part of the secondary store. The primary memory for CELLSCAN was magnetic tape and, in the other subarray machines, was furnished by the main memory of a host minicomputer. This relatively simple architecture is shown in Fig. 2a.

As time progressed, another architecture emerged (Fig. 2b) which used multiple primary stores with a secondary store that furnished data to many processing elements [35]. These processing elements operated upon many data values simultaneously, all of which were extracted from the secondary store. Currently this is a popular architecture and hundreds of machines using it are employed worldwide. Another architecture, called the *pipeline* architecture (Fig. 2c), has been under development by the Environmental Research Institute of Michigan [36] and elsewhere [37]. In this so-called cytocomputer system, many subarray processors are pipelined into a string of identical CELLSCAN-like stages, wherein the output of one is coupled directly to the input of the next. Each machine has associated with it the full complement of CELLSCAN-like secondary storage registers. An alternative to this architecture is that given in Fig. 2d, wherein the secondary stores are multiplexed to several processing elements in parallel. Finally, the full-array machine (represented by ILLIAC, CLIP, DAP, and MPP) is shown in Fig. 2e. Even in this case there exists an off-line primary store as well as secondary storage directly associated with the processing elements of the array.

## IV   CELLULAR ARRAY LOGIC MACHINES

The majority of cellular array logic machines built during 1960–1979 were subarray machines. Their construction was driven by two forces: one relating to research on how to make computers reproduce themselves; the other to producing practical applications in image pattern recognition, especially as applied to the recognition of printed characters and simple computer vision tasks in hematology and cytology. In this chapter, the applications of the machines are omitted, and the text concentrates on architectural considerations. The significant features of each system are highlighted. Comparisons are summarized in the final section following a section on programming methods.

**CELLSCAN   A**

| | | | |
|---|---|---|---|
| *Type*: | 3 × 3 subarray | *Frame time*: | 5 sec |
| *PEs*: | One | *Rate*: | $3.7 \times 10^3$ pixops/sec |
| *Image size*: | 300 × 63/63 × 63 | *Host*: | None (autonomous system) |

CELLSCAN (Fig. 3) was a true Turing machine that both read from and wrote on an endless magnetic tape at 3720 picture elements/sec. This tape formed the primary store. The image input was a Dage Data-Vision slow-scan television system operating at a rate of 60 horizontal lines/sec and producing a frame consisting of 300 lines with a resolution of 300 picture elements/line. CELLSCAN used a video-rate, one-dimensional reduction algorithm (see Taylor [38]) to reduce negative-going (dark-polarity) video signals by five picture elements while simultaneously lengthening positive-going (bright-polarity) signals by an equal amount. This reduced primary storage to only 63 binary picture elements/line. Image data was recorded using a pair of data tracks on an ordinary audio tape deck. Synchronizing signals were generated from this data in order to clock the serial transfer to the secondary storage registers.

The block diagram of CELLSCAN (Fig. 4) shows that CELLSCAN was self-contained (using no host computer). The original design was by Preston [13], thus reducing to practice the invention of Golay [39] filed in 1959 with the U.S. Patent Office (Fig. 5). Details of the CELLSCAN subarray processor are shown in Fig. 6. The CELLSCAN computer used a semiconductor memory as the secondary store, consisting of two 60-bit shift registers holding the incoming picture element values ($A, \ldots, X, \ldots, H$) and another 60-bit shift register holding the values of the picture elements after processing ($X_p, \ldots, H_p, \ldots, A_p$). The 3 × 3 subarray data values and the five values of the processed information were used to address the processing element, which consisted of hard-wired image processing logic (whose functions were controlled by sense switches) which generated the 1-bit output value ($X_p$). At the time of construction (1960–1961), all circuitry was built from discrete-component transistor logic.

The CELLSCAN algorithms included those for (1) image complementation, (2) reduction *without* the retention of residues, and (3) reduction *with* the retention of residues. The switches on the control console of CELLSCAN not only selected the algorithm but also selected the number of iterations by an amount geometrically variable from 4 to 128. When the specified number of iterations had been executed, CELLSCAN reverted to an image retention and display mode in which the magnetic tape was continuously read, the binary image data was displayed, and identical data were rewritten periodically on the endless magnetic tape without further processing. Finally, the CELLSCAN computer could be instructed, at any time during the image processing cycle, to generate a count of the number of residues in the image

**Fig. 3.** The world's first cellular logic array machine (CELLSCAN), built by the Navigation Computer Corporation (Pennsylvania) under contract to the Perkin–Elmer Corporation (Connecticut) in accordance with the design of Preston [14].

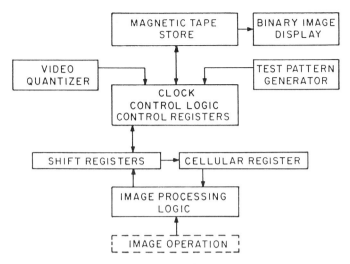

**Fig. 4.** Overall block diagram of the CELLSCAN system.

array. By generating counts each iteration, the residue histogram was produced. Further details on these operations and the circuits by which they were executed is provided by Izzo and Coles [32].

**GLOPR (Golay LOgic PRocessor)   B**

| | | | |
|---|---|---|---|
| *Type*: | Hexagonal subarray | *Frame time*: | 50 msec; 25 msec; |
| *PEs*: | One | | 13 msec |
| *Image size*: | 128 × 128; 64 × 64; | *Rate*: | 3.3 × 10$^5$ pixops/sec |
| | 32 × 32 | *Host*: | Varian 620i |

While CELLSCAN was the first reduction to practice Golay's hard-wired, square-tessellation cellular logic subarray machine, GLOPR was the reduction to practice of a hexagonal-tessellation cellular logic subarray machine based on Golay's invention of the hexagonal parallel pattern transform [40]. The image input device to GLOPR was an oscillating-mirror television scanner which rastered the image past a 25-$\mu$m aperture beyond which light was collected by an RCA 8645 10-stage photomultiplier. The horizontal scan rate was 40 Hz, with a total scan time of 3 sec.

The GLOPR architecture introduced several major innovations which took it far beyond the original CELLSCAN architecture. First, the image was transferred in groups of either 128, 64, or 32 elements to primary storage in a host minicomputer at approximately 30,000 image elements/sec. During mirror retrace, the host computer binarized the image (originally digitized at 8 bits/element) and stored the result as either a 128 × 128, 64 × 64, or

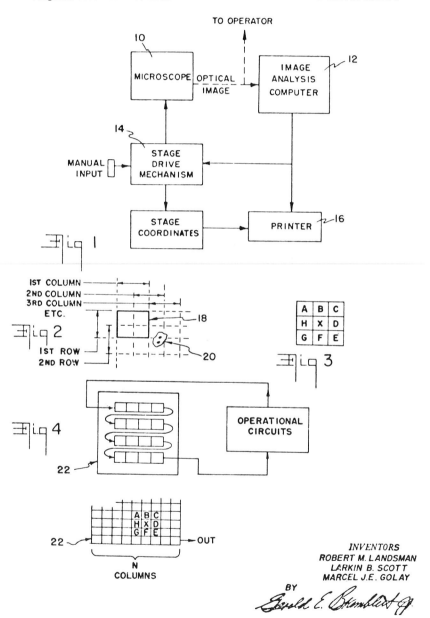

Oct. 26, 1965                R. M. LANDSMAN ETAL                3,214,574
APPARATUS FOR COUNTING BI-NUCLEATE LYMPHOCYTES IN BLOOD
Original Filed Oct. 8, 1959                                    5 Sheets-Sheet 1

**Fig. 5.** The basic patent on cellular logic array computers as awarded to Golay and his colleagues in 1965. Golay's concept followed what is now called the *systolic* computer architecture.

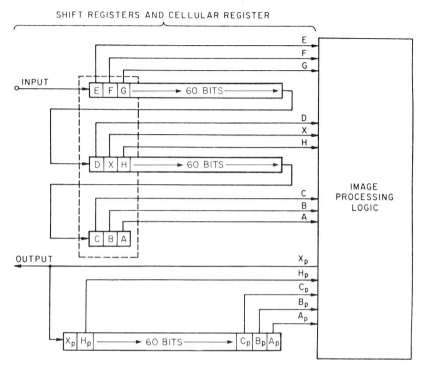

**Fig. 6.** The CELLSCAN processing element including shift registers for incoming binary image data as well as a shift register for one line of processed data. Contents of these registers were delivered to a sense-switch-programmable combinational logic circuit for use in executing certain specific Golay transforms in the square tessellation. Dashed lines indicate the 3 × 3 subarray, all of whose contents were processed in parallel.

32 × 32 binary data field in from 2K to 128 bytes of main magnetic core memory. Since the image acquisition and image processing systems operated asynchronously (unlike CELLSCAN), image processing could operate at a totally different rate than that used during image acquisition. Referring to the block diagram of Fig. 7, it can be seen that GLOPR contained five 16-bit registers for use in parallel-serial transfers to the host. Two registers held microde control words for selection of the Golay primitives and determination of the image size and subfield order. Two registers were used for transfers (16-elements at a time) of both the direct image and the template image from the host. The final register was an output register for either the computed image or data from the television microscope.

GLOPR used variable-length image shift registers (including the subarray register), which comprised secondary storage. These operated at 500 kHz and, after each shift, the six hexagonal neighboring elements were transferred to an 8-MHz circular shift register which addressed (at each shift) 14 comparators in parallel. The comparators were matched with the 14 Golay primitives and,

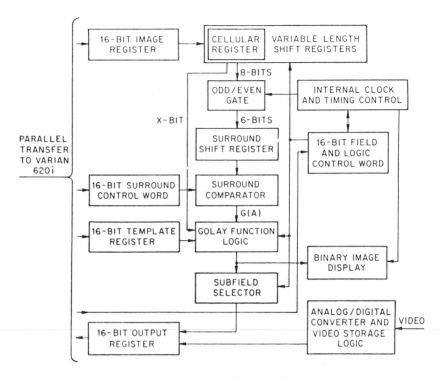

**Fig. 7.** Block diagram showing the operation of the GLOPR cellular logic array computer in the hexagonal tessellation. It was microcoded for the general Golay hexagonal parallel transform by means of the 16-bit surround control word and the 16-bit field and logic control word and the 16-bit field and logic control word. Binary image data and the binary template were delivered 16 elements at a time and were processed at the rate of 1 Golay transform each 2 μsec, with the result entered in the output register.

when subfields were employed, comparators were disabled except when the proper subfield was positioned in the circular shift register. The circular shift register, the accompanying comparators, and the subfield logic comprised the fundamental processing element of GLOPR. One neighborhood operation was conducted each 2 μsec, resulting in a peak pixel operation rate of 500 kHz. Input/output overhead reduced this to an average processing rate of 330 kHz .

Further innovations in GLOPR were that it could be microcoded and vectored so that merely two microcode words were all the instruction data necessary to process the entire image array using the Golay hexagonal parallel transform. Image archiving was provided by means of a seven-track read–write magnetic tape interfaced to the host. The system was user programmable using a high-level language (GLOL), which is described in Section V. Image displays included a binary image display, an analog gray-level display, and a contourograph display for image-analytic purposes [41].

Of historical interest is that the success of this general-purpose cellular logic machine performing ultrahigh-speed image processing led to the first commercially produced cellular logic array system, the diff3-series machines of the Perkin–Elmer Corporation and Coulter Electronics, Inc. (see Section IV.E).

## BIP (Binary Image Processor)   C

| *Type*: | $3 \times 3$ subarray | *Frame time*: | 1.8 msec |
|---|---|---|---|
| *PEs*: | One | *Rate*: | $10^7$ pixops/sec |
| *Image size*: | $36 \times 511$ | *Host*: | Digital equipment PDP-10 |

The BIP (Binary Image Processor) combined features of both CELLSPAN and GLOPR and showed a speed increase of a factor of 30 over GLOPR. It was a square-array machine rather than hexagonal and, instead of decoding all orientation-dependent pattern primitives, it decoded only those that were specific to area, perimeter, and connectivity number. The BIP, rather than using a full-field template image (like GLOPR), used a $36 \times 36$ template against which binary correlations could be executed. The correlation value was then transferred to the host computer. The purpose of this mode of operation was to utilize a series of templates, each corresponding to a particular character in a type font, in character recognition applications. (The BIP was part of the GRAFIX 1 system manufactured by Information International, Inc. for this purpose.)

An overall block diagram is provided in Fig. 8, where it is seen that, instead of a single-user system like GLOPR, the BIP was part of a multi-user system

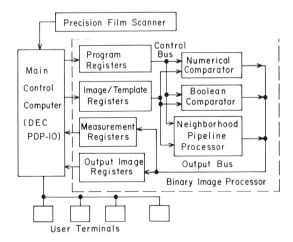

**Fig. 8.** Block diagram of the binary image processor (BIP) of Image International, Inc.

running under the time-sharing operating system of the host Digital Equipment PDP-10. The BIP, in addition to having cellular logic array hardware, also included a numerical arithmetic logic unit for executing integer calculations. (This aspect of BIP is not treated here.) The BIP operated serially and received, as with GLOPR, input from the central element value and neighborhood element values of the binary image to be processed and the central element value of the template image. The basic cellular array logic operation executed by BIP was to do nine simultaneous Boolean comparisons of the binary image against the binary template. A direct comparison plus eight other comparisons with the binary template, obtained by shifting the template by one element value (either plus or minus) in the horizontal, vertical, and $\pm 45°$ directions, could be handled at once. The results from these nine comparisons were counted separately for each element of the image, and these values were stored in nine correlation counters in BIP.

Information International considered, but rejected, the full decoding of all $2^9 = 512$ possible binary input patterns over the $3 \times 3$ kernel and, instead, used the subarray logic schemes described earlier [42]. The hardware operations were pipelined (Fig. 9), with the first stage of the pipeline selecting either the eight neighborhood inputs (as in GLOPR) or selecting previously computed data (like CELLSCAN). The element values selected were then directly decoded or sent to the next stage for counting. The translator used for counting produced a one-out-of-nine result which was delivered to nine separate output channels. These signals were separately gated in the count combiner by a 9-bit control word and then ORed to produce what was called the "processed bit" (P-bit). This permitted BIP to generate several connectivity or neighborhood count conditions simultaneously, just as all Golay primitives could be monitored simultaneously in GLOPR. Next, the P-bit and the central bits from both the incoming image and the template image were combined by output logic to produce what was called the "result bit" (R-bit). The output logic was controlled by means of an 8-bit "Boolean

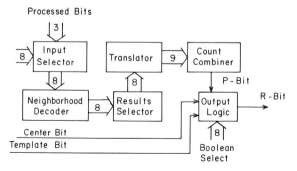

**Fig. 9.** Processing element of the BIP consisting of a six-stage pipeline which receives inputs from both the image and template. (See text for details.)

select" word, whose condition selected the combinations of the three input variables to be enabled. Correlation counts and result counts were passed to the host computer via nine registers (each 36-bit). Using this data, the host calculated such quantities as total area and total number of connected regions.

Other functions carried out by the BIP were to use its real-time histogramming capabilities for selecting a threshold to generate binary images and carry out such operations as shading correction, image scaling and rotation. By suitable programming of the host computer, image montages larger than $36 \times 511$ could be processed.

Control of the BIP operations were microcoded, as in GLOPR, and vectored. The microcode consisted of six 36-bit words stored in registers that were part of BIP. The first control word provided control information to the cellular logic array; the next indicated one of approximately 30 operational codes; the others provided addresses and control information for the various geometric transforms which could be executed.

**ILLIAC IV   D**

| | | | |
|---|---|---|---|
| *Type*: | Full $8 \times 8$ array | *Frame time*: | 0.65 $\mu$sec |
| *PEs*: | 64 | *Rate*: | $9.6 \cdot 10^7$ pixops/sec |
| *Image size*: | $8 \times 8$ | *Host*: | Burroughs B6500 |

The ILLIAC IV was the first full-array machine built in the United States. It consisted of 64 processing elements [27]. Each processing element had a full 64-bit fixed or floating-point arithmetic unit with direct electrical connections to its four neighbors and contained 2K words of memory. There were some 100,000 transistors per processing element and, therefore, over 6 million such devices in the array itself. The operation of each processing element was conditional, based upon its "mode flag." A mode value of 0 turned the processing element off so that it did not take part in the computation performed by the "on" elements of the array.

Control of the array was from the host computer, having 1 MBytes of main memory. An input/output subsystem also accessed 125 MBytes of rotating memory. An archival memory for "write-once" operations (using a laser) was available with a capacity of 125 gigabytes. The ILLIAC IV control circuitry was SSI (small scale integration), custom-designed by Texas Instruments, Inc., using 34-transistor chips. The memory chips (made by the Semiconductor Division, Fairchild Camera and Instrument Corporation) contained 2485 devices each and provided a storage capacity of 265 bits. Use in image analysis was limited by a lack of any video input/output capability.

## E  diff3

| Type: | 28-element hexagonal subarray | Frame time: | 100 $\mu$sec |
|---|---|---|---|
| PEs: | Eight | Rate: | $4.1 \times 10^7$ pixops/sec |
| Image size: | $64 \times 64$ | Host: | Data General Nova4 |

The GLOPR in the diff3 of Coulter Electronics, Inc. was the first cellular logic computer to go into volume production [43]. It is part of a computer vision system for hematology. The diff3 system is, in fact, a robot microscope capable of handling human blood smears on microscope slides. The slides are searched for objects of interest (white blood cells). The white blood cell images are analyzed in full color at approximately 5000 per hour. Instead of a single subarray processor addressing a single neighborhood, central element, and template central element simultaneously, the GLOPR of the diff3 uses eight complete processing elements to operate on eight neighborhoods and their associated central and template elements in parallel. The rotating neighborhood shift register of the original Perkin–Elmer GLOPR was replaced by a look-up table consisting of a single ROM having $2^6 = 64$ addresses used to decode and thereby recognize each of the 14 Golay primitives. The diff3 GLOPR uses eight parallel ROMS. Each generates a one-out-of-fourteen signal according to the Golay primitive contained in the corresponding input image neighborhood. The output signals from all eight ROMs are simultaneously compared with the contents of one of the microcoded control words, the present value of eight central elements, and the corresponding template elements in parallel so as to determine eight values of the output binary image.

The architecture of the diff3 GLOPR is similar to that shown in Fig. 2b. There are four primary stores, with each holding a different $64 \times 64$ binary image. The secondary store is a 512-stage 8-level shift register. The processing element architecture has the advantage that a single microcoded control word, with a length equal to the total number of Golay primitives, replaces the alternative look-up table, which would consist of $2^7 = 128$ microcode words. The final computational stage of the diff3 GLOPR is performed in a set of eight combinational logic circuits, with inputs consisting of the eight central elements from the image and the central element from the template. The resultant image is placed on an 8-bit bus connecting to the secondary register. As output data are generated, eight counters are used to total the 1s in the output. At the end of a cycle, the contents of these counters are summed to produce the final output count. This measurement data is then transferred from the diff3 GLOPR to the host, a Data General Nova4.

The microcode in the diff3 GLOPR consists of three 16-bit words specifying five control functions, as follows:

(1)   the designation of two primary source image stores (input and template) and the destination image store;

(2)   the Boolean Golay function specifications supporting all possible combinations of data from the two source stores;

(3)   the 14 Golay primitives;

(4)   the number of iterations for which the transform is to be formed;

(5)   the subfield and the subfield sequence specification.

Three data-transfer cycles are required to pass the microcode to the diff3 GLOPR. The diff3 GLOPR requires 100 $\mu$sec to execute a 64 × 64 transform; meanwhile, the host is free to perform other functions. Thus, the diff3 GLOPR is a vectored, microcoded cellular logic array machine, as with the original GLOPR.

The entire system (Fig. 10) is composed of many other parts, including the automated mechanism for mechanically moving the microscope slide, an illumination source, relay optics to a television camera tube (Plumbicon), a video-rate digitizer, a video-rate histogrammer, and the primary image store multiplexor. The latter directs the digitized image to one of four integer image stores, which then transfers image data to one of four primary binary image stores which are part of the diff3 GLOPR. A further feature of the system is that any of the binary image stores may be used as a template to gate the video-rate histogrammer. This permits real-time histogramming and analysis

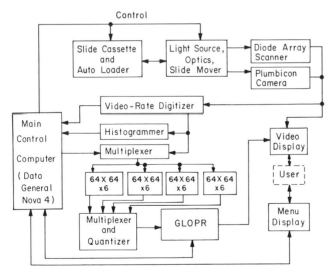

**Fig. 10.** Diagram of the diff3-50 system of Coulter Electronics (Florida), the world's first programmable robot microscope to include a cellular logic array computer (GLOPR). Four primary gray-level image stores delivered data via a multiplexer to four secondary binary stores in the GLOPR. The processing rate is 40 megapixels/sec.

of a particular region of the image, disregarding all image data not within the region defined by the template.

## F   Cytocomputer

| | |
|---|---|
| *Type*: | Eighty 3 × 3 subarrays |
| *PEs*: | Eighty |
| *Image size*: | 512 × ∞ |
| *Frame time*: | 170 msec (512 × 512) |
| *Rate*: | 1.5 × 10⁶ (minimum) pipops/sec |
| | 120 × 10⁶ (maximum) pixops/sec |
| *Host*: | Digital Equipment PDP 11 and VAX 11 |

The Cytocomputer [37] was structured as shown in Fig. 2c by connecting a series of CELLSCAN-like processing elements in series. In the Cytocomputer, each processing element contains secondary storage in the form of two fixed-length shift registers, each with 509 stages plus the 3 × 3 subarray register. The nine elements of this register deliver their signals as a 9-bit word to a 512-position look-up table. Thus, the data flow is identical to CELLSCAN (Fig. 4) as developed in the Golay patent (Fig. 5), but the hard-wired logic of CELLSCAN is replaced by a complete look-up table requiring the loading of 512 one-bit words. Thus, in effect, an infinite number ($2^{512}$) of cellular logic transforms may be programmed. In such a pipeline structure, each look-up table must be loaded separately. This mode of programming of the cellular logic array should be compared with the original GLOPR, which used only two 16-bit words of microcode for programming purposes, and with the diff3 GLOPR, which used three 16-bit words of microcode. The 80-stage cytocomputer uses approximately 40K 1-bit words of microcode to fill all 80 tables.

In the Cytocomputer, the host provides primary image storage and delivers the image data as a stream of multibit words from which the desired bits are gated to the look-up tables of a given stage (Fig. 11). This architecture is excellent when executing a known algorithm repetitively, in which case the contents of the look-up tables can remain unchanged. A major use is in reconnaissance, where a continuously scanning system interrogates the gray-level information of the terrain, submitting data pixel-by-pixel to the cyto-computer. However, when used in a research mode with variable algorithms, there is significant overhead in look-up table loading. Furthermore, the fixed-length shift register has the disadvantage that variable-width images are not readily processed (this is also true of CELLSCAN and the diff3 GLOPR but not of the original GLOPR). Finally, it should be pointed out that an algorithm having less than 80 iterations does not use this architecture

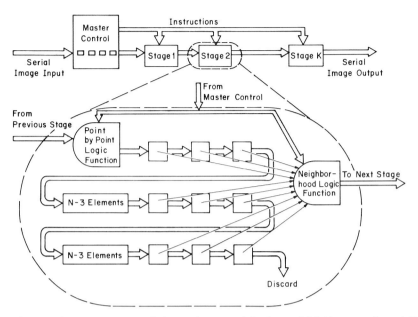

**Fig. 11.** The Cytocomputer of the Environmental Institute of Michigan consists of 80 CELLSCAN-like stages configured as a pipeline. Unlike CELLSCAN, the nine-element contents of each subarray are fully decoded by the corresponding $2^9 = 512$ address look-up table. The table for each stage defines the transform to be performed. Tables are loaded into the Cytocomputer from the host computer.

efficiently. A one-step cellular logic transform will run at only 1.5 MHz. Only an 80-transform procedure uses the full pipeline and would operate effectively at 120 MHz.

### PHP (Preston–Herron Processor)     **G**

| | | | |
|---|---|---|---|
| *Type*: | 54-element subarray | *Frame time*: | 200 msec (512 × 512) |
| *PEs*: | Sixteen | *Rate*: | $1.5 \times 10^6$ pixops/sec |
| *Image size*: | 6 × 3 (minimum) | *Host*: | Perkin–Elmer 3230 |
| | 10714 × ∞(maximum) | | |

The PHP uses a cellular logic array architecture having fully configured look-up tables. This architecture (Fig. 2d) combines the advantages of both the Cytocomputer and the diff3 GLOPR. The data flow in this machine is shown in Fig. 12. There are 16 identical processing elements that act in parallel (as in the diff3 GLOPR). Data is delivered to them from three secondary image stores which receive *identical* image data from the primary image store. Unlike CELLSCAN and the Cytocomputer, these memories are

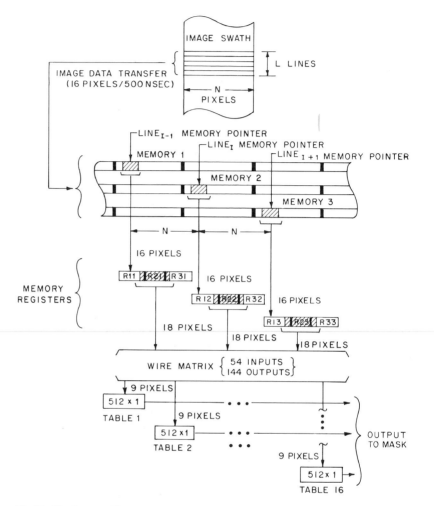

**Fig. 12.** The Preston Herron processor of Carnegie-Mellon University and the University of Pittsburgh is the first cellular logic array computer to permit a wide variation in image swath width. Fifty-four inputs are fetched simultaneously to the 16 processing elements. Each processing element consists of a fully decoded $2^9 = 512$ entry look-up table. All look-up tables are identical so that processing is uniform across the image field. Precomputed tables are stored in the host computer and loaded by the user under program control.

not shift-register stages. Instead, they are RAMs so that image information stored in them may be extracted in parallel from three separate lines of the image. The line length is determined by three offset addresses (set electronically by the host computer) which point to the desired data in the three image lines simultaneously. Since 16 processing elements must be serviced in parallel with data from three lines in the image, 54 bits of image data are delivered simultaneously from a set of buffers associated with the processing elements. As shown in Fig. 12, these buffers present 54 inputs to a distribution matrix. The 144 outputs of this matrix furnish the 16 processing elements with 16 9-bit addresses. The outputs of the processing elements are gated within the PHP to the host computer via a subfield mask.

The contents of the look-up tables are loaded in parallel by the host prior to the execution of an image processing transform. In the present design of the PHP, the three identical image-slice memories are each 2048 × 16. Since offset addresses are variable over the full range of the image-slice memories, there is no restriction on image width as in the Cytocomputer, and an image as small as 16 × 3 may be processed as well as an image slice as large as 10,714 × 3. Image slices of intermediate size may be handled as long as the number of picture elements per line are modulo 16.

The PHP is designed so that the host computer can load the image-slice memories at 40 million picture elements/sec. This would permit an image slice consisting of 32K 1-bit elements to be processed in 1.6 msec, that is, the cycle time required to complete one cycle to load the image-slice data and to process it. Thus, a 1024 × 1024 image could be transformed in 50 msec. To this time must be added the time required for the host computer to load the look-up tables and extract the image data from the primary image store.

It is worth noting that the triply redundant image-slice memory concept has been extended to a three-dimensional cellular logic array processor having an architecture identical to the PHP but with seven identical image-slice memories, each of which can contain eight planes of a 64 × 64 × 64 binary volume. This processor is the TRO [44] which, as with the PHP, utilizes 16 processing elements operating in parallel. Each processing element is addressed by the binary values of the 13 voxels of the tetradecahedral neighborhood (the extension of Golay's hexagonal neighborhood into three dimensions [45]). Thus, each look-up table has 8192 positions. As with the PHP, these tables are loaded in parallel from the host computer, after which the image transformation is generated. Use of the TRO in three-dimensional skeletonization and information on the use of the PHP in image analysis are given by Hafford and Preston [46] and Herron et al. [47] in

### PICAP (PICture Array Processor)   H

| | | | |
|---|---|---|---|
| *Type*: | 3 × 3 subarray | *Frame time*: | Variable |
| *PEs*: | One | *Rate*: | 8.3 × $10^5$ pixops/sec |
| *Image size*: | 64 × 64 | *Host*: | Swedish 16-bit minicomputer |

The PICAP represents a major design departure in the architecture of cellular logic arrays. It is the first machine to employ "condition templates" operating on the $3 \times 3$ subarray. PICAP uses a nine-element integer condition vector which maps nine conditions to the nine positions in the $3 \times 3$ subarray. These are tested in parallel for all nine elements. The conditions which can be examined by the PICAP condition template circuitry are the logical statements "less than," "greater than," and "equal to." Any element of the nine-element vector can also store a "don't care" condition. In the case where all conditions are true, the output value for the central image data point being interrogated is set to a specified "transition" value [48]. Otherwise, the image data element value remains unchanged.

PICAP is capable of storing up to eight condition templates which may be used in one image processing cycle. The templates are examined sequentially using a template "priority list." When the first full match occurs, the transition state associated with that template becomes the state of the output picture element. If no match occurs for any of the templates, then the picture element value is unchanged. Cellular logic transforms are performed by PICAP by using binary images and the conditions "equal to," "less than one," and "greater than zero." These cellular logic operations may be performed directly in the square tessellation. If the hexagonal tessellation is to be employed, then "don't care" conditions are inserted in two of the eight neighborhood positions in the nine-element condition vector.

The architecture of PICAP is shown in Fig. 13 with a detailed block diagram of the template matching unit given in Fig. 14. Image input to PICAP is from an elaborate video system that includes both a television microscope and a television scanner for reading images recorded on photographic transparencies. The PICAP video input system extracts a $64 \times 64$ array of 4-bit integers selected arbitrarily (both in position and scale) from

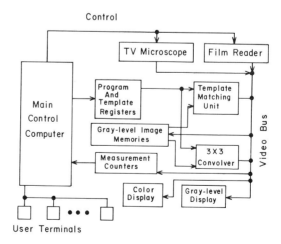

**Fig. 13.** Block diagram of the PICAP cellular logic array computer of the University of Linkoping (Sweden).

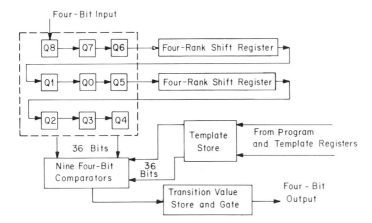

**Fig. 14.** Processing element of the PICAP, consisting of nine 4-bit comparators which make parallel conditional comparisons between the template and the contents of the 3 × 3 subarray in order to produce a 4-bit output word.

the full television frame. This permits the user to screen images at low resolution and, after processing the resultant data, to select specific "windows" for high-resolution analysis, thus providing telescopic processing [49]. Note that in Fig. 13 the image data bus is 4 bits wide, so that the cellular logic array receives 4-bit words, that is, the video image data digitized in its original form.

PICAP, as with BIP, is a multi-user, dedicated image processing system having nine 64 × 64 4-bit primary image data stores as well as storage for eight condition templates. Transfer from the image memories is multiplexed in many different ways. When a single primary store is accessed, the nine 4-bit words associated with the 3 × 3 subarray are transferred to the template matching unit. However, all nine image memories can also be accessed in parallel with each memory contributing a 4-bit element to the nine-element template matching unit. Furthermore, using the "rotational control bit," a single template can be simultaneously interrogated with either four-fold or eight-fold rotational symmetry. Thus, the eight-template store can be used to emulate as many as 32 or 64 templates, respectively. The time required for a single template match is 1.2 μs. Statistical data generated by the template matching unit is tabulated using measurement registers that count all matches between each of the eight templates. Sixteen of a total of 32 registers are used as counters to generate the histogram of the image data. Three additional registers store the maximum value, minimum value, and mean value over the 4096-element image array. Finally, four other registers are used to store the minimum and maximum values in the vertical and horizontal directions.

A new version of PICAP has been constructed (PICAP II) which is an instruction-set processor considerably different from the original [50]. The instruction processors in PICAP II are the video input processor, the template matching processor, the cellular logic processor, the filter processor, and the region analysis processor. Only the cellular logic processor carries out cellular array logic with either the square or hexagonal kernel. It receives a high-speed bit stream generated from thesholded images. Image data may be stored in as many as 16 $512 \times 512$ 8-bit primary image stores. Bus transfer rates are at 40 MB/secs. Little detailed information is available on the speed of the cellular logic array portion of the system.

## DIP (Delft Image Processor)

| | | | |
|---|---|---|---|
| *Type:* | $3 \times 3$ subarray | *Rate:* | $6.6 \times 10^5$ pixops/sec (maximum) |
| *PEs:* | One | | $2.4 \times 10^5$ pixops/sec (minimum) |
| *Image size:* | $256 \times \infty$ | *Host:* | Hewlitt-Packard 1000 |
| *Frame time:* | 100 msec (minimum), | | |
| | 280 msec (maximum) | | |
| | for a $256 \times 256$ image | | |

The DIP combines traditional computing technology with the concept of the cellular logic array machine for image analysis. A block diagram of the DIP environment is given in Fig. 15. Unlike PICAP, there is no video input processor but rather three separate video input devices: (1) a television microscope, (2) a Plumbicon, and (3) a flying-spot scanner. The host computer is the Hewlitt-Packard 1000. DIP has 0.5 MBytes of main memory

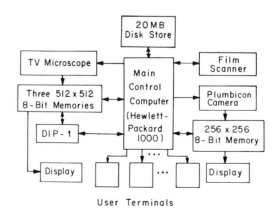

**Fig. 15.** Block diagram of the DIP of the University of Delft (Holland).

and 20 MBytes rotating memory. The dedicated DIP hardware has the attractive feature that it contains a writeable control store whose contents are selected by a program sequencer. The contents of both store and sequencer are loaded from the host computer. The noncellular portion of the DIP consists of two traditional arithmetic logic units (ALUs) and a multiplier. The ALUs and the multiplier may operate in either floating-point mode (12-bit mantissa and 6-bit exponent) or in integer mode. Images themselves can be represented either as 8-bit integer picture element values or as real values in floating-point notation. The relationship between these traditional computing units and the cellular logic array portion of the machine are illustrated in Fig. 16.

The cellular logic array portion of the machine is capable of storing eight look-up tables. Each look-up table is fully configured with 512 positions. Only one is activated for a particular image transform and is selected under program control. If desired, the user may specify the output of the look-up table as input to one of the ALUs. Approximately 40 msec is required to load a (precomputed) look-up table from the host computer. The cellular logic

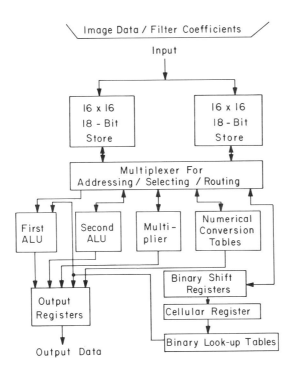

**Fig. 16.** Image processing system for DIP consisting not only of a cellular logic array with electronically selectible, fully decoded look-up tables but also traditional multipliers, conversion tables, and arithmetic logic units. Provision is made for 16 × 16 convolutions in parallel.

array also incorporates, as secondary image data stores, two 256-bit, incoming data, binary shift registers plus another 256-bit shift register which may be used for recursive operations (exactly as in CELLSCAN). In addition, there are two $3 \times 3$ cellular registers for storing both the incoming image data and the incoming template. The primary image store is in the host minicomputer.

In the numerical portion of the DIP, 256-position conversion tables are provided to convert from integer to floating-point format. Each of these conversion tables consists of 4096 words of 18 bits each. These may also be utilized to execute real-time gray-level picture point operations and are either loaded from the host computer or from within the image data loop. Finally, these tables may also be used as row or column buffers for the temporary storage of intermediate results from the various image data manipulation modules and have both autoincrement and autodecrement features using both absolute and relative addressing. In addition, there are 256-position tables that store the filter coefficients for convolutions. Convolutions may use kernels as large as $16 \times 16$.

## J   DAP (Distributed Array Processor)

| | | | |
|---|---|---|---|
| *Type*: | Full array | *Frame time*: | 0.2 μsec |
| *PEs*: | 1024 | *Rate*: | $5 \times 10^9$ pixops/sec |
| *Image size*: | $32 \times 32$ | *Host*: | International Computers Ltd. 2900 |

Discounting the rather small ILLIAC IV, the $32 \times 32$ DAP was the first large (more than 1000 PEs) cellular array machine implemented. The almost prohibitive cost (about two million dollars) has limited sales to only a small number of machines. Since the primary use of the DAP is not image processing, neither a video input device nor a video display device is supplied. (The primary application for the DAP is in solving two- or three-dimensional array data analysis problems in meteorology, finite element analysis, operations research, and related areas.)

The memory of the DAP is shared between the host computer and the array of 1024 processing elements (4096 in one commercial version). This is illustrated in Fig. 17. Thus, both primary memory and secondary memory are physically the same. Stored in the same memory module are the control words used as instructions for operating the DAP. Before execution, these instructions must be transferred from their initial locations to the main control unit of the host computer. The DAP is designed to carry out both matrix operations, where each matrix element is stored within one 4K-bit module (the memory of a single processing element), as well as vector operations, where the value of a vector is spread over one row or column of processing elements.

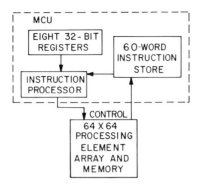

**Fig. 17.** Block diagram of the DAP of International Computers Ltd. (England).


The processing element itself is diagrammed in Fig. 18. It consists of a 1-bit full adder which receives its inputs from $Q$ (a 1-bit accumulator), $C$ (a 1-bit carry register), and the output of $P$ (the input multiplexer that receives the carry outputs from four neighboring processors). Thus, the DAP is a four-connected machine and must be altered by software to carry out hexagonal or square cellular array transformations. The input multiplexer may also receive a signal from the local output multiplexer (either direct or inverted). Furthermore, the $Q$ input may be set to a binary 0 or 1 and either $Q$, $C$, or $O$

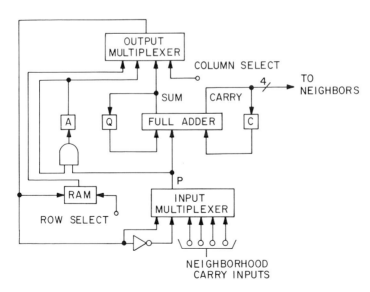

**Fig. 18.** The processing element of the DAP receives inputs from all four neighbors in a square 32 × 32 array.

may receive the "carry" input. Finally, the output from the full adder returns the sum to the accumulator and the carry to $C$. This same carry output is propagated to the input multiplexers of four neighbors.

All data paths within the DAP processing element are 1 bit wide. Besides being connected to the input of the full adder, the input multiplexer is also connected to an AND gate. The other input of this gate is the output of the activity register $A$. The state of this register is used to indicate the status of the processing element and controls the storage of data generated by this processing element in main memory. The output multiplexer is used to specify the output from (1) the 4K-bit random access memory, (2) the sum output of the full adder, (3) a column select signal used for broadcasting to the array, or (4) the state of the activity register. The output from this multiplexer also returns to the input multiplexer and is gateable both to memory and to the main control unit. (The row select signal enters the processing element from the random access memory.)

In order to perform eight-connected cellular logic array operations on the DAP, the $3 \times 3$ neighborhood must be synthesized by moving image data diagonally in the array using column and row shift operations. A single picture point operation requires nine instruction cycles in order to test a single template. A more complex operation, such as the Golay transform using as many as 14 templates, would need approximately 100 cycles. This implies that the speed of the DAP is far slower than its 0.2-$\mu$sec single instruction cycle would imply. Even when doing simple logical functions between binary images, the full adder must be employed for separate AND and NOT operations since there is no Boolean logic unit. Each of these operations requires a full instruction cycle, thus doubling processing time.

## K  CLIP (Cellular Logic Image Processor)

| | | | |
|---|---|---|---|
| *Type*: | Full array | *Frame time*: | 10 $\mu$sec |
| *PEs*: | 9216 | *Rate*: | $9.2 \times 10^8$ pixops/sec |
| *Image size*: | $96 \times 96$ | *Host*: | PDP11/35 |

The CLIP series of cellular logic arrays is a series of systems of which CLIP4 is described here as being of the most importance. The overall CLIP system is shown in Fig. 19, which shows the video input system as well as the host computer. Primary image data storage is located between the video camera and the array. It consists of both input and output shift registers, each having 9216 stages. From the shift registers, image data flows over a 96-bit bus into secondary stores in the array by propagating horizontally long rows. The entry of one binary image takes 96 instruction cycles (0.96 msec). A similar technique is used for extracting binary image data from the array.

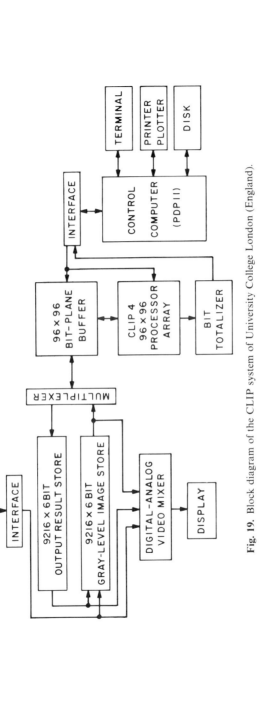

**Fig. 19.** Block diagram of the CLIP system of University College London (England).

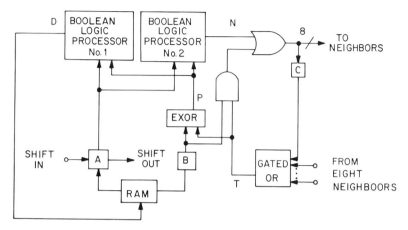

**Fig. 20.** The processing element of the CLIP receives inputs from all eight neighbors in a square 96 × 96 array. Two Boolean processors are furnished in addition to 32 bits of local memory (RAM).

The processing element for CLIP4 is shown in Fig. 20. It is fabricated as a custom-designed, large-scale integrated circuit. Eight of the CLIP4 processing elements are integrated per chip so that 1152 chips comprise the entire processor. The structure of the CLIP4 processing element is arranged with 32 bits of secondary image data storage per element. Each processing element contains two identical Boolean processors, each of which has two inputs defined as $P$ and $A$, and can generate any of the 16 possible Boolean functions of its two inputs. The particular function generated is determined by four control lines which are common to all processors. One of the Boolean processors uses an output $D$ to store data in any one of the 32 possible memory locations. The other Boolean processor produces an output $N$ for transmission to all eight neighboring processing elements in the array. The output $N$ is also stored in the 1-bit register $C$. Each processing element receives eight inputs from its eight neighbors. These inputs are individually gated into an OR gate with the value contained in the register $C$. The output of this gate is designated as $T$ and is EXORed with the signal designated as $D$ in order to generate $B$.

A general CLIP4 operation consists of (1) loading a single bit of image data from the specified location (out of 32) into the 1-bit $A$ register, (2) loading a single bit of image data similarly into the 1-bit $B$ register, (3) conducting the specified Boolean functions using the Boolean processors and the neighborhood interconnections specified by the OR gate, and (4) enabling the array interconnections and clocking the output $D$ into the selected storage location as well as, if desired, storing $N$ in the 1-bit register $C$. In addition to point operations executed between images and cellular operations on neighborhood functions, CLIP4 may conduct what are called "propagation operations" using a "ripple through" technique. Here the state of a processing element is propagated from neighbor to neighbor until stability is achieved. Propagation operations are particularly useful for region labeling in binary images. These operations occur rapidly on the CLIP4 and may be conducted in either the square, hexagonal, or four-connected tessellations.

Image input is from a television camera via a 6-bit digitizer. The system transfers images into the primary storage buffers using multiple bit planes and then into secondary storage, one bit at a time, using the 96 independent row shift registers. A controller sequences instructions to the array and handles the registers that control looping and image memory indexing. The D outputs of all elements are hierarchically interconnected through an OR gate tree for the purpose of detecting the "empty state" of the array. Finally, a tree of parallel adders is utilized to sum the 1-elements in a particular bit plane. This operation takes 96 clock cycles since bits are counted as the image data is shifted across the array.

### MPP (Massively Parallel Processor)  L

| | | | |
|---|---|---|---|
| *Type*: | Full array | *Frame time*: | $0.1 \mu sec$ |
| *PEs*: | 16384 | *Rate*: | $1.6 \times 10^{11}$ pixops/sec |
| *Image size*: | $128 \times 128$ | *Host*: | PDP11/VAX11 |

The MPP was designed as a cellular array with both numerical and Boolean processing capabilities. Although there is no direct video input, the MPP was designed with image processing in mind. Image data is transferred from magnetic tape primary storage in the host computer. This computer was initially a Digital Equipment Corporation PDP11 and later augmented by a VAX11/780. Between the control computer and the processing elements is another memory called the "staging memory." This and the array operate under control of an independent "array control unit" (Fig. 21).

The processing element of the MPP is shown in Fig. 22. Eight of these processing elements are integrated per chip. The processing element memories (each 1K-bit) for one chip are contained in two additional memory chips which are each 1K × 4. The processor incorporates a full adder to perform 1-bit arithmetic operations. There are three 1-bit inputs stored in the registers, designated as $A$, $P$, and $C$. The output of the full adder is stored in the 1-bit register $B$. The carry output is stored in the 1-bit register $C$. A variable-length shift register (2, 6, . . . , or 30 bits) is provided in order to avoid the extra instruction cycles required for returning partial sums to local storage. Logical operations are performed in a logic unit which is associated with the 1-bit register $P$. A data bus, designated by $D$, interconnects all 1-bit registers in the processing element and forms an interface to the random access memory. The quantity $P$ can be loaded from the data bus or from any

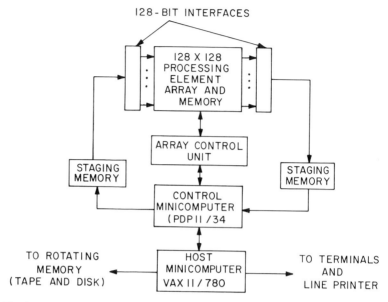

**Fig. 21.** Block diagram of the MPP of the Goodyear Aerospace Corporation (Ohio).

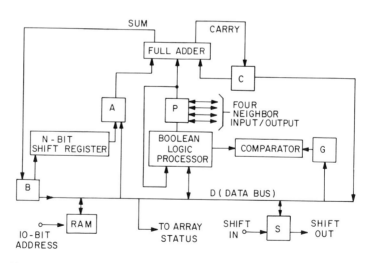

**Fig. 22.** Processing element of the MPP, which is directly connected to four neighbors in the 96 × 96 array. In addition to a full adder, each element incorporates an accumulator (*N*-bit shift register), a Boolean logic processor, and a comparator. Off-chip memory of 4096 bits is also available.

of the four-connected neighbors. The logical unit may then be used to form one of the 16 possible Boolean functions of the current states of $P$ and $D$. The result of this operation is returned to the 1-bit register $P$. When required, data can be returned via the data bus to the 1 K random access memory associated with the processor. There is also a 1-bit activity register $G$ which is used for conditional operations, that is, the contents of this register determine whether the processing element takes part in a particular calculation. A hierarchical OR gate connects all data buses in order to detect the "array empty" condition.

Input and output to the array is produced by shifting columns of 1-bit data through row shift registers consisting of the 1-bit elements designated $S$ in each processing element. This shifting action may be done independently without interrupting the action of the processing elements themselves. Transfers to the 1-bit register $D$ are made in a single parallel operation requiring one instruction cycle. This occurs once the full array of 1-bit data has been shifted to the appropriate $S$ locations. The array control unit (ACU) is used for input/output control and control of the processing elements. It is also used to perform all scalar arithmetic for purposes of addressing. The staging memories are a table-controlled system used to rearrange and reformat the image data during input/output. These memories are capable of serial-to-parallel and parallel-to-serial conversion as well as image data windowing and montaging. The role of the host minicomputer(s) is to perform program management and to coordinate the activities of the staging memories and the ACU.

## CELLULAR ARRAY PROGRAMMING    V

Dozens of languages have been developed for programming cellular logic arrays. Examples are DEFPRO and PPL, used by the University of Linkoping in programming PICAP; C3PL, used at the Environmental Research Institute of Michigan for programming the Cytocomputer; GLOL, used for programming both the Perkin-Elmer GLOPR and the Coulter diff3-50 GLOPR; and SUPRPIC, written at Carnegie-Mellon University for the PHP. Surveys of many such languages are given by Preston [51]. Some of these languages were written as autonomous software systems composed of an operating system for controlling the computer environment, an editor for preparing program code and subroutines, an interpreter or compiler for converting program statements into executable machine language, and some sort of file management system. Other languages have been coded in high-level languages (e.g., FORTRAN) and require compilation using subroutine libraries. Still others use the command substitution systems now available as part of most modern operating systems which call subroutines and pass arguments to them in a sequential or chained manner without the necessity of task compilation and subroutine linkage. A complete analysis and tabulation of languages and programming methods for cellular logic arrays is beyond the scope of this chapter. Therefore, a summary is provided in the following sections, giving specific examples taken from five different languages.

## A    GLOL

GLOL is the language used for programming the Perkin–Elmer research GLOPR as well as the Coulter diff3, diff3-50, and diff4 GLOPRs. The data type of all arrays is binary. Array operations do not require indexing. Rather, the user specifies the size of the image within the constraints that it be $32 \times 32$, $64 \times 64$, or $128 \times 128$. The other data types supported by GLOL are scalars (constants) and vectors (generated by sequences of image measurement commands). These data are 16-bit integers stored in 2s complement format. GLOL uses an editor which permits the user to name strings of GLOL commands (called "procedures") and then to execute a procedure by typing EX PROC ABC, where ABC is the procedure name. GLOL prohibits the GOTO statement and uses no program labels. This leads to highly structured programming with all code in-line so as to permit easy debugging. GLOL runs on the Varian 620i, Data General Nova, and Intel 8086. It is written entirely in assembly language.

An example of the use of GLOL to carry out a Boolean exclusive OR between two binary arrays is given below.

| Command | Description |
|---|---|
| SET SYS 64 | Dimension image to $64 \times 64$ |
| DEF A,B,C | Name the images A,B,C |
| SEARCH A,N1 | Put image labeled N1 in A |
| SEARCH B,N2 | Put image labeled N2 in B |
| C = A − B | Exclusive OR of A,B stored in C |

## B    C3PL

C3PL runs under a command substitution system and allows the user to call any of a long list of subroutines. These subroutines constitute the commands of the language. Thus, the language is not part of an autonomous software system but is embedded in the host computer software. The language was developed to control the Cytocomputer at the Environmental Research Institute of Michigan, which is a pipelined cellular logic array (see Section IV.F). The Cytocomputer requires that look-up tables be loaded in each stage of the pipeline corresponding to each step of the procedure to be executed. C3PL automatically computes these look-up tables according to the command issued by the user and the arguments submitted to parameterize this command.

An example of the program required to perform the Boolean exclusive OR in this language is given below.

| Command | Description |
|---------|-------------|
| TAPEIN | Reads first image from tape (autodimensioned) |
| SAVE 1 | Stores image file in disk file 1 |
| TAPEIN | Reads second image |
| SAVE 2 | Stores image file in disk file 2 |
| COMBINED 1,2 | Combines images into an active file |
| BITXOR 2, 1 | Performs exclusive OR |

## PPL  C

PPL is the language used to manipulate the PICAP of the University of Linkoping. There are two primary versions of this language (PPL I and PPL II). This section treats the second version only. PPL is similar to C3PL in that it is not autonomous but is embedded in the software of the host minicomputer. PPL II has commands for manipulating video input and output interfaces as well as controlling the various processors of the PICAP system (see Section IV.H). An example of the use of this language in performing the Boolean exclusive OR follows.

| Command | Description |
|---------|-------------|
| PROGRAM EXOR | |
| BPICT P1,P2(64,64) | Dimension the image array |
| BEGIN | |
| P1 = XOR(P1,P2) | Perform the exclusive OR |
| DISP(P1,4) | Display the result on monitor 4 |
| END | |

## CAP4  D

CAP4 is an assembly-like language used to program the CLIP series of computers developed at University College London. (A new high-level language, IPC, has recently been coded for CLIP4 but is not covered in this chapter.) CAP4 commands exist as a subroutine library accessible under the operating system (UNIX) of the main control computer of the CLIP (a DEC

PDP11/35). The major instruction carried out in the CLIP cellular logic array is the SET instruction, which determines the operation to be executed. The three other primary instructions are LOAD, PROCESS, and STORE, which are concerned only with data transfers within the array.

Five main classes of operations may be performed in CLIP. There are "point operations" for executing simple Boolean functions between binary images; "local operations" for selecting data lying on the array edge; "propagation operations" for transmitting connectivity information across the array; "labeled propagations," which gate the propagation operation with a template; and "arithmetic operations," which carry out integer arithmetic between integer arrays.

An example of using CAP4 for performing the Boolean exclusive OR between two binary arrays is as follows.

| Command | Description |
|---|---|
| *CSIN* | Input image 0 |
| .WORD 1 | |
| SET A | |
| PST 0 | Save image 0 |
| CSIN | Input image 1 |
| .WORD 2 | |
| SET A | |
| PST 1 | Save image 1 |
| ; | |
| SET P&A | Setup the EXOR function |
| LDA 0 | |
| LDA 1 | |
| PST 2 | Execute the function |
| .END | |

## E   DAP-FORTRAN

DAP-FORTRAN is the FORTRAN extension written by International Computers Ltd. to manipulate the DAP. It can be used for image processing algorithms using both Boolean and numerical operators. Subroutines are written in a lower-level assembly language (APAL) which permits the construction of macros. DAP-FORTRAN supports both matrices and vectors as data types as well as scalars. DO-loop facilities are available as well as all other standard FORTRAN operators. DAP-FORTRAN and APAL can be mixed at the subroutine level for ease of coding. An example of the execution of the Boolean exclusive OR follows.

| *Command* | *Description* |
|---|---|
| Host Program (for the ICL2960 processor): | |
|     COMMON/IMAGE/A(64,64,4),B(64,64,4) | Dimension the image arrays |
|     LOGICAL A(64,64,4),B(64,64,4) | Declare the array type |
|     READ (5,100)A,B | Read the images |
| 100  FORMAT (L1) | Specify format |
|     CALL DAPXOR | Call DAP XOR subroutine |
|     WRITE (6,100)A | Write the result |
| Image Processor Program (for the DAP): | |
|     SUBROUTINE DAPXOR | |
|     COMMON/IMAGE/A(,,4),B(,,4) | Use four subarrays |
|     DO 10 I = 1,4 | |
|     CALL CONVMFL(A(,,I)) | Convert "horizontal" to "vertical" format |
|     CALL CONVMFL(B(,,I)) | |
|     A(,,I) = A(,,I).LNEQB),,I) | Execute the exclusive OR |
|     CALL CONVMFL(A(,,I)) | Convert the data format |
| 10   CONTINUE | |
|     RETURN | |
|     END | |

### Comparing the Programming Methods   **F**

The languages described in this section illustrates the variety of current means for programming cellular logic array machines. GLOL, which was the first cellular logic array language devised, has a relatively small command repertoire and concentrates on the manipulation of binary image data. This facilitates its use in that the repertoire is easily memorized. Boolean logic and the Golay hexagonal parallel pattern transform are the only image processing operators available. GLOL is coded entirely in assembly language (including its monitor, interpreter, supervisor, and editor) and resides in only 12 K Bytes of main memory in the host minicomputer.

Like GLOL, C3PL and PPL reside in a host minicomputer but, unlike GLOL, do not incorporate an autonomous operating system. On the other hand, they provide a far greater range of image manipulative capabilities. C3PL, through appropriate subroutines, permits the utilization of an essentially infinite number of look-up tables to program the operations in the multiple stages of the Cytocomputer. PPL, through the mechanism of both the choice of template and the choice of template matching conditions, permits the user to carry out both binary and integer transforms over the 3 × 3 PICAP subarray.

CAP4 and DAP-FORTRAN are true full-array programming languages. CAP4 is a simple, machine-oriented language whose assembly-like instructions relate directly to the functions executed by the CLIP processing element. Hence, the user has direct control over the step-by-step operations of the cellular logic array. In contrast, the user of DAP-FORTRAN is not conscious of the specific data manipulations being made. The contents of the DAP processing elements are automatically shifted and the results combined using both the numerical and Boolean capabilities of the machine. DAP-FORTRAN forms a bridge with standard FORTRAN repertoire by adding extensions which include commands useful in manipulating data in a full-array machine.

The use of CAP4 is centered in the Image Processing Group at University College London and a small group of other research laboratories in Great Britain. GLOL has few programmers but is in use in hundreds of installations worldwide due to the wide dissemination of the Coulter diff3 series of robot microscopes. The user community for DAP-FORTRAN is primarily restricted to users of the few DAP machines that have been installed. Often users employ these machines on a service basis using dial-up connections. Since the DAP has no method for displaying the contents of the array, use in interactive image processing is difficult. C3PL and PPL are restricted in their use to those communities employing the facilities of the Environmental Research Institute of Michigan (ERIM) and the University of Linkoping, respectively. With the proliferation of spin-offs from ERIM in the United States and the foundation of IMTEC in Sweden, the user community for Cytocomputer-like and PICAP-like machines using these languages is growing.

## VI  SUMMARY

Previous sections in this chapter introduced and diagrammed the five basic architectures currently used in cellular logic array systems. Most of the important examples of such systems which have been built to date were then discussed in detail, accompanied by both system and structural block diagrams. One limitation of the discussion is that, for some of the newer multipurpose machines, that is, those which are partly cellular and partly not, the description has been limited to the cellular logic array aspects. The machines described show both an enormous variety and great ingenuity in

TABLE I

Cellular Logic Array Systems

| Name | Type | Connectivity | Speed | Speed/cost ratio |
|------|------|--------------|-------|------------------|
| CELLSCAN | $a$ | 8 | $4 \times 10^3$ | $10^{-1}$ |
| GLOPR | $a$ | 6 | $3 \times 10^5$ | $10^1$ |
| BIP | $a$ | var. | $2 \times 10^7$ | $10^2$ |
| ILLIAC IV | $e$ | 4 | $10^6$ | $10^1$ |
| Cytocomputer | $c$ | 8 | $2 \times 10^6$ | $10^1$ |
| PHP | $d$ | var. | $10^6$ | $10^3$ |
| PICAP | $a$ | var. | $8 \times 10^5$ | $10^1$ |
| DIP | $d$ | var. | $4 \times 10^5$ | $10^1$ |
| diff3 | $b$ | 6 | $4 \times 10^7$ | $10^3$ |
| DAP | $e$ | 4 | $10^{10}$ | $10^4$ |
| CLIP | $e$ | var. | $10^9$ | $10^4$ |
| MPP | $e$ | 4 | $10^{11}$ | $10^4$ |

their design. It is the purpose of this section to tabulate and summarize their salient features.

Table I list the cellular logic array systems in more or less chronological order. As can be seen, type $a$ systems, having a single processing element, predominated initially. These systems were replaced by multiprocessing-element systems, of which the Cytocomputer is the only type $c$ (pipelined) machine. The two type $d$ systems (DIP and PHP) used a multiplicity of secondary image stores and either a single processing element (DIP) or multiple processing elements (PHP). The diff3-50 cellular logic machine is the only type $b$ system listed, in that multiple primary image stores are provided as part of the processor. The other cellular logic array systems shown in Table I are all full array (type $e$).

As mentioned in the introduction (see Fig. 1), speed has increased by almost eight orders of magnitude from the year 1961, when CELLSCAN was first operational, to 1984, when MPP was delivered and in operation at NASA Goddard Laboratories. Cost performance is also important (see Table I) and is indicated as the ratio of the entry in column 1 to the estimated cost (in dollars) of the cellular logic array machine in question. CELLSCAN is rated at only 0.1 picture point operations per second per dollar, whereas the more modern machines range between 1000 and 10,000 picture point operations per second per dollar. There is not as much diversity in this figure of merit as in the speed figure of merit alone. Furthermore, the speed figure of merit is based solely on a simple Boolean operation in the cellular logic array. For more complex operations, certain cellular logic array systems are at a significant disadvantage in comparison with others. For example, in the CLIP-series machines, there are direct connections to all eight neighbors, making eight-neighbor cellular computations possible within one instruction cycle. This is not true in the four-connected cellular logic arrays, which thus require several instruction cycles to execute the same operation. Furthermore, even in the CLIP-series machines, all fourteen Golay primitives cannot be coded in one instruction cycle, as is possible using the diff3-50. Therefore, a comparison of the operational characteristics of cellular logic array machines, in general, requires extensive benchmarking. Some benchmark tasks have been coded and executed, but, as a whole, far more extensive testing is needed [52]. This is one of the most important tasks for the future.

## REFERENCES

1. H. H. Goldstine, "The Computer from Pascal to von Neumann." Princeton Univ. Press, Princeton, New Jersey, 1972.
2. W. S. McCulloch and W. Pitts, A logical calculus of the ideas immanent in nervous activity, *Bull. Math. Biophys.* **5**, 115–133 (1943).
3. E. L. Post, Finite combinatory processes—Formulation I, *J. Symbol. Logic* **1**, 103–105 (1936).
4. A. M. Turing, On computable numbers, with an application to the Entscheidungs-problem, *Proc. London Math. Soc., Series 2* **42**, 230–265 (1936).
5. S. M. Ulam, On some mathematical problems connected with patterns of growth of figures, *Proc. Symposia Appl. Math., Amer. Math. Soc.* **11**, 214–224 (1962).
6. J. G. Kemeny, Man viewed as a machine, *Sci. Amer.* **192**, 58–67 (1955).
7. W. H. Walton, Automatic counting of microscopic particles, *Nature (London)* **169**, 518–520 (1952).
8. D. Causley and J. Z. Young, The flying spot microscope—Use in particle analysis, *Research* **8**, 430–434 (1953).
9. G. A. Moore, Applications of computers to the quantitative analysis of microstructures, *U.S. Natl. Bureau Stds. Rpt.*, No. 9428 (1966).
10. R. A. Kirsch, Experiments in processing information with a digital computer, *Proc. Eastern Joint Comput. Conf., Washington D.C.*, pp. 221–229 (1957).
11. G. P. Dinneen, Programming pattern recognition, *Proc. Western Joint Comput. Conf., Los Angeles*, pp. 94–100 (1955).
12. S. H. Unger, A computer oriented toward spatial problems, *Proc. IRE* **46**, 1744–1750 (1958).
13. M. J. E. Golay, Hexagonal parallel pattern transformation, *IEEE Trans. Comput.* **C-18**, 733–740 (1969).
14. K. Preston, Jr., The CELLSCAN system—A leucocyte pattern analyzer, *Proc. Western Joint Comput. Conf., Los Angeles*, pp. 175–178 (1961).
15. M. Gardner, On cellular automata, self-reproduction, the Garden of Eden and the game 'life', *Sci. Amer.* **224**(2), 112–117 (1971).
16. E. R. Banks, Universality in cellular automata, *Proc. 11th Switch, Automata Th. Conf.*, pp. 216–224 (1970).
17. R. G. Schrandt, and S. M. Ulam, On patterns of growth of figures in two dmensions, *N. Amer. Math. Soc.* **1**, 642–651 (1960).
18. H. Yamada and S. M. Amoroso, Structural and behavioral equivalences of tessellation atuomata, *Inform. Control* **18**, 1–31 (1971).
19. A. R. Smith, III, Simple computation—Universal cellular spaces, *J. Assoc. Comput. Mach.* **18**, 339–353 (1971).
20. A. Tojo, Pattern description with a highly parallel information processing unit, *Bull. Electrotech. Lab.* **31**(8), 930–946 (1967).

21. A. Tojo, Distance functions and minimum path connections, *Bull. Electrotech. Lab.* **32**(9), 1930–1942 (1968).

22. A. Tojo, T. Yamaguchi, and H. Aoyama, Pattern description with highly parallel information processing unit. VI—Construction and simulation, *Bull. Electrotech. Lab.* **33**(5), 479–505 (1970).

23. *Proc. Intl. Symp. Uniformly Structured Automata and Logic* (IEEE 75 CH1052-6C) (1975), Tokyo.

24. "*Cellular Automata*" (D. Farmer, T. Toffoli, and S. Wolfram, eds.). North-Holland, Amsterdam (1984).

25. D. L. Slotnick, W. C. Borck, and R. C. McReynolds, The Solomon computer, *Proc. Western Joint Comput. Conf., Los Angeles*, pp. 87–107 (1962).

26. B. H. McCormick, The Illinois pattern recognition computer—ILLIAC III, *IEEE Trans. Electron. Comput.* **EC-12**(6), 791–813 (1963).

27. D. L. Slotnick, The fastest computer, *Sci. Amer.* **224**(2), 76–87 (1971).

28. M. J. B. Duff and D. M. Watson, CLIP3: A cellular logic image processor, *in* "New Concepts and Technologies in Parallel Information Processing" E. R. Caianiello, ed.), pp. 75–86, Noordhoff, Leyden, 1975.

29. T. J. Fountain, A survey of bit-serial array processor circuits, *in* "Computing structures for Image Processing" (M. J. B. Duff, ed.) pp. 1–14. Academic Press, London, 1983.

30. D. J. Hunt, The ICL DAP and its application to image processing, *in* "Languages and Architectures for Image Processing" (M. J. B. Duff and S. Levialdi, eds.) pp. 275–282, Academic Press, London, 1981.

31. K. E. Batcher, Design of a massively parallel processor, *IEEE Trans. Comput.* **C-29**, 836–840 (1980).

32. K. Preston, Jr., Automatic differentiation of white blood cells, *in* "Image Processing in Biomedical Science" (D. M. Ramsey, ed.), pp. 97–117. Univ. of California Press, Berkeley, 1969.

33. S. B. Gray, The binary image processor and its applications, Rpt. 90365-5C (unpublished), Informational International Inc., Los Angeles, 1972.

34. B. Kruse, A parallel picture processing machine, *IEEE Trans. Comput.* **C-22**(12), 1075–1087 (1973).

35. M. D. Graham and P. E. Norgren, The diff3 analyzer: A parallel/serial Golay image processor, *in* "Real-Time Medical Image Processing" (M. Onoe, K. Preston, Jr., and A. Rosenfeld, eds.), pp. 168–182. Plenum, New York, 1980.

36. S. R. Sternberg, Parallel architectures for image processing, *in* "Real/Time Parallel Computers" (M. Onoe, K. Preston, Jr., and A. Rosenfeld, eds.) pp. 347–359 Plenum, New York, 1981.

37. R. Nawrath and J. Serra, Quantitative image analysis: Theory and instrumentation, *Microsc. Acta* **82**(2), 101–111 (1979).

38. W. K. Taylor, An automatic system for obtaining particle size distributions with the aid of the flying-spot microscope, *Brit. J. Appl. Phys.*, Supp. 3, 173–180 (1954).

39. M. J. E. Golay, Apparatus for counting bi-nucleate lymphocytes in blood, U.S. Patent 3,214,574 (1965).

40. K. Preston, Jr., Use of the Golay logic processor in pattern-recognition studies using hexagonal neighborhood logic, *Proc. Symp. Comput. Automata*, Polytechnic Press (Polytechnic Institute of Brooklyn) (1971).

41. K. Preston, Jr., and J. Carvalko, Jr., Use of the contourograph to evaluate a high resolution television microscope, *Proc. IEEE* **57**(1), 104–106 (1969).

42. S. B. Gray, Local properties of binary images in two dimensions, *IEEE Trans. Comput.* **C-20**(5), 551–561 (1971).

43. M. D. Graham, The diff4: A second-generation slide analyzer, *in* "Computing Structures for Image Processing" (M. J. B. Duff, ed.) pp. 179–194. Academic Press, London, 1983.

44.  K. Preston, Jr., Cellular architectures for image processing, *Inter. Conf. Comput. Design: VLSI in Comput., New York.* IEEE Publication No. CH1935-6/83 (1983).

45.  K. Preston, Jr., The crossing number of a three-dimensional dodecamino, *J. Combin. Info. Sys. Sci.* **5**(4), 281–286 (1980).

46.  K. J. Hafford and K. Preston, Jr., Three-dimensional skeletonization of elongated solids, *Comput. Vision Graph. Image Proc.* **27**(1), 78–91. (1984).

47.  J. M. Herron, J. Farley, K. Preston, Jr., and H. Sellner, A general-purpose high-speed logical transform image processor, *IEEE Trans. Comput.* **C-31**(8), 795–800 (1982).

48.  B. Kruse, System architecture for image analysis, *in* "Structured Computer Vision" (S. Tanimoto and A. Klinger, eds.), pp. 169–212. Academic Press, New York, 1980.

49.  K. Preston, Jr., Multiresolution microscopy, *in* "Multi-Resolution Image Processing and Analysis" (A. Rosenfeld, ed.). Springer-Verlag, Heidelberg, 1983.

50.  B. Kruse, P. E. Danielsson, and S. Gudmundsson, From PICAP I to PICAP II, *in* "Special Computer Architectures for Pattern Processing" (K. S. Fu and T. Ichikawa, eds.), pp. 127–155, CRC Press, Boca Raton Florida, 1982.

51.  K. Preston, Jr., Progress in image processing languages, *in* "Computing Structures for Image Processing" (M. J. B. Duff, ed.) pp. 195–211. Academic Press, London, 1983.

52.  K. Preston, Jr., Comparison of parallel processing machines: A proposal, *in* "Languages and Architectures for Image Processing" (M. J. B. Duff and S. Levialdi, eds.) pp. 305–324. Academic Press, London, 1981.

# Chapter **18**

# Parallel Architectures for Image Processing, Computer Vision, and Pattern Perception

LEONARD UHR

Department of Computer Sciences
University of Wisconsin
Madison, Wisconsin

HANDBOOK OF PATTERN RECOGNITION
AND IMAGE PROCESSING

## I  INTRODUCTION

This chapter examines the wide range of parallel multicomputer architectures that have already been developed and explores the far wider range of architectures that will soon become feasible, and attractive, because of the rapid explosion of very-large-scale integration (VLSI) technologies.

First, we briefly describe the human visual system as an existence proof that massively parallel perception is possible. Then we examine the technological and design possibilities and constraints that underlie the development of very large multicomputers. Next, we describe a variety of the proposed multicomputer architectures, exploring the strengths and weaknesses of each. These include (a) algorithm-structured architectures, (b) attempts to design generally usable multicomputers, and (c) algorithm-structured, generally usable architectures.

## II  THE PERCEPTION PROBLEMS POSED AND SOLVED BY MASSIVELY PARALLEL BRAINS

A good general perception program should be able to recognize and describe any complex real-world scene that contains a number of independent objects. It should further be able to do this in real time, as some of these objects move about, by processing the images input continuously to it by a TV camera or similar transducing device. Parallel algorithms, and very large multicomputer architectures that handle these algorithms efficiently, are absolutely necessary.

The human brain is a highly parallel multicomputer built from roughly 12 billion components, the neurons, linked to one another over the synapses. It takes roughly 1.5 msec to fire a neuron (that is, for one or more neurons to fire into and across a synaptic junction, thus firing the neuron on the other side). Therefore the brain's cycle time for a basic operation is 1–2 msec. This contrasts sharply with the microsecond and nanosecond cycle times of today's computers.

When each frame in a scene of moving objects is processed in 30 msec, the maximum possible serial depth is 15 to 30. When the many objects in a complex scene are perceived in substantially less than 1 sec, the maximum serial depth is a few hundred. These astoundingly small numbers document a serial depth so shallow that they can be achieved only by massively parallel systems. They are existence proofs of the enormous speedups that are possible.

## THE IMMINENT POSSIBILITIES OFFERED BY  III
## VLSI AND WSI TECHNOLOGIES

During the next 5, 10, and 20 years successively more powerful multicomputers will rapidly become feasible at reasonable prices. This is because of the technology of the very high-density VLSI chips from which modern computers are constructed. We can begin to think about the following set of practicable computer topologies: any graph whose nodes are basic devices (e.g., transistors) and whose links are wires, that contain 1–100,000 clusters each of which has 1–10,000,000 nodes (these probably need to be linked in near planar fashion), with from 16 to 500 wires linking into each of these clusters. This offers an overwhelming range of possibilities for networks with many thousands, or even millions, of individual computers, as we shall now see.

A multicomputer is built from processors and memories and the connector wires that link them together, plus input transducers, output transducers, and controllers.

(1)   Each processor often contains a number of special-purpose circuits for the fast computation of particular frequently executed operations.

(2)   Several different types, speeds, and sizes of memories are often used, from highest-speed individual registers and small caches through the high-speed main memories to successively slower bulk memories, disks, and tapes.

(3)   Connectors can range in bandwidth from hundreds to billions of bits per second.

(4)   Input and output transducers can be thought of as connectors to the outside world (often, as with a TV camera or TV screen, this entails analog–digital or digital–analog tranductions).

(5)   Controllers handle a variety of functions, including the fetching, decoding, and execution of instructions, the handling of input and output, and the general flow of processes.

Today's basic computer component is a rectangular chip roughly 4–6 mm on each side. Today's largest chips contain 100,000–500,000 devices (transistors and logic gates—today these terms are often used interchangeably). Chips have been doubling in size every 12 to 18 months for the past 20–30 years, and this doubling should continue (possibly at a slightly slower rate) until at least 1,000,000-device and then 10,000,000-device or even larger chips are achieved. (These are conservative extrapolations into the future. Chips with a million transistors have already been fabricated experimentally. And, new technologies, for example, wafer-scale integration, three-dimensional chips or stacked wafers, optical fiber processors, and biological computers, may well vault us substantially beyond these figures.)

Essentially, the designer develops a graph whose nodes are devices and whose links are wires, arranges this graph so that it fills as small as possible a two-dimensional Euclidean space, and embeds it into the rectangular chip's surface. Usually the chip is treated as though it were a square grid, with no diagonal wires allowed; this chiefly serves to simplify the design process. The embedding entails the printing of a number of layers (much like a color silkscreen); this makes it possible to have wires cross one another occasionally, by burrowing them down into different layers. But such crossings are expensive, and therefore the embedded graph should be "almost planar."

A reasonable rule of thumb is that the feasible limit to the size of a computer is the number of separate basic components (today these are the chips) that must be handled individually and wired together. One thousand components give a large minicomputer; 10,000 give a very large computer; several hundred thousand components give a buildable but extremely large supercomputer.

A traditional computer needs roughly 50–500 devices for a 1-bit processor, 2000–5000 devices for an 8-bit processor, and 10,000–100,000 or more devices for a 32-bit processor [1]. Memory needs 1 or 2 devices for slow dynamic RAMs (random access memory chips) and 4–12 devices for faster static RAMs. A traditional single-processor serial computer might have 16K–16,000K words of memory. See Table I for a few examples.

It should be emphasized that no matter how large and how densely packed with devices future chips may be, it is very unlikely that a single chip can be fabricated that contains a powerful conventional 32-bit computer plus all its memory. For, although a powerful CPU might even today be built on one corner of one chip, its memory would need several chips. A 10,000,000-device chip will at most hold 1 MByte of memory, but a powerful conventional computer needs from 4 to 64 MBytes (or more). Thus several million chips would be needed for a network with a million conventional computers.

TABLE I

**Examples of Device Counts for Various Kinds of Computers**[a]

| Computer type | Devices in | | Computers in |
|---|---|---|---|
| | Processor | Memory | $10^8$–$10^{11}$ devices |
| 1-bit | 50 | 50 | $10^6$–$10^9$ |
| 1-bit | 400 | 600 | $10^5$–$10^8$ |
| 8-bit | 2,000 | 8,000 | $10^4$–$10^7$ |
| 32-bit | 10,000 | 90,000 | $10^3$–$10^6$ |

[a] Memory has been minimized for each computer—to make possible large numbers of computers—and the total memory is large.

Note that this argument holds only for conventional computers with their traditionally large memories. As we shall see, different types of computers can make very large networks feasible without such heroic efforts. It is probably more reasonable to think in terms of the total size of the memory for the whole set of computers that are working on a single problem, rather than the size of each computer's memory.

It is important to mention the emerging possibilities of wafer-scale integration (WSI). The 4-mm square chip is diced from a wafer that might be from 3 to 6 in. in diameter. It is becoming feasible to use the entire wafer, which is the equivalent of several hundred chips. Even more exciting is the possibility of stacking wafers, to build a three-dimensional structure [2].

## BASIC TOPOLOGIES OF PARALLEL SYSTEMS THAT BREAK IV
## OUT OF THE SINGLE-CPU SHELL

It is instructive to use relatively simple graphs to examine the basic structure of multicomputers. The detailed parts of a computer will be far more complex, but simple graphs can illuminate the basic structure. At the highest level the graph will simply be a set of abstract nodes connected with links, for example $\bigcirc-\bigcirc-\bigcirc$. At successively lower levels, the type of node can be designated, for example, $P-M-P$ (indicating a memory linked to two processors). An arrow indicates that information can flow in only one direction over a link, for example, $I \rightarrow C1 \rightarrow C1 \rightarrow O$ (indicating input to C1 then C2 then output).

A traditional Von Neumann computer can be diagrammed as a single node, as in Fig. 1a, although we can blow this up to show successively more detail, as in Fig. 1b. A multiprocessor system is diagrammed in Fig. 2.

To get substantial increases in power, we must somehow or other multiply computers. The simplest thing to do is to add a second computer, as shown in Fig. 3. More computers can be added (for example, see Fig. 4).

$$
\begin{array}{cc}
C & P-M \\
(a) & (b)
\end{array}
$$

**Fig. 1.** Simple traditional single-CPU computer: (a) a single-CPU computer and (b) a single-CPU computer in more detail.

$$
\begin{array}{cccc}
P & P & P & P \\
| \_ & | \_ & | \_ & | \\
& & T & \\
& M & &
\end{array}
$$

**Fig. 2.** Multiprocessor computer.

```
        o—o              P   P
                         |   |
        C—C              R—R
                         |   |
                         M   M
```

**Fig. 3.** Multicomputer with two computers. The high-level, two-node diagram ○—○ can link two computers, or, as shown, in more detail, the processors can be linked to their memories and to each other via registers.

The line topology is more commonly called a "bus." A high-speed bus is probably the most widely used way to link together a small number (2, 3, ..., 8, ..., 16, and possibly up to 32 or 64) of computers. Since all information passed between any pair of computers must travel over the single common bus, bandwidth problems quickly grow worse as $N$ grows.

A star topology might in theory have any number of computers linked to the single device at its center, but in actuality the single central node can quickly become a bottleneck. This central node might be another computer, but often it is a large shared memory, or a bus (in which case Figs. 4a and 4b are identical).

A complete topology graph (that is, a graph where every node is directly linked to very other node) needs $N - 1$ links to each node. But only 2, 3, 4 or up to only 8 or so computers can be linked in this way, since the number of wires and interfaces quickly becomes excessive.

A polygon topology is simply a line topology with one link added, between the first and the last nodes. This can serve several useful purposes—the diameter of the graph is cut in half. Information can be made to cycle, for

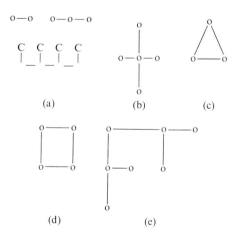

**Fig. 4.** Several topologies for small multicomputer structures: (a) line, (b) star, (c) complete, (d) polygon, and (e) tree. Usually each mode is a separate computer, but it might be a processor, memory, or some other device.

example, from one node through all the others and back to that node. Polygons are frequently implemented in multicomputers; they are usually called rings.

Note that the four-node polygon drawn in Fig. 4d is also a two-cube (an $N$-dimensional binary cube where $N = 2$). The two-node line is a one-cube topology, our familiar eight-node "cube" is a three-cube, and so on.

A tree topology starts from a root, which links to two or more nodes, which in turn link to two or more nodes, and so on, ending with a link into each leaf node (leaves have no other links). The example drawn in Fig. 4e is a binary tree. Note that a star is actually a tree, but with only one ply that directly links the root to all other nodes, which are all leaves.

The simple basic topologies examined so far already account for most of the multicomputers that have actually been built to date. This will probably continue to be the case so long as these multicomputers are very small, with only a few dozen, or at most a few hundred, computers in toto. However, a large number of different parallel architectures have been proposed, both for general-purpose systems and also for a variety of specialized applications. An explosively larger number of architectures are possible—all the possible graphs that can be drawn with several hundred, thousand, or million nodes.

Several of these have been examined and developed to the point where they appear to have, potentially, the size and power needed for large artificial intelligence (AI) problems. To date only prototypes have actually been built. Most have only 4, 8, or 16 or so computers. Only a handful of systems have actually been built with more—several asynchronous networks (that is, where each computer works independently) that have 50 to 65 computers, one pipeline with 113 processors, one almost completely synchronized network with 256 microcomputers, and 3 synchronized arrays of very simple (albeit general-purpose) computers with 4000 to 16,000.

### Complete Connectivity, Actual and Approximate    A

Many researchers suggest that the ideal topology would directly link every computer to every other computer, that is, forming a complete graph. However, that is a true ideal, since it can never be realized. For only very small graphs can be linked in this way.

Most of the small prototype networks have linked their separate computers together via either a common bus or ring (i.e., a line or polygon of big high-bandwidth wires) (DeWitt et al. [3], Farber and Larson [4]), a shared memory (i.e., a star whose center is a memory) (Wulf et al. [5]), or (as diagrammed in Fig. 5) a cross-bar grid of switches (an array of wires, with each of $N$ computers linked to one row and one column, and a switch at every wire crossing (i.e., $N*N$ switches) (Hwang and Briggs [6]).

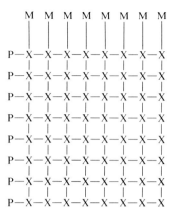

**Fig. 5.** Array topology of the cross-bar switch. An 8 × 8 cross bar links eight processors to eight memories.

Bus, ring, shared memory, and cross-bar switch are probably the simplest ways to connect computers, but they are feasible only for very small networks of 4, 8, 16, or, possible in special cases, a few more. The single bus, ring, or shared memory experiences increasing problems of contention and overload as the number of computers linked to it increases.

The cross-bar switch, which needs $N \times N$ $B$-bit switches (where $B$ is usually 32), rapidly becomes too expensive. The largest cross-bar-based system being proposed is the very powerful and very expensive S-1 multicomputer under development at Lawrence Livermore Laboratories [7], where it is contemplated that 64 Cray-equivalent supercomputers will be linked. Each of these computers will itself be so powerful and so expensive that the cost of the expensive cross bar should not be relatively excessive; however, 64 is probably the limit.

The ZMOB [8] is to some extent a clever exception. It will have 256 Z-80 processors, all linked in a ring via a (very expensive) 256-stage shift register that is 256 times as fast as the relatively slow Z-80s, and hence needs only one Z-80 instruction cycle to shift information once around the ring. Each processor can send two 8-bit words of information and receive two 8-bit words of information at each cycle. Thus, the ZMOB's ring is roughly equivalent to a cross bar that would have to have 256 × 256 16-bit switches.

## B  Reconfiguring Networks for Virtual Complete Connectivity

The cross-bar linkage can be approximated with a shuffle-exchange reconfiguring network [9-13] that links $N$ nodes to $N$ (either the same or different) nodes using log $N$ banks each with $N$ switches (see Fig. 6).

```
0    0 0   0 0   0 0    0
1    4 4   2 2   1 1    1

2    1 1   4 4   2 2    2
3    5 5   6 6   3 3    3

4    2 2   1 1   4 4    4
5    6 6   3 3   5 5    5

6    3 3   5 5   6 6    6
7    7 7   7 7   7 7    7
```

**Fig. 6.** Shuffle-exchange reconfiguring network (links not shown). Information shuffles left to right through three banks of $2 \times 2$ switches.

This kind of network reduces the $N \times N$ switches needed in a cross bar to $N \log N$ switches. Now, whereas 1,000,000 switches would need to link 1000 computers using a cross bar, only (sic) 10,000 would be needed using a flip network. This kind of system has been designed by Lipovski [14, 15] at Texas, Siegel [11, 16], and Briggs *et al.* [17], at Purdue. At least two, Lipovski's TRAC and Siegel's PASM, are now being built in prototype form with 16 computers. Siegel contemplates a full-blown system with 1024 computers. The goal for the utracomputer being designed at NYU [18] is 8096 processors linked over a reconfiguring network (augmented with buffers and processors) to 8096 large memory banks, so that programs can be coded and executed as though each processor has direct access to all these memories.

Reconfiguring networks were originally developed for problems where $N$ pieces of data must be shuffled around—probably the primary example is the fast Fourier transform. They can also be used, as in the ultracomputer, so $N$ processors can access $N$ pieces of data spread out in different memories, or, as in Siegel's PASM, so $N$ processors can send messages to one another.

## ALGORITHM-STRUCTURED ARCHITECTURES: PIPELINES, ARRAYS, V AND PYRAMIDS

### Assembly-Line Pipelines of Workers (Computers or Processors) A

Rather than establish an anarchy of independent computers, as is essentially the case when several conventional computers are linked together via a cross-bar, bus, ring, or reconfiguring network, various kinds of coordination and control can be superimposed.

Possibly the simplest structure, and among the most powerful, is a small pipeline of independent computers (see Fig. 7). Now information is input to

$$I \to C \to C \to C \to C \to C \to C \to C \to 0$$

**Fig. 7.** Pipeline multicomputer.

the first computer, which acts upon it and sends its results to the second, and so on, until the pipe is filled—at which point its results are output. A short pipeline of very powerful processors gives the Cray supercomputer much of its power. Pipelines are also useful, as we shall see, whenever images can fruitfully be transformed as they stream by.

Figure 8 examines some of the ways in which the basic structure of a line can be used.

In Fig. 8a, the pipeline can in effect be turned over onto its side and made into a one-dimensional array. In Fig. 8b, this one-dimensional array can be used as a two-dimensional pipeline simply by streaming information through each single-processor pipeline, storing intermediate results in a register or memory cell as appropriate. In Fig. 8c, a two-dimensional pipeline can be constructed so that a different computer executes each process. This reduces the time $P$ needed for a single computer to execute the whole sequence of processes to $(P/C) + C$ (since all of the $C$ computers are working together in parallel; and it also takes $C$ steps to fill and empty the pipe).

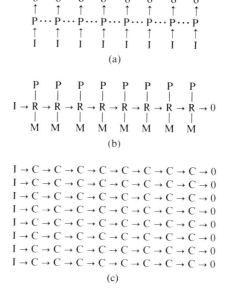

(a)

(b)

(c)

**Fig. 8.** Linking a line of computer components. (a) Information is input to and output from a computer; many computers (possibly linked) work side-by-side. (b) Information is input to and output from a line of registers that also serve to link each computer's processor and memory. (c) Information is streamed through a one-dimensional array of one-dimensional pipelines.

Input device → C1 → C2 → C3 → C4 → C5 → C6 → C7 → Output device
Data:                     9      8      7      6      5      4      3      2, 1

**Fig. 9.** A pipeline of $N$ computers through which data flow. At time 1, C1 will execute the first instruction on the first piece of data; at time 2, C2 will execute the second instruction on the first piece of data and C1 will execute the first instruction on the second piece of data, and so on. The data row shows the state of the system at time 9: C7 (the last stage in a seven-stage pipeline) is executing the seventh process on data job 3; C1 is executing the first process on job 9, which is just starting; jobs 1 and 2 are finished and have been output (probably to some memory storage device).

Several pipelines of processors or computers have been built. These are much in the spirit of an assembly line of workers, with the major restriction that all processors link in a single line, that is, each processor inputs information from only one other processor and outputs to only one other processor. Each processor in the pipe repeatedly executes the same instruction on a sequence of data flowing through that pipe. This means that if the same sequence of instructions is to be executed on a large number of different pieces of data—this is the case whenever the data stored in an array are to be operated on in parallel—a pipeline as long as the sequence of instructions can be built, and information (e.g., TV images or information stored in the cells of an array) can be flowed through the pipeline's processors. Figure 9 explains in more detail the actual step-by-step processing carried out by a pipeline.

If the pipeline has $N$ processors, then (once the pipe is full) the program will execute up to approximately $dN$ times as fast as a single-processor computer ($d$ is the often appreciable additional saving from not having to fetch and decode the next instruction, since each processor fetches only once, then keeps executing the same instruction). The processor that needs the longest time will determine the system's speed, since all the other processors must wait for it to finish. Therefore, the ideal mapping of a program into a pipeline would have each processor do exactly the same amount of work (in terms of time taken).

### *Examples of the Most Powerful and the Largest Pipelines* **1**

The fastest of today's "supercomputers," Seymour Cray's Cray [19, 20] and the Cyber-205 [21], use such pipelines, with up to several dozen very powerful and expensive processors, to execute vector operations on arrays of data for "number-crunching" purposes.

Bjorn Kruse's [22–25] PICAP uses a pipeline of processors specially designed to effect local $3 \times 3$ "window" functions that compute any logical or arithmetic operation whose operands are the center cell of the window plus whichever of the 1–8 of the neighbor is computed everywhere, with each cell in the large array centered under the 3 × 3 window array.

The longest pipeline built to data is in Stanley Sternberg's [26, 27] Cytocomputer, a multicomputer specialized to execute image processing operations. The Cytocomputer has two types of processors—one that computes Boolean (that is, 1-bit "true" or "false") functions over the center cell and its 8 neighbors, and a second that computes 3-bit arithmetic—useful in perception programs for handling gray-scale images and weights. (Note that the 1-bit processor can compute $N$-bit functions, but only bit serially, which means it needs at least $N$ times as much time.) Each processor is much simpler and smaller than those found in a Cray; but the largest Cytocomputer has 113 processors in toto. Even more are possible in projected future systems that might be built using VLSI chips (one processor to each chip) that can be linked together to, in theory, make arbitrarily long pipelines (S. R. Sternberg, personal communication).

## 2  Pipeline Array Processors that Simulate Parallel Processing

The term "array processor" is commonly used for a number of commercially available pipelines. These systems have been developed in two different varieties, each specialized for a different problem domain.

The first system, exemplified by the floating-point systems (FPS) processors, is usually built and sold as add-on devices to be interfaced to a conventional computer's high-speed bus. They rapidly stream a vector or array of numerical data through a small pipe of processors that have been specialized to their task. Typically, therefore, each processor is optimized to compute 32-bit floating-point operations.

The second system, built by Vicom, deAnza, and a number of other manufacturers, is specialized for image processing. Whereas the numerical processors iterate a pipe of powerful floating-point operations over a set of numbers that might be of any size, the image processors stream a fixed-size array (usually 512 × 512) of 8-bit numbers or 1-bit values through a pipe that computes 8-bit fixed-point arithmetic or 1-bit logical and matching operations. Often special-purpose boards with built-in hardware can be added for fast computation of histograms, 3 × 3 mask operations (usually convolutions), or other commonly used image processing functions. Several companies are now building Cytocomputers with small pipelines, and Cytocomputer boards can be purchased as add-ons for the Vicom.

## 3  Special-Purchase Chips for Frequently Computed Functions

Custom chips can be designed and fabricated to speed up key, frequently computed processes. A single chip that computes a relatively large convolution, for example, $7 \times 7$, $11 \times 11$, $17 \times 17$, or even larger, can enormously speed up processing (where convolutions are frequently used). One chip of special interest computes the convolution and zero crossing (that is, thresholding) used by Marr [28] and his associates as a key part in turning the raw image into a "primal sketch." A more elegant version of such a chip can be achieved by carefully designing a "systolic" system [29, 30], whose whole structure of gates has been carefully designed to compute with minimum waste, in true pipeline, assembly-line fashion. Kung has developed a very fast special-purposed systolic convolution chip [31].

## Arrays of Very Large Numbers of Computers   B

A two-dimensional array of computers can be built and used to process images by having the pixels (picture elements) in an image or the entries in a matrix spread uniformly throughout their memories, so that all the array's computers can participate in processing the array of information. Assume an $N \times N$ grid of computers and an $n \times n$ image array. If $n = N$, each computer can be assigned a single pixel of the large image. If $n = kN$ ($k$ is a small integer), a $k \times k$ subarray of the image can be stored in each computer's memory.

An array multicomputer will execute instructions, and sequences of instructions, in parallel everywhere, at each processor. It can execute local window operations with extreme speed and power. It is one of the most promising candidate components of vision systems fast enough to execute in real time, and it is instructive to examine this kind of system in some detail.

### Today's Very Large Parallel Arrays  1

Several very large two-dimensional arrays of this sort have been built in recent years.

These include the $64 \times 64$ DAP (distributed array processor) designed by Reddaway [32, 33] at ICL; the $96 \times 96$ CLIP4 (cellular logic information processor), designed by Duff [34–36] at University College London; and the $128 \times 128$ MPP (massively parallel processor), designed by Batcher [37, 38] along with Schaefer [39] and others at Goodyear-Aerospace and NASA Goddard. A VLSI chip (containing roughly 100,000 devices) with an $8 \times 8$ array of processors has been fabricated by the Japanese Telephone Company [40], but an array using these chips has not yet been completed.

Each of these systems' thousands of computers executes the same instruction, but on a different set of data. The data to be processed are input to a large array (for example, the same size as the array of computers) so that each computer has one subset of those data in its own memory (for example, one

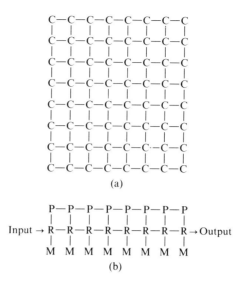

(a)

```
P—P—P—P—P—P—P—P
        |   |   |   |   |   |   |   |
Input → R—R—R—R—R—R—R—R →Output
        |   |   |   |   |   |   |   |
        M   M   M   M   M   M   M   M
```

(b)

**Fig. 10.** Arrays of computers. (a) Two-dimensional 8 × 8 array of computers, viewed from above. Each is directly linked to its four square neighbors. Each computer's processor also links directly to that computer's memory (not shown in this view), and also, via the links shown, to the memories of its four square neighbors. (b) 1 × 8 array, with each processor linked to its own memory and to input and output via registers. (Alternatively, this diagrams the 8 × 8 array viewed from one side, showing how each computer's processor in a 1 × 8 one-dimensional subarray links to its own memory and to input/output via registers.)

pixel from the total image). Each computer then operates on data stored in its own memory and also on near-neighbor data (see Fig. 10).

## 2 Earlier Arrays

CLIP and the MPP are quite similar to two earlier 32 × 32 bit arrays of 1-bit processors: the almost-completed Illiac-III [41], which was destroyed by fire, and Solomon 1 [42, 43], which was the precursor of the Illiac-IV supercomputer, an 8 × 8 array of 64-bit computers [44]. Unger [45, 46] appears to be the first person who proposed a parallel array of this sort (for pattern recognition).

The development of cellular automata by Von Neumann, Burks, Thatcher, Codd, and others [47, 48] was a major influence on the CLIP design. In sharp contrast, Reddaway designed the DAP as a number-crunching super-computer and was completely unaware of any of the other array computers or cellular automata.

An important, but somewhat smaller, precursor was Batcher's STARAN [49, 50]. STARAN was designed to be built using from 1 to 12 modules. Each module has 256 processors linked via a reconfiguring network (the "flip" network [9]) to a bank of memories. The largest STRATAN evert built had 1024 processors. A VLSI version of STARAN has recently been built to fit in a 1-ft$^3$ box in the nose of a radar surveillance airplane. This ASPRO system [51], with 32 processors plus their memories and a flip network on each chip, has 1024 processors in toto.

Following along a slightly divergent line of development, Slotnick's Solomon 1 array of 1-bit processors evolved into Solomon 2, an array of 24-bit processors, and, finally, Illiac-IV, which was designed to contain a $2 \times 2$ array of $8 \times 8$ arrays of very powerful 64-bit processors. Only one of the four $8 \times 8$ arrays was finally built. Illiac-IV was judged to be the most powerful computer running during the late 1970s—and also the most expensive computer ever built.

### Some Details as to How the Large Arrays Operate    3

The DAP and MPP link each computer to its four square neighbors. CLIP links each computer to its eight square and diagonal neighbors; CLIP (under program control) also can be reconfigured to be a hexagonal array, with each computer linked to its six surrounding neighbors.

A basic CLIP4 machine-language instruction has (in 11 μsec) every computer fetch (in parallel) and operate on information from its own memory and also from any or all of the eight immediately surrounding near-neighbor computers' memories, that is, from the $3 \times 3$ window that surrounds and includes it. This instruction is quite similar to the window operations executed by PICAP and the Cytocomputer. However, it is important to emphasize that the actual hardware embodiment is radically different since CLIP *executes the entire window operation everywhere in the array in one 11-μsec instruction*, whereas the pipeline systems must flow each pixel and its surrounding window through the sequence of processors that execute this information and thus take 30 msec or so.

The DAP and MPP do not have built-in window operations. Their basic instructions consist of "fetch–add," "fetch–or," or some other sequence of one fetch followed by an arithmetic or logic operation on that (1-bit) piece of data and a second piece of data presently in an accumulator. This means DAP and MPP must use a sequence of up to 12 operations to execute a single window operation. A basic instruction takes 250 nsec on the DAP and 100 nsec on the MPP. So a window operation that needs 4, 8, or even 12 instructions will be executed in a microsecond or two. It is important to emphasize that this operation will be executed by *several thousand different* processors during that *same* microsecond or two.

Today's arrays have from 4000 to 16,000 computers. However, well within current technology and current economics is the capability to build much larger arrays, with 256 × 256, 512 × 512, 1024 × 1024, or even more computers.

These very large arrays of many thousands of computers have become feasible largely because each computer has been made as simple as possible and all execute the same instruction (which means that only one controller is needed for the entire system).

Today's large arrays use processors that compute 1 bit at a time. This is entirely appropriate and efficient for logical operations. Logic operations include at least two very important classes of picture processing operations —those where two things (images, models, graphs, etc.) are matched; and those where several features are examined together and combined, and the resulting characteristic (often called a "label") is represented as being either "present" or "absent" at each cell.

Arithmetic and string-matching operations that must be executed on pieces of data longer than 1 bit are quite straightforwardly carried out by 1-bit processors, but only serially, 1 bit at a time, in what is called *bit-serial mode*. This means that, for example, when 8-bit, 21-bit, and 89-bit arithmetic or match operations must be executed, they will take 8, 21, and 89 times as long as the 1-bit operation. Thus, at the price of occasional 8-fold, 64-fold, or even greater degradations when large numbers and strings must be handled serially, today's arrays gain 4000-16,000-fold increases in speed. Tomorrow's systems, with hundreds of thousands or millions of computers, will achieve five, six, or even more orders of magnitude increases in speed.

## 4  The Prospect of Increasingly Large, Cheap Micromodular Arrays

Probably the most important feature of the array, a feature that will become increasingly compelling over the next 10 to 20 years, is the fact that the size of the total array can be increased with relative ease. A 512 × 512 array equals 16 128 × 128 arrays combined into one single array. Along with this come major economies of scale, since mass production savings are achieved as larger numbers of identical chips are fabricated and as larger numbers of identical boards and other modules are tied together.

Roughly, it appears that a 32 × 32 array (that is, 1024) of this kind of simple 1-bit computer will cost the same amount [52] as a single traditional 32-bit computer. This is so chiefly because, although the CPU of a conventional serial computer can fit easily on a single VLSI chip, the many millions of bits of memory that it must be given to keep it busy will need at least a small handful of additional chips.

In sharp contrast, a 200-device processor with an 800-device memory of 800 bits (these are typical sizes for 1-bit computers) should, because of its highly micromodular and simple design, pack extremely well into future

VLSI chips. So a 1,000,000-transistor chip containing a $32 \times 32$ array of 1024 such computers appears to be a reasonably conservative goal.

With future VLSI technologies these parallel arrays will almost certainly become increasingly attractive because their simple micromodular and highly iterated structure makes them especially easy to design and fabricate. By 1990 and probably before, when it becomes possible to fabricate several million devices on a single chip, it will become possible to put a relatively large $32 \times 32$ or $64 \times 64$ subarray on each chip and use only a small number of such chips to build a large array (or, as we shall see, a pyramid of arrays).

In addition, several important further parallelizations can be built into the hardware:

(1)  The entire window or other region surrounding the cell that each computer processes can be fetched and examined in parallel (as done by CLIP for the surrounding $3 \times 3$ window).

(2)  The entire transform can in many cases be further parallelized with additional hardware (for example, to evaluate in parallel the several parts in a compound and imply several acts).

(3)  $N$ processors can be placed in each cell, so that $N$ transforms can be executed in parallel.

(4)  More powerful 8-bit, 32-bit, or other-sized processors can be used (when costs have gone down sufficiently to justify this) to replace the 1-bit processors found in todays' arrays.

## Converging–Diverging Pyramid and Lattice Structures   C

An especially attractive multicomputer structure for image processing and pattern perception is a pyramid whose base is a large array, with successively smaller arrays on top of it. Pyramid architectures have been examined and designed by Dyer [53, 54], Tanimoto [55–58], Schaefer [59], and Uhr [60]. Tanimoto and Schaefer are now building such structures.

### *The Basic Pyramid Structure and Variations*   1

A pyramid can be built from a set of successively smaller arrays as follows (see Fig. 11). Each processor links to its near neighbors in its own array (usually four square neighbors, or eight square and diagonal neighbors, or six hexagonal neigbors), exactly as in an array like CLIP, DAP, or the MPP. Each processor also links to nearby offspring in the next-larger array below it (usually a $2 \times 2$ subarray of four offspring) and to one or several parent nodes in the next-smaller array above (with the exception of the top array,

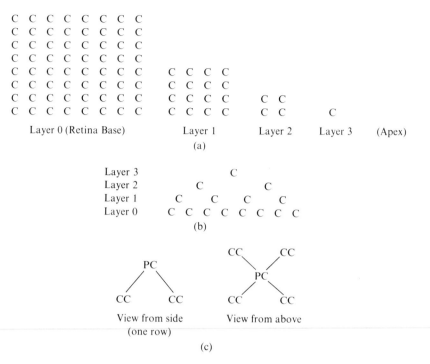

**Fig. 11.** Building a pyramid from successively smaller arrays: a four-layer pyyramid with an 8 × 8 "retinal" base and 2 × 2 convergence from each layer to the next, until a 1 × 1 "apex" is achieved. (a) Four arrays of computers are first constructed, thus forming the layers of the pyramid. (b) These array/layers are stacked, each successively smaller layer above the last (side views are given, showing only one row of each layer). (c) Computers are linked from layer to layer so that each parent (PC) has enough children (CC) so all children have parents.

which has no parents, and the bottom array, which has no children). An image array is input to the memory stores at the base of the pyramid. A pyramid can also be thought of as a tree linked at its buds to an array and (possibly) with its interior nodes linked to nearest-neighbor siblings to form interior arrays at every level (often called "ply").

A number of variations on this converging hierarchical local-neighborhood pyramid architecture are possible.

(1)  Each processor can be linked to four or eight neighbors in a square array, or to six neighbors in a hexagonal array (or, if more wires can be handled, to any desired number of other processors in a more complex topology).

(2)  Each layer, each subarray at each layer, each pyramid, or any other desired substructure of computers, can be given its own controller.

(3)  Each processor can be made more powerful, for example, 8- or 32-bit processors can be used.

(4)   As the arrays become smaller, the individual processors can be made more powerful. For example, 4-, 8-, 16-, 32-, or 64-bit processors can be used. Each can be given its own controller, for more flexibility.

(5)   At higher levels different kinds of interconnection topologies can be added to the array tree linkage or can replace them.

(6)   Processors can have more than one parent, giving "overlap."

(7)   A layer of processors can be sandwiched between two layers of memories, each processor linked to a $2 \times 2$ subarray of four (or a $3 \times 3$ subarray of nine) offspring memories and to one parent memory, or (to give overlap) four parent memories.

(8)   A network of traditional computers can be linked to pyramid nodes (probably at higher layers), or a common dual-ported memory can be used to link pyramid and network.

A pyramid architecture allows information to be converged and merged together as the image is successively transformed. It also effects an important reduction in the distances over which information is transferred and messages are passed. For example, a $1024 \times 1024$ four-square-connected array needs 2046 operations to send data or any other kind of message from one of its corners to the opposite corner. (Some arrays are augmented by linking their left row of processors to their right row and their top column to their bottom column; this cuts the worst distance to half, from 2046 to 1023. However, when a $1024 \times 1024$ array is used as the base array of a pyramid, only 20 operations are needed, since the message can be passed up to the apex of the pyramid and then back down. To state this more generally, whereas the diameter (that is, the worst-case message-passing distance) of an $N \times N$ array is $O(N)$, the diameter of a pyramid that includes that array is $O(\log N)$. It is important to emphasize that a pyramid is at most only $1/3d$ bigger.

A number of researchers have been developing computer vision systems that have multilayer converging structures of the sort that map naturally into pyramid multicomputers [61–75]. Indeed, these systems have been the primary impetus toward the specification and development of hardware pyramids.

## Augmented Pyramids   2

Pyramids can handle the wide variety of local processes typically applied at every cell in an image that array multicomputers like CLIP, DAP, and the MPP can handle so well—if only because pyramids are built from sets of successively smaller arrays. Pyramids can also handle a wide variety of other important processes, where information must be gathered together, coalesced, or abstracted.

However, there are a number of processes—especially those that appear to be useful at the higher, more cognitive levels of perception—that should be executed more independently of one another or may be inherently serial. For example, the program might be trying to recognize different objects in different regions of an image. These can be handled by executing the different processes one at a time, serially, but this would be very inefficient. OR serial procedures can be reformulated into equivalent, or near equivalent, parallel –serial pyramid procedures of appropriate power. OR/AND pyramids can be augmented with additional appropriate hardware (e.g., a network of appropriately configured computers, each more independent and more powerful). For examinations of pyramid augmentations, see Ahuja and Swami [76] and Uhr [52, 77–79].

## VI  (HOPED TO BE) GENERALLY USABLE ARCHITECTURES

The structures examined so far have all been designed for specific types of problems. Each tends to have a particular more or less specialized structure and an overall control that coordinates and synchronizes the individual computers. A far larger set of possibilities opens up when separate computers are linked and asked to work together on the same problem—but without any built-in overall control. These will be examined now.

## A  The Enormous Variety of Possible Asynchronous Network Structures

Because of the limits on arrays (which, ultimately, are imposed by considerations of costs)—their 1-bit processors, the single controller, and the near-neighbor connectivity between processors—and the specialized aspects of other more or less synchronized designs such as pipelines, systolic systems, and pyramids, many people would prefer to see other kinds of asynchronous networks built. A large number of asynchronous networks have been described or designed, including variations on the ring, star, cluster, clustered clusters, snowflake, lens, $N$-cube, lattice, tree, $X$-tree, hypertree, and a variety of other graph structures [6, 52, 80, 81].

However, very few such networks have actually been built. Only two have more than 50 processors: Cm* [82], a cluster of clusters, and the Genoa machine [83], which flows information through an appropriately structured network to read portions of addresses on envelopes for the Postal Service. Trees have been suggested by several researchers [84–88]. Trees augmented with additional links (usually at the leaves but often at a middle interior level) that really turn them into graphs with cycles are being investigated by a number of people [89–91]. *N*-cubes have been examined by Wittie [92], Sullivan *et al.* [93], Preparata and Vuillemin [94], and others.

The possibilities for different topologies are in fact potentially infinite since they include all conceivable interconnections among (as technology continues to improve and grow cheaper) a continually growing number of processor components, that is, all possible graphs. However, the problems are enormous. Today people are just beginning to attack the very difficult problems of designing such multicomputers; developing parallel algorithms, programming and mapping these algorithms properly into the network, and coordinating the many different processors that are executing the same program to work with reasonable efficiency (see Uhr [52] for an examination of these interrelated aspects of the problem).

### *Criteria for Evaluating Topologies* **1**

Not merely the relatively small handful that have been explored or proposed so far but *any* *N*-node graph can form the basis of an *N*-node multicomputer topology. It is not at all clear how to evaluate and choose among this enormous set of possible topologies. The most common criterion that researchers have suggested [95] is the minimization of the diameter (the longest shortest distance between processors). A variant on this is the minimization of the average distance [90]. Other criteria that have been suggested include easy addressibility and finding of alternative paths, connectivity (the minimum number of vertices that can be eliminated before the graph is disconnected), edge connectivity (the minimum number of edges that can be eliminated before the graph is disconnected), and various symmetries.

Topologies are often judged chiefly on the basis of diameter distance (possible simply because that is the most common measure, and a good bit is known about it), but almost certainly preferable is average distance, or even a weighted average that emphasizes nearby distances, on the assumption that most interactions in a well-structured program that is properly mapped into an appropriately structured network [52, 96] will be between near neighbors, if not nearest neighbors.

*N*-cubes, which are often characterized as quite dense and desirable from this point of view, are actually rather poor. In contrast, trees are among the denser known topologies. And augmented trees (A-trees), e.g., *X*-trees, hypertrees, Moore graphs, and De Bruijn networks, are among the very densest known. The lens [97] has the same topology as a reconfiguring network where a processor replaces each of the $M \log N$ switches. It is a reasonably good topology from the point of view of density, although not one of the best.

## 2  *Approaching Optimal Graphs*

There is actually an upper bound, the Moore bound [98, 99], on the minimum diameter of a graph with a given number of nodes and a given degree:

$$N_{(d,k)} = (d(d-1)^k - 2)/(d-1) \qquad (d > 2)$$

where $N$ is the number of nodes, $d$ the degree, and $k$ the diameter. This is most simply visualized by starting with a tree that has $d$ links from each and every node (except the leaves, which have 1 link, and the root, which can have either $d$ or $d - 1$ links) and has all leaves equidistant from the root. The distance from any leaf to the root is the tree's "radius." The diameter of such a tree is twice the radius since for some pairs of leaves the only path goes through the root. The Moore bound states that if we add links until all leaves have $d$ rather than 1 link, at best the diameter can be reduced to the radius.

It turns out that only three nontrivial graphs can possibly achieve this Moore bound—one with 10 nodes, degree 3, and diameter 2; one with 50 nodes, degree 7, and diameter 2; and one that may exist but has not yet been discovered, with 3250 nodes, degree 57, and diameter 2.

The 10- and 50-node graphs are relatively small and are attractive candidates for several purposes.

(1)   Each might be used for a small network.

(2)   Each might be used to augment some other type of network (e.g., a pyramid or an array) or as part of a larger heterogenous network.

(3)   Each might be compounded into a larger compound-of-compounds topology. For example, 51 copies of (7, 2) will compound into a graph with 2550 nodes, degree 8, and diameter 5, which is the densest graph yet discovered for (8, 5).

The densest known graphs for more than a few thousand nodes [100] is the de Bruijn network [101]. A number of other new, dense graphs have been discovered in the past few years [102]. It seems likely that these discoveries will continue, since except for very small graphs with fewer than 100 or so nodes, the best graphs discovered to date are far smaller than the Moore bound (which is probably an overbound, but it remains the best bound that we have).

These kinds of asynchronous networks raise extremely difficult and as yet little understood problems, revolving around the transmission of information from one computer to another. Systems that use a single controller (e.g., arrays) or in other ways synchronize all computers (e.g., pipelines and ZMOB) evade most of these problems. To demonstrate the severity of the problem, in today's asynchronous multicomputers the operating system executes many thousands of instructions to transmit a packet of information, where each packet is typically on the order of 1–80, or occasionally up to

2000 bytes [3, 92, 103–105]. Thus, it takes thousands of times longer to transmit information than to operate upon that information. In striking contrast, in a synchronous array each computer can receive information from one (or in the case of the CLIP array any subset) of its 4, 6, or 8 nearest neighbors in one instruction time. Essentially what is often called "message passing" is reduced to the same speed and virtually the same operation as a "fetch."

### Toward Asynchronous Networks with Millions of Computers    B

Several researchers have proposed building "mega-micronetworks" [104] containing millions of computers each. Wittie [92, 104] and Sullivan *et al.* [93] were among the first to point out that such enormous sizes may soon be technologically feasible and are desirable for a variety of important applications. Wittie's Micronet is a 20-cube, Sullivan's system is a 17-cube with each node a cluster of 8 computers. Wittie designed and built a 16-computer prototype system; Sullivan's system has, apparently, not yet been started.

More recently, Wittie has lowered his sights. He appears to feel that a thousand or so computers is all that might be realistically feasible—apparently chiefly because of the complexity of each of his computers.

Schaefer and Strong [106] proposed an optical computer made from fiber optics with 10,000 processors in each of 10,000 bundles. This proved to be technologically unfeasible for the state of the art at that time; but it led to the design and construction of the MPP. They then proposed that a next generation super-MPP might be built using VLSI with a large MPP array of 1-bit computers on a single wafer and a whole stack of wafers forming a three-dimensional multicomputer. Thus, for example, 100 wafers might be used to pipeline images through successive $128 \times 128$ or larger arrays.

Hillis [107] and Christman [108] have proposed "connection machines" with millions of computers. These systems appear to be designed to attempt to handle a wide range of problems, including image processing, computer vision, and semantic memory searches of the sort Fahlman's 1979 NETL is designed to handle [109]. It appears that a full connection machine is intended to be $1024 \times 1024$ array (much like an MPP) that is also linked into a 14-cube. Apparently 64 processors will be fabricated on a chip, with each chip forming one node of the 14-cube, and with the 64 processors on each chip linked over a cross-bar switch. All processors appear to be 1-bit, each with only a small local memory, apparently all working in single-instruction completely synchronized lock-step mode, but with message-passing periods interspersed between processing periods. These message-passing intervals are apparently expected to take thousands of times longer than processing instructions, so it appears a conventional multicomputer operating system is planned.

Shaw [91] has described the ultimate version of his non-Von multicomputer as consisting of millions of computers. The general architecture of the non-Von is a binary tree whose size will be determined by the number of computers (each with an 8-bit processor and a relatively small amount, probably a few hundred bits, of memory) that can be fabricated onto a single chip. Input/output to the chip will be through the root of this local tree. (Stolfo [110] is developing a similar tree structure to handle expert production systems.)

## VII TOWARD GENERALLY USABLE ALGORITHM-STRUCTURED ARCHITECTURES

The systems designed to be generally usable are excessively slow. The algorithm-structured systems can be very wasteful where not appropriate. There are several virtually unexplored possibilities for combining their advantages only.

## A Reconfiguring Switches to Enrich Structures

Reconfiguring switches can play a number of potentially very important purposes, in addition to shuffling data between two sets of nodes.

### 1 Local, Partial Reconfiguring

Reconfiguring networks have primarily been used in $N \log N$ banks of switches to allow $N$ pieces of information to be shuffled around among $N$ major components (computers, processors, memories), as just described. However, much smaller sets of switches can also be interspersed, at a variety of levels, to effect some partial reconfiguration.

Possibly the simplest example is the CLIP array, which can be reconfigured, under programmer control, so that each cell is directly linked to either eight square + diagonal neighbors or six hexagonal neighbors. This turns out to be very easy to do, since a square array becomes a hexagonal array if the odd rows are shifted by $\frac{1}{2}$ column, as shown in Fig. 12a. Another interesting example is a tree that can be reconfigured into an array, as shown Fig. 12b. In VLSI chips trees are often embedded (with more regularity) into square arrays.

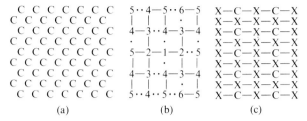

```
C  C  C  C  C  C  C      5··4—5··6—5        X—C—X—C—X
C  C  C  C  C  C  C      |  |  |   ·  |      X—X—X—X—X
  C  C  C  C  C  C  C    4—3··4—3—4         X—C—X—C—X
C  C  C  C  C  C  C         ·  |  ·  |  ·   X—X—X—X—X
  C  C  C  C  C  C  C    5—2—1—2··5         X—C—X—C—X
C  C  C  C  C  C  C      |  |  ·  |  |      X—X—X—X—X
  C  C  C  C  C  C  C    4—3··4—3—4         X—C—X—C—X
C  C  C  C  C  C  C      |  |  |   ·  |      X—X—X—X—X
  C  C  C  C  C  C  C    5··4··5··6—5        X—C—X—C—X
         (a)                  (b)                (c)
```

**Fig. 12.** Examples of local switches for partial reconfiguring. (a) Square–hexagonal array (links between computers are not shown). (b) Array–tree ( · indicates array; — and | indicate tree links). (c) Blue chip grid [X indicates switches, where an array of switches surrounds an array of computers (vertical links are not shown)].

The Blue Chip system [111] reconfigures at still another level. Here an array of computers, much like CLIP, DAP, or the MPP, has a row of switches between each of its rows and a column of switches between each of its columns (in toto forming an array of switches), as shown in Fig. 12c.

## Partial Reconfiguring at the Global Level    2

Siegel's [16, 17] PASM makes very interesting uses of reconfiguring at several levels. The full 1024-processor PASM will have 64 controllers and a capability to reconfigure the linkages between controllers and processors so that a variety of different groupings can be made. In addition, the basic linkages between processors is also effected via a reconfiguring network.

This means that many different topologies and data flows can be achieved. For example, PASM can emulate an array by assigning subarrays of a large image to different processors and passing data from one to another as needed over the reconfiguring network. PASM can also emulate a pyramid simply by passing information originally processed by four different computers to a single computer (reducing it along the way). In general, PASM appears to combine many of the virtues of the synchronized, specialized structures like arrays and pyramids with asynchronous systems like Cm* and Crystal. It appears to minimize the message-passing problems and delays of the asynchronous systems.

## Information Flowed through an Appropriately Structured Network    B

A very attractive concept is the following: use a data-flow programming language to build a "data-flow graph" that shows exactly how processes will operate on and transmit data. Ideally, the program would actually be executed by flowing information through a multicomputer with an isomorphic configuration. Unfortunately, today that can be done in only a few very simple situations. A pipeline can effect this kind of process, but only when the stream of information and transformations forms a simple line. Other examples are an array that carries out a sequence of local operations and a pyramid that pipes and transforms a sequence of moving images. A good traditional example is a structure of gates carefully designed for fast execution of some basic function (e.g., a parallel adder). Good examples in VLSI design are the special-purpose systolic chips [29–31], where data are pumped into an appropriate structure of gates that computes the results and pumps out answers.

However, all these examples require carefully and appropriately structured if not special-purpose hardware, and they assume that this hardware will be dedicated to a steady, continuing stream of appropriately structured information. The ideal would be a topology for the hardware that was general enough so that most, if not all, of the programs' data-flow topologies could easily be embedded in it. Such complete generality would not be necessary; such a system might contain local reconfiguring switches that could change the hardware topology as needed, and, of course, if perfect mappings cannot be achieved the system would still work, at the cost of lower efficiency.

It would appear to be extremely difficult to achieve such general structures. For the general case the operating system would have to figure out how to embed any graph into any other graph, using reconfiguring switches that we had figured out how to add that would change any graph to any other graph. However, it may well be that a relatively small number of basic structures can be used to compose the much larger and more complex structures needed for most programs, and that if these were known they would be desirable structures to use.

For example, at the moment only a surprisingly small number of structures appear to have special virtues—arrays for local operations, trees for broadcasting and converging information, reconfiguring networks for shuffling, systems based on lines and polygons for piping and circulating information, but virtually nothing has been done to date to try to find good basic structures and techniques to combine them into larger data-flow structures, map data-flow program graphs into appropriately structured multicomputer hardware, and partially reconfigure one hardware topology into another.

## C   Different Kinds of Gradiented and Heterogeneous Systems

To the extent that different kinds of specialized architectures appear to be indicated for different perceptual or cognitive functions, it would appear that an integrated hardware system capable of computing these several different functions might best be specialized in one way in one region of the multicomputer and in a different way in another. Several such systems have been designed, including the following.

McCormick's Illiac-III [41] was planned to combine three different types of computer: (a) the two-dimensional array described earlier (for image processing), (b) a conventional CPU (designed to handle statistical and numerical problems), and (c) a list-processing computer (designed to manipulate symbolic information structured into graphs).

An attractive design for a pyramid is some variant on the following. At the lowest retinal layer there is a large array of 1-bit processors, all synchronized to execute the same instruction stream (since nothing is yet known about the sensed image, there is no reason to do different things in different regions). Moving up through the layers of the pyramid, computers can gradually be made more and more powerful, for example, using 4-bit, 8-bit, 16-bit, and 32-bit processors. The number of controllers per layer can go up, with each controller responsible for a smaller and smaller subarray, subpyramid, or other substructure, until each processor has a separate controller.

Pyramids augmented with networks of more powerful and more independent computers are still another good example of heterogeneous systems. Here the two might be linked directly to one another or via an $N \log N$ reconfiguring network. An attractive local use of an $N \log N$ network might be to link local subarrays together and to link the nodes within a subarray.

Several special-purpose systolic chips might be combined into a general-purpose total system, in any of the following ways.

(1)   Add these chips to a serial computer's high-speed bus.

(2)   Build a network whose nodes are systolic chips, each type scattered uniformly throughout.

(3)   Build a network whose nodes are specialized sets of systolic chips; send information to be processed to a chip in the appropriate node.

## THE MAJOR TYPES OF PARALLEL ARCHITECTURES SUMMARIZED   VIII

The following attempts to categorize and summarize the major types of parallel architectures, both those already developed and future possibilities.

(1)   A super-1-CPU computer might be specialized for image processing and pattern perception.

(2)   A small number (up to a few dozen) of conventional computers or supercomputers might be linked over a cross bar, bus, ring, or reconfiguring network into a (virtual) complete graph.

(3)   A serial pipeline of processors can be used to iteratively execute complex sequence of operations.

(4)   An array of computers can be built with each computer linked to its near neighbors.

(5)   A network can be constructed with potentially any number of computers. Among the topologies people have found most interesting are $N$-cubes, trees, and augmented trees (e.g., $X$-trees and de Bruijn networks).

(6)   An especially important topology is a cluster of clusters, used so that communication between clusters is rare.

(7)   A pyramid can be built that combines the good near-neighbor properties of the array with the diverging–converging capabilities of a tree.

(8)   A pyramid (or an array) can be augmented with a network of asynchronous computers.

(9)   A more of less special-purpose systolic system can be used to transform information pipeline flowed through it.

(10)   Micromodular processors might be used in a network reminiscent of the brain's many synapsing neurons.

(11)   Partial reconfiguring can be used, globally and/or locally, to reconfigure the system from one set of basic structures to another.

(12)   Structures might contain different types of substructures, either scattered throughout or concentrated in different regions.

(13)   Data-flow networks might be constructed, and information flowed through them. It seems likely that partial reconfiguring capabilities are needed to achieve the necessary adaptability.

The only hope of massively parallel multicomputers, capable of the million-fold speedups needed to perceive scenes of moving objects in real time, appears to lie in developing systems in which many different more or less independent processors work in parallel. Traditional serial computers can have small amounts of parallel capabilities, as in the parallel fetch and operation on a 32-bit word. Pipelines can make good use of a few dozen, or even a few hundred, processors working in parallel; but it seems unlikely that programs can be achieved that keep substantially larger numbers busy. Arrays and pyramids appear to be the simplest structures to build to massively parallel size. A wide variety of other topologies are possible, but at least today they must either be carefully designed for a special problem or the need to coordinate processors degrades performance substantially. Topologies are needed that can be reconfigured to different algorithms.

## REFERENCES

1.  D. J. Kuck, "The Structure of Computers and Computation," Vol. 1. Wiley, New York, 1978.
2.  R. D. Etchells, J. Grinberg, and G. R. Nudd, The development of a novel three-dimensional microelectronic processor with ultrahigh performance, *Proc. Soc. Photo-Optical Instrumentation Engin.* (1981).

3. D. J. DeWitt, R. Finkel, and M. Solomon, The CRYSTAL multicomputer: design and implementation experience, *Computer Sci. Dept. Tech. Rept.*, Univ. of Wisconsin, Madison, 1984.

4. D. J. Farber and K. C. Larson, The system architecture of the distributed computer system—the communications system, *Symposium on Computer Networks*, Polytechnic Institute of Brooklyn, New York, April, 1972.

5. W. A. Wulf and C. G. Bell, C.mmp—a multi-mini processor, *Proc. AFIPS NCC, 41 part II*, 765–777 (1972).

6. K. Hwang and F. A. Briggs, "Computer Architecture and Parallel Processing." McGraw-Hill, New York, 1984.

7. L. C. Widdoes, The S-1 project: developing high-speed digital computers, *Proc. Compon 80*, 282–291 (1980).

8. C. Rieger, J. Bane, and R. Trigg, A highly parallel multiprocessor, *Proc. IEEE Workshop on Picture Data Description and Management*, pp. 298–304 (1980).

9. K. E. Batcher, The flip network in STARAN, *Proc. 1976 Int. Conf. on Parallel Processing*, pp. 65–71 (1976).

10. M. C. Pease, The indirect binary *n*-cube microprocessor array, *IEEE Trans. Computers* **26**, 458–473 (1977).

11. H. J. Siegel, A model of SIMD machines and a comparison of various interconnection networks, *IEEE Trans. Computers* **28**, 907–917 (1979).

12. H. J. Siegel, "Interconnection Networks for Large Scale Parallel Processing." Lexington, Lexington, Massachusetts, 1984.

13. V. E. Benes, "Mathematical Theory of Connecting Networks and Telephone Traffic." Academic Press, New York, 1965.

14. J. Lipovski, On a varistructured array of microprocessors, *IEEE Trans. Computers* **26**, 125–138 (1977).

15. G. J. Lipovski and A. Tripathi, A reconfigurable varistructure array processor, *Proc. 1977 Int. Conf. on Parallel Processing*, 165–174 (1977).

16. H. J. Siegel, PASM: a reconfigurable multimicrocomputer system for image processing, *in* "Languages and Architectures for Image Processing" (M. J. B. Duff and S. Levialdi, eds), pp. 257–265. Academic Press, New York, 1981; PASM: A partitionable multimicrocomputer, SIMD/MIMD system for image processing and pattern recognition, *TR-EE* 79-40, School of Electrical Engineering, Purdue Univ., West Lafayette, Indiana, 1979.

17. F. Briggs, K. S. Fu, K. Hwang, and J. Patel, PMY—a reconfigurable multimicroprocessor system for pattern recognition and image processing, *Proc. AFIPS NCC*, 255–265 (1979).

18. J. T. Schwartz, Ultra-Computers, *ACM Trans. Programming Languages and Systems* **2**, 484–521 (1980).

19. R. M. Russell, The Cray-1 computer system, *Comm. ACM* **21**, 63–72 (1978).

20. S. S. Chen, J. J. Dongarra, and C. Hsiung, Multiprocessing linear algebra algorithms on the CRAY X-MP-2, *J. Parallel Distributed Computing* **1**, 22–31 (1984).

21. E. W. Kozdrowicki and D. J. Thies, Second generation of vector supercomputers, *Computers* **13**, 71–83 (November 1980).

22. B. Kruse, A parallel picture processing machine, *IEEE Trans. Computers* **22**, 1075–1087 (1973).

23. B. Kruse, The PICAP picture processing laboratory, *Proc. IJCPR-3*, **4**, 875–881 (1976).

24. B. Kruse, Experience with a picture processor in pattern recognition processing, *Proc. AFIPS NCC*, pp. 1015–1022 (1976).

25. B. Kruse, System architecture for image analysis. *in* "Structured Computer Vision: Machine Perception through Hierarchical Computation Structures" (S. Tanimoto and A. Klinger, (eds.), pp. 169–212. Academic Press, New York, 1980.

26. S. R. Sternberg, Cytocomputer real-time pattern recognition, paper presented at *8th Pattern Recognition Symp.*, National Bureau of Standards, 1978.

27. S. R. Sternberg, Language and architecture for parallel image processing, *Proc. Conf. on Pattern Recognition in Practice* (E. S. Gelsema and L. N. Kanal, eds.). North-Holland Publ., Amsterdam, 1980.

28. D. Marr, "Vision." Freeman, San Francisco, California, 1982.

29. H. T. Kung, Special-purpose devices for signal and image processing: an opportunity in VLSI, *Computer Sci. Dept. Tech. Rept.* 80-132, *Carnegie-Mellon Univ., Pittsburgh, Pennsylvania,* 1980.

30. H. T. Kung and M. S. Lam, Wafer-scale integration and two-level pipelined implementations of systolic arrays, *J. Parallel and Distributed Computing* **1**, 32–63 (1984).

31. H. T. Kung and S. W. Song, A systolic 2-d convolution chip, *in* "Multi-Computer Algorithms for Image Processing" (K. Preston, Jr., and L. Uhr, eds.), 373–384. Academic Press, New York, 1982.

32. S. F. Reddaway, DAP—a flexible number cruncher, *Proc. 1978 LASL Workshop on Vector and Parallel Processors, Los Alamos,* pp. 233–234 (1978).

33. S. F. Reddaway, Revolutionary array processors, in "Electronics to Microelectronics" (W. A. Kaiser and W. E. Proebster eds.), pp. 730–734. North-Holland Publ., Amsterdam, 1980.

34. M. J. B. Duff, CLIP4: a large scale integrated circuit array parallel processor, *Proc. IJCPR-3* **4**, 728–733 (1976).

35. M. J. B. Duff, Review of the CLIP image processing system, *Proc. AFIPS NCC,* pp. 1055–1060 (1978).

36. M. J. B. Duff, "Parallel algorithms and their influence on the specification of application problems, *in* "Multi-Computer Algorithms and Image Processing" (K. Preston, Jr., and L. Uhr, eds.), pp. 261–274. Academic Press, New York, 1982.

37. K. E. Batcher, Design of a massively parallel processor, *IEEE Trans. Computers* **29**, 836–840 (1980).

38. K. E. Batcher, Bit-serial parallel processing systems, *IEEE Trans. Computers* **31**, 377–384 (1982).

39. D. H. Schaefer, J. R. Fischer, and K. R. Wallgren, The massively parallel processor, *J. Guidance, Control and Dynamics,* 5 (1982).

40. T. Kondo, T. Nakashima, M. Aoki, and T. Sudo, An LSI adaptive array processor, *IEEE J. Solid-State Circuits* **18**, 147–155 (1983).

41. B. H. McCormick, The Illinois pattern recognition computer ILLIAC III, *IEEE Trans. Computers* **12**, 791–813 (1963).

42. D. L. Slotnik, W. C. Borck, and R. C. McReynolds, The Solomon computer, *Proc. AFIPS FJCC,* 97–107 (1962).

43. J. Gregory and M. McReynolds, The SOLOMON computer, *IEEE Trans. Computers* **12**, 774–780 (1963).

44. G. H. Barnes, R. M. Brown, M. Kato, D. J. Kuck, D. L. Slotnick, and R. A. Stokes, The ILLIAC IV computer, *IEEE Trans. Computers* **17**, 746–757 (1968).

45. S. H. Unger, A computer oriented toward spatial problems, *Proc. IRE* **46**, 1744–1750 (1958).

46. S. H. Unger, Pattern detection and recognition, *Proc. IRE* **47**, 1732–1752 (1959).

47. A. Burks, (ed.), "Theory of Self-Reproduction Automata." Univ. of Illinois Press, Urbanna, 1966.

48. E. F. Codd, "Cellular Automata." Academic Press, New York, 1968.

49. K. E. Batcher, STARAN/RADCAP hardware architecture, *Proc. 1973 Sagamore Computer Conf. on Parallel Processing,* pp. 147–152 (1973).

50. K. E. Batcher, STARAN parallel processor system hardware, *Proc. AFIPS NCC* **43**, 405–410 (1974).

51. Anonymous, Untitled unpublished paper on ASPRO, Goodyear-Aerospace, Akron, Ohio, 1979.

52. L. Uhr, "Algorithm-Structured Computer Arrays and Networks: Architectures and Processes for Images, Percepts and Information." Academic Press, New York, 1984.

53. C. R. Dyer, A quadtree machine for parallel image processing, *Information Engin. Dept. Tech. Rept.* KSL 51, University of Illinois at Chicago, 1981.

54. C. R. Dyer, Pyramid algorithms and machines, *in* "Multicomputers and Image Processing" (K. Preston and L. Uhr, eds.), pp. 409–420. Academic Press, New York, 1982.

55. S. L. Tanimoto, Towards hierarchical cellular logic: design considerations for pyramid machines, *Computer Science Dept. Tech. Rept.* 81-02-01, Univ. of Washington, Seattle, 1981.

56. S. L. Tanimoto, Programming techniques for hierarchical image processors, *in* "Multi-Computer Algorithms and Image Processing (K. Preston, Jr., and L. Uhr, eds.), pp. 421–429. Academic Press, New York, 1982.

57. S. L. Tanimoto, A pyramidal approach to parallel processing, *Proc. 10th Annual Intl. Symposium on Computer Architecure, Stockholm,* pp. 372–378 (1983).

58. S. L. Tanimoto, A hierarchical cellular logic for pyramid computers, *J. Parallel and Distributed Computing* 1, 105–132 (1984).

59. D. H. Schaefer, A pyramid of MPP processing elements—experiences and plans, *Proc. 18th Int. Conf. on System Sciences, Honolulu* (1985).

60. L. Uhr, Converging pyramids of arrays, *Proc. Workshop on Computer Architecture for Pattern Analysis and Image Data Base Management,* pp. 31–34 IEEE Computer Society Press (1981).

61. A. R. Hanson and E. M. Riseman, Pre-processing cones: a computational structure for scene analysis, *COINS Tech. Rept.* 74C-7, Univ. of Massachusetts, Amherst, 1974.

62. A. R. Hanson and E. M. Riseman, A progress report on VISIONS, *COINS Tech. Rept.* 76-79, Univ. of Massachusetts, Amherst, 1976.

63. A. R. Hanson and E. M. Riseman, Visions: A computer system for interpreting scenes, *in* "Computer Vision Systems" (A. R. Hanson and E. M. Riseman, eds.), pp. 303–334. Academic Press, New York, 1978.

64. A. R. Hanson and E. M. Riseman, Processing cones: a computational structure for image analysis, *in* "Structured Computer Vision" (S. L. Tanimoto and A. Klinger, eds.), pp. 101–131. Academic Press, New York, 1980.

65. M. D. Levine, A knowledge-based computer vision system, *in* "Computer Vision Systems" (A. Hanson and E. Riseman, eds.), pp. 335–352. Academic Press, New York, 1978.

66. M. D. Levine, Region analysis with a pyramid data structure, *in* "Structured Computer Vision," (S. L. Tanimoto and A. Klinger, eds.), pp. 57–100. Academic Press, New York, 1980.

67. S. L. Tanimoto, Pictorial feature distortion in a pyramid, *Comp. Graphics Image Proc.* 5, 333–352 (1976).

68. S. L. Tanimoto, Regular hierarchical image and processing structures in machine vision, *in* "Computer Vision Systems" (A. R. Hanson and E. M. Riseman, eds.), pp. 165–174. Academic Press, New York, 1978.

69. S. L. Tanimoto, Algorithms for median filtering of images on a pyramid machine, *in* "Computing Structures for Image Processing," (M. J. B. Duff, ed.), pp. 123–141. Academic Press, London, 1983.

70. L. Uhr, Layered "recognition cone" networks that preprocess, classify and describe, *IEEE Trans. Computers* 21, 758–768 (1972).

71. L. Uhr, "Recognition cones" that perceive and describe scenes that move and change over time, *Proc. Intl. Joint Conf. on Pattern Recognition,* 4, 287–293 (1976).

72. L. Uhr, "Recognition cones" and some test results, *in* "Computer Vision Systems" (A. Hanson and E. Riseman, eds.), pp. 363–372. Academic Press, New York, 1978.

73. Nevin, Chin and Dyer, (1984).

74. S. Tanimoto and A. Klinger, (eds), "Structured Computer Vision." Academic Press, New York, 1980.

75. A. Rosenfeld, (ed.), "Multi-Resolution Systems for Image Processing." North-Holland Publ., Amsterdam, 1984.

76. N. Ahuja and S. Swami, Multiprocessor pyramid architectures for bottom-up image analysis, *in* "Multiresolution Image Processing and Analysis" (A. Rosenfeld, ed.), pp. 38 59. Springer-Verlag, Berlin, 1984.

77. L. Uhr, Pyramid multi-computer structures, and augmented pyramids, *in* "Computing Structures for Image Processing" (M. Duff, ed.), pp. 95 112. Academic Press, London, 1983.

78. L. Uhr, Augmenting pyramids and arrays by compounding them with networks, *Proc. Workshop on Computer Architectures for Pattern Analysis and Image Data Base Management*, pp. 162 169. IEEE Computer Society Press (1983).

79. L. Uhr, Pyramid multi-computers, and extensions and augmentations, *in* "Algorithmically Specialized Parallel Computers" (L. Snyder, L. M. Jamieson, D. B. Gronnon, and H. J. Siegel, eds.), Academic Press, New York, 1984, pp. 177 186.

80. K. J. Thurber, "Large Scale Computer Architecture." Hayden, Rochelle Park, New Jersey, 1976.

81. H. S. Stone, (ed.), "Introduction to Computer Architecture." SRA, Chicago, 1980.

82. R. J. Swan, S. H. Fuller, and D. P. Siewiorek, Cm* A modular, multi-microprocessor, *Proc. AFIPS NCC*, pp. 637 663 (1977).

83. R. Manara and L. Stringa, The EMMA system: An industrial experience on a multiprocessor, *in* "Languages and Architectures for Image Processing" (M. J. B. Duff and S. Levialdi, eds.). Academic Press, London, 1981.

84. W. Handler, A unified associative and Von Neumann processor EGPP and EGPP array, *in* "Lecture Notes in Computer Science Parallel Processing," pp. 97 99, Springer-Verlag, Berlin and New York, 1975.

85. W. Handler, Aspects of parallelism in computer architecture, *in* "Parallel Computers Parallel Mathematics" (M. Feilmeier, ed.). Intl. Assoc. for Mathematics and Computers in Simulation, 1977.

86. W. Handler, H. Schreiber, and V. Sigmund, Computation structures reflected in general purpose and special purpose multiprocessor systems, *Proc. 1979 Int. Conf. on Parallel Processing*, pp. 95 102 (1979).

87. S. A. Browning, The tree machine: a highly concurrent programming environment, Unpublished Ph.D. dissertation, Computer Science Dept., California Inst. Technology, 1980.

88. G. A. Mago, A cellular computer architecture for functional programming, *Proc. COMPCON Spring 1980*, pp. 179 187 (1980).

89. A. M. Despain and D. A. Patterson, X-tree: a tree structured multi-processor computer archotecure, *Proc. 5th Ann. Symp. Computer Arch.*, pp. 144 151 (1978).

90. J. R. Goodman and C. H. Sequin, Hypertree, a multiprocessor interconnection topology, *Computer Sci. Dept. Tech. Rept.* 427, Univ. of Wisconsin, Madison, 1981.

91. D. W. Shaw, The NON-VON Supercomputer, *Computer Sci. Dept. Tech. Rept.*, Columbia University, August 1982.

92. L. D. Wittie, MICRONET: A reconfigurable microcomputer network for distributed systems research, *Simulation* 31, 145 153 (1978).

93. H. Sullivan, T. Bashkov, and D. Klappholz, A large scale, homogeneous, fully distributed parallel machine. *Proc. 4th Annu. Symp. on Computer Arch.*, pp. 105 124 (1977).

94. F. P. Preparata and J. Vuillemin, The cube-connected-cycles: a versatile network for parallel computation, *Proc. 20th Ann. Symp. on Foundations of Computer Sci.*, pp. 140 147 (1979).

95. R. A. Finkel and M. H. Solomon, Processor interconnection strategies, *Computer Sci. Dept. Tech. Rept.* 301, Univ. of Wisconsin, Madison, 1977.

96. S. H. Bokhari, On the mapping problem, *IEEE Trans. Computers* 30, 207 214 (1981).

97. R. A. Finkel and M. H. Solomon, The Lens interconnection strategy, *Computer Sci. Dept. Tech. Rept.* 387, Univ. of Wisconsin, Madison, 1980.

98. A. J. Hoffman and R. R. Singleton, On Moore graphs with diameter 2 and 3, *IBM J. Res. Devel.* **4**, 497 504 (1960).

99.  J. A. Bondy and U. S. R. Murty, "Graph Theory with Applications." Elsevier, New York, 1976.

100.  M. Imase and M. Itoh, Design to minimize diameter on building-block network, *IEEE Trans. Computers* **30**, 439–442 (1981).

101.  D. G. De Bruijn, A combinatorial problem, *Koninklijke Nederlandsche Academie van wetenschappen et Amsterdam, Proc. Section of Sciences* **49**, 7, 758–764 (1946).

102.  J-C. Bermond, C. Delorme, and J.-J. Quisquater, Grands graphes non diriges de degre et diameter fixes, *Technical Report*, Phillips Research Laboratory, Brussels, Belgium, 1982.

103.  R. A. Finkel and M. H. Solomon, The Arachne kernel, *Computer Sci. Dept. Tech. Rept.* 380, Univ. of Wisconsin, 1980.

104.  L. D. Wittie, Efficient message routing in mega-micro-computer networks, *Proc. 3rd Annu. Symp. on Computer Arch., New York*, IEEE (1976).

105.  L. D. Wittie and A. M. van Tilborg, MICROS, a distributed operating system for MICRONET, a reconfigurable network computer, *IEEE Trans. Computers* **29**, 1133–1144 (1980).

106.  D. H. Schaeffer and J. P. Strong, TSE Computers, *Proc. IEEE* **65**, 129–38 (1977).

107.  W. D. Hillis, The connection machine, *A. I. Memo* 646, MIT AI Lab., 1981.

108.  D. P. Christman, Programming the connection machine, unpublished M.S. thesis, Dept. of Electrical Engineering and Computer Science, MIT, Cambridge, Massachusetts, 1984.

109.  S. Fahlman, "NETL: a System for Representing and Using Real-World Knowledge." MIT Press, Cambridge, Massachusetts, 1979.

110.  S. Stolfo and D. Miranker, DADO: A parallel processor for expert systems, *Proc. 1984 Intl. Conf. Parallel Proc.*, IEEE Comp. Soc. Press, 1984.

111.  L. Snyder, Introduction to the configurable highly parallel computer, *IEEE Computer*, 47–64 (January 1982).

# Chapter **19**

# VLSI Array Architecture for Pattern Analysis and Image Processing

TZAY Y. YOUNG and PHILIP S. LIU

Department of Electrical and Computer Engineering
University of Miami
Coral Gables, Florida

## INTRODUCTION I

With recent advances in VLSI technology, it is feasible to fabricate hundreds of thousands of switching devices on a single chip. Computation throughput can be increased significantly by parallel processing and pipe-lining, using specially designed VLSI chips for applications that require extensive computation.

A digital image consists of the gray levels of a large number of pixels, and many image processing operations are performed repeatedly over the pixels.

471

The major functions of image processing systems may be divided into four categories, preprocessing, segmentation, description and recognition. Both preprocessing and segmentation are high throughput operations, processing speed can be improved significantly by parallel processing and pipelining. Description and recognition require sophisticated techniques to perform feature extraction, region description, scene analysis, and object identification by statistical or syntactic methods. VLSI algorithms and arrays for pattern recognition have received attention in recent years. The arrays are special-purpose devices that can be attached or interfaced to a host computer system through the system bus.

## II  VLSI ARRAY ARCHITECTURE

VLSI architecture and design are based on the following principles and considerations: (1) the processing array should consist of only a few types of simple processing elements, (2) communication structure should be kept simple and regular, and (3) data streams and control flow should be simple and regular, and branching and decision making should be kept to minimum. A major difficulty in VLSI design is the limitation in the number of I/O pins on a chip, and it may be necessary to execute a pattern analysis operation on several interconnected VLSI chips.

## A  Systolic Arrays

A systolic array [1, 2] consists of interconnected processing elements (PEs) or cells. Each PE is capable of performing some simple operations. Data streams and control commands flow between PEs in a pipelined fashion, and communication with the outside world occurs only at the boundary PEs. A linear systolic array with its memory shared by the PEs is shown in Fig. 1.

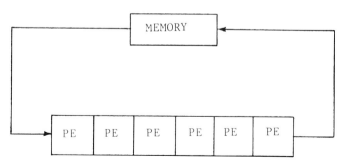

**Fig. 1.**  Linear systolic array. (From Kung [2]. © 1981 IEEE.)

The memory functions in a manner similar to the heart; it pumps the data synchronously through the array of PEs.

Commonly used array configurations include linear, square, triangular, and hexagonal arrays and the binary tree. For example, one-dimensional convolution can be implemented on a linear systolic array. Matrix multiplication can be implemented on a hexagonal array with the two matrices $\mathbf{A}$ and $\mathbf{B}$ entering the array from two separate directions and the product $\mathbf{Z} = \mathbf{AB}$ leaving the array in the third direction. The hexagonal array with three-directional data flow may also be used for matrix triangularization [1–3].

*Orthogonally connected systolic arrays.* If one of the two matrices to be multiplied is stored in the array, matrix multiplication can be executed on an orthogonally connected square array with two-directional data flow [4, 5]. Consider the multiplication of two $n \times n$ matrices, $\mathbf{Z} = \mathbf{AB}$. In terms of matrix elements, it can be expressed as the following recurrences:

$$z_{ij}^{(0)} = 0$$
$$z_{ij}^{(k)} = z_{ij}^{(k-1)} + a_{ik}b_{kj} \tag{1}$$
$$z_{ij} = z_{ij}^{(n)}$$

Assuming the matrix $\mathbf{A}$ is already inside a square array, as shown in Fig. 2, $\mathbf{B}$ can be piped in to interact with $\mathbf{A}$ to produce the multiplication result. During each computation cycle, all the PEs in the array perform the same multiplication step: each PE takes the sum of partial products from its left neighbor and adds it to its partial product of $a \times b$, and then passes the sum to its right neighbor for the next multiplication step. The computation time required is $4n - 2$ units, including $n$ units of matrix $\mathbf{A}$ loading time. It is interesting to note that a two-dimensional discrete Fourier transform for image processing may be implemented using a matrix multiplication array [5].

A symmetric nonsingular covariance matrix $\mathbf{R} = [r_{ij}]$ can be decomposed into an upper triangular matrix $\mathbf{U} = [u_{ij}]$ and a lower triangular matrix $\mathbf{L} = [l_{ij}]$, using an orthogonally connected triangular array with two-directional data flow [4, 6]. The recurrence procedure for L–U decomposition is as follows:

$$c_{ij}^{(1)} = r_{ij}$$
$$c_{ij}^{(k+1)} = c_{ij}^{(k)} - l_{ik}u_{kj}$$
$$l_{ik} = \begin{cases} 0 & \text{if } i < k \\ 1 & \text{if } i = k \\ c_{ik}^{(k)}u_{kk}^{-1} & \text{if } i > k \end{cases} \tag{2}$$
$$u_{kj} = \begin{cases} 0 & \text{if } k > j \\ c_{kj}^{(k)} & \text{if } k \leq j \end{cases}$$

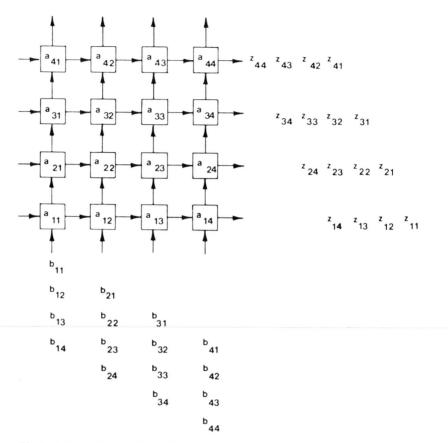

**Fig. 2.** Data flow in an orthogonally connected multiplication array. (From Liu and Young [4]. © 1983 IEEE.)

The operations required of each PE and data movement of the array are shown in Fig. 3, assuming a $4 \times 4$ covariance matrix. The PE has two inputs $c_{in}$ and $u_{in}$ and two outputs $c_{out}$ and $u_{out}$ which are buffered or latched internally, and it has an internal storage register $l$. Each PE operates in two modes, the multiplication mode and the division mode. It is assumed that each operation takes one unit of time to complete. The multiplication mode allows the PEs in the array to implement the recurrence $c_{ij}^{(k+1)} = c_{ij}^{(k)} - l_{ik}u_{kj}$ in the decomposition and at the same time move $u_{kj}$ upward. The division mode allows a PE to calculate $l_{ik} = c_{ik}^{(k)}u_{kk}^{-1}$ when necessary and store the result in the internal register $l$. With alternating multiplication and division cycles, the computation time required is $6n - 3$ units.

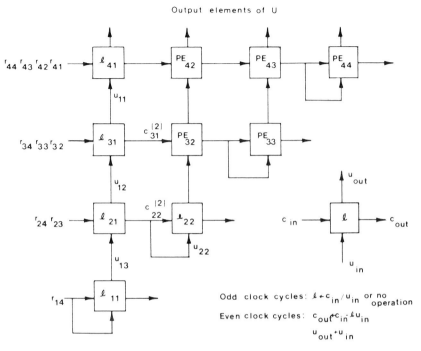

**Fig. 3.** Triangular array for L–U decomposition. Odd clock cycles: $l \leftarrow c_{in}/u_{in}$ or no operation. Even clock cycles: $c_{out} \leftarrow c_{in} - lu_{in}$, $u_{out} \leftarrow u_{in}$. (From Liu and Young [4]. © 1983 IEEE.)

## Reconfigurable Arrays  **B**

A general reconfigurable processor array is constructed with three types of components: a set of PEs, a switch lattice, and an array controller [7]. The PEs are not directly connected to each other but are connected indirectly through the switches. The switch lattice is a regular structure formed from programmable switches. Each switch contains local memory capable of storing several configuration settings. The controller is responsible for loading the switch memory with appropriate settings. The two structures in Fig. 4 show a switch lattice configured into a mesh pattern and a binary tree, respectively.

*Reconfigurable array for matrix operations.* Matrix inversion involves several computation steps which can be implemented on a reconfigurable array [4]. There are two potentially important advantages. First, it replaces several specialized arrays, one for each computation step. Probably more

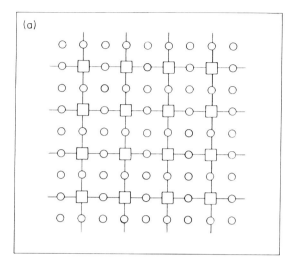

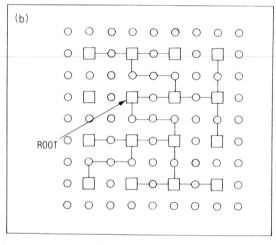

**Fig. 4.** (a) Switch lattice configured into a mesh pattern. (b) Lattice reconfigured into a binary tree. (From Snyder, [7]. © 1982 IEEE.)

important, it allows one processing task to follow another without the data leaving the array; in other words, there is no I/O between computation steps.

The block diagram of a reconfigurable array for covariance matrix inversion is shown in Fig. 5a. In Fig. 5b, the orthogonally connected square array is reconfigured along the diagonal to become an upper triangular array for **L**–**U** decomposition. The next step is the computation of $\mathbf{V} = \mathbf{U}^{-1}$, which can be implemented on a reconfigured lower triangular array. The matrix **U** is piped back without delay to the bottom of the array for the computation of

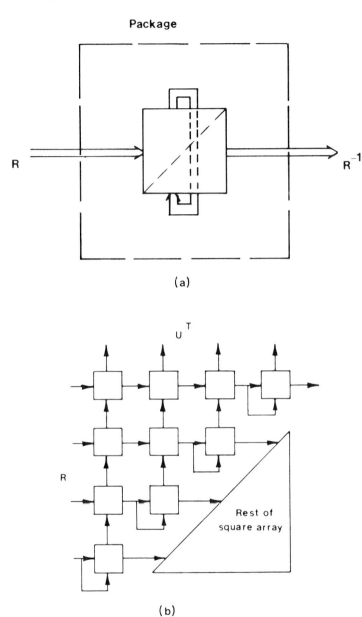

**Fig. 5.** (a) Reconfigurable array for covariance matrix inversion. (b) Array reconfigured into an upper triangular array for L–U decomposition. (From Liu and Young [4]. © 1983 IEEE.)

**V**; the latter remains in the triangular array after the computation. Step 3 is the computation of the inverse of **L**, which is denoted by $\mathbf{M} = [m_{ij}]$. Since **R** is symmetric, $m_{ji} = v_{ij}u_{jj}$ and **M** can be easily computed from **V**. The last step is the computation of $\mathbf{R}^{-1} = \mathbf{U}^{-1}\mathbf{L}^{-1} = \mathbf{VM}$ using the square array as a multiplication array. Clearly, switches are needed along the diagonal and at the boundary of the array to divert data flow. With computation overlap of the steps accounted for, the total computation time of the four steps for covariance matrix inversion is $13n - 4$ units.

## C  Wavefront Arrays

In a wavefront array [8], waves of data and computation activities advance continuously in a manner resembling a wave propagation phenomenon (see Fig. 6). Computation will not be initiated until the arrival of the data wavefront. The array is programmable, and the wavefront notion reduces the complexity in the description of parallel algorithms. A matrix data-flow language has been developed that allows the programmer to address an entire front of processors.

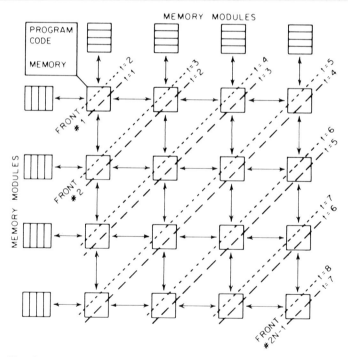

**Fig. 6.** Wavefront array processor. ——, First wave; ---, second wave. (From Kung *et al.* [8]. © 1982 IEEE.)

The processors in a wavefront array are more complex than the PEs of systolic arrays. Each processor has a relatively conventional architecture consisting of an internal program memory, a control unit, an ALU, and a set of registers. It allows data to flow in four directions using a bidirectional buffer and four bidirectional buses. Interprocessor communication is implemented by a simple handshaking protocol. Therefore, the wavefront architecture provides asynchronous waiting capability and can cope with timing uncertainties. The array is, in a sense, a trade-off between the globally synchronous systolic array and the asynchronous general-purpose data-flow multiprocessors [8].

## VLSI ARCHITECTURE FOR STATISTICAL PATTERN RECOGNITION   III

In statistical pattern classification (see Chapter 1 and Young and Calvert [9]), a set of $n$ measurements is regarded as an $n$-dimensional vector in a vector space. The vector space is divided into several regions based on statistical analysis or decision theory, with each region corresponding to one class of patterns. The required computations are mostly matrix operations, and systolic and wavefront arrays may be adopted to improve computation throughput.

### Discriminant Functions   A

Pattern classification can be divided into two phases, the training phase and the classification phase. If the probability distributions of the classes are known except for some parameter values to be estimated, Bayes decision rules may be adopted, and the resulting discriminant functions are essentially log-likelihood functions. Often the probability distributions are assumed to be Gaussian; then the discriminant functions are linear or quadratic depending on whether or not the covariance matrices of the different classes are identical. During the training phase, covariance matrices and mean vectors are estimated from sample vectors of known classifications. Discriminant functions are obtained and new samples of unknown classifications are classified using the discriminant functions.

*Quadratic discriminant functions.* Let $\mathbf{x}$ be an $n$-dimensional column vector. With a Gaussian distribution for each class, the discriminant function for class $s$ may be expressed as [9]:

$$D_s(\mathbf{x}) = -2 \log p_s(x)$$
$$= (\mathbf{x} - \boldsymbol{\mu}_s)^{\mathrm{T}} \mathbf{R}_s^{-1} (\mathbf{x} - \boldsymbol{\mu}_s) + \log(2\pi)^n |\mathbf{R}_s| \tag{3}$$

where $\mathbf{R}_s$ and $\boldsymbol{\mu}_s$ are the covariance matrix and mean vector, respectively. This is a quadratic discriminant function, and the pattern vector $\mathbf{x}$ will be assigned to class $s$ if $D_s(\mathbf{x})$ is minimum among the values of discriminant functions of all classes.

*Linear discriminant functions.* If the covariance matrices are identical, the pairwise discriminant function for class $s$ and class $t$ is linear:

$$D_{st}(\mathbf{x}) = D_s(\mathbf{x}) - D_t(\mathbf{x})$$
$$= 2\mathbf{x}^T\mathbf{R}^{-1}(\boldsymbol{\mu}_t - \boldsymbol{\mu}_s) - \boldsymbol{\mu}_t^T\mathbf{R}^{-1}\boldsymbol{\mu}_t + \boldsymbol{\mu}_s^T\mathbf{R}^{-1}\boldsymbol{\mu}_s \tag{4}$$

Class $s$ is preferred if $D_{st}(\mathbf{x}) < 0$.

The *Fisher's linear discriminant* seeks the projections of the $\mathbf{x}$ vectors in a direction that minimizes the average variance of the two classes subject to the constraint that the difference in mean values is constant. The resulting discriminant function is [9]

$$F_{st}(\mathbf{x}) = \mathbf{x}^T(\mathbf{R}_t + \mathbf{R}_s)^{-1}(\boldsymbol{\mu}_t - \boldsymbol{\mu}_s) + \alpha \tag{5}$$

where $\alpha$ is a threshold value for classification. It is noted that if $\mathbf{R}_s = \mathbf{R}_t = \mathbf{R}$, then (5) reduces to (4) with an appropriate value of $\alpha$.

*Estimation of the covariance matrix.* During the training phase, it is necessary to estimate covariance matrices and mean vectors for each class from a set of training samples of known classification. Let us assume for convenience that $\mathbf{x}_1, \mathbf{x}_2, \ldots, \mathbf{x}_m$ belong to the same class $s$. Then

$$\boldsymbol{\mu}_s = \frac{1}{m}\sum_{i=1}^{m}\mathbf{x}_i$$

$$\mathbf{R}_s = \frac{1}{m}\sum_{i=1}^{m}\mathbf{x}_i\mathbf{x}_i^T - \boldsymbol{\mu}_s\boldsymbol{\mu}_s^T, \qquad \mathbf{x}_i \in \text{class } s. \tag{6}$$

## B  Modular System for Pattern Classification

Pattern classification involves a number of computation steps. Therefore, it is natural to consider VLSI implementation using several VLSI modules. We discuss in the following a specific modular system. It should be clear that a modular approach may be adopted for almost any statistical pattern classification scheme.

*Modular pattern classifier.* Shown in Fig. 7 is a modular pattern classifier using Fischer's linear discriminant [10]. There are two inputs to the system, one for the training samples of the two classes and the other for new samples to be classified. Module A in Fig. 7 computes from sample vectors of class $s$ the mean vector $\boldsymbol{\mu}_s$ and an $n \times m$ matrix

$$\mathbf{Y}_s = [\mathbf{x}_1 - \boldsymbol{\mu}_s, \mathbf{x}_2 - \boldsymbol{\mu}_s, \ldots, x_m - \boldsymbol{\mu}_s] \tag{7}$$

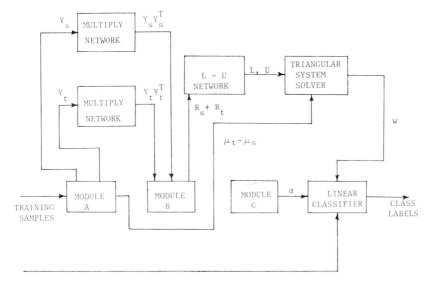

SAMPLES TO BE CLASSIFIED

**Fig. 7.** Modular pattern classifier using Fisher's linear discriminant. (From Huang and Su [10]. © 1981 IEEE.)

and in a similar manner, it computes $\boldsymbol{\mu}_t$ and $\mathbf{Y}_t$ for class $t$. The two multiply networks perform matrix multiplications $\mathbf{Y}_s\mathbf{Y}_s^T$ and $\mathbf{Y}_t\mathbf{Y}_t^T$, and module B divides the two resulting $n \times n$ matrices by the numbers of samples in class $s$ and class $t$, respectively, and then adds them to form the sum of two covariance matrices $(\mathbf{R}_s + \mathbf{R}_t)$. The vector $\mathbf{w} = (\mathbf{R}_s + \mathbf{R}_t)^{-1} (\boldsymbol{\mu}_t - \boldsymbol{\mu}_s)$ is then calculated using the L–U decomposition network and the triangular solver, and it is stored in the linear classifier. Module C is responsible for calculating the threshold value $\alpha$. Finally, the classifier computes $\Gamma_{st}(\mathbf{x})$ for a sample $\mathbf{x}$ and decides which class, $s$ or $t$, $\mathbf{x}$ belongs to.

*Partitioned matrix algorithms.* If the dimension $n$ of the pattern space is large, it may be impractical to fabricate an $n \times n$ systolic array on a monolithic chip due to I/O bandwidth limitation. A partitioned approach [10, 11] will circumvent this problem by using $k \times k$ VLSI array modules, where $k$ is smaller than $n$. Several types of $k \times k$ array modules have been described. The D-type module is for submatrix L–U decomposition. Similarly, the I-type module is for triangular submatrix inversion, and the M-type for submatrix multiplication. Partitioned L–U decomposition of an $n \times n$ nonsingular matrix may be implemented using all three types of modular chips with a chip count of $O(n^2/k^2)$ and computing time of $O(n)$. For partitioned inversion of an $n \times n$ nonsingular triangular matrix, I-type and M-type chips are needed.

## C  Reconfigurable Pattern Analysis Array

A statistical pattern analysis array that consists of a square array and a linear array is shown in Fig. 8. The proposed array processor [12, 13] is reconfigurable in the sense that data paths can be changed by modifying the communication structure between the two arrays and/or the structures among the PEs. Each PE of the square array has two inputs and two outputs, and a PE may have several internal storage registers. It can perform three types of operations: (1) data transfer and loading, (2) multiplication-and-addition (or subtraction), and (3) division. For the linear array, each PE has three inputs and two outputs, and its operations are very similar to that of the PEs of the square array.

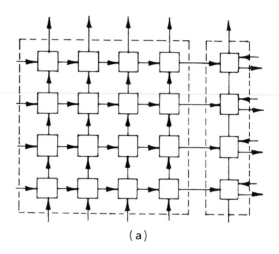

(a)

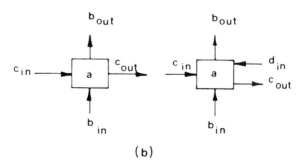

(b)

**Fig. 8.** (a) Statistical pattern analysis array and (b) its processing elements. (From Young *et al.* [12]. © 1983 IEEE.)

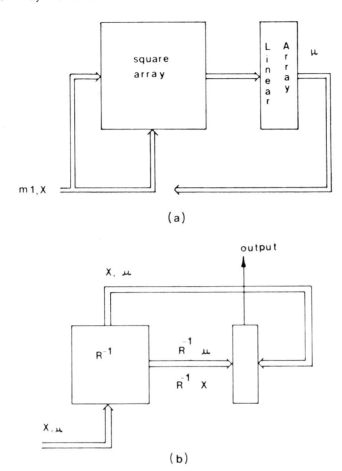

**Fig. 9.** (a) Computation of covariance matrices and mean vectors. (b) Computation of the quadratic discriminant function. (From Young *et al.* [12]. © 1983 IEEE.)

*Computation of covariance matrices.* The covariance matrix and the mean vector of class *s* is calculated from a set of *m* samples belonging to that class. Let

$$\mathbf{X} = [\mathbf{x}_1, \mathbf{x}_2, \ldots, \mathbf{x}_m] \qquad (8)$$

and omit the subscript *s* for simplicity of notation. The skewed input data **X** are piped into the array from two directions, as shown in Fig. 9a. The computation can be divided into three steps. In the first step, $PE_{jk}$ of the square array computes recursively $a \leftarrow a + x_{ji}x_{ki}$ as the data streams arrive, and $PE_j$ of the linear array calculates $a \leftarrow a + x_{ji}$. After the data streams of **X** have passed through a PE, the content of the register *a* is divided by *m* so that $(\Sigma\, x_{ji}x_{ki})/m$ is stored in $PE_{jk}$ of the square array. The vector *m*1, after passing through the square array, enters the linear array for the computation of $\mu_j = (\Sigma \, x_{ji})/m$. The last step is to pipe $\boldsymbol{\mu}$ back into the square array from two directions and to compute at $\mathrm{PE}_{jk} \; a \leftarrow a - \mu_j\mu_k$. Thus, after the last step of computation, we have the matrix $\mathbf{R}$ stored in the square array and the vector $\boldsymbol{\mu}$ stored in the linear array. Since the input data streams are skewed, the total computation time is $2n + m + 1$ units.

*Computation of discriminant functions.* The computation of $\mathbf{R}^{-1}$ using the reconfigurable square array has been discussed in Section II, and the determinant $|\mathbf{R}| = |\mathbf{L}||\mathbf{U}| = 1 \times |\mathbf{U}| = \Pi \, u_{jj}$ can be computed on the linear array. The block diagram for computing the quadratic term of the quadratic discriminant function is shown in Fig. 9b, where $\mathbf{X}$ represents $m$ sample vectors being classified. The quadratic term may be expressed as $(\mathbf{x} - \boldsymbol{\mu})^{\mathrm{T}}(\mathbf{R}^{-1}\mathbf{x} - \mathbf{R}^{-1}\boldsymbol{\mu})$. With $\mathbf{R}^{-1}$ stored in the square array, the array essentially performs matrix multiplication. Its skewed outputs, $\mathbf{R}^{-1}\boldsymbol{\mu}$ and $\mathbf{R}^{-1}\mathbf{X}$, are piped into the linear array, and at the same time, the skewed data streams $\boldsymbol{\mu}$ and $\mathbf{X}$, having passed through the square array enter the linear array from the other side. The vectors $\boldsymbol{\mu}$ and $\mathbf{R}^{-1}\boldsymbol{\mu}$ are stored in internal registers of the linear array, before the array executes the appropriate multiplication-and-subtraction operations. The computation time is $2n + m$ units.

Since there are several classes of patterns, local memory is needed to store the data $\mathbf{X}$ and the several covariance matrices and mean vectors. Comparison of the several $D_s(\mathbf{x})$ may be carried out in a special linear "compare" processor [14] or in the host computer. Pairwise linear discriminant functions, $D_{st}(\mathbf{x})$ and $F_{st}(\mathbf{x})$, can also be computed using the pattern analysis array [12, 13].

## D   Pipelined Systolic Array for Cluster Analysis

Clustering algorithms can be broadly classified into one of two types: (1) hierarchical and (2) partitional (see Chapter 2). A majority of partitional techniques seek a partition that minimizes some criterion function. Finding an optimal partition is, in general, computationally not feasible. Therefore, most partitional techniques use heuristics to reduce the amount of computation, and they usually yield only suboptimal partitions.

*Square-error clustering.* Given a set of $m$ pattern vectors $\mathbf{x}_i, i = 1, 2, \ldots, m$, and a partition of this data into $C$ clusters, the square error for cluster $s$ is defined as

$$e_s^2 = \sum_i (\mathbf{x}_i - \boldsymbol{\mu}_s)^{\mathrm{T}}(\mathbf{x}_i - \boldsymbol{\mu}_s), \qquad \mathbf{x}_i \in \text{Cluster } s \qquad (9)$$

where $\boldsymbol{\mu}_s$ is the mean vector (cluster center) of cluster $s$. The square error for the partition of the pattern vectors into $C$ clusters is

$$E_C^2 = \sum_{s=1}^{C} e_s^2 \qquad (10)$$

After an initial partition, an iterative procedure assigns $\mathbf{x}_i$ to cluster $t$ if the Euclidean distance $d(\mathbf{x}_i, \boldsymbol{\mu}_t)$ is minimum for $t = 1, 2, \ldots, C$. With the $m$ pattern vectors reassigned, new cluster centers are calculated. The iteration continues until either the cluster labels do not change or the number of iterations exceeds a certain limit. Thus, the two major computation-extensive tasks are the label reassignment process and the cluster center updating process. A flowchart for the iterative procedure can be found in Ni and Jain [15] and in Chapter 2.

*Systolic clustering array.* The iterative square-error algorithm involves vector operations that can be classified into four primitive types: $f_1: V \to V$, $f_2: V \to S$, $f_3: V \times V \to V$, and $f_4: V \times S \to V$, where $V$ and $S$ denote vector and scalar operands, respectively. For example, summation of vector elements is an $f_2$ operation, and vector addition is an $f_3$ operation. Each type of operations can be implemented using one of the four basic primitive pipeline organizations.

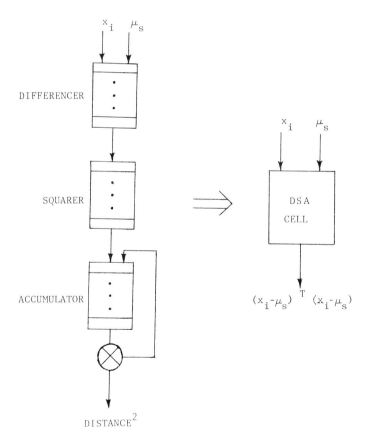

**Fig. 10.** Pipeline organization and the logic symbol of a DSA cell. (From Ni and Jain [15]. © 1983 IEEE.)

A two-level pipelined architecture is adopted for the clustering array [15]. The upper level is for the label reassignment process. It includes $C$ difference–square–accumulate (DSA) cells in parallel for the computation of squared distances between $\mathbf{x}_i$ and the $C$ cluster centers. The pipeline organization of the DSA cell is shown in Fig. 10. The pipeline differencer, squarer, and accumulator are $f_3$, $f_1$, and $f_2$ operations, respectively. The DSA cells are followed by a pipeline comparator for comparison of the squared distances. The lower level of the array consists of pipeline accumulators and dividers for updating the $C$ cluster centers. The speedup of this design over a sequential clustering processor is approximately $3CN_s$, where $N_s$ is the number of segments in a primitive pipeline organization.

## IV  VLSI ARRAY FOR SYNTACTIC PATTERN RECOGNITION

In syntactic pattern recognition (see Chapter 4) an input pattern is converted into a string of primitives, the string is syntax analyzed, and the result shows whether the input pattern is rejected or accepted by the parser. In general, the process is very slow because of the tedious calculation involved in the parser. A very popular parsing algorithm for general context-free languages is Earley's algorithm, which is basically a dynamic programming procedure.

A context-free grammar is a 4-tuple $G = (V, \Sigma, P, S)$, where $V$ is a finite set called the vocabulary, $\Sigma$ is the set of terminal symbols, and $N = V - \Sigma$ is the set of nonterminals. The set of all finite-length strings over $V$ is $V^*$; $P$ is the set of production rules, and $S$ is the starting symbol. In this section, capital letters $A$, $B$, ... denote elements of $N$, while lowercase letters $a$, $b$, ... are elements of $\Sigma$. Greek letters $\alpha$, $\beta$, ... are elements of $V^*$, and $\lambda$ denotes the null string. For any production rule $A \to \beta$ in $P$, $A \to \alpha \cdot \beta$ is called a dotted rule. The dot is a symbol not in $V$ and is used as a marker to indicate that the $\alpha$ part is consistent with the input string while the $\beta$ part remains to be considered.

*Parallel Earley's algorithm.* The algorithm constructs a parsing matrix $\mathbf{T} = [t(i,j)]$, and the matrix elements are sets of dotted rules. The string is correctly recognized if $S \to \alpha \cdot \in t(0, n)$, where $n$ is the string length. The computation of weakened Earley's algorithm is shown in Fig. 11 [16, 17].

The parallel algorithm is described in terms of an $\times *$ operation. Let $Q$ be a set of dotted rules and

$$Y = \text{PREDICT}(N)$$
$$= \{C \to \gamma \cdot \delta \,|\, C \to \gamma\delta \text{ is in } P, \gamma \xrightarrow{*} \lambda, B \xrightarrow{*} C\eta$$
$$\text{for some } B \text{ in } N \text{ and some } \eta\} \tag{11}$$

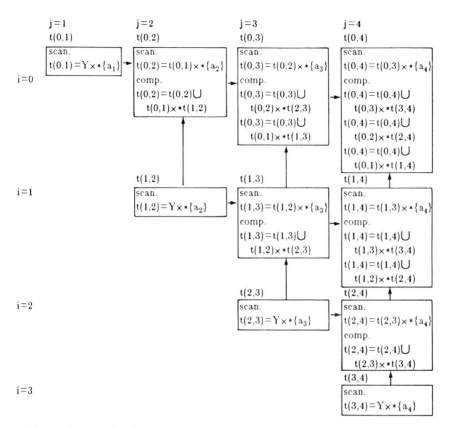

**Fig. 11.** Computation of weakened Earley's algorithm. (From Chiang and Fu [16]. © 1984 IEEE.)

which replaces the central diagonal elements of the matrix **T**. The $\times *$ operation is defined as follows:

if $R$ is a set of dotted rules, then

$$Q \times * R = \{A \to \alpha U \beta \cdot \gamma \,|\, A \to \alpha \cdot U \beta \gamma \in Q, \beta \overset{*}{\to} \lambda, \text{ and } U \to \delta \cdot \in R\}$$

and

$$\{B \to \delta C \xi \cdot \eta \,|\, \gamma = \lambda, B \to \delta \cdot C \xi \eta \in Y, \text{ and } \xi \overset{*}{\to} \lambda, C \overset{*}{\to} A\};$$

if $R \subseteq V$, then

$$Q \times * R = \{A \to \alpha U \beta \cdot \gamma \,|\, A \to \alpha \cdot U \beta \gamma \in Q, \beta \overset{*}{\to} \lambda, U \in R\}$$

and

$$\{B \to \delta C \xi \cdot \eta \,|\, \gamma = \lambda, B \to \delta \cdot C \xi \eta \in Y, \text{ and } \xi \overset{*}{\to} \lambda, C \overset{*}{\to} A\} \qquad (12)$$

*Algorithm 1*:

    **for** $i = 1$ **to** $n$ **do in parallel**

        $t(i - 1, i) = Y \times * \{a_i\};$

    **for** $j = $  2 **to** $n$ **do**

        **for** $i = 0$ **to** $n - j$ **do in parallel**

        **begin**

        [Scanner:]
        $t(i, i + j) = t(i, i + j - 1) \times * \{a_{i+j}\};$

        [Completer:]

        **for** $k = 1$ **to** $j - 1$ **do in parallel**

        $t(i, i + j) = t(i, i + j) \cup t(i, i + k) \times * t(i + k, i + j);$

    **end**

*VLSI implementation of Earley's algorithm.* A direct implementation on a VLSI system is to assign each matrix element a processing cell [16, 17]. Note from Fig. 11 that in the computation of $t(0, 2)$, two data items $t(0, 1)$ and $t(1, 2)$, and an input symbol $a_2$ are needed; on the other hand, computation of $t(0, 4)$ requires six data items plus an input symbol. This problem is solved by using slow and fast buses. The VLSI architecture is shown in Fig. 12, where each processing cell of the triangular array has identical structure. It is assumed that within each system unit time, every cell can complete its

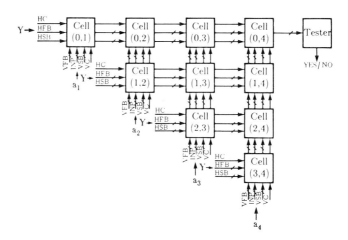

**Fig. 12.** VLSI architecture for the computation of Algorithm 1. (From Chiang and Fu [16]. © 1984 IEEE.)

computation. There are three vertical buses, VFB (vertical fast bus), VSB (vertical slow bus), and INP (input symbol bus); and two horizontal buses, HFB (horizontal fast bus) and HSB (horizontal slow bus). The fast buses transfer data at a rate one cell per unit time, while the slow buses and INP bus have a rate one cell every two unit times. Each cell has three functions, namely, computing the $\times *$ operation, loading data onto fast buses, and shifting the data from the fast buses to the slow buses. The last two functions are essential for keeping the bus system working and are controlled by two control lines, VC (vertical control) and HC (horizontal control).

Bit vectors are used to represent symbols in $V$ and the matrix element $t(i, j)$; the latter is a set of dotted rules. Each dotted rule conveys the information about a production rule and its associated dot position. Since the production rules are given in the grammar, the matrix elements only need to memorize the dot position via bit vectors. The execution time for the $\times *$ operation is data dependent. This is due to the fact that the length of $\beta$ in (12) is unknown, and it is necessary to check the following symbols until a decision is made. It is always possible to compensate different execution times by using a synchronizer; however, this approach often slows down the whole system. If the grammar is restricted to be $\lambda$ free, then the $\times *$ operation becomes data independent and can be implemented on dedicated hardware.

*Computation of string distances.* When pattern grammars are not readily available or a complete description is not required, decision theoretical approaches based on string distances may be applied in a manner similar to statistical pattern recognition. With syntactic representation, the distance between two strings is defined as the smallest number of insertions, deletions, and substitution of string symbols required to derive one string from the other. For two strings $x_1, x_2, \ldots, x_n$ and $y_1, y_2, \ldots, y_n$, the partial distance at the $(i, j)$th step is $\delta(i, j) = \min\{\delta(i, j - 1) + I(y_j),\ \delta(i - 1, j - 1) + S(x_i, y_j),\ \delta(i - 1, j) + D(x_i)\}$, where $I$, $S$, and $D$ stand for insertion, substitution, and deletion, respectively. An orthogonally connected, $m \times n$ systolic array may be used to compute string distances [14].

## VLSI ARRAYS FOR IMAGE PROCESSING  V

There are two types of techniques for preprocessing of images: frequency-domain methods based on the two-dimensional discrete Fourier transform (DFT) and spatial domain operations, which usually depend on the values of a pixel and its neighboring pixels only. Segmentation techniques are mostly spatial-domain operations. The choice of object and/or regional description methods is often problem dependent; its computation speed can be improved by distributing the tasks to several processors in a multiprocessor system.

## A    Systolic Arrays for Discrete Fourier Transform

Let $\mathbf{G} = [g_{ij}] = [g(i,j)]$ represent the gray levels of the pixels of an $n \times n$ image. A two-dimensional discrete Fourier transform (DFT) may be defined as

$$f_{kl} = \sum_{i=0}^{n-1} \sum_{j=0}^{n-1} g_{ij} \exp[-j2\pi(ki + jl)/n] \qquad (13)$$

where we have used $j$ to represent both the unit imaginary number and an index. Clearly, we may define a matrix

$$\mathbf{A} = [a(k, i)] = [\exp(-j2\pi ki/n)] \qquad (14)$$

and express (13) in the matrix form

$$\mathbf{F} = \mathbf{AGA} \qquad (15)$$

The inverse transform can be expressed in a similar manner.

*Fast Fourier transform algorithms.* Fast Fourier transform (FFT) promises significant reduction in the number of multiplications required for calculating DFTs. LSI processors for one-dimensional FFTs are available commercially [5]. The heart of an FFT processor is a high-speed multiplier–accumulator (MAC) that will perform the basic butterfly computations in FFT. A single-chip MAC has been developed by TRW which is capable of performing a $16 \times 16$ bit multiplication in 100 nsec. With a single MAC, the total computation of a one-dimensional 1024-point FFT takes less than 6 msec. A two-dimensional FFT can be computed by first calculating one-dimensional row FFTs and then column FFTs [18]. If $n^2/2$ PEs are used, a two-dimensional FFT requires only $2 \log n$ units of time. The FFT algorithm sends the outputs of its PEs back to the inputs of the same set of PEs, and it requires rather complicated branching or switching circuits.

*DFT computation by matrix multiplication.* It is clear from (15) that computation of a DFT can be implemented on an $n \times n$ matrix multiplication array [5, 19]. It is assumed that both $\mathbf{G}$, the image, and $\mathbf{A}$, the Fourier matrix, have been loaded into an orthogonally connected square array. The matrix $\mathbf{A}$ is taken out from the top of the array and piped back from below so that it interacts with $\mathbf{G}$ to form a matrix product $\mathbf{GA}$. The next step is to feed $\mathbf{GA}$ back into the array to interact with the stored $\mathbf{A}$ for the computation of $\mathbf{AGA}$. The two-dimensional inverse DFT can be calculated in a similar manner. We note that the DFT array is slower than a properly designed FFT array, but it has a regular data-flow pattern and simple communication and control structure. Thus, the choice of DFT or FFT for future VLSI image processing is a matter of the trade-off between computation costs and communication and control costs.

*Image filtering.* The two-dimensional DFT is a frequency-domain representation of an image. Frequency-domain methods for image enhancement modify the DFT of an image by two-dimensional filtering followed by inverse DFT. Two-dimensional filters can be easily specified in the frequency domain. In this way, smoothing filters and high-frequency emphasis filters for image enhancement can be implemented on DFT arrays.

### Arrays for Spatial Domain Operations  B

A popular approach to segmentation is the detection of the edges of an object by template matching. To match a $3 \times 3$ template or window, $\mathbf{W} = [w(k, l)]$, we need to compute

$$\hat{g}(i, j) = \sum_{k=-1}^{1} \sum_{l=-1}^{1} w(k, l)g(i + k, j + l) \qquad (16)$$

and then compare the result with a predetermined decision threshold. By selecting the weighting coefficients $w(k, l)$ properly, template matching may be used for various spatial tasks, including line detection and edge detection [20]. Template matching may also be used for image enhancement. Several approaches to VLSI implementation of template matching have been proposed.

*Kernel cells.* A kernel cell for a $3 \times 3$ template consists of nine basic PEs to form three linear arrays, plus a row interface PE to add the results emanated from the linear arrays. A total of $n - 2$ cells are used [21]. Three data streams enter a kernel cell, two of which exit from the cell after necessary computations and then enter the next kernel cell. If the template size is large, computation speed can be improved by using a single kernel cell. At the Jet Propulsion Laboratory, a $35 \times 35$ element pipelined convolution kernel has been fabricated using VLSI chips, each containing 5 PEs [22]. Two hundred forty-five chips are connected together to represent a $35 \times 35$ template.

*Matrix multiplication for template matching.* It may be desirable to implement frequency-domain and spatial-domain operations on the same VLSI systolic array. It has been shown [5, 19] that template matching can be implemented using matrix multiplications, and hence the computation is somewhat similar to computing DFTs. As many as four matrix multiplication operations are needed for a $3 \times 3$ template. The values of the matrix elements must be precomputed from the given weighting coefficients, possibly at the host computer.

*Two-dimensional parallel pipelines.* With this approach, the image is stored in an $n \times n$ orthogonally connected square array, and the array is conceived as overlapping templates [12, 13]. With $3 \times 3$ templates, the $(i, j)$th template computation involves nine PEs in the following order: $\text{PE}_{i-1,j-1} - \text{PE}_{i-1,j} - \text{PE}_{i-1,j+1} - \text{PE}_{i,j+1} - \text{PE}_{i+1,j+1} - \text{PE}_{i+1,j} - \text{PE}_{i+1,j-1} - \text{PE}_{i,j-1} - \text{PE}_{i,j}$. All $n^2$ PEs perform multiply-and-add operations at the same time and pass the results to one of their neighbors. It takes only nine units of time to complete the template matching computation of the image. Each coefficient is presented to all PEs simultaneously, and all PEs are required to be active right from the beginning. This implies broadcasting of weighting coefficients and control commands to the PEs. Thus, the method is based on a combination of systolic and cellular array concepts.

## C  Three-Dimensional VLSI Architecture

Most existing parallel image processing systems are cellular array processors which are basically SIMD (single instruction stream, multiple data streams) machines (see Chapter 17). The array consists of a number of identical processing cells which may have some form of topological interconnections. The interconnections allow data to be passed from one processing

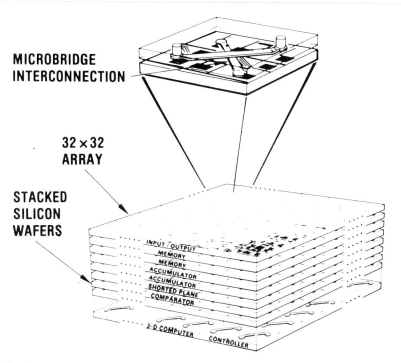

**Fig. 13.** Basic structure of a three-dimensional computer. (From Grinberg *et al.* [23]. © 1984 IEEE.)

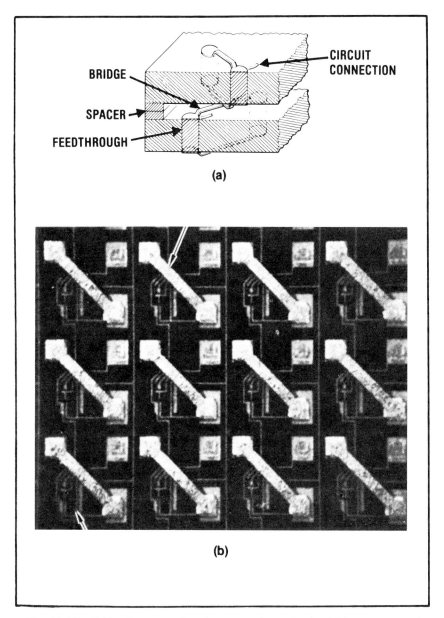

**Fig. 14.** Microbridge interconnections between wafers: (a) microbridge connector; (b) CMOS circuitry of processing element, 20 mil. (From Grinberg *et al.* [23]. © 1984 IEEE.)

cell to a number of other cells. There is a single control unit which broadcasts instructions one at a time to all processing cells. By connecting every processing cell to its four, six, or eight nearest neighbors, spatial-domain operations for image enhancement and segmentation can be executed in parallel for each pixel in the array processor.

The three-dimensional VLSI architecture proposed at Hughes Research Laboratories [23, 24] is an SIMD machine. It differs from existing cellular arrays in its degree of integration and the three-dimensional organization of the processing circuitry. The three-dimensional microelectronic mapping provides significant advantages in packing density and the average length of interconnect. The three-dimensional computer consists of $n \times n$ identical processors contained on a stack of silicon wafers. As shown in Fig. 13, the array of processors is arranged horizontally, with the elements of each processor in the array assembled vertically. Microbridge interconnections between wafers are shown in Fig. 14.

Each wafer in the stack contains a complete $n \times n$ array of one particular type of processing element. Five elemental wafer types (memory, accumulator, replicator, counter, and comparator) are required for efficient implementation of image processing algorithms. The majority of the processing takes place in the memory and accumulator wafers. The replicator plane wafer allows rapid communication by broadcasting data values to the processors in the array. The counter plane is particularly useful for calculating histograms of gray-level values of images. To implement a certain operation, an image is moved up and down the stack to the appropriate processing planes using the parallel $n \times n$ array of bus lines. Data flow and instruction streams are controlled by a stored program control unit. Data-dependent branching is achieved by using a masking plane. The three-dimensional computer can be

TABLE I

Projected Processing Times for Various Operations Assuming a 10-MHz Clock[a]

| Operation | Time |
|---|---|
| Data move (MEM → MEM) | 1.8 $\mu$sec |
| ADD (ACC + MEM → ACC) | 1.8 $\mu$sec |
| MULTIPLY (ACC × MEM → ACC) | 42.2 $\mu$sec |
| DIVIDE (ACC ÷ MEM → ACC) | 127.1 $\mu$sec |
| SQUARE ROOT ($\sqrt{ACC}$ → ACC) | 152.6 $\mu$sec |
| Sobel edge operator | 54.3 $\mu$sec |
| 256 × 256 matrix multiply | 12.0 msec |
| 256 × 256 8-bit histogram | 1.7 msec |
| 256 × 256 matrix inversion | 10.2 msec |

[a] From Grinberg et al. [23]. © 1984 IEEE.

programmed for high-speed image processing. Table I shows the projected performance of various operations.

## REFERENCES

1. H. T. Kung and C. E. Leiserson, Algorithms for VLSI processor arrays, *in* "Introduction to VLSI Systems" (C. A. Mead and L. Conway, aus.), pp. 271 292. Addison-Wesley, Reading, Massachusetts, 1980.
2. H. T. Kung, Why systolic architectures? *Computer* **15**, 37–46 (January 1982).
3. L. Johnson, VLSI algorithms for Doolittle's, Crout's and Cholesky's methods, *Proc. IEEE International Conf. Circuits Computers, Sept. 1982*, pp. 372–376 (1982).
4. P. S. Liu and T. Y. Young, VLSI array design under constraint of limited I/O bandwidth, *IEEE Trans. Computers* **C-32**, 1160–1170 (1983).
5. T. Y. Young and P. S. Liu, Impact of VLSI on pattern recognition and image processing, *in* "VLSI Electronics: Microstructure Science" (N. G. Einspruch, ed.), Vol. 4, pp. 319–360. Academic Press, New York, 1982.
6. H. M. Ahmed, J. M. Delsome, and M. Morf, Highly concurrent computing structure for matrix arithematic and signal processing, *Computer* **15**, 65–82 (January 1982).
7. L. Snyder, Introduction to the configurable, highly parallel computer, *Computer* **15**, 47–56 (January 1982).
8. S. Y. Kung, K. S. Arun, R. J. Gal-Ezer, and D. V. Bhaskar Rao, Wavefront array processor: language, architecture, and applications, *IEEE Trans. Computers* **C-31**, 1054–1066 (1982).
9. T. Y. Young and T. W. Calvert, "Classification, Estimation and Pattern Recognition." Elsevier, New York, 1974.
10. K. Hwang, and S. P. Su, A partitioned matrix approach to VLSI pattern classification, *Proc. Workshop Comp. Arch. Pattern Analysis Image Database Management, Nov. 1981*, pp. 168–177 (1981).
11. K. Hwang and Y.-H. Cheng, Partitioned matrix algorithm for VLSI arithematic systems, *IEEE Trans. Computers* **C-31**, 1215–1224 (1982).
12. T. Y. Young, P. S. Liu, and Y. Gao, Reconfigurable VLSI arrays for pattern analysis and image processing, *Proc. Workshop Comp. Arch. Pattern Analysis Image Database Management, Oct. 1983*, pp. 118–124 (1983).
13. T. Y. Young and P. S. Liu, VLSI arrays for pattern recognition and image processing: I/O bandwidth considerations, *in* "VLSI for Pattern Recognition and Image Processing" (K. S. Fu, ed.), pp. 25–42. Springer-Verlag, New York, 1984.
14. H. H. Liu and K. S. Fu, VLSI arrays for minimum distance classifications, *in* "VLSI for Pattern Recognition and Image Processing" (K. S. Fu, ed.), pp. 45–63. Springer-Verlag, New York, 1984.
15. L. M. Ni and A. K. Jain, A VLSI systolic architecture for pattern clustering, *Proc. Workshop Comp. Arch. Pattern Analysis Image Database Management, Oct. 1983*, pp. 110–117 (1983).
16. Y. T. Chiang and K. S. Fu, Parallel parsing algorithm and VLSI implementations for syntactic pattern recognition, *IEEE Trans. Pattern Analysis Machine Intelligence* **PAMI-6**, 302–314 (1984).
17. Y. P. Chiang and K. S. Fu, VLSI arrays for syntactic pattern recognition, *in* "VLSI for Pattern Recognition and Image Processing" (K. S. Fu, ed.), pp. 85–104. Springer-Verlag, New York, 1984.
18. P. T. Muller, Jr., L. J. Siegel, and H. J. Siegel, Parallel algorithms for the two-dimensional FFT, *Proc. 5th Intl. Conf. Pattern Recognition, Dec. 1980*, pp. 497–503 (1980).
19. T. Y. Young and P. S. Liu, VLSI arrays and control structure for image processing, *Proc. Workshop Comp. Arch. Pattern Analysis Image Database Management, Nov. 1981*, pp. 257–264 (1981).
20. M. J. Clarke and C. R. Dyer, Curve detection in VLSI, *in* "VLSI for Pattern Recognition and Image Processing" (K. S. Fu, ed.), pp. 157–173. Springer-Verlag, New York, 1984.

21. H. T. Kung, Special-Purpose Devices for Signal and Image Processing: An Opportunity in VLSI. Tech. Rep. CS-80-132, Dept. Computer Science, Carnegie-Mellon University, Pittsburgh, Pennsylvania, 1980.

22. R. Nathan, Large array VLSI filter, *Proc. Workshop Comp. Arch. Pattern Analysis and Image Database Management, Oct. 1983*, pp. 15–21 (1983).

23. J. Grinberg, G. R. Nudd, and R. D. Etchells, A cellular VLSI architecture, *Computer* **17**, 69–81 (January 1984).

24. G. R. Nudd, Concurrent systems for image analysis, *in* "VLSI for Pattern Recognition and Image Processing" (K. S. Fu, ed.), pp. 107–132. Springer-Verlag, New York, 1984.

Part **IV**

Applications

# Chapter **20**

# Computer Recognition of Speech*

RENATO DE MORI and DAVID PROBST

Department of Computer Science
Concordia University
Montreal, Quebec

## INTRODUCTION I

At present, a number of scientists and engineers seem to be quite interested in doing research in the area of speech recognition by computer. Different workers in the field have different approaches and might even describe their motivations for doing speech recognition research somewhat differently. A very common position, for example, is that the main goal of speech recognition research is to develop techniques and systems for speech input to machines. If we consider machines that are real computers, rather than mere automatic dictation devices, this makes speech recognition an instance of the general problem of designing a convenient and pleasant human–computer interface, the ultimate goal being the ability to talk to computers in much the same way we now talk to fellow human beings. Indeed, if both speech recognition and general machine intelligence make sufficient progress in our lifetimes, we could conceivably encounter computers that not only listen but also reply sensibly.

* This chapter is dedicated to the memory of Eva De Mori.

**HANDBOOK OF PATTERN RECOGNITION
AND IMAGE PROCESSING**

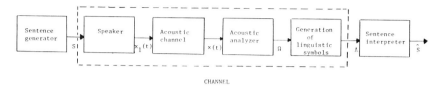

CHANNEL

**Fig. 1.**   Transformations of information in speech communication. $S$, sentence representation; $x_1(t)$, generated signal; $x(t)$, received signal; $\Omega$, acoustic pattern, $\Lambda$, lattice of hypotheses composed of linguistic symbols; $\hat{S}$, interpretation.

Even so, this ambitious desire to make spoken input part of the human–computer interface, while undoubtedly deeply rooted in genuine practical concerns, is only one of several possible motivations; we would also argue that speech recognition is not only useful but also interesting.

Figure 1 shows the essential transformations of information involved in speech communication. Initially, a sentence generator produces an abstract representation $S$ of the sentence to be transmitted. This abstract representation $S$ is then converted by the speaker into a sequence of sets of discrete articulatory commands which drive the vocal tract actuators, producing a continuously time-varying pressure signal $x_1(t)$. The signal $x_1(t)$ is transmitted through a noisy acoustic channel, resulting in a different signal $x(t)$ which is perceived by the listener. The listener transforms the signal $x(t)$ into an acoustic pattern $\Omega$. The acoustic pattern is then interpreted by a recognition–understanding system which first transforms the acoustic information in $\Omega$ into an abstract, linguistic representation $\Lambda$. Unfortunately $\Lambda$ is not $S$. Rather, it may be a continuous string or a lattice of characters or of word hypotheses which must be interpreted in order to produce $\hat{S}$, the recognition system's final interpretation of $x(t)$. In a satisfactory recognition system, the self-correcting mechanisms of perception function well enough to produce an $\hat{S}$ which is $S$ most of the time.

Some speech recognition workers have chosen to apply the discipline of information theory to the construction of recognizers [1]. That theory as originally conceived is a mathematical theory designed to measure the amount of information necessary to reduce the receiver's doubt concerning given alternatives.

A second approach consists in matching sequences of feature vectors with prototypes [2]. This matching must take into account the fact that words and sentences can be enunciated at different speeds. Dynamic programming is an excellent tool for performing the associated nonlinear time warping.

These methods are usually speaker dependent and are made speaker independent by clustering prototypes obtained from many speakers. The classifier is not capable of making reliable decisions about phonemes or phonetic features; rather, it generates scored competing hypotheses that are combined together to form scored word and sentence candidates.

If the protocol exhibits enough redundancy, it is likely that the cumulative score of the right candidate is significantly higher than the scores of competing candidates. If, however, there is little redundancy in the protocols, as in the case of connected letters or digits or in the case of a large lexicon, then it is important that ambiguities at the phonetic level are resolved before hypotheses are generated. Examples of these difficulties have been reported in the recent literature [3, 4]. For example, in the case of connected letters, in order to distinguish between /p/ and /t/ the place of articulation is the only distinctive feature, and its detection may require the execution of special sensory procedures on a limited portion of the signal.

For this purpose a third approach may be used where the sentence interpreter is conceived as a rule-based system, and the rules encode the a priori knowledge we have about human speech generation and understanding. This chapter will review the three approaches mentioned earlier.

There are very few books on computer recognition of speech. Some of them are monographs on particular projects [5, 6], while others are collections of chapters by different authors reflecting a variety of views [7–11]. A paper by Doddington [12] discusses the performance of some commercially available products. Speech databases for English [13] and French [14] have been developed for helping in comparing the performances of new products.

## DYNAMIC PROGRAMMING METHODS  II

One approach to computer recognition of speech requires that we compare two sequences of elements and compute the distance between them by finding an optimal alignment or correspondence between the elements of one sequence and those of the other. In speech research, these sequence comparison methods are capable of performing nonuniform *time warping* using *dynamic programming* (DP). The name refers to allowing nonlinear distortions of time scales in computing the acoustic similarity between a reference prototype and features extracted from the input utterance, thereby taking into account speaking rate variability as well as substitution, insertion, and deletion errors; dynamic programming is an efficient algorithm by which both optimal alignments and the resulting distances are computed at the same time. Data and prototypes to be matched are represented by discrete sequences produced after either synchronous or asynchronous sampling of the continuous speech signal; due to normal speech variability, two sequences arising from two utterances of the same word may exhibit a number of local differences.

These local differences may be that one element has been substituted for another, that an element has been inserted, or that an element has been deleted. Other local difference models are conceivable, for example, one that allows expansion of a single element into several elements or compression of several elements into a single element, as independent types of local difference; for the moment, we restrict our attention to substitutions, insertions, and deletions. Given two sequences and costs (or weights) of the local differences, an alignment is assigned a cost equal to the sum of the costs of the local differences in it; the distance between the two sequences is the least cost of any alignment. A formal account follows.

Let $\mathbf{a} = \langle a_1, a_2, \ldots, a_m \rangle$ be a *source sequence* of length $m$ and let $\mathbf{b} = \langle b_1, b_2, \ldots, b_n \rangle$ be a *target sequence* of length $n$. For the moment, we suppose that $a_i$ and $b_j$ are symbols taken from a finite alphabet; the sequence $\mathbf{a}$ is a representation of the speech pattern of a template or prototype, while $\mathbf{b}$ is a representation of an unknown word or training instance. The two sequences are connected by an *alignment* or *matching* if there are two monotonically nondecreasing integer sequences $\mathbf{i} = \langle i_1, i_2, \ldots, i_k \rangle$ and $\mathbf{j} = \langle j_1, j_2, \ldots, j_k \rangle$ both of length $k$ (and subject to certain continuity constraints) with the convention that, for any $1 \leq h \leq k$, if $i = i_h$ and $j = j_h$, then $a_i$ is made to correspond to $b_j$ of both $i$ and $j$ have increased in the last step, $a_i$ to ø (the null element) if only $u_i$ has increased, and ø to $b_j$ if only $j$ has increased. In the case where an element of $\mathbf{a}$ corresponds, in the final matching, to a null element, a *deletion* is said to have occurred. In the case where an element of $\mathbf{b}$ corresponds to a null element, an *insertion* is said to have occurred. Finally, in the case where an element $a_i$ of $\mathbf{a}$ corresponds to an element $b_j$ of $\mathbf{b}$, a *substitution* is said to have occurred; if $a_i = b_j$, then this substitution is a *continuation*.

We can display these correspondences graphically in matrix form with the source sequence $\mathbf{a}$ running vertically upward and the target sequence $\mathbf{b}$ running horizontally to the right; in this representation, a substitution is shown by a diagonal arc in the box indexed by $a_i$ and $b_j$. Deletions are shown by vertical arcs indexed by the deleted $a_i$, while insertions are shown by horizontal arcs indexed by the inserted $b_j$ (see Fig. 2).

The number of arcs may vary from $\max(m, n)$ to $m + n - 1$; this number is the length $k$. These arcs lead from the origin through a sequence of points $\mathbf{c} = \langle c_1, c_2, \ldots, c_k \rangle$, where $c_h = \langle j_h, i_h \rangle$. This sequence of points expresses the warping of time scales between the source $\mathbf{a}$ and the target $\mathbf{b}$. In the discussion so far, a point $\langle j, i \rangle$ has the possible successors $\langle j + 1, i \rangle$, $\langle j, i + 1 \rangle$, and $\langle j + 1, i + 1 \rangle$.

We seek the optimal alignment between sequence $\mathbf{a}$ and sequence $\mathbf{b}$; the distance $d(\mathbf{a}, \mathbf{b})$ between the two sequences is defined to be the cost of the optimal alignment. We shall consider a weighted Levenshtein distance [15] in which $D(a_i)$ is the cost of deleting $a_i$, $I(b_j)$ is the cost of inserting $b_j$, and $S(a_i, b_j)$ is the cost of substituting $b_j$ for $a_i$. When $a_i = b_j$, $S(a_i, b_j) = 0$. The cost of an alignment is the sum of the costs of the deletions, insertions, and substitutions contained within it; the optimal alignment is the one with the

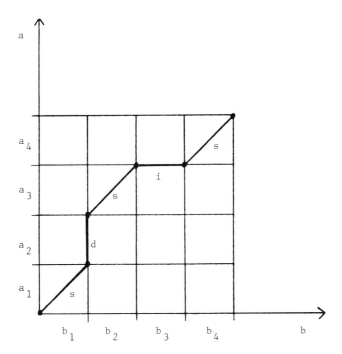

**Fig. 2.** Local differences in DP matching.

least cost and this cost, by definition, is $d(\mathbf{a}, \mathbf{b})$. Given sequences $\mathbf{a}$ and $\mathbf{b}$, and cost functions $D$, $I$, and $S$, an efficient dynamic programming algorithm simultaneously computes the optimal alignment and the distance $d(\mathbf{a}, \mathbf{b})$.

Let $\mathbf{a}^i$ and $\mathbf{b}^j$ denote $\langle a_1, a_2, \dots, a_i \rangle$ and $\langle b_1, b_2, \dots, b_j \rangle$, respectively. We have $\mathbf{a}^m = \mathbf{a}$ and $\mathbf{b}^n = \mathbf{b}$. A matching is a path from $\langle 0, 0 \rangle$ to $\langle n, m \rangle$. With the weighted Levenshtein scheme under consideration, the distance $d(\mathbf{a}, \mathbf{b})$ and the final matching may be determined by successively computing

$$d(\mathbf{a}^i, \mathbf{b}^j) = \min \begin{cases} d(\mathbf{a}^{i-1}, \mathbf{b}^j) + D(a_i) \\ d(\mathbf{a}^{i-1}, \mathbf{b}^{j-1}) + S(a_i, b_j) \\ d(\mathbf{a}^i, \mathbf{b}^{j-1}) + I(b_j) \end{cases}$$

and recording whether point $\langle j, i \rangle$ was reached from point $\langle j, i-1 \rangle$, point $\langle j-1, i-1 \rangle$, or point $\langle j-1, i \rangle$. The idea here is that optimal alignments are obtained by extending optimal alignments involving less of sequence $\mathbf{a}$, less of sequence $\mathbf{b}$, or less of both sequences; this idea is known as the "principle of optimality."

This is only one of several possible schemes; others may be more appropriate in certain contexts for either theoretical or practical reasons. For example, we may wish to define pattern distance so that $d(\mathbf{a}, \mathbf{b})$ possesses certain desirable properties. One possible list of desirable properties is as follows.

(1)  Positive semidefinite: $d(\mathbf{a}, \mathbf{b}) \geq 0$, $d(\mathbf{a}, \mathbf{a}) = 0$.
(2)  Symmetric: $d(\mathbf{a}, \mathbf{b}) = d(\mathbf{b}, \mathbf{a})$.
(3)  Time reversible: $d(\mathbf{a}, \mathbf{b}) = d(\mathbf{a}', \mathbf{b}')$, where $\mathbf{a}' = \langle a_m, a_{m-1}, \ldots, a_1 \rangle$ and $\mathbf{b}' = \langle b_n, b_{n-1}, \ldots, b_1 \rangle$.
(4)  Linear matching consistent: when $m = n$ and optimal alignment is linear,

$$d(\mathbf{a}, \mathbf{b}) = \sum_i \frac{w(a_i, b_i)}{m}$$

As alternatives to the basic scheme, we quote one rectangular DP matching scheme and one trapezoidal DP matching scheme.

*Rectangular scheme*:

$$g(1, 1) = 2w(1, 1)$$

$$g(i, j) = \min \begin{cases} g(i, j-1) + w(i, j) \\ g(i-1, j) + w(i, j) \\ g(i-1, j-1) + 2w(i, j) \end{cases}$$

$$d(m, n) = g(m, n)/(m + n)$$

*Trapezoidal scheme*:

$$g(1, 1) = 2w(1, 1)$$

$$g(i, j) = \min \begin{cases} g(i, j-1) + w(i, j-1) + w(i, j) \\ g(i-1, j) + w(i-j, j) + w(i, j) \\ g(i-1, j-1) + 2w(i-1, j-1) + 2w(i, j) \end{cases}$$

$$d(m, n) = [g(m, n) + 2w(m, n)]/2(m + n)$$

In this notation $w(i, j)$ is a local distance measure defining a measure of dissimilarity between the corresponding acoustic events. Also, $d(m, n) = d(\mathbf{a}^m, \mathbf{b}^n) = d(\mathbf{a}, \mathbf{b})$. Our basic scheme does not possess property (4). The first scheme does not possess property (3). The second scheme possesses, apart from property (1), all three desirable properties, that is, (2), (3), and (4). For more discussion of this matter, see Sakoe and Chiba [16] and Sakai [17].

In Fig. 3, we show a DP matching between a prototype source and a trainee target; here, the word is the digit zero and the sequence elements are drawn from a finite alphabet of primary phonetic features. This alphabet is defined in Table III, shown in Section IV. Here, $\mathbf{a} = \langle NA, VF, SON, VB \rangle$ and $\mathbf{b} = \langle NA, VF, SON, VB, VC \rangle$. The DP matching algorithm discovers four continuations and one insertion. The sequence of points is: $\langle 0, 0 \rangle$,

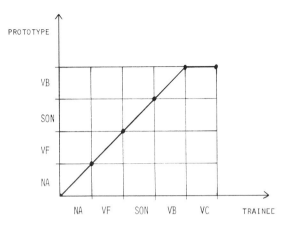

Fig. 3. DP matching of the digit zero.

$\langle 1, 1 \rangle$, $\langle 2, 2 \rangle$, $\langle 3, 3 \rangle$, $\langle 4, 4 \rangle$, $\langle 5, 4 \rangle$. The total distance $d(\mathbf{a}, \mathbf{b})$ depends on distances between the elements of Table III. These distances can be based on phonetic considerations and error statistics.

When the elements of the sequences to be compared are elements from a finite alphabet, then we need only possess tables of the various costs $D(a_i)$, $I(b_j)$, and $S(a_i, b_j)$. Analyzing a substitution cost $S(a_i, b_j)$ is actually computing the "distance" between a set of features in frame $i$ of the source and another set in frame $j$ of the target. If, however, the frames of features are spectra, then a spectral distance must be defined; the sum of distances becomes an integral. One spectral distance is the Itakura–Saito distortion measure [18], given by

$$d(|X|^2; |G|^2) \doteq \int_{-\pi}^{\pi} [|X/G|^2 - \ln(|X/G|^2) - 1] \frac{d\theta}{2\pi}$$

where $X(z)$ is the $z$ transform of the windowed speech data, which have been modeled by an all-pole filter $G(z)$.

In general, these dynamic programming algorithms have quadratic time complexity. The computational requirements are measured as the number of local distance calculations; in the worst case, matching a sequence $\mathbf{a}$ of length $m$ against a sequence $\mathbf{b}$ of length $n$ could have cost $mn$. The cost is therefore the area of the matrix or grid which is formed by the sequences $\mathbf{a}$ and $\mathbf{b}$. If $N$ is the number of time frames in the input pattern, and if $N_j$ is the number of frames in the $j$th prototype, then matching the input against $J$ prototypes has a worst-case cost of $N \sum_{j=1}^{J} N_j$. The worst-case running time can be reduced by various heuristics, including introducing a matching window so that optimal paths through the grid are only sought within a subset of the grid; this may be accomplished by requiring that $|j - i| \le r$, where $r$ is the window size. This defines a strip around the diagonal line.

Dynamic programming techniques originally developed for isolated word recognition have also been applied to the problem of recognizing connected words. Here, the spoken input is a sequence of words from a specified vocabulary, and matching occurs against isolated word reference templates. We are given an input pattern with some number of time frames. We also possess a set of reference templates, where each template has a length equal to the number of frames in that template. The goal is to find that sequence of templates that best matches the input pattern for a particular match criterion. The concatenation of templates is referred to as a "super" reference pattern. We discuss two proposed solutions to this problem, the two-level algorithm of Sakoe [19] and the level-building algorithm of Myers and Rabiner [20]. Also worth mentioning in this context is the one-stage dynamic programming algorithm of Ney [21].

We give a very brief description of Sakoe's two-level DP matching algorithm for finding the "best" match to a given test string of words. The two levels are word-level matching followed by phrase-level matching. On the first level, all reference patterns are systematically matched against all possible subsections of the test pattern; we compute the word distances that describe how well a contiguous region of the test pattern (some number of frames) matches some reference template. We store the distance and the index of the best template for each of the possible portions of the test pattern. When phrase-level matching begins, the distance scores generated in the previous phase are used to obtain an optimal estimate of the unknown sequence of words by minimizing the total distance of all possible word sequences. Both distances between test pattern sections and reference patterns and distances between initial segments of the test pattern and concatenations of reference templates are calculated using dynamic programming techniques.

We now move on to a brief description of Myers and Rabiner's level-building dynamic time-warping (DTW) algorithm for connected word recognition; the underlying idea is that the matching of all possible word sequences can be performed by successive concatenation of reference patterns. At the beginning, the time registration of the test pattern against a given super reference pattern is considered; it is observed that the algorithm can be implemented in levels, that is, one reference (of the super reference pattern) at a time. The computation matches test frames only against frames within a particular reference; the set of accumulated distances between different segments of the test pattern and that reference are saved and used as a set of initial distances for the next level. This idea is then extended to a level-building algorithm with multiple reference patterns, that is, when each reference of the super reference pattern is one of a set of reference patterns. A more formal account follows.

Assume we have an $L$-word connected word sequence which is represented as an input test pattern $\mathbf{b} = \langle b_1, b_2, \ldots, b_n \rangle$. The goal of the level-building DTW algorithm is to find a sequence $\mathbf{R} = \langle R_1, R_2, \ldots, R_L \rangle$ of $L$ reference patterns such that each $R_i$ is one of a fixed set of reference patterns and such that $R_1$, $R_2$, etc. have been chosen to minimize the distance $d(\mathbf{a}, \mathbf{b})$ between the sequence $\mathbf{a} = \langle a_1, a_2, \ldots, a_m \rangle$ formed by concatenating the frames of $R_1$, $R_2$, etc. given the choices for $R_1$, $R_2$, etc. and the input test pattern $\mathbf{b}$. In other words, we construct the optimal sequence $\mathbf{a}$.

We will consistently use constrained DTW algorithms in which the slope of the warping function lies within a certain range, that is, grid paths will lie between upper and lower warping constraint lines.

We build up all possible $L$-word matches one level (word) at a time; at each level, information about accumulated distances, best word candidates, and backtracking pointers is retained and used at the next level of the algorithm. Only at the end of the final level is backtracking used to recover the optimal sequence $\mathbf{a}$.

On the first level, we find matches between initial portions $\mathbf{b}^j$ of $\mathbf{b}$ and reference patterns $R_k$; for a particular $R_k$, its length in frames and the warping constraint lines will force the values of $j$ to lie within a certain range. Let $J_1$ (for level 1) denote the union over $k$ of these ranges. For each $j \in J_1$, we determine both the reference pattern $R^{(j)}$ which best matches $\mathbf{b}^j$ and the distance $d(\mathbf{a}^{(j)}, \mathbf{b}^j)$, where $\mathbf{a}^{(j)}$ is the sequence of frames of $R^{(j)}$. For each $j \in J_1$, the backtracking pointers indicate that the portions $\mathbf{b}^j$ start from $b_1$.

On the second level, we will find matches between embedded portions $\mathbf{b}^{j',j}$ of $\mathbf{b}$ and reference patterns $R_k$; here $j'$ is the initial index of the portion and $j$ is the final index. In contrast to level 1, where portions automatically begin at $b_1$, on level 2, a portion $\mathbf{b}^{j',j}$ may begin at any $j'$ for which $j' - 1 \in J_1$. As on level 1, there will be a global range $J_2$ determined by $J_1$, the length of the $R_k$, and the warping constraint lines. In general, $J_l$ is the ending range for paths on level $l$. For each $j \in J_2$, using the accumulated distances from level 1, we determine both the reference pattern $R^{(j)}$ which best matches $\mathbf{b}^{j',j}$ and the distance $d(\mathbf{a}^{(j)}, \mathbf{b}^j)$, where $\mathbf{a}^{(j)}$ is now the concatenation of the best match for $\mathbf{b}^{j'-1}$ and the best match for $\mathbf{b}^{j',j}$. For each $j \in J_2$, the backtracking pointers indicate that the best match to frame $b_j$ at level 2 comes from a particular portion $\mathbf{b}^{j',j}$, that is, it records the value of $j'$. In other words, for each $j$, the optimal $j'$ is determined.

On level $l$, for each $j \in J_l$, we determine the minimum accumulated distance for matching $\mathbf{b}^j$, the best reference pattern $R_k$ for the match at level $l$, and a backtracking pointer which expresses that the best path to $b_j$ at level $l$ arises from matching a particular embedded portion $\mathbf{b}^{j',j}$. In other words, for each ending frame, we have a minimum distance, a best pattern, and an optimal portion. On the last level, only a single path is retained, as this is the path that yields the solution to the original minimization problem. We backtrack as follows. The last word is the best word on the last level. The last portion is of the form $\mathbf{b}^{j+1,n}$. This determines an optimal ending frame, namely, $b_j$, on the previous level. The second to the last word is the best word for this ending frame on this level. The process continues until the entire sequence of words has been recovered. A segmentation of the test string into appropriate matching regions is also produced.

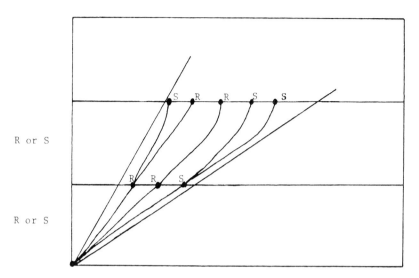

**Fig. 4.** Lower stages of the level-building algorithm.

Assuming only two reference patterns, $R$ and $S$, both of equal length, we can diagram the first two levels of the algorithm in Fig. 4. We find optimal paths from the origin to each of the three possible ending points of level 1; then, for each possible ending point of level 2, we find both an optimal starting point and an optimal path from the starting point to the ending point.

We now present a more general framework which allows a simpler presentation of algorithms such as the level-building algorithm. Consider a directed network **a** (with a single source and a single sink) such that we need to find the best match between a sequence **b** and any possible alternative sequence in the network **a** (which runs from the source to the sink). Let the elements from both the network **a** and the sequence **b**, as before, be taken from a finite alphabet. As directed cycles are excluded, we can number the nodes of the network so that every node is assigned a larger number than any of its predecessors. The goal is to obtain a best match between the network $\mathbf{a} = \langle a_1, a_2, \ldots, a_m \rangle$ and the sequence $\mathbf{b} = \langle b_1, b_2, \ldots, b_n \rangle$; the crucial fact is that, while the predecessor of $b_j$ in **b** is $b_{j-1}$, the predecessors of $a_i$ in **a**, in general, form a set $\{a_{i*} | i^* \text{ indexes a predecessor of } a_i\}$ determined by the network **a**.

We can now obtain the direct analog of our basic scheme by successively computing

$$
d(\mathbf{a}^i, \mathbf{b}^j) = \min_{i^*} \begin{cases} d(\mathbf{a}^{i*}, \mathbf{b}^j) + D(a_i) \\ d(\mathbf{a}^{i*}, \mathbf{b}^{j-1}) + S(a_i, b_j) \\ d(\mathbf{a}^i, \mathbf{b}^{j-1}) + I(b_j) \end{cases}
$$

and recording whether point $\langle j, i \rangle$ was reached from a particular point $\langle j, i^* \rangle$, a particular point $\langle j - 1, i^* \rangle$, or point $\langle j - 1, i \rangle$. Optimal alignments between network **a** and sequence **b** are obtained by extending optimal alignments involving less of a particular sequence through **a**, less of sequence **b**, or less of both. When this computation finishes, we have determined both the optimal sequence through **a** which best matches sequence **b** and also the distance $d(\mathbf{a}, \mathbf{b})$.

The level-building algorithm is an easy special case. The set of reference templates, i.e., reference sequences, with a dummy common predecessor source and a dummy common successor sink forms a directed network whose possible paths include all one-word sequences from the vocabulary. Adding a null path to each network and then concatenating $L$ networks gives us a super network whose possible paths are all possible super reference patterns of length up to $L$. Using directed-network DP matching as described, we easily compute the optimal super reference pattern.

The implicit goal of each of the algorithms considered is to escape from the combinatorial explosion that would occur if we tried matching all combinations of reference patterns one after the other. The time complexity of the network algorithm is linear in the number of templates and quadratic in the number of frames of the test pattern. It is also worth noting that when moving through the level-building network, $a_i$ will have multiple predecessors only at template boundaries; this allows a clear distinction to be made between within-template transition rules and transition rules at template boundaries.

Interesting improvements in the DP matching algorithm have been proposed by Bridle *et al.* [22]. A VLSI implementation of the DP matching algorithm is given by Weste *et al.* [23]. Experimental results for the recognition of 200 Russian words are reported by Velichiko and Zagoruiko [24], for the recognition of isolated English digits by Rosenberg and Shipley [25], for the recognition of connected English digits by Rabuner *et al.* [26], and for speaker-independent connected word recognition by Myers and Levinson [27].

### NETWORK-BASED SYSTEMS III

In the previous section we studied dynamic time-warping systems originally developed for isolated word recognition and later extended to recognition of strings of connected words. In this section we look at two representative network-based systems, CMU's Harpy system and IBM's Markov modeling system, which are directed toward the more difficult problem of continuous speech recognition. In the general form of this problem we are interested in large-vocabulary, speaker-independent recognition; the two systems under consideration restrict the problem considerably by introducing grammatical and/or task constraints so that a simple finite-state model may be built of the entire language to be recognized.

Both systems compile knowledge at different levels of the language model into an integrated network. In the Harpy system, phonetic, phonological, lexical, and syntactic constraints have been combined into a single model which generates all acceptable pronunciations of all recognizable sentences; in the IBM system, each word of the top-level language model is replaced by a phonetic subsource, and then each phone is replaced by an acoustic sub-source, yielding a model of all acoustical realizations of sentences in the language. An important difference between the two networks is the fact that, in the IBM system, all sources and subsources are Markov models, while in Harpy, Markov networks have given way to transition networks with no a priori probabilities associated to symbols that label transitions; as already mentioned, in both cases the integrated language models are finite-state models.

Another important difference is that Harpy uses segmentation while the IBM system does not. In Harpy, the acoustic signal is divided into variable-length segments that represent "stable" portions of the acoustic signal; spectral characteristics of each segment are then determined for use in phone template matching. The assumption here is that, given enough allophone templates, it is reasonable to attempt labeling of segments using pattern matching techniques. Asynchronous segmentation is performed top-down and then the network is used to select prototypes to be matched with the data. In the IBM system, no attempt is made to try to segment the speech into phoneme-like units; instead, a time-synchronous acoustic processor produces parameter vectors computed from successive fixed-length intervals of the speech waveform. A parameter vector coming from a 10-msec frame is matched against a set of prototypes; the parameter vector is then labeled by giving it the name of the prototype to which it is closest. Another possibility is that of using the input vector for retrieving a priori probabilities of different labels.

We now give a brief account of the CMU Harpy speech recognition system [28]. The Harpy system is an attempt to combine the best features of the Hearsay I system and the Dragon system [29]. The most significant aspects of the system design are an *integrated network* language model (knowledge representation) and use of *beam search* through the network during recognition. Segmentation is attempted, phonetic classification depends on unique templates, and word juncture knowledge is an integral part of the network. A word network exists such that any path through the network gives an acceptable sentence. Each word is replaced by a pronunciation network which represents expected pronunciations of the word. After words have been replaced by their subnetworks, word juncture rules are applied to the network to model phone string variations due to influences of neighboring words.

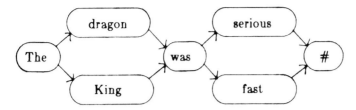

Fig. 5. Nonredundant grammar network.

During compilation into the composite network, various optimization heuristics are applied to yield an efficient phone network, that is, a network of acceptable pronunciations. During the recognition process, Harpy attempts to find an optimal sequence of phones satisfying two criteria: (a) the sequence must represent a legal path through the network and (b) the sequence should consist of phones with high acoustic match probabilities. It is possible that the best fit to a particular segment in the left-to-right search does not correspond to the correct interpretation; to compensate for this, a beam-search strategy is used in which a group of near-miss alternatives around the best path is examined. When the end of the sentence is reached, the phone sequence with the lowest total distance is selected; backtracing through the globally best sequence obtained at the end of forward searching yields the desired phone and word assignments.

In Harpy, a grammar network is initially specified by a BNF grammar, and then null states and redundant paths are removed. A grammar (or word) network is illustrated in Fig. 5.

A pronunciation dictionary and phone characteristics allow us to replace words with their subnetworks. A simplified subnetwork for the word *was* is shown in Fig. 6. As before, redundant paths are removed; phonetic symbols are taken from the ARPAbet [8].

So far we have seen illustrations of syntactic knowledge and lexical knowledge, although information about phone duration has been deliberately omitted from the latter. The phonetic network attempts to capture intraword phonological phenomena; word boundary phonological phenomena, on the other hand, are represented by word juncture rules, which contain examples of insertion, deletion, and substitution of phones at word

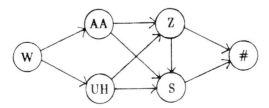

Fig. 6. Nonredundant phonetic network.

boundaries. The word juncture rules are expressed as graph rewriting rules, which are then applied to the network as it exists so far. Finally, as before, redundant paths are removed.

Harpy's front end performs rough segmentation based on zero-crossing rates and peaks in smoothed and differenced waveform parameters (called "zapdash" parameters). Quasi-stationary segments derived from the zapdash parameters are matched against phone templates. These phone templates are linear prediction spectral templates, and comparison is based on Itakura's minimum prediction residual error measure, which computes similarity in spectral shape. The spectral templates are talker specific but new templates may be learned automatically, for example, by adapting speaker-independent templates. The beam-search strategy for searching the finite-state graph prunes from further consideration paths scoring less than a variable threshold; rather than using a priori probabilities to find the most likely path through the network, Harpy relies only on spectral distance. By beam searching many alternatives simultaneously, the need for backtracking is eliminated.

Before going on to the stochastic models used in the IBM continuous speech recognition system, it may be useful to say a few words about spectral vector quantization. In systems like Harpy and Hearsay II [30], segments are detected asynchronously and then labeled; labeling a variable-length segment consists of recording, for each allophonic template, the probability that the segment represents an occurrence of that particular template. In contrast, synchronous nonsegmenting systems consider successive fixed-length frames of the speech signal. For each frame, we obtain a vector $\mathbf{x}$ of parameters representing the spectrum of that frame of speech. In vector quantization, our problem, for each such $\mathbf{x}$, is to find that codeword $\mathbf{x}_i$ in a codebook of stored prototypes whose spectral distance from $\mathbf{x}$ is minimum. In this speech coding technique, we have the collection of possible reproduction vectors $\mathbf{x}_1$, $\mathbf{x}_2, \ldots, \mathbf{x}_n$, which is stored in the reproduction codebook or simply the codebook of the quantizer; the reproduction vectors are called codewords (or templates). Moreover, we have a distance classifier which allows us to compare vectors according to a spectral distance. The encoding is illustrated in Fig. 7. Problems in constructing a good vector quantizer include choosing a good spectral representation, choosing a good spectral distance, and choosing a good set of spectral representatives in the codebook, usually through training. For more details see Ref. 31.

We now describe IBM's maximum-likelihood approach to continuous speech recognition [1]. The system is based on Markov models of language and has been implemented using two control strategies: (a) a Viterbi algorithm and (b) a left-to-right stack decoder algorithm that estimates the probability that a given partial hypothesis can be extended to yield the actual sentence. Important aspects of the system design include the presence of a priori transition probabilities in the finite-state language model and formula-

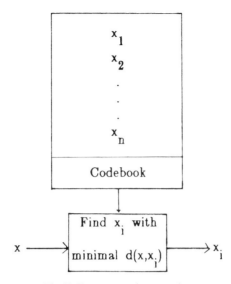

**Fig. 7.** Vector quantizer encoder.

tion of speech recognition as a problem of maximum-likelihood decoding. As such, statistical models of the speech production process are required. The choice between the two control strategies or decoding methods mentioned earlier is a function of degree of task constraint, that is, the size of the state space.

In the IBM approach, the allowed sentences are either described *a priori* by an artificial grammar or else limited by a vocabulary and a task domain in which models may be constructed from observed data. The distinctive feature of the IBM approach is that speech recognition is formulated as a problem in *communication theory*. The speaker and the acoustic processor are conceptually combined into a single unit, the *acoustic channel*. Fig. 8 shows the relation between the text generator, the acoustic channel, and the linguistic decoder.

In this diagram, **w** is a string of words generated by the text generator, **y** is a string of acoustic processor output symbols (more specifically, a string of prototype identifiers, one for each 10 msec of speech), and **ŵ** is the word string produced by the linguistic decoder as an estimate of the word string **w**. The acoustic channel provides the linguistic decoder with a noisy string from which it must attempt to recover the original message. The linguistic decoder

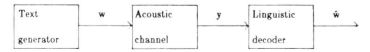

**Fig. 8.** Speech recognition as a communications problem.

searches for a word string **w** which maximizes the probability $P(\mathbf{w}, \mathbf{y})$ of the joint observation of $\langle \mathbf{w}, \mathbf{y} \rangle$ at the two ends of the channel.

We are interested in maximizing the likelihood $P(\mathbf{w}, \mathbf{y}) = P(\mathbf{w})P(\mathbf{y}|\mathbf{w})$ over **w** for fixed **y**; this is equivalent to maximizing $P(\mathbf{w}|\mathbf{y})$ since $P(\mathbf{y})$ is equal for all the candidates. Here $P(\mathbf{w})$ is the a priori probability that the word sequence **w** is produced by the text generator; the computation therefore requires a stochastic model of the text generator. On the other hand, $P(\mathbf{y}|\mathbf{w})$ is the probability that the speaker together with the acoustic processor will transform the word string **w** into the acoustic processor output string **y**. A stochastic model of the acoustic channel will account for both the speaker's phonological and acoustic–phonetic variations and for the unvarying (deterministic) performance of the acoustic processor. Given models that specify both $P(\mathbf{w})$ and $P(\mathbf{y}|\mathbf{w})$, the linguistic decoder may determine **w** using some algorithm which is appropriate to the size of the language.

The model of text generation is a language model. Whether the text is generated from an artificial grammar or naturally generated within a limited task domain, the model has the form of a Markov source consisting of states connected by transitions; with each transition there is an associated output word. A probability is attached to each transition. In natural tasks, these probabilities or parameters may be estimated from a large sample of text. The model of the acoustic channel is also a Markov source. If we first model the channel performance for each word in the vocabulary, we can then model the effect on a word string **w** by concatenating the models for the individual words. Ultimately, we will embed acoustic channel word models in the Markov source specifying the language model. This will be explained later.

A *Markov source* is a stochastic automaton $\langle S, T, A, M \rangle$, where $S$ is a finite set of states (with designated initial and final states $s_I$ and $s_F$), $T$ a finite set of transitions, $A$ a finite alphabet of output symbols, and $M$ a map $T \rightarrow S \times A \times S, t \mapsto (l, a, r)$. Moreover, there is a probability $q_s(t)$ associated with each transition $t$. When $s \neq l$, $q_s(t) = 0$. Occasionally, we will abbreviate $q_l(t)$ as $q(t)$. Here $q_s(t)$ is the probability that transition $t$ will be chosen next when state $s$ is reached. Figure 9 shows a Markov source.

A sequence of transitions $\mathbf{t}^n = \langle t_1, t_2, \ldots, t_n \rangle$ for which $l_1$ is the initial state is called a path; if $r_n$ is the final state, it is called a complete path. The

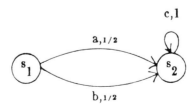

**Fig. 9.** Markov source.

probability of a completely general path $\mathbf{t}^n$, that is, one which may have an $i > 1$ for which $r_{i-1} \neq l_i$, must be expressed as

$$P(\mathbf{t}^n) = \prod_i q_{l_i}(t_i)$$

For paths in which the successor state of a transition is always the predecessor state of the following transition, we may write more simply

$$P(\mathbf{t}^n) = \prod_i q(t_i)$$

With each path $\mathbf{t}^n$ there is an associated output symbol string $\mathbf{a}^n$. Since a given $\mathbf{a}^n$ may result from more than one $\mathbf{t}_n$, its probability is given by

$$P(\mathbf{a}^n) = \sum_{\mathbf{t}^n \to \mathbf{a}^n} P(\mathbf{t}^n)$$

In the IBM system, the language model must assign probabilities to strings of words; the other model is the acoustic channel model. We now consider the problem of modeling the acoustic channel for single words. With each word, we associate a phonetic Markov subsource whose possible output strings, drawn from an alphabet of phones, are all the different phonetic pronunciations of the word. An example is shown in Fig. 10. Just as we have a set of *phonetic subsources*, one for each word, so we also have a set of *acoustic subsources*, one for each phone. An acoustic subsource for a phone is a Markov source whose output alphabet contains the output symbols of the acoustic processor and which specifies both possible acoustic processor outputs for each phone and their probabilities.

We have described Markov models for the language, the individual words, and the individual phones; we are now in a position to describe how these three levels of description can be integrated into a single global Markov source. Replace each transition in the language model by the phonetic subsource for the corresponding word. Now, replace each transition in the resulting network by the acoustic subsource for the corresponding phone. The resulting network is a global Markov source which models the entire process of text generation, speech production, and acoustic processor transformation.

When the state space is not prohibitively large, the linguistic decoder may employ a dynamic programming algorithm known as the *Viterbi algorithm*.

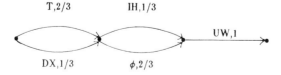

**Fig. 10.** Phonetic Markov subsource for the word "two." (Phones taken from the ARPAbet.)

Each complete path $\mathbf{t}^n$ through the global Markov source determines both a unique word sequence $\mathbf{w}^k$ and a unique acoustic processor output string $\mathbf{y}^m$. (If transitions with null output are allowed, then $m \le n$.) The Viterbi linguistic decoding problem is to determine, for given $\mathbf{y}^m$, the complete path $\mathbf{t}^n$ which maximizes the probability $P(\mathbf{t}^n)$ such that $\mathbf{t}^n$ produces $\mathbf{y}^m$. Although this decoding strategy is not optimal, because of the many $\mathbf{t}$ consistent with a given $\mathbf{w}$ and a given $\mathbf{y}$, good recognition results have been obtained.

We now describe the Viterbi algorithm and show how it may be applied to this problem. The essential observation is that well-known, minimum-cost, path-finding algorithms may be used to find the most probable path in the global Markov source. For simplicity of exposition, we restrict ourselves to situations where a path $\mathbf{t}^k$ of $k$ transitions always yields an output string $\mathbf{y}^k$ of $k$ symbols, that is, each transition produces one output symbol.

Let $\mathbf{t}_*^k(s) = \langle t_1, t_2, \ldots, t_k \rangle$ denote the most probable path such that $r_k = s$ and such that $a_i = y_i$, $1 \le i \le k$. In a Markov process, the probability of being in state $s$ at time $k$ depends only on the state $s'$ at time $k-1$. It follows that there exists a state $s'$ such that $\mathbf{t}_*^{k-1}(s') = \langle t_1, t_2, \ldots, t_{k-1} \rangle$, that is, $\mathbf{t}_*^k(s)$ may be obtained by adjoining $t_k$ to $\mathbf{t}_*^{k-1}(s')$. Moreover, $P(\mathbf{t}_*^k(s)) = P(\mathbf{t}_*^{k-1}(s')) * q(t_k)$. *Proof*: Take $s' = l_k$. If $\langle t_1, t_2, \ldots, t_{k-1} \rangle$ is not the most probable path to state $s'$, then $\langle t_1, t_2, \ldots, t_k \rangle$ cannot be the most probable path to state $s$. (We could substitute a more probable path to $s'$.) The result is that $\mathbf{t}_*^k(s)$ and $P(\mathbf{t}_*^k(s))$ may be computed from the set, for $s' \in S$, of $\mathbf{t}_*^{k-1}(s')$ and $P(\mathbf{t}_*^{k-1}(s'))$. Let $E(s, y) = \{t | r = s \text{ and } a = y\}$. Then

$$P(\mathbf{t}_*^k(s)) = \max_{t \in E(s, y_k)} P(\mathbf{t}_*^{k-1}(l)) * q(t)$$

That is, consider all transitions which both lead to state $s$ and yield output symbol $y_k$; choose the one which gives the best cumulative probability given the most probable paths to each predecessor in this set of transitions.

A complete path $\mathbf{t}^n$ through the Markov source corresponds to a sequence of states which may be shown graphically as a path through a network called a *trellis*; the nodes in column $k+1$ of the trellis are the states the source can be in after transition $k$, while the arcs are the transitions themselves. Figure 11 shows a trellis to illustrate the operation of the Viterbi algorithm. In this trellis, only (partial) paths consistent with the output sequence $\langle a, b, a \rangle$ are represented.

Suppose that $\mathbf{t}_*^2(s)$ and $P(\mathbf{t}_*^2(s))$ are known for $s = s_1, s_2$, and $s_3$, and that we wish to compute $\mathbf{t}_*^3(s_2)$ and $P(\mathbf{t}_*^3(s_2))$. The most probable two-transition paths have been marked with asterisks. The set $E(s_2, a)$ for the third transition has two members, say, $t_3$ and $t'_3$, with predecessors $s_2$ and $s_3$, respectively. Suppose that $P(\mathbf{t}_*^2(s_3)) * q(t'_3) > P(\mathbf{t}_*^2(s_2)) * q(t_3)$; in that case we record that $\mathbf{t}_*^3(s_2)$ corresponds to the state sequence $\langle s_1, s_3, s_3, s_2 \rangle$ and we delete the other path to $s_2$.

When the state space is quite large, Viterbi search is not computationally

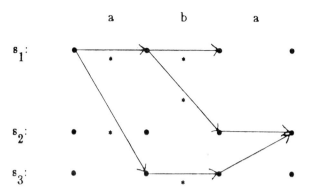

**Fig. 11.** Finding $t_i^3(s_2)$ with the Viterbi algorithm.

feasible. The alternative is to use a stack decoding algorithm which only looks at the most promising word sequences. The stack contains partial sentences ordered as to their likelihood of being portions of the actual sentence spoken. The algorithm proceeds by estimating the likelihoods of one-word extensions of partial sentences on top of the stack until a complete sentence is found.

More details on stochastic decoding and its performance can be found in Jelinek [32] and Bahl *et al.* [1]. Interesting work in network-based systems is described by Lowerre [28] and Bush and Kopec [33]. Architectures for these systems are proposed by Bisiani *et al.* [34]. Performance comparisons between vector quantization with stochastic decoding and dynamic programming using word templates are discussed by Rabiner *et al.* [35].

## KNOWLEDGE-BASED FOCUSING OF ATTENTION    IV

In the network-based systems considered in the previous section, there is a uniform strategy of feature extraction and classification which precedes the stage of linguistic decoding. For example, in the Harpy system, once segmentation has occurred, spectral characteristics of *each* segment are determined by using linear prediction coefficient (LPC) analysis at the midpoint of the segment. Similarly, in the IBM system, the same set of features is extracted at fixed time intervals (every 10 msec) and labels are generated by matching centisecond speech patterns to prototypes. In a system built around knowledge-based focusing of attention, data along the time axis are treated in a *nonuniform* manner: different features are extracted from different frames of the speech signal as specifically required by the recognition process. We say that attention has been *focused*, leading to directed explorations of the speech signal arising out of rule-based mechanisms to pay attention to distinctive acoustic information, detailed phonetic features, and the like.

An intuitive example is the interaction of lexical and sublexical levels in a speech understanding system. We might, for example, access the lexicon with a set of phonetic features not rich enough for generating a lexical hypothesis but capable of focusing attention on a set of words compatible with syntactic and semantic predictions. The existence of this set would lead to requests for hypothesizing phonetic features characterizing differences between the words. These phonetic feature hypotheses would be evaluated by extracting new acoustic cues from the data and even from the waveform. In the present treatment, for space reasons, we shall limit ourselves to discussing an analogous example, that of how phonetic features are related to acoustic cues.

We now provide an outline of an expert system for interpreting speech patterns in which both the extraction of acoustic properties and the generation of syllabic hypotheses result from the collaboration of several distinct processes. The system is organized as a society of experts. Experts are computing agents which execute reasoning programs using structural and procedural knowledge. The knowledge of each expert is expressed by a set of *plans*, some of which can be executed in parallel. Communication between cooperating tasks is performed by message passing. The novelty of the knowledge-based approach under discussion is that descriptions of acoustic properties are extracted and related to phonetic feature interpretations using plans which have been learned. Figure 12 shows the structure of the expert system society.

$EXP_1$ is the acoustic expert (AE). It has the task of sampling and quantizing the signal, performing various types of signal transformations, and extracting and describing acoustic cues. The term *acoustic cues* will be used for indicating spectral or signal properties describing aspects that are

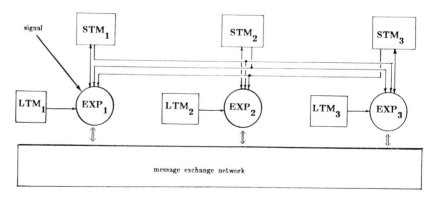

**Fig. 12.** Structure of the expert system society.

relevant for hypothesizing phonetic features. Examples of acoustic cues are formant loci, characteristics of burst spectra like compactness, and peaks and valleys of signal energy.

$EXP_1$ can perform, for example, an analysis based on linear prediction coefficients for segments labeled with vocalic hypotheses in order to find formant loci capable of describing the place and manner of articulation. $EXP_1$ can also perform a broadband spectral analysis based on the fast Fourier transformation (FFT) when hypotheses of nonsonorant continuant sounds have been made. Like other experts, $EXP_1$ may carry out both spontaneous *data-driven* activities and *expectation-driven* activities arising out of requests issued by other experts.

Requests and control messages are exchanged among experts through the message exchange network shown in Fig. 12. Data, cues, descriptions, and hypotheses are written by an expert into its own short-term memory (STM). Only the expert that owns the STM can write into it, but any expert can read any STM.

$EXP_2$ is the phonetic and syllabic expert (PSE). It translates descriptions of acoustic cues into *phonetic feature hypotheses*. These features describe the *manner* and the *place* of articulation of each segment of the spoken utterance. This translation may involve the extraction of new acoustic cues by asking $EXP_1$ to execute sensory procedures.

There are some acoustic cues, such as peaks and valleys of time evolutions of energies in fixed bands of the signal, that can be extracted by context-independent algorithms. These acoustic cues will be called *primary acoustic cues* (PACs) and the phonetic features related to them will be called *primary phonetic features* (PPFs). A definition of the primary cues and features used in the system described here is given in Tables I–III. These algorithms for extracting PACs generate descriptions of a time interval of the signal without being constrained by contextual information extracted from adjacent segments.

Other functions of $EXP_2$ include segmenting the speech signal into pseudosyllabic segments (PSSs) and checking or evaluating phonetic hypotheses. In $EXP_2$, the activity of generating PPFs is *data driven*, while the activities of extracting other phonetic features are *expectation driven*. Expectations may arise from a strategy inside $EXP_2$ or they can be requests transmitted by $EXP_3$. $EXP_3$ is the lexical expert (LE), which generates lexical hypotheses based on prosodic features, phonetic hypotheses, and syntactic and semantic constraints.

Relations of phonetic features to acoustic properties are embedded in *plans* which are executed by the expert system. With this approach a phoneme $PH_i$ is expressed by a set of phonetic features, that is,

$$PH_i = (pf_{i1}, pf_{i2}, \ldots, pf_{ij}, \ldots, pf_{iJ}) \tag{1}$$

**TABLE I**

**Primary Acoustic Cues**

| Symbol | Attributes | Description |
|---|---|---|
| LPK | tb, te, m1, zx | Long peak of total energy (TE) |
| SPK | | Short peak of TE |
| MPK | | Peak of TE of medium duration |
| LOWP | | Low-energy peak of TE |
| LNS | tb, te, zx | Long nonsonorant tract |
| MNS | | Medium nonsonorant tract |
| LVI | tb, te, m1, zx | Long vocalic tract adjacent to a LNS or an MNS in a TE peak |
| MVI | tb, te, m1, zx | Medium vocalic tract adjacent to a LNS or an MNS in a TE peak |
| LDD | emin, tb, te, zx | Long, deep dip of TE |
| SDD | | Short, deep dip of TE |
| LMD | | Long dip of TE with medium depth |
| SMD | | Short dip of TE with medium depth |
| LHD | | Long, non-deep dip of TE |
| SHD | | Short, non-deep dip of TE |

Each phonetic feature $pf_x$ is represented by a relation $R_x$ to a set of acoustic properties $ap_x$, that is,

$$pf_x = R_x(ap_{x1}, ap_{x2}, \ldots, ap_{xk}, \ldots, ap_{xK}) \qquad (2)$$

For example, the phoneme /p/ is represented as follows:

/p/ = (nonsonorant-interrupted-consonant, tense, labial) = (nit, labial)

The phonetic feature "labial" in the context of "nit" features is represented by the following relation $R_k$:

> (*relation* $R_k$
> (*left-side*
> (*feature* (labial))
>         (*feature context* (nit))
>         (*temporal context* (*followed-by* front vowel))) $\qquad$ (3)
> (*right-side*
> (suprasegmental and time-domain properties)
> (formant-transition properties)
> (burst—spectra properties)))

The rule for "labial" takes into account different types of *contextual dependencies*. One contextual dependency is represented by the other features that appear with "labial" in a plosive phoneme. The other contextual dependences are represented by the class of phonemes that can follow or

**TABLE II**

**Attribute Description**

| Attribute | Description |
|-----------|-------------|
| tb | Time of beginning |
| te | Time of end |
| m1 | Maximum signal energy in the peak |
| emin | Minimum total energy in a dip |
| zx | Maximum zero-crossing density of the signal derivative in the tract |

precede the plosive phoneme under consideration. Relations are used by *plans* executed by the expert system.

In many cases, acoustic property extraction is context dependent; for example, we may be forced to impose precedence relations on the extraction processes. Thus, burst properties are useful for hypothesizing the place of articulation of plosive sounds, but the operator that extracts them can be applied only after the successful application of another operator that detects and locates a plosive burst.

A *plan* is a sequence of items. Each item may contain a *precondition expression* for applying rules of the type $R_k$, *operators* containing sensory procedures for extracting the properties used by $R_k$, and an *algorithm* for evaluating the evidence of the hypothesis generated by $R_k$. In practice, a plan is a sequence of operators. Each operator is associated with a precondition and an action.

The application of a sequence of operators produces a redundant set of descriptions of acoustic properties. Positive and negative examples of phonetic features are sets of descriptions of acoustic properties. *Discriminant*

**TABLE III**

**Primary Phonetic Features**

| Symbol | Primary phonetic feature |
|--------|--------------------------|
| VF | Front vowel |
| VC | Central vowel |
| VB | Back vowel |
| VFC | Front or central vowel |
| VCB | Central or back vowel |
| VW | Uncertain vowel |
| NI | Nonsonorant interrupted consonant |
| NA | Nonsonorant affricate consonant |
| NC | Nonsonorant continuant consonant |
| SON | Sonorant consonant |
| SONV | A sonorant or the /v/ consonant |

*descriptions* are learned using *inductive inference* on the basis of positive and negative examples and their statistics. The generation of phonetic hypotheses can be seen as a *vector quantization process* in which labels for speech segments are generated by a knowledge source capable of extracting acoustic properties and interpreting them by taking into account their statistics.

We now describe the application of the planning concept to the recognition of spoken connected letters belonging to the following set, called the $E1$ set:

$$E1 := \{P, T, K, B, D, G, C, V, E, 3\}.$$

The speech signal is first analyzed on the basis of loudness, zero-crossing rates, and broadband energies using an expert system. The result of this analysis is a string of symbols and attributes. Symbols belong to an alphabet of primary acoustic cues (PACs) whose definition is recalled in Table I.

Figure 13 shows the loudness curve (——) and the zero crossing rate of the first derivative of the signal (---) for a sequence of elements from the $E1$ set. This particular sequence is the sequence E3KBCV. The PAC description is also shown in Fig. 13.

A semantic syntax-directed translation scheme operates on PAC descriptions and, through the use of sensory procedures, identifies the vocalic and the consonantal segments of syllable nuclei and hypothesizes the place of articulation of the vowel for the vocalic segments. Plans are then applied for

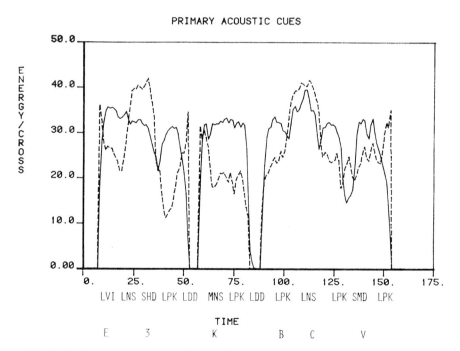

**Fig. 13.** Total energy and zero-crossing rates for the pronunciation of the sequence E3KBCV.

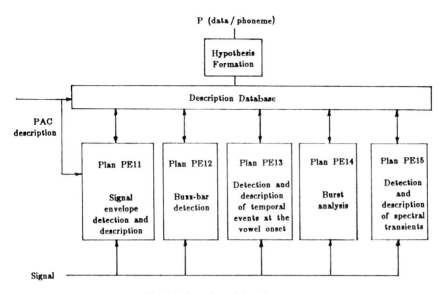

Fig. 14. Overview of the plan *PE*1.

interpreting the consonantal segment of every syllable. An overview of the plan *PE*1 for the recognition of the *E*1 set is shown in Fig. 14.

The purpose of *PE*1 is that of discriminating among the elements of the *E*1 set. As can be seen from Fig. 14, the plan is subdivided into subplans (*PE*11, *PE*12, *PE*13, *PE*14, *PE*15). *PE*11 produces an envelope description by analyzing the signal amplitude before and after preemphasis. *PE*12 describes the buzz-bar by analyzing the shape of the time waveform and the spectra before the voice onset. *PE*13 analyzes temporal events related to voice onset time. *PE*14 performs burst detection and analysis. *PE*14 also detects friction intervals at the voice onset. *PE*15 describes transitions of the second and third formant at the voice onset.

More details concerning the subplans, additional references describing the expert system, and recent experimental results can be found in Ref. 36; an extended treatment of the knowledge-based approach and the learning algorithms is contained in Schroeder [10].

Expressions made of symbols extracted by subplans *PE*11 and *PE*12 and representing positive and negative examples have been inferred for each PAC description and for each phoneme using a learning algorithm. Examples of such rules are given in the following:

$$E := \text{NOB} \quad \text{NBP} \quad \text{NBZ} \quad \text{NST} \quad \text{NBU} \quad \text{NPB}$$

$$B := \text{BU} \quad \text{BP} \quad \text{BZ} \quad \text{NST} \quad \text{NBU} \quad \text{PBU}$$

The symbols in these rules describe such things as degrees of buzz-bar evidence and characteristics of steps in the envelope curve. There are 96 such rules in the system.

A PAC description is used for indexing a set of rules that is matched against the input description produced by the plan. Since rules and descriptions contain the same number of symbols, a similarity index between a rule and a description is computed in closed form.

The parameters extracted by $PE13$, $PE14$, and $PE15$ are used in fuzzy relations. There is a fuzzy relation for each phoneme and the invocation of a fuzzy relation is conditioned by PAC, $PE11$, and $PE12$ descriptions. Fuzzy relations are conjunctions of disjunctions of fuzzy sets. A fuzzy relation computes another similarity index between phonemes and data.

The proposed approach has been tested on a protocol of 1000 connected pronunciations of symbols of the $E1$ set in strings of five symbols each. The strings were pronounced by five male speakers and five female speakers whose voices were not used for deriving the rules. Since the recognition algorithm is syllable based, it is not constrained by the number of syllables.

The idea of using a number of phonetically significant properties in a recognition system based on the planning paradigm appears very promising. The analysis of the behavior of each plan and of the errors generated by their application suggests the actions that must be taken in order to improve recognition accuracy.

## V  CONCLUSION

Computer recognition of speech is a very difficult problem. The same word can produce a large variety of different waveforms and it is not yet completely known how the essential information common to different pronunciations of the same word can be extracted. One way for solving this problem is to avoid the extraction of the essential information and to match data to be interpreted with prototypes. Although some experimental comparisons have been performed on different methods using this approach, it is not clear which one is the best. Probably, on limited tasks, different algorithms may perform equally well. Word prototypes are highly speaker dependent and cannot easily incorporate word boundary coarticulation effects. In order to cope with these difficulties, multiple templates can be collected, thus increasing the computational complexity of the recognition task even if dynamic programming algorithms are suitable to be implemented with very efficient systolic arrays in VLSI chips.

Systems based on stochastic models rely heavily on probability distributions that are speaker dependent, although coarticulation effects can be easily incorporated into the knowledge-representing networks. Feature-based approaches seem to be appropriate for representing essential information but they can exhibit low performance if the features are not well chosen and/or not well extracted.

Certainly a lot of research work still has to be done, even if the results obtained in the past 10 years are an encouraging sign of real progress.

## ACKNOWLEDGEMENT

This research was supported by the Natural Sciences and Engineering Research Council of Canada with grant No. A2439.

## REFERENCES

1. L. Bahl, F. Jelinek, and R. Mercer, *IEEE Trans. on PAMI* **PAMI-5**, 179–190 (1983).
2. S. Levinson and L. Rabiner, *IEEE Trans. on Comm.* **COM-29**, 621–659 (1981).
3. L. Bahl, S. Das, P. De Souza, F. Jelinek, S. Katz, R. Mercer, and M. Pichenx, *Proc. ICASSP* **84**, 2651–2653 (1984).
4. L. Rabiner, J. Wilpon, and S. Terrace, *Proc. ICASSP* **84**, 3541–3544 (1984).
5. R. De Mori, "Computer Models of Speech Using Fuzzy Algorithms." Plenum, New York, 1983.
6. D. Walker, (ed.) "Understanding Spoken Language." Elsevier, New York, 1978.
7. N. Dixon and T. Martin, (eds.) "Automatic Speech and Speaker Recognition." IEEE Press, New York, 1979.
8. W. Lea, (ed.) "Trends in Speech Recognition." Prentice-Hall, Englewood Cliffs, New Jersey, 1980.
9. R. Reddy, "Speech Recognition—Invited Papers of the 1974 IEEE Symposium." Academic Press, New York, 1975.
10. M. Schroeder, (ed.) "Speech Recognition." Karger, Basel, 1985.
11. C. Suen and R. De Mori (eds.) "Computer Analysis and Perception of Visual and Auditory Signals." CRC Press, Boca Raton, Florida, 1982.
12. G. Doddington and T. Schalk, *IEEE Spectrum* **18**, 26–32 (1981).
13. R. Leonard, *Proc. ICASSP* **84**, 42.11.1–42.11.4 (1984).
14. R. Carre, R. Descout, M. Eskenazi, J. Mariani, and M. Rossi, *Proc. ICASSP* **84**, 42.10.1–42.10.4 (1984).
15. V. Levenshtein, *Soviet Physics-Doklady* **10**, 707–710 (1966).
16. H. Sakoe and S. Chiba, *IEEE Trans. on ASSP* **ASSP-26**, 43–49 (1978).
17. T. Sakai, *in* "Spoken Language Generation and Understanding" (J. Simon, ed.) pp. 147–190. Nordoff, Leyden, 1980.
18. F. Itakura, *IEEE Trans. on ASSP* **ASSP-23**, 67–72 (1975).
19. H. Sakoe, *IEEE Trans. on ASSP* **ASSP-27,** 588–595 (1979).
20. C. Myers and L. Rabiner, *IEEE Trans. on ASSP* **ASSP-29**, 284–297 (1981).
21. H. Ney, *IEEE Trans. on ASSP* **ASSP-32**, 263–271 (1984).
22. J. Bridle, M. Brown, and R. Chamberlain, *Proc. ICASSP* **82**, 899–902 (1982).
23. N. Weste, D. Burr, and B. Ackland, *IEEE Trans. on Comp.* **C-32**, 731–744 (1983).
24. V. Velichiko and N. Zagoruiko, *Intl. J. of Man–Machine Studies* **2**, 223–234 (1970).
25. A. Rosenberg and K. Shipley, *Proc. ICASSP* **84**, 9.5.1–9.5.3 (1984).
26. L. Rabiner, J. Wilpon, A. Quinn, and S. Terrace, *IEEE Trans. on ASSP* **ASSP-32**, 272–280 (1984).
27. C. Myers and S. Levinson, *IEEE Trans. on ASSP* **ASSP-30**, 561–565 (1982).
28. B. Lowerre and R. Reddy, *in* "Trends in Speech Recognition" (W. Lea, ed.), pp. 340–360. Prentice-Hall, Englewood Cliffs, New Jersey, 1980.
29. J. Baker, *IEEE Trans. on ASSP* **ASSP-23**, 24–29 (1975).

30.  L. Erman, F. Hayes-Roth, V. Lesser, and R. Reddy, *Comp. Surv.* **12**, 213–253 (1980).
31.  A. Buzo, A. Gray, R. Gray, and J. Markel, *IEEE Trans. on ASSP* **ASSP-28**, 562–574 (1980).
32.  F. Jelinek, *Proc. of the IEEE* **64**, 532–556 (1976).
33.  M. Bush, G. Kopec, and N. Lauritzen, *Proc. ICASSP* **84**, 17.11.1–17.11.5 (1984).
34.  R. Bisiani, H. Mauersberg, and R. Reddy, *Proc. of the IEEE* **71**, 885–898 (1983).
35.  L. Rabiner, M. Sondhi, and S. Levinson, *Proc. ICASSP* **84**, 17.1.1–17.1.4 (1984).
36.  R. De Mori, G. Rossi, and J. Sun, *Proc. ICASSP* **85**, 1225–1229 (1985).

# Chapter **21**

# Seismic and Underwater Acoustic Waveform Analysis

C. H. CHEN

Department of Electrical and Computer Engineering
Southeastern Massachusetts University
North Dartmouth, Massachusetts

## INTRODUCTION I

Much effort has been made in the past 15 years to apply pattern recognition and image processing to seismic and underwater acoustic waveform analysis. There are three major classes of seismic waveforms. The first is the exploration seismic waveform from which detection is made of petroleum and natural gas. This includes both inland and offshore explorations. The second is the teleseismic waveform from which discrimination of underground nuclear explosions from natural earthquakes is made. The third is the earthquake data from which the properties and effects of the earthquakes are studied. Recently there has been intense interest in the automatic recognition of exploration seismic waveforms or seismograms. For the teleseismic data the feasibility of automatic recognition has been established. Automatic earthquake analysis is a relatively new effort. Both statistical and syntactic–structural pattern recognition techniques have been successfully employed in automatic seismic waveform analysis for the three classes of seismic data

527

described. A fourth class of seismic data is marine seismic reflection–refraction profiles for geological study of the ocean floor. However, the main concern here is filtering for removal of multipaths so that the enhanced seismic profiles can be more easily interpreted by experienced marine geologists.

Figure 1 shows typical short-period nuclear explosion waveforms and earthquake waveforms. The frequency range is usually 0 to 10 Hz. These are typical teleseismic waveforms for discrimination study. Figure 2 is a typical seismogram for exploration study. Another class of seismic waveform is footstep signals taken by seismic sensors for intrusion detection. Figure 3 is a typical example of such a signal. To improve event detection, adaptive digital filtering is frequently employed. Figure 3 also shows a result of such filtering.

For underwater acoustic data, pattern recognition analysis is a new area of study. There are two important topics for underwater acoustics. One is the contact motion analysis in which target (contact) parameters including range, range rate, bearing, etc., are determined from passive sonar data. The

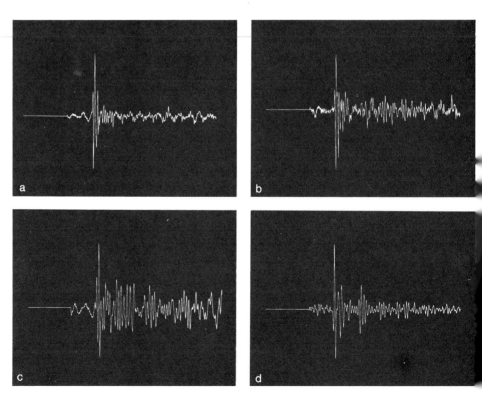

**Fig. 1.** Typical short-period nuclear explosions: (a) explosion No. 0040; (b) explosion No. 0070. Natural earthquake waveforms: (c) earthquake No. 0211; (d) earthquake No. 0220.

SEISMIC SECTION

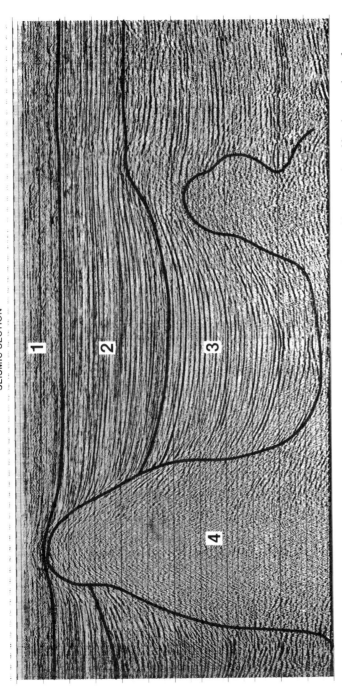

**Fig. 2.** Typical seismogram showing a piece of a stacked section from the Gulf of Mexico. A manual interpretation of four large regions of common characteristics is shown by the dark lines. (Courtesy P. L. Love, Gulf Research and Development Co., Houston, Texas.)

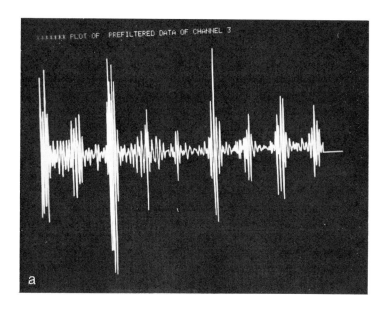

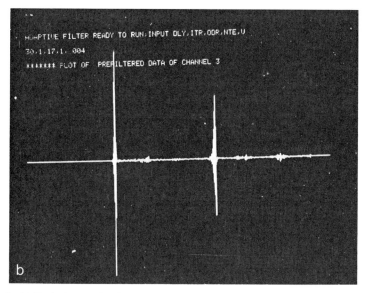

**Fig. 3.** (a) Typical example of a footstep seismic sensor signal and (b) the adaptive digital filtering result.

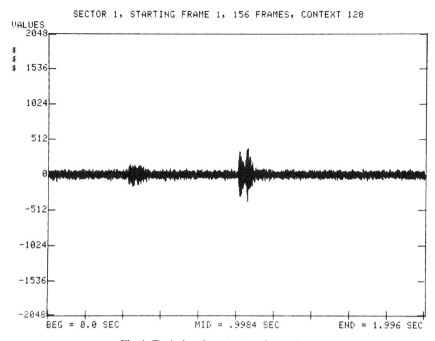

**Fig. 4.** Typical underwater transient pattern.

problem here is mainly effective estimation and filtering. One well-established procedure is the extended Kalman filtering. The second topic is the underwater transient signal analysis. Most transients are mechanically induced waveforms or flow-related noise, which exist in the ever-present instrument noise in submarines. Underwater transient studies are most needed for vulnerability assessment of vessels due to radiated noise transients, diagnostics for transient noise control, and characterization of self-noise pertinent to a passive sonar transient processor. The transient pattern is basically a sound and thus almost all analysis performed so far makes use of speech processing and recognition techniques. Figure 4 is a typical transient pattern resulting from a mechanically induced event. Although classification of transient events appears to be a well-defined pattern recognition problem, very limited success has been reported so far. This is in part due to the complex ocean environment.

## FEATURE ANALYSIS  II

For discrimination, classification, or detection of seismic and acoustic events, effective features must be extracted. This has been a difficult task, as in most other pattern recognition problems. Generally speaking, physical features, namely, features with good physical meaning or representing some physical characteristics, are intuitively appealing, but they may not be effective for automatic recognition of interpretation unless they can be properly quantified. Purely mathematical features obtained through feature-space transformations are often too general to be effective in specific applications. In this section effective features are identified for seismic and underwater acoustic waveforms.

For short-period teleseismic data, spectral-domain features have been extensively examined for discrimination between two classes: explosions and earthquakes. Let $x(t)$ be the seismic signal trace with corresponding Fourier transform $X(f)$. Three useful discriminants (or features) developed in the early 1970s are complexity $C$, spectral ratio SR, and third moment of frequency TMF, as defined in the following with time $t$ in seconds and frequency $f$ in Hertz:

$$C = \int_0^5 x^2(t)\, dt \bigg/ \int_5^{35} x^2(t)\, dt \tag{1}$$

$$\mathrm{SR} = \int_{L1}^{L2} |X(f)|\, df \bigg/ \int_{H1}^{H2} |X(f)|\, df \tag{2}$$

where the limits of the low- and high-frequency bands have been selected as follows:

|              | L1   | L2   | H1   | H2   |
|--------------|------|------|------|------|
| U.S. events  | 0.55 | 0.94 | 1.48 | 1.87 |
| U.S.S.R. events | 0.66 | 0.94 | 2.19 | 2.89 |

$$\mathrm{TMF} = \left[ \int_{0.32}^{5.0} |X(f) - Y(f)|\, f^3\, df \bigg/ \int_{0.32}^{5.0} |X(f) - Y(f)|\, df \right]^{1/3} \tag{3}$$

where $Y(f)$ is the spectrum of the instrument noise alone. The integrals are replaced by summations for digitized data. Each of these three features may be paired with the body wave magnitude to provide a scatter plot of available seismic traces.

The noise compensation idea suggested in TMF can be extended to the energy estimate in general. Let $X_i$ be the frequency estimate at the $i$th frequency. The following are two energy estimates:

$$\text{conventional energy estimator} = \sum |X_i|^2 \tag{4}$$

ALPHA-C energy estimator

$$= \sum \left[ |X_i| - c\sigma_i \exp - (\alpha |X_i|^2/\sigma_i^2) \right]^2 \tag{5}$$

where $c$ and $\alpha$ are arbitrary constants and $2\sigma_i^2$ is the noise power at the $i$th frequency component. Here the summation can be taken over any frequency range of interest. Note that the ALPHA-C estimator is a function of the observed value as well as the noise statistics. A typical choice of constants are $c = 1.45$ and $\alpha = 0.1$.

A dynamic spectral ratio is a generalization of the spectral ratio in that frequency range of integration or summation, and the inverval of the signal trace from which the Fourier transform is taken can be adjusted. A feature set can be formed with several dynamic spectral-ratio features. Other effective features, obtained by signal processing, are the autocovariance features (autocorrelation with zero-mean process) and the power cepstrum features with the ALPHA-C energy estimate. For performance comparison, a typical multichannel teleseismic database is used that consists of 214 earthquake and 113 explosion events. These seismic events, all recorded at the LASA (large-aperture seismic array) facility in Montana, have a wide variety of source origins, including central Asia, Turkey, and Western China. The three discriminants (1)–(3) can only provide up to 80% correct recognition. Better performing features are tabulated as follows:

| Feature type | Percentage correct |
| --- | --- |
| Autocovariance | 89.32 |
| Power cepstrum with $\alpha C$ energy estimate | 87.06 |
| Normalized power cepstrum | 88.04 |
| Dynamic spectral ratios | 94.24 |

For the first three feature types, 16 features, 7 best training samples per class, and the nearest-neighbor decision rules are employed. The last feature type is defined as the ratio of signal energy above 0.5 Hz to that below 0.5 Hz for a 200-sample duration. Two ratios are computed as features for a nearest-neighbor decision-rule classification. One ratio covers the duration of sample numbers 550 to 749 and the other ratio covers the duration of sample numbers 750 and 949. Forty randomly selected events from each class are used for learning and the remaining events are used for classification.

For the explosion seismology, data are gathered in the form of time samples by an array of geophones. To increase the signal-to-noise ratio, a stacking method is used. Each trace in the resulting seismogram is a collection of time samples in the vertical direction, the values (amplitude) of the sample signifying reflectance from an embedded element and its position with respect to the depth of the element in the ground. In the case of lateral homogeneity, similar samples occur in consecutive traces in the horizontal direction. In the presence of a fault, the samples are shifted laterally upward or downward.

One pattern recognition problem is recognizing reservoirs. One can fit an autoregressive (AR) model to the raw seismic trace, and the model parameters can be used as features in clustering analysis. Each waveform is represented by a point in the feature space. Points belonging to the same reservoir tend to cluster. The determination of the boundaries separating the clusters serves to indicate the nature of the reservoir by comparison with the known nature of a reservoir which has been drilled.

Another pattern recognition problem is classifying individual samples of the seismic trace rather than the trace itself. For a typical section with a 4-msec sampling time, a sample represents about 40 ft of earth. For layers of thin beds, changes in lithology can occur within a thickness as small as 80 ft. A properly digitized waveform is processed via the Hilbert transform to obtain the analytic signal given by

$$a(t) = x(t) + jx'(t)$$

where $x'(t)$ is the Hilbert transform of seismic trace $x(t)$. The following are effective features which must be used together:

(1)   raw trace amplitude $x(t)$:
(2)   envelope amplitude $|a(t)| = \sqrt{x^2(t) + x'^2(t)}$;
(3)   instantaneous phase $\phi(t) = \cos^{-1}\lfloor x(t)/|a(t)| \rfloor$;
(4)   instantaneous frequency $f(t) = (1/2\pi)(d\phi(t)/dt)$;
(5)   pseudo-interval velocity, using one of the conventional processing and velocity analysis methods.

Thus each sample can be represented as a vector of five features. The rationale for using these features is as follows. The envelope amplitude is associated with the reflection strength of the signal. A large value of envelope amplitude usually indicates major changes in the subsurface layers. If there is a discontinuity in the layer structure, it will be detected from the instantaneous phase even when the signal strength is not high. The dominant frequency derived from the phase can be used to detect rapid changes in layers which may be associated with pinch-outs and hydrocarbon–water interfaces. Pseudo-interval velocities are indicators of changes in the characteristics of the medium.

For underwater acoustic transient signal classification, well-accepted features have not been developed. It is generally recognized, however, that significant separability among transient classes can be generated through combination of time-domain and frequency-domain feature sets. Some potentially valuable features are transient duration, short-term bandwidth, variation of spectral peaks as a function of time throughout the event duration (which may be unique to each event type), energy distribution with time, and frequency structure, including harmonic content and coherency.

Basic transient signal parameters are instantaneous amplitude, instantaneous phase (though noisy) and its derivative, and the instantaneous frequency, as well as the transient duration (epoch). Sixteen features of the envelope and frequency histogram data have been identified. The first six are mean, variance, and skewness for both the envelope and frequency data. The next six are cross moments between envelope and frequency data, and the remaining four are the moments of the time distribution of envelope or amplitude. Feature-space transformation such as the principal component analysis may then be used to compress the feature-vector dimension.

## SIGNAL MODELS  III

A good parametric model for the time-series data, including the digitized seismic and underwater acoustic waveforms, is given by the linear prediction theory. Basically, the model describes the waveform in the frequency domain by a pole-zero model with the filter transfer function

$$H(Z) = \frac{Y(Z)}{X(Z)} = \frac{1 + b_1 Z^{-1} + b_2 Z^{-2} + \cdots + b_q Z^{-q}}{1 + a_1 Z^{-1} + a_2 Z^{-2} + \cdots + a_p Z^{-p}} \tag{6}$$

where $Z$ denotes a $Z$-transform variable. Equation (6) does indeed model the signal generation process to a good approximation. For example, in seismic signal analysis the earth, consisting of a number of layers, can be modeled as a lumped parameter system. Equation (6) then represents the transfer function of a normal-incidence reflection seismogram (with $p = q$). A further approximation is the AR or all-pole model,

$$H(Z) = \frac{Y(Z)}{X(Z)} = \frac{1}{1 + a_1 Z^{-1} + a_2^{-2} + \cdots + a_p Z^{-p}} \tag{7}$$

in which the model coefficients $a_i$ can be much more easily determined. For example, the Burg's maximum-entropy spectral analysis technique provides an efficient algorithm for computing the $a_i$ values. It is noted that both AR and ARMA models are based on the assumption of stationary underlying processes. Both seismic and underwater acoustic waveforms are nonstationary. Thus, the model can only fit into segments which can be considered as piecewise stationary. This is particularly important for underwater transients in which the AR model is fitted only to extracted transient segments which tend to have short duration. Signal segmentation thus becomes necessary before the signal is modeled. Also, proper choice of the model order $p$ is essential. Criteria for model order selection, such as Akaike's information criterion, can be employed. Such criteria depend on the data characteristics rather than the parameter estimation technique.

The AR model coefficients are useful features in pattern classification and cluster analysis. These features are empoyed in reservoir recognition, as described in the previous section. For underwater transient event classification, such features taken from the extracted transient segments are very effective.

The ARMA model provides a better model of the real data than the AR model and generally requires a lower-order model to fit the data. Recently several effective techniques to calculate the ARMA model coefficients have been developed even though the required computation is still considerably more than that for the AR model.

In this section only linear ARMA and AR signal models have been considered. Nonstationary ARMA models have been examined, but their application so far has been limited to speech. Other models such as nonlinear and adaptive models are less developed. For a more complete modeling, the multipath and other environmental factors which frequently exist in underwater acoustic waveforms must be taken into account.

## IV  STATISTICAL METHODS IN SEISMIC PATTERN RECOGNITION

Statistical decision-making techniques have been employed to classify, discriminate, or detect seismic events or regions. A proper utilization of statistical decision theory can lead to very good classification. Fisher's linear discriminant, maximum-likelihood decision rule, Bayes decision rule, and the nearest-neighbor decision rule are most typically used. For the maximum-likelihood decision rule and the Bayes decision rule, a probability density must often be estimated from properly selected seismic traces. The multivariate Gaussian density is most often employed since the seismic noise follows the Gaussian distribution quite well. The *a priori* probability required in the Bayes classification can have a significant effect on performance. *A priori* knowledge should be used in determining such a probability.

If the available number of training samples is small and there is insufficient confidence in the Gaussian assumption, the nearest-neighbor decision rule should be used. Computational algorithms are available to reduce the amount of computation and storage with this nonparametric decision rule. The recognition results of the maximum-likelihood decision rule with properly chosen probability density and the nearest-neighbor decision rule are very much the same in practice for a limited number, say, 100, of training samples (traces).

Features can have different orders of importance. A tree classifier that processes features sequentially in multistages can have a much simpler classifier structure but performance comparable to an optimum (Bayes)

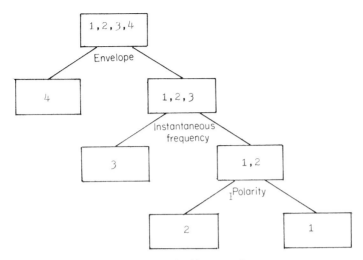

**Fig. 5.** Tree classifier example.

classifier. As an example, consider a tree classification of a Ricker wavelet using three features: envelope, instantaneous frequency, and polarity. A tree classifier, as shown in Fig. 5, may be designed from the training traces for each feature with the aid of scatter diagrams of pairs of features. For the data in a scatter diagram of envelope versus instantaneous frequency, which are above the envelope threshold, the threshold of the instantaneous frequency is determined, and the process continues until all features are processed.

## SYNTACTIC—STRUCTURAL METHODS IN SEISMIC ANALYSIS    V

In syntactic methods of seismic analysis, the one-dimensional waveform is represented by sentences, that is, strings of primitives. Three steps are required to obtain such representations: pattern segmentation, feature selection, and primitive recognition. A variable-length segmentation is more efficient and precise in representation, but it is usually difficult and time consuming to find an appropriate segmentation. A fixed-length segmentation is much easier to implement. The segments should be sufficiently short for good representation accuracy but long enough to maintain analysis efficiency. For the seismic records shown in Fig. 1, which contain 1200 sample points, each at a sampling rate of 10 samples per second, a proper choice is 60 samples per segment for 20 segments.

An advantage of syntactic analysis is that features can be fairly simple. For discrimination of teleseismic waveforms, a pair of commonly used features are the zero-crossing count and log energy of each segment, which are easy to compute and contain significant information. After segmentation and feature selection, primitives can be recognized from the analysis of training segments, and an identifier can be assigned to each segment. Automatic clustering analysis, such as the $K$-means algorithm or hierarchical clustering algorithm, can be used to classify each segment. After each segment is identified, the seismic waves are converted into strings of primitives, or sentences.

A syntax analysis can then be performed on the sentences constructed. If the classification of the whole sentence is all we need, then the nearest-neighbor decision rule is recommended because of its computation efficiency. If, however, a complete description of the waveform structure is desired, we must use error-correcting parsing. An error-correcting parser instead of a regular parser is required for seismic recognition since noises and errors in seismic signal processing usually cause regular parsers to fail.

The concept of the nearest-neighbor decision rule in the syntactic approach is the same as that in the decision–theoretic approach. The only difference is in distance calculation. The distance between two strings is sometimes called the Levenshtein distance, which is the minimum number of symbol insertions, deletions, and substitutions required in order to transform one string into the other. If different weights are assigned to different symbols and/or operations, then the distance becomes a weighted Levenshtein distance. These distances can be computed using a dynamic programming method.

For error-correcting parsing, a grammar must first be available either by inference or construction. The pattern grammar is then transformed into a covering grammar that generates the correct sentences as well as all the possible erroneous sentences. The errors in string patterns are substitution errors, deletion errors, and insertion errors. Different weights can be assigned to each error production, resulting in a minimum-cost, error-correcting parser. For a finite-state grammar, which is represented bvy a transition diagram, minimum-cost, error-correcting parsing is equivalent to finding a minimum-cost path from the initial state to the final state. The parsing time is proportional to the length of the sentences.

For the teleseismic database described in Section II, the syntactic recognition result using the nearest-neighbor decision rule is 90.5 % correct recognition (200 records correctly classified out of 221; the other 106 records are for training) at an average time of 0.07 sec for one string. The available syntactic recognition result of the error-correcting parser is also 90.5 % correct, with an average parsing time of 2.6 sec per string.

Syntactic pattern recognition techniques have also been applied to the analysis of one-dimensional seismic traces and two-dimensional seismograms for the detection of bright spots. The detected bright-spot patterns should be continuous and represent the reflection layer in the two-dimensional seismogram. The recognition steps include preprocessing that provides encoded strings, string distance computation, and thresholding to test bright spots.

In structural methods of seismic analysis, the preprocessing result is usually a linear approximation of waveforms. Signal smoothing is necessary since the seismic waves are noisy. The morphological structure of seismic waves can be determined by using clustering analysis or an affinity algorithm. The teleseismic wave maintains a time structure (e.g., the $P$ wave occurs before the $S$ wave). The final representation of the waveform can be a tree structure that links the morphs. The tree structure will also facilitate the development of rules and grammars that describe the structural properties of the seismic waveforms.

A descriptive method of seismic analysis makes use of specific shape as a feature to distinguish between seismic and nonseismic events. The shape of a seismic sequence is described by selected pseudo-envelopes that give rough representations of local and global regions of the waveform. Additional structural information includes the slope and relative amplitudes of signal variation, onset time, and signal duration. Classification can be performed by matching with stored references.

## UNDERWATER TRANSIENT SIGNAL ANALAYSIS VI

As described in Section II, segmentation to extract transient portions of an underwater transient signal is the necessary first step in signal analysis. An effective segmentation procedure is to compute an entropy distance, which is compared to some threshold. The waveform is first divided into a number of finite-length sections. Consider two adjacent sections, called reference and testing sections, with each section modeled by a $p$th-order autoregressive series. Under a multivariate Gaussian density assumption of the AR series, the likelihood functions of the two sections under the null hypothesis that they are identical and under the alternative that they are different can be computed. The logarithm of the ratio of the two likelihood functions is the entropy distance. Those sections of the waveform whose entropy distance exceeds some threshold are identified. For such sections, smaller subsections are examined by using the entropy distance. This process continues until single-point boundaries are established. Each segment between two adjacent boundaries is represented by a $p$th-order AR model that has different parameters from its adjacent segments. Extensive experimental results have indicated that the optimum order $p$ is 2 or 3, which implies a simple, generalized likelihood-ratio detection for segmentation use.

Figure 6 shows the segmentation (in vertical dashed lines) of (a) flow-radiated and (b) mechanically induced underwater transient signals. The segmentation algorithm is also useful for detecting the onset of seismic events. it is particularly effective in determining correctly the beginning of a segment. By reversing the data sequence, however, there is essentially no change in the

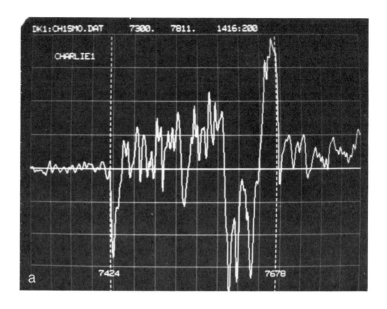

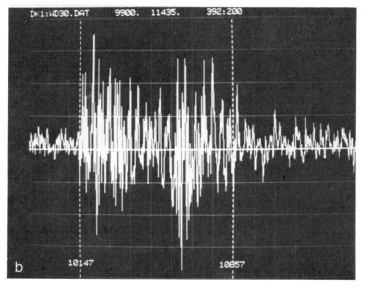

**Fig. 6.** Segmentation of (a) flow-radiated and (b) mechanically induced transient waveforms.

detection of the ending point of an event. The algorithm is quite insensitive to additive noise. Experiments with artificial data indicate that the error in segment boundary estimates remains very small until the signal-to-noise ratio is decreased to 0.1, below which the error becomes large.

Although only the use of a low-order AR model is required for segmentation, a much higher-order model is needed for spectral characterization of the transient data. Even for the actual transient portion only, a 15th-order (or higher) model is required in the Burg's maximum entropy spectrum, as shown in Fig. 7, which corresponds to the transient portion of Fig. 6b.

For clustering analysis and event classification, the low-order AR model parameters have been useful for separating different events. An 8th-order AR model compressed to two dimensions by principal component analysis can result in good separation of four different transient events, as shown in Fig. 8, which is plotted by using an ILS (Interactive Laboratory Systems) software package. Another effective signal processing software package, I*S*P, is available from Bedford Research.

As a concluding note, it is interesting to compare underwater transients with speech. The major difference appears to be in the spectral characteristics and the contextual information. The effectiveness of AR modeling is common to both. An interesting comparison is the use of a second-order AR model, which is very useful for transient signal segmentation. In the speech area, a low-order (second-order) model has also been proposed for speech segmentation and gross representation of the spectrum. Many segment boundaries,

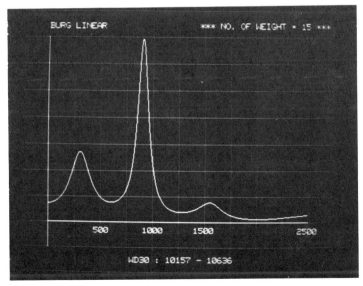

**Fig. 7.** 15th-order Burg's maximum entropy spectrum of Fig. 6b.

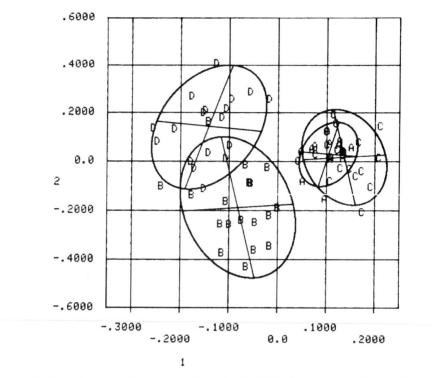

**Fig. 8.** Scatter plot of four classes (denoted A, B, C, D) of transient waveforms, with each letter representing one sample waveform of a class. The first two components of principal component analysis are shown.

particularly those where a change of manner of articulation takes place, are clearly marked by abrupt or rapid change in the two-pole frequencies. The position of the two-pole frequency can be a good differentiation between sonorant and nonsonorant sounds. The underwater transients, however, have much less contextual or structural information and a much more limited choice of features.

## VII    KNOWLEDGE-BASED SIGNAL INTERPRETATION

The artificial intelligence area is rapidly entering seismic and underwater acoustic waveform analysis. Some powerful and low-cost workstations are expected to be a reality in the near future. Some existing work reported in the literature includes the following:

(1)    the HASP/SIAP system for ocean surveillance based on passive sonar data, as developed by the Heuristic Programming Project of Stanford University;

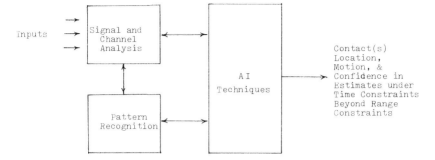

**Fig. 9.** Block diagram of an expert system for contact motion analysis.

(2) the INTERSENSOR expert system, also for machine interpretation of sonar signals, as developed by the Defence Research Establishment Atlantic in Canada;

(3) the RESOLVER algorithm, a LISP program that aids the classification process by modeling heuristic constraints that a human interpreter would use while segmenting a seismic section, as developed by the Gulf Research and Development Co.

Basically, an expert system consists of knowledge (data, rules) and a control strategy. The system allows integration and intelligent utilization of diverse sources of knowledge typically experienced in complex seismic and underwater acoustic waveform analysis problems. A knowledge-based signal interpretation system is an expert system that integrates signal processing, pattern recognition, and artificial intelligence and provides much greater capability in waveform analysis than can be provided by the signal processing or pattern recognition system alone. For a contact motion analysis expert system, Fig. 9 shows a general block diagram in which the outputs are all the required information of a contact (target). Efforts like this and other signal interpretation systems are expected to be reported in the literature in the near future.

## BIBLIOGRAPHY

C. H. Chen, Seismic pattern recognition, *Geoexploration* **16**, 133–146 (1978).

C. H. Chen, Application of pattern recognition to seismic wave interpretation, *in* "Applications of Pattern Recognition" (K. S. Fu, ed.), Chap. 4. CRC Press, Boca Raton, Florida, 1981.

C. H. Chen, *Proceedings of the 2nd International Symposium on Computer-aided Seismic Analysis and Discrimination*, IEEE Computer Society Press, August 1981.

C. H. Chen, Adaptive and learning algorithms for intrusion-detection with seismic sensor data, *IEEE Trans. on Pattern Analysis and Machine Intelligence* (March 1982).

C. H. Chen (ed.), *Proceedings of the 3rd International Symposium on Computer-aided Seismic Analysis and Discrimination*, IEEE Computer Society Press, June 1983.

C. H. Chen, Applications of signal processing and pattern recognition to underwater acoustics, *in* "Issues in Acoustic Signal/Image Processing and Recognition" (C. H. Chen, ed.). Springer-Verlag, Berlin and New York, 1983.

C. H. Chen, Pattern recognition processing in underwater acoustics, *Pattern Recognition* (December 1983).

C. H. Chen, Characterization and analysis of underwater transient signals, *IEEE International Conference on Acoustics, Speech, and Signal Processing, San Diego, California*, March 1984.

C. H. Chen "Seismic Signal Analysis and Discrimination III." Elsevier, 1985.

C. H. Chen (ed.), Application of artificial intelligence and signal processing to underwater acoustics and geophysics problems, *Pattern Recognition*, Special Issue (1985).

# Chapter **22**

# Methods of Biological Signal Processing

Richard G. Shiavi and John R. Bourne

Department of Electrical and Biomedical Engineering
Vanderbilt University
Nashville, Tennesee

545

**HANDBOOK OF PATTERN RECOGNITION
AND IMAGE PROCESSING**

# I  INTRODUCTION

This chapter describes a series of methods that have been used for biological signal processing. Methodologies presented span the range from more traditional multivariate and syntactic methods to newer semantic approaches to the analysis of biological signals. Attention is focused on the three bioelectric measurements that have extensive utility; the electroencephalogram (EEG), the electrocardiogram (ECG) and the electromyogram (EMG). The organization is by technique not by application area; thus, methods explained in different sections can be implemented in the same application.

# II  TIME-SERIES METHODS

## A  Overview

Classical and modern time-series methods are commonly used in pattern recognition applications. Correlation, power spectral analysis, Kalman filtering, autoregressive moving average (ARMA) modeling, etc., not only provide valuable information directly, but also provide variables for features, that is, they are also feature extraction methods.

All of the formulas and algorithms for time signals are described using discrete time representation $y(n)$, where real time $t$ is $n * T$ and $T$ is the sampling interval. Similarly, the frequency and power spectra are denoted using capital letters, $Y(m)$ or $Y(f)$. For the discrete frequency representation $Y(m)$, $m$ is the frequency number and the actual frequency $f$ is $m$ times the frequency spacing.

## B  Correlation

Cross correlation or matched filtering is a valuable technique for waveform detection in a single signal channel [1] and alignment of unknown wavelets in a multiple signal channel [2]. Given a template $s(n)$ and a measured signal $x(n)$, the cross correlation is given by

$$y(n) = \sum_{m=1}^{N} s(m) * x(m - n) \tag{1}$$

where $N$ is the number of points in the template. In the single signal situation, a wavelet of form $s(n)$ exists when $y(n)$ is maximized above a designated threshold. When multiple signals exist, as when detecting motor unit action potentials (MUAPs) or nerve action potentials (NAPs), operation (1) is performed between all of the reference templates and the unknown wavelet over a range of lag values of $n$. The lag value producing the maximum value of $y(n)$ indicates the point of alignment for comparison. The wavelet is assigned to the template yielding the largest cross correlation.

This technique has become utilized more recently for detecting the arrival time of EEG- and EMG-evoked responses. Ordinarily, the templates are selected from the measured data immediately to be analyzed or, less often, from population averages. The underlying assumption until recently has been that the signals are time invariant. Studies of the calculated cross-correlation functions and application of piece-wise cross correlation show definitely that in many situations the generated signals vary with time [3, 4].

## Signal Estimation   C

Often the signal-to-noise ratio is small and the signal waveform is not discernable. Several techniques are available for estimating the signal depending on the underlying signal and noise properties. Most of these techniques assume additive and independent noise. For a deterministic signal, one that never changes, ensemble averaging is appropriate. This is a common approach with evoked potentials; the fiducial mark is the stimulus time. For a stationary stochastic signal, one whose statistical properties are time invariant, Weiner filtering is valid. The frequency-domain structure of the filter is

$$H(f) = \frac{S(f)}{S(f) + N(f)} \tag{2}$$

where $S(f)$ and $N(f)$ are the power spectral densities (PSDs) of the signal and noise, respectively. These spectra must be known *a priori* or estimated from experimental measurements. Note that $H(f)$ emphasizes more those frequency ranges that contain greater signal power [5]. Another approach is Kalman filtering. However, this requires knowledge of the signal model and second-order statistical properties of the signal and noise [6]. The recursive estimator is

$$\hat{s}(k) = \phi\hat{s}(k - 1) + K(k)[x(k) - H\phi\hat{s}(k - 1)] \tag{3}$$

where $\hat{s}(k)$, $x(k)$, $K(k)$, $\phi$, and $H$ represent the signal estimate, measurement, time-varying gain, system matrix, and observation matrix, respectively. One recent application uses Kalman filtering to estimate the EMG control signal for powered protheses [7].

In many situations the signal waveform changes with time. Common reasons are electrode motion, changing physiological conditions, habituation, etc. Thus, some adaptive filtering or estimation scheme is needed. The most commonly used approach in wavelet detection of ECG and EMG potentials is to update the templates sequentially as each new wavelet is detected and classified [8]. For the $i$th template and the $M$th occurrence, the updated template is

$$s_i(k) = \frac{M-1}{M} s_{i-1}(k) + \frac{1}{M} x(k), \qquad 0 \le k \le N \tag{4}$$

## D   Power Spectral Density

The estimation of PSD is often used for many applications, including signal modeling, filter specifications, and feature extraction [9, 10]. There are two basic approaches to PSD estimation. One is the classical periodogram, whose formula is

$$S(m) = \frac{X(m)X^*(m)}{N}, \qquad X(m) = \sum_{k=1}^{N} x(k) \exp(-j2\pi mk/N) \tag{5}$$

The number of signal points is $N$, $S(f)$ is the PSD, and $X(f)$ is the discrete Fourier transform of the measured signal $x(k)$. The fast transform techniques have made this operation easy and feasible. Windowing of $x(k)$ or $S(m)$ is mandatory to reduce estimation variance and leakage effects. The second estimation procedure is based on ARMA modeling. The number of references on these topics is almost endless and will not be elaborated [11, 12].

The coherence spectrum $K(m)$ has been used as a frequency-domain measure of functional similarity of separate parts of the cortex in investigations of higher cortical function. The squared coherency is

$$K^2(m) = \frac{S_{12}^2(m)}{S_1(m)S_2(m)}, \qquad 0 \le K(m) \le 1 \tag{6}$$

where $S_{12}^2(m)$ is the cross PSD of any two EEG recordings and $S_1(m)$ and $S_2(m)$ are the individual PSDs. Different frequency ranges of $K(m)$ have been found sensitive to mental tasks [13].

## E   Envelope Detection

Envelope detection is used primarily in EMG processing to derive an estimate of the intensity of the EMG since it is a function of muscular force. Essentially it is a nonlinear operation followed by linear filtering, as shown in

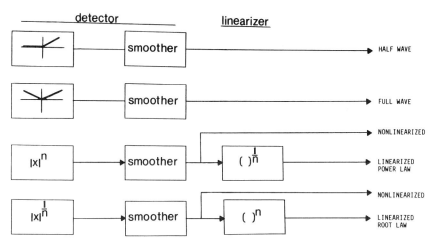

**Fig. 1.** Block diagram of the processors evaluated in linearized and nonlinearized forms. The exponent was either 2 or 4. (From Kreifeldt and Yao [14]. Copyright © 1974 IEEE.)

Figure 1 [14]. Presently the EMG envelopes are used to derive control signals for powered prostheses [15] and to estimate muscle patterns in locomotion [16].

### Waveform Detection and Recognition    F

Waveform detection systems have become very important in certain applications where the shape and time of occurrence of different wavelets are needed to discriminate between normal and pathologic conditions. The applications include studying NAPs and MUAPs, normal and arrythmic cardiac activity, and spike EEG activity.

The first phase of these systems, waveform detection, is the easiest. Low error rate detection algorithms include finding amplitude threshold exceedure for indicating action potential waveforms and finding wavelets with short durations or large rates of change in amplitude for indicating ECG and EEG complexes. Once a wavelet is detected, it is classified by either template matching or position in parameter feature space. For this to be accurate, the epoch of the wavelet must be delineated and the baseline identified. In each physiologic area there are heuristics that are too numerous to mention here [2, 8].

### Autoregressive Modeling    G

Autoregressive (AR) modeling or linear prediction has become used more prevalently within the last decade in EEG and EMG applications. The underlying concept is to develop several signal models which correspond to different activities or situations. Then, given the ongoing signal epoch, decide which model best describes it. In other words, it is a signal classification technique. Specifically, the models are used to detect different levels of muscle activity for EMG control [17], or to segment periods of EEG activity into normal background, epileptic, or other states [18].

The AR model has the form

$$x(k) = \sum_{i=1}^{N} a_i x(k - i) + w(k) \tag{7}$$

where $x(k)$ is the signal, $a_i$ the model coefficients, $N$ the model order, and $w(k)$ a zero-mean white-noise process. The coefficients are derived by minimizing the mean-square error (MSE) between $x(k)$ and the linear prediction based on Eq. (7). The prediction error is

$$e(k) = x(k) - \hat{x}(k) = x(k) - \sum_{i=1}^{N} a_i x(k - i) \tag{8}$$

The minimization produces the Yule–Walker equations which are, in matrix form,

$$\begin{bmatrix} R(0) & R(1) & \cdots & R(N) \\ R(1) & R(0) & \cdots & R(N-1) \\ \vdots & & & \vdots \\ R(N) & & \cdots & R(0) \end{bmatrix} \begin{bmatrix} 1 \\ -a_1 \\ \vdots \\ -a_N \end{bmatrix} = \begin{bmatrix} \sigma_w^2 \\ 0 \\ \vdots \\ 0 \end{bmatrix} \tag{9}$$

where $R(k)$ is the autocorrelation of $x(k)$ and $\sigma_w^2$ is both the variance of $w(k)$ and the MSE. The solution of matrix equation (9) provides the AR coefficients. There are many references describing AR modeling and order selection algorithms in detail [19].

Two different approaches are used for signal identification. One is for off-line classification. A signal is divided into epochs of equal length and the coefficients are calculated for each epoch and used as feature vectors. One of the many standard classifier algorithms is then applied to classify the epochs into predetermined groups. The other is for on-line classification and is based on the prediction error. As the signal is measured, the prediction error of all the models is calculated simultaneously for a finite time. Naturally, the signal is classified as that for which it has the least MSE.

The segmentation of EEG signals is a variation of the on-line approach designed to classify epochs of variable duration. An initial model is calculated and the MSE is continuously calculated. When the MSE exceeds a designated threshold, the signal is demarcated, and a new set of coefficients is estimated on the next $N$ signal points. The MSE calculation then resumes and the process continues until the entire measurement is segmented. Figure 2 illustrates this procedure [18].

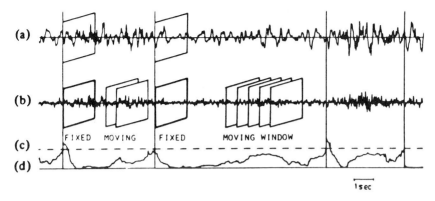

**Fig. 2.** Segmentation procedure. (a) Raw EEG. The slab indicates the section to which the LP filter is adapted. (b) Resulting prediction error. The initial PE ACF is computed from the fixed window; the running ACF corresponds to the moving window. (c) Segmentation threshold. (d) SEM. (From Bodenstein and Praetorius [18]. Copyright © 1977 IEEE.)

## TRADITIONAL METHODS  III

### Feature Extraction  A

There are two general types of features, explicit and derived, which comprise feature vectors. The explicit features are those which are waveform parameters, whereas the derived features are calculated from some mathematical transformation. The features for wavelets, that is, action potentials, spikes, and ECG complexes, are generally the same. Parameters of descriptive value are maxima, minima, slopes, durations, etc. Additional parameters pertaining to action potentials are number of phases and to ECG complexes are time durations between the P and Q waves, etc. For other signals with a more random quality, like the interference EMG, general characteristics are utilized. The rates of zero crossings and turns in amplitude have been found to be valid measures that distinguish between normal and pathologic states in EMGs and EEGs. Trends in the mean frequency of the EMG PSD is an indicator of muscular fatigue [10, 20].

The derived features emanate from orthogonal transformations. The most used mathematical transformation is the Fourier transform in the form of the PSD. All of the components or energy within certain bands have been valuable [1, 21]. Exponential and Hermite polynomial basis sets have been applied to a lesser extent [22]. If $N$ is the dimension of the basis set $\{\mathbf{f}_i\}$, then the set is orthogonal if

$$\mathbf{f}_i \cdot \mathbf{f}_j = \begin{cases} 0, & i \neq j \\ \lambda_i \neq 0, & i = j \end{cases} \tag{10}$$

The new features, $y_i$, are

$$y_i = \mathbf{x'} \cdot \mathbf{f}_i \qquad (11)$$

The new feature vector is the vector of $y_i$ values.

The method of principal components or the Karhunen–Loéve transformation (KLT) is by far the most prevalently used database transformation. Applications are found in such diverse areas as gait analysis [23], evoked EEG potentials [24], and MUAP description [25]. The essential steps for utilizing this technique are outlined [26]. Briefly, for all data vectors $\mathbf{x}$ in a measurement set, form a grand mean vector $\mathbf{m}$ and a covariance matrix $\mathbf{S}$. Perform an eigenanalysis on $\mathbf{S}$. Order the eigenvectors according to the descending magnitude of the eigenvalues $e_i$. The first basis vector, $\mathbf{a}_1$, is associated with the largest eigenvalue, $e_1$, and so on. These eigenvectors form a new basis set. Form a matrix $\mathbf{A}$ of these eigenvectors. The new feature vector of equal dimension for each data vector is

$$\mathbf{z} = \mathbf{A'}(\mathbf{x} - \mathbf{m}) \qquad (12)$$

## B   Feature Vector Dimension Reduction

Because of the large dimension of some feature vectors, dimension reduction techniques are a prominent part of analysis. For instance, harmonic analysis can produce vectors of 256 elements and signal-space epochs of easily 125 or more elements [27]. The KLT is also used for reduction, as is stepwise discriminant analysis (SWDA) [28]. A dimensionality reduction is effected with the KLT by retaining the first $K$ eigenvalues which account for a significant amount of data variance. The dimension of $\mathbf{z}$ is $K$ and its variance is

$$\mathrm{var}(\mathbf{z}) = \sum_{i=1}^{K} e_i \qquad (13)$$

A summary of SWDA is described [29], but to understand the concept consider the general linear discriminant function

$$d_i = \sum_{j=1}^{N} w_{ij} x_j + w_{i0} \qquad (14)$$

where the set $(w_{in}, \ldots, w_{i0})$ is the weight vector for the $i$th class using the full $N$-dimensional feature vector. The SWDA procedure finds the best subset of lower dimension, $K$, of the features for classifying the training data. It operates by finding sequentially the best features by minimizing the within-group variance; an $F$ statistic is the measure of goodness. Selection ceases when further improvement is minimal.

Clustering Techniques **C**

Clustering or unsupervised learning has been used to learn the number of classes in data sets. These techniques are described in Chapter 2. Please refer to it; however, an excellent reference is [30]. Examples of an application of a K-MEANS algorithm are in EMG gait analysis [16] and MUAP classification [31]. The nearest-neighbor (NN) algorithm has been useful in EEG studies of higher cortical function [28].

Classification **D**

Classification algorithms are abundant [32, 33]. Naturally, all assume a valid feature vector and a learned set of clusters.

One general type of algorithm is based on a distance meassure between the unclassed feature vector and some property of the known clusters. Of all the geometric distance measures the Euclidean distance, or squared error, is the most prevalent. Give an unknown feature vector $\mathbf{x}$ of dimension $N$ and all the $K$ cluster center vectors (means) $\mathbf{m}_i$, the squared distance from any cluster is

$$d_i^2 = \sum_{j=1}^{N} (x_j - m_{ji})^2, \qquad 1 \le i \le K \tag{15}$$

where $j$ is the element index. The vector $\mathbf{x}$ belongs to the cluster with minimum $d_i^2$. Action potential wavelets and QRS complexes are assigned in this fashion. The centers are average or adaptive templates [2, 8]. A variation of this measure is the Mahalanobis distance

$$d_i^2 = \sum_{j=1}^{N} \frac{(x_j - m_{ji})^2}{\sigma_i^2} \tag{16}$$

where $\sigma_i^2$ is the variance of cluster $i$. Event-related potentials are classified this way [27].

Another distance measure is the nearest neighbor. This algorithm uses (15), where $\mathbf{m}_i$ now represents any member of the entire data set. The minimum $d_i^2$ is found and its corresponding data vector $\mathbf{u}_j$ noted. Vector $\mathbf{x}$ is assigned to the same cluster as $\mathbf{u}_j$. Practically this can be unfeasible, so a constrained data set is selected. Such an approach works well in EMG control of prosthesis [34].

The workhorse technique seems to be the linear discriminant function (LDF). The feature vectors are usually waveform parameters. The LDFs are important in their own right. They are a particularization of the multivariate Gaussian variable with equal covariances in decision theory. Applications include discerning renal function from AR parameters of the EEG [35] and depth of anesthesia from ECG and EEG waveform parameters [36]. The mathematics of discriminant functions are summarized for only one of several forms [33]. Let $\mathbf{w}_i$ be a set of $K$ weight vectors for a $K$ class situation. The decision value for it is

$$d_i = \mathbf{w}_i \cdot [x:1] \tag{17}$$

The feature vector $\mathbf{x}$ is assigned to the class with the largest $d_i$.

## IV  SYNTACTIC METHODS

### A  General Synopsis

In grammar, syntax deals with the structure of sentences and the rules of arrangement of words in sentences. Similarly, in the processing of biological signals, syntactic analysis deals with rule-driven amalgamation of fundamental units of information about a signal into an interpretation of the characteristics of the signal. These fundamental elements of information are often referred to as tokens, primitives, or morphs. A syntactic pattern recognition system can be considered to have three main parts: (a) feature selection and extraction, (b) representation of basic elements, and (c) syntax analysis.

### B  Feature Selection and Extraction

The selection of features for syntactic pattern recognition of biological signals is similar to the feature selection procedures described earlier. However, the selection and extraction paradigm is guided by the need to secure features that closely describe the fundamental elements of the biological signal under study. Some signals have features that are predominantly observable in the time domain, while others have characteristics more suitable for observation in the frequency or other domains.

*Carotid pulse-wave (CPW) feature selection.* One technique for selecting features from a pulse wave is shown in Fig. 3 [37]. Eight primitive elements are extracted, as shown. These elements provide a reasonably complete description of the fundamental activity in the time domain. For repetitive, well-defined signals such as the CPW, a best-fit algorithm can be used to match the prespecified elements to the waveform.

*ECG features.* ECG features can be reasonably selected in the time

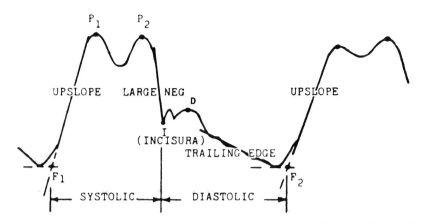

**Fig. 3.** Carotid pulse wave showing primitive elements. (From Klein and Davis [36]. Copyright © 1976 IEEE).

domain. Various levels of granularity are possible. A rather coarse representation of the waveform can be achieved by simply coding the signal into the amplitude of the QRS complex [38]. A more detailed representation might use primitives such as positive, negative, or zero slope line segments [39].

*EEG features.* Both time- and frequency-domain features can be used to characterize this signal. Frequency-domain techniques allow extraction of information about activity in frequency ranges [40], while time-domain features for activity such as spikes can also be useful [41].

*Representation of basic elements.* In general, labels that describe basic primitive elements in the signal should be selected. For example, in EEG analysis the label "A" might be selected to represent a segment of the signal with artifactual activity, or an "S" may represent slow wave activity [40]. The important point is to decide on the granularity of representation and choose a representational strategy that allows representation of the important elements in the waveform while retaining computational simplicity. Primitive elements are normally assigned to contiguous elements in a waveform, and the concatenation of these elements is a string that represents all we know about the waveform. Thus, low granularity produces short strings with often inadequate information and high granularity produces long strings with redundant information. The selection of grain size (i.e., how much information a primitive element describes) is left to the individual researcher.

*Syntax analysis.* In the analysis of biological signals, parsing is the process of analyzing the fundamental elements or tokens in a string that represents the biological waveform. In many cases, a string of fundamental elements can be digested according to a series of rules. Consider the following simplified example from the EEG analysis domain.

Given:  a string $S$ that represents a waveform

$S = [\text{A A A A A A A S S S S S S S S N N N N A A A}]$

Where:  Twenty tokens represent 100 sec of data in 5-sec epochs

Three token types are defined:

A = artifactual
S = slow
N = normal

Task:  Reduce the string to a simple representation by applying the following rules:

Artifact: [A A][Artifact A][A Artifact]
Slow: [S S][Slow S][S Slow]
Normal: [N N][Normal N][N Normal]

where any of the elemental combinations in braces on the right-hand side of the rule that are found in the string are replaced by the element (called a nonterminal) on the left during repeated application of the rules

Result:  For this simple example, $S$ would be replaced by

$S = [\text{Artifact Slow Normal Artifact}]$

if there were any particular meaning associated with the syntax of these four elements, $S$ could be further operated upon by another rule to achieve additional reductions. In practice, one might design a rule set to produce outcomes such as "normal" or "abnormal" or any other desired evaluation. The application of rules as demonstrated earlier is called data-driven or forward chaining and is typical of most syntactic pattern recognition control strategies.

*Example.* Figure 4 displays an example taken from the analysis of EEG signals [40]. As shown, the EEG is split into contiguous segments and each segment is transformed into the frequency domain. Using discriminant analysis, each epoch is classified into one of the following categories: N (normal), S (slow), L (low amplitude), A (artifactual), NL (normal low), AL (artifactual low), or SL (slow low). Next, rules are applied to attempt to classify the signal as normal or abnormal. The concatenation of tokens by rules in tree form illustrates reaching normal and abnormal conclusions in Figs. 5 and 6 [41].

*Implementation languages.* The ideas described can be implemented in virtually any computer language from Basic to LISP. As in other endeavors, languages such as Basic, FORTRAN, and C that do not have robust string or list handling capabilities require users to add such functionality to the system created. As an alternative, one might consider the LISP language, in which

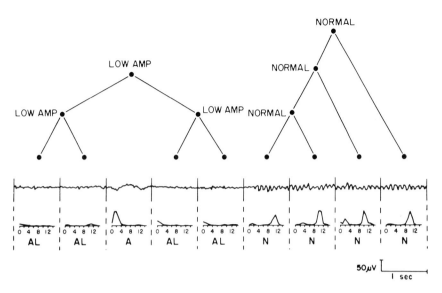

Fig. 4. Amalgamation of adjacent labels in a single-channel EEG. The first 5 sec are identified as "LOW AMP" and the remaining 4 sec as "NORMAL." The artifact is ignored. (From Horowitz [39]. Copyright © 1981 Elsevier Biomedical Press.)

most needed functions for string and list manipulation are provided. Simple systems for parsing lists of tokens, as described earlier, can be written in about one page of LISP code.

*Advantages and disadvantages.* There are obvious problems with the use of the techniques described previously. First, rather deep knowledge about the problem is required in order to successfully identify features and write rules. While it is conceptually interesting to consider the possibility of using some automated type of grammatical inference to produce the rules, in practice no technique of grammatical inference has proved robust enough to be used with real problems involving biological waveforms. Hence, the writing of rules is incumbent on the designer of the analysis system. Similarly, the selection of features must be accomplished essentially by hand since automated techniques usually cannot provide the guidance necessary to make a useful feature selection. Second, the control strategy of typical parsing systems is relatively trivial and cannot deal with very difficult problems. Typical parsing techniques consist of simple repeated application of a list of rules, which is often equivalent to forward chaining, an elementary concept in knowledge-based rule systems. Formation of a robust control strategy for guiding syntactic parsing of strings appears somewhat problematic. However, if rather straightforward amalgamation of constituent elementary tokens in a waveform will suffice to secure an identification or evaluation, then this technique will work rather well.

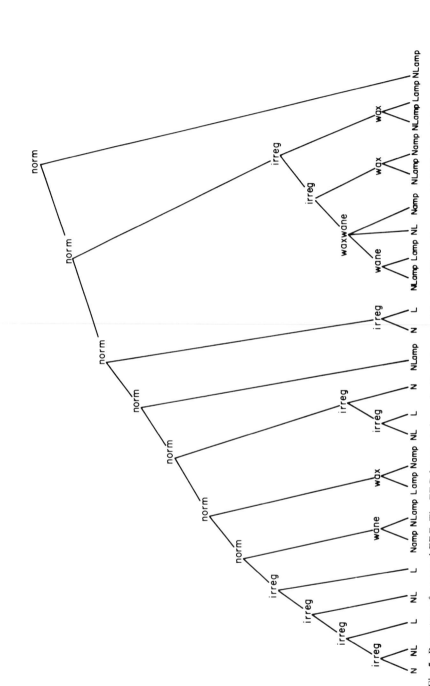

Fig. 5. Parse tree of a normal EEG. The EEG fragment shown in Fig. 4 is part of the tree. (From Bourne et al. [40]. Copyright © 1979 IEEE).

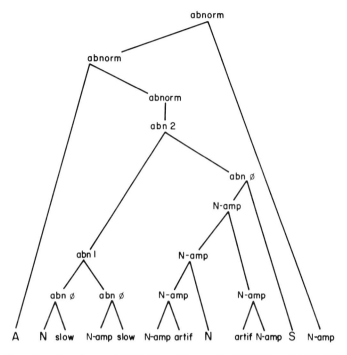

**Fig. 6.** Parse tree of an abnormal EEG. (From Bourne *et al.* [40]. Copyright © 1979 IEEE.)

## SEMANTIC METHODS   V

### General Synopsis   A

Semantic methods (also referred to as knowledge-based methods) of waveform evaluation deal with the use of knowledge to guide the evaluation of waveforms. Knowledge and solution strategies may be heuristic or procedural or a combination of both. Consider how an expert physician evaluates biological waveforms. When evaluating EEGs, EMGs, or ECGs, the performance of the expert physician is apt to significantly outperform any computer program. Why is this so? Most likely, it is because the reasoning processes that a physician uses requires a large database of past history that he can call on (so-called common-sense knowledge), an accumulated store of rules to apply to the problem, the knowledge of how to control rule application, and when to back up and try something else. This sort of knowledge is difficult to code in either algorithmic or syntactic systems but can be dealt with using knowledge-based methods.

## B  Expert Systems

Expert systems that mimic human problem-solving capabilities have been built in many areas of medicine [42–45] and other fields. The concepts used are applicable to processing of biological waveforms.

## C  Inference Engine

The term *inference engine* refers to a general-purpose implementation of control strategies that can be used with rules and data in differing domains without modification of the software.

## D  Knowledge Representation

*Rules.* Typically, dynamic knowledge about a domain is coded in the form of if–then rules. Control is specified in the form of agendas (procedural specifications; also called scripts) or metarules. Metarules are rules that control the application of rules and, as such, define the strategy for working a problem. One might consider the following rule in an EEG domain.

Rule 1:   *Ifall* (The frequency of the waveform is dominantly around 10 Hz)
              (There are no slow waves present (or slow waves have been shown to be caused by drowsiness))
              (Artifacts in the record have been eliminated)
              (The patient is an adult, age less than 70)
         *then*
              (The record is likely to be normal)

The consequent part of this rule (i.e., the *then* part) contains a conclusion which becomes true only if all the parts of the antecedent (the *if* part) become true. Typical rule systems consist of many rules of this type, often with different *if* types (e.g., *ifall*, *ifsome*).

*Control structures.* Two basic control strategies are frequently used in expert systems. Forward chaining is the technique most similar to the rule application method found in syntactic systems in which rules are tried one by one until no more fire. Backward chaining requires that the system designer specify a list of hypotheses (e.g., "The record is normal," "The record is abnormal"). Usually, hypotheses are tested by collecting all rules which could contribute to the successful conclusion of the hypothesis. These rules are then evaluated. If any are found that require other rules to be evaluated, these rules are collected and then tried. This procedure continues backward until there are no more rules and the data are reached. If data do not exist, then either the user is asked, a default value used, or a value guessed by the system. In practice, forward and backward control strategies are frequently mixed and combined with heuristic search methods that are either procedurally specified or implemented using metarules.

*Frames.* Frames provide ways of organizing knowledge hierarchically. As a data structure, they allow information to be broken down into more and more refined elements. In biological signal processing, representing waveforms using this technique allows varying granularity.

A frame is a generalized property list in which an object can take on a series of descriptors, which in turn can be described by subdescriptors. The tree-like organization assists in organization of both prototypical and common-sense static knowledge. Prototypical knowledge is useful in designating the type of analysis to be carried out. If one determines by analyzing the basic data that there is suggestive evidence that the waveform belongs to an abnormal class, a prototype knowledge base could contain a slot that suggests that an evaluation procedure be used that is appropriate for this class. Similarly, there is often a large store of knowledge that one might refer to as "common sense." To create a truly useful biological waveform analysis system, one needs to include a large store of common-sense knowledge about the domain of interest and more general information about biological signal analysis. For example, consider the problem of aliasing in which too low sampling rates produce signals in the power spectrum that are obviously bogus. The expert human signal evaluator can immediately spot this problem and properly recommend the corrective action of increasing the sampling rate to a level commensurate with the content of the signal. In contrast, few biological waveform analysis systems can presently accomplish this task. An automated knowledge-based system would contain common-sense knowledge about the appropriate sampling rate for the class of signals studied and would understand how to raise the sampling rate and test the results of the change.

*Semantic and associative nets.* These networks provide means of organizing knowledge that are not necessarily hierarchical. The term "semantic" deals with the meaning as contrasted with form.

### Knowledge Acquisition    E

To build knowledge-based systems for processing biological signals, one must acquire knowledge about how signals are processed.

*Knowledge engineering.* A typical method for acquiring knowledge is to involve a person familiar with both the problem and methods of building knowledge-based systems. Such a person is called a knowledge engineer. The task of this person is to translate information from an expert in the domain into rules, frames, or other representations that can be used with a general inference engine.

*Knowledge engineering assistant programs.* A knowledge engineering assistant program is a program that essentially replaces the knowledge engineer as previously described.

## F Languages

Most expert systems are built using the LISP language [46] due to the heavy reliance on list processing techniques. PROLOG [47] is also a reasonable choice, providing many of the same capabilities as LISP and one prespecified control strategy (backward chaining) as well. Naturally, other languages may be used, but they usually produce difficulties.

## G Examples

*EEG.* Figure 7 shows an outline of a semantic system created for the evaluation of EEGs [48]. This system converts spectral data in 5-sec epochs to a list of attributes (e.g., "alpha is high"), tests hypotheses temporally and spatially, and finally generates conclusions. Figure 8 displays an example of how rules in this system are used to evaluate EEGs. An analogous system has also been created on a microprocessor-based instrument [49] and on larger computer systems [50].

*GAIT.* GAITSPERT [51, 52] is a system designed to be a clinical tool that produces an evaluation of abnormal human locomotion arising from stroke. EMG signals are acquired and, including other patient information, diagnoses and thereapeutic recommendations are made. Figures 9 and 10 show a diagram of this system and a typical rule.

*Serum protein electrophoresis.* A microprocessor system that implements semantic interpretation methods has been developed for analyzing signals acquired from a scanning densitometer [53]. This system provides an interpretation of peaks contained in the waveform produced by a scanning densitometer.

## H Advantages and Disadvantages

The use of knowledge-based systems for biological signal processing is relatively new but shows great promise for combining traditional signal processing techniques with heuristic knowledge. Improved analysis systems

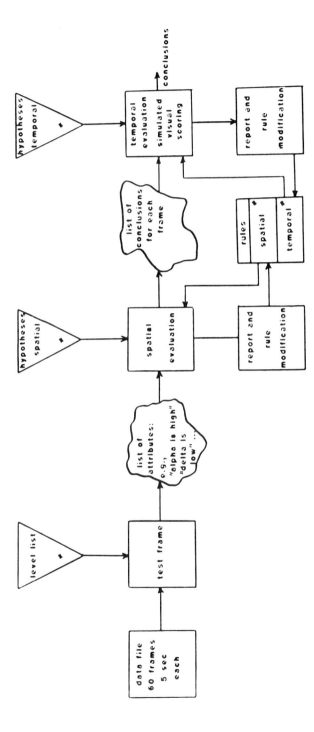

Fig. 7. Block diagram of an expert system used for the evaluation of electroencephalograms. (From Clocksin and Mellish [47]. Copyright © 1983 IEEE.)

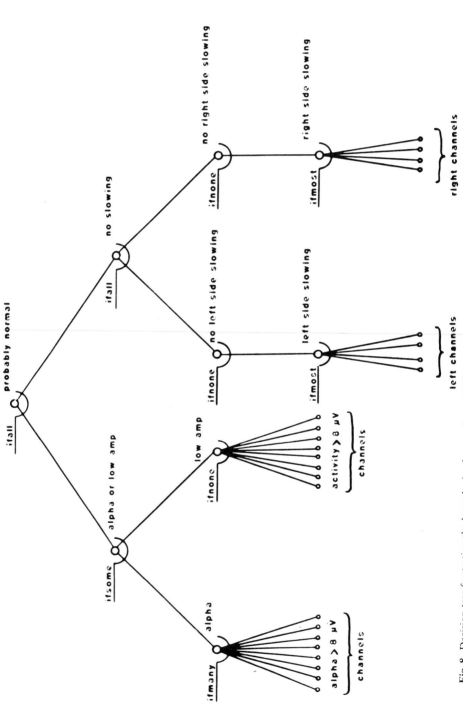

**Fig. 8.** Decision tree for testing the hypothesis of normality in EEG analysis. (From Clocksin and Mellish [47]. Copyright © 1983 IEEE.)

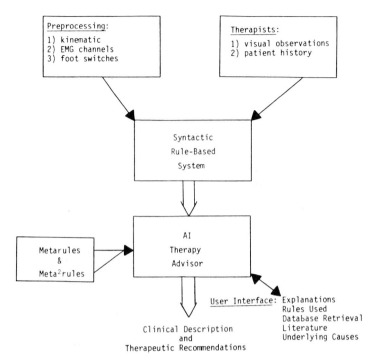

**Fig. 9.** Block diagram of system used for syntactic and semantic evaluation. (From Dzierzanowski *et al.* [51]. Copyright © 1983 IEEE.)

```
CLINICAL_rule2
    ifall
        (PSM suggested_therapy) member (synonym neuro)
        (PSM general_description date_of_stroke) <= 6
        (PSM patient_state) = cooperative
        (PSM patient_state) = hearing_ok
        (PSM patient_state) = speech_ok
        not
            (PSM patient_state) = incontinent
        not
            (PSM patient_state) = over_weight
    then
        conclude:  (PSM recommended_therapy)
            with values:
            all of: (PSM suggested_therapy)
            that occur in: (synonym neuro)
    else
        conclude: (PSM not_recommended_therapy)
            with values:
            all of: (PSM suggested_therapy)
            that occur in: (synonym neuro)
```

**Fig. 10.** Example of a rule used in GAITSPERT.

can be realized using these combined techniques rather than selecting a single method. Most problems require rather deep semantic knowledge for proper evaluation; hence, methods that allow simulation of such knowledge are more likely to succeed than other methods.

## REFERENCES

1.  P. Ktonas, Automated analysis of abnormal electroencephalograms, *CRC Critical Reviews Biomed. Engr.* **9**, 39–97 (1983).
2.  B. Mambrito and C. DeLuca, Acquisition and decomposition of the EMG signal, *in* "Computer-Aided Electromyography" (*Prog. Clin. Neurophysiol.*, Vol. 10) (J. E. Desmedt, Ed.), pp. 52–72. Karger, Basel, 1983.
3.  M. Berger, Analysis of sensory evoked potentials using normalized cross-correlation functions, *Med. Biol. Engr. Comp.* **21**, 149–157 (1983).
4.  S. Hecht and J. Vidal, Generation of ECG prototype waveforms by piecewise correlational averaging, *IEEE Trans. Pat. Anal. Mach. Intell.* **2**, 415–420 (1980).
5.  J. deWeerd, A posteriori "Weiner" filtering, *IEEE Trans. Biomed. Engr.* **28**, 252–257 (1981).
6.  J. Meditch, "Stochastic Optimal Linear Estimation and Control." McGraw-Hill, New York, 1969.
7.  H. Evans, Z. Pan, P. Parker, and R. Scott, Signal processing for proportional myoelectric control, *IEEE Trans. Biomed. Engr.* **31**, 207–211 (1984).
8.  L. Thomas, K. Clark, C. Mead, K. Ripley, B. Spenner, and G. Oliver, Automated cardiac dysrhythmia analysis, *Proc. IEEE* **67**, 1322–1327 (1979).
9.  L. Lindstrom and R. Magnusson, Interpretation of myoelectric power spectra: A model and its applications, *Proc. IEEE* **65**, 653–662 (1977).
10. E. Richfield, B. Cohen, and J. Albers, Review of quantitative and automated needle electromyographic analysis, *IEEE Trans. Biomed. Engr.* **28**, 506–514 (1981).
11. D. Childers, "Modern Spectrum Analysis." IEEE Press, New York, 1978.
12. N. Geckinli and D. Yavus, "Discrete Fourier Transformation and Its Applications to Power Spectra Estimations." Elsevier, New York, 1983.
13. T. Yunck and F. Tuteur, Comparison of decision rules for automatic EEG classification, *IEEE Trans. Pat. Anal. Mach. Intell.* **2**, 420–428 (1980).
14. J. Kreifeldt and S. Yao, A signal-to-noise investigation of nonlinear electromyographic processors, *IEEE Trans. Biomed. Engr.* **21**, 298–308 (1974).
15. P. Parker, J. Stuller, and R. Scott, Signal processing for the multistate myoelectric channel, *Proc. IEEE* **65**, 662–647 (1977).
16. R. Shiavi and N. Green, Ensemble averaging of locomotor electromyographic patterns using interpolation, *Med. Biol. Engr. Comput.* **21**, 573–578 (1983).
17. D. Graupe and W. Cline, Functional separation of EMG signals via ARMA identification methods for prosthesis control purposes, *IEEE Trans. Sys., Man and Cybernetics* **5**, 252–259 (1975).
18. G. Bodenstein and M. Praetorius, Feature extraction from the electroencephalogram by adaptive segmentation, *Proc. IEEE* **65**, 642–652 (1977).
19. D. Childers, J. Aunon, and C. McGillem, Spectral analysis: Prediction and extrapolation, *CRC Critical Reviews Bioengr.* **6**, 133–175 (1981).
20. J. Jenkins, Computerized electrocardiography, *CRC Critical Reviews Bioengr.* **6**, 307–350 (1981).
21. K. Roberts, P. Lawrence, and A. Eisen, Dispersion of somatosensory evoked potential (SEP) in multiple sclerosis, *IEEE Trans. Biomed. Engr.* **30**, 360–364 (1983).
22. S. Nandedkar and D. Sanders, Special-purpose orthonormal basis functions—application to motor unit action potentials, *IEEE Trans. Biomed. Engr.* **31**, 374–377 (1984).

23. R. Shiavi and P. Griffin, Representing and clustering electromyographic gait patterns with multivariate techniques, *Med. Biol. Engr. Comput.* **19**, 605–611 (1981).
24. J. Aunon, C. McGillem, and D. Childers, Signal processing in evoked potential research; averaging and modeling, *CRC Critical Reviews in Bioengr.*, **5**, 323–367 (1981).
25. B. Wheeler and W. Heetderks, A comparison of techniques for classification of multiple neural signals *IEEE Trans. Biomed. Engr.* **29**, 752–759 (1982).
26. E. Glaser and D. Ruchkin, "Principles of Neurobiological Signal Analysis." Academic Press, New York, 1976.
27. J. Vidal, Real-time detection of brain events in EEG, *Proc. IEEE* **65**, 633–641 (1977).
28. A. Gevins, Pattern recognition of human brain electric potentials, *IEEE Trans. Pat. Anal. Mach. Intell.* **2**, 383–484 (1980).
29. A. Afifi and S. Azen, "Statistical Analysis—A Computer Oriented Approach." Academic Press, New York, 1979.
30. J. Hartigan, "Clustering Algorithms." Wiley, New York, 1975.
31. G. Dinning and A. Sanderson, Real-time classification of multiunit neural signals using reduced feature sets, *IEEE Trans. Biomed. Engr.* **28**, 804–812 (1981).
32. M. Anderberg, "Cluster Analysis for Applications." Academic Press, New York, 1973.
33. J. Tou and R. Gonzalez, "Pattern Recognition Principles." Addison-Wesley, Reading, Massachusetts, 1974.
34. D. Denning, F. Gray, and R. Haralick, Prosthesis control using a nearest neighbor electromyographic pattern classifier, *IEEE Trans. Biomed. Engr.* **30**, 356–360 (1983).
35. B. Jansen, J. Bourne, and J. Ward, Autoregressive estimation of short segment spectra for computerized EEG analysis, *IEEE Trans. Biomed. Engr.* **28**, 630–638 (1981).
36. F. Klein and D. Davis, The use of time domain analyzed EEG in conjunction with cardiovascular parameters for monitoring anesthetic levels, *IEEE Trans. Biomed. Engr.* **28**, 36–40 (1981).
37. G. Stockman, L. Kanal, and M. Kyle, Structural pattern recognition of carotid pulse waves using a general waveform parsing system, *Commun. ACM* **19**, 688–695 (December 1976).
38. G. Belforte, R. DeMori, and F. Ferraris, A contribution to the automatic processing of electrocardiograms using syntactic methods, *IEEE Trans. Biomed. Engr.* **26**, 125–136 (March 1979).
39. S. Horowitz, Peak recognition in waveforms, *in* "Syntactic Pattern Recognition, Applications" (K. S. Fu, ed.), pp. 31–49. Springer-Verlag, Berlin and New York, 1977.
40. J. Bourne, V. Jagannathan, B. Hamel, B. Jansen, J. Ward, J. Hughes, and C. Erwin, Evaluation of a syntactic pattern recognition approach to quantitative electroencephalographic analysis, *Electroenceph. Clin. Neurophys.* **52**, 57–64 (1981).
41. D. Giese, J. Bourne, and J. Ward, Syntactic analysis of the electroencephalogram, *IEEE Trans. Sys., Man and Cybernetics* **9**, 429–435 (1979).
42. J. Aikins, J. Kunz, E. Shortliffe, and R. Fallat, PUFF: An expert system for interpretation of pulmonary function data, *Comp. Biomed. Res.* **16**, 199–208 (1983).
43. M. First, B. Weimer, S. McLinden, and R. Miller, "LOCALIZE: computer-assisted localization of peripheral nervous system lesions, *Comp. Biomed. Res.* **15**, 525–543 (1982).
44. R. Miller, H. Pople, and J. Myers, INTERNIST-I, An experimental computer-based diagnostic consultant for general internal medicine, *New England J. Med.* **307**, 468–476 (August 1982).
45. E. Shortliffe, "Computer Based Medical Consultations: MYCIN." Elsevier, New York, 1976.
46. P. Winston and B. Horn, "LISP." Addison-Wesley, Reading, Massachusetts, 1981.
47. W. Clocksin and C. Mellish, "Programming in PROLOG." Springer-Verlag, Berlin and New York, 1981.
48. J. Bourne, M. Matousek, S. Friberg, and A. Arvidsson, "SEER-I: The semantic EEG evaluation regimen," *IEEE Trans. Biomed. Engr.* **30**, 239–244 (April, 1983).

49. L. Baas and J. Bourne, A rule-based microcomputer system for electroencephalogram evaluation, *IEEE Trans. Biomed. Engr.* **31**, 660–664 (October 1984).
50. V. Jagannathan, J. Bourne, B. Jansen, and J. Ward, Artificial intelligence methods in quantitative electroencephalogram analysis, *Comp. Progs. Biomed.* **15**, 249–258 (1982).
51. J. Dzierzanowski, J. Bourne, and R. Shiavi, GAITSPERT: A knowledge-based expert system for evaluation of human gait abnormalities *Proc. 6th Annu. Conf. IEEE Engr. Med. Biol. Soc. Los Angeles, California*, 62–65 (1984).
52. J. Dzierzanowski, R. Shiavi, and J. Bourne, A syntactic method for evaluation of abnormalities in human gait, *Proc. 5th Annu. Conf. IEEE Engr. Med. Biol. Soc., Columbus, Ohio, Sept. 1983*, pp. 12–14, (1983).
53. C. Kulikowski, Artificial intelligence methods and systems for medical consultation, *IEEE Trans. Pat. Anal. Mach. Intell.* **2**, 464–476 (September 1980).

# Chapter **23**

# Character Recognition by Computer and Applications

CHING Y. SUEN

Department of Computer Science
Concordia University
Montreal, Quebec

## INTRODUCTION I

Optical character recognition (OCR) has been a subject of great interest to many computer scientists, engineers, and people from other disciplines. Intensive research has made OCR an efficient means of entering data directly into the computer and capturing information from data sheets, books, and other machine-printed or handwritten materials. Such capabilities greatly widen the applications of computers in areas like automatic reading of texts

569

**HANDBOOK OF PATTERN RECOGNITION
AND IMAGE PROCESSING**

and data, man–computer communications, language processing, and machine translation. Indeed, present OCR machines have been used to process very large volumes of type- and handwritten and printed data generated by large corporations and government agencies, for example, bank and postal services, credit card and insurance companies, telephone and electricity companies, and medical, taxation, and finance departments, which handle millions of accounts and payments each year. While data can be processed very quickly by computers, the input of data into them is still very slow and tedious and has been considered as the real bottleneck in data processing. Throughout the entire history of computing, keypunches, largely developed in the 1920s and 1930s, have dominated the data entry market. Keypunching is not only slow and cumbersome, but is also error prone due to keying errors. As technology advances, so is the technique of data entry. Optical character recognition and key-to-disk/tape systems have become the most prominent types of new stand-alone data entry equipment. These new systems provide data capture plus preprocessing capabilities such as editing, verifying, sorting, merging, reformatting, and balancing, offering significantly more advantages than punch card equipment. The cost effectiveness as analyzed by several independent parties shows that for large volumes of data in excess of half a million cards, both OCR and key-to-disk/tape systems start to pay off and can be operated more economically than keypunching. Hence, it is not surprising that shipments of these new data entry devices have been increasing, while shipments of keypunches have declined. Actually, keypunches are now gradually being replaced by on-line terminals. OCR has the additional advantages of little human intervention and higher speed in both data entry and text processing, especially when the data already exist in machine-readable fonts. In fact, OCR has become one of the most successful applications of modern technology in the field of applied pattern recognition and artificial intelligence.

This chapter gives a brief description of the functions and operations of the major building blocks of the OCR system, including (a) digitization, preprocessing and smoothing, (b) standardization and feature extraction, and (c) classification of characters. It also presents a brief survey of the challenging problems of recognition of handwritten characters, special symbols, and ideographs and their applications. Owing to the limitation of space allowed, this chapter is confined to the subject of OCR, which is often referred as an off-line process, as opposed to real-time recognition of characters. Those readers who are interested in on-line recognition may refer to Suen et al. [1] or Berthod [2], which cover the generation of handwriting and its characteristics and techniques to preprocess and recognize handwritten words and cursive scripts and Yhap et al. [3] on Chinese characters.

We conclude by summarizing the implications of modern technologies on OCR hardware and software. Finally, it attempts to foretell the future trends of this branch of applied pattern recognition.

## OCR SYSTEM AND PRACTICAL APPLICATIONS  II

A block diagram of an OCR system is shown in Fig. 1. At the input end, characters typed or written on documents are scanned and digitized by an optical scanner to produce a digitized image. At this stage, the OCR system will start to locate the regions (usually guided by marks preprinted on the input document) in which data have been entered, typed, printed, or written on the input documents. Once these regions are found, the data blocks are then segmented into character images. Instead of keeping the images in multi-gray levels, it is common practice to convert them into binary matrices to save memory space and computational effort. Depending on the complexity of the character shapes and the vocabulary involved, the size of the matrix, which reflects the resolution of a digitized character, varies to achieve speed and accuracy. Typically, a character size of 8 (wide) by 10 (high) pixels is sufficient for recognizing stylized type fonts such as OCRA and OCRB [4] and those imprinted by credit cards. Slightly bigger matrix sizes are required for the regular type fonts such as Elite, Courier, and Gothic. For handwritten alphanumerics and Chinese characters, the dimensions of the matrix have to be much larger so that detailed features can be extracted from the complex patterns. Typical matrix sizes are presented in Table I.

After digitization, location, and segmentation, characters in the form of binary matrices go through the preprocessor to eliminate random noise, voids, bumps, and other spurious components which might still be with them.

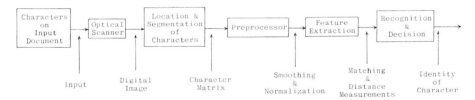

**Fig. 1.** Block diagram of a typical OCR system.

TABLE I

**Matrix Sizes of Binarized Characters (Width and Length)**

| Stylized type fonts | Regular type fonts | Handprinted alphanumerics | Printed Chinese characters | Handprinted Chinese characters |
|---|---|---|---|---|
| 8 × 10 | 12 × 15 | 15 × 20 | 25 × 32 | 30 × 40 |
| ↓ | ↓ | ↓ | ↓ | ↓ |
| 12 × 15 | 20 × 25 | 30 × 40 | 35 × 45 | 60 × 80 |

In some cases, normalizations in size, orientation, position ; well as other operations are performed to facilitate the extraction of distinctive features in the subsequent stage. More details concerning preprocessing and smoothing are described in the next section. Once the characteristics (see the section on features) of the cleaned characters have been extracted, they are matched to a list of references and a knowledge base built during the learning process to classify the characters. In addition, distance measurements are used, as well as shape derivation, shape matching, and hierarchical feature matching in the form of decision trees. Note that the decision-maker is strongly influenced by the types of features detected. A successful recognition system is built on the joint operations and performances of the feature detector and the classifier. More details about classification schemes are provided in Section VII on features and recognition.

In practical applications, for economical and technological reasons, data are usually typed on OCR forms by typists in special type fonts. The most common font used in North America is OCRA. Developed by the American National Standards Institute (ANSI), OCRA has been designed for easy recognition by OCR machines [4]. Alphanumeric characters of this font are presented below:

A  B  C  D  E  F  G  H  I  J  K  L

M  N  O  P  Q  R  S  T  U  V  W  X

Y  Z  1  2  3  4  5  6  7  8  9  0

Another common font is the OCRB, developed by the European Manufacturers Association (ECMA) [4]. Its character shapes are shown below:

A  B  C  D  E  F  G  H  I  J  K  L

M  N  O  P  Q  R  S  T  U  V  W  X

Y  Z  1  2  3  4  5  6  7  8  9  0

In looking at the character shapes of the OCRA and OCRB fonts, it is worthwhile to note that each character has a unique shape to avoid ambiguity with other characters similar in shape. Using these character sets, it is quite common for commercial OCR machines to achieve a recognition accuracy as high as 99.99% with a high reading speed of over 100 characters per second. Apart from these standardized fonts, special fonts have been designed for credit card slips and cashier tapes (called journal tapes) produced by cash registers. Through standardization of type fonts, OCR has become an important means of processing the ever-increasing volumes of water bills, medicare slips, insurance forms, and others.

In addition to the OCRA and OCRB fonts, others such as OCR-1403, 7B, 3/16 Gothic, MICR, etc. have also been used with a limited vocabulary (mainly numbers) by banks, credit companies, and others. Apart from OCR type fonts, standards on handprints have also been developed for OCR applications; more details will be given later in Section V. The way input data are processed commercially is described.

After the data have been typed, each character is brought under a scanner which either digitizes the character or traces it. The extracted image is compared with stored templates or features for identification. Identified characters are coded and stored on disk or tape for subsequent processing. Unidentified characters can be viewed via the console and corrected on line. Some systems use minicomputers and others make use of large computers to recognize the characters. The sophistication of the recognition process depends on the type and number of fonts used and the number of characters in the alphabet, for example, numeric or alphanumeric. Some systems can read several typefonts and handprinted numerals as well. Like the key-to-disk/tape system, software has been developed in some OCR systems to provide editing capability, data validation, and balancing. The chief advantage of an OCR system is its high reading speed. For simple fonts such as the OCRA font shown above, a reading speed higher than 3000 numerals/sec has been reported. The drawback of previous OCR systems lies in the area of errors. However, most systems now can read data with a substitution rate of less than 0.01 %. Further, in more elaborate systems, the software generates a scannable error-correction document which lists the document number, the field description, and the unreadable characters. The rejected characters can be keyed in and merged into the files of correct data.

## PREPROCESSING AND FEATURE EXTRACTION III

When patterns are scanned and digitized, the raw data may carry a certain amount of noise, for example, a scanner with low resolution will produce touching line segments and smeared images. In order to eliminate unwanted noise which may cause severe distortions in the digital image and hence ambiguous features and poor recognition rates, a preprocessor is used to smooth the digitized characters. Most smoothing algorithms are based on a technique which moves a window (e.g., $3 \times 3$) across the binary matrix of the character. The main operations of a preprocessor are shown in Table II. Essentially, smoothing performs the functions of both filling and thinning [6] to eliminate noise, isolated pixels, breaks, or bumps or to reduce the matrix character into a skeleton. Normalization is applied to produce patterns of

**TABLE II**

**Smoothing and Normalization in Preprocessing**

| Technique | Operation | Purpose |
|-----------|-----------|---------|
| Smoothing | Filling | To eliminate small breaks, gaps, and holes |
|  | Thinning | To remove noise, bumps, and isolated pixels |
|  |  | To reduce the character matrix to a skeleton so that line ends, lengths, directions, etc. can be extracted easily |
|  | Size | To produce character matrices of a uniform size |
|  | Position | To move the character matrix to a preferred position, e.g., centering, top-left justification, etc. |
| Normalization | Skew | To orient the characters in an upright direction |
|  | Linewidth | To produce characters with more or less the same width in all line segments |
|  |  | To reduce characters to skeletons whose lines are uniformly one unit wide |

uniform size or linewidth, fixed boundaries along certain edges (e.g., top-left justification), or a preferred orientation (e.g., vertical). The end results are ease in data handling and feature extraction and an improved recognition rate. More details can be found in Ref. 6.

## IV  FEATURE EXTRACTION

Feature extraction plays a very important role in all pattern recognition systems. In OCR applications, it is best to extract those features which will enable the system to discriminate correctly one class of characters from the others. Since characters are formed from line segments, many different types of shape features can be extracted and used to recognize the characters. With reference to Suen's work on distinctive features [6], we can classify features into two main groups through global and structural analyses. These two groups are composed of six feature families, as presented in Table III. Usually, some of these families are combined to produce more distinctive and/or effective features. According to our analysis [1], structural features can describe the topology of a character more easily and accurately; hence they are more tolerant to the deformation of the image than the global features. On the other hand, global features can be detected more easily and are more immune to noise and minor local distortions than structural features. As a result, a proper combination of both types of features can produce a powerful character recognizer.

**TABLE III**

**Distinctive Features which Can Be Extracted from Character Matrices**

| Group | Feature families | Features | Method of extraction |
|---|---|---|---|
| Global analysis | Distribution of points | a. Positions of points and their distances from a reference point (e.g., center of gravity, origin of coordinate system) | Locating the points in the $x$–$y$ coordinate system and recording those in specific zones |
| | | b. Crossing counts | Counting along certain directions, e.g., $0°$, $45°$, $90°$, and $135°$ |
| | | c. Density of the matrix | Counting the points in different locations |
| | Transformations | Series, spectra vectors | Fourier, Haar, Hadamard, Walsh, etc. |
| | Physical measurements | Width, height, length of different limbs and between line segments | Recording the first and last rows/columns of the character matrix or measuring length of lines |
| Structural analysis | Edges and lines | Straight and inclined lines, line lengths, line tips | Edge/line detection, window moving across character matrix |
| | Outline of character | Line directions, line intersections | Contour tracing by rules |
| | Center line of character | Line discontinuities, curves, loops, perimeters, areas, centers of gravity | Thinning by gradually peeling off the outermost layers |

## MULTIFONT AND HANDWRITING RECOGNITION   V

There exists hundreds of type fonts and thousands of printfonts in the world, each having its own distinctive style and peculiarities, such as serifs, shapes, curvatures, sizes, pitch, line thickness, etc. As a result of the great variety of fonts, machine recognition of multifont and handwritten characters is far from being solved. The main problems are as follows.

(1)  Variations in character shapes, for example,

```
Prestige Elite       Courier          Letter Gothic
g  Q  1                g  Q  1          g  Q  1
```

Also, in some type fonts there are no distinctions between "oh" and "zero" or "one" and "lower case el".

(2)  Variations in sizes, for example, 10 pitch characters are usually bigger in both width and height than those in 12 pitch and 15 pitch.

(3)  Variations in pitch, for example, 10, 12, 15 pitch, which corresponds to 10, 12, and 15 characters/in, and proportional spacing. These variations affect the location and segmentation of characters in a typewritten or printed text.

(4)  Ornaments and serifs of the characters, for example, the great differences between sans serif fonts like Gothic and Orator and serif fonts such as Courier and Elite.

(5)  Variations in line thickness, for example bold fonts are thicker than regular fonts, while sans serif characters have more uniform widths than those with serifs.

Apart from the above basic differences, there exist

(a)  italics whose characters are all tilted to the right,
(b)  script, which has a cursive type style that simulates handwriting, and
(c)  some characters which may touch each other, for example, the wide characters m and w may touch their neighbors.

In order to recognize characters printed in books and magazines, the optical reader must be able to handle touching characters (e.g., i is usually housed under f in words like five and first), proportional spacing, variable line spacing, change of type styles in the same text, and text and figures, in addition to those problems for multifonts listed above. Several manufacturers have already announced machines which can read a limited number of fonts or print fonts with limited vocabulary and accuracy, for example, AM ECRM, Burroughs Corp., Dest Corp., ELSAG Inc., Fujitsu Ltd., IBM Corp., Kurzweil Computer Products, Inc., Nippon Electrics Co., Recognition Equipment Inc., and Scan Data Ltd.

Variations in handwritten characters are even greater than those in type fonts because they can be written in an immensely different number of ways. Since each person has his/her own ways and styles of writing and character samples written by the same hand are never identical in shape or in size, there are an infinite number of possible character shapes. Actually, the problem of handprint recognition is of great interest and challenge to researchers because even human beings, who possess the best trained optical readers (their eyes) and interpreters (their minds), would make about 4% mistakes when reading handprinting in the absence of context [1]. The characters 6/G, D/O, I/1, S/5, 2/Z, and U/V are the most confusing pairs, especially when they are written sloppily, because they have very similar topological structures.

The great variability in handprinting may be attributed to writing habits, style and care in writing, education, region of origin, mood, health, and other conditions of the writer. Apart from these human factors, writing instruments writing surfaces and scanning equipment and methods, as well as machine recognition algorithms, also play an important role in explaining the recognition rate [1].

Over the years, the state of the art in this field has advanced from the use of primitive schemes to recognize stylized numerals to the application of sophisticated techniques to recognize a large vocabulary of symbols printed by man, including FORTRAN, Katakana, Hiragana, and Chinese characters.

Similar to the recognition of type fonts, in order to establish a common frame of reference for the application of machine recognition of handprinted characters, standards have also been developed. For obvious reasons, more emphasis has been placed on accuracy of machine reading rather than on speed and flexibility of writing. They include standards developed by the OCR Committees of the American National Standards Institute, the Japanese Standards Society, and the Canadian Standards Association [4]. Standard handprint shapes recently developed by the author for the Canadian Standards Association are shown in Fig. 2 [7]. Character shapes and sizes, height and width, allowed deviations in stroke widths and slopes, character separation and clear area for OCR, as well as guidelines and aids for forming characters, preprinted guidelines, and spacing are contained in these standards.

Apart from the above standards, OCR manufacturers have also invented their own handprint shapes to achieve acceptable recognition rate and speed. Hence many OCR machines currently available in the market can read constrained numeric handprint and some can read stylized or standardized alphanumeric handprints [1, 6]. Needless to say, most of these manufacturers have put forth immense efforts in research and development on their products.

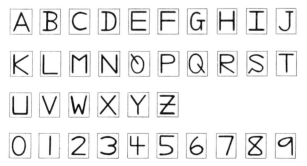

**Fig. 2.** Alphanumeric character shapes of the Canadian handprint standard [7]. (Copies may be obtained from the Canadian Standards Association, 178 Rexdale Boulevard, Rexdale, Ontario M9W 1R3, Canada.)

In parallel with the research efforts of the OCR manufacturers, active research has also been conducted at academic and government institutions focusing on handwriting recognition. Indeed, significant advancements have been reported in the field of handprint recognition. Encouraging results were achieved in the recognition of constrained handprinted FORTRAN characters, and an accuracy of 99 % has been reported [1, 6]. Recognition of less-constrained handwritten characters are still under investigation.

## VI   RECOGNITION OF SPECIAL SYMBOLS AND IDEOGRAPHS

Human beings are trained to recognize all sorts of characters, symbols, and patterns. As the OCR field progresses, considerable research has been done on algorithms, software, and hardware to recognize not only the numerals and Roman letters, but also special symbols such as those used in commands and computer languages like FORTRAN (see, e.g., Suen *et al.* [1], including Chinese ideographs [8–10], Korean [5], Indian, and Arabic alphabets, mathematical and electronic circuit symbols, and even shorthand [8, 11–20]. Owing to the limitation of space provided for this chapter, the following section will deal with the subject of recognition of purely Chinese ideographs, which has become the most challenging subject to researchers because of the complexity of shapes and the large vocabulary of the Chinese language.

Following the advances in automatic recognition of handprinted alphanumeric and Katakana characters [1], many scientists have now embarked on the more challenging subject of recognition of a large set of characters including machine and handwritten Kanji (in this section, Kanji and Chinese characters will be used interchangeably). Recognition of Kanji differs significantly from that of alphanumerics in the following aspects.

(1)  *Large number of characters.* In Japanese, more than 2000 Kanji are used in daily newspapers and business letters. In Chinese, 2500–3000 characters are commonly used in newspapers and up to about 6000 in books and literature. A number of rare characters are used in people's names. Small dictionaries usually hold 8000–9000 characters, while large ones contain 10–15 thousand Chinese characters. Hence one approach in Chinese character recognition is preclassification, which first reduces the number of categories of candidate characters for more precise classification subsequently.

(2)  *Composition.* Ideographs have complex structures. A lot of them contain many line segments (strokes), for example,

On the other hand, the line segments are mainly oriented horizontally, vertically, or diagonally, and they bear certain relations to each other. Thus Chinese characters contain a great deal of structural information which is conducive to recognition. However, most characters have two or more components (sometimes called radicals) which, depending on the type font, may or may not touch each other. This means that many Chinese characters contain isolated parts and yet some line segments of various parts may touch one another, complicating any structural analysis of such characters, whether by contour tracing or skeletonization. Furthermore, some look very similar to others and can only be distinguished by minute features, for example,

己 已 巳, 大 太 犬, 日 曰,
土 士, 未 末, 戊 戌 戍

(3)  *Fonts and shapes.* Like Roman alphabets, Chinese characters can be printed in many different fonts by varying the stroke widths, their orientations and sizes, and positions and shapes. The Soong ( 宋 ) font is characterized by a great difference in stroke width horizontally (thin) and vertically (thick). The black ( 黑 ) font has strokes more or less of uniform width. The Kai ( 楷 ) font is close to handwriting by brush. Though certain characteristics of some fonts are known and the artistic (aesthetic) component has already been built into the character, there do not appear to be standards which specify the widths, sizes, and shapes of the strokes or their locations, orientation, and relations to each other in the character. This means that appearance, style, and legibility of Chinese characters have somewhat been taken into consideration, but little has been done to standardize the fonts for reading by human beings and computers. At least to the best of this author's knowledge, there is no such standard yet for this purpose.

(4)  *Quality.* It is well known that handwritten characters are poorer in quality than machine-printed ones, although they vary with the writer, style, the printing process, types of ink, paper, etc. Characters of poor quality need more sophisticated preprocessing techniques to clean them and more powerful recognition algorithms to identify them.

As described above, recognition of Chinese characters by computer is a formidable task. Educated Chinese and Japanese people may find it easy to recognize a basic vocabulary of Kanji characters. But to most Westerners, Kanji remains difficult to learn and recognize. However, just like research in any other discipline, human intelligence has made a lot of progress in this area in recent years. Some features used in recognition will be described.

## VII  FEATURES AND RECOGNITION

Since Chinese characters are rich in texture, many different types of features can be extracted and used in the classification process. Table IV summarizes the features used in the recognition of printed Chinese characters during the past 10 years [9].

In the recognition of handwritten ideographs, the following features, as presented in Table V, have been described in survey papers written by Mori [10] and Mori et al. [21], covering the recognition schemes and the results (mainly for a repertoire of less than 1000 categories) obtained by several leading industries and government research laboratories in Japan.

With regard to the matching techniques, correlation, shift similarity, complex similarity, and relaxation matching have been used. More details can be found in Refs. 10 and 21.

Apart from those features and the classification schemes listed in Table I, other features have also been explored, for example, the following.

(1)  Phase features extracted from the fast Fourier transform (FFT) of an $8 \times 8$ mesh with $8 \times 8$ gray levels of digitized Chinese characters [22, 23].

(2)  A new clustering algorithm (called ISOETRP) with new objectives in minimizing overlap between pattern class groups, minimizing entropy, and keeping balance between these groups [23].

In both cases, a tree classifier was designed. A recognition rate of 99.8% was obtained when tested with noisy data of 3200 categories [23]. Further research includes the design of tree classifiers, the determination and extraction of more distinctive features and efficient means of combining them, and fuzzy logic search for the closest candidate character.

### TABLE IV

#### Features Described in Papers Published in the Past Decade

| | |
|---|---|
| Projection profiles | Fourier transform |
| Ratios of overall stroke lengths in horizontal and vertical directions to their respective spread values | Hadamard transform, rapid transform, Walsh transform |
| Belt patterns and density of points in four strips surrounding the character | Edges and line segments, center line of strokes of characters, contours of four corner parts of character |
| Distribution of points in an $8 \times 8$ mesh of the character | |

**TABLE V**

**Features Used in the Recognition of Handprinted Ideographs**

| | |
|---|---|
| Orthogonal expansion | K-L expansion |
| Stroke distribution | Line direction, crossing counts, stroke length, stroke length matrix, direction continuity density |
| Stroke analysis | Stroke extraction, polygonal approximation |
| Background feature distribution | Modified Glucksman's stroke density, Glucksman's line stroke density |
| Background analysis | Edge propagation, line direction propagation |
| Combination | Crossing count and projection, stroke density and line direction propagation |

## ABNORMALITIES AND STYLISTIC PECULIARITIES  VIII
## OF CHINESE CHARACTERS

To illustrate the problems involved in computer recognition of printed Chinese characters, we present Figs. 3–12, which contain characters cut out from various magazines and newspapers.

(1)  Some examples of characters whose strokes touch one another are shown in Fig. 3. As pointed out before, this will complicate tremendously any structural methods which recognize characters by identifying the various components (structures) of the characters. Apart from that, it also affects, though to a lesser extent, other recognition methods based on a global analysis.

(2)  Some examples of shapes which differ from the traditional way of writing are shown in Fig. 4.

Note that some of the discrepancies are attributed to artistic and/or aesthetic appearances. We can further classify the shape variations into the following categories.

(a)  abnormal stroke representation (Fig. 5),

(b)  serifs and ornaments (Fig. 6),

(c)  strokes placed in abnormal positions (Fig. 7),

(d)  shapes not used in handwriting (Fig. 8),

(e)  omission of parts of strokes (Fig. 9),

(f)  disproportionate sizes of the different parts of the characters (Fig. 10),

(g)  parts touching where they should not (Fig. 11),

(h)  characters that have become smeared patterns because they contain too many strokes or they are poorly printed (Fig. 12).

暑 會 關 說
假 傾 基 性
萬 停 認 洲

**Fig. 3.** Characters with strokes touching one another.

解 即 糈 社 瑜

**Fig. 4.** Character shapes that differ from traditional ways of writing.

主 刊 領 逾 禮

**Fig. 5.** Abnormal stroke representations.

全 肉 叉 之 晨

**Fig. 6.** Unnecessary serifs and ornaments.

向 訊 寶 北

**Fig. 7.** Strokes placed in abnormal positions.

角 令 眞 囘 悅

**Fig. 8.** Shapes not used in handwriting.

您 觸 東 未

**Fig. 9.** Omissions of parts of strokes.

邱 出 舉 豐

**Fig. 10.** Disproportionate sizes of the different parts of the characters.

經 謙 柏堅斯

**Fig. 11.** Parts touching where they should not.

優鐵　槍歐　廠獨

**Fig. 12.** Smeared patterns due to too many strokes or poor printing.

(3) *Shape variations due to font styles.* Stylistic variations are great because Chinese ideographs have been written with a brush for several thousand years. The pressure controlled by the hand can produce different stylistic corners, ➔, narrowing of stroke tips ノ, ノ, 丿, 乀, artistic dots ✔, ➘, ➘, narrow horizontal and thick vertical strokes ┼, termination bulges ➖, and various flurries and ornaments. In addition, some fonts emphasize symmetry at the sacrifice of correct positioning of the strokes, for example, 火 員 美. Others make the width of all strokes uniform throughout the entire character, for example 同. In both cases the character shapes undergo some kind of distortion which is detrimental to the recognition rate.

## IX  CONCLUDING REMARKS

The idea of making a machine read printed material the way human beings do goes as far back as the 1930s. Judging from the ease with which humans read, it appeared at first that the problem of machine recognition of characters could be solved quite easily. However, as research went on, the difficulties of correctly identifying characters, no matter whether they are printed or handwritten, become apparent due to the infinite variety of character shapes and styles. In spite of this, substantial research and development efforts have been devoted to OCR, resulting in a rich accumulation of technical reports, papers, patents, books, industrial brochures, and manuals. It appears that the most significant OCR efforts in the 1970s lie in the work of standardization and the realization by scientists of the interplay between machine characteristics and the quality of data. A large number of OCR standards have been developed by the standards committees established in various countries throughout the world and the International Standards Organization (ISO) [4], composed of experts and representatives from manufacturers, users, scientific, technical and professional communities, and government agencies. As a result, OCR has become a reliable, and actually indispensable, means of entering large volumes of data into computers. Standardized type fonts and handprints play a vital role in its success.

As the OCR field advances, more and more research efforts have been directed toward the recognition of less-constrained and totally unconstrained characters handwritten by the public (e.g., characters and symbols written on checks, maps, engineering drawings, and charts; application, sale, account forms; and other types of handwritten notes and records), characters and symbols in languages other than the common Roman letters, and complex ideographic characters and symbols. Supporting this trend are active research and development work in search of better and more cost-effective scanning and preprocessing techniques, feature extraction, and classification methods. From research and practical experience gained in the past, it appears to the author that the most promising approach is to divide the recognition process into various stages, including the following:

(1) a *prerecognition stage* which uses more general features for example, those based on the distribution of points, to reduce the number of possible choices;

(2) an *intermediate recognition stage* which makes use of geometrical and topological features to limit the identity of the character–symbol to only a few choices;

(3) a *discriminant stage* which focuses on the detection of detailed features to discriminate confusing groups and/or pairs of characters;

(4)   a *final stage* which makes use of linguistic, contextual, or statistical information, leading to the correct identity of characters, symbols, words, or even groups of words, or phrases, clauses, and sentences.

While the software aspects of character recognition are making giant strides toward more accurate and reliable recognition and high speed, impressive progress in OCR hardware is also marching forward. Modern OCR systems have already entered the microcomputer and microelectronic age. With that, many complex and sophisticated algorithms can be implemented with VLSI circuit technology and supermicrocomputers, enabling the implementation of powerful and effective feature extraction schemes, enhancing both accuracy and speed and reducing both size and cost. Future OCR systems may take the form of portable terminals which can be connected to either a computer or built-in multiprocessor.

With rapid progress in nanosecond and the approach of picosecond microelectronics, there is a good chance that OCR may one day outperform the blinking mechanism human beings are endowed with at birth.

## ACKNOWLEDGEMENT

This work was supported by the Natural Sciences and Engineering Research Council of Canada and the Department of Education of Quebec.

## REFERENCES

1.  C. Y. Suen, M. Berthod, and S. Mori, Automatic recognition of handprinted characters—the state of the art, *Proc. IEEE* **68**, 469–487 (April 1980).
2.  M. Berthod, On-line analysis of cursive writing, *in* "Computer Analysis and Perception: Vol. 1, Visual Signals" (C. Y. Suen and R. De Mori, eds.), pp. 55–81. CRC Press, Boca Raton, Florida, 1982.
3.  E. F. Yhap and E. C. Greanias, An on-line Chinese character recognition system, *IBM J. Res. Develop.* **25**, 187–195 (May 1981).
4.  C. Y. Suen and S. Mori, Standardization and automatic recognition of handprinted characters, *in* "Computer Analysis and Perception: Vol. 1, Visual Signals" (C. Y. Suen and R. De Mori, eds.), pp. 41–53. CRC Press, Boca Raton, Florida. 1982.
5.  C. Y. Suen (ed.), *Proceedings International Conference of the Chinese Language Computer Society, Washington D. C., Sept. 1982.*
6.  C. Y. Suen, Distinctive features in automatic recognition of handprinted characters, *Signal Processing* **4**, 193–207 (April 1982).
7.  Alphanumeric character set for handprinting, Canadian Standards Association, Standard Z 243.34—M1983, July 1983.
8.  *Proceedings of the International Conferences on Pattern Recognition*, July–August 1984, Oct. 1982, and December 1980.
9.  C. Y. Suen, Computer recognition of Kanji characters, *Proc. Intl. Conf. on Text Processing with a Large Character Set, Oct. 1983*, pp. 429–435 (1983).
10. S. Mori, Research on machine recognition of handprinted characters, *Computer Processing of Chinese and Oriental Languages* **1**, 24–39 (July 1983).
11. P. Ahmed and C. Y. Suen, Segmentation of unconstrained handwritten numeric postal zip codes, *Proc. Intl. Conf. Pattern Recognition, Oct. 1982*, pp. 545–547 (1982).
12. R. Bozinovic and S. N. Srihari, Knowledge based cursive script interpretation, *Proc. Intl. Conf. Pattern Recognition, July–August 1984*, pp. 774–776 (1984).

13. F. Kimura, T. Harada, S. Tsuruoka, and Y. Miyake, Modified quadratic discriminant functions and the application to Chinese character recognition, *Proc. Intl. Conf. Pattern Recognition, July–August 1984*, pp. 377–380 (1984).

14. C. G. Leedham and A. C. Downton, On-line recognition of shortforms in Pitman's handwritten shorthand, *Proc. Intl. Conf. Pattern Recognition, July–August 1984*, pp. 1058–1060 (1984).

15. K. Maeda, Y. Korosawa, H. Asada, K. Sakai, and S. Watanabe, Handprinted Kanji recognition by pattern matching method, *Proc. 6th Intl. Jt. Conf. Pattern Recognition, Oct. 1982*, pp. 782–792 (1982).

16. S. Mori and T. Sakakura, Line filtering and its application to stroke segmentation of handprinted Chinese characters, *Proc. Intl. Conf. Pattern Recognition, July–August 1984*, pp. 336–369 (1984).

17. T. Sagawa, E. Tanaka, M. Suzuki, and M. Fujita, An unsupervised learning of hand-printed characters with linguistic information, *Proc. Intl. Conf. Pattern Recognition, July–August 1984*, pp. 766–769 (1984).

18. J. Tsukumo and K. Asai, Non-linear matching method for handprinted character recognition, *Proc. Intl. Conf. Pattern Recognition, July–August 1984*, pp. 770–773 (1984).

19. H. Yamada, Contour DP matching method and its application to handprinted Chinese character recognition, *Proc. Intl. Conf. Pattern Recognition, July–August 1984*, pp. 389–392 (1984).

20. K. Yamamoto, H. Yamada, T. Saito, and R. I. Oka, Recognition of handprinted Chinese characters and Japanese cursive syllabary, *Proc. Intl. Conf. Pattern Recognition, July–August 1984*, pp. 385–388 (1984).

21. S. Mori, K. Yamamoto, and M. Yasuda, Research on machine recognition of handprinted characters, *IEEE Trans. Pattern Analysis and Machine Intelligence* **PAMI-6**, 386–405 (July 1984).

22. Q. R. Wang and C. Y. Suen, Analysis and design of a decision tree based on entropy reduction and its application to large character set recognition, *IEEE Trans. Pattern Analysis and Machine Intelligence* **PAMI-6**, 406–417 (July 1984).

23. Q. R. Wang and C. Y. Suen, Classification of Chinese characters by phase features and fuzzy logic search, *Proc. Intl. Conf. Chinese Information Processing, Oct. 1983*, pp. 327–331 (1983).

Chapter **24**

# Algorithms and Techniques for Automated Visual Inspection*

ROLAND T. CHIN

Electrical and Computer Sciences and Computer Engineering
University of Wisconsin
Madison, Wisconsin

* This work was supported by the National Science Foundation under Grant ECS-8352356 and General Motors Foundation, Inc., Detroit, Michigan.

# I  INTRODUCTION

## A  Motivations of Automated Visual Inspection

In most mass-production manufacturing facilities, an attempt is often made to achieve 100% quality assurance of all parts, subassemblies, and finished products. One of the most difficult tasks in this process is that of inspecting for visual appearance—an inspection that seeks to identify both functional and cosmetic defects. Undoubtedly, the automation of visual inspection will increase productivity and improve product quality.

Advances in computer technology, image processing, pattern recognition, and artificial intelligence have resulted in better and cheaper industrial image analysis equipment. Automated visual inspection for manufacturing is now of broad and rapidly expanding commercial use. A recent study has estimated that 1400 vision systems are in operation in manufacturing industries in the United States, most of them performing visual inspection tasks. The electronics industry is the most active one in applying automated visual inspection to such products as printed circuit boards, integrated circuit chips, and photomasks. Other industries—automobile, lumber, textiles, and packaging—use similar procedures and systems. The latest addition to this growing technology is that of off-the-shelf, programmable visual inspection systems for broad-based industrial applications. These versatile vision systems can be programmed to perform a number of different inspections. Their inspection utilization rate, and the ease with which their inspection roles can be extended, make them economical for many industries.

## B  Definitions

The automated visual inspection process involves observing the same type of object repeatedly to detect anomalies. Figure 1 shows a greatly simplified diagram of an automated visual inspection station. The transport moves the objects to be inspected into the scanning station, where the sensor collects visual data describing the object and sends them to the processor to be analyzed. The analysis includes the processing of the imagery to enhance relevant features and the detection of defects. After the analysis, decisions are made and the processor directs the sorter to reject the defective item.

## C  Chapter Summary

In this chapter, a variety of algorithms and techniques for the automated inspection of industrial products will be examined. Discussions will be concentrated on image analysis techniques and detection strategies. Topics such as sensing technology, hardware implementation, and other implemen-

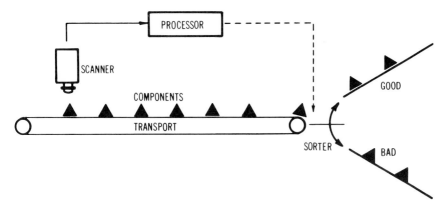

Fig. 1. Simple pictorial diagram of an automated visual inspection system.

tation issues will not be discussed here. The inspection methodologies examined here are selected on the basis of their success. Some of the representative systems are R & D systems from industrial laboratories, research institutions, and universities related to the development of concepts and algorithms for inspection. The others are production-line, one-of-a-kind installations used in manufacturing. In this chapter a survey will be presented of state-of-the-art visual inspection technology, and some fresh insights and tutorial information will be provided for those interested in this field.

Various algorithms and applications will be examined in detail. The chapter is organized according to the methods of inspection, including image subtraction, feature matching, dimensional verification, differential scanning, spatial filtering, color separation, and syntactic approach. Three central issues common to each technique are examined: feature extraction, modeling, and matching. The inspection of printed circuit patterns is used as a common example in the discussion. Finally, limitations of current inspection systems are summarized.

## MODEL-BASED VISUAL INSPECTION    II

All visual inspection algorithms, although seemingly diverse, utilize *a priori* knowledge. This *a priori* knowledge is organized into *models* which provide strategies and standards for the inspection process. These systems are referred to as *model-based* or *model-driven* systems. They perform inspection by matching the part under inspection with a set of predefined models. A typical inspection procedure of such systems is first to precompile a description (or measurement) of each of a known set of defects, and then to use these defect models to detect in an image each instance of a defect and to specify its location. For example, the defect model of a printed circuit board may consist of the description of nicks, cracks, and short circuits. Another typical

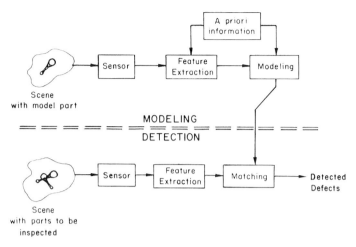

**Fig. 2.** Components of a model-based inspection system.

procedure is to model the part by its normal, expected features and then to use the part model to verify in an image that the part under inspection has all the expected features. For example, the part model of a printed circuit board may consist of the description of conducting patterns and pads and their dimensions, with various engineering tolerance standards.

In general, an automated visual inspection system is broken down into a training (modeling) phase and a detection phase, as illustrated in Fig. 2. The three major components of the system are *feature extraction, modeling,* and *detection.* These components will be examined in detail and their properties will be illustrated by case studies.

## A    Features

In many inspection applications, the first problem is to determine which feature measurements should be taken from the input patterns. Features are less sensitive with respect to the encountered variations of the original noisy gray-scale images and provide data reduction while preserving the information required for the inspection. Usually, the decision regarding what to measure is rather subjective and depends on practical situations.

Features such as corner, line, curve, hole, etc. define geometric characteristics of a part under inspection; see Fig. 3 for some examples. Other features common to inspection problems are dimensions, locations, and orientations. These features are used to generate the part model in the modeling phase and are again extracted from parts under inspection in the detection phase for the detection of anomalies.

Most existing industrial vision systems and inspection algorithms require

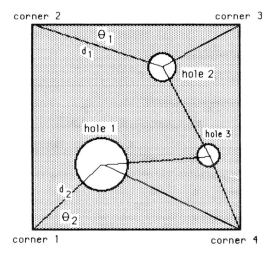

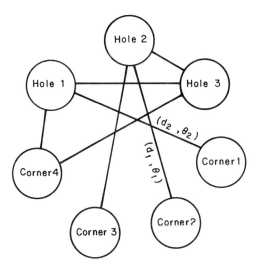

**Fig. 3.** Model–graph representation of a machine part. The nodes contain geometric descriptions of the features and the arcs contain relations between the features.

their applications to industrial parts to be against a high-contrast background with controlled lighting to eliminate shadows, highlights, and noisy backgrounds. The process of feature extraction usually begins with the generation of a binary image from the original gray-scale image using simple thresholding, or simply a sensor that produces binary images. The use of a binary representation reduces the amount of data that must be handled. This simplification might meet the cost requirement of most industrial inspection applications, but it places certain limitations on the capabilities of the system. For example, physical surface properties such as surface reflectance, surface orientation, and textures are lost in reducing the gray-scale image to a binary image. Most image feature extraction algorithms used in these binary visual inspection systems are simple edge-detection and line-tracing algorithms, and the extracted features are functions of silhouettes. For inspecting part surfaces and complex industrial parts, there exist only a few gray-scale vision systems and algorithms that are capable of extracting useful features from complex industrial scenes with considerable noise caused by dirt and unfavorable lighting conditions. The most important drawback of gray-scale image processing is the slow processing rate in extracting features.

## B   Models

A model is an organized representation of features extracted from a part from which adequate descriptions and information for the inspection are provided. Most part models for inspection are based on geometric properties of a part's silhouette. In a simple example, one of inspecting drilled holes on a machine part for their correct placements (see Fig. 3), the model may constitute three circular blobs with known radii and four corner patterns representing the corners of the part. In addition, the model may contain interrelations between the seven features. This example can be generalized as a model consisting of a graph structure in which nodes represent geometric features (i.e., circles and corners) and arcs the spatial relations between these features (i.e., distances and angles between features). *A priori* information concerning the industrial part (e.g., dimensional tolerances) can also be part of the model.

From another point of view, the modeling can be interpreted as a syntactic pattern recognition approach in which geometric features are transformed into primitives and their spatial relations are transformed into a string grammar.

Most modeling processes involve the "training by showing" procedure, in which the user uses a model part to teach the system the features to be examined, their relations, and their acceptable tolerances. Interaction between the system and the user is usually carried out to construct and fine tune the model. The resulting model, in the form of a graph or table, is stored in easily accessible devices. Figure 4 shows a simple example of an interactive training-by-showing process. In this step, the operator is presented with an image of a part to be modeled and uses an interactive device to select windows and remove unwanted regions. After the interaction, the system will define the model and encode it in compact data structures. In some applications, the model can be automatically constructed without any user intervention by accessing and processing information obtained from available computer-aided design (CAD) databases. In these situations, the CAD database must be an integrated part of the vision system.

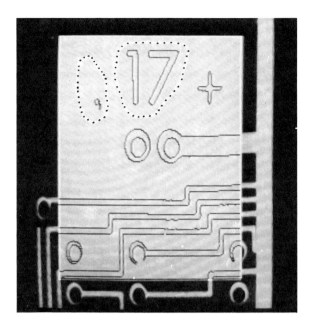

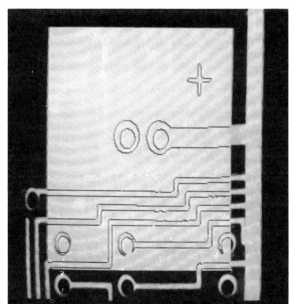

**Fig. 4.** Example of the interactive training-by-showing procedure.

Most industrial inspection applications involve the inspection of planar (flat) patterns (e.g., circuit boards, labels on packages). These patterns can be well represented by models containing two-dimensional features. The inspection of three-dimension parts requires the construction of three-dimensional models. In one example, an approach to model three-dimensional industrial parts was developed by computing the two-dimensional projections of all the possible stable positions of the part with respect to the sensor's viewpoint [1]. Figure 5 shows a set of stable orientations of a part and their corresponding two-dimensional models. In this case the part model is a set of two-dimensional models. Another approach to inspecting simple three-dimensional objects is the use of multiple sensors. Figure 6 shows such a setup with a sensor inspecting the top view and a second sensor looking at the side. In this multisensor configuration, the model again consists of a number of two-dimensional models, each describing a different view of the part. The inspection of complex three-dimensional industrial objects has not yet been fully developed for industrial applications. Therefore, discussions in this chapter will mainly be focused on the inspectison of two-dimensional parts.

## C   Detection

After the modeling procedure, the system contains a model that describes all required aspects of the part that is to be inspected. The process of defect detection then consists of matching the extracted features from the part under inspection with those of the model. Some of the detection methods rely on total image matching, or cross-correlation type of measures applied to image intensities, or coefficients of some mathematical transforms (e.g., the Fourier transform). In these cases, the model is simply an image of an ideal part, or a transformed version of it, and the required detection is a simple comparison. These methods are very computationally intensive if computed digitally. Moreover, if the image of the part under inspection is noisy and it is located at random positions, the detection will be very ineffective. Detection algorithms of this type have serious limitations in industrial inspection applications.

Detection techniques using representative features and their relationships (i.e., a highly structured model) provide a way to inspect a part and locate defects on the basis of measurements taken from key features. This type of algorithm is more robust and effective. The training of the model in this case is of ultimate importance. Using the example in Fig. 3, the detection process involves locating the features from the image under inspection that match with the nodes in the model graph, checking their specifications, and measuring their relations as specified as arcs in the model graph. If all the measurements agree with the model, the part passes the inspection.

The general problem of detection may be formulated by two approaches: (a) finding defects in the given part that match the model's definition of

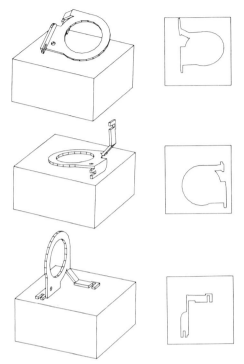

**Fig. 5.** Three stable orientations of a three-dimensional part and their corresponding two-dimensional models viewed from directly overhead. (From Lieberman [1].)

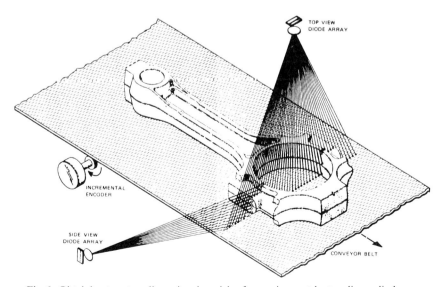

**Fig. 6.** Obtaining two two-dimensional models of a moving part by two linear diode arrays. (From Rosen and Nitzan [2].)

defects; (b) verifying all extracted features in the given part to be normal, expected features as those defined by the part model. The former approach is a true defect-detection procedure, while the latter one is a verification process. The choice of detection process is highly dependent on the type of model used and the nature of the part to be inspected. The verification approach is more commonly used in industrial inspection because the training of the part model can be easily done by "showing" the system a normal prototype part, whereas the detection approach requires the generation of a set of defective patterns. The number of possible defective patterns might be large, making the detection process computationally intensive. Moreover, it is almost impossible to come up with all possible defective patterns to construct a defect model for reliable detection. Of course, both approaches can be combined into an inspection strategy for more accurate and efficient inspection.

The requirement of precise registration between the model and the part under test during the detection phase is a common problem to many inspection systems. The registration problem is usually handled either by moving the part physically by a mechanical stage or by positioning it electronically by shifting and rotating. Again, this requirement is highly dependent on the model and the nature of the part. Detection techniques using well-designed model and well-chosen features are usually invariant to translation and rotation and are not very sensitive to noise and image distortion. This type of system can handle parts that are randomly placed under the sensor without the trouble of registering their precise placements.

## III  VISUAL INSPECTION SYSTEMS AND ALGORITHMS

In the following sections, various inspection algorithms and systems will be examined. The discussion will be focused on the three components (features, models, and detection) described above. The inspection of printed circuit boards (PCBs) will be used in most cases as the example to illustrate the similarities, strengths, and weaknesses of the various approaches.

## A  Image Subtraction

Image subtraction is the most simple approach to the visual inspection problem. In this approach, the part to be inspected is scanned and its image is compared against the image of an ideal part. The "feature" is an intensity function of the part at all locations $(x, y)$; the "model" is simply another intensity function of a perfect part; and the "detection" is a subtraction

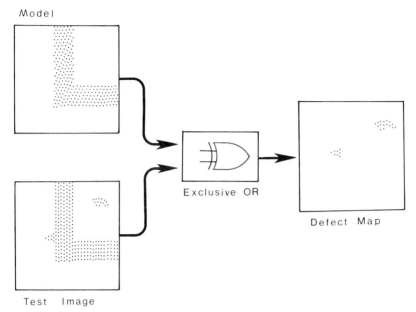

Fig. 7. Image subtraction process.

operation performed at all $(x, y)$. The subtracted image, showing defects, can subsequently be displayed and analyzed. Figure 7 shows the subtraction process as a logical operation when the feature and the model are both binary functions.

This approach has a variation of implementation techniques depending on the application. In one experiment, two cameras were used to inspect PCBs at video rate. The model that is used as the ideal standard circuit is stored in analog form as a coded gray-scale image and not in digital form. The subtraction is done by scanning the PCB to be inspected by one camera and the coded model by the other in synchronism so inspection is performed at high speed. In another setup, the subtraction is implemented using a video processor, where the model is stored on a video disk. Yet another implementation performs PCB inspection at the speed of light. In this case, the model is a mask with a light-blocking pattern corresponding to the perfect PCB patterns. The detection is performed by illuminating the PCB through the mask with the light of a color complementary to the color of the PCB. With the mask in registry with the PCB, defects are readily apparent as bright spots on a dark surface.

The image subtraction approach has several limitations: large data storage needs for the model, the need for precise alignment, sensitivity to illumination and sensor conditions, and the lack of flexibility. The data storage requirement and inspection speed can usually be dealt with by smart implementation approaches. The sensitivity problem is the major drawback of image subtraction, and it is due to the fact that many, and perhaps most, acceptable PCBs do not match point-by-point because of shrinking or swelling of the board. The same condition may occur in many other products. In addition, variations in lighting during inspection will generate undesirable effects on the subtraction algorithm similar to those generated because of product variations. In these situations, the use of correction schemes to compensate for such problems is necessary and may result in systems which become impractical. Another drawback of the subtraction method is its inspection versatility. Versatility refers to the number of different inspections the system can perform. In most image subtraction implementations special-purpose apparatuses are required to speed up the processing of the large amount of data; such systems are thus very difficult to adapt to handle other products.

All these limitations together represent a serious drawback for the practical application of image subtraction to industrial visual inspection.

## B   Image Subtraction via Pseudomodeling

Ejiri *et al.* [3], from Hitachi Ltd., Japan, have developed a somewhat unique method for inspecting PCBs. The inspection involves the *expansion–contraction* process, which does not require any predefined model of perfect patterns. Starting with a binary image of the PCB to be inspected, areas identified as conductor are first enlarged uniformly in all directions. The enlargement eliminates all small-scale features on the conductor. Here, small-scale features smaller than a certain size are considered to be defects and are eliminated from the input pattern. This enlarged pattern is then reduced by the same factor to eliminate small features within the substrate. The pattern derived from this expansion–contraction process is used as the model in an image subtraction process in which the input PCB pattern is compared with the derived model. Since this model is generated from the image pattern under inspection without using any perfect patterns, the term *pseudomodel* is used. Figure 8 illustrates this pseudomodeling and the subsequent image subtraction process.

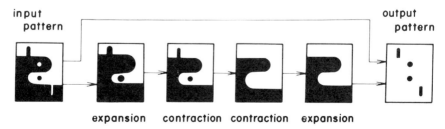

input                                                              output
pattern                                                            pattern

expansion    contraction    contraction    expansion

**Fig. 8.** Principle of the expansion–contraction method for detecting small defects. (From Ejiri *et al.* [3].)

The unique characteristic of this method is its generation of the pseudo-model. The feature is a set of small-scale objects (e.g., nicks and dots) found on the PCB. This feature is used only for the modeling process and not during the detection; the detection is an image subtraction process operating on two binary arrays. This method eliminates the problem of positioning between the input and the model as well as the need to train the model manually before the inspection process begins. However, it detects only small defects.

## Differential Scanning  C

In the manufacture of integrated circuits (ICs), the inspection of IC photomasks is very important. The function of the photomask is to transfer the desired pattern to the wafer for the semiconductor lithographic process. Examples of defects include registration errors, dimension variations, and random defects. The most common photomask inspection technique used today is *differential scanning*. This method can in principle provide reliable inspection with high efficiency.

Differential scanning is a slight variation of the image subtraction method. This method scans and compares adjacent chip patterns of the photomask. This conceptually simple approach uses the fact that IC photomasks contain a periodic array of nominally identical chip images, so that defects on a chip image can be detected by comparing it with a neighboring image. A simplified system is shown in Fig. 9. In this method, the feature is an intensity pattern of a chip image and the detection is a simple subtraction. The model is not a predefined version of a perfect pattern, but rather an intensity pattern of one of the neighboring chips.

One example of an automated photomask inspection system is the AMIS system, which routinely measures defect counts on various types of IC photomasks at Bell Laboratories. A differential laser scanning system scans two adjacent and identical patterns, and a processor compares their outputs; any deviations found are defects. The system is composed of a flying spot laser with two optically deflected laser beams, photodetectors to measure the light transmitted through the photomask, a mechanical table driven by a stepping motor to align and step through the repeated IC patterns, a signal processor to measure the analog difference between outputs of the two photodetectors and to detect and classify defects, and TV monitors to display the defect map. The scanning and defect detection reportedly take about 3 min for a 50 × 50 mm mask area with a detection limit down to 2 $\mu$m [4]. A recent addition to the photomask inspection field is a number of commerically available photomask inspection systems using differential scanning. The data acquisition of these systems is similar to that of the system described above. The optical information which comes from two adjacent dice is first

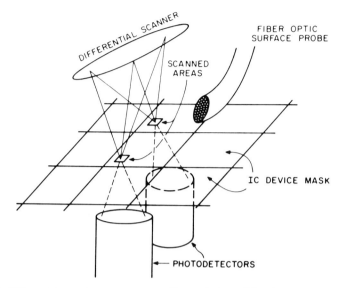

**Fig. 9.** Differential scanning system scans adjacent devices of the photomask and compares their outputs.

converted to digital data and then stored and processed for alignment corrections. Random defects are detected by simple subtraction.

Differential scanning has been shown to be quite successful in photomask inspection. However, it is applicable only to applications that have step-and-repeat patterns. Moreover, this method of inspection does not detect repeated defects, and one must rely on additional inspection to ensure that there are no repeated defects. Optical and mechanical alignment is also a difficult requirement to meet when using this method.

## D  Color Separation

Color separation is a different scanning method that uses color information to detect defects on photomasks. Three identical photomasks are illuminated side-by-side, and the transmitted light is filtered to give complementary colors. The three color images are then superimposed precisely. Assuming that defects can rarely occur at the same place in the three photomasks, the locations of defects in each of the three photomask patterns can be determined by identifying the superimposed color.

The model and detection are of the same forms as those in the differential scanning method. The feature in this case is a trichromatic luminance measure instead of a monochrome intensity value. Similar to differential scanning, this method requires precise optical alignment. Furthermore, since the three photomasks are separated in space, the mechanical registration requirement is another major problem.

### Optical Spatial Filtering  E

Optical spatial filtering is another method for inspecting microcircuit photomasks. This approach is based on one of the most important assets of coherent optical processing—the ease with which a lens can perform the Fourier transformation of an image. Perhaps even more essential to the inspection problem is the fact that the spectrum of the input pattern is physically accessible and therefore can be manipulated by simply placing optical spatial filters in the Fourier transform plane. As illustrated in Fig. 10, an input transparency (the photomask) of amplitude transmittance $g(x, y)$ is

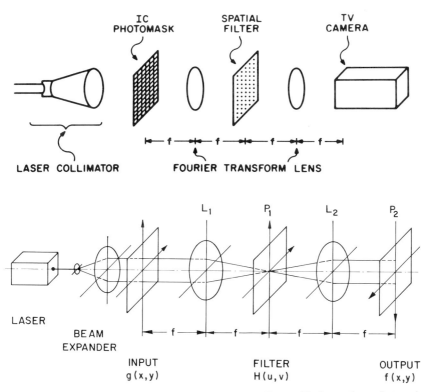

**Fig. 10.** Fourier optics inspection system uses a spatial filter to block out the perfect-mask array in the Fourier plane, leaving only defects on the output plane.

placed in the front focal plane of lens L1 and illuminated by a collimated laser beam. The amplitude in the back focal plane P1 of the lens is represented by the Fourier transform $G(u, v) = F[g(x, y)]$ of the input. If a filter transparency of amplitude transmittance $H(u, v)$ is placed in the plane P1, the amplitude distribution just behind the transparency becomes $G(u, v) \times H(u, v)$. The second lens L2 performs a second Fourier transform of $G(u, v) \times H(u, v)$, leading to an image in its back focal plane P2 given by $f(x, y) = F[G \times H]$. Equivalently, the output can be represented as the convolution of the input, with a filter function taking the form $f(x, y) = g(x, y) * h(x, y)$, where $h(x, y) = F[H(u, v)]$ and $*$ denotes a convolution operator. It can also be shown that if a photomask is placed at $g(x, y)$ and the filter $H(u, v)$ is removed from the optical processor, then the output $f(x, y)$ is the reconstruction of the original photomask image.

The Fourier transform of the step-and-repeat die arrays of a photomask consists of a two-dimensional array of bright spots. The spacing of these spots depends only on the spacing of the die on the photomask, and the amplitude and shape of these spots depends upon the individual device pattern. If any defects are present on the photomask, a different transformed pattern will appear, one which is not confined to the array of bright spots generated by the perfect photomask. The simplest way to use these properties to inspect photomasks is to design a spatial filter which is placed at $H(u, v)$ to block out the spectrum of the perfect-mask array, leaving only the spectrum of the defects. The Fourier transform of the defects at the output of the spatial filter is transformed again to produce a defect map at the output plane $f(x, y)$.

The model in this approach is a negative of the two-dimensional spectrum of a perfect photomask. The feature is the amplitude transmittance of an image spectrum, and the detection is implemented by a simple optical blocking filter. This approach has the usual drawbacks of image subtraction. Making the spatial filter $H(u, v)$ is both difficult and time consuming and, in addition, there are problems with respect to focusing and aligning the filter with the image spectrum. In addition, this technique is very sensitive to surface and thickness irregularities in the photomask.

A number of studies have been performed based on the approach described above. In one study, two apertures were used to select two portions of the illuminated periodic photomask pattern, and a grating at the Fourier plane was used for the detection. In another study, the two-dimensional spatial filtering process was simplified by comparing patterns of one-dimensional optical Fourier transforms. This simplification avoids the inconvenient process of producing a spatial filter for each photomask. In one system, the spatial filter is in the form of a set of directional filters. The directional filter masking the particular angular components, such as $0°$, $45°$, $90°$, and $135°$, is used as the spatial filter in the optical system. The filtered output shows the pattern distribution, which contains directional components other than the particular directions defined by the filter. Random defects such as pinholes, nicks, and cracks are usually not of particular directions, and are therefore displayed as defects in the output image plane.

### Feature Matching   F

Feature matching is an improved form of the image subtraction method. Instead of comparing the image of the part under inspection with that of a perfect part, the features extracted from the part and those defined by the model are compared. The extracted features are in most cases geometrical patterns such as corners, lines, holes, etc. In this approach, the extraction of salient features and their organization into models for efficient matching govern the success of the inspection. This approach greatly compresses the image data for storage, and at the same time reduces the sensitivity of the input intensity data and enhances the robustness of the system. In image processing terminology, the matching process is called *template matching*.

Let $f(x, y)$ be the image field containing the part to be inspected, and let $t(x, y)$ be the template of a defective pattern. The template $t(x, y)$ is rarely ever matched exactly with defects in $f(x, y)$, because of image noise, quantization effects, and *a priori* uncertainty as to the exact shape and structure of the defect to be detected. Consequently, the matching is commonly done by computing a similarity measure $C(x, y)$ between $f(x, y)$ and $t(x, y)$ at all $(x, y)$ in $f(x, y)$, and then designating detection whenever the similarity is larger than some established threshold level. One common similarity measure is the cross correlation (or a variation of the cross correlation), defined as $C(x, y) = \sum_i \sum_j f(i, j)t(i - x, j - y)$. To be practical, $t(x, y)$ is usually zero outside a small window. At each $(x, y)$, the match is restricted to the overlap region between the translated window of $t(x, y)$ and the image field $f(x, y)$. At the coordinate location of a good match, that is, a detected defect, $C(x, y)$ should become large, indicating a small difference. Figure 11 shows the extracted features (edges) of a PCB and the templates of four possible configurations of a nick with a width of one pixel along the extracted edges. The defect detected by using cross correlation is enclosed by the square.

One of the major limitations of template matching for inspection is that an enormous number of templates must often be used, making the procedure computationally expensive. In the example in Fig. 11, a number of templates are required for a single defect to account for changes in rotation. Another set will be required if one wants to account for changes in size of that particular defect. For this reason, template matching is usually limited to smaller local features, which are invariant to size and shape variations. In the following, various extensions of template matching for part inspection will be discussed. It should be noted that the template $t(x, y)$ can be defined either as a defect template for defect detection or as a template containing normal patterns for the verification of normal features (i.e., the detection of the flawless part).

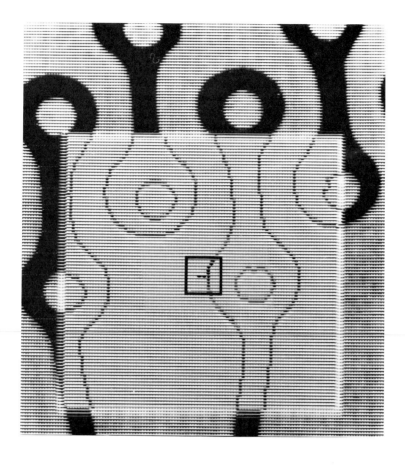

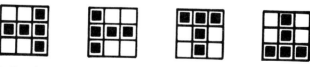

**Fig. 11.** Template matching. Extracted edges are matched with a set of four defect templates. The detected defect is enclosed by a window.

## 1   Inspection of PCBs by Feature Matching

In Ref. 5 a two-stage strategy for PCB inspection is described. The feature in this approach consists of edge patterns and measurements derived from edges. The model includes a set of binary templates used in the first stage and a set of tolerant standards used in the second. The detection is a cross-correlation-type template matching followed by a scalar subtraction between measurements and tolerant standards if the template matching is not successful. The method preselects a list of local $5 \times 5$ binary templates which describe the normal conductor-substrate boundary (edge) derived from a perfect PCB. In the first stage of the inspection, each boundary from the PCB being inspected is matched with the templates from the prepared list. Those boundary areas not found in this list are subjected to the second-stage process, which employs scalar subtraction to verify defects. These supplemental tests include the extraction of such features as the area of conductor paths, the length between boundaries, the ratio of area to length, and others. It was found in the reported example that 99% of the possible normal $5 \times 5$ boundary patterns could be enumerated by preparing less than a few hundred binary templates and only a small percentage of the boundaries were subject to the second-stage process. It should be noted that this method eliminates the need for precise alignment for the test board but requires careful generation of the set of binary templates.

In another PCB inspection experiment, a somewhat different matching approach was used [6]. The feature is the location of the conductor boundary. The model is a structured set of these edge locations with respect to a reference point on the PCB. The detection is not the traditional correlation-type matching that searches for patterns throughout the entire image; instead, it accesses the model for expected edge locations and then directs the scanner to look for edges only at expected locations in the test image. Unlike most of the other feature-matching methods, this procedure does not require the scanning-processing of the entire image. However, it requires precise registration, and isolated defects far away from the expected edge will be missed.

At General Motors, a system was developed to inspect and align IC chips using a multiple template-matching method. First, the system approximates the orientation of the IC chip by determining the highest relative frequency of edge occurrence among all edge directions. Next, all possible corners of the chip are located by matching the image with corner templates. Then, the actual four corners are determined by applying a global relational template to match with all the possible corners. Finally, the chip's structural integrity is inspected by examining the boundaries of the located chip. After this, the system directs the alignment of test probes to desired locations for functional tests.

### Inspection of IC Photomasks by Feature Matching    2

Feature extraction and template matching have been used to detect defects on IC photomasks. The fundamental concepts of the approach used in this application are very similar to those used in PCB inspection. The following describes examples using this and variations of it.

A system at Hitachi, Ltd., Japan, inspects photomasks by extracting local features from two die patterns of the photomask and comparing them. The local features include corner, curvature, width, orientation, and density. Implementation of the feature extraction and matching are realized in hard-wired circuits. Another system which utilizes local features was developed at Toshiba Research and Development Center, Japan. Local features are defined by $3 \times 3$ digital templates, including normal local patterns and defective patterns. Applying inspection at different levels of detail (multiple levels of spatial resolution), the detection is a hierarchical inspection scheme using a coarse-and-fine procedure. Large defects are detected from a coarse image with less information in parallel with small-defect detection from a fine image representation. The system was hardware implemented and was reported to have a detection capability of 1 $\mu$m and an inspection time of less than 1 hr for 4-in. photomasks.

In one approach, the template used for matching is not a two-dimensional pattern representing geometrical features of the photomask. Instead, the features are projections of the two-dimensional geometrical features in a fixed number of directions, including the horizontal and vertical. The detection using these features no longer requires the correlation-type template matching, but entails only simple comparison with some predefined parameters. In a specific case, the number of contour lines of each direction within a window is counted. The introduction of defects within the window will change the predefined number of counts. The contour direction counts then determine whether or not there is a defective pattern in the window. This method has the advantage that defects can be extracted without any stored templates and precise alignment requirements, but the exact locations of defects cannot be pinpointed.

## G    Dimensional Verification

In many applications, the feature extraction or template-matching method is simplified to dimensional verification (distance checking). The task is to make a determination, for each measurement, as to whether it falls within the previously established standards. In general terminologies, the feature is a set of linear measurements (e.g., length and width) usually measured as the distance between edges. Figure 12 illustrates the simple idea. The model is a set of predefined tolerance standards, with each component corresponding to a component in the feature set. The detection is a vector subtraction between the model set and the feature set. Several systems of this type will be described.

In one system based on dimensional verification, a special detector array was designed and used to inspect PCBs. This detector array, containing a

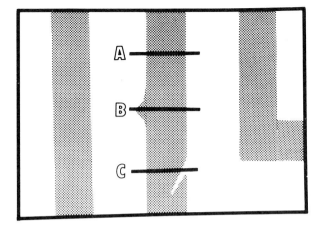

**Fig. 12.** Basic idea of dimensional verification: measurement A is acceptable; B and C are rejected.

total of 38 detector elements, is arranged in three circular rings centered at one point so that it can detect flaws by minimum conductor width and minimum conductor spacing criteria. The bright conductor areas detected by the array will turn the detectors *on* while the detectors imaging the board substrate remain *off*. Checking the placement of *on* and *off* detectors is equivalent to measuring the linear dimension. Dimensional verification is performed by analyzing the detector's output patterns by logic circuitry. It should be noted that precise registration is not required.

Another system worth mentioning is the proposed PCB inspection system reported in Ref. 7 that uses a charge-coupled-device (CCD) linear-array sensor and a video preprocessor. Predefined dimensions such as width and length are used as criteria to determine defects. The unique characteristic of this system is the use of run-length encoding. The image is first scanned in a line-by-line fashion. Then the signal is processed by the video preprocessor to generate a binary signal, to remove edge artifacts, and to encode a run-length code. The encoding permits the determination of relative positions of the edges of the conductor on each scan and the linkage of edge information on a scan line to the previous scan lines. In addition, the code contains sufficient dimensional information of the two-dimensional image, even though the image analysis is based on the processing of one-dimensional video pulses. After the encoding, the detection process involves the tracking of regions (conductor and substrate) from scan line to scan line, the extraction of topological features for dimensional measurements, and the detection of anomalies by imposing local constraints, such as minimum or maximum width. All dimensions are measured as relative distances between edges; thus precise alignment is not required.

A PCB inspection system using the center-line method was developed by Philips Research Laboratories, The Netherlands [8]. The center line of a track (a track is the conductor path or the substrate strip between the conductors) is a line that runs parallel to the boundary of the conductor that lies midway between the two boundaries. In other words, the center line is a skeleton of the track. The model in this method is a set of center lines, each with a test criterion that indicates the minimum required width of the track and whether it belongs to a conductor track or a substrate track. When the width of a track in the ideal pattern varies along a center line, different dimensional criteria are defined in the model for the various portions of the center line. During inspection, the PCB is aligned and a determination for each center-line point is made as to whether there is sufficient clearance around it.

The generalization of various dimensional verification methods to PCB inspection was presented in Ref. 9. The investigated algorithms are all based on the perpendicular distance measured from one boundary point to another. The author performed detailed analyses and comparative studies as well as exploring hardware realization issues concerning these algorithms.

## H  Syntactic Approach

Another method of inspection is the syntactic pattern recognition approach (also referred to as the structural approach). This approach to inspection offers a possibility for describing a complex object using a small set of simple subpatterns and structural rules. The existence of a recognizable structure of the part being inspected with known interrelationships between the subpatterns of that structure is essential for the success of the syntactic approach. For this reason, syntactic pattern recognition can be applied to most industrial inspection problems. This section examines some of the inspection methods that have been developed from recent research using syntactic approaches. Much of the present research using this approach is still evolving. See Ref. 10 for the fundamentals and other applications of this approach.

Syntactic pattern recognition uses an analogy between the structure of pictorial patterns and the syntax or grammar of languages. Pictorial patterns, such as PCB patterns, are specified by composing subpatterns together in various ways of composition, just as phrases and sentences are built up by concatenating words, and words are built up by characters. The simplest subpatterns are called *primitives*. The next level of description is called the *sentence*, which is a concatenation of primitives using composition operations relating the primitives. See Fig. 13 for four pattern primitives of a PCB and a simple sentence composed from the primitives. In general terms, a *language*

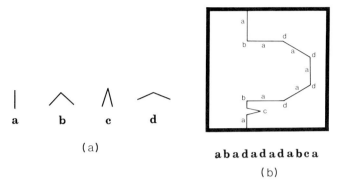

**Fig. 13.** Illustration of boundary description by syntax: (a) primitives of a PCB grammar and (b) boundary pattern and its string representation.

with a specified *grammar* can be defined to provide the structural description of pictorial patterns in terms of a set of primitives and the rules governing the composition of primitives. Using inspection terminologies, the features in this approach are the primitives. The model is the language with a well-specified grammar governing the correctness of a sentence (a flawless pattern) and detecting the error of a sentence (a defect). After each primitive (feature) is identified, and the language (model) is established, the detection is accomplished by performing a syntax analysis, or *parsing*, of the sentence describing the given pattern to determine whether or not it is syntactically (or grammatically) correct with respect to the specified grammatical rules.

In the inspection of PCBs, corners, simple curves, and lines are the primitives. The grammar is a set of rules defining all valid situations under which defective patterns such as "aca" (a sharp angle between two lines) can be detected among normal, valid patterns. In most cases, a great deal of preprocessing is required before the parsing can be done, making the procedure unattractive for some industrial applications.

Various syntactic techniques for shape analysis and boundary tracing have been studied, and some have been applied to the problem of PCB inspection. In one experiment [11], a PCB image was encoded into primitives. The procedure involves a boundary tracer which produces ordered lists of boundary points, a polygonal approximation program which attains data compaction and noise removal, and a syntactic shape analyzer which produces descriptions of the shape. The descriptions are then composed into an expression. The detection of defects then involves the detection of local defective features expressed in the expression.

In Ref. 12, an algorithm using *regular expression language* was developed to inspect PCBs. A regular expression is a specification for a finite-state automaton which recognizes the occurrence of the specified pattern of text in an input stream of sentences. Initially, a set of common PCB defects is expressed in regular expressions. Later in the inspection, conductor boundaries are extracted from the PCB image and expressed in regular expressions via chain coding. Specified defects are then detected by searching the text stream for the occurrences of the defective pattern expressions.

## I  Other Inspection Applications

The applications of automated visual inspection are very diverse. The electronics industry is one of the major driving forces in the investigation of visual inspection because miniaturized solid-state components and other electrical devices are increasingly complex and beyond human inspection capability. A variety of inspection tasks other than PCB and photomasks have been automated to relieve the human inspector of the tedious search for defects. Applications include the inspection of contact switches, hybrid circuits, light bulb filaments, bubble memory overlay patterns, etc.

Automated visual inspection to improve productivity is needed in many nonelectronic industrial applications. These include the inspection of automobile parts, fabrics, pharmaceutical products, paper products, military equipment, railroad tracks, food and packaging goods, glass and ceramic products, metal surfaces, etc. For a more extensive survey on automated visual inspection, see Ref. 13.

## IV  CONCLUDING REMARKS

Since the mid-1970s, a large number of vision systems and algorithms for industrial inspection have been developed. Since then, the number of production-line vision systems operating in various manufacturing processes has increased many-fold and is still growing. This chapter has summarized various inspection techniques and algorithms, using PCB inspection as an example to illustrate their similarities and differences. The systems and techniques examined here also allow us to point out various limitations and weaknesses of present industrial systems. These limitations are discused below.

To be acceptable by industry, vision systems must be inexpensive and yet have the following requirements:

(1) *Speed.* The duration required for processing the image and detecting defects has to agree with the speed of the production-line flow. Often, the required rate is less than some fraction of a second per part.

(2) *Accuracy*. The percentage of successful detection of defects must be high.

(3) *Flexibility*. The system must be flexible enough to accommodate changes in products and competent enough to inspect parts in an uncontrolled environment.

With these industrial requirements, inspection systems today are still very limited when their capabilities are compared with human vision. There are many important industrial vision applications that might seem simple for humans to fulfill but are still well beyond the ability of any existing machine.

Most existing systems are binary image processing systems requiring well-positioned, isolated parts against a high-contrast, clean background. This alone places serious limitations on the capability and flexibility of the system. The development of more sophisticated gray-scale processing inspection algorithms will enhance their performance. Another limitation is the inability to deal with three-dimensional objects. This problem can be solved by using more than one image sensor and the development of three-dimensional models. Most current vision systems are custom-engineered systems with only one specific task in mind. They represent *ad hoc* approaches to a single problem. As more complex industrial parts must be handled, the vision system has to be flexible and more versatile. Until recently, we have not seen a strong desire for general-purpose machine vision systems. The capital costs of general systems are relatively high because they are difficult to design, but they can be justified in the long run by their utilization rate.

To summarize, the following are some limitations of current industrial inspection systems:

(1) Require controlled environment for binary processing
(2) Unable to handle shadows and highlights
(3) Unable to handle occlusion
(4) Unable to inspect surface properties
(5) Require precise positioning
(6) Use two-dimensional models for three-dimensional objects
(7) Employ *ad hoc* approaches and limited applications
(8) Are inflexible and nonversatile

## REFERENCES

1. L. Lieberman, Model-driven vision for industrial automation, *in* "Advances in Digital Image Processing-Theory, Applications, Implementation" (P. Stucki, ed.), pp. 235–246. Plenum, New York, 1979.
2. C. A. Rosen and D. Nitzan, Use of sensors in programmable automation, *Computer*, 12–23 (December 1977).
3. M. Ejiri, T. Uno, M. Mese, and S. Ikeda, A process for detecting defects in complicated patterns, *Computer Graphics and Image Processing* **2**, 326–339 (1973).
4. J. H. Bruning, M. Feldman, T. S. Kinsel, E. K. Sittig, and R. L. Townsend, An automated mask inspection system—AMIS, *IEEE Trans. Electronics Devices* **ED-22**, (July 1975).

5.  J. F. Jarvis, A method for automating the visual inspection of printed wiring boards, *IEEE Trans. Pattern Anal. Machine Intell.* **PAMI-2**, 77–82 (January 1980).
6.  R. T. Chin, C. A. Harlow, and S. J. Dwyer, III, Automatic visual inspection of printed circuit boards, *Proc. SPIE, Image Understanding Syst. and Industrial Applications* **155**, 199–213 (1978).
7.  W. M. Sterling, Automatic non-reference inspection of printed wiring boards, *Proc. IEEE Comput. Soc. Conf. Pattern Recognition and Image Processing, Aug. 1979*, pp. 93–100 (1979).
8.  F. L. A. M. Thissen, An equipment for automatic optical inspection of connecting-lead patterns for integrated circuits, *Philips Tech. Rev.* **37**, No. 2, 77–78 (1977).
9.  P.-E. Danielsson and B. Kruse, Distance checking algorithms, *Computer Graphics and Image Processing* **11**, 349–376 (1979).
10. K. S. Fu, "Syntactic Pattern Recognition and Applications." Prentice-Hall, Englewood Cliffs, New Jersey, 1982.
11. C. M. Bjorklund and T. Pavlidis, On the automated inspection and description of printed wiring boards, *Proc. Int. Conf. Cybern. Soc., 1977*, pp. 690–693 (1977).
12. J. F. Jarvis, Feature recognition in line drawing using regular expression, *Proc. 3rd Int. Joint Conf. Pattern Recognition, Nov. 1976*, pp. 189–192 (1976).
13. R. T. Chin and C. A. Harlow, Automated visual inspection: a survey, *IEEE Pattern Analysis and Machine Intelligence* **PAMI-4**, No. 6, 557–573 (November 1982).

# Chapter **25**

# Remote Sensing

PHILIP H. SWAIN

School of Electrical Engineering and
Laboratory for Applications of Remote Sensing
Purdue University
West Lafayette, Indiana

## INTRODUCTION   I

### Perspective   A

The origins of remote sensing date back to the invention of the photographic camera. The term denotes the sensing and recording of physical phenomena related to and characteristic of an object of interest, from a distance, without coming into contact with the object [1]. Operations which

HANDBOOK OF PATTERN RECOGNITION
AND IMAGE PROCESSING

subsequently are used to extract information from the sensed data often are considered part of the remote sensing process. Some forms of remote sensing do not involve the formation of an image (for example, radar altimetry), but many modern applications of the technology make extensive use of photography and other types of image-forming sensors, image processing, and image pattern recognition (for example, earth resources surveys). This chapter is concerned exclusively with image-related remote sensing. Furthermore, emphasis is given to remote sensing of the Earth; strictly speaking, all applications of imaging science could be considered "remote sensing."

## B    Overview of the Technology

Key elements in understanding modern remote sensing include the general goals of the remote sensing user, the nature of the sensing process, and the steps used in transforming remotely sensed data into useful information.

(1)  *Goals of the user.* Typically, the user is interested in extracting from the remotely sensed data information which will assist in decision-making related to the geographic area surveyed. Major subgoals often include classification of the area and production of a thematic map.

(2)  *The sensing process.* Multispectral sensor systems aboard aircraft and spacecraft are often used to measure and record the data [1]. Examples include photographic and electronic cameras, multispectral scanners, and radars. Multiple images of the survey area may be recorded, thus representing the scene in different regions of the electromagnetic spectrum (e.g., ultraviolet, visible, infrared, and microwave) and at different times (e.g., different seasons of the year). Figure 1 shows an example of imagery from the Landsat Multispectral Scanner (MSS), which is used principally for remote sensing of the Earth's resources.

(3)  *Geometric registration and rectification.* These image preprocessing steps ensure that multiple images of the scene coincide geometrically and represent faithfully the geometry of the actual ground area [2]. Once registration has been accomplished, the ensemble of measurements related to each ground resolution element comprises a multivariate pixel (picture element). The number of measurements per pixel is referred to as the dimensionality of the image data.

(4)  *Transformations.*   The components of each pixel may be subjected to a number of transformations before the information extraction process actually begins. The purpose of such transformations may be to enhance the visual representation of the image (to facilitate manual interpretation), to improve its signal-to-noise properties, or to reduce the dimensionality of the data [3].

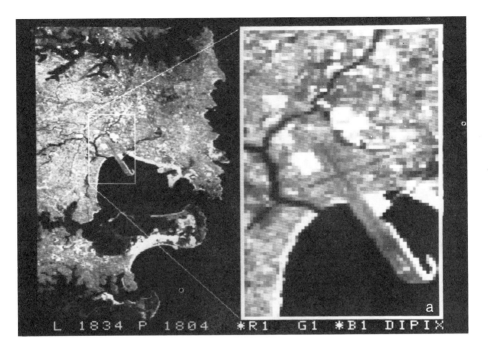

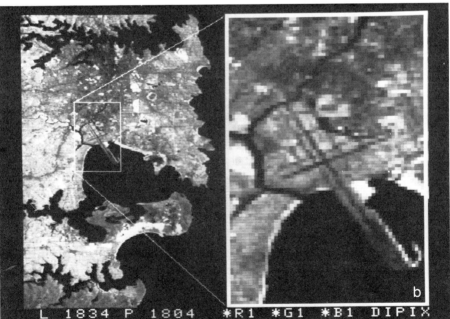

**Fig. 1.** Landsat view of the Sydney, Australia, area in two spectral bands: (a) 0.6–0.7 μm (red) and (b) 0.8–1.1 μm (infrared). Part of Landsat Scene No. 2215323005, December 14, 1980. The Sydney harbor is near the top of the scene. The right side shows an enlargement of the Sydney International Airport, with one runway extending into Botany Bay. (Photos courtesy of the Centre for Remote Sensing, The University of New South Wales, Sydney, Australia.)

(5) A *Pattern recognition.* Remote sensing data are usually classified using the techniques of image pattern recognition; that is, each pixel is assigned a label which describes the ground cover category or condition inferred from its component values. The results of the classification may be used to make thematic maps or may be entered into a geographic information system and subjected to higher-level information extraction operations.

(6) *Geographic information extraction.* Much of the useful information derivable from remotely sensed data is of a regional nature and often requires inferences to be drawn involving various sources of data used in conjunction with classifications of the scene. Such higher-level information extraction operations may be referred to collectively as geographic information extraction. They include map-algebraic operations [4] and methods based on the art and science of image understanding.

Possibly the most characteristic aspects of this application of image processing and pattern recognition are the high dimensionality of the data, the relatively coarse resolution of the imagery, and the very large number of pixels in a scene (typically several million). The data are often multivariate, consisting of 4, sometimes 12, possibly hundreds of spectral (and other) variables per pixel. Although a "scene" may consist of several million pixels, an individual "object" in the scene may consist of a dozen or fewer pixels and be only a pixel or so across its smallest dimension. Under these circumstances, extracting information from remotely sensed image data may be difficult, expensive, and time consuming.

Remote sensing imagery is analyzed by both manual and computerized techniques. This chapter emphasizes the latter. In either case, however, the computer has important roles to play. Computers and digital imagery have made feasible image processing operations which are vital in remote sensing applications, such as meaningful calibrations, geometric manipulations, and mathematical transformations which greatly enhance the interpretability of the imagery and the usefulness of the final product.

## II  IMAGE PROCESSING

The image data produced by multispectral scanner systems are usually subjected to numerous forms of "preprocessing" before manual or digital interpretation of the imagery is attempted. In the main, these are not substantially different from the operations used in other applications of image processing, although the mix of operations employed is, of course, somewhat specialized. A useful overview of image processing in the remote sensing context, with attention to the special qualities of the imagery arising from sensor characteristics, may be found in Ref. 3.

## Image Sampling and Reconstruction    A

In remote sensing, the matter of sampling arises in several ways. In converting the essentially two-dimensional image into a one-dimensional data stream, the sensor system must sample the scene. The optimal rate at which this sampling is performed depends on the instantaneous field of view of the sensor and the spatial frequency distribution of the scene [3]. Sensor designers must understand the nature of this dependency in order to maximize the capture of scene detail on the one hand while minimizing the load on the system communication channels on the other.

After the image is "on the ground," so to speak, it is often necessary to resample the image in order to bring it into coincidence with other images having a different grid structure (different scale, orientation, map projection, etc.). Many methods are available to accomplish this; computation cost considerations tend to drive the selection of the method. The simplest method is nearest-neighbor resampling. Under this method, the output pixel at location $(i, j)$ is determined by computing the precisely located input position $(x, y)$ and then selecting the pixel at the actual input location $(m, n)$, where $m$ is the integer part of $x + 0.5$ and $n$ is the integer part of $y + 0.5$. A spectrum of two-dimensional interpolation techniques is available which provides greater image fidelity than nearest-neighbor resampling, but these techniques require considerable computational effort [5]. Cubic methods are perhaps the most popular, providing a good compromise between image fidelity and computation cost [3].

## Image Encoding    B

Encoding of remote sensing image data is necessary for data transmission and archiving, in both cases in order to minimize the quantity of data which must be dealt with. The dominating considerations are three: to minimize the required transmission bandwidth, to achieve maximum freedom from the degrading effects of noise, and to minimize effects which would tend to degrade subsequent analyses. These considerations impose constraints which greatly narrow the choice of encoding methods.

The principal methods used to encode remote sensing image data fall into three classes [3]:

(1)  direct encoding in the spatial domain, for example, pulse code modulation, delta modulation, and noiseless coding;

(2)  transform techniques, for example, Fourier, Walsh–Hadamard, and cosine transforms;

(3)  multispectral encoding, for example, principal components, and cluster encoding.

The most effective encoding methods are often hybrids of techniques from these three classes. There are fixed and adaptive versions of practically every method. Within limits, it is possible to trade off the degree of compression against the complexity of the method. In general, greater complexity implies more computations required for encoding and decoding the data.

Optimal encoding methods take into account the statistical nature of the images, the properties of the communication channel and/or storage medium, the analysis procedures to be applied to the data, and the requirements of the application(s) in which the data are to be used.

## C   Geometric Processing

There are numerous sources of geometric distortion in remote sensing imagery, related both to the sensor system and to the nature of the scene [2, 3]. Some of these are well characterized, through either understanding the viewing geometry or prelaunch geometric calibration of the sensor. Examples include image skew due to rotation of the Earth during the period in which a scene is scanned and the variation in distance between pixel centers with variation in view angle. Other causes of distortion are of a more transient and random nature. An example is the aberrations due to unpredictable irregularities in the positioning of the sensor platform due to, for instance, wind or minor orbital variations. In either case, it is first necessary to model the distortions present, develop an image-warping function based on the model, then apply this function to reverse the distorting effects in the image.

When there is prior knowledge of the nature of the distortions, the required image-warping function can be generated directly and applied to remove the distortions. This is referred to as *systematic* correction.

However, most of the geometric corrections of remote sensing imagery are not of this systematic type, and the modeling process must be accomplished through the use of control points. Control points are precisely located coordinates in the scene which can be identified in the image. Control points may be located in the image by manual, semiautomatic, or automatic methods involving image-to-image correlation [6]. Roughly speaking, the correction process involves warping or modifying the geometry of the image so that a network of control points in the image is made to have the same spatial relationship as the control points on the ground. (Actually, the relationships will differ by a geometric transformation called a map projection, which accounts for the fact that the image is a planar representation of the approximately spherical surface of the Earth [2].) In practice, the image to be corrected is usually adjusted relative to another, already "rectified," image of the same scene.

Up to fifth-degree bivariate polynomials typically are used to model distortions over large scenes, such as those produced by the Landsat system. The actual correction process involves resampling, as described earlier. These operations are sufficiently complex to have warranted the development of special-purpose computer systems for their routine execution [2].

A very important use of these techniques is to achieve geometric registration of multiple images of the same scene, often from the same sensor system but collected at different times. Such multitemporal and multisource data sets are proving to be of great value in Earth resources monitoring and other applications of remote sensing.

### Radiometric Processing    D

Radiometric (intensity) adjustments are also applied to remote sensing imagery, both to improve the fidelity with which the image represents the scene and to enhance the interpretability of the image. Here we are concerned principally with the former category. Examples include atmospheric correction, compensation for the point-spread function of the sensor, and radiance calibration.

Although effects of the atmosphere, especially a nonuniform atmosphere, on remote sensing imagery can severely degrade its interpretability, atmospheric corrections are not routinely performed. Modeling the effects of the atmosphere on remote sensing data remains an area of intensive research.

Similar comments pertain to corrections for the blurring effect of the sensor system's point-spread function. Techniques for modeling the point-spread function have been developed and shown effective for improving the visual quality of the imagery [3], but this correction is only rarely applied in practice, at least in part due to the computation cost involved.

Radiance calibrations are used routinely. One application is to adjust for the effects of aging of the sensor detectors and system electronics so that, over time, a given data value represents a constant scene radiance value, within prescribed system tolerances. Another important application arises from the fact that many orbiting multispectral sensors use clusters of solid-state detectors for each spectral band. The outputs of all the detectors in a given spectral band must be precisely calibrated relative to each other; otherwise, the imagery will contain horizontal striping, which is cosmetically annoying and has deleterious effects on subsequent image processing operations.

### Mosaicking    E

Mosaicking, the operation of joining together images from contiguous scenes to form a contiguous image, deserves special mention because of its importance to many applications of remote sensing. Producing a high-quality mosaic requires that the component images be made both geometrically and radiometrically compatible. Many of the adjustments described earlier are used [2]. Mosaics of Landsat images have been produced covering several states and even the entire continental United States.

## F   Image Enhancements

The geometric and radiometric image transformations described earlier are used to improve the fidelity with which the image represents the scene. Many other transformations are employed which actually degrade the fidelity of the image but enhance the processes, manual or digital, which are used to interpret the image. Chief among these are filtering operations used to smooth the image, to accentuate edges, etc. These are performed using either convolutional filtering in the image domain or various operations in the spatial frequency domain. Other image enhancements commonly employed involve the arithmetic combination of spectral bands, typically linear combinations, ratios, and ratios of linear combinations of spectral bands. These transformations may be used to suppress incidental variations in the image due to, for example, differences in view angle, or to accentuate the interactions among selected spectral bands. These transformations tend to be highly application specific.

Additional enhancements used for feature extraction in conjunction with pattern recognition are discussed later.

## III   PATTERN RECOGNITION

## A   Spectral Pattern Recognition

Multispectral remotely sensed imagery may be subjected to either supervised or unsupervised analysis or, more typically, a hybrid of the two approaches. Supervised analysis is used if sufficient "ground truth" is available and readily locatable in the data to permit accurate characterization of the ground cover classes of interest. Otherwise, unsupervised analysis using clustering is employed to partition the feature space, after which the analyst must identify the ground cover class corresponding to each of the cluster classes (often called spectral classes). Since at least some of the classes in the scene may not be contained in the ground truth, the analyst will often choose to use a combination of supervised and unsupervised analysis [1].

Both statistical and nonstatistical pattern recognition methods are employed. The most commonly used of these methods are now discussed.

### *Parallelipiped Classifier (Multivariate Level Slicing)* **1**

This nonstatistical parallelepiped classifier is most often used for qualitative or "quick look" scene analysis, particularly when a good interactive color image display system is available for training the classifier. In a supervised mode of operation, the analyst locates a few regions in the image (e.g., agricultural fields) representative of each of the apparent ground cover types. To define the feature-space parallelepipeds corresponding to each ground cover class, the system determines the maximum and minimum data values in each of the specified spectral bands for each of the selected regions. More than one parallelepiped may be required for a given class, depending on the degree of spectral heterogeneity of the class. Recognition proceeds by assigning a given pixel to any class having a parallelepiped which contains that pixel.

This classifier has the advantages of being easy to train and able to classify a large area very rapidly. However, the results are highly prone to analyst bias and it is possible, even likely, for pixels to be ambiguously classified into more than one class since parallelepipeds of different classes may overlap. It is also possible for some pixels to lie outside all defined parallelepipeds and thereby be impossible to classify.

### *Minimum Distance Classifier* **2**

The minimum distance classifier is the simplest of the statistical classifiers commonly used for remote sensing applications. Class means are determined from training data by either supervised or unsupervised methods. Each pixel is then assigned to the class with the nearest class mean. This classifier requires a moderate amount of training data, that is, sufficient to compute reliable estimates of the multivariate class means, and the results it produces are not optimal if the class covariance matrices are not equal. However, it is relatively fast compared to other statistical methods and does not suffer the problems of the parallelepiped classifier in permitting pixels to be classified ambiguously or to not be classified at all.

### *Gaussian Maximum, Likelihood Classifier* **3**

The Gaussian maximum-likelihood statistical classifier is by far the classifier most commonly used in remote sensing. The mean vectors and covariance matrices of the classes required to compute the class-conditional density functions as part of the recognition process are estimated by supervised or unsupervised methods. When it is determined that some of the classes grossly violate the underlying multivariate Gaussian (normal) assumption, the problem is usually dealt with by subdividing the offending classes into subclasses, each represented by its own mean vector and covariance matrix. In practice, the classes tend to have Gaussian distributions, and, moreover, the classifier is relatively tolerant of deviations from normality.

The principal disadvantages of this classifier are two. Because second-order statistics are required, more training data are needed to characterize the classes adequately than are needed by the minimum-distance classifier. The recognition process is comparatively slow and the computation time varies approximately as the square of the number of features used (the variation is linear for the other two classifiers described). This can be a serious disadvantage because large areas often must be classified, but where operational use of this classifier is made, this problem is attacked through clever software implementation or implementation on an array processor.

Generalizations of the Gaussian maximum-likelihood classifier are employed. When reasonable estimates of the class prior probabilities are available, the classification may be based on maximizing posterior probabilities, which are proportional to the product of the prior probabilities and the class-conditional density functions. When some classes in the scene are of greater importance than others, a minimum risk strategy may be adopted which weights the classification in favor of the more important classes.

It cannot be overemphasized that the success of applying pattern recognition to remote sensing data (as with any other type of data) depends critically on the use of an effective classifier training procedure. A training procedure is considered effective if it produces characterizations of the classes which are truly representative of the scene(s) to be classified. The reader is referred to the literature (e.g., Refs. 7–9) for examples specific to remote sensing.

## B  Clustering

Clustering is widely employed in remote sensing data analysis for unsupervised classification, primarily as part of the training process [1]. Unsupervised classification allows the analyst to utilize any natural structure which may be present in the data as an aid to appropriately partitioning the feature space into regions corresponding to the classes.

Multivariate clustering algorithms of the iterative "migrating means" variety, typically variants of ISODATA [10], are most commonly used. Others are related to histogram peak selection [11]. Many of these algorithms attempt to determine automatically the proper number of clusters contained in the data set being analyzed. However, no completely satisfactory method is known for accomplishing this.

**Contextual Pattern Recognition   C**

The pattern recognition methods described so far are pixel specific, that is, they make no use of the context of each pixel in the process of classifying that pixel. As in all image data, the pixels in remote sensing image data have spatial context; in addition, they may have temporal and other types of context as well.

*Spatial Context*   *1*

Many fundamentally different approaches have been taken to the use of spatial context in remote sensing. These range from simple neighborhood relations including co-occurrence probabilities and texture to more global relations involving the structure or pictorial syntax of the image.

Texture has been the local spatial feature most intensively studied for remote sensing applications. The most successful, but also the most computationally demanding, have been the gray-tone co-occurrence relations [12, 13]. Often the computed textural feature values are simply appended to the spectral components of the pixel and used conjointly with them to classify the pixel. Texture has also been used to segment the image into regions [14], after which other forms of analysis generally follow.

For example, it may be assumed that each region in a segmented scene consists of pixels from the same ground cover class. In this case, sample classification [15] may be used to classify simultaneously all of the pixels in a given region. If the homogeneous ground regions are, on the average, large compared to the resolution of the remote sensor, thus resulting in a relatively large number of pixels per region, then sample classification has the dual advantages of being both faster and more accurate than pixel-at-a-time classification.

Compound decision theory has been invoked to provide a neighborhood-based generalization of the minimum risk or Bayesian classification [16]. This approach is based on the co-occurence probabilities of classes rather than gray tones. Its use depends on the availability of information sufficient to characterize the relative frequencies with which classes co-occur in a given neighborhood configuration. The amounts of computation and memory required by this type of classifier are substantial.

Syntactic pattern recognition, which uses spatial structural properties of the classes to characterize and recognize their occurrence [17], incorporates contextual information of a more global nature. This method employs grammars that must be capable of generating the patterns in a given class; learning these grammars from examples contained in the available data, called grammatical inference, is a difficult problem which is still the subject of considerable research.

## 2  *Temporal Context*

The availability of data from repetitive coverage of the same ground area makes it possible to exploit information in the temporal domain. The "stacked vector" approach to multitemporal data analysis is based on the formation of a spectrotemporal data vector by concatenating data components from a sequence of sensor passes. Analysis may proceed as in the purely spectral case. However, this direct approach leads to data of very high dimensionality, so that feature extraction methods, such as those described later in this chapter, are very important.

Scene changes, either changes in spectral characteristics or changes in classification, are of immediate interest in many applications. Often images of the same scene, measured at different times, are compared pixel by pixel; regional comparisons are also important. Comparison of spectral characteristics requires that the data first be normalized, for example, calibrated in units of radiance or reflectance, in order to be comparable. When classified images are to be compared, care is required that the classes in the different scenes are truly comparable. In general, change detection by digital methods is very sensitive to the accuracy of registration of the images involved.

## 3  *Generalized Contextual Reasoning*

In addition to spatial and temporal relations, other factors may contribute to the contextual knowledge about the remote sensing data to be analyzed [18]. Some examples include terrain (topography), climatological variables, and geopolitical information. These often can have a significant influence on the utility of the information derivable from the remote sensing data and should be used to the extent possible. At the current state of the art, the methods used to do this are largely ad hoc, but research into analytical tools for geographic information systems will yield more systematic approaches.

## D  Feature Extraction

Feature extraction in remote sensing applications of pattern recognition has three main purposes:

(1)  to reduce the high dimensionality of multivariate image data to two or three components in order to plot them on paper, render them in image form photographically, or view them on a color image display screen;

(2)  to reduce the data dimensionality in order to gain processing speed; and

(3)   to extract and enhance features characteristic of the classes of interest which would otherwise be obscured by the high dimensionality of the data or by incidental environmental variations.

Many of the transformations which have been developed for this purpose have been derived on a purely empirical basis. Simple ratios and ratios of sums and differences of multispectral bands, on a pixel-by-pixel basis, have been found to emphasize ground characteristics of particular interest in applications such as agricultural surveys and geological studies. Where multiseasonal data are available, the temporal trajectories of some of these features have also been found to be particularly useful [19].

The linear transformation based on the Karhunen-Loève expansion [20] (also called principal components analysis) has been found useful for mono-chrome and color image enhancement in a broad range of applications. It is usually used in an unsupervised mode in that the transformation is deter-mined from the multivariate image data without regard to ground cover discrimination. Another method, called canonical analysis, which also uses eigenanalysis to determine a dimensionality-reducing linear transformation, is more useful for maximizing class discriminability [21]. This method is used in a supervised mode; the transformation is based on the second-order statistics of the ground cover classes as determined from training data.

Another entire family of supervised methods for deriving optimal, dimen-sionality-reducing transformations has been developed specifically in the context of remote sensing applications [22]. These methods are based on the concept of directly minimizing the probability of classifier error or maximiz-ing a measure of interclass statistical separability, such as divergence or Bhattacharyya distance.

A number of spatial features, including texture and syntax (structure), have already been discussed. Shape, like texture, has been characterized by a great number of different approaches, one of the most successful being Fourier analysis of object boundaries. The resulting spatial frequency representation tends to be invariant to rotation and translation, an extremely important property in applications based on shape discrimination.

**Evaluation of Results   E**

The spatial aspect of an image, which enriches its potential information content, also complicates greatly the task of assessing the accuracy with which it has been classified. Properly determining the accuracy of a classified image or, more particularly, a thematic map, requires statistical sampling of the area which has been classified. In general, both a level of accuracy and a confidence interval for that level are needed. For some applications, these results may be obtained solely in terms of overall accuracy, but in others accuracy results are needed for some or all of the individual categories represented by the image or thematic map. Valid methods for obtaining these results are discussed in Refs. 23 and 24.

## IV  GEOGRAPHIC INFORMATION EXTRACTION

The image processing and pattern recognition operations described usually do not produce the end product sought by the user. Typically, applying these operations to remotely sensed data provides only a subset of the information on which the user must draw in order to formulate a plan or make a decision. Computer technology has made it possible to integrate remote sensing data into comprehensive geographic information systems which significantly automate the compilation of geographic data and facilitate the extraction of information from such data [4].

Geographic information systems differ markedly from other information systems in their explicit focus on spatial entities and relations. The efficient storage and handling of extremely large volumes of data are particularly critical issues in such systems, as are the merging of multiple sources of data, which involves interfacing multiple forms and formats of data.

The principal classes of operations which must be implemented in a geographic information system include the following.

(1)  *Data input*: manual and automatic digitizing, encoding, and editing of data.

(2)  *Storage and retrieval*: registration and cross referencing, cataloging, updating, query processing.

(3)  *Analysis*: scene modeling, classification, overlay, neighborhood and regional computations, distance and area measurements.

(4)  *Report generation*: summarization, generation of map overlays, including themes and annotation, tabular formatting.

The state of the technology of geographic information systems which use remote sensing data and image analysis techniques is well presented in Ref. 4.

## REFERENCES

1.  P. H. Swain and S. M. Davis (eds.), "Remote Sensing: The Quantitative Approach." McGraw-Hill, New York, 1978.
2.  R. Bernstein, Image geometry and rectification, *in* "Manual of Remote Sensing" (R. N. Colwell, ed.), 2nd ed., Chap. 21. American Society of Photogrammetry, Falls Church, Virginia, 1983.

3.  F. C. Billingsley, Data processing and reprocessing, *in* "Manual of Remote Sensing" (R. N. Colwell, ed.), 2nd ed., Chap. 17. American Society of Photogrammetry, Falls Church, Virginia 1983.

4.  D. F. Marble and D. J. Peuquet, Geographic information systems and remote sensing, "Manual of Remote sensing" (R. N. Colwell, ed.), 2nd ed., Chap. 22. American Society of Photogrammetry, Falls Church, Virginia 1983.

5.  S. Shlien, Geometric correction, registration, and resampling of Landsat imagery, *Canadian Journal of Remote Sensing* **5**, 74–89 (May 1979).

6.  M. Swedlow, C. D. McGillem, and P. E. Anuta, Image resgistration: Similarity measure and preprocessing method comparisons, *IEEE Trans. Aerospace Electronics Systems* **AES-14**, 141–150 (1978).

7.  *IEEE Transactions on Geoscience and Remote Sensing*, IEEE, New York.

8.  *Photogrammetric Engineering and Remote Sensing*, American Society of Photogrammetry, Falls Church, Virginia.

9.  *Remote Sensing of Environment*, Elsevier, New York.

10. R. O. Duda and P. E. Hart, "Pattern Classification and Scene Analysis," Wiley, New York, 1973.

11. K. Matsumoto, M. Naka, and H. Yamamoto, A new clustering method for Landsat images using local maximums of a multidimensional histogram, *Proc. Symp. Machine Processing Remotely Sensed Data, Purdue University, 1981*, pp. 321–326 (1981).

12. R. M. Haralick, K. Shanmugan, and I. Dinstein, Textural features for image classification, *IEEE Trans. Systems, Man Cybernetics* **SMC-3**, 610–621 (1973).

13. J. S. Weszka, C. R. Dyer, and A. Rosenfeld, A comparative study of texture measures for terrain classification, *IEEE Trans. Systems, Man Cybernetics* **SMC-6**, 269–285 (1976).

14. O. R. Mitchell and S. G. Carlton, Image segmentation using a local extrema texture measure, *Pattern Recognition* **10**, 205–210 (1981).

15. D. A. Landgrebe, The development of a spectral-spatial classifier for Earth observational data, *Pattern Recognition* **12**, 165–175 (1980).

16. J. C. Tilton, S. B. Vardeman, and P. H. Swain, Estimation of context for statistical classification of multispectral image data, *IEEE Trans. Geoscience Remote Sensing* **GE-20**, 445–452 (1982).

17. J. M. Brayer, P. H. Swain, and K. S. Fu, Modeling earth resources satellite data, *in* "Syntactic Pattern Recognition: Applications (K. S. Fu, ed.), Chap. 9, Springer-Verlag, New York, 1977.

18. R. M. Haralick, J. B. Campbell, and S. Wang, Automatic inference of elevation and drainage models from a satellite image, *Proc. IEEE* **73**, 1040–1053 (1985).

19. G. D. Badhwar, J. C. Carnes, and W. W. Austin, Use of Landsat derived temporal profiles for corn–soybean feature extraction, *Remote Sensing of Environment* **12**, 57–59 (1982).

20. J. Kitler and Y. C. Young, A new approach to feature selection based on the Karhunen-Loève expansion, *Pattern Recognition* **5**, 335–352 (1973).

21. B. F. Merembeck and B. J. Turner, Directed canonical analysis and the performance of classifiers under its associated linear transformation, *Proc. Symp. Machine Processing Remotely Sensed Data, Purdue University, 1979*, pp. 314–322 (1979).

22. H. P. Decell and L. F. Guseman, Jr., Linear feature selection with applications, *Pattern Recognition* **11**, 55–63 (1979).

23. R. M. Hord and W. Brooner, Land use accuracy criteria, *Photogrammetric Engineering Remote Sensing* **42**, 671–677 (1976).

Chapter **26**

# Biomedical Image Analysis

J. SKLANSKY, P. V. SANKAR,
and
R. J. WALTER, JR.

University of California
Irvine, California

## INTRODUCTION: THE GROWTH OF IMAGE ENGINEERING I

The past decade has witnessed a tremendous development of new, powerful instruments for detecting, storing, transmitting, analyzing, and displaying images. These instruments are greatly amplifying the ability of biochemists, biologists, medical scientists, and physicians to see their objects of study and to obtain quantitative measurements to support scientific hypotheses and medical diagnoses. In this chapter we summarize developments in those aspects of biomedical imaging that are closest to the themes of this book: pattern recognition and image processing, that is, computer-aided analysis of images. In addition, we describe several exciting new developments in the *formation* of images. This chapter is divided in two parts: microscopic and macroscopic.

## II  MICROSCOPIC IMAGE ANALYSIS: BIOLOGY AND PATHOLOGY

### A  Overview

The study of microscopically small objects is a necessary and historically important part of the sciences of biology and medicine. All living organisms are composed of cells, and the critical examination of living material at the cellular level is important to an understanding of biological processes, both normal and abnormal, that influence growth, development, disease, or malignancy. Many of the great advances that have been made in the biomedical sciences over the past several decades can be at least partially attributed to the development of new imaging techniques that have allowed previously hidden aspects of microscopic biological material to be viewed for the first time.

Present-day clinical and biological laboratories may employ many micro-scopic imaging devices that each produce unique information about the material under study. An awareness of the power of computer analytical techniques, coupled with a continuing need to derive more information from these microscope images, has led to a growing application of digital process-ing techniques to the problems of biology and medicine. In the research laboratory digital image processing techniques are being used to improve the clarity of microscope images using histogram manipulations, filtering, or related techniques [1-4]; to derive quantitative and morphometric data from the microscope image [5-10]; and to produce three-dimensional image reconstruction from an ensemble of two-dimensional images [1, 11-13]. In the clinical laboratory, digital image processing techniques are used to automate and standardize diagnostic tests performed on blood cells [14-17], histological samples [18-21], cervical smears [22-25], chromosome prepara-tions [26, 27], and other types of microscopic images [28-30]. These applica-tions of digital techniques are not meant to be a substitute for the skills of a pathologist, but instead are meant to augment the speed and reliability with which the pathologist makes his or her diagnosis.

In spite of these and other examples of the usefulness of computerized analysis, digital image processing has not yet been widely used in either the clinical or research laboratory. This reluctance is due in part to the relatively high capital cost of such equipment. However, it is also due to other limitations relating to the types of analysis digital techniques are asked to perform. In the research laboratory digital analysis is used with images that are highly unique and may differ significantly over time as the focus of research projects change. The uniqueness of such images frequently means that appropriate instrumentation and routines for their analysis is not available commercially [31]. The alternative is to develop such instrumentation in-house, a task for which most biological researchers have neither the training or inclination. At present, most image processing devices targeted for the research laboratory are described as general-purpose processors, being able to perform a variety of basic routines common to many types of image analysis, but which rarely have sufficient software to analyze specific types of images without extensive further development and testing.

In the clinical laboratory, computerized image analyzers have not been widely used for other reasons. Image processors for clinical use are required to analyze complex scenes that may contain scores of different cell types, plus additional objects such as fragmented cells or other debris. From this complexity the automated analyzer is required to identify and classify each cell type, prepare a population distribution, and possibly identify abnormal populations based on previously determined distributions. Ideally, these machines would perform such analysis quickly with zero error (no false positives and no false negatives). However, in practice this result has not been achieved. At the present time automated clinical image analysis is either too slow in comparison to the speed of a trained pathologist or suffers from unacceptably high error rates.

## Optical Microscopy  *1*

Many different kinds of imaging systems can and have been used with digital image analysis techniques. It is important to understand the differences between these imaging techniques, since each will affect the information content of the image and several produce information that is unique to that imaging system and cannot be duplicated by other means. Further details on optical microscopy can be found in Spencer [32].

The *brightfield microscope* is widely used to observe microscopic material that is opaque or highly pigmented. Most cells and tissues lack natural pigments; consequently, they must first be chemically stained to produce a specimen suitable for viewing under this microscope. Over the years numerous staining procedures have been developed that specifically label biologically important structures such as nuclei, chromosomes, or nerve fibers in such a way that they become visible using brightfield techniques. These chemical stains often bind stoichiometrically to their target molecules. Consequently, optical density measurements made through the microscope can sometimes be used as a quantitative measure of chemical concentration [30]. Brightfield microscopy is the type most often used in clinical image analysis, where the specimen being visualized has been previously stained with specific dyes, typically heomotoxylin and eosin (abbreviated H & E), which stain the cell nucleus blue–purple and the cytoplasm pinkish red. Most chemical treatments used to fix and stain biological material result in cell death. Consequently, the brightfield microscope generally cannot be used to observe living specimens.

The *phase contrast microscope* is commonly used to observe living material without the need for prior chemical staining. This microscope, which utilizes an optical Fourier filtering technique, produces an image that is a function of the variations of refractive index within the specimen being observed. Objects will appear light or dark in a phase contrast image depending on whether their refractive index is higher or lower than that of the bulk medium. The largest variations in refractive index in biological material are found at cell boundaries or within dense structures such as cell nuclei or chromosomes. Consequently, these structures most clearly visualized using this technique. Not all structures of biological interest have significantly different refractive indexes; consequently not all structures of interest can be visualized using this microscope. The phase contrast microscope has made it possible to use image processing techniques to study the properties of living cells such as cell motion [33] and cell shape [21, 34].

*Polarization microscopy* (POL) and *differential interference contrast* (DIC) *microscope* can also be used to observe living, unstained biological material. These techniques, which are modifications of the brightfield microscope, utilize high-intensity illumination with cross-polarizing filters to produce an image of the specimen. Polarization microscopy is used in biology to examine structure with natural birefringence, such as the highly organized "paracrystalline" fiber arrays found in muscle tissue or the mitotic spindle of dividing cells. Only those structures that interact with polarized light are visible in POL microscopy.

DIC microscopy utilizes special prisms to introduce optical shear into the microscope image [32]. The DIC technique produces images that are related to the *gradient* of refractive index within the specimen (in the direction of the optical shear), which have an unusual three-dimensional appearance. Like phase contrast, DIC microscopy is useful for detecting cellular boundaries and highly refractive objects. The DIC microscope has an extremely shallow depth of focus which can be used to take "optical sections" of biological material at slightly different focal points within a specimen. Such images can then be used for three-dimensional image reconstruction.

The images produced by POL and DIC techniques are often poorly matched to the visual sensitivity of the human eye, and the high-intensity illumination can often damage living material. Several techniques have been recently reported for enhancing DIC and POL images using video imaging and computer processing techniques [3 and references therein].

Biological material that has been stained with fluorescent compounds can be visualized using a *fluorescence microscope* equipped with the appropriate excitation light source and colored filters. Fluorescent images generally have a higher signal-to-noise ratio than the equivalent brightfield technique, consequently the fluorescence microscope can be used to detect compounds at much lower light levels than are possible using brightfield techniques. Fluorescent techniques can also be used to visualize fluorescently labeled ligands that have been incorporated into living cells and tissue.

### Electron Microscopy 2

Electron microscopes are used to produce images of biological material with a resolution on the order of a few angstroms, compared to the 0.25–0.5-$\mu$m resolution limit possible using the light microscope. Biological material must be specifically stained with salts of lead, osmium, uranium, or other heavy metals before they can be imaged using this technique. The images produced in the electron microscope correspond to the electron density of the heavy metal stain(s) used during specimen preparation. The image output of an electron microscope is either a video raster display or a photographic negative exposed directly by the interrogating electron beam. Digital analysis techniques are frequently applied to electron microscope images for the purpose of morphometric measurement [7, 11, 21, 36], image reconstruction [5, 37, 38], and visualization of crystalline structures [14, 39].

The transmission electron microscope (TEM) is analogous to the bright-field microscope and is used to examine biological material that has been physically sliced into ultrathin sections of less than 10 nm in thickness. Several thousand such sections may pass through a single cell. Consequently, it is frequently difficult to visualize structures using the TEM that cannot be confined to a few contiguous sections. In some instances this problem can be overcome by using a special TEM with a very high-energy electron beam (high voltage EM, or HVEM). This instrument can be used to image specimens with a thickness approaching that of a single cell.

The scanning electron microscope (SEM) is used to examine whole-mounted biological specimens that have been dried and coated with an electron-dense metal film. The preparation is then placed under vacuum and scanned in a raster fashion by an electron beam. The image produces by the SEM represents the surface features of the specimen (as revealed by the heavy metal coating) and does not reveal information concerning internal structures of the specimen.

## 3  Autoradiography

It is frequently advantageous to use radioactive molecules to label biological material for subsequent analysis under the light or electron microscope. The labeled specimen is placed in direct contact with an appropriate photographic film or emulsion, which is subsequently developed to produce an image of the specimen (the autoradiograph) that reveals the location of the radiolabeled molecule. Autoradiographs are analyzed to determine ligand concentration in the original specimen by either measuring the average film density per unit area or by individually tabulating the number of exposed silver grains per unit area [6, 30, 40].

## 4  Gel Electrophoresis and Chromotography

The chemical constituents of biological material can be identified using several chemical sorting techniques. A widely used technique is that of polyacrylamide gel electrophoresis (PAGE), which separates macromolecules into a linear pattern of bands according to their relative mobility in an electric field. After application of the field, the gel is stained with a specific dye which reveals the location of the migrating molecules as a pattern of spots or bands. The separation between the individual bands and a point of origin can be used as a measure of molecular charge and/or molecular weight, depending on the conditions of the experiment. The density of an individual band can be used as a measure of molecular concentration using densitometric techniques. Classical chromatography utilizing a solid phase (agarose gels, cellulose acetate, etc.) and a solvent phase is used in a similar manner to separate mixtures of smaller molecules according to their differential solubilities.

Mixtures if proteins that have been separated in one dimension on a gel according to electrical charge can be separated in a second dimension according to molecular weight. These preparations, called *two-dimensional gels* or *electrophorograms*, can be used to distinguish individual proteins with a resolution that exceeds that possible in any one dimension. Such gels, which may contain tens of thousands of individual spots, are subject to a high degree of technical variability, making it difficult to accurately compare different gels from different laboratories. Several automated techniques have been proposed for converting electrophorograms into uniform format so that they may be directly compared [6, 28, 31, 41–44].

## 5  Digitizing Systems in Biology

Several strategies have been used for digitizing biological images. The simplest technique, used for morphometric analysis, is to digitize shape parameters manually from a photograph or projected image using a digitizing tablet [10, 12, 13]. Such techniques are invariably slow and tedious but can benefit from the expertise of the operator in distinguishing image features that may be difficult to classify in a fully automated system. Tablet systems are also relatively inexpensive and easy to master. Consequently, they are widely used.

Gray-scale digitization can be accomplished using spot digitizers that measure density from photographic film or directly through a microscope using a photodiode or other light-sensitive device [40]. An array of image density is produced by moving the sensor, the specimen itself [24, 25], or a focused illuminating beam in a raster fashion [45]. The sensors used in scanning digitizers are selected for a highly linear light sensitivity and produce minimal spatial distortion due to the mechanical nature of the scanning device. Scanning digitizers are limited in speed and cannot be used in real-time or fast-response applications.

The development of high-speed analog-to-digital converters has led to an increasing use of video cameras as imaging–digitizing tools in biology. The video camera–digitizer combination can be used in applications where real-time or near real-time analysis is required or where other properties of the video camera (such as low light sensitivity) can be used to advantage. Unfortunately, video digitizing systems are subject to several sources of image degradation and distortion [107]. Consequently, their suitability for a specific application must be carefully determined. However, the speed, low cost, and ease of use of these devices have made them the device for choice for many applications in biology where their drawbacks are not absolutely prohibitive [3, 6, 35, 41, 46, 47].

## Analysis of Optical Microscope Images   B

### Preprocessing   1

The complexity of biological material viewed under the microscope often limits the usefulness of digital processing techniques to routines of image preprocessing and enhancement for the benefit of a human operator. Digital techniques can be used to optimize the image for human vision through gray-scale, pseudocolor, or histogram manipulations, using predefined or interactively defined look-up functions [4, 6]. Image integration or spatial averaging can be used to reduce the effects of statistical noise, particularly in video applications where such noise may be significant [38].

Digital preprocessing techniques can also be used to improve the visibility or object boundaries that may be poorly resolved because of high magnification or low contrast. Spatial filtering using sharpening filters or Laplacian operators can be used to enhance object boundaries, as can zonal filtering techniques [36, 46]. Simple histogram transforms can often be used to enhance object boundaries in phase contrast and DIC images because these boundaries are often found at the gray-value extremes in these images [4, 107].

Microscope images often contain shading irregularities that result from uneven illumination, shading distortion in the imaging system, or out-of-focus debris on the optics. Digital processing techniques can be used to compensate for this distortion by comparing an acquired image to a previously stored image of a blank (empty) microscope field. The distortion can be minimized by using techniques of image subtraction, image division, or other techniques [6, 46, 107]. These techniques can be conveniently implemented on multi-image parallel processing systems, where such corrections can be performed automatically at or near real time.

## 2  Morphometry

Descriptors of size and shape, for example, area, radius, or perimeter, are useful for describing biological objects and traditionally have been obtained manually from photographic records. Digital processing techniques can be used to increase the speed and accuracy of such measurements and can also be used to derive other descriptors that are difficult to obtain through other means. Computerized morphometric techniques are often required to classify complex biological objects such as single cells, where repetitive measurements on large sample sets are required for accuracy.

Object boundaries must be identified before morphometric analysis can be performed. Such boundaries can be derived manually using a digitizing tablet or other interactive device, thus yielding a map of edge elements which can be used for subsequent computer processing. Automated routines exist for deriving edge maps from binary images using gray-level thresholding techniques [9, 14, 46].

Numerous shape descriptors have been used to classify biological objects based on simple measurements of size, length, circularity, and so on [14–17]. Many automated image processors are equipped with preprogrammed routines for calculating these descriptors from interactively determined binary images [31].

## 3  Image Analysis in Pathology

Over 300 million clinical tests are performed every year on blood smears, cervical smears, urine sediments, and other cell-containing preparations [15]. These samples typically contain many different cells which can be classified into distinct types such as red blood cells, lymphocytes, granulocytes, platelets, etc. It must be determined if any of these cell types show abnormalities, or if any cell class occurs in unusual frequency compared to normal samples. The pathologist relies on a well-trained eye to examine and characterize such cellular preparations, using criteria based on nuclear shape, quantity and color of the cellular cytoplasm, size and color of cytoplasmic particles, overall cell shape, cell–cell contacts, and so on. Normal and abnormal cells may differ so slightly in these parameters that such differences can only be reliably detected after examining many cells. Conversely, abnormal cells may only represent a small fraction of a larger population of normal cells.

The pathologist's job could be made much simpler if automated techniques could be used to detect and classify cell types from a clinical sample. Automated techniques have been developed for the purpose of detecting and classifying bone marrow smears [17] red blood cells [14, 16], cervical smears [22–25], histological preparations [9, 18, 20, 21], urine sediments [29], and chromosome preparations [26, 27].

Each of these applications involves the detection and segmentation of individul cellular images, followed by the calculation of relatively simple morphometric measurements such as cell and nuclear diameter, P/A ratio, integrated optical density, or the ratio of nuclear and cytoplasmic volume. These parameters are then used to classify each cell based on a classification matrix determined from a learning set [34, 48, 49]. At present such classification schemes are rarely 100% successful, particularly when high throughput speed is required, with error rates for false positives and false negatives being on the order of 5 to 20% [20, 23–25]. The accepted strategy for such devices at the present time is not the fully automated analysis of clinical samples, but the rejection of clearly normal cell types so that only cells and tissues that may be suspected of abnormality can be brought to the attention of the pathologist.

Clinical samples are usually chemically treated with polychromatic dyes before examination. However, many automated techniques utilize monochrome images captured with a particular colored filter selected for high contrast. The colored properties of the stained cells are often used for classification by a human observer. However, this information can be lost in a monochrome image. Several attempts have been made to utilize the color information in stained material for the purpose of automated analysis [19, 20, 22].

A particular type of abnormal cell or tissue is often classified along a continuum from slightly abnormal up to higher degrees of abnormality. Although the differences between different grades of abnormality may be slight, the distinction is often of importance because the classification may be used to indicate greatly different clinical therapies, for example, drug treatment versus major surgery for a suspected malignant growth. Although pathologists can usually be expected to agree on a diagnosis of a clinical specimen, there can often be disagreement in the classification along the continuum, leading to disagreements in the recommended therapy. Digital analysis techniques can be used in an attempt to quantify different stages carefully along this classification continuum so that such classification can be performed more reproducibly. In several examples given by Baak [18], it is shown that careful analysis of preselected abnormal specimens can be used reproducibly to classify tissue preparations representing cancerous or precancerous states. We believe such analysis and classification may be useful for standardizing the analyses among various medical groups and may be particularly useful in classifying abnormalities that are rarely seen by a given pathologist.

## III  MACROSCOPIC IMAGE ANALYSIS: RADIOLOGY, PSYCHIATRY, CARDIOLOGY, AND OPHTHALMOLOGY

Macroscopic images, for example, images of human organs such as the heart, brain, and eye, play major roles in diagnostic radiology, psychiatry, cardiology, and ophthalmology. In this section we summarize several recent applications of image analysis to these disciplines. For further details on medical imaging, see Wells [50], Nudelman [51], and Macovski [52].

### A  Overview of Medical Image Analysis

The basic image processing operations on medical images (usually performed by computers) are conveniently placed in four categories: filtering, shape modeling, segmentation, and classification.

*Filtering* includes enhancement, deblurring, and edge detection. Enhancement techniques may consist of linear or nonlinear, local or global filters [53]. Deblurring techniques may consist of inverse or Weiner filters. Edge-detection techniques may include local operators [54] and/or classification techniques [55].

*Segmentation* includes clustering, object detection, and boundary detections. Simple histogram or thresholding techniques are used to segment objects of interest [56]. When adequate prior information is available, matched filters can be used effectively [57, 58]. Heuristic techniques are useful for tracing contours in the presence of highly structured background noise, such as in chest radiographs [59].

*Shape modeling* includes three-dimensional representation and graphics manipulation, such as three-dimensional contours of the spinal column [60], the coronary artery [61], or shaded images [62].

*Classification* includes feature selection, texture characterization [63], and pattern recognition [64]. Current medical image engineering includes a broad range of image-formation modalities, several of which are described below. For each of these modalities we indicate the role of the preceding four categories to the extent they appear in various applications.

## Computer-Aided Conventional Radiography   B

The development of automated analysis of medical images has taken place in stationary as well as in time-varying medical images. The stationary images are exemplified by chest radiographs; the time-varying images by digital subtraction cineangiograms.

## Time-Varying Images   C

Digital subtraction techniques for enhancing the visibility of medically significant details in cineangiograms and for the detection and measurement of stenoses in arteries have been successfully demonstrated in recent years. Among the recent publications on this subject, we recommend Ort [65] for the use of matched filtering techniques; Brown [66] for measurement of stenoses; Ovitt [67] for the use of image intensifiers tied to image processors; Bursch [68] for blood flow measurement; Radtke [69] and Sayre [70] for the measurement of ventricular muscle volume; Spears [71] for the measurement of vessel diameter; Borgen [72] for the detection of cardiac lesions with left-to-right shunting; Slutsky [73] for the analysis of pulmonary circulation; Enzmann [74] for the integration of mask and contrast images in intracranial intravenous subtraction angiography; Bogren [75] for histogram equalization of axial projections; Nakatsuka [76] for the measurement of valvular regurgitant flow ratio; Shaw [77], Nalcioglu [78], and Sasayama [79] for corrections of scatter and glare; and Sayre [70] for the imaging of three-dimensional angiograms.

## Stationary Noninvasive Images   D

Many forms of medical images, especially radiographs, are poorly matched to human vision due to low contrast, noisy background, obscured portions in foreground, wide dynamic range, and blurred edges. To suppress these defects, notch filters and zonal filters have been successfully used [80, 81]. These techniques are especially amenable for implementation by parallel multimicroprocessor architecture [82]. Considerable work on automated lung nodule detection has been done at U.C. Irvine [83]. For a recent technique on three-dimensional reconstruction of a coronary arterial network from a small number of projections, see Blume [61].

## E  Tomographic Reconstruction

While computerized tomography (CT) revolutionized medical radiography techniques, nuclear magnetic resonance imaging (NMR or, equivalently, MRI) is outriding some of the earlier advances made by CT. For the first time the physician can see changes in chemical composition in three-dimensional slices of anatomic structures and can visualize organ metabolism. For explanations of the principles underlying CT and NMR, see Wells [50].

## F  X-Ray Computed Tomography

Since the quality of CT images is usually good to start with, one needs little or no preprocessing for CT images. However, for segmentation of tumors or other regions of interest, simple edge-detection techniques have been used [79]. Since only few CT scans are collected to avoid overdose, there is a tremendous mismatch in resolution of CT scans along the scan plane versus the line perpendicular to the CT scans. To overcome this problem, Rhodes [60] devised a fast contour-generation program which stacks three-dimensional contours and builds network models of the spinal column and ventricles. Robb [62] at Mayo Clinic devised an alternative approach based on shaded surface generation in a CT system with 28 x-ray tubes, thereby obtaining a three-dimensional volume reconstruction. Bajcsy [84] developed a computerized system for the elastic matching of deformed radiographic images to idealized atlas images. For further discussion of computerized tomography, see Chapter 27 by A. C. Kak in this book.

## G  Positron Emission Tomography

Recent research has shown that positron emission tomography (PET) can discriminate schizophrenic from normal individuals [85]. Thus PET has become a major imaging tool in psychiatry and has amplified the interest in this form of medical imaging.

Medical PET images are produced by introducing into human tissue a selected chemical compound that has a positron-emitting radionuclide. The distribution of the radionuclide in the tissue is imaged by detecting the nearly collinear oppositely moving pair of photons generated by each annihilation of an electron–positron pair. By the use of algorithms similar to those used in transmission computerized tomography, one may obtain quantitative images of the distribution of these pairs. PET imaging enables the *in vivo* analysis of several biochemical processes essential to life.

In the analysis of schizophrenia by PET, digital image processing yields a reconstruction of the brain's lateral cortical surface. The results lend support to the use of image analysis for producing a brain atlas of each patient.

## Nuclear Magnetic Resonance Imaging   H

Nuclear magnetic resonance imaging (NMR or MRI) is a new form of radiographic imaging with enormous potential for medical science and practice because it seems to produce negligible damage in the patient and because it provides three-dimensional chemical and metabolic information as well as structural information on the patient's anatomy and physiology. The technology of NMR imaging is in its infancy; consequently, an effective use of image processing for NMR has not yet been reported. For an overview of NMR imaging techniques, see Cho [108].

## Volume Image Reconstruction   I

Most image reconstruction methods for the representation of three-dimensional structures are based on stacking two-dimensional images that are constructed by computerized tomography. In some medical applications, however, the statistics of the data (e.g., signal-to-noise ratio) are so poor that the direct reconstruction of three-dimensional volume images offers an advantage. An example of such a potential application is positron emission radiography. A recent overview of three-dimensional volume reconstruction methods is presented by Z. H. Cho [86].

## Nuclear Medicine   J

King [87] describes an optimal filter for improving the quality of digitally recorded nuclear images. Conventional gamma camera systems are not ideally suited for image processing. Richardson [88] discusses hardware modifications of a Gamma 11 system to facilitate image processing. Oshai [89] describes a new adrenal computer imaging technique using radio-isotopes. Davis [90] describes a microprocessor-based simulator for gamma camera image processors.

## K    Ultrasonic Imaging

A recent study by Skorton [91] reveals that using simple image analysis techniques such as low-pass filtering, threshold segmentation, and boundary detection can lead to left ventricular measurements that correlate more closely with M mode measurements than do measurements derived from unprocessed two-dimensional echo cardiography. Itoh [92] has constructed a three-dimensional display system for ultrasonic diagnosis of a breast tumor. The use of pattern classification techniques in ultrasound is described by Finette [93], Good [94], Green [95], and Towfiq [96]. Dickinson presents an interesting use of digital image processing for reducing speckle in ultrasonic images [97].

## L    Diaphonography

Diaphonography is a new noninvasive method for examining the breast using visible and/or infrared light. This technique seems to provide some useful diagnostic information without exposing the patient to any harmful radiation. For details, see Barbrum [98] and Marshall [99].

## M    Opthalmography

The extent of use of image analysis techniques in opthalmology has been relatively small compared to other forms of medical imaging; yet the results are interesting and useful. Miszalok [100] describes an image analysis technique for enhancing capillary networks in optical images of the fundus. Cornsweet [101] discusses techniques for quantification of shape and color of the optic nerve head.

## N    Electroencephalographic Topography

For a recent review on computerized clinical electroencephalography, see Barlow [102]. Bourne [103] discusses the use of syntactic pattern recognition for the analysis of electroencephalograms (EEGs). For discussions of the analysis of two-dimensional representations of electrical activity in the brain, see Sandini [104] and Buchsbaum [105]. Buchsbaum [106] describes the use of simultaneous cerebral glucography with positron emission tomography and topographic quantitative electroencephalography.

## REFERENCES

1. D. A. Agard and J. W. Sedat, Three-dimensional architecture of the polytene nucleus, *Nature (London)* **301**, 676–671 (1983).
2. T. S. Baker, D. L. Caspar, and W. T. Murakami, Polyoma virus hexamer tubes consist of paired pentamers, *Nature (London)* **303**, 406–448 (1983).
3. S. Inoue, Video image processing greatly enhances contrast, quality and speed in polarization-based microscopy, *J. Cell. Biol.* **89**, 346–356 (1981).
4. R. J. Walter and M. W. Berns, Computer-enhanced video microscopy: Digitally processed microscope images can be produced in real time, *Proc. Natl. Acad. Sci. U.S.A.* **78**, 6927–6931 (1981).
5. U. Aebi, W. E. Fowler, and P. R. Smith, Three dimensional structure of proteins determined by electron microscopy, *Ultramicroscopy* **9**, 191–206 (1982).
6. C. A. Altar, R. J. Walter, K. A. Neve, and J. F. Marshall, Computer-assisted video analysis of $^3$H-spiroperidol binding auto-radiographs, *J. Neurosci. Methods* **10**, 173–188 (1984).
7. C. F. Chang, R. C. Williams, D. A. Grano, K. H. Downing, and R. M. Glaeser, Quantitative evaluation of high resolution features in images of negatively stained tobacco mosaic virus, *Ultramicroscopy* **11**, 3–11 (1983).
8. D. J. Forbes and R. W. Petry, Computer assisted mapping with the light microscope, *J. Neurosci. Methods* **1**, 77–94 (1979).
9. R. P. Rigaut, P. Berggren, and B. Robertson, Automated techniques for the study of lung alveolar stereological parameters with the IBAS image analyser on optical microscopy sections, *J. Microsc.* **130**, 53–61 (1983).
10. K. Saito and K. Niki, Morphometric synaptology of a whole neuron profile using a semiautomatic interactive computer system, *Cytometry* **4**, 20–30 (1983).
11. E. M. Johnson and J. J. Capowski, A system for the 3-D reconstruction of biological structures, *Comp. Biomed. Res.* **16**, 78–87 (1983).
12. R. R. Mize, A computer electron microscope plotter for mapping spatial distributions in biological tissues, *J. Neurosci. Methods* **8**, 183–195 (1983).
13. J. Yelnik, G. Percheron, J. Perbos, and C. Francois, A computer-aided method for the quantitative analysis of dendritic arborizations reconstructed from series sections, *J. Neurosci. Methods* **4**, 347–364 (1981).
14. J. W. Bacus and J. H. Weens, An automated method of differential red blood cell classification with application to the diagnosis of anemia, *J. Histochem. and Cytochem.* **25**, 614–632 (1977).
15. F. H. Deindoerfer, W. B. Boris, J. R. Gangwer, C. W. Laird, J. W. Tittsler, Automated intelligent microscopy (AIM) and its potential application in the clinical laboratory, *Clin. Chem.* **28**, 1910–1916 (1982).
16. J. K. Mui, K. S. Fu, and J. W. Bacus, Automated classification of blood cell neutrophils, *J. Histochem. Cytochem.* **25**, 633–640 (1977).
17. G. Zajicek, M. Shohat, Y. Melnick, and A. Yegeuz, Image analysis of nucleated red blood cells, *Comp. Biomed. Res.* **16**, 347–356 (1983).
18. J. P. Baak, P. H. Kurver, and M. E. Boon, Computer aided application of quantitative microscopy in diagnostic pathology, *Pathol. Annual* **17**, 287–306 (1982).
19. C. Garbay, G. Baugal, and C. Choquet, Application of colored image analysis to bone marrow cell recognition, *Anal. Quant. Cytol.* **3**, 272–278 (1981).
20. Y. Noguchi, Y. Tenjin, and T. Sugishita, Cancer-cell detection system based on multispectral images, *Anal. Quant. Cytol.* **5**, 143–151 (1983).
21. P. I. Polimeni, S. Williams, and H. Weisman, Application of an automatic electron image and analyzer to the measurement of myocardian extracellular space, *Comp. Biomed. Res.* **16**, 522–530 (1983).
22. R. K. Aggarwal and J. W. Bacus, A multispectral approach for scene analysis of cytological smears, *J. Histol. Cytol.* **25**, 668–680 (1977).

23. A. Mukawa, Y. Kamitsuma, F. Jisaki, N. Tanaka, H. Ishida, T. Ueno, and S. Tsunehawa, Progress report on experimental use of Cybest model 2 for practical gynecologic mass screening. Alterations of the specimen rejection threshold and specimen preparation, *Anal. Quant. Cytol.* **5**, 31–34 (1983).

24. J. H. Tucker and O. A. N. Husain, Trials with the Cerviscan experimental prescreening device on polyserine prepared slides, *Anal. Quant. Cytol.* **3**, 117–120 (1981).

25. J. H. Tucker and G. Shippey, Basic performance test on the CERVIFIP linear array prescreener, *Anal. Quant. Cytol.* **5**, 129–137 (1983).

26. K. R. Castleman, J. Melnyk, H. J. Frieden, G. W. Persinger, and R. J. Wall, Computer-assisted karyotyping, *J. Reproductive Med.* **17**, 53–57 (1976).

27. L. Koss, A. B. Sherman, and S. E. Adams, The use of hierarchic classification in the image analysis of a complex cell population. Experience with the sedimentation of voided urine, *Anal. Quant. Cytol.* **5**, 159–164 (1983).

28. N. G. Anderson and L. Anderson, The human protein index, *Clin. Chem.* **28**, 739–748 (1982).

29. K. D. Kunze, V. Dimmer, and G. Hardske, Differentiation of human T and B peripheral blood lymphocytes by high resolution cell image analysis, *Anal. Quant. Cytol.* **5**, 167–172 (1983).

30. R. J. Sklarew, Simultaneous Feulgen densitometry and autoradiographic grain counting with the Quantimet 720D image-analysis system. III. Improvement in Feulgen densitometry, *J. Histochem. Cytochem.* **31**, 1224–1232 (1983).

31. S. Bradbury, Commercial image analyzers and the characterization of microscope images, *J. Microsc.* **131**, 203–210 (1983).

32. M. Spencer, "Fundaments of Light Microscopy." Cambridge Univ. Press, Oxford, 1982.

33. G. S. Berns and M. W. Berns, Computer-based tracking of living cells, *Exp. Cell Res.* **142**, 103–109 (1982).

34. J. E. Bowie and I. T. Young, An analysis technique for biological shape—III, *Acta Cytol.* **21**, 739–746 (1977).

35. L. R. Jarvis, Microdensitometry with image analyser video scanners, *J. Microsc.* **121**, 337–346 (1981).

36. L. Lipkin, P. Lempkin, B. Shapiro, and J. Sklansky, Preprocessing of electron micrographs of nucleic acid molecules for automated analysis by computer, *Comp. Biomed. Res.* **12**, 279–289 (1979).

37. R. A. Crowther and P. K. Leuther, Three dimensional reconstruction from a single oblique section of fish muscle M-band, *Nature* (*London*) **307**, 569–570 (1984).

38. C. Nicolini, B. Cavazza, V. Trefiletti, F. Pioli, F. Beltrame, G. Brambilla, N. Maraldi, and E. Patrone, Higher order structure of chromatin from resting cells. II. High resolution computer analysis of native chromatin fibers and freeze etching of nuclei from rat liver cells, *J. Cell. Sci.* **62**, 103–115 (1983).

39. M. Ohtsuki and A. V. Crewc, Evidence for a central substructure in a *Lumricus terrestris* hemoglobin obtained with STEM low-dose and digital processing techniques, *J. Ultrastruct. Res.* **83**, 312–318 (1983).

40. H. J. Bryant and F. A. Kutyna, The development and evaluation of a low-cost microdensitometer for use with the 2-deoxyglucose method of functional brain mapping, *J. Neurosci. Methods* **8**, 61–72 (1983).

41. T. S. Ford-Holevinski, B. W. Agranoff, and N. S. Radin, An inexpensive microcomputer based video densitometer for quantitating thin-layer chromatographic spots, *Anal. Biochem.* **132**, 132–136 (1983).

42. D. M. Gersten, E. J. Zapolski, and R. S. Ledley, Computer applications in analysis, mapping and cataloging of proteins separated by two dimensional gel electrophoresis, *Comp. Biol. Med.* **13**, 175–187 (1983).

43. P. F. Lemkin, L. E. Lipkin, and E. P. Lester, Some extensions to the GELLAB two-dimensional electrophoretic gel analysis system, *Clin. Chem.* **28**, 840–849 (1982).

44. M. M. Skolnick, An approach to completely automatic comparison of two-dimensional electrophoresis gels, *Clin. Chem.* **28**, 966 979 (1982).

45. R. L. Shoemaker, P. H. Bartels, D. W. Hillman, J. Jonas, D. Kessler, Shack, R. V., and D. Vukobratovich, An ultrafast laser scanning microscope for digital image analysis, *IEEE Trans. Biomed. Engr.* **29**, 82 91 (1982).

46. B. F. Aycock, D. E. Weil, D. V. Sinicropi, and D. L. McLlwain, Television based densitometric analysis of proteins separated by two-dimensional gel electrophoresis, *Comp. Biomed. Res.* **14**, 314 326 (1981).

47. R. P. Tracy and D. S. Young, A densitometer based on a microcomputer and TV camera, for use in the clinical laboratory, *Clin. Chem.* **20**, 462 465 (1984).

48. A. C. Olson, N. M. Larson, and C. A. Hechman, Classification of cultured mammalian cells by shape analysis and pattern recognition, *Proc. Natl. Acad. Sci. U.S.A.* **77**, 1516 1520 (1980).

49. J. M. S. Prewitt and M. L. Mendelsohn, The analysis of cell images, *Annals N.Y. Acad. Sci.* **128**, 1035 1051 (1965).

50. P. N. T. Wells (ed.), "Scientific Basis of Medical Imaging." Churchill Livingston, London, 1982.

51. S. Nudelman and D. D. Patton (eds.), "Imaging for Medicine," Vol. 1. Plenum, New York, 1980.

52. A. Macovski, "Medical Imaging Systems." Prentice Hall, Englewood Cliffs, New Jersey, 1983.

53. W. Pratt, "Digital Image Processing." Wiley, New York, 1977.

54. A. Rosenfeld and A. Kak, "Digital Image Processing." Academic Press, New York, 1980.

55. M. Hashimoto, P. V. Sankar, and J. Sklansky, Detecting the edges of lung tumors by classification techniques, *Proc. 6th International Conference Pattern Recognition, Munich, 1982*, pp. 276 279 (October 1982).

56. C. K. Chow and T. Kaneko, Automatic boundary detection of the left ventricle from cineangiograms, *Computers and Biomedical Research* **5**, 388–410 (1972).

57. D. Ballard and J. Sklansky, A ladder structured decision tree for recognizing tumors in chest radiographs, *IEEE Trans. Computers* **C-25**, No. 5, 503 515.

58. J. Sklansky, On the Hough technique for curve detection, *IEEE Trans. Computers* **C-27**, No. 10, 923 926.

59. P. V. Sankar and J. Sklansky, A gestalt-guided heuristic boundary for lung nodules of x-ray images, *IEEE Trans. Pattern Analysis Machine Intelligence* **PAMI** (1979).

60. J. Rhodes, Towards fast edge detection for clinical 3-D applications of CT, *Proc. 6th Conference Computer Applications Radiology, Newport Beach, California, June 18–21*, pp. 321 327

61. W. Blume, P. V. Sankar, and J. Sklansky, Reconstructing a network of three-dimensional curves from a small number of projections, *Proc. 7th International Conf. Pattern Recognition, Montreal, 1984*, pp. 1292–1294 (1984).

62. L. D. Harris, R. A. Robb, and E. L. Ritman, Visual enhancement and display of three-dimensional reconstructed anatomic morphology, *Proc. 6th Conference Computer Applications Radiology, Newport Beach, California, June 18–21*, pp. 278 284.

63. R. M. Haralick, Statistical and structural approach to texture, *Proc. 4th International Joint Conference Pattern Recognition, Kyoto, 1978*, pp. 45 69 (1978).

64. J. Sklansky, "Pattern Classification and Trainable Machines." Springer-Verlag, New York, 1980.

65. M. Ort, *et al.*, Subtraction radiography; techniques and limitations, *Radiology* **124**, 65 (1977).

66. G. B. Brown, *et al.*, Computer-assisted measurement of coronary arteries from cineangiograms: present technologies and clinical applications, *in* "Biomedical Images and Computers" (J. Sklansky and J. C. Bisconte, eds.), pp. 102 111. Springer-Verlag, Berlin, 1982.

67.  T. W. Ovitt, Ideal configurations for intravenous digital subtraction angiography machine, *Cardiovasc. Intervent. Radiol.* **6**, 300–302 (1983).
68.  J. H. Bursch, *et al.*, Digital function angiography, a method of measuring arterial blood flow, *Radiology* **23**, 202–207 (May 1983).
69.  W. Radtke, *et al.*, Assessment of left ventricular muscle volume by digital angiocardiography, *Invert. Radiol.* **18**, 149–154 (April 1983).
70.  R. E. Sayre, *et al.*, Quantitative three-dimensional angiograms: applications, including augmentation of computer tomograms, *Proc. 6th Conference Computer Applications Radiology, Newport Beach, California, June 18–21*, pp. 95–102 (1979).
71.  J. R. Spears, *et al.*, Computerized image analysis for quantitative measurement of vessel diameter from cineangiograms, *Circulation* **68**, 453–461 (August 1983).
72.  H. G. Borgen, *et al.*, Intravenous angiocardiography using digital image processing, Detection of left-to-right shunts in an animal model, *Invest. Radiol.* **18**, 11–17 (January 1983).
73.  R. A. Slutsky and C. B. Higgins, Analysis of the pulmonary circulation using digital intravenous angiography, *Radiology* **146**, 219–221 (January 1983).
74.  D. R. Enzmann, *et al.*, Intracranial intravenous digital subtraction angiography, *Neuro Radiology* **23**, 241–251 (1982).
75.  H. G. Bogren, *et al.*, Intravenous angiocardiography using digital image processing: I. Experience with axial projections in normal pigs, *Invest. Radiol.* **17**, 216–223 (May 1982).
76.  T. Nakatsuka, *et al.*, Quantitative cineangiographic evaluations of the valvular regurgitant flow ratio by digital image processing technique, *J. Cardiogr.* **11**, 911–919 (1981).
77.  C. G. Shaw, *et al.*, A technique of scatter and glare corrections for video densitometric studies in digital subtraction videoangiography, *Radiology* 142, 209–213 (January 1982).
78.  T. Siebert, O. Nalcioglu, and W. Roeck, Deconvolution technique for the improvement of image intensifiers, *SPIE Proceedings on Digital Radiography* **314**, 310–318 (1981).
79.  S. Sasayama, *et al.*, Automated method for left ventricular volume measurement by cineventriculograph with minimal dose of contrast medium, *Am J. Cardiol.* **48**, 746–753 (1981).
80.  J. Sklansky, Medical radiographic image processing and pattern recognition, *Proc. 5th International Conference on Pattern Recognition, IEEE Computer Society* **1**, 374–382 (1980).
81.  A. A. Schwartz and J. M. Soha, Variable threshold zonal filtering, *Applied Optics* **16**, 1779–1781 (1977).
82.  L. M. Chen and J, Sklansky, A parallel multimicroprocessor image processing architecture.
83.  P. V. Sankar, *et al.*, An experiment on computed detection of lung tumors, *Proc. International Workshop on Physics and Engineering in Medical Imaging, March*, pp. 106–114 (1982).
84.  R. Bajcsy, *et al.*, A computerized system for the elastic matching of deformed radiographic images to idealized atlas images, *J. Comp. Ass. Tomography* **7**, 618–625 (August 1983).
85.  M. S. Buchsbaum, *et al.*, Positron emission tomographic image measurement in schizophrenia and affective disorders, *Annals of Neurology* **15**, 157–165 (April 1984).
86.  Z. H. Cho and J. B. Ra, Methods and algorithms toward three-dimensional volume image reconstruction with projections, "Selected Topics in Image Science" (O. Nalcioglu and Z. H. Cho, eds.), pp. 1–39. Springer-Verlag, New York, 1983.
87.  M. A. King, "Fast-count dependent digital filtering of nuclear medicine images: concise communication, *J. Nuc. Med.* **24**, 1039–1045 (November 1983).
88.  R. L. Richardson and W. H. Bettinger, A modified composite video signal generator for the gamma II computative system, *J. Nuc. Med.* **24**, 838–840 (September 1983).
89.  T. Oshai, *et al.*, A new adrenal computer imaging technique using radio isotopes, *Acta Med. Okayaua* **35**, 165–172 (June 1981).
90.  O. J. Davis and F. Lombardi, Microprocessor based simulators for gamma camera image processors, *Med. Biol. Eng. Comput.* **18**, 479–480 (1980).

91. D. J. Skorton, Digital image processing of two dimensional echo cardiograms; identification of the endocardium, *Am. J. Cardiol.* **48**, 479–486 (September 1981).

92. M. Itoh, A computer-aided three dimensional display system for ultrasonic diagnosis of a breast tumor, *Ultrasonics* **17**, 261–268 (1979).

93. S. Finette, *et al.*, Breast tissue classification using diagnostic ultrasound and pattern recognition techniques: methods of pattern recognition, **5**, 55–70 (January 1983).

94. M. S. Good *et al.*, Application of pattern recognition to breast cancer detection: ultrasonic analysis of 100 pathologically confirmed tissue areas, *Ultrasonic Imaging* **4**, 378–396 (October 1982).

95. F. M. Green, Jr., *et al.*, Computer based pattern recognition of carotid arterial disease using Doppler ultrasound, *Ultrasound Med. Biol.* **8**, 161–176 (1982).

96. F. Towfiq, F. W. Barnes, and E. J. Pisa, Tissue classification on autoregressive models for ultrasound pulse echo data, *Acta Electronica* **26**(4) (1983).

97. R. J. Dickinson, Reduction of speckle in ultrasound B scans by digital filtering, *Ultrasonics Symposium, IEEE, New York*, pp. 655–658 (1984).

98. R. J. Bartrum and H. C. Crow, Transillumination light scanning to diagnose breast cancer: a feasibility study, *Amer. J. Radiol.* **142**, 409–414 (February 1984).

99. V. Marshall, *et al.*, Diaphonography as a means of detecting breast cancer, *Radiology* **150**, No. 2, 339–343 (1984).

100. V. Miszalok and J. Wollensak, Investigations on the optic nerve head by computer; graphics, *Fortschy. Opthalmol.* **79**, 1–4 (1982).

101. T. N. Cornsweet, *et al.*, Quantification of the shape and color of the optic nerve head, in *Advances in Diagnostic Visual Optics, Proc. 2nd Intl. Symposium, Tucson, Arizona, Oct. 23–25*, pp. 141–149 (1983).

102. J. S. Barlow, Computerized clinical electroencephalography in perspective, *IEEE Trans. Biomed. Eng.* **26**, 377–391 (July 1979).

103. J. R. Bourne, *et al.*, Evaluation of a syntactic pattern recognition approach to quantitative electroencephalographic analysis, *Electroencephalography Clin. neurophysiol* **52**, 57–64 (July 1981).

104. G. Sandini, *et al.*, Topography of brain electrical activity: a bioengineering approach, *Med. Prog. Technol.* **10**, 5–18 (1983).

105. M. S. Buchsbaum, *et al.*, A new system for gray level surface distribution maps of electrical activity, *Electroencephalography and Clinical neurophysiol.* **53**, 237–242 (1982).

106. M. S. Buchsbaum, *et al.*, Simultaneous cerebral glucography with positron emission tomography and topographic electroencephalography, private correspondence, 1984.

107. S. Inoué, "Video Microscopy," Plenum Press, New York, 1986.

108. Z. H. Cho, C. H. Oh, II. W. Park, and S. W. Lee, "NMR Imaging—principles, algorithms, and systems," in "Selected Topics in Image Science" (O. Nalcioglu and Z. H. Cho, eds.), pp. 277–308. Springer-Verlag, New York, 1984.

# Chapter **27**

# Reconstruction from Projections: Applications in Computerized Tomography

A. C. KAK and B. A. ROBERTS

School of Electrical Engineering
Purdue University
West Lafayette, Indiana

**INTRODUCTION  I**

Of the many applications that exist for reconstructing images from their projections, computerized tomography has definitely been the most revolutionizing. Tomographic imaging consists of illuminating an object from various directions and for each direction, recording the transmitted fields. Each transmitted recording is an integrated measure of some parameter of the object along a particular path of propagation. For example, in x-ray tomographic imaging, the body is illuminated with x-rays which propagate in straight lines (Fig. 1). A measurement of the transmitted photons allows us to calculate the line integral of the x-ray attenuation coefficient along a straight

HANDBOOK OF PATTERN RECOGNITION
AND IMAGE PROCESSING

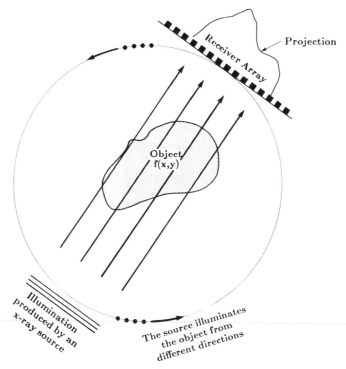

**Fig. 1.** Case of transmission tomography, in which the object is illuminated by the source at many different directions since the source–receiver array combination moves about the object.

line connecting the source and the detector. From a mathematical standpoint, the data collected in this fashion constitute a projection of the object $f(x, y)$ (shown in Fig. 1), the problem then being to reconstruct the object from the projections taken from different directions.

Transmission tomography has uses besides those in medical imaging. For example, in Fig. 2 we show how it might be used in earth resources imaging via cross-bore hole measurements employing either electromagnetic or acoustic sources. In this application, first investigated by Dines and Lytle [1], for each position of the transmitter in one bore hole, the transmitted fields are measured at a large number of locations in the other bore hole, and the procedure is repeated for different positions of the transmitter in its bore hole. As it happens, this application is also a classic example of the violation of the assumption of straight-line propagation of energy in the object (caused by refraction and diffraction created by object inhomogeneities] that makes reconstruction algorithms so easy to derive. For this reason, the magnitude of the inhomogeneities must be small if one wants to successfully image the interior of the medium. For large inhomogeneities, strictly speaking, recourse

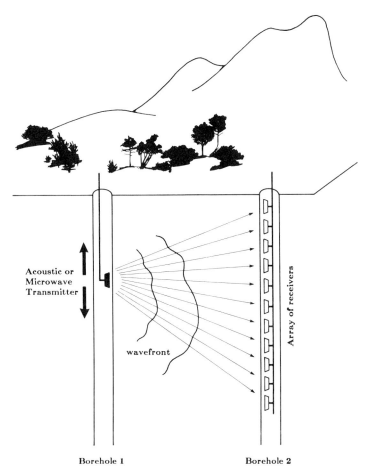

**Fig. 2.** Illustration of the sensor configuration used in earth resources applications of computerized tomography. The stationary array of receivers records the wavefront emanating from the transmitter for each of its positions within borehole No. 1.

must be made to diffraction tomography, which is still under development as a research area.

One of the first practical applications of tomographic imaging was due to Bracewell *et al.* [2] in radio astronomy for determining the brightness distribution over the celestial sphere, the sun, and the radio stars. In these applications, a radio telescope with a long narrow aperture in one direction was used to generate strip integrals of the emitted radio intensities. The scan required for generating a series of such integrals for a projection was provided by the earth's rotation. Reorienting the radio telescope yielded the projections at different angles.

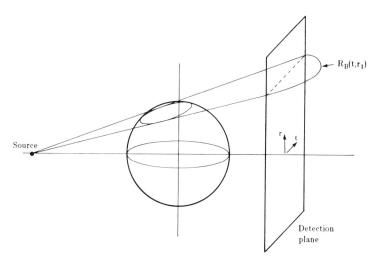

**Fig. 3.** Case of cone-beam projections, in which the projection line becomes a plane and allows the data necessary for approximate three-dimensional reconstruction to be recorded all at once.

Another important application of tomographic imaging that has come of age is in electron microscopy [3]. A transmission electron micrograph is essentially a projection of the specimen onto a plane. Projections taken at different directions can be fed into a tomographic reconstruction algorithm for displaying the interior structure of the specimen.

In the area of algorithm development, the most recent work in tomographic imaging has focused on reconstructing three-dimensional objects from their two-dimensional projections (Fig. 3). This is in contrast with

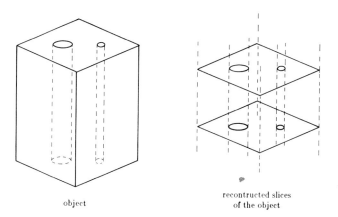

object                         recontructed slices
                               of the object

**Fig. 4.** Three-dimensional object reconstruction can be done by repetitively applying the two-dimensional reconstruction algorithms at various heights along the $z$ axis.

conventional tomography, where the images are made of one cross section at a time for the given object, and if the need exists for a three-dimensional composite, the cross-sectional reconstructions can be stacked for that purpose (Fig. 4). The advantage of direct three-dimensional reconstruction is the reduction in data-collection time, since all the projections can be measured in the same time that it takes to record the transmission data for a single cross-sectional slice. This is due to the fact that x-ray sources emanate radiation in all directions in a semihermispherical space, which makes it possible to illuminate a volume of an object in a single flash and record its two-dimensional projection in one instant. Algorithms for reconstructing from such data must take into account the three-dimensional divergent of sources used for this type of imaging.

## DEFINITIONS AND THEORETICAL PRELIMINARIES  II

Before the discussion of reconstruction algorithms can begin, various terms must be defined and the underlying general concepts of tomographic imaging must be explained. The goal of the imaging process is to reconstruct a slice, $f(x, y, 0)$ of a three-dimensional object represented by $f(x, y, z)$. Data necessary to reconstruct $f(x, y, 0)$ consist of sets of line integrals along rays that pass through the object.

The line $AB$ in Fig. 5 connecting the source at point $A$ and the detector at point $B$ represents a ray passing through the object. Integration of the object function along such a ray constitutes a line integral. Such line integrals repeated along rays parallel to $\overline{AB}$ constitute a parallel projection. In Fig. 5 the source and detector pair are moved in unison along lines $L$ and $L'$, respectively, to construct the parallel projection. Note that the parallel lines $L$ and $L'$ make an angle $\theta$ with the $x$ axis which is reflected in the expression $P_\theta(t)$, that is used to represent a projection. The variable $t$ represents the position of the detector on the line $L$. In Fig. 6 two such parallel projections are illustrated.

Repeated projection measurements recorded for $\theta$, $0 < \theta < \pi$, constitute the Radon transform of the object. Given the projection data, the object can be reconstructed by inverse Radon transforming, as will be described in subsequent sections.

The important point of this discussion lies in the type of data obtained from projection measurements. If an x-ray source is used, the integral along the line $\overline{AB}$ is equivalent to the line integral of the attenuation coefficient of the object. Hence a reconstruction algorithm operating on the x-ray-generated projection measurements would reconstruct the attenuation coefficient function of the object. In the case of ultrasound used to image

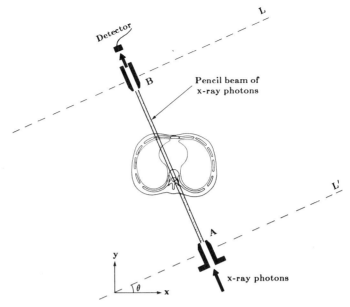

**Fig. 5.** Logarithm of the ratio of the beam intensity at $B$ to the incident intensity at $A$ is proportional to the line integral of the x-ray attenuation coefficient from $A$ to $B$.

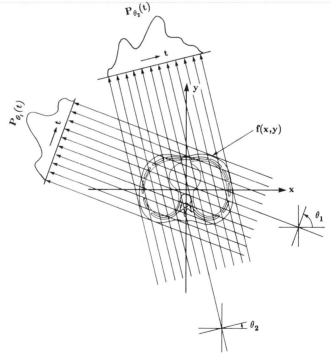

**Fig. 6.** Two parallel projections of an object whose cross section is represented mathematically by the function $f(x, y)$.

nondiffracting objects such as soft tissue, the time of propation of an ultrasound pulse from the source to detector is recorded in place of a line integral. The time of propagation through the tissue is directly related to the line integral of the refractive index of the object. As before, when a reconstruction algorithm is applied to the time-of-flight measurement projections, the result is an image which is a depiction of the refractive index of the object.

In general, a ray in the $z = 0$ plane, such as the ray $AB$ in Fig. 7, can be mathematically expressed as

$$t_1 = x \cos \theta + y \sin \theta \qquad (1)$$

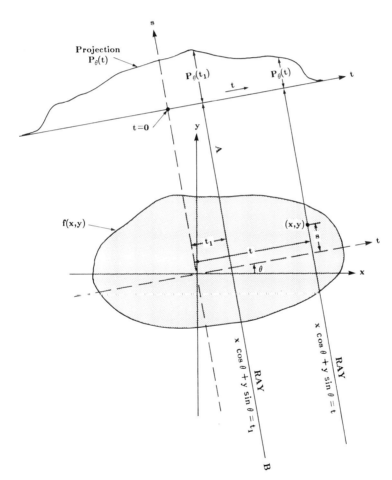

**Fig. 7.** Function $P_\theta(t)$ is a parallel projection of $f(x, y)$. Also shown in this figure is the rotated coordinate system represented by the $s$ and $t$ axes.

where $t_1$ is the perpendicular distance of the line from the origin. With the use of this ray equation, the ray integral becomes

$$P_\theta(t_1) = \int_{\text{ray } AB} f(x, y, 0)\, dx\, dy$$

$$= \int_{-y_m - x_m}^{y_m x_m} f(x, y, 0)\, \delta(x \cos \theta + y \sin \theta - t_1)\, dx\, dy \qquad (2)$$

If the $x$ coordinate axis is rotated about the $z$ axis by an angle $\theta$, the $t$ axis is formed and the projection can be written more simply as

$$P_\theta(t_1) = \int_{-s_m}^{s_m} f(t_1, s, 0)\, ds \qquad (3)$$

where $t = x \cos \theta + y \sin \theta$ and $s = -x \sin \theta + y \cos \theta$.

As previously noted, $P_{\theta_i}(t)$, which is a function of $t$, is the parallel projection at an angle $\theta_i$. Also, for continuous $\theta$, the function $P_\theta(t)$ is the Radon transform of $f(x, y, 0)$. Note that in the remainder of this chapter the projections will always be recorded parallel to the rotated $x$ axis, which we label $t$.

In three dimensions a ray may be described by the intersection of the two planes

$$t_1 = x \cos \theta + y \sin \theta, \qquad r_1 = -(-x \sin \theta + y \cos \theta) \sin \gamma + z \cos \gamma \qquad (4)$$

in the rotated coordinate system $(t, s', r)$. This new coordinate system is obtained by two rotations of the $(x, y, z)$ coordinate axes. The first rotation is the same as in the two-dimensional case, which is $\theta$ degrees about the $z$ axis, resulting in the $(t, s, z)$ axes as illustrated in Fig. 8. The second rotation is of $\gamma$ degrees about the new $t$ axis, resulting in $(t, s', r)$. In matrix form the required rotation is described as

$$\begin{bmatrix} t \\ s' \\ r \end{bmatrix} = \begin{bmatrix} 1 & 0 & 0 \\ 0 & \cos \gamma & \sin \gamma \\ 0 & -\sin \gamma & \cos \gamma \end{bmatrix} \begin{bmatrix} \cos \theta & \sin \theta & 0 \\ -\sin \theta & \cos \theta & 0 \\ 0 & 0 & 1 \end{bmatrix} \begin{bmatrix} x \\ y \\ z \end{bmatrix} \qquad (5)$$

A three-dimensional parallel projection can now be expressed as

$$P_{\theta, \gamma}(t_1, r_1) = \int_{-s_m}^{s_m} f(t_1, s', r_1)\, ds'$$

The resulting projection is now two dimensional and is obtained by integrating along lines parallel to the $s'$ axis. Note that any line integral can be mathematically expressed in this manner.

The computer simulation results presented in this chapter will use the image in Fig. 9, which is the well-known Shepp and Logan [4] "head phantom." The parameters of the head phantom are listed in Table I. For the

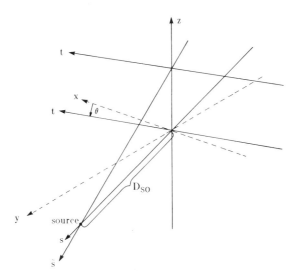

**Fig. 8.** New coordinate axes $(t, s, z)$ generated by rotating the $(x, y, z)$ axes about the $z$ axis by an angle of $\theta$ degrees.

three-dimensional reconstruction algorithm presented herein, the 10 ellipses which constitute the phantom have been made ellipsoids and have been repositioned. Figure 10 illustrates the modified head phantom used in this chapter and Table II provides the parameters of the phantom.

The advantage of using an image like Fig. 10 for computer simulation is that one can write analytical expressions for each of the ellipsoids. Due to the linearity of the Radon transform, a projection of an image composed of a number of ellipsoids is simply the sum of the projections for each of the ellipsoids. In the following, expressions will be presented for the projections of a single ellipsoid. If the object is a constant, $f(x, y, z)$ can be expressed as

$$f(x, y, z) = \begin{cases} \rho, & (x^2/A^2) + (y^2/B^2) + (z^2/C^2) \le 1 \\ 0, & \text{otherwise} \end{cases} \tag{6}$$

It can be shown, although the algebra for doing so is tedius, that the projections of such an object are given by

$$P_{\theta, \gamma}(t, r) = \frac{2\rho ABC}{a^2(\theta, \gamma)}$$

$$\times \left[ a^2(\theta, \gamma) - t^2(C^2 \cos^2 \gamma + (B^2 \cos^2 \theta + A^2 \sin^2 \theta) \sin^2 \gamma) \right.$$

$$- r^2(A^2 \cos^2 \theta + B^2 \sin^2 \theta)$$

$$\times \left. \left( \frac{7 + \cos 4\gamma}{8} \right) - tr \sin \gamma \cos \theta \sin \theta \, (B^2 - A^2) \right]^{1/2} \tag{7}$$

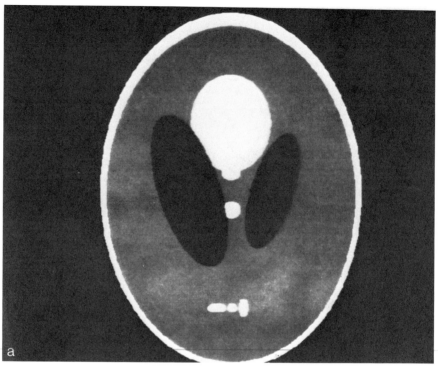

a

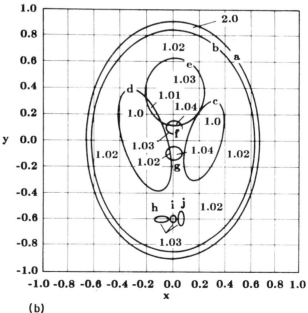

(b)

**Fig. 9.** (a) Image used for testing the accuracy of reconstruction algorithms for tomographic imaging with nondiffracting sources. (b) The test image of (a) is a superposition of the 10 ellipses shown here. On a scale of 0 to 2, the gray-scale distribution of the test image is also shown.

**TABLE I**

**Parameters of the Ellipses that Constitute the Two-Dimensional Phantom**

| Ellipse | Coordinates of the center, $(x, y)$ | Axis lengths $(A, B)$ | Rotation angle $\alpha$ (deg) | Gray level $\rho$ |
|---------|--------------------------|------------------------|-------------------------------|-------------------|
| a | (0, 0) | (0.92, 0.69) | 90 | 2.0 |
| b | (0, −0.0184) | (0.874, 0.662) | 90 | −0.98 |
| c | (0.22, 0) | (0.31, 0.11) | 72 | −0.02 |
| d | (−0.22, 0) | (0.41, 0.16) | 108 | −0.02 |
| e | (0, 0.35) | (0.25, 0.21) | 0 | 0.01 |
| f | (0, 0.1) | (0.046, 0.046) | 0 | 0.01 |
| g | (0, −0.1) | (0.046, 0.046) | 0 | 0.01 |
| h | (−0.08, −0.605) | (0.046, 0.046) | 0 | 0.01 |
| i | (0, −0.605) | (0.023, 0.023) | 0 | 0.01 |
| j | (0.06, −0.605) | (0.046, 0.023) | 90 | 0.01 |

where

$$a^2(\theta, \gamma) = C^2(B^2 \sin^2 \theta + A^2 \cos^2 \theta) \cos^2 \gamma + A^2 B^2 \sin^2 \gamma$$

If the angle $\gamma$ is zero degrees, the projection formula reduces to the more manageable form

$$P_{\theta, 0}(t, 0) = \begin{cases} \dfrac{2\rho AB}{a^2(\theta, 0)} \sqrt{a^2(\theta, 0) - t^2} & \text{for} \quad |t| < a(\theta, 0) \\ 0 & \text{for} \quad |t| > a(\theta, 0) \end{cases} \tag{8}$$

**TABLE II**

**Parameters of the Ellipsoids that Constitute the Three-Dimensional Phantom**

| Ellipsoid | Coordinates of the center, $(x, y, z)$ | Axis lengths $(A, B, C)$ | Rotation angle $\beta$ (deg) | Gray level $\rho$ |
|-----------|-----------------------------------------|---------------------------|------------------------------|-------------------|
| a | (0, 0, 0) | (0.69, 0.92, 0.9) | 0 | 2.0 |
| b | (0, 0, 0,) | (0.6624, 0.874, 0.88) | 0 | −0.98 |
| c | (−0.22, 0, −0.25) | (0.41, 0.16, 0.21) | 108 | −0.02 |
| d | (0.22, 0, −0.25) | (0.31, 0.11, 0.22) | 72 | −0.02 |
| e | (0, 0.35, −0.25) | (0.21, 0.25, 0.5) | 0 | 0.01 |
| f | (0, 0.1, −0.25) | (0.046, 0.046, 0.046) | 0 | 0.02 |
| g | (−0.8, −0.65, −0.25) | (0.046, 0.023, 0.02) | 0 | 0.01 |
| h | (0.06, −0.605, −0.25) | (0.046, 0.023, 0.02) | 90 | 0.01 |
| i | (0.06, −0.105, 0.625) | (0.056, 0.04, 0.1) | 90 | 0.02 |
| j | (0, 0.1, −0.625) | (0.056, 0.056, 0.1) | 0 | −0.02 |

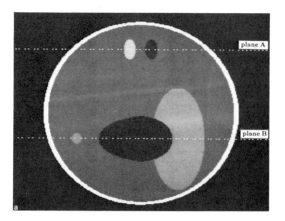

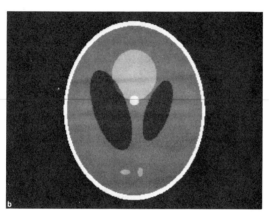

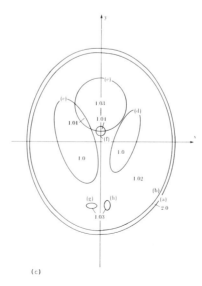

(c)                                                                Fig. 10a–c.

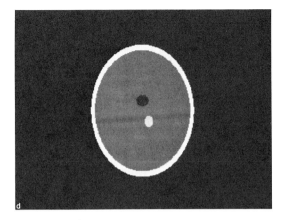

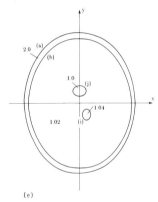

**Fig. 10d, e.**

**Fig. 10.** Three-dimensional mathematical phantom used to test the cone-beam reconstruction algorithm constructed by the 10 separate ellipsoids whose parameters appear in Table II. (a) A picture inside of the "skull" of the phantom, which illustrates the positioning of the six visible ellipsoids. $y = -0.605$ line. (b) A slice of the phantom at plane $B$ ($z = -0.25$). (c) An illustration of the gray levels within the slice at plane $B$. (d) A slice of the phantom at plane $A$ ($z = 0.625$). (e) An illustration of the gray levels within the slice at plane $A$.

where $a^2(\theta, 0) = A^2 \cos^2 \theta + B^2 \sin^2 \theta$. The quantity $a(\theta, 0)$ is equal to the projection half-width, as shown in Fig. 11a.

If the center of the ellipse is moved to $(x_1, y_1)$ and its orientation rotated by an angle $\alpha$ as shown in Fig. 11b, the resulting projections ($\gamma = 0°$), denoted by $P'_\theta(t)$, are related to the original $P_\theta(t)$ by

$$P'_\theta(t) = P_{\theta - \alpha}(t - s \cos(\alpha - \theta)) \qquad (9)$$

where $s = \sqrt{x_1^2 + y_1^2}$ and $\alpha = \tan^{-1}(y_1/x_1)$.

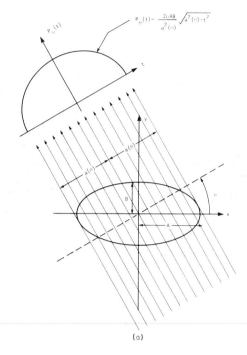

$$P_{\theta}(t) = \frac{2\rho AB}{a^2(\theta)} \sqrt{a^2(\theta) - t^2}$$

(a)

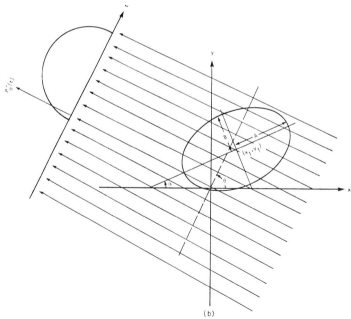

(b)

**Fig. 11.** (a) Projection of an ellipse. The gray level in the interior of the ellipse is $\rho$ and is zero outside of the ellipse. (b) Ellipse with its center located at $(x_1, y_1)$ and its major axis rotated by $\alpha$.

## FOURIER SLICE THEOREM FOR TOMOGRAPHIC IMAGING   III

In this section the underlying theory behind the convolution-back-projection algorithms will be presented. In the next section comutational procedures which implement the algorithms will be derived.

The *Fourier slice theorem* is the basis of the reconstruction techniques for most reconstruction algorithms. With the use of this theorem the one-dimensional Fourier transform of a function $g(x, y)$ is mathematically related to its two-dimensional Fourier transform. The theorem can be stated as follows. The Fourier transform of a parallel projection of an image $g(x, y)$ taken at an angle $\theta$ is equivalent to a slice of the two-dimensional transform of $g(x, y)$, $G(\omega_1, \omega_2)$, subtending an angle $\theta$ with the $\omega_1$ axis. In other words, the Fourier transform of $P_\theta(t)$ provides the values of $G(\omega_1, \omega_2)$ along line $BB$ shown in Fig. 12.

The theorem implies that if sufficiently many different projections are recorded at many different positions around the object, the object's Fourier transform could be generated. Once all of the projections are obtained, the object could be reconstructed by direct Fourier inversion. Typically, reconstruction is not done in this manner; rather, filtered-backprojection algorithms are used for reconstruction because of their greater accuracy and ease of implementation. Such filtered-backprojection algorithms will be derived in the following sections with the use of the Fourier slice theorem.

To quickly prove the theorem, also known as the *projection slice theorem*, let $G(\omega_1, \omega_2)$ be the Fourier transform of the image $g(x, y)$, which implies that

$$G(\omega_1, \omega_2) = \int_{-\infty}^{\infty} \int_{-\infty}^{\infty} g(x, y) \exp[-j2\pi(\omega_1 x + \omega_2 y)] \, dx \, dy \qquad (10)$$

and

$$g(x, y) = \int_{-\infty}^{\infty} \int_{-\infty}^{\infty} G(\omega_1, \omega_2) \exp[j2\pi(\omega_1 x + \omega_2 y)] \, d\omega_1 \, d\omega_2 \qquad (11)$$

Next, let us consider the values of $G(\omega_1, \omega_2)$ on the line $\omega_2 = 0$ in the $(\omega_1, \omega_2)$ plane. From (10), $G(\omega_1, 0)$ is expressed as

$$G(\omega_1, 0) = \int_{-\infty}^{\infty} \int_{-\infty}^{\infty} g(x, y) e^{-j\omega_1 x} \, dx \, dy = \int_{-\infty}^{\infty} \left[ \int_{-\infty}^{\infty} g(x, y) \, dy \right] e^{-j\omega_1 x} \, dx$$

$$= \int_{-\infty}^{\infty} P_0(t) e^{-j\omega_1 t} \, dt = S_0(\omega_1) \qquad (12)$$

which results due to $P_0(t) = (\int_{-\infty}^{\infty} g(x, y) \, dy)$, in which $\theta = 0$ and therefore $t = x$. Note that $S_\theta(\omega)$ is the Fourier transform of the projection $P_\theta(t)$. The preceding result, $G(\omega_1, 0) = S_0(\omega_1)$, implies that the Fourier transform of the projection measured perpendicular to the $y$ axis, $S_0(\omega_1)$, is equal to the Fourier transform of the object function on the $\omega_1$ axis. This result can be expanded to obtain a similar result for $\theta$ not equal to zero.

First let us rotate the $(x, y)$ coordinate axes by an angle $\theta$ to form the $t$, $s$ axes. The $(t, s)$ and $(x, y)$ coordinates are related as described in the previous section:

$$\begin{bmatrix} x \\ y \end{bmatrix} = \begin{bmatrix} \cos\theta & \sin\theta \\ -\sin\theta & \cos\theta \end{bmatrix} \begin{bmatrix} t \\ s \end{bmatrix} \tag{13}$$

Next we rewrite (10) in terms of $t$ and $s$, where $g(t, s)$ represents the object function in the rotated coordinate system:

$$S_\theta(w) = \int_{-\infty}^{\infty} P_\theta(t)\, e^{-jwt}\, dt = \int_{-\infty}^{\infty}\int_{-\infty}^{\infty} g(t, s)\, ds\, e^{-jwt}\, dt \tag{14}$$

Converting to $(x, y)$ coordinates yields

$$S_\theta(w) = \int_{-\infty}^{\infty}\int_{-\infty}^{\infty} g(x, y)\, \exp[-j(xw\cos\theta + yw\sin\theta)]\, dx\, dy$$

$$= G(w\cos\theta, w\sin\theta)$$

At this point it is obvious that a rotation by $\theta$ degrees in the time domain corresponds to a rotation by $\theta$ degrees in the frequency domain. Hence our

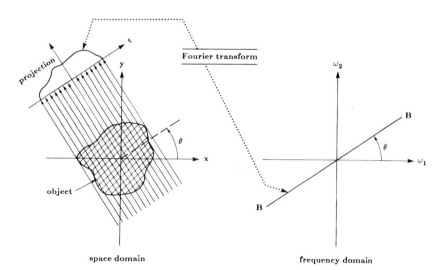

**Fig. 12.** Fourier slice theorem. In the left half of the figure, $P_\theta(t)$ is a parallel projection of $f(x, y)$ at angle $\theta$. The Fourier transform of $P_\theta(t)$ gives values of $F(\omega_1, \omega_2)$ on line $BB$ shown on the right.

desired generalized relationship, written in the polar coordinates $(\omega, \theta)$, becomes

$$G(\omega, \theta) = S_\theta(\omega) \tag{15}$$

This result is illustrated in Fig. 12. The Fourier transform of the projection $P_\theta(t)$ corresponds to the frequency-domain values of $G(\omega_1, \omega_2)$ on the line $BB$ (the $u$ axis).

**FILTERED-BACKPROJECTION ALGORITHMS   IV**
**FOR TWO-DIMENSIONAL RECONSTRUCTION**

**Reconstruction Algorithm for Parallel Projection Data   A**

The algorithm most widely utilized in applications using nondiffracting sources is the filtered-backprojection algorithm. This algorithm has gained its popularity due to its extreme accuracy, quickness, and easy implementation. It is presented in this section only for the case of parallel projection data, with the case of fan projection data to be presented in Section IV.B. Also in this section we will discuss various aspects of actual implementation of the algorithm and how the fast Fourier transform (FFT) can be used to speed up the necessary filtering.

The derivation of this algorithm will utilize the Fourier slice theorem and end up with an implementation that is very different from what the theorem might basically suggest. To start the derivation let us make use of the polar coordinates $(\omega, \theta)$ in the $(\omega_1, \omega_2)$ plane to rewrite the relationship of Eq. (11):

$$g(x, y) = \int_0^{2\pi} \int_0^\infty G(\omega, \theta) \exp[j\omega(x \cos \theta + y \sin \theta)] \omega \, d\omega \, d\theta$$

$$= \int_0^{2\pi} \int_0^\infty G(\omega, \theta) \exp[j\omega(x \cos \theta + y \sin \theta)] \omega \, d\omega \, d\theta$$

$$+ \int_0^\pi \int_0^\infty G(\omega, \theta + 180°)$$

$$\times \exp[j\omega(x \cos(\theta + 180°) + y \sin(\theta + 180°))] \omega \, d\omega \, d\theta \tag{16}$$

By using the relationships

$$G(\omega, \theta + 180°) = G(-\omega, \theta) \quad \text{and} \quad t = x \cos \theta + y \sin \theta \tag{17}$$

in (16) we may write $g(x, y)$ as

$$g(x, y) = \int_0^\pi \left[ \int_{-\infty}^\infty G(\omega, \theta)|\omega|e^{j\omega t} \, d\omega \right] d\theta$$

$$= \int_0^\pi \left[ \int_{-\infty}^\infty S_\theta(\omega)|\omega|e^{j\omega t} \, d\omega \right] d\theta \qquad (18)$$

with the help of the Fourier slice theorem as stated in (15) and the expression for $t$ in terms of $x$ and $y$ as written in (3). To make (18) appear in its filtered-backprojection form, it is necessary to separate the equation into two different operations. The first operation is the filtering of the projection data at each angle $\theta$, as follows:

$$Q_\theta(t) = \int_{-\infty}^\infty S_\theta(\omega)|\omega|e^{j\omega t} \, d\omega \qquad (19)$$

Second the "filtered projections" are backprojected to obtain the original object function

$$g(x, y) = \int_0^\pi Q_\theta(x \cos \theta + y \sin \theta) \, d\theta \qquad (20)$$

The filtering described in (19) would be physically impossible if it were not for the fact that the projections are in practice bandlimited to a maximum frequency of $W$ radians/sec. The frequency $W$ is defined as the frequency above which any spectral energy in a projection may be considered negligible. By virtue of the sampling theorem, the value of $W$ will bound the sampling frequency $\omega_s$ as follows:

$$2W \le \omega_s = 2\pi/\tau \qquad (21)$$

If the projection data are sampled with the sampling interval $\tau$, the sampled data should not suffer greatly from aliasing errors. By making the bandlimited projection assumption, (19) may be expressed with the use of the filter transfer function, $H(\omega)$, as follows:

$$H(\omega) = \begin{cases} |\omega|, & |\omega| < W \\ 0, & \text{otherwise} \end{cases} \qquad (22)$$

as illustrated in Fig. 13. Substitution of $H(\omega)$ into (19) yields

$$Q_\theta(t) = \int_{-\infty}^\infty S_\theta(\omega)H(\omega)e^{j\omega t} \, d\omega \qquad (23)$$

The filter's impulse response, $h(t)$, is obtained by inverse Fourier transforming $H(\omega)$ as written below with the use of (21):

$$h(t) = \int_{-\infty}^\infty H(\omega)e^{j\omega t} \, d\omega \qquad (24)$$

$$= \frac{1}{2\tau^2}\left[ \frac{\sin(2\pi t/2\tau)}{2\pi t/2\tau} \right] - \frac{1}{4\tau^2}\left[ \frac{\sin(\pi t/2\tau)}{\pi t/2\tau} \right]^2 \qquad (25)$$

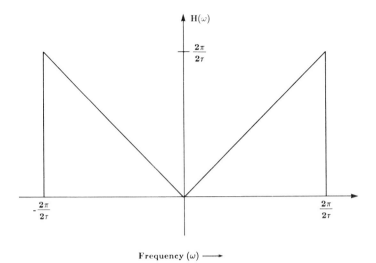

**Fig. 13.** Transfer function of the filter with which the projection must be processed prior to back projection.

The sampled version of the impulse response, which is all we need to know for the digital filtering of the sampled projection data, is given by

$$h(n\tau) = \begin{cases} 1/4\tau^2, & n = 0 \\ 0, & n \text{ even} \\ -1/n^2\pi^2\tau^2, & n \text{ odd} \end{cases} \tag{26}$$

which is illustrated in Fig. 14.

By using the convolution theorem, (23) may be written as

$$Q_\theta(t) = \int_{-\infty}^{\infty} P_\theta(\zeta)h(t-\zeta)\,d\zeta \tag{27}$$

which is discretely implemented as

$$Q_\theta(n\tau) = \tau \sum_{k=-\infty}^{\infty} h(n\tau - k\tau)P_\theta(k\tau) \tag{28}$$

In actual implementation each projection is finite in extent, which leads to a truncated version of (28):

$$Q_\theta(n\tau) = \tau \sum_{k=0}^{N-1} h(n\tau - k\tau)P_\theta(k\tau), \qquad n = 0, 1, 2, \ldots, N-1 \tag{29}$$

where $P_\theta(k\tau) = 0$ for $k < 0$ and $k > N - 1$. This filtering of the projection data may be accomplished as a discrete convolution in the time domain or as a multiplication in the frequency domain. In this discussion we will use the

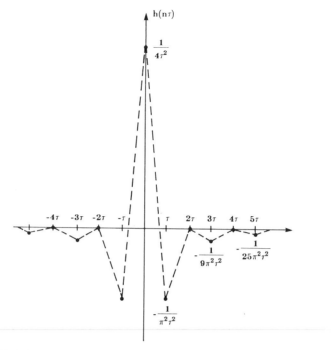

**Fig. 14.** Unit sample response corresponding to the transfer function of Fig. 13.

frequency-domain method, which is faster than time-domain convolution due to the use of the FFT algorithm. The problem next encountered is the periodic nature of the frequency-domain-implemented filtering. Note that the space-domain convolution in (28) is aperiodic; unless precautions are taken, its implementation in the frequency domain, although faster, would suffer from interperiod interference. To eliminate this problem associated with the use of the FFT algorithm for computing convolutions, the data sequences $P_\theta(n\tau)$ and $h(n\tau)$ are padded with zeros before being Fourier transformed. If an $N$-element projection is zero padded to make it $2N - 1$ elements long, it can be shown that the interperiod interference would not occur. Usually, further padding may become necessary to make the sequence lengths a power of 2, if a standard power-of-2 FFT algorithm is used.

To recapitulate in equation form, the frequency-domain implementation is expressed as

$$Q_\theta(n\tau) = \tau \times \text{IFFT}\{\text{FFT}[P_\theta(n\tau) \text{ with ZP}] \times \text{FFT}[h(n\tau) \text{ with ZP}]\} \qquad (30\text{a})$$

where FFT and IFFT denote the fast Fourier transform and the inverse fast Fourier transform, respectively, and ZP stands for zero padding. Superior reconstructions are usually obtained when some smoothing is also incorporated in (29) and (30a). For that purpose, we multiply the product of the two FFTs by a Hamming window, as follows:

$$Q_\theta(n\tau) = \tau \times IFFT\{FFT[P_\theta(n\tau) \text{ with ZP}] \times FFT[h(n\tau) \text{ with ZP}]$$
$$\times [\text{smoothing window}]\} \qquad (30b)$$

The next step in the reconstruction algorithm is the backprojection of the filtered projections as described by (20). The discrete approximation to (20) is

$$\hat{g}(x, y) = \frac{\pi}{K} \sum_{i=1}^{K} Q_{\theta_i}(x \cos \theta_i + y \sin \theta_i) \qquad (31)$$

where the $K$ angles $\theta_i$ are the discrete values of $\theta$ at which $P_\theta(t)$ is known. Note that the function $\hat{g}(x, y)$ is only a discrete version of $g(x, y)$.

In the process of backprojection each point $(x, y)$ in the reconstruction plane that lies on the line $t = x \cos \theta_i + y \sin \theta_i$ is given the value of $Q_{\theta_i}(t)$. The addition of all such values of $Q_{\theta_i}(t)$ at the point $(x, y)$ as $i$ varies from 1 to $K$ constitutes the reconstructed value at $(x, y)$ after a scaling of $\pi/K$. An illustration of this process is provided in Fig. 15 Note that the value of $Q_{\theta_i}(t)$ is a constant on the line $LM$ and each point in the reconstruction plane lying on that line has the value of $Q_{\theta_i}(t)$ added to it. In a similar fashion, each $t$ value of $Q_{\theta_i}(t)$ is smeared back over the image plane for each value of $\theta_i$. The sum of all smearings multiplied by $\pi/K$ results in the reconstruction image.

When the value of $t$ calculated with $(x \cos \theta_i + y \sin \theta_i)$ does not correspond to any of the values of $t$ in the discretized function $Q_{\theta_i}(t)$, the need

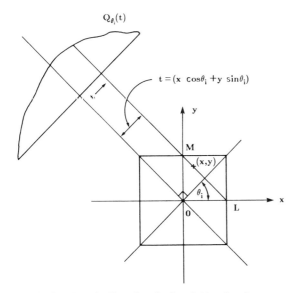

**Fig. 15.** When we backproject, the filtered projection $Q_\theta(t)$ makes the same contribution to all the pixels on line $LM$ in the image frame.

for interpolation arises. In most cases linear interpolation is good enough, but there is a better technique which preinterpolates the function $Q_{\theta_i}(\cdot)$. Preinterpolation is done by zero padding in the frequency domain before inverse Fourier transforming to obtain $Q_{\theta_i}(\cdot)$. This implies adding zeros to the product sequence in (30a) before the IFFT step. The result is the $Q_{\theta_i}(\cdot)$ function known at a smaller sampling interval depending upon the number of zeros in the padding procedure. Interpolation is no longer needed, due to the dense sampling, and the nearest-neighbor values are used to approximate $Q_{\theta_i}(t)$.

To illustrate how accurate the algorithm is, we will next present a computer-generated reconstruction of the test image in Fig. 9, as discussed in Section II. Most of the useful information in the image is contained in the 1% variations in gray levels within the "skull."

Using the implementation in (30b), Fig. 16b shows the reconstructed values on the line $y = -0.605$ for the test image and Fig. 16a shows the complete reconstruction. For this reconstruction 127 rays constituted each of the 100 projections, which were zero padded to 256-element sequences for the filtering process. Figure 16 demonstrates the remarkable accuracy of this method.

## B    Reconstruction Algorithms for Fan-Beam Projections

Up to this point only reconstruction from parallel ray projections has been discussed. In this section an alternate geometry for collecting projection data will be discussed. Collecting parallel projections requires either an array of sources which are pulsed sequentially or a single source which scans the length of the receiving line of detectors. This arrangement can result in a very long data collection time. With the use of a fan-beam of x rays, as in Fig. 17, only one stationary source is required for one projection; the source may then be rotated to another location for another projection. Scanning around the object in this manner reduces considerably the data collection time. See Fig. 18 for a depiction of data collection with fan beams.

The fan data can be rearranged into parallel projection data if the angles at which the fan projections are measured and the angular intervals between the rays within each fan projection are constrained. With such constraints it is possible to immediately convert the fan data into equivalent parallel form by *rebinning* or, in other words, reindexing. The resulting parallel projection data still might not be uniformly spaced, this problem being rectifiable with suitable interpolation. The interested reader is referred to Refs. 5 and 6 for further information on this rebinning technique. In the following paragraphs a direct filtered-backprojection algorithm for fan-beam projection data will be discussed. This algorithm will prove to be more complex than the parallel ray algorithm but will be just as accurate and elegant.

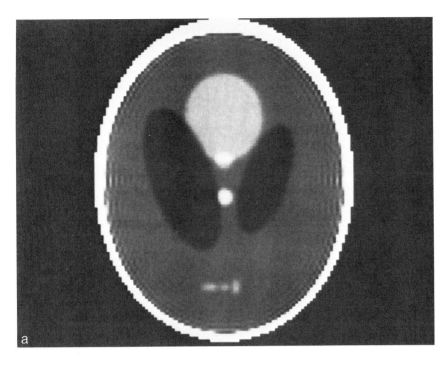

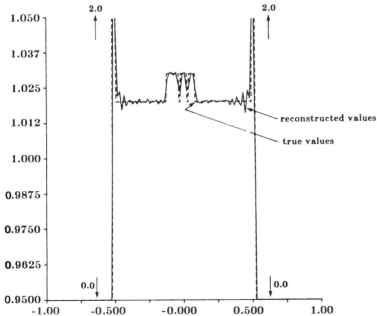

**Fig. 16.** (a) 128 × 128 filtered-backprojection reconstruction of the test image in Fig. 9 from 100 parallel projections over 180° and 127 rays in each projection. (b) A numerical comparison of the true and reconstructed values on line $y = -0.605$.

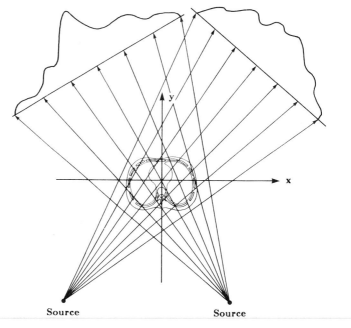

**Fig. 17.** Fan-beam scanner of Fig. 19 produces fan projections like those shown here.

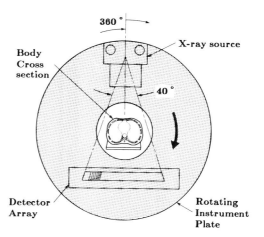

**Fig. 18.** Fan-beam scanner. An x-ray source illuminates a cross section of the body, and the transmitted photons are measured by an array of detectors. The measurement system is mounted on a gantry which rotates rapidly around the patient.

The approach to the derivation of a fan-beam reconstruction algorithm taken here will consist of replacing the variables in the parallel-beam algorithm with their corresponding fan-beam geometry equivalents. These substitutions and subsequent algebraic manipulations will lead to a filtered-backprojection algorithm for the fan-beam case.

The two predominant types of fan-beam geometries currently used are referred to as *equiangular* and *equispaced*. The difference between the two lies in the spacing of the detectors along the projection line. This difference is illustrated in Fig. 19. Note that for the equiangular case in Fig 19a, the projection line is drawn as an arc. To keep the discussion brief, the equispaced geometry is the only one that will be explored and for which a reconstruction algorithm will be derived. A similar derivation for the case of equiangular fan data may be found in Refs. 5 and 6.

The projection function for the fan-beam case will be expressed as $R_\beta(p)$ and is illustrated in Fig. 20a, where $p$ is the distance along the straight line that represents the detector bank. To simplify the geometry of the derivation, we will assume that the projections are measured on the line $D'_1 D'_2$ in Fig. 20a. The resulting projection will have the same values as the original projection on the line $D_1 D_2$ except that the distance between detectors will decrease. As a result, the ray integral along $SB$ is recorded at point $A$ on $D'_1 D'_2$ instead of point $B$ on $D_1 D_2$.

The first step in the derivation will be to examine Fig. 20 in an effort to determine the relationships between an equispaced fan-beam projection and a parallel ray projection. In Fig. 20b the axis $t$ is the line upon which the detectors lie. Hence the projection value corresponding to ray $SB$ is recorded at position $p(=OA)$ on the $t$ axis. If the ray $SB$ were a part of a parallel ray projection, the detector bank would lie on the dashed line and the ray would intersect that line at the point $t'$. The projection would then be represented by $P_\theta(t')$, where $\theta$ is the angle between the dashed line and the $x$ axis. From the figure the following relationships between fan- and parallel-beam variables are evident:

$$t' = p \cos \gamma = p \, D_{SO}/\sqrt{D_{SO}^2 + p^2}$$
$$\theta = \beta + \gamma = \beta + \tan^{-1}(p/D_{SO})$$

(32)

The net result of the last subsection was the reconstruction algorithm for the parallel ray projections which is described by (20) and (27). If those two operations were combined into one, we would have

$$g(x, y) = \int_0^\pi \int_{-t_m}^{t_m} P_\theta(t) h(x \cos \theta + y \sin \theta - t) \, dt \, d\theta$$

(33)

where $(t_m < t < -t_m)$ is the range of $t$ outside of which $P_\theta(t) = 0$ in all projections. Please note that the parallel projections are collected only over a

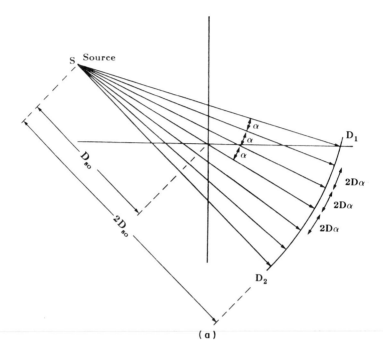

(a)

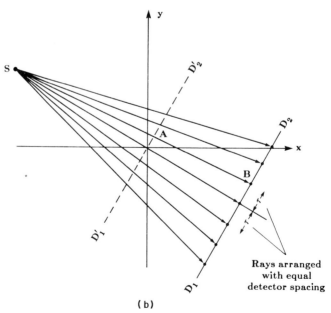

(b)

**Fig. 19.** Fan-beam projection taken with either (a) equiangular rays or (b) with rays that result in equispaced detectors on a line.

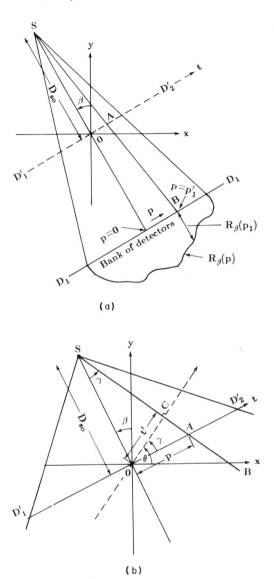

**Fig. 20.** (a) For the case of a fan beam with equispaced detectors, each projection is denoted by the function $R_\beta(s)$. (b) Various parameters used in the derivation of the fan-beam reconstruction algorithm.

range of 180°. To make subsequent manipulations easier, let us modify (33) such that projections will be taken over 360°. Hence let us start the derivation by rewriting (33) as

$$g(x, y) = \frac{1}{2} \int_0^{2\pi} \int_{-t_m}^{t_m} P_\theta(t) h(x \cos \theta + y \sin \theta - t) \, dt \, d\theta \qquad (34)$$

and converting the coordinates $(x, y)$ to their polar form $(r, \phi)$:

$$x = r \cos \phi, \qquad y = r \sin \phi \qquad (35)$$

In polar form, (34) can be written as

$$g(r, \phi) = \frac{1}{2} \int_0^{2\pi} \int_{-t_m}^{t_m} P_\theta(t') h(r \cos(\theta - \phi) - t') \, dt' \, d\theta \qquad (36)$$

At this point the relationships in (32) can be used to convert (36) into a fan-beam reconstruction algorithm. With the substitution of the transformation relationships in (32) and the use of the Jacobian of the transformation,

$$dt' \, d\theta = \frac{D_{SO}^3}{(D_{SO}^2 + p^2)^{3/2}} \, dp \, d\beta \qquad (37)$$

the reconstruction algorithm may be expressed as

$$g(r, \phi) = \frac{1}{2} \int_{\beta_1}^{\beta_2} \int_{-p_m}^{p_m} P_{\beta + \gamma} \left( \frac{p D_{SO}}{\sqrt{D_{SO}^2 + p^2}} \right)$$

$$\times h \left[ r \cos \left( \beta + \tan^{-1} \left( \frac{p}{D_{SO}} \right) - \phi \right) - \frac{D_{SO} p}{\sqrt{D_{SO}^2 + p^2}} \right]$$

$$\times \frac{D^3}{(D^2 + p^2)^{3/2}} \, dp \, d\beta \qquad (38)$$

The values of $\beta_1$ and $\beta_2$ are

$$\beta_1 = -\tan^{-1} \left( \frac{p_m}{D} \right), \qquad \beta_2 = 2\pi - \tan^{-1} \left( \frac{p_m}{D} \right) \qquad (39)$$

but since the effective range of integration remains 360°, $\beta_1$ and $\beta_2$ will be replaced by 0 and $2\pi$, respectively. The value of $p_m$, as used in (38) and (39), is the largest value of $p$ within each projection and serves the same purpose as $t_m$ in the parallel projection algorithm.

Further simplification of (38) occurs with the use of the equation

$$R_\beta(p) = P_{\beta + \gamma}(p D_{SO} / \sqrt{D_{SO}^2 + p^2})$$

which relates the fan-beam projection to the parallel ray projection. Hence (38) becomes

$$g(r, \phi) = \frac{1}{2} \int_0^{2\pi} \int_{p_m}^{p_m} R_\beta(p) h\left[ r \cos\left( \beta + \tan^{-1}\left(\frac{p}{D_{so}}\right) - \phi \right) \right.$$
$$\left. - \frac{D_{so}p}{\sqrt{D_{SO}^2 + p^2}} \right] \frac{D_{so}^3}{(D_{SO}^2 + p^2)^{3/2}} \, dp \, d\beta \tag{40}$$

To bring the algorithm closer to a filtered-backprojection form, let us examine the argument of the filter function, $h(\cdot)$, and define two new variables. The argument of $h(\cdot)$ can be rewritten by breaking the $\cos(\cdot)$ term into its equivalent form:

$$r \cos\left( \beta + \tan^{-1}\left(\frac{p}{D_{so}}\right) - \phi \right) - \frac{D_{so}p}{\sqrt{D_{SO}^2 + p^2}}$$
$$= r \cos(\beta - \phi) \frac{D_{so}}{\sqrt{D_{SO}^2 + p^2}} - (D_{so} + r \sin(\beta - \phi)) \frac{p}{\sqrt{D_{SO}^2 + p^2}} \tag{41}$$

At this point let us define a new variable, $U(r, \phi, \beta)$, which is the ratio of the distance $\overline{SP}$, illustrated in Fig. 21, to $D_{SO}$:

$$U(r, \phi, \beta) = \frac{\overline{SP}}{D_{so}} = \frac{\overline{SO} + \overline{OP}}{D_{so}} = \frac{D_{so} + r \sin(\beta - \phi)}{D_{so}} \tag{42}$$

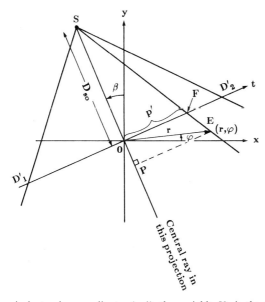

**Fig. 21.** For a pixel at polar coordinates $(r, \phi)$, the variable $U_r$ is the ratio of $SP$ to the source-to-origin distance.

Note that $\overline{SP}$ is equal to $D_{so}$ plus the projection of the pixel location onto the central ray of the projection. Second, an expression is needed that defines the point at which the ray passing through the pixel under consideration, $(r, \phi)$, intersects the projection plane. In Fig. 21 this point is labeled as $p'$ and is defined as

$$\frac{p'}{D_{so}} = \frac{\overline{EP}}{D_{so} + \overline{OP}}$$

which can be written in terms of $\beta$, $\phi$, and $r$ as

$$p' = D_{so} \frac{r \cos(\beta - \phi)}{D_{so} + r \sin(\beta - \phi)} \tag{43}$$

The substitution of (42) and (43) into (41) yields a new form for the argument of $h(\cdot)$:

$$r \cos\left( \beta + \tan^{-1}\left(\frac{p}{D_{so}}\right) - \phi \right) - \frac{D_{so}p}{\sqrt{D_{so}^2 + p^2}} = \frac{p'UD_{so}}{\sqrt{D_{so}^2 + p^2}} - \frac{pUD_{so}}{\sqrt{D_{so}^2 + p^2}} \tag{44}$$

This result leads to a new form for the fan-beam reconstruction algorithm:

$$g(r, \phi) = \frac{1}{2} \int_0^{2\pi} \int_{-p_m}^{p_m} R_\beta(p) h\left( (p' - p) \frac{UD_{so}}{\sqrt{D_{so}^2 + p^2}} \right) \frac{D_{so}^3}{(D_{so}^2 + p^2)^{3/2}} \, dp \, d\beta \tag{45}$$

One more modification to (45) is needed to place the algorithm fully into its filtered-backprojection form. Let us examine the filtering process in the frequency domain without taking into account the bandlimited nature of the filtering. As will be evident, when the $|\omega|$ filter is not bandlimited, we have an infinite energy filter, but this exploration is being made only to find an alternate form of the filter's impulse response. After carrying out frequency-domain manipulations, we will immediately return to the spatial domain.

The transfer function of the filter, as shown in (22), is related to the function $h(t)$ by the equation

$$h(t) = \int_{-\infty}^{\infty} |\omega| e^{j\omega t} \, d\omega \tag{46}$$

which leads to

$$h\left( (p' - p) \frac{UD_{so}}{\sqrt{D_{so}^2 + p^2}} \right) = \int_{-\infty}^{\infty} |\omega| \exp\left[ j\omega(p' - p) \frac{UD_{so}}{\sqrt{D_{so}^2 + p^2}} \right] d\omega \tag{47}$$

With the use of the following frequency scaling,

$$\omega' = \omega \frac{UD_{so}}{\sqrt{D_{so}^2 + p^2}} \tag{48}$$

(47) can rewritten as

$$h\left((p' - p)\frac{UD_{SO}}{\sqrt{D_{SO}^2 + p^2}}\right) = \frac{D_{SO}^2 + p^2}{U^2 D_{SO}^2} \int_{-\infty}^{\infty} |\omega'| \exp[j(p' - p)\omega'] \, d\omega$$

$$= \frac{D_{SO}^2 + p^2}{U^2 D_{SO}^2} h(p' - p) \qquad (49)$$

which, upon substitution into (45), yields

$$g(r, \phi) = \frac{1}{2} \int_0^{2\pi} \frac{1}{U^2} \int_{-\infty}^{\infty} R_\beta(p) h(p' - p) \frac{D_{SO}}{\sqrt{D_{SO}^2 + p^2}} \, dp \, d\beta \qquad (50)$$

This is the final form for the fan-beam reconstruction algorithm. Note the weighting factors in this algorithm, which are not a part of the filtered-backprojection algorithm for parallel ray projections.

To illustrate the steps involved, we break up the reconstruction algorithm as follows. The first step weights the fan-beam projections, resulting in $R(p)$:

$$\tilde{R}_\beta(p) = R_\beta(p) \frac{D_{SO}}{\sqrt{D_{SO}^2 + p^2}} \qquad (51)$$

Second, the weighted projections are filtered with $h(p)/2$:

$$Q_\beta(p) = \tilde{R}_\beta(p) * h(p)/2 \qquad (52)$$

The last step is the backprojection of the filtered and weighted projections:

$$g(r, \phi) = \int_0^{2\pi} \frac{1}{U^2} Q_\beta(p') \, d\beta \qquad (53)$$

The symbol $*$ denotes the operation of convolution.

For actual computer implementation, (51)–(53) must be discretized, and in the following, the process is described one step at a time.

*Step 1.* Here we will assume that each projection $R_\beta(p)$ is sampled with a sampling interval of $\Delta$. Then the known data are $R_{\beta_i}(n\Delta)$, where $n$ is an integer, with $n = 0$ corresponding to the central ray passing through the origin, and $\beta_i$ are the angles for which fan projections are known. As in (51), the weighting is implemented by the equation

$$\tilde{R}_{\beta_i}(n\Delta) = R_{\beta_i}(n\Delta) \frac{D_{SO}}{\sqrt{D_{SO}^2 + n^2\Delta^2}} \qquad (54)$$

*Step 2.* Convolve each modified projection $\tilde{R}_{\beta_i}(n\Delta)$ with $g(n\Delta)$ to generate the corresponding filtered projection:

$$Q_{\beta_i}(n\Delta) = \tilde{R}_{\beta_i}(n\Delta) * g(n\Delta) \qquad (55)$$

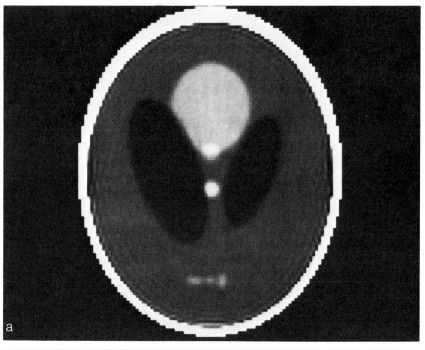

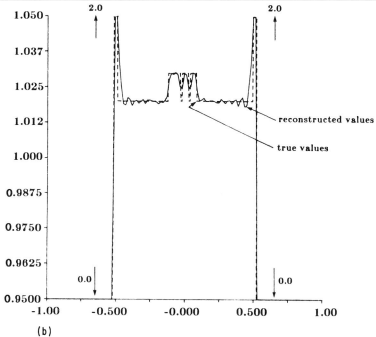

**Fig. 22.** (a) Fan-beam reconstruction of the image of Fig. 9. The fan angle is 45° with 200 projections over 360° and 100 rays in each projection. (b) Numerical comparison of the true and reconstructed values on the $y = -0.605$ line.

where

$$g(n\Delta) = \tfrac{1}{2}h(n\Delta) \qquad (56)$$

Substitution of $h(n\Delta)$, given in (26), into (56) yields

$$g(n\Delta) = \begin{cases} \tfrac{1}{8}\Delta^2, & n = 0 \\ 0, & n \text{ even} \\ -1/2n^2\pi^2\Delta^2, & n \text{ odd} \end{cases} \qquad (57)$$

Remember to zero pad the data sequences before implementing the FFT algorithm to carry out the filtering process as discussed previously. Also remember to add a smoothing window, as indicated in (30b).

*Step 3.* Last of all, backproject the weighted and filtered projections. The sum of all the backprojections is the reconstructed image

$$g(x, y) = \Delta\beta \sum_{i=1}^{M} \frac{1}{U^2(x, y, \beta_i)} Q_{\beta_i}(p') \qquad (58)$$

The value of $p'$ identifies the ray passing through $(x, y)$ for the central ray of the projection rotated by an angle $\beta_i$ from the $y$ axis. If the value of $p'$ does not correspond to one of the sampled values of $Q_{\beta_i}(\cdot)$, then some form of interpolation between values must be used.

Our computer-generated reconstruction of the test image in Fig. 9 appears in Fig. 22a. In this reconstruction we have used 100 projections of 127 elements each and a beamwidth of $45°$. The graph in Fig. 22b illustrates the accuracy of the reconstructed values on the line $y = -0.605$.

## FILTERED-BACKPROJECTION ALGORITHM V
## FOR THREE-DIMENSIONAL RECONSTRUCTION

In this section an approximation to a three-dimensional reconstruction algorithm for use with cone-beam x rays will be presented. The geometry chosen for this algorithm is very similar to that used in fan-beam reconstruction algorithms for equispaced collinear detectors. Hence the work is made easier by the results presented in Section IV.B.

In many cases "three-dimensional" reconstruction of an object is accomplished simply by applying the standard two-dimensional reconstruction algorithms repetitively at different heights along the $z$ axis, as illustrated in Fig. 4. In this section we will present an algorithm which will take us one step further by expanding the projection line into a *projection plane* and by using a *cone beam* of x rays. There has already been a lot of work done on the use of cone beams in computerized tomography, and the interested reader is referred to Refs. 7–9. The approach used in the derivation of a cone-beam reconstruction algorithm approximation, presented in the following, was first taken by Feldkamp *et al.* [7]. The resulting algorithm closely resembles that in Ref. 7 with only minor differences. Hopefully the following derivation will be more clear and concise since it builds directly upon the results of the last section, which derived a two-dimensional fan-beam reconstruction formula.

To begin the derivation, let us first recall the fan-beam reconstruction formula in (50), which will be repeated here for convenience:

$$g(r, \phi) = \frac{1}{2} \int_0^{2\pi} \frac{1}{U^2} \int_{-\infty}^{\infty} R_\beta(p) h(p' - p) \frac{D_{SO}}{\sqrt{D_{SO}^2 + p^2}} \, dp \, d\beta \qquad (59)$$

$$p' = \frac{D_{SO} r \cos(\beta - \phi)}{D_{SO} + r \sin(\beta - \phi)}, \qquad h(p) = \int_{-w}^{w} |\omega| e^{j\omega p} \, d\omega \qquad (60)$$

$$U(r, \phi, \beta) = \frac{D_{SO} + r \sin(\beta - \phi)}{D_{SO}}$$

Before continuing, let us convert the values of $r$ and $\phi$ into their equivalent values on the $t$ and $s$ axes. The $(t, s)$ coordinate axes are the $(x, y)$ axes rotated by an angle $\beta$, which represents an angular position of the source-detector gantry as it is being rotated about the object to record projection planes. Hence the following is true:

$$t = x \cos \beta + y \sin \beta, \qquad s = -x \sin \beta + y \cos \beta$$

$$x = r \cos \phi, \qquad y = r \sin \phi$$

which leads to new expressions for $U$ and $p'$:

$$p' = D_{SO} t / (D_{SO} - s), \qquad U(x, y, \beta) = (D_{SO} - s) / D_{SO}$$

Substitution of these relationships into (59) yields

$$g(t, s) = \frac{1}{2} \int_0^{2\pi} \frac{D_{SO}^2}{(D_{SO} - s)^2} \int_{-\infty}^{\infty} R_\beta(p) h\left(\frac{D_{SO} t}{D_{SO} - s} - p\right) \frac{D_{SO}}{\sqrt{D_{SO}^2 + p^2}} \, dp \, d\beta \qquad (61)$$

In this equation one can directly see how the location specified by the rectangular coordinates $(t, s)$ is reconstructed.

To arrive at a cone-beam reconstruction formula, it is first necessary to consider reconstructing a plane tilted about the source location. The key to the derivation of the cone-beam algorithm is the way in which the fan-beam reconstruction is carried out in the tilted plane with the origin remaining on the $z$ axis. Figure 8 illustrates the tilted plane in which the coordinate axes are $\tilde{t}$ and $\tilde{s}$. The fact that the origin of the tilted plane remains on the $z$ axis results in the projection plane lying in the $t, z$ plane. This is a result of Section IV.B, in which the projection line was moved to the $t$ axis for convenience, as noted in Fig. 20a. Since the intersection point of the tilted plane and the $z$ axis varies, one can see from Fig. 8 that the projection line always stays in the $t, z$ plane, hence the projection plane becomes the $t, z$ plane.

Our first step is to derive the filtered-backprojection algorithm to use in a tilted plane, which is accomplished by a change in variables. Also, a change in the coordinate system and a scaling of $D_{SO}$ and $d\beta$ occurs in the tilted plane. The distance $D_{SO}$ becomes $D'_{SO}$,

$$D'^2_{SO} = D^2_{SO} + \zeta^2$$

and $d\beta$, the differential angle of rotation, is changed to $d\beta'$ in the tilted plane. The change in the differential angle of rotation is demonstrated by the corresponding differential arc lengths:

$$D_{SO}\, d\beta = D'_{SO}\, d\beta', \qquad d\beta' = \frac{d\beta\, D_{SO}}{\sqrt{D^2_{SO} + \zeta^2}}$$

By making use of these new variables, (61) can be rewritten in the form

$$g(\tilde{t}, \tilde{s}) = \frac{1}{2} \int_0^{2\pi} \frac{D'^2_{SO}}{(D'_{SO} - \tilde{s})^2} \int_{-\infty}^{\infty} R_{\beta'}(p, \zeta) h\left(\frac{D'_{SO}\tilde{t}}{D'_{SO} - \tilde{s}} - p\right) \frac{D'_{SO}}{\sqrt{D'^2_{SO} + p^2}}\, dp\, d\beta' \tag{62}$$

which is the reconstruction algorithm in the tilted plane. Notice that the projection $R_\beta(\cdot)$ has taken on a height variable, $\zeta$.

The next step in the derivation is to put the algorithm in (62) back into terms of $\beta$, $D_{SO}$, and the $(t, s, z)$ coordinates. Note that in the tilted plane a point $(t_1, \hat{s}_1)$ can be represented by the vector $\mathbf{r}$, which can be broken into components, as illustrated in Fig. 23:

$$\mathbf{r} = r_t \hat{a}_t + r_s \hat{a}_s + r_z \hat{a}_z$$

The relationships between the components of $\mathbf{r}$ and the variables of $(t_1, \hat{s}_1)$ are expressed as

$$t_1 = r_t, \qquad \hat{s}_1/D'_{SO} = r_s/D_{SO}, \qquad \zeta/D_{SO} = r_z/(D_{SO} - r_s) \tag{63}$$

The substitution of (63) into (62) will eliminate the tilted plane variables from the algorithm and leave it dependent only upon $D_{SO}$, $\beta$, $r_s$, $r_t$, and $r_z$. Hence (62) becomes

$$g(r_t, r_s) = \frac{1}{2} \int_0^{2\pi} \frac{D^2_{SO}}{(D_{SO} - r_s)^2} \int_{-\infty}^{\infty} R_\beta(p, \zeta) h\left(\frac{D_{SO} r_t}{D_{SO} - r_s} - p\right)$$

$$\times \frac{D_{SO}}{\sqrt{D^2_{SO} + \zeta^2 + p^2}}\, dp\, d\beta \tag{64}$$

which is the desired weighted, filtered-backprojection algorithm.

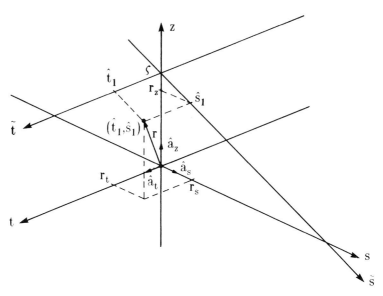

**Fig. 23.** Vector **r** in the $(t, s, z)$ coordinate system representing the point $(\tilde{t}_1, \tilde{s}_1)$ in the tilted reconstruction plane.

This algorithm can be broken down into the following three steps.

*Step 1.* Multiply each projection $R_\beta(p, \zeta)$ by the weighting function $(D_{so}/\sqrt{D_{so}^2 + \zeta^2 + p^2})$ to obtain $\tilde{R}_\beta(p, \zeta)$:

$$\tilde{R}_\beta(p, \zeta) = \frac{D_{so}}{\sqrt{D_{so}^2 + \zeta^2 + p^2}} R_\beta(p, \zeta) \qquad (65)$$

*Step 2.* Implement the convolution with $h(p)/2$ by multiplying, for each value of $\zeta$, the Fourier transform of $h(p)/2$ and the one-dimensional Fourier transform of $\tilde{R}_\beta(p, \zeta)$ with respect to $p$. Inverse transforming this product leaves us with $Q_\beta(p, \zeta)$:

$$Q_\beta(p, \zeta) = \tilde{R}_\beta(p, \zeta) * \tfrac{1}{2}h(p)$$

Note that no filtering of the projection in the $z$ direction is being implemented.

*Step 3.* The final step is the weighted backprojection:

$$g(\mathbf{r}) = \int_0^{2\pi} \frac{D_{so}^2}{(D_{so} - r_s)^2} Q_\beta\left(\frac{D_{so}r_t}{D_{so} - r_s}, \frac{D_{so}r_z}{D_{so} - r_s}\right) d\beta \qquad (66)$$

The two arguments of $Q_\beta$ specify the coordinates of the projection plane element that are attributed to the ray passing through the point represented by $\mathbf{r} = r_t\hat{a}_t + r_s\hat{a}_s + r_z\hat{a}_z$.

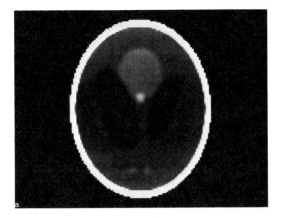

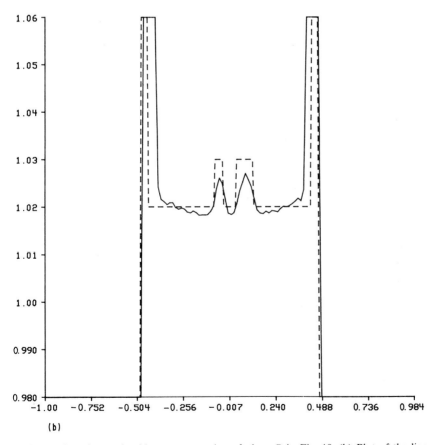

(b)

**Fig. 24.** Cone-beam algorithm reconstruction of plane $B$ in Fig. 10. (b) Plot of the line $y = -0.105$ in the reconstruction compared to the original.

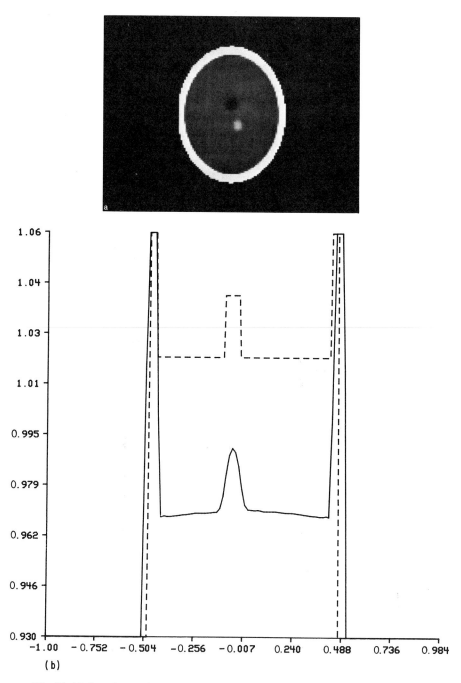

**Fig. 25.** (a) Cone-beam algorithm reconstruction of plane $A$ in Fig. 10. (b) Plot of the line $y = -0.605$ in the reconstruction compared to the original.

Due to the shape of the cone-beam projections, as described herein, only the portion of the object contained within the x-ray beam can be reconstructed. As the gantry, on which the source and the projection plane are mounted, rotates around the object, a "reconstruction region" is defined by the cone beam. Only the portion of the object totally inside of the region will be reconstructed with confidence. Outside of this region the reconstruction algorithm will not function properly due to an incomplete coverage of that area within each projection. As a result, only the contents of the object totally contained within the sphere of radius $D_{SO} \sin(\Gamma_m)$, where $\Gamma_m$ is half of the beamwidth angle, will be accurately reconstructed.

To test the cone-beam algorithm, 100 projections of $127 \times 127$ elements, each of the phantom illustrated in Fig. 10, were taken and two planes within the object have been reconstructed. The reconstructed planes are the $z = 0.625$ and $z = -0.25$ planes, which are marked A and B, respectively, in Fig. 10a.

The reconstruction of plane $B$ appears in Fig. 24a, with a plot of the $y = -0.605$ slice of the reconstruction appearing in Fig. 24b. The quality of this plane is acceptable as compared with the two-dimensional reconstructions of the previous sections. The reconstruction of plane $A$ appears in Fig. 25a, with a plot of the $y = -0.105$ slice of the reconstruction appearing in Fig. 25b. In this reconstruction a dc shift of 0.06 occurred, although the general shape and position of the ellipses appeared correct. Of course, finer resolution can be obtained by increasing the number of projections, but such an increase causes the memory requirements to increase rapidly.

From the studies performed up to this point, it seems as if the quality of the reconstruction algorithm degrades with distance of the reconstruction plane away from the $z = 0$ plane. The degradation seems to be attributable to an incomplete coverage of the object by the projection set, even though the object is completely irradiated by the cone beam. If a two-dimensional reconstruction of a tilted plane, as described earlier, were to be attempted, we would normally rotate the source-detector gantry around the normal to the center of the plane. In this cone-beam algorithm the source-detector gantry only rotates about the $z$ axis. The result is a loss of some low-frequency information in all reconstructions off of the $z = 0$ plane. The amount of loss varies with the distance away from the $z = 0$ plane.

## BIBLIOGRAPHIC NOTES    VI

The first mathematical solution to the problem of reconstructing a function from its projections was given by Radon [10] in 1917. More recently, some of the first investigators to examine this problem either theoretically or experimentally (and often independently) include (in a roughly chronological order): Bracewell [2, 11], Oldendorf [12], Cormack [13, 14], Kuhl and

Edwards [15], DeRosier and Klug [16], Tretiak *et al.* [17], Rowley [18], Berry and Gibbs [19], Ramachandran and Lakshminarayanan [20], Bender *et al.* [21], and Bates and Peters [22]. A detailed survey of the work done in computerized tomographic imaging up to 1979 appears in Ref. 23. More recent surveys emphasizing the algorithms aspect of tomographic imaging appear in Refs. 5 and 24-26.

The concept of filtered backprojection was first proposed by Bracewell [8] and later independently by Ramachandran and Lakshminarayanan [20]; the proposed algorithms were meant for parallel projection data. A similar algorithm for fan-beam data collected with an array of equispaced collinear detectors was proposed by Lakshminarayanan [27]; its extension to equiangular fan-beam data was made by Herman and Naperstek [28]. The fan-beam derivation presented in this chapter was first developed by Scudder [29]. Many authors [17, 30-33] have proposed variations on the filter function of the filtered-backprojection algorithms discussed in this chapter. When fan beams are used for data generation, images may also be reconstructed by first sorting the recorded data into parallel projections, the aim being to then use the relatively simple and fast algorithms for parallel data. Fast algorithms for ray sorting of fan-beam data have been developed by Wang [34], Dreike and Boyd [35], and Peters and Lewitt [36]. The reader is referred to Refs. 37 and 38 for algorithms for nonuniformly sampled projections data; to Refs. 39-43 for reconstructions from incomplete and limited projections; and to Refs. 44 and 45 for circular transform approaches to image reconstruction.

The success of tomographic imaging with x rays has sparked an interest in using other energy sources that are less harmful, such as ultrasound and low-power microwaves. The difficulty with these other sources is that they refract and diffract; in other words, they violate the basic assumption of straight line propagation employed in the derivation of algorithms presented in this chapter. For objects that are only lightly refracting, a combination of algebraic reconstruction and digital ray tracing may be the best approach to obtaining high-quality reconstructions [46, 47]. Some early ultrasonic reconstructions using this approach were reported by Glover and Sharp [48]. As shown by Dines and Kak [49], Kak [23], and Crawford and Kak [50], in such ultrasonic reconstructions it is possible to maintain the basic x-ray type of algorithm, yet introduce artifact-removing features such as corrections for multipath effects, frequency-dependent attenuation, and so on.

When the object inhomogeneities become comparable in size to a wavelength, it is not appropriate to talk about propagation along lines and rays, and energy transmission must be discussed in terms of wavefronts and fields scattered by inhomogeneities, which is what is done in diffraction tomography. The paper by Mueller *et al.* [51] was responsible for focusing the interest of many researchers on the area of diffraction tomography, although from a purely scientific standpoint the technique can be traced back to the now classic paper by Wolf [52] and a subsequent article by Iwata and Nagata [53]. For recent developments in the field of diffraction tomography, and also more chronological accounts of the developments by various investigators in this field, the reader is referred to Refs 54–57.

Tomographic imaging may also be accomplished, although less accurately, by direct Fourier inversion instead of the filtered-backprojection methods discussed in this chapter. This was first shown by Bracewell [21] for radioastronomy, later independently by DeRosier and Klug [16] in electron microscopy, and Rowley [18] in optical holography. Several workers who applied this method to radiography include Tretiak *et al.* [58], Bates and Peters [22], Mersereau and Oppenheim [59], and Stark *et al.* [60]. One source of errors in the direct approach is the interpolation in the frequency domain from polar coordinates to rectangular coordinates. Wernecke and D'Addario [61] have proposed a maximum-entropy approach to direct Fourier inversion. Their procedure is especially applicable if for some reason the projection data are insufficient.

Aliasing artifacts in tomographic imaging have been studied by Brooks *et al.* [62] and Crawford and Kak [50]. With regard to the properties of noise in images reconstructed with filtered backpropagation, Shepp and Logan [4] first showed that the variance of noise is directly proportional to the area under the square of the filter function. This derivation was based on the assumption that the variance of the measurement is the same for all the rays in the projection data, a condition that is usually not satisfied. A more general expression (not using this assumption) for the noise variance was derived by Kak [23], who has also introduced the concept of "the relative uncertainty image." For tomographic imaging with x-rays, Tretiak [63] has derived an algorithm-independent lower bound on the noise variance in a reconstructed image. Noise properties of x-ray tomograms have also been discussed by Chesler *et al.* [64].

An entirely different approach to image reconstruction is found in algebraic reconstruction algorithms in which the cross section of an object is considered to be an array of unknowns. These unknowns are recovered by solving algebraic equations in terms of the measured projection data. The algebraic techniques are discussed in great detail by Gordon *et al.* [65–67], Herman and Rowland [68], Herman *et al.* [69], Budinger and Gullberg [70], Gilbert [71], Oppenheim [41], Ramakrishnan *et al.* [72], and Andersen and Kak [47].

Much work has been done in the development of cone-beam reconstruction algorithms for three-dimensional reconstruction. Some of these algorithms are derived by using the exact three-dimensional Radon transform inversion formula, as done by Minerbo [8] and Denton *et al.* [9]. Although these derivations tend to be elegant and precise, the results do not lend themselves to easy implementation. The cone-beam algorithm presented in this chapter was derived by Feldkamp *et al.* [7] and possesses an easy implementation, which yields reasonably accurate three-dimensional reconstructions. Three-dimensional cone-beam algorithms for use in medical nuclear emission tomography are presented in Ref. 73.

## ACKNOWLEDGEMENTS

The continuing collaboration and exchange of ideas with Malcolm Slaney and Mani Azimi has made possible the more recent developments made by the authors in the field of tomographic imaging. During the past few years, our work in this area has been supported by the National Institutes of Health and the Walter Reed Army Institute of Research.

## REFERENCES

1. K. A. Dines and R. J. Lytle, Computerized geophysical tomography, *Proc. IEEE* **67**, 1065–1073 (1979).
2. R. N. Bracewell, Strip integration in radio astronomy, *Aust. J. Phys.* **9**, 198–217 (1956).
3. R. A. Crowther, D. J. DeRosier, and A. Klug, The reconstruction of a three-dimensional structure from projections and its applications to electron microscopy, *Proc. Roy. Soc. Lond.* **A317**, 319–340 (1970).
4. L. A. Shepp and B. F. Logan, The Fourier reconstruction of a head section, *IEEE Trans. Nucl. Sci.* **NS-21**, 21–43 (1974).
5. A. C. Kak, Image reconstruction from projections, *in* "Digital Image Processing Techniques" (M. P. Ekstrom, ed.). Academic Press, New York, 1984.
6. A. Rosenfeld and A. C. Kak, "Digital Picture Processing," 2nd ed., Vol. 1. Academic Press, New York, 1982.
7. L. A. Feldkamp, L. C. Davis, and J. W. Kress, Practical cone-beam algorithm, *J. Opt. Soc. Am. A* **1**, No. 6, 612–619 (June 1984).
8. G. N. Minerbo, Convolution reconstruction from cone-beam projection data, *IEEE Trans. Nuc. Sci.* **NS-26**, No. 2, 2682–2684 (April 1979).
9. R. V. Denton, B. Friedlander, and A. J. Rockmore, Direct three-dimensional image reconstruction from divergent rays, *IEEE Trans. Nuc. Sci.* **NS-26**, No. 2, 4695–4703 (October 1979).
10. J. Radon, Uber die bestimmung von funktionen durch ihre intergralwerte langs gewisser mannigfaltigkeiten (On the determination of functions from their integrals along certain manifolds), *Ber. Saechsische Akademie der Wissenschaften* **29**, 262–279 (1917).
11. R. N. Bracewell and A. C. Riddle, Inversion of fan-beam scans in radio astronomy, *Astrophys. J.* **150**, 427–434 (1967).
12. W. H. Oldendorf, Isolated flying spot detection of radiodensity discontinuities displaying the internal structural pattern of a complex object, *IRE Trans. Biomed. Eng.* **BME-8**, 68–72 (1961).
13. A. M. Cormack, Representation of a function by its line integrals with some radiological applications, *J. Appl. Phys.* **34**, 2722–2727 (1963).
14. A. M. Cormack, Representation of a function by its line integrals with some radiological applications, II, *J. Appl. Phys.* **35**, 2908–2913 (1964).
15. D. E. Kuhl and R. Q. Edwards, Image separation radio-isotope scanning, *Radiology* **80**, 653–661 (1963).
16. D. J. DeRosier and A. Klug, Reconstruction of three dimensional structures from electron micrographs, *Nature (London)* **217**, 130–134 (1968).
17. E. Tanaka and T. A. Iinuma, Correction functions for optimizing the reconstructed image in transverse section scan, *Physiol. Med. Biol.* **20**, 789–798 (1975).
18. P. D. Rowley, Quantitative interpretation of three dimensional weakly refractive phase objects using holographic interferometry, *J. Opt. Soc. Amer.* **59**, 1496–1498 (1969).

19. M. V. Berry and D. F. Gibbs, The interpretation of optical projections, *Proc. Roy. Soc. London* **A314**, 143–152 (1970).

20. G. N. Ramachandran and A. V. Lakshminarayanan, Three dimensional reconstructions from radiographs and electron micrographs: Application of convolution instead of Fourier transforms, *Proc. Nat. Acad. Sci. USA* **68**, 2236–2240 (1971).

21. R. Bender, S. H. Bellman, and R. Gordon, ART and the ribosome: A preliminary report on the three-dimensional structure of individual ribosomes determined by an algebraic reconstruction technique, *J. Theor. Biol.* **29**, 483–487 (1970).

22. R. H. T. Bates and T. M. Peters, Towards improvements in tomography, *New Zealand J. Sci.* **14**, 883–896 (1971).

23. A. C. Kak, Computerized tomography with x-ray, emission and ultrasound sources, *Proc. IEEE* **67**, 1245–1272 (1979).

24. S. R. Dean, "The Random Transform and Some of Its Applications." Wiley, New York, 1983.

25. A. C. Kak, (Guest ed.) Computerized medical imaging, *IEEE Trans. Biomed. Engrg.*, Special Issue (February 1981).

26. A. C. Kak, Tomographic imaging with diffracting and non-diffracting sources, *in* "Array Signal Processing" (S. Haykin, ed.) pp. 351–428. Prentice-Hall, Engelwood Cliffs, New Jersey, 1984.

27. A. V. Lakshminarayanan, Reconstruction from divergent ray data, Dept. of Computer Science, State Univ. of New York at Buffalo, Technical Report 92, 1975.

28. G. T. Herman and A. Naparstek, Fast image reconstruction based on a Radon inversion formula appropriate for rapidly collected data, *SIAM J. Appl. Math.* **33**, 511–533 (1977).

29. H. J. Scudder, Introduction to computer aided tomography, *Proc. IEEE* **66**, 628–637 (June 1978).

30. N. Baba and K. Murata, Filtering for image reconstruction from projections, *J. Opt. Soc. Amer.* **67**, 662–668 (1977).

31. S. K. Kenue and J. F. Greenleaf, Efficient convolution kernels for computerized tomography, *Ultrasonic Imaging* **1**, 232–244 (1979).

32. Y. S. Kwoh, I. S. Reed, and T. K. Truong, A generalized |w|-filter for 3-D reconstruction, *IEEE Trans. Nucl. Sci.* **NS-24**, 1990–1998 (1977).

33. R. M. Lewitt, Ultra-fast convolution approximation for computerized tomography, *IEEE Trans. Nucl. Sci.* **NS-26**, 2678–2681 (1979).

34. L. Wang, Cross-section reconstruction with a fan-beam scanning geometry, *IEEE Trans. Comput.* **C-26**, 264–268 (1977).

35. P. Dreike and D. P. Boyd, Convolution reconstruction of fan-beam reconstructions, *Comp. Graph. Image Proc.* **5**, 459–469 (1977).

36. T. M. Peters and R. M. Lewitt, Computed tomography with fan-beam geometry, *J. Comput. Assist. Tomog.* **1**, 429–436 (1977).

37. B. K. P. Horn, Density reconstructions using arbitrary ray sampling schemes, *Proc. IEEE* **66**, 551–562 (1978).

38. B. K. P. Horn, Fan-beam reconstruction methods, *Proc. IEEE* **67**, 1616–1623 (1979).

39. R. N. Bracewell and S. J. Wernecke, Image reconstruction over a finite field of view, *J. Opt. Soc. Amer.* **65**, 1342–1346 (1975).

40. R. M. Lewitt and R. H. T. Bates, Image reconstruction from projections, *Optik* **50**, Part I: 19–33; Part II: 85–109; Part III: 189–204; Part IV: 269–278 (1978).

41. B. E. Oppenheim, Reconstruction tomography from incomplete projections, *in* "Reconstruction Tomography in Diagnostic Radiology and Nuclear Medicine" (M. M. Ter-Pogossian *et al.* eds.). Univ. Park Press, Balitmore, Maryland, 1975.

42. T. Sato, S. J. Norton, M. Linzer, O. Ikeda, and M. Hirama, Tomographic image reconstruction from limited projections using iterative revisions in image and transform spaces, *Applied Optics* **20**, 395–399 (February 1980).

43. K. C. Tam and V. Perez-Mendez, Tomographical imaging with limited angle input, *J. Opt. Soc. Amer.* **71**, 582–592 (May 1981).

44. E. W. Hansen, Theory of circular image reconstruction, *J. Opt. Soc. Amer.* **71**, 304–308. (March 1981).

45. E. W. Hansen, Circular harmonic image reconstruction: experiments, *Applied Optics* **20**, 2266–2274 (July 1981).

46. A. H. Andersen and A. C. Kak, Digital ray tracing in two-dimensional refractive fields, *J. Acoust. Soc. Am.* **72**, 1593–1606 (November 1982).

47. A. H. Andersen and A. C. Kak, Simultaneous algebraic reconstruction technique: A new implementation of the ART algorithm, *Ultrasonic Imaging* **6**, 81–94 (January 1984).

48. G. H. Glover, and J. L. Sharp, Reconstruction of ultrasound propagation speed distribution in soft tissue: time-of-flight tomography, *IEEE Trans. Sonics Ultrasonics* **SU-24**, 229–234 (1977).

49. K. A. Dines and A. C. Kak, Ultrasonic attenuation tomography of soft biological tissues, *Ultrasonic Imaging* **1**, 16–33 (1979).

50. C. R. Crawford and A. C. Kak, Multipath artifact corrections in ultrasonic transmission tomography, *Ultrasonic Imaging* **4**, 234–266 (1982).

51. R. K. Mueller, M. Kaveh, and G. Wade, Reconstructive tomography and applications to ultrasonics, *Proc. IEEE* **67**, 567–587 (1979).

52. E. Wolf, Three-dimensional structure determination of semi-transparent objects from holographic data, *Optics Communications* **1**, no. 4, 153–156 (1969).

53. K. Iwata and R. Nagata, Calculation of refractive index distribution from interferograms using Born and Rytov's approximation, *Jap. J. Appl. Phys.* **14**, Suppl. 14-1, 383 (1975).

54. M. Azimi and A. C. Kak, Distortion in diffraction tomography caused by multiple scattering, *IEEE Trans. Med. Imaging* **MI-2**, 176–195 (December 1983).

55. D. Nahamoo, S. X. Pan, and A. C. Kak, Synthetic aperture diffraction tomography and its interpolation-free computer implementation, *IEEE Trans. Sonics Ultrasonics* **SU-31**, 218–230 (1984).

56. S. X. Pan and A. C. Kak, A computational study of reconstruction algorithms for diffraction tomography: Interpolation vs. filtered-backpropagation, *IEEE Trans. Acous. Sp. Sig. Proc.* **ASSP-31**(5), 1262–1275 (October 1983).

57. M. Slaney, A. C. Kak, and L. E. Larsen, Limitations of imaging with first-order diffraction tomography, *IEEE Trans. Microsc. Theory Tech.* **MTT-32**, 860–874 (1984).

58. O. Tretiak, M. Eden, and M. Simon, Internal structures for three dimensional images, *Proc. 8th Int. Conf. Med. Biol. Eng., Chicago* (1969).

59. R. M. Mersereau and A. V. Oppenheim, Digital reconstruction of multidimensional signals from their projections, *Proc. IEEE* **62**, 1319–1338 (1974).

60. H. Stark, J. W. Woods, I. Paul, and R. Hingorani, Direct fourier reconstruction in computer tomography, *IEEE Trans. Acoust. Speech Sig. Proc.* **ASSP-29**, 237–244 (1981).

61. S. J. Wernecke and L. R. D'Addario, Maximum entropy image reconstruction, *IEEE Trans. Comput.* **C-26**, 351–364 (1977).

62. R. A. Brooks, G. H. Weiss, and A. J. Talbert, A new approach to interpolation in computed tomography, *J. Comput. Assist. Tomogr.* **2**, 577–585 (1978).

63. O. J. Tretiak, Noise limitations in x-ray computed tomography, *J. Compt. Assist. Tomogr.* **2**, 477–480 (1978).

64. D. A. Chesler, S. J. Riederer, and N. J. Pele, Noise due to photon counting statistics in computer x-ray tomography, *J. Comput. Assist. Tomog.* **1**, 64–74 (1977).

65. R. Gordon, R. Bender, and G. T. Herman, Algebraic reconstruction techniques (ART) for three-dimensional electron microscopy and X-ray photography, *J. Theor. Biol.* **29**, 470–481 (1971).

66. R. Gordon, A tutorial on ART (algebra reconstruction techniques), *IEEE Trans. Nucl. Sci.* **NS-21** 78–93 (1974).

67. R. Gordon and G. T. Herman, Reconstruction of pictures from their projections, *Commun. Assoc. Comp. Mach.* **14**, 759–768 (1971).

68. G. T. Herman and S. Rowland, Resolution in ART: An experimental investigation of the resolving power of an algebraic picture reconstruction, *J. Theor. Biol.* **33**, 213–233 (1971).

69.  G. T. Herman, A. Lent, and S. Rowland, ART: mathematics and applications: A report on the mathematical foundations and on applicability to real data of the algebraic reconstruction techniques, *J. Theor. Biol.* **43**, 1–32 (1973).

70.  T. F. Budinger and G. T. Gullberg, Three-dimensional reconstruction in nuclear medicine emission imaging, *IEEE Trans. Nucl. Sci.* **NS-21**, 2–21 (1974).

71.  P. Gilbert, Iterative methods for the reconstruction of three-dimensional objects from their projections, *J. Theor. Biol.* **36**, 105–117 (1972).

72.  R. S. Ramakrishnan, S. K. Mullick, R. K. S. Rathore, and R. Subramanian, Orthogonalization, Bernstein polynomials, and image restoration, *Appl. Opt.* **18**, 464–468 (1979).

73.  Z. H. Cho, J. B. RA, and S. K. Hilal, True three-dimensional reconstruction (TTR)—application of algorithm toward full utilization of oblique rays, *IEEE Trans. Med. Imag.* **MI-2**, no. 1 (March 1983).

# Index

695